Philippe Verdier
615 Victoria Avenue
Westmount 217
P. Q. Canada

# NORMAN ILLUMINATION AT MONT ST MICHEL

966–1100

# NORMAN ILLUMINATION AT MONT ST MICHEL 966–1100

J. J. G. ALEXANDER

CLARENDON PRESS · OXFORD
1970

*Oxford University Press, Ely House, London W.1*
GLASGOW NEW YORK TORONTO MELBOURNE WELLINGTON
CAPE TOWN SALISBURY IBADAN NAIROBI DAR ES SALAAM LUSAKA
ADDIS ABABA BOMBAY CALCUTTA MADRAS KARACHI LAHORE
DACCA KUALA LUMPUR SINGAPORE HONG KONG TOKYO



PRINTED IN GREAT BRITAIN
BY W. S. COWELL LTD,
AT THE BUTTER MARKET, IPSWICH

TO
PROFESSOR OTTO PÄCHT

# PREFACE

The present study has been undertaken first because an examination of the stylistic development of manuscript illumination in Normandy in the late tenth and the eleventh centuries can be expected to shed light, as part of a more general movement, on the emergence of the new style of the period, the Romanesque.

Secondly, the Norman achievement in manuscript illumination has a special importance for the understanding of the development of pictorial art in England from the Conquest until the end of the twelfth century. By examining in detail Norman illumination on the eve of the Conquest, it is possible to get a better idea of what the Conquest meant for art in England. This has long been the subject of controversy and of the views held in the past none can be entirely satisfactory. The picture of a *tabula rasa*, a cultural disaster by which the immense achievements of the civilized Saxons were swept away by the vandal invaders, was replaced by the view that there was after all a great deal of continuity of the Anglo-Saxon tradition.[1] This, in turn, it could be pointed out, was not only a genuine continuity but due also to the fact of Norman dependence on Anglo-Saxon art. Norman art was therefore by implication derivative and provincial.[2]

There was continuity and Norman art was deeply imbued with Anglo-Saxon art. But to judge the Conquest as a cultural catastrophe is to ignore the fact that what the Normans brought was not something

[1] F. Wormald, 'The Survival of Anglo-Saxon illumination after the Norman Conquest', *Proceedings of the British Academy*, xxx (1944), 127–45.

[2] Dodwell, *Canterbury School*, 6–20. 'Norman illumination is to some extent a provincialization of English art. It does not compare in quality with English illumination, though from English art it partly derives', p. 8. Dodwell does however recognize that 'the copyist produces something more progressive than the creative artist', p. 9, and that there are other influences. See also for North French influence and the emerging Romanesque his paper, 'Un manuscrit enluminé de Jumièges au British Museum', *Jumièges, Congrès Scientifique du XIIIe Centenaire* (1955), 740.

inferior to but something different from what went before.[1] If the Norman methods of book production and illumination, therefore, are looked on as in part a forerunner of the twelfth-century achievement in England (there were, of course, many other factors and many Norman experiments were discarded), then the Conquest can no longer be viewed as an unmitigated disaster. Out of it emerged something new.

Amongst Norman abbeys Mont St Michel has a special place. There had been no great centre of book production in Normandy during the Carolingian period. Even apart from the Norman destructions there was, therefore, no indigenous tradition to influence scriptoria. Normandy stood between the two great centres of manuscript production of the tenth century, Anglo-Saxon England and Ottonian Germany, particularly the western schools of Reichenau, Trier, Echternach and Liège. As the centre of a famous pilgrimage and with widely scattered property as the result of it, Mont St Michel was perhaps better able to feel and absorb the different artistic currents of the time than any of the other Norman abbeys. In blending these and in making its own experiments the scriptorium was remarkably perceptive and original.

Finally Mont St Michel has been fortunate in that a large number of manuscripts from this period have been preserved. Not only that but the majority of them are still together at Avranches a few miles from where they were produced. This, of course, makes them far easier to study particularly as regards their script, than if they were widely scattered.

In October 1966, a Congress was held at Mont St Michel to celebrate the Millenary of the refoundation of the abbey as a regular Benedictine community in 966. The Benedictine monks had returned after nearly two hundred years and the abbey seemed again to be a living institution, the hospitable sanctuary and place of pilgrimage it must have been in the Middle Ages. Unfortunately it will be impossible for me to take full advantage of all the various studies which are to be published in connection with the celebrations, though I am grateful for the privilege of being

[1] The importance of Norman experiments towards the Romanesque in sculpture before the Conquest has recently been emphasized by G. Zarnecki, '1066 and architectural sculpture', *Proceedings of the British Academy*, lii (1962), 87–104. Anglo-Saxon sculptors on the contrary, even after the Conquest, did not understand the new principles of architectural sculpture.

present at the Congress. Six volumes are planned including the much needed edition of Robert de Torigni's cartulary. Two have appeared already which add much to our knowledge of the abbey's history, and of its spiritual, intellectual and artistic life.

It is a pleasant duty to acknowledge the help of teachers and friends. I should particularly like to thank Mr F. Avril, Professor B. Bischoff, Mr T. A. M. Bishop, Dr T. S. R. Boase, Professor M. de Bouard, Dr W. Cahn, Mr P. Chaplais, Miss Rosalie Green, Dr M. Gibson, Dr K. Hoffmann, Dr R. W. Hunt, Mr N. R. Ker, Dom J. Laporte, Dr R. W. Pfaff, and Professor F. Wormald for help and information. Dr John Plummer of the Pierpont Morgan Library, New York, Dr H. Lülfling of the Deutsche Staatsbibliothek, East Berlin, and Dr P. F. J. Obbema, Leiden, kindly answered questions about the Mont St Michel manuscripts in their custody.

For the travelling necessary to see manuscripts the Colt Fund of the Society for Mediaeval Archaeology made a generous grant and Magdalen College, Oxford, gave me a Senior Mackinnon scholarship which was used for the same purpose. I am also grateful to the Curators of the Bodleian Library for giving me study leave to complete revisions of my text. The authorities of the following institutions have kindly given me permission to reproduce objects in their care: Alençon, Bibliothèque municipale, Amiens, Bibliothèque municipale, Angers, Bibliothèque municipale, Arras, Bibliothèque municipale, Avranches, Bibliothèque municipale, Bamberg, Staatsbibliothek, Bayeux, Bibliothèque du chapitre, Berlin, Deutsche Staatsbibliothek and Staatsbibliothek Preussischer Kulturbesitz, Bordeaux, Bibliothèque municipale, Boulogne-sur-mer, Bibliothèque municipale, Brussels, Bibliothèque royale de Belgique, Cambrai, Bibliothèque municipale, Cambridge, Master and Fellows of Corpus Christi College, Master and Fellows of Trinity College, the University Library, Einsiedeln, Stiftsbibliothek, El Escorial, Biblioteca del monasterio, Göttingen Niedersächsische Staats- und Universitätsbibliothek, Ivrea, Biblioteca capitolare, Leiden, Bibliotheek der Rijksuniversiteit, Leipzig, Museum der Kunshandwerks, Le Mans, Bibliothèque municipale, London, Trustees of the British Museum, Milan, Biblioteca Ambrosiana, Munich, Bayerische Staatsbibliothek, New York,

Pierpont Morgan Library, Orléans, Bibliothèque municipale, Oxford, Bodleian Library, Master and Fellows of University College, Paris, Bibliothèque de l'Arsenal, Bibliothèque nationale, Rouen, Bibliothèque municipale, St Gall, Stiftsbibliothek, St Omer, Bibliothèque municipale, Tours, Bibliothèque municipale, Trier, Stadtbibliothek, Troyes, Bibliothèque municipale, Valenciennes, Bibliothèque municipale, Vatican, Biblioteca Apostolica, York Minster, Dean and Chapter.

I am most grateful to those of the above institutions who have allowed me to examine manuscripts and particularly to the two librarians at Avranches, first Mlle Desmier and then her successor M. Pierre Delalonde. They were most generous with their time and I owe a very special debt to their kindness and patience. The libraries which I have used most for my researches are the Fine Arts Library of the Ashmolean Museum, Oxford, and the Bodleian Library, Oxford. To the librarians and staff of both I am most grateful for their help and kindness. The photographic collections of the Warburg and Courtauld Institutes have been essential sources, and at the latter Mrs Joan Waissen and Dr Peter Kidson have continually helped me with the problem of illustrations.

Finally I have to thank my supervisor Professor Otto Pächt. Without him this work would not have been begun or ended. It owes everything to his guidance and inspiration.

J.J.G.A.

*Oxford, February 1968.*

# CONTENTS

# LIST OF ILLUSTRATIONS

## PLATE 46



## PLATE 47



## PLATE 48



## PLATE 49



## PLATE 50

# ABBREVIATIONS

Where a manuscript is referred to as MS. and a number or as Avranches and a number, e.g. MS. 72 or Avranches 72, this is to be found in the Bibliothèque Municipale, Avranches, Manche. The number is that given in the 'Catalogue Général', Volume x by H. Omont (1889).

| | |
| --- | --- |
| Avril, *Notes* (1) and (2) | Fr. Avril, 'Notes sur quelques manuscrits bénédictins normands du XIe et du XIIe siècle', *Mélanges d'Archéologie et d'Histoire*, lxxvi (1964), 491–525, and lxxvii (1965), 209–48. |
| Boinet | A. Boinet, *La Miniature carolingienne* (Paris, 1913). |
| *D.A.C.L.* | F. Cabrol, H. Leclercq, *Dictionnaire d'Archéologie chrétienne et de Liturgie* (Paris, 1903–53). |
| Dodwell, *Canterbury School* | C. R. Dodwell, *The Canterbury School of Illumination, 1066–1200* (Cambridge, 1954). |
| Exh., *Karl der Grosse* | *Karl der Grosse. Werk und Wirkung*, 10th Council of Europe exhibition (Aachen, 1965). |
| Exh., *Millénaire* | *Millénaire du Mont-Saint-Michel 966–1966, Exposition, Paris, Mont-Saint Michel, 18 mars–1 octobre, Caisse Nationale des monuments historiques* (Paris, 1966). |
| Goldschmidt, *Elfenbeinskulpturen* (1) and (2) | A. Goldschmidt, *Die Elfenbeinskulpturen aus der Zeit des Karolingischen und sächsischen Kaiser*, 2 vols. (Berlin, 1914–18). |
| Goldschmidt, *Elfenbeinskulpturen* (3) and (4) | A. Goldschmidt, *Die Elfenbeinskulpturen aus der romanischen Zeit XI-XIII Jahrhundert*, 2 vols. (Berlin, 1923–6). |
| Goldschmidt, *German illumination* (1) and (2) | A. Goldschmidt, *German illumination. Vol. i. The Carolingian period. Vol. ii. The Ottonian period.* (Florence and Paris, 1928). |
| Gout | P. Gout, *Le Mont-Saint-Michel*, 2 vols. (Paris, 1910). |
| Kendrick, *Late Saxon* | T. D. Kendrick, *Late Saxon and Viking Art* (London, 1949). |
| Köhler (1), (2) and (3) | W. Köhler, *Die Karolingischen Miniaturen*. I. *Die Schule von Tours*. II. *Die Hofschule Karls des Grossen*. III. 1. *Die Gruppe des Wiener Krönungs-Evangeliars*, 2. *Metzer Handschriften*, Deutscher Verein für Kunstwissenschaft (Berlin, 1963, 1958, 1960). |
| Lauer, *Enluminures romanes* | Ph. Lauer, *Les Enluminures romanes des manuscrits de la Bibliothèque Nationale* (Paris, 1927). |
| Leroquais, *Psautiers* | V. Leroquais, *Les Psautiers manuscrits des bibliothèques publiques de France*, 3 vols. (Paris, 1937). |

| | |
|---|---|
| Leroquais, *Sacramentaires* | V. Leroquais, *Les Sacramentaires et les missels manuscrits des bibliothèques publiques de France*, 4 vols. (Paris, 1924). |
| *MSS. à peintures* | *Les Manuscrits à peintures en France du VIIe au XIIe siècle*, Bibliothèque Nationale (Paris, exhibition catalogue, 1954). |
| Martin | J.-P. Martin, 'La Bibliothèque d'Avranches. Ses origines et ses richesses', *Normannia*, vi (1933), 551–64. |
| Micheli, *L'Enluminure* | G. L. Micheli, *L'Enluminure du Haut Moyen Age et les influences irlandaises* (Brussels, 1939). |
| *Millénaire* (1) and (2) | *Millénaire monastique du Mont Saint-Michel*. I. *Histoire et vie montoise*, ed. J. Laporte (Paris, 1967). II. *Vie montoise et rayonnement intellectuel*, ed. R. Foreville (Paris, 1967). |
| *P.L.* | *Patrologia Latina*, ed. J. P. Migne, 221 vols. (Paris, 1844–64). |
| Porcher, *French Miniatures* | J. Porcher, *French Miniatures from Illuminated Manuscripts*, transl. J. Brown (London, 1960). |
| *R.D.K.* | *Reallexicon zur deutschen Kunstgeschichte*, ed. O. Schmitt, H. M. von Erffa (Stuttgart, 1937 – in progress). |
| Rickert | M. Rickert, *Painting in Britain. The Middle Ages* (2nd edn., London, 1965). |
| *St Albans Psalter* | *The St Albans Psalter* 1. *The full-page miniatures* by Otto Pächt. 2. *The initials*, by C. R. Dodwell. 3. *Preface and description of the manuscript*, by Francis Wormald (Warburg Institute, London, 1960). |
| Schardt, *Das Initial* | A. Schardt, *Das Initial. Phantasie und Buchstabenmalerei des frühen Mittelalters* (Berlin, 1938). |
| Swarzenski, *Monuments* | H. Swarzenski, *Monuments of Romanesque Art. The art of Church Treasures in north-western Europe* (2nd edn., London, 1967). |
| Talbot Rice | D. Talbot Rice, *English Art 871–1100*, Oxford History of English Art, vol. ii (Oxford, 1952). |
| Van Moé, *Illuminated initials* | E. A. van Moé, *Illuminated initials in Medieval Manuscripts*, transl. J. Evans (London, 1950). |
| Volbach, *Elfenbeinarbeiten* | W. F. Volbach, *Elfenbeinarbeiten der Spätantike und des frühen Mittelalters* (Mainz, 1952). |
| Wormald, *Decorated initials* | F. Wormald, 'Decorated initials in English MSS. from A.D. 900 to 1100', *Archaeologia*, xci (1945), 107–135. |
| Wormald, *English Drawings* | F. Wormald, *English Drawings of the Tenth and Eleventh Centuries* (London, 1952). |
| Zimmermann | E. H. Zimmermann, *Vorkarolingische Miniaturen* (Berlin, 1916). |

# I

# HISTORY OF THE ABBEY TO *c.* 1100

THE abbey of Mont St Michel claimed in its Annals and Chronicles to have been founded in 708.[1] The area had been Christian earlier[2] and the first bishop of Avranches recorded is Nepos present at the Council of Orleans in 511.[3] In 708 the bishop was Autbert,[4] and it was to him that the Archangel Michael was said to have appeared with a command to build a church on the summit of the Mons Tumba. The legends of the foundation[5] closely follow those of Monte Gargano, the most famous shrine of St Michael in the west, whose church was dedicated in

[1] Annals of Mont St Michel are found in Avranches MS. 211, fols. 67–77 of the early twelfth century, published by L. Delisle, 'Chronique de Robert de Torigni, Abbé du Mont-Saint-Michel suivie de diverses opuscules historiques', *Société de l'histoire de Normandie*, 2 vols. (Rouen, 1872–3); and in Avranches MS. 213 of the fifteenth and sixteenth centuries, printed by P. Labbe, *Novae Bibliothecae Manuscriptorum Librorum*, i (1657), 347–52. The earliest surviving account of the foundation from Mont St Michel itself is in Avranches MS. 211, fols. 156–210, late tenth century; it has been printed as Appendix I of 'Les Curieuses Recherches du Mont-Saint-Michel' by Dom Thomas Le Roy, written between 1647 and 1648 and published by E. de Beaurepaire, *Mémoires de la Société des Antiquaires de Normandie*, ix (1877), 225–947. The chronicle and cartulary of Robert de Torigni, Avranches MS. 210, mid-twelfth century, will be published in full to commemorate the millenary of 1966. Later histories have been largely based on the researches of Le Roy and the earlier 'Histoire Générale de l'Abbaye du Mont-Saint-Michel', by Dom J. Huynes, finished in 1639, edited by E. de Beaurepaire, *Société de l'histoire de Normandie*, 2 vols. (1872–3). But see now *Millénaire* (1) especially the articles by Dom Hourlier and Dom Laporte.

[2] See Dom J. Laporte, 'Les origines du monachisme dans la province de Rouen,' *Revue Mabillon*, xxxi (1941), 22–41 and 49–68. The Avranchin and the Cotentin are the areas of Normandy for which most evidence of monasticism in the sixth century survives.

[3] *Gallia Christiana*, ed. P. Piolin, xi (1874), col. 468.

[4] Referred to as 'Le mythique Saint Aubert prétendu évêque d'Avranches . . .' by Dom J. Laporte, 'Gérard de Brogne à S. Wandrille et à S. Riquier', *Revue Bénédictine*, lxx (1960), 164. Nearly everything concerning Mont St Michel before the introduction of the community in 966 is uncertain and disputed. For a masterly account of this early period see J. Hourlier, 'Le Mont Saint-Michel avant 966', *Millénaire* (1), 13–28. For St Aubert see M. Lelegard, ibid, 29–52.

[5] These legends are contained already in the chronicle of Avranches, MS. 211, late tenth century, ed. de Beaurepaire, op. cit.

494 after the Archangel's appearance there in 492.[1] The church which was to be built at Mont St Michel was to be an hollowed-out cavern, as at Monte Gargano, sufficient to hold about a hundred people, and the site was revealed, according to one story at least, by the discovery of a tethered bull. St Autbert sent off at once to the older foundation for relics and when his messengers returned they found the church completed, having been dedicated on 16 October 709,[2] and everything ready for the twelve monks of the foundation to begin their new life.[3] The messengers brought back with them as relics of the Archangel a piece of his scarlet cloak and a fragment of the rock on which he had impressed his footprint.

For the next two hundred years there is little information about the Mont. In 870 the monk Bernard made his pilgrimage to Jerusalem and after his return visited 'Sanctum Michaelem ad duas Tumbas', where he found a church on the top of the hill which he unfortunately does not describe.[4] He does, however, say that it was surrounded by the sea, and tells of the miraculous way the waters stand back in walls so that the pilgrims can pass on the feast of St Michael.[5]

If this passage is really of this date, it shows that already in the ninth century the Mont was a common place of pilgrimage. Another interesting piece of information is that contained in the story of the wanderings of the monks of Glanveuil during the Norman invasions.[6] In 863 on their way to Fossez they met, at the crossing of a river, a band of pilgrims from Rome. The Abbot Odo questioned these men about the Holy Places and what they had seen and done. Eventually he asked them if they had any

1 *Acta Sanctorum, September t.VIII* (1762), 54 ff.

2 Avranches 211, ed. de Beaurepaire, op. cit.

3 Hourlier, op. cit., argues that the foundation consisted of monks (though not following the rule of St Benedict) not secular canons, though perhaps by the late tenth century they were canons.

4 T. Tobler, A. Molinier, *Itinera hierosoloymitana* (Publications de la Société de l'Orient latin), i (1879), 319. Incomplete text in *P.L.*, cxxi 569. Before leaving Rome Bernard and his two companions visited Monte Gargano which is more fully described.

5 The passage of the chronicle describing the return of the messengers from Monte Gargano in 709, 'quasi novum ingressi sunt orbem quem primum veprium densitate reliquerant plenum', seems to be at the base of the theory that the Mont once stood in the midst of a forest. Whether it became 'in periculo maris' as a result of a tidal wave or of a gradual encroachment has been endlessly discussed. See H. Elhai, 'Le Mont Saint-Michel. Le cadre naturel et les vicissitudes du site jusqu'au VIII$^{e}$ siecle', *Millénaire* (2), 14–29.

6 This is in Abbot Odo's letter to Adalmodus of Le Mans, *Acta Sanctorum, January*, i (1643), 1052.

books. And a clerk named Peter who was from Mont St Michel answered that he had. He had been away for two years and was now carrying back some old manuscripts written in an ancient hand, which contained the lives of St Benedict and five of his disciples, Honoratus, Simplicius, Theodorus, Valentianus and Maurus.[1] These Odo eventually managed to buy for 'no small sum'. There follows an interesting passage on the difficulties involved in deciphering and correcting the text. It was then rendered easier to understand without, of course, altering the sense.[2]

Would the monks of Mont St Michel have been able to read and copy these texts, how learned were they, and what sort of library would they have had? There is only one entry for the library at Avranches in the corpus publication of older Latin manuscripts.[3] This is various fragments of an eighth-century Insular Gospel book, with no indication of how or when it reached Mont St Michel. Of the other manuscripts of the tenth century or earlier, eight cannot be connected with the earliest productions of the scriptorium of the reformed community.[4] One of these comes

1 '. . . quaterniunculos nimia pene vetustate consumptos, antiquaria et obtunsa olim descriptos manu . . .'

2 '. . . salva fide dictorum ac miraculorum inibi repertorum.' For critical views of the text of the Life of St Maur and Odo's correction of it, see P. B. F. Adlhoch, 'Zur Vita S. Mauri', *Studien und Mitteilungen aus dem Benedicter-und dem Cistercienser-Orden*, xxvi (1905), 4–22 and 207–226.

3 *Codices Latini Antiquiores*, ed. E. A. Lowe, vi (1953), no. 730, and E. A. Lowe, *English Uncial* (1960), pl. xxix. The fragments are in Avranches, MSS. 48, 66 and 71, and in Leningrad. They are uncial, saec. viii, written in England. For arguments for a provenance from St Augustine's, Canterbury, see D. H. Wright, *The Vespasian Psalter* (Early English Manuscripts in facsimile) (1967), 58. Scollandus' abbacy of St Augustine's would then be a possible occasion for the manuscript to reach Normandy.

4 MS. 29, Homilies on Epistles of St Paul. Southern England, tenth century; MS. 32, fols. 37–267, Origen on Epistle to Romans. St Mesmin de Micy, diocese Chartres, late ninth or ninth-tenth century; MS. 87, St Augustine, Speculum. Tours or area, first half ninth century; this has two early Tours school type of initials; MS. 108, Liber scintillarum etc. French, ninth century, middle or second half; MS. 109, fols. 77–end, Isidore, Augustine, Jerome, etc. Rheims, ninth century middle; MS. 229, fols. 193–end, Poem on the categories etc. Close to Brittany, *c.* 900 or tenth century first half; MS. 236, Boethius, Musica, English, tenth to eleventh centuries; MS. 238, Cicero, de Oratore and Orator. Mid-ninth century.

Of these, MSS. 29 and 236 have additions of the eleventh century in what are perhaps Mont St Michel hands. There are no early marks of provenance. I am very grateful to Professor B. Bischoff for allowing me to quote his opinions on the dates and places assigned to these MSS. For the history and contents of the library see G. Nortier, 'Les Bibliothèques médiévales des abbayes bénédictines de Normandie. La Bibliothèque du Mont Saint-Michel', *Revue Mabillon*, 3e sér. xlvii (1957), 135–71.

from St Mesmin de Micy, in the diocese of Chartres, a monastery with connections with Jumièges. Some of the others could have perhaps belonged to the canons, but there is no positive evidence for this. They could equally well have been brought in by the new community, or acquired later. Dom Hourlier concludes that the *Revelatio*, MS. 211, copies an earlier text belonging to the canons.[1] They would surely also have had some form of liturgical books.

Mont St Michel seems to have avoided destruction in the Norman invasions. Besides the canons' cells presumably there were pilgrim hostelries and some sort of hamlet. Its site was strong, of course, and people from around may have fled there for protection. Or perhaps there was little to plunder anyway.

In 911, by the agreement of St Clair-sur-Epte, a *terra* in Normandy was ceded to Rollo, the leader of a band of Northmen, by Charles the Simple, and Rollo became a Christian.[2] Rollo added other territories and by 933 the Avranchin and Cotentin had become part of the Duchy. Perhaps at some time after this the church, which later was to form a crypt of the Romanesque church, was built to replace the oratory of St Autbert.[3]

The most recent study of this church (now known as Notre-Dame-sous-Terre) by M. Vallery-Radot supposes that there were three stages in the building. Of the original building of uncertain date the north and south walls survive. To this was added a central arcade of two arches built of brick and the west wall, possibly after a fire in 992. A third stage was the addition of a further ante-chamber to the west and other building

[1] *Millénaire* (2), 124–8.

[2] For the early history of the Duchy see M. de Bouard, 'Le Duché de Normandie', *Histoire des Institutions Françaises au Moyen Age*, I (1957).

[3] For the summary of the architectural history of Mont St Michel given below I have followed Paul Gout, *Le Mont-Saint-Michel* (Paris, 1910). For a review of this by E. Mâle see *Journal des Savants*, 9e Année, nouvelle série, no. 6 (June, 1911), pp. 260–75. It is also corrected and supplemented in important respects by G. Bazin, *Le Mont-Saint-Michel* (1933).

For the Carolingian church of Notre-Dame-sous-Terre see M. de Bouard, 'L'église Notre-Dame-sous-Terre au Mont Saint-Michel. Essai de datation', *Journal des Savants* (January–March, 1961), 10–27. Y. Froidevaux, 'L'église Notre-Dame-sous-terre de l'abbaye du Mont Saint-Michel', *Les Monuments historiques de la France* (1961), 145–66. J. Vallery-Radot, 'Quelques remarques sur l'église Notre-Dame-sous-Terre au Mont-Saint-Michel', *Bulletin de la Société Nationale des Antiquaires de France* (1962), 100–6. There are no known parallels to the building to help in dating it. Cf. E. G. Carlson, 'Religious architecture in Normandy 911–1100', *Gesta*, v (1966), 27–33.

to the south. This was in connection with the plan for the Romanesque church begun in 1023, the north-west aisle wall and nave piers of which rested on the walls of the church below. Additional support for the piers had to be built below. After the destruction of the three western bays of the nave in 1776 a wall was built across the lower church to support the new façade. This it has only recently been possible to remove, using a reinforced concrete support to replace it.

De Bouard and Vallery-Radot have made the further important suggestion that there was an upper church to the east of Notre-Dame-sous-Terre. The evidence for this in the sources, the record of miracles at the main altar and the account of the chronicle in MS. 211 stating that the churches (plural) were burnt in 992, is supported by the foundations found by Gout, which he wrongly supposed to be those of the conventual buildings. Another important discovery made by Froidevaux is of a rounded wall of masonry at the east end of the south chancel of Notre-Dame-sous-Terre. His suggestion that this may be a relic of St Autbert's oratory modelled on the round end of Monte Gargano is very plausible, explaining, as he points out, the trouble taken to preserve Notre-Dame-sous-Terre when the Romanesque church was built. There were two windows on the south and west sides of the building and one on the north. At the east end were two bays under arches and in each, on their north and south sides, niches with stone benches. The church got its name of Notre-Dame-sous-Terre after the removal there in the seventeenth century of a statue of the Virgin from the north crypt chapel of the main church. Gout saw traces of murals in the north chapel – a border formed by a series of juxtaposed 'M's. The south chapel was dedicated to the Trinity and traditionally St Autbert had celebrated at its altar. The recess above the altar was probably the treasury and would have been a very suitable place for exposure of the relics to the pilgrims where they could easily be seen but were quite safe.

In 911 Rollo was said to have recalled the canons who had fled, returned their possessions to them and added others.[1] Between 933 and

[1] Dudo of St Quentin, *De moribus et actis primorum Normanniae Ducum*, ed. J. Lair (Caen, 1865), Bk. I, ch. 30, p. 170. Also interpolations of Ordericus Vitalis in William of Jumièges 'Gesta Normannorum Ducum', ed. J. Marx, *Société de l'histoire de Normandie* (1914), Bk. II, ch. 17, p. 151.

942 William Longsword gave them various villages[1]. He was succeeded after his assassination in 943, by Duke Richard I, who was still a boy. Duke Richard's visits to Mont St Michel are said to have been frequent and it was he who in 966 decided to replace the canons by a regular Benedictine community. According to the cartulary the canons employed clerks to take their services and spent their time in hunting and other pleasures, in spite of the prayers and threats of Richard.[2] His decision to replace them was taken in conjunction with Hugo, archbishop of Rouen, and Raoul of Ivry, and confirmed by King Lothair.[3] Only two of the canons remained. Durandus, repenting his errors, asked to become a monk, was accepted by the abbot and given the office of *capellanus*. Bernerius, who was too ill to be moved, was kept under guard. But in spite of the Duke's precautions the canons evidently managed to conceal their most precious possession, the relics of St Autbert.

Duke Richard chose as the first abbot Mainard, a monk originally of St Peter, Mons Blandiniensis, at Ghent, whom he had in 960 made abbot of St Wandrille.[4] The monasticism he thus introduced was the reformed monasticism of Lotharingia, which had spread from Gérard of Brogne's abbey near Namur to Flanders and in particular to the monasteries at Ghent and St Omer.[5] The cartulary says that Duke Richard decorated the altars, enriched the treasury with a piece of precious goldsmith's

[1] See M. Fauroux, *Recueil des actes des ducs de Normandie de 911 à 1066* (1961), 21, no. 8.

[2] Avranches MS. 210, twelfth century, '. . . solis conversationibus, venationibus ceterisque intenti erant voluptatibus . . .'

[3] L. Halphen and F. Lot, 'Recueil des actes de Lothaire et de Louis V, rois de France (959–87)', *Académie des inscriptions et belles-lettres* (1908), no. 24. A spurious bull of Pope John XIII was later interpolated. See below, p. 15.

[4] 'Inventio et Miracula Sancti Vulfranni', ed. Dom J. Laporte, *Mélanges, Société de l'histoire de Normandie* (1938), ch. 12, p. 30. It is curious that in the obituaries it is St Bavon not St Peter's with which there seem to be close ties. Cf. J. Laporte, 'Les obituaires du Mont Saint-Michel', *Millénaire* (1), 728–9.

[5] For Gérard of Brogne see various articles in *Revue Bénédictine*, lxx, no. 1 (1960), resulting from the Congress held at Maredsous in 1959, the millenary of St Gérard's death; and particularly Dom J. Laporte, 'Gérard de Brogne à S. Wandrille et à S. Riquier'. He suggests, p. 162–3, that Mainard, according to the 'Inventio Sancti Wulfrani,' op. cit., ch. 12, 'alto parentum sanguine oriundus', was of the family of Wichmann II, Count of Hamaland. Wichmann II married the daughter of Arnulf of Flanders. This connection would explain Mainard's success at St Wandrille where St Gérard had failed. See also J. Laporte, 'L'abbaye du Mont Saint-Michel aux X^e^ et XI^e^ siècles', *Millénaire* (1), 53–80.

work, built new quarters for the monks and added a wall around the buildings.[1] The new buildings for the monks would be to make possible communal existence required by the rule of St Benedict. Abbot Mainard probably also brought books, ornaments and relics from his old monastery as he had to St Wandrille.[2]

Abbot Mainard I died on 16 April 991, and his funeral was attended by the Duke. He was succeeded by his nephew, Mainard II, who had been prior at St Wandrille earlier. In the following year occurred the fire which led to the replacement of the wooden roof of the church by barrel vaults to reduce the risk in future. This fire was connected by Rodulfus Glaber with the appearance of a comet at this time.[3] His description of the abbey, in a passage of his history written between 1046 and 1049, as one which is widely venerated, is an indication of the importance it had already achieved in the mid-eleventh century.[4] Another such indication is Ethelred's instructions to his troops raiding the French coast about the year 1000 to spare Mont St Michel lest 'they should burn down a place of such sanctity and religion'.[5]

The abbey's property continued to grow. Gonnor, Richard I's wife, gave the villages of Bretteville and Domjean in 1015.[6] Richard himself is said to have confirmed the Canons' possessions and added others.[7] Conan of Brittany gave the parish of Villamée in 990.[8] Under Mainard II, Geoffrey of Brittany made further grants and St Maieul, abbot of Cluny, *c.* 906–94, gave lands in Touraine.[9] Other gifts are recorded by Rodulfus, viscount of Maine, about 994, and Hugo I, count

1 As Dom J. Laporte, op. cit., *Rev. Bén*, lxx (1960), 164, says, among the Duke's motives was no doubt the wish to have a firm base on the Mont for the reconquest of the area from the Bretons.

2 'Inventio sci Wulfrani', op. cit., ch. 14, p. 32, '. . . libros quoque et cartas et quaedam ornamenta sed et filacteria cum preciosis sanctorum pigneribus ab abbate suo et fratribus sibi indulta illuc [sc. St Wandrille] convexit'.

3 Rodulfus Glaber, *Historiarum Libri Quinque*, ed. M. Prou (1886), Bk. III, ch. 3, p. 60.

4 'toto orbe nunc usque habetur venerabilis.'

5 See William of Jumièges, op. cit. Bk. V, ch. 4, p. 76 '. . . ne tantae sanctitatis et religionis locum igne concremarent'.

6 See Fauroux, op. cit., no. 17, p. 98.

7 *Gallia Christiana*, xi (1874), col. 513D.

8 *Gallia Christiana*, xi (1874), col. 513E.

9 *Gallia Christiana*, xi (1874), col. 514A.

of Maine between 955 and 1015,[1] and in 997 the priory of L'Abbayette was founded with grants by Ivo and Guy on the borders of Maine and the Avranchin.[2] Also in this early period, Heriwardus, a monk of the abbey, succeeded his brother Herluin as abbot of Gembloux in 987.[3] Both Conan I of Brittany and Geoffrey his son and successor, were buried in the abbey. And about this time Norgaudus, bishop of Avranches, is said to have become a monk.[4]

Abbot Mainard II died on 14 July 1009. It is from the period of his abbacy that a list survives of the monks of the abbey, fifty that are alive and thirty-eight that are dead, including the former canons Bernerius and Durandus. This is written on the end leaves of Orléans, Bibliothèque Municipale, MS. 105, an Anglo-Saxon Sacramentary of the late tenth century, probably from Winchcombe, which was at Fleury in the early eleventh century.[5] The hand which wrote the list is almost certainly the same as that found in several of the Mont St Michel manuscripts still at Avranches, and thus gives a dating for them.

In 1001 an event of some importance for the future history of the abbey was Duke Richard II's summons to William of Volpiano, abbot of St Bénigne at Dijon, to Normandy to reform the abbey of the Holy Trinity,

[1] *Cartulaire de Saint-Victeur au Mans*, ed. Bertrand de Broussillon (1895), nos. 1–3, with photographs of some of the original charters destroyed with the Archives de la Manche at St Lô in 1944.

[2] *Cartulaire de l'Abbayette*, ed. Bertrand de Broussillon (1894), nos. 1–2, with facsimiles. Ivo belonged to the family of Bellême. Laporte, *Millénaire* (1), 66.

[3] *Gallia Christiana*, xi (1874), col. 513E.

[4] Known from charters in favour of Fécamp. Fauroux, op. cit., no. 4 in 990, and in favour of Mont St Michel, ibid. no. 16, *c.* 1015. See also *Gallia Christiana*, xi (1874), col. 514A.

[5] Published by L. Delisle, 'Mémoire sur des anciens Sacramentaires' (1886), no. lxxix, 211–18 and Appx. XVI, 389–91. See D. Gremont, L. Donnat, 'Fleury, Le Mont Saint-Michel et l'Angleterre à la fin du Xe et au début du XIe siècle à propos du manuscrit d'Orléans No. 127(105),' *Millénaire* (1), 751–93, pl. xiv, for a detailed examination of the manuscript and of links with Fleury. In whatever way it reached Fleury, it seems more likely to me that the list of monks was written in at Fleury by a Mont St Michel monk who had gone there to copy manuscripts. See below p. 35 for a visit to Corbie by the same scribe for this purpose. No contemporary record of connections with Fleury survives but it appears in later lists of affiliated houses. See J. Laporte, 'Les associations spirituelles entre les monastères', *Cahiers Léopold Delisle*, xii (1963), 29–38, publishing lists from Avranches MSS. 214 and 211 of *c.* 1300–14, 1326 and *c.* 1400. These affiliations certainly in some cases go back to a much earlier date.

Fécamp, which was still occupied by canons.[1] Richard I had earlier appealed to St Maieul of Cluny for monks but had been refused.[2] According to both Robert de Torigni and the 'Life of St. William' by Rodulfus Glaber, William of Volpiano became 'custos' besides of Jumièges, St Ouen, and Bernay, also of Mont St Michel.[3] When this was exactly is not clear, but perhaps at the accession as abbot of Hildebertus I. This was before the death of Mainard II who was too old to continue to rule. Hildebertus, who was a monk of the abbey, is described as though young, of exceptional intelligence and moral worth.[4] This then might have been an occasion for St William's supervision.

Hildebertus I's rule was notable for the discovery of the relics of St Autbert concealed in the wall of the canon Bernerius' cell against the church.[5] Their translation was celebrated by the monks of all the priories 'Abbatiae obnoxii'. Hildebert I died in 1017 and was succeeded by his nephew Hildebert II, who only ruled for five years until his death on 30 September 1023. But it was in the last year of his life, according to the twelfth-century Annals and to Robert de Torigni, that work was begun on the building of a new abbey church.[6] In 1026 when Duke Richard II died on 23 August, little more than the foundations seem to have been

[1] For William of Volpiano see especially E. Sackur, *Die Cluniacenser* (1892); W. Williams, 'William of Dijon: a monastic reformer of the early XIth century', *Downside Review*, lii (1934), 520–45; M. Chaume, 'Les origines paternelles de Guillaume de Volpiano', *Revue Mabillon*, xiv (1924), 68–77; J. Depoin, 'Un problème éclairci. L'agnation restituée de Saint Guillaume', *Revue Mabillon*, xiv (1924), 243–7.

[2] 'Excerpta ex libro de revelatione, aedificatione et auctoritate monasterie fiscannensis', *P.L.*, cxli, 848. On the reasons for St Maieul's refusal see Laporte, op. cit., *Revue Mabillon*, xxxi (1941), 52.

[3] Rodulfus Glaber, 'Vita Sancti Guillelmi', *P.L.*, cxli, 865 §23. Robert de Torigni, 'De immutatione ordinis monachorum', ed. Delisle, op. cit. vol. ii, 192–3.

[4] 'Juvenili aevo floridus, sed acumine vivacis ingenii praeclarus, morumque maturitate gravidus.' See Fauroux, op. cit., no. 12, p. 85. Richard II's designation of Hildebertus as abbot, dated 1009 but only in the copies. The original or an ancient copy was lost in the disastrous destruction of the Archives of the Manche at St Lô in 1944. There is a copy in the twelfth-century cartulary, Avranches MS. 210, fol. 71^v^.

[5] Lelegard, *Millénaire* (1), 42–52.

[6] Avranches MS. 211, fols. 67–77, published by L. Delisle, 'Chronique de Robert de Torigni', op. cit., ii, 219. Gout, thinking erroneously that Richard II married Judith in 1017, says that it was in that year that plans for the new church were laid. Laporte, however, *Millénaire* (1), 271, considers that Hildebert I lived until 1023 and his nephew was then elected by the monks but replaced by the Duke's orders.

laid, though it must be remembered that this, in view of the site, was a task of great difficulty.

Hildebert II was succeeded by Theodoricus,[1] a monk of St Bénigne, Dijon, who ruled at the same time both Jumièges and Bernay, and had been formerly prior of Fécamp.[2] His custody of Jumièges explains the similarities between the two churches both of which have a choir with deambulatory but no radiating chapels.[3] Theodoricus died in 1027 or early 1028 and was succeeded by Almodus, who had been born at Le Mans. However in 1033 Almodus was replaced. This event is perhaps to be connected with the expedition of Alan III of Brittany into the Avranchin in 1032, and the Duke's reprisals. As a result Alan came to Mont St Michel to be reconciled to Duke Robert through their mutual uncle, Robert, Archbishop of Rouen (987–1037),[4] and to do homage for his lands.[5] Almodus was made abbot of St Vigor, at Cerisy-la-forêt, a foundation of Duke Robert's own,[6] and was still alive in 1049.[7]

Further indications of the abbey's growing importance and wealth are found in these years. Duke Richard II had married Judith, daughter of Geoffrey of Brittany, in the abbey some time before 1008.[8] In 1015 he confirmed his mother Gonnor's grant to the abbey and also the grant of Tissey by Robert of Mortain.[9] Under Hildebert I, Hugo, count of Maine, gave land at 'Vedobris'.[10] Amongst Richard II's gifts were, between 1017

1 The question of the order of succession of Almodus and Theodoricus, a muddle going back to the Annals in Avranches MS. 211 (see Delisle, op. cit.), has been cleared up by H. Chanteux, 'L'Abbé Thierry et les églises de Jumièges, du Mont Saint-Michel et de Bernay', *Bulletin Monumental*, xcviii (1939), 67–72.

2 Chronicon S. Benigni, *P.L.*, clxii, 824, and the 'Vita Sancti Guillelmi', by Rodulfus Glaber, *P.L.*, cxli, 861.

3 See Bazin, op. cit., p. 111, and Chanteux, op. cit., p. 70.

4 See William of Jumièges, op. cit., Bk. VI, chs. 8 and 10, pp. 105–110.

5 Gout, op. cit., makes various conjectures as to these events but gives no evidence for them. Further gifts of land in Brittany were received at this time. See Laporte, *Millénaire* (1), 73–4.

6 See Laporte, op. cit., *Revue Mabillon*, xxxi (1941), 56.

7 See Chanteux, op. cit., p. 69.

8 See William of Jumièges, op. cit., Bk. V, ch. 13, p. 88.

9 See Fauroux, op. cit., nos. 16, 17. The original of no. 16 survived until the destruction of the Archives de la Manche. Both are known also from the twelfth-century cartulary, Avranches, MS. 210.

10 Bertrand de Broussillon, 'Cartulaire de Saint-Victeur', op. cit., no. 4 with facsimile of the original destroyed in 1944.

and 1026, his domaine at Verson in the Bessin and, between 1022–26, the abbey of St Pair in the Cotentin with its dependencies. He also confirmed the abbey's earlier possessions.[1] These grants are no doubt as Gout has suggested to be connected with the plans for building the new abbey church. Between 1027 and 1033 Duke Robert again confirmed the abbey's titles and between 1032 and 1035 made new gifts including half the island of Guernsey.[2]

Almodus was replaced in 1033 by Suppo who was by birth a Roman and had been abbot of William of Volpiano's foundation of Fruttuaria in northern Italy in the diocese of Ivrea.[3] William of Volpiano had died in 1031 on 1 January at Fécamp, but Suppo had been 'in omni sanctitate educatus' by him and it was William's successor at Fécamp, Abbot John, according to Rodulfus Glaber, who made him abbot.[4] There is some evidence that he had been nominated to the abbey in 1023, but whether because he could not leave Fruttuaria or for some other reason, he did not take up the office till ten years later.[5] He brought with him from Italy relics of St Lawrence, St Agapitus and St Innocent, also gold and silver vessels for the church, the inscriptions on two of which are recorded, books and two silver angels.[6] It is in the years of his abbacy and of his two successors that the scriptorium reaches its highest point of activity and excellence. It is, therefore, the more curious to find that in 1048 Suppo resigned the abbacy and returned to Fruttuaria.

1 See Fauroux, op. cit., nos. 47 and 49.

2 See Fauroux, op. cit., nos. 65 and 73. The original of this latter grant was destroyed in 1944 but a facsimile exists in V. Hunger, *Histoire de Verson* (Caen, 1908). It is a curious document with a charter of William the Conqueror included between the text and the witnesses' signatures: Fauroux, op. cit., no. 111. However both parts are accepted as genuine by Mme Fauroux.

3 For the foundation of Fruttuaria see bibliography of William of Volpiano, above and also Dom A. Wilmart, 'Jean l'Homme de Dieu. Auteur d'un traité attribué à S. Bernard', *Revue Mabillon*, xv (1925), 5–29.

4 'Vita Sancti Willelmi', *P.L.*, cxli, 865.

5 This in the List of Abbots from Avranches MS. 213, fol. 178, fifteenth and sixteenth centuries, printed by P. Labbe, *Novae Bibliothecae Manuscriptorum Librorum* (1657), 350–2. '1033. Ordinatus fuit Suppo Abbas. Multa bona contulit Abbatiae et propter odium monachorum recessit et reversus est ad solum proprium.'

6 J. Mabillon, *Annales Ordinis S. Benedicti*, iv (1707), 496. For a list of the abbey's relics in the seventeenth century see the 'Histoire Générale', by Dom J. Huynes, ed. de Beaurepaire, op. cit., ii, pp. 36ff. Robert de Torigni tells us he remounted Suppo's relics, ed. Delisle, op. cit., i, p. 358.

According to the Annals in Avranches MS. 213 Suppo left because of the hostility of the monks. The earlier Annals, fols. 67–77 of Avranches MS. 211, of the twelfth century, only says under 1048 that Radulfus became abbot 'vivente Suppone'.[1] *Gallia Christiana* suggests that the charge was 'dilapidatio bonorum',[2] which might be substantiated by a manuscript made in the scriptorium at Suppo's orders for Fécamp surviving at Rouen,[3] and by a charter in which lands at Dol given by Suppo to Rivalo are returned by his son William in about 1060.[4]

However, it seems possible that Suppo's departure is connected with Gui de Brionne's rebellion in 1047, which was crushed by the Conqueror at the Battle of Val-les-Dunes. Gui's main support came from lower Normandy, particularly from Rannulf of Bayeux and Niel of St Sauveur, viscount of the Cotentin.[5] Since, however, he was also the grandson of Otto William I of Burgundy to whom it has been shown William of Volpiano was related,[6] it is not at all unlikely that William's disciple Suppo had aided him.[7] If this is so, it would have a bearing on the part played by Cluny in Normandy after this date.

Two monks noted at the time for their learning entered the monastery probably during Suppo's rule. One was Robert of Tombelaine, who

[1] 'Chronique de Robert de Torigni', ed. Delisle, op. cit., ii, p. 220. Suppo's death is noted in 1061. Rodulfus Glaber, *P.L.*, cxli, 865 says Suppo left 'quibusdam contrarietatibus exortis.'

[2] *Gallia Christiana*, xi (1874), col. 515C.

[3] Rouen, Bib. Mun., MS. A.143. For other manuscripts of which the same may be true, now in Paris, see below, App. IV.

[4] *Cartulaire de l'Abbayette*, ed. Bertrand de Broussillon, no. 5.

[5] Gout, op. cit., i, pp. 120–21, following Dom Huynes, says that Niel gave all his possessions in the island of Sercq to Mont St Michel and became a monk there in 1048. It is not clear what his evidence is for this. By a charter of 1035–48 (Fauroux, op. cit., no. 111) William the Conqueror gave Mont St Michel the islands of Sercq and Aurigny in exchange for half of Guernsey given them by his father Duke Robert. In 1054 or possibly 1055 William confirmed a gift made by the priest Niellus of Ste Colombe to Mont St Michel, see Fauroux, op. cit., no. 132. Niellus is called 'presbiter' in the Mont St Michel cartulary, Avranches MS. 210. But in a leaf from a fifteenth-century cartulary lost at St Lô in 1944, but copied by G. de Beausse, a seventeenth- or eighteenth-century hand added 'vicecomes' in red ink. According to William of Poitiers, ed. R. Foreville (1952), Bk. I, ch. 9, Niel of St Sauveur was exiled. Robert de Torigni, ed. Delisle, op. cit., i, p. 44, says of the conspirators only 'quosdam exulavit, quosdam corpore minuit'.

[6] Chaume, op. cit., *Revue Mabillon*, xiv (1924), 68ff.

[7] Laporte and others, *Millénaire* (1), 76 etc., are inclined to see the troubles as resulting from rivalries between the local monks and outsiders from upper Normandy. The close connections witnessed by the manuscripts give no support to theories of quarrels with Fécamp.

wrote a commentary on the Song of Songs dedicated to Ansfrid of Préaux.[1] He was made abbot of his new foundation of St Vigor, Bayeux, by bishop Odo in 1066, but after Odo's imprisonment by the Conqueror returned either to Mont St Michel or to Italy.[2]

He refers in the preface of his commentary to Anastasius, 'dilectissimus frater et dominus meus', at whose request he undertook it. Anastasius was identified by Mabillon with a monk whose life he printed from a manuscript obtained at the church of St Martin, Doydes, diocese of Rieux. This Anastasius had been born at Venice[3] and from there, after a good education which left him with a thorough knowledge of Greek as well as Latin,[4] he travelled north until he came to Mont St Michel, where he became a monk. However, on learning that the abbot was simonaical – for this reason assumed to be Suppo[5] – he retired to a deserted island near by, which was probably Tombelaine. From there he was persuaded to go to Cluny by Abbot Hugh[6] and later at the order of Gregory VII he was sent to preach in Spain. He died at Doydes on his way back to Cluny again after a second period as a hermit in the Pyrenees, and his biographer seems to have written his life about 1100–1120 some thirty years after his death. The Anastasius who wrote a letter on the subject of the real presence to abbot Gerard, perhaps of St Aubin, Angers,[7] and the Anastasius referred to by St Anselm in one of his letters to Robert of Tombelaine are also perhaps the same man.[8] The few phrases of Greek, transliterated and with a Latin translation, which seem designed for a pilgrim to the East (added to Avranches MS. 236 on fol. 97[v]) may possibly be connected with him.[9]

1 *P.L.*, cl, 1361. F. Stegmüller, *Repertorium Biblicum Medii Aevi*, v (1955), 163–5.

2 *Ordericus Vitalis*, ed. Prévost, vol. iii, pp. 264 and 429, Bk. VIII, chs. 1 and 25. See also *Histoire litéraire de la France*, viii (1747), 334–41, and P. Quivy, J. Thiron, 'Robert de Tombelaine et son commentaire sur le Cantique des Cantiques', *Millénaire* (2), 347–56.

3 J. Mabillon, *Annales Ordinis S. Benedicti*, iv (1707), 497.

4 'tam Graecis quam Latinis litteris omnibus ad unguem . . . imbutus.'

5 *Acta Sanctorum, October t.VII* (1845), 1136 with discussion of various questions involved in the Life. Also printed *P.L.*, cxliii, 425ff.

6 This might connect with the possibility of Suppo's removal for political reasons.

7 Printed from a manuscript belonging to the abbey of Sts Sergius and Bacchus, Angers, by Dom L. D'Achery, *Lanfranci Opera Omnia* (1648), 21–22.

8 *P.L.*, clviii, 1067. F. S. Schmitt, *S. Amselmi Opera Omnia*, iii (1946), 102–3.

9 As Mme Nortier suggests, op. cit., *Revue Mabillon*, xlvii (1957), 138. MS. 107 contains a glossary in Hebrew, Greek and Latin found elsewhere. See Bischoff, op. cit., Appx. II.

Also during Suppo's abbacy Lanfranc is said to have taught at Avranches. The evidence for this is late,[1] but further support for the existence of a school there is in an addition to Eadmer's Life of St Anselm, which appears to derive from the Bec tradition.[2] For St Anselm also is said to have visited the schools at Avranches before going to Bec.

In 1040 the knight Raginaldus and his mother Hersinde gave the monastery of St Victor which had been destroyed in the Norman invasions and which was in the suburbium of Le Mans, to the abbey.[3] This is important in view of stylistic connections with Le Mans manuscripts later in the century. About this time also King Edward the Confessor is said to have given the abbey St Michael's Mount, Cornwall with the manors of 'Vennesire', possibly Winnianton, and 'Ruminella,' possibly Treiwall.[4] The evidence is a charter copied into Robert de Torigni's cartulary of the mid-twelfth century, now Avranches MS. 210. However, one of the witnesses is Robert, Archbishop of Rouen, who died in 1037, and Edward signs as King. As P. L. Hull says, 'the grant could only be made if Edward was King *de facto* or *de jure* and there is no evidence for this before 1042'.[5] Unfortunately the evidence of Domesday book is not conclusive either, as to whether Mont St Michel had lands in the area or not at King Edward's death.[6] After the Conquest there were disputes with

[1] Milo Crispin, Life of Lanfranc, *P.L.*, cl, 30.

[2] *The Life of St. Anselm Archbishop of Canterbury by Eadmer*, ed. R. W. Southern (1962), pp. xiv and 8 n.1.

[3] Bertrand de Broussillon, *Cartulaire de Saint-Victeur*, no. 6 with facsimile, pl. iv, of the original charter destroyed at St Lô in 1944. See also no. 8.

[4] The question is fully discussed in 'The Cartulary of St. Michael's Mount, Hatfield House MS. 315', edited with introduction by P. L. Hull, *Devon and Cornwall Record Society*, new series vol. 5 (1962). Also P. L. Hull, 'The foundation of St. Michael's Mount in Cornwall', *Millénaire* (1), 703–24.

[5] op. cit., 1962, p. xiii, and Appx I. Mme Fauroux, op. cit., no. 76, on the other hand accepts the charter and dates it 1033–4, connecting it with Edward's abortive invasion of England.

[6] The Exon Domesday, *Victoria County History*, *A History of the County of Cornwall*, Part 8 (1924), 'The Domesday Survey for Cornwall', L. F. Salzman and T. Taylor, fol. 208b: 'St. Michael has 1 manor which is called Treiwal which Brismar held T.R.E. Therein are two hides of land which have never rendered geld . . .'. On fol. 508v, however, the entry runs: 'St Michael has one manor which is called Treiwal from which the Count of Mortain has taken away 1 hide which was in the demesne of the Saint T.R.E. . . .' Hull, op. cit., p. xi, concludes 'the manor of Treiwal was undoubtedly the land of St. Michael in 1066'. D. J. A. Matthew, *The Norman Monasteries and their English Possessions* (1962), 24, on the other hand, says: 'the evidence for any grants of lands in Cornwall to the Norman Mont St. Michel before the Conquest is unconvincing'. This was also E. Dupont's opinion, 'Les possessions du Mont St Michel en Angleterre', *Revue d'études Normandes*, ii (1908), 341–2. To the contrary see also Hull, *Millénaire* (1), 709.

Robert, Count of Mortain, who eventually gave the Mount to the abbey, and these may have been an inducement to forge a charter.[1] There is no evidence for the establishment of a priory at the Mount before 1135.[2]

Suppo was replaced by Radulfus who was brother of Roger de Beaumont, and therefore related to the Duke.[3] Originally a monk of Fécamp, he continued the building of the church and in 1048 a start was made on the four great pillars of the crossing.[4] These and the high parts of the choir were finished with the arches and vaults in the succeeding ten years. This date is confirmed by the discovery of two coins of Eudes de Penthièvre of Rennes (1040–7) under the paving of the crossing.

Radulfus died after his return from a pilgrimage to Jerusalem, sometime between *c.* 1055 and 1058.[5] During his rule Duke William had confirmed the gift of William Pichenoht, who gave Perelle in Guernsey to the abbey on becoming a monk on 25 December 1054. This is the only original charter of the abbey to survive from this period.[6] Radulfus' successor was Rannulfus I, by birth from Bayeux, but a monk of the abbey. Both the year of Radulfus' death and the year of Rannulfus' succession are uncertain. There seems to have been a dispute between Duke William and the monks as to the election of the new abbot, causing an interregnum. It is on this supposition that Halphen and Lot date the interpolation of the spurious bull of Pope John XIII (confirming the monks' right to elect an abbot from amongst themselves) in the act of Lothair confirming the

1 Hull accepts a grant of *c.* 1070 by Robert of Mortain, cartulary no. 1. There was certainly a later grant 1087–91. Hull, op. cit. (1962), Appx II and *Millénaire* (1), 722.

2 Hull, op. cit. (1962), pp. xvii–xviii and *Millénaire* (1), 720.

3 For the connections of Radulfus see L. Grodecki, 'Les débuts de la sculpture romane en Normandie: Bernay', *Bulletin Monumental*, cviii (1950), 11ff., correcting an error in Robert de Torigni, ed. Delisle, op. cit., ii, 194.

4 See P. Gout, op. cit., ii, 406, based on Dom Le Roy.

5 In the Annals of MS. 211 printed by Delisle, op. cit., p. 220, the date is given as 1060 and Rannulfus is added in a later hand as ninth abbot in 1063. The other Annals (p. 232) gives Radulfus' death as 1053 (perhaps a copyist's error, MLIII for MLVIII?). The MS. 213 list of abbots printed by Labbe, op. cit., i, 351, says that he died 'in itinere Hierusalem' in 1058 and that there was a two-year gap before Rannulfus succeeded. Laporte, *Millénaire* (1), 273 argues that Radulfus died in 1055 and Rannulfus succeeded *c.* 1057.

6 See Fauroux, op. cit., no. 133. It is in the Archives de la Manche, H. fonds du Mont St Michel, and a facsimile will be published in V. H. Galbraith and P. Chaplais, *Facsimiles of Norman and Anglo-Norman Charters*.

foundation, to the years 1058–60.[1] Rannulfus ruled until 1085 and he set about finishing the nave of the church. At the east end of the new church, three crypt chapels had been built, the Chapel of St Martin on the south side, the Chapel of the Virgin, called from the thirteenth century of the 'Trente Cierges' on the north, and in the middle an absidial crypt. All three had semi-circular vaults, though the North Chapel was revaulted in the thirteenth century. The choir built above collapsed in 1421, the supporting buttresses evidently not being strong enough. It ended with an apse, and was slightly higher than the nave.[2] It had a deambulatory and an absidial chapel was built probably later, in the twelfth century.[3] The triforium was similar to that of the nave. The transepts had barrel vaults remarkable at this date, of which that on the south is original and that to the north rebuilt in 1899.[4] Whether the crossing was vaulted or not is uncertain. Probably there was a wooden roof in preparation for a lantern. At this stage the arches of the choir and the two side aisles would have been filled, so that the roof of the Carolingian church could be pulled down and the services held in the new church. At his death in 1085 Abbot Rannulfus left the nave almost completed, and he had also begun to replace the wooden conventual buildings which had been erected temporarily after the destruction of Duke Richard's buildings. The nave was built over the Carolingian church and unwisely two of the pillars of the north aisle were placed on its central arcade. The wall of the north aisle rested on the wall of the Carolingian Church. To the west a system of arcades had been built to support the extended nave which both increased the size of the lower church and made a succession of galleries covering the approach to the abbey entrance. Though little idea of the church's appearance can be gained from the earliest representation of it,

[1] Halphen and Lot, 'Recueil des Actes de Lothaire', op. cit., p. 53.

[2] J. Vallery Radot, 'La Crypte du choeur roman de l'abbatiale du Mont-Saint-Michel', *Bulletin de la Société nationale des antiquaires de France* (1965), 70–7.

[3] G. Bazin, op. cit., p. 111, had already made this very important correction of Gout using the miniature of the Mont by the Limbourg brothers in the 'Tres Riches Heures' of the Duc de Berry, now at Chantilly, painted before the choir collapsed, as evidence. The archaeological evidence has now confirmed his conjecture. See Vallery-Radot, op. cit.

[4] 'Le berceau du transept du Mont est l'une des plus anciennes voûtes de haute nef que nous rencontrions au XI$^{e}$ siècle, concues originellement et non ajoutées après coup', Bazin, op. cit., p. 254.

that on the Bayeux Tapestry, this system of support seems to be alluded to and to have caught the artist's attention.[1]

The nave consisted of seven bays of which the three westernmost were destroyed after the fire of 1776. The present façade was erected in 1780.[2] The nave had a panelled wooden ceiling. The triforium stage consisted of a 'false tribune' between the arcade and the high windows, of twin arches to each bay divided by a single column.[3] To the south the aisle was built on a platform which was part of the earlier constructions. This was doubled in size and a vault built to cover the steps which led to the south door of Notre-Dame-sous-Terre. Both side aisles had groin vaults. Gout says of this whole construction 'elle dénote de la part du constructeur des connaissances qu'on s'étonne de rencontrer dans cette période de l'art Roman'.

Further gifts are recorded under Rannulfus. The abbey benefited from the Conquest as did many other Norman houses. Robert of Mortain either gave, or confirmed, the abbey's possession of St Michel's Mount with further grants later,[4] and Domesday also records land at Otterton in Devon, at Basingstoke in Hampshire and elsewhere.[5] Rannulfus had sent six ships to Duke William after the Battle of Hastings, and with them went a number of monks from the abbey. Four of these became abbots of English houses: Rualdus of Hyde Abbey, Winchester; Scollandus of St Augustine's, Canterbury, 1072–87; Serlo of Gloucester, ?1072–1104; and William of Agorn of St. Peter's, Cerne.[6] Amongst the colophons in Mont St Michel manuscripts still at Avranches is one in MS. 103, St Gregory's Dialogues, stating it to have been written by six

[1] *The Bayeux Tapestry*, ed. Sir Frank Stenton, 2nd edn. (1965), fig. 21. Mont Saint Michel is shown in the background at the beginning of Duke William's expedition with Harold into Brittany, which probably took place in 1064.

[2] The design of the façade is known from an early eighteenth-century engraving. See Bazin, op. cit., fig. 19. It was very simple. Two flanking towers were added by Abbot Robert de Torigni (1154–86).

[3] The north and south sides of the nave differ, owing to the rebuilding of the north side finished in 1136 by Abbot Bernard of Bec, 1131–49. See Bazin, op. cit., p. 116–17. For the Norman 'false tribune' see M. Anfray, *L'architecture Normande* (1939), 131ff.

[4] P. L. Hull, 'The Cartulary of St. Michael's Mount', op. cit. Robert's charters contain the information that he carried the 'vexillum sancti Michaelis' at Hastings.

[5] D. Matthew, 'Mont Saint-Michel and England,' *Millénaire* (1), 678–9.

[6] Labbe, op. cit., i, 351.

scribes amongst whom is Scollandus, 'prefulgens dogmate cuncto'. Manuscripts from St Augustine's decorated with Mont St Michel style initials show either that he brought gifts with him or that other Mont St Michel monks accompanied him. At Gloucester the similarity of the design of the triforium in Serlo's new church, dedicated in 1100, to that of Mont St Michel is noteworthy.[1] It is built in the thickness of the wall and the proportions are different, but twin arches to each bay in the triforium are very uncommon in Norman churches.

Rannulfus died in 1085 and was succeeded by Roger I, a monk of St Étienne de Caen from the King's chaplaincy, who was later present at King William's funeral. In 1091 Henry was besieged by his brothers William II and Duke Robert for fifteen days in the Mont, finally fleeing to Brittany.[2] In 1088 Duke Robert, by a charter which still exists,[3] granted the abbey a market in the village of Ardevon near Pontorson, for the repose of his own soul and that of his brother Henry, and gave Roger permission to build a house in Rouen. Shortly before 1094 the north wall of the nave collapsed, and in 1103 the same part of the church collapsed and destroyed the monks' dormitory on the north side of the church, though miraculously no one was hurt.[4] The north side of the church had to be reconstructed and under Roger I and his successor Roger II, 1106–23, formerly prior of Jumièges (who was appointed by Henry I after the monks had complained to him of Roger I's dispersal of their numbers to various monasteries in Normandy), the conventual buildings were increased and the defences of the abbey strengthened.

It is unnecessary for our purpose to follow the history of the abbey any further. It will be seen that there was continuous building activity at the Mont from 1023 to the end of the century, that the possessions of the abbey and its reputation as a place of pilgrimage continued to grow, and that on the whole it avoided both internal and external quarrels, even the

[1] For Serlo's achievement in increasing the numbers of his monks, see William of Malmesbury, 'De gestis pontificum Anglorum', *Rolls Society*, 52 (1870), 292–3.

[2] See *Ordericus Vitalis*, ed. Prévost, vol. iii, p. 378, Bk. VIII, ch. 18.

[3] See L. Delisle, 'La commémoration du Domesday Book à Londres en 1886. Charte Normande communiquée au comité de cette fête', *Société de l'Histoire de France* (1886), facsimile. The charter is now in Paris, Bib. Nat., nouv. acq. lat. 1674, fol. 4. Exh., *Millénaire*, no. 123.

[4] Bazin, op. cit., p. 65–66, corrects Gout as to the two separate falls.

dismissals of abbots Almodus and Suppo seeming to result in little permanent harm to the abbey's progress.

The circumstances were propitious, therefore, for the activity of a flourishing scriptorium – a reformed community which included men of learning, combined with the material resources necessary for the production of fine books. The abbey's wealth was based on widely scattered possessions and these together with the celebrity of the Mont as a place of pilgrimage (to which, of course, the dispersion of its property was largely due) meant that it was exposed to an unusual variety of influences. The way in which the artists combined, assimilated, and, in making their own contributions, altered their different sources, gives the products of the scriptorium their particular character and their particular interest and importance.

A short account of the fortunes of the library may be added here.[1] This was notably increased in the twelfth century under the abbacy of Robert de Torigni, 1154–86, formerly prior of Bec, who besides himself being an historian and important source for the period was active in procuring books and having them copied. His cartulary, now Avranches MS. 210, shows a high standard of calligraphy and decoration.[2] An important figure in the abbey's later history, Pierre le Roy, abbot 1386–1410, further enriched the library. In the fifteenth century *ex libris* inscriptions and lists of contents were added to many of the manuscripts, which suggests some systematic care for the library.

Of the great collection, however, now only a part survives. Already in 1582 Nicolas le Fèvre, in a letter of 18 November in which he mentions a number of the library's treasures,[3] says that Cujas[4] has had permission

[1] See G. Nortier, op. cit., *Revue Mabillon*, xlvii (1957), 135ff. M. Delalonde, 'Petite histoire des manuscrits du Mont-Saint-Michel', *Art de Basse Normandie*, xl (1966), 19–25.

[2] A. Boinet, 'L'illustration du Cartulaire du Mont-Saint-Michel', *Bibliothèque de l'école des chartes*, lxx (1909), 335–43. *Manuscrits à peintures*, no. 195. Swarzenski, *Monuments*, figs. 294–5. Exh., *Millénaire*, no. 139, pls. 7–9. F. Avril, 'La décoration des manuscrits du Mont Saint-Michel (XIe et XIIe siècles),' *Millénaire* (2), 61–66.

[3] These include the copy of Pliny's Natural History written for Robert de Torigni with his prologue, which is so often mentioned as one of the finest of the abbey's manuscripts (Delisle, *Robert de Torigni*, op. cit., ii, 343), and also copies of the Epistles of Pliny, of Symmachus, and of Ivo of Chartres, the works of Ovid and various works of Cicero, the *de Fato, de Divinatione, de Universitate* (sic) and some of the Philippics. Nortier, op. cit., 153.

[4] Jacques Cujas, the famous jurist (1522–90). His library was sold in 1593.

to take what he likes, from M. Do and M. de Coutances (Arthur de Cossé-Brissac, bishop of Coutances 1561–87, and abbot of Mont St Michel 1570–87). Cujas' books are dispersed and lost, and most of the books mentioned by Le Fèvre had disappeared when the Congregation of St Maur was established at the Mont in 1622. They looked after their books more carefully, and when Colbert's emissary, Charpentier, arrived in 1678 he was unable to look at them, as the key to the grille was unfortunately lost! In 1639 they were arranged and catalogued by Le Michel[1] and they appear to have been bound somewhat later as they are today. Certain manuscripts were sent to St Germain-des-Prés for the editions, particularly of St Augustine, which the Maurists were preparing. A list survives of books sent to St Germain about 1670, including a Bible said to have been written more than a thousand years earlier.[2] A frustrating reference is to the manuscript seen by Dom Julien Bellaise in 1687, which contained catalogues of the libraries of Savigny, Mont St Michel, Caen, Le Bec and Jumièges. This according to Dom Bellaise was written in 1210, but it has disappeared.[3]

At the Revolution the abbey was secularized. It had long been used as a prison and continued to be so, though now with the name of 'Mont Libre'! The manuscripts which survived were transferred to Avranches when Napoleon established a central school there for the département. Some disappeared after the Revolution but over two hundred and forty still remain.[4] The conservation and cataloguing of the manuscripts were due to the librarians, M. Saint Victor from 1815 and M. Motet from 1821. The former's itemised catalogue made in 1820 is printed at the end of M. Raoul's *Histoire Pittoresque du Mont St. Michel*, 1833. In 1840 the Abbé Desroches printed a notice of most of the manuscripts at Avran-

[1] Le Michel's catalogue numbers, with a concordance of the manuscripts listed by Montfaucon, *Bibliotheca Bibliothecarum*, ii (1739), and by Omont, are given by Nortier, op. cit., Appx. II.

[2] Quoted by Nortier, op. cit., p. 170, 'pièces justificatives, iii'. The list of books is in Paris, Bib. Nat., Latin 13074, fol. 55.

[3] Letter to Mabillon quoted by L. Delisle, *Le Cabinet des Manuscrits*, i (1868), 527. Du Molinet, who saw it in 1678, says it was written in 1240.

[4] The Catalogue of the manuscripts deposited at Avranches after the Revolution is contained in Avranches MS. 246. The librarian at Avranches, M.M. Delalonde, drew my attention to this. He has counted the items and found a total of two hundred and fifty-three.

ches,[1] and in the next year Ravaisson dealt with forty-five manuscripts in his *Rapports au Ministre de l'Instruction Publique sur les bibliothèques des départements de l'Ouest.* In 1872 Léopold Delisle published a corrected version of a catalogue made by Taranne in 1841 as Vol. IV of the *Catalogue général des Manuscrits des Bibliothèques publiques des Départements.* In the new series of the *Catalogue général*, Vol. X published in 1889, the the manuscripts were catalogued by H. Omont.

As for the illuminated eleventh-century manuscripts, some of them were studied and reproduced by J.-P. Martin, 'La Bibliothèque d'Avranches. Ses origines et ses richesses'.[2] A number of the most important were exhibited in Paris in 1954.[3] Most recently the manuscripts have been studied by F. Avril in a thesis entitled 'La décoration des manuscrits dans les abbayes bénédictines de Normandie aux XIe et XIIe siècles'.[4] He has also contributed an important paper to the *Millénaire* studies.[5]

The manuscripts are now kept in the Hôtel de Ville at Avranches and, in spite of all losses, still provide an impressive indication of the scriptorium's activity from the foundation in 966 to *c.* 1100, with a total of nearly fifty manuscripts or fragments of manuscripts.

[1] *Mémoires de la société des Antiquaires de Normandie*, 2è ser. i (1840), 70–156.

[2] *Normannia*, vi (1933), 551–64.

[3] See the catalogue, *Bibliothèque Nationale, Les Manuscrits à peintures en France du VIIe au XIIe siècle* (1954), nos. 186–95. Also Porcher, *French Miniatures*, 19–20, pls. ix and x.

[4] For an abstract see *École nationale des Chartes, Position des Thèses* (1963). I am most grateful to M. Avril for sending me a copy of the abstract, for allowing me to read his thesis in Paris, and for discussions of the Mont St Michel manuscripts. On many points we have been glad to find we have reached agreement independently. On some we differ. On very many others – too many for me to acknowledge them all separately – I have learnt from his suggestions and discoveries. I should again like to thank him most warmly for his habitual generosity and kindness.

[5] F. Avril, 'La décoration des manuscrits au Mont Saint-Michel (XIe–XIIe siècles)', *Millénaire* (2), 203–38, pls. xxxvii–liv. See also M. Bourgeois-Lechartier, 'A la recherche du scriptorium de l'abbaye du Mont Saint-Michel', *Millénaire* (2), 171–202, pls. i–xxxvi.

# II

## THE SCRIPT OF THE TENTH- AND ELEVENTH-CENTURY MANUSCRIPTS OF MONT ST MICHEL

OVER sixty manuscripts or fragments of manuscripts attributable to the scriptorium of Mont St Michel and belonging to the eleventh century and the last years of the tenth century now survive. The majority of them are still in the Bibliothèque Municipale at Avranches, to which they were transferred after the secularisation of the abbey at the French Revolution.

Four manuscripts at Avranches and one at Rouen have colophons which make it certain that they were written in the abbey scriptorium,[1] and similarities of script and decoration make it possible to group the remaining manuscripts around these. Besides the colophons there are not many mediaeval marks of ownership surviving, due, probably, to the rebinding.[2] In addition to the manuscripts preserved at Avranches nineteen others now dispersed to other libraries, which on the evidence of script and decoration were either made at Mont St Michel or are closely connected with the abbey's production, will be discussed.

In this chapter an examination of the development of the script of the surviving manuscripts will be attempted to give a relative chronology. Then, whatever other evidence survives will be used to suggest an absolute chronological framework. This is admittedly far less exact than could

[1] MSS. 98, 91, 77 and 103. Rouen, Bib. Mun., MS. A.178(425).

[2] How the manuscripts were catalogued or shelf-marked before Le Michel made his catalogue in 1639 is unknown. His shelf-marks written on small pieces of paper or leather are preserved and pasted into many of the manuscripts. For a concordance see Nortier, op. cit., Appx. MS. 78 contains a late eleventh-century ownership mark inscription and MSS. 61 and 109 twelfth-century inscriptions. In MSS. 51, 58, 59, 75, 91, 97, 98, 101, 115, 163 and 229, there are fifteenth-century lists of contents or ownership marks entered by the same hand.

be wished. The loss of most of the charters of Mont St Michel is a great handicap in this respect.

## A: THE SCRIPT

The manuscripts can be divided for convenience into four groups: early, transitional, middle and late. Naturally different scripts in the same book written by scribes belonging probably to different generations, may mean that a book will seem to overlap these divisions. At the beginning of the period the temptation is to feel that a book was written by a multitude of different scribes. At the end, it is to think that only one scribe was at work in the scriptorium writing all the books. In other words from irregularity of writing in letter forms and general scribal practice the scriptorium progresses to great uniformity. This is exactly the case with the initial decoration where a number of different styles and methods give way finally to one uniform one. It will be convenient to discuss the script of each of the four groups separately and then to turn to the scribal practice in which is included the size of the manuscript, the gatherings of the folios, and the pricking and ruling of the page, as it develops over the whole period.

### *The early group*

Pls. 1–2 This group comprises eleven manuscripts still at Avranches[1] and five others attributed to Mont St Michel on grounds of script and decoration.[2] The general impression given by the script of these manuscripts is one of exuberant haste. The words look as if they had been written very fast and with a careless bravado. Thus the abbreviation and punctuation marks are long dashes, ascenders and descenders tend to be long and to be flourished, and descenders from the last line of script are often carried right down into the margin.

[1] MSS. 35(2), 50, 69, 78, 95, 97, 98, 109(1), 211, 229, 240. See the catalogue of manuscripts for descriptions, Appx. II.

[2] Bayeux, Bib. Cap., MS. 56; Rome, Biblioteca Vaticana, Reg. Lat. 2043; Paris, Bib. Nat., Latin 8055 and 8070; Leiden, Bib. Univ., Voss. lat. fol. 39 with Paris, Bib. Nat., Latin 5920, one manuscript originally.

*Letter forms*. The script is a form of Carolingian minuscule. Noticeable letters are 'a' which is open in MSS.78 and 97 and very commonly round regardless of whether it is medial or initial; 'g' which has a long stem connecting the bowl with the tail of the letter, and 'n' which is written in Pl. 1*a*
uncial form, particularly before 't', but also frequently at the ends of words and before vowels. In 't' the minim curves into the head stroke and Pl. 1*b*
round 'r' is used after 'o'. In MS. 78 tailed 'e' is found – ę – and in the same manuscript the Tironian 'et' – ⁊ – occurs. 'Et' is sometimes written in full, but the ampersand is usually used and frequently for verb terminations – e.g. dec & – and even in the middle of words – e.g. a& ternam. The abbreviation ÷ for 'est' is also found.

Ligatures for 'ct' and 'st' are used and in MS. 50 there is the biting 'ae' – æ . In MS. 98 the ligature ns for 'ns' occurs. The tail of long 's' tends to project below the line. The ascenders are still mostly club-like. Seriphs appear irregularly in MS. 50. The descenders slant to a point to the left.

*Spacing*. The words are written on the ruled lines and are well spaced vertically, but tend to run together horizontally. Vertically the ascenders and descenders, as has been said, are long, being frequently twice or three times, sometimes as much as four times as long as a minim (MS. 97, fol. Pl. 1*b*
92). The interlinear space[1] is commonly between three and four times the height of a minim, so ascenders and descenders constantly overlap. A clash between the bow of a 'g' and the 'st' ligature is solved by hunching up the 'g' and restraining the 'st' ligature (MS. 97, fol. 92 column 2, line 25-26). The script is not heavy on the page and evidently the quill is cut thin. The ink has mostly faded to a brown sometimes very pale.

*Abbreviation*. Abbreviation is limited. Final '-m', final '-us' and '-ur', and -oꝝ for '-orum' are common abbreviations by suspension. The use of the ampersand has been noticed. The mark of abbreviation by contraction is usually cup-shaped – ~.

*Punctuation*. The scribes use the point, and the point and tick, the *punctus elevatus*, within the sentence, and the 'semi-colon' mark at the end. The latter is used too in abbreviations of final '-bus' and '-que', a potential source of confusion. The interrogative mark is also rather similar to the

1 The space between the top of a minim in one line and the bottom of a minim in the line above.

abbreviation mark for final '-ur'. The punctuation has frequently been
Pl. *1b* corrected later, notably by the addition or erasure of ticks to points (MS. 97).

## *The transitional group*

Pls. *2c–3a* Eleven manuscripts still at Avranches[1] and one in the Vatican Library[2] belong to this group, not counting overlappings of hands from the early group (e.g. Bayeux 56) at one end and from the middle group at the other (e.g. Avranches 59). The script generally has a neater appearance. It is written larger and heavier with broader strokes. There seem to be two tendencies, one to a more angular hand, sharpening as it were the forms of
Pl. *3a* the earlier script (MS. 61, MS. 128); another to a rounder hand (MS. 91,
Pls. *2c, 9d* MS. 105). It is this second which becomes dominant, but for a time they seem to run parallel.

*Letter forms.* Characteristic letter forms are again 'a' which is written with a square top – ɑ – (MSS. 91, 105, 68, 128) open – u – (MSS. 105 and 61), and round – a – (MSS. 115 and 99), and in MS. 91 also with a trailing head – a ; also 'g' which remains long-tailed in some manuscripts. (MS. 128) but more commonly becomes 'three shaped', with the top bowl open. Seriphs, usually slanting, are the rule now, and many ascenders curve forward slightly at their ends – see particularly MS. 105.

*Spacing.* Spacing is still wide vertically and since ascenders and descenders are shorter, seldom more than twice the size of a minim, there is not much overlapping. Horizontally words still run into each other but not commonly. One hand in MS. 91 has short ascenders only about three quarters of a minim. MS. 68 is particularly widely spaced vertically.

*Abbreviation and Punctuation.* Abbreviation is, if anything, less common than in the early group. MS. 68 does not even abbreviate final '-em' or '-um'. MS. 128, an Homiliary, writes, folio 53, gaudiorū. MS. 91 uses a very distinctive cedilla to 'e' for 'ae' – ę . Only the ampersand abbreviation for 'et' is used, but the word is sometimes written out (MS. 68). The point and comma, 'semi-colon' mark, at the end of a sentence is fading

[1] MSS. 38, 61(2), 68, 70, 79, 91, 99, 105, 115, 128 and 129.

[2] Vat. Lat. 9668. Avril, *Notes* (1), 492–504, *Notes* (2), 246–7.

out. Where it is used, as in MS. 128, it is a 'point and seven' rather – ȷ̇ . The point, and the point and tick are the common punctuation marks.

## *The middle group*

There are ten manuscripts of the middle group still at Avranches.[1] To these can be added as an appendix four books written wholly or in part by the scribe Antonius, probably for (and perhaps at) Fécamp, one now in Rouen and three in Paris.[2] Pls. 3*b*-4

The middle group scripts continue the two trends noticed already in the transitional group. The angular script is exemplified in MS. 72, written by Frotmundus, and in MSS. 59, 76, and 101. The rounder hand is becoming dominant and as written by Gyraldus the scribe of MSS. 90 and 77 is of great beauty. Pl. 3*c* Pl. 3*b* Pls. 4*a*-*b*

*Letter forms*. In the 'angular' manuscripts the three-shaped 'g' continues to be used. Final 's' written round not tall is also noticeable. In the rounder hands the amply curving tail of 'g' slightly hunched but no longer with a stem is characteristic. The script is generally written smaller, and this is noticeable in the fineness of the bowls of 'a' and 'e'. Ascenders and descenders are straight and end with an oblique point. Pl. 3*c* Pl. 4*a*

*Spacing*. Ascenders and descenders are further reduced in length. Ascenders are now the same height as, or even less than, the height of a minim, though a ligature 'st' will protrude above the general level, for instance. The lines of script still appear very widely spaced, however, and the reduction of the 'body' of the script does not seem to be intended to save space. Rather, by removing the distracting loops and flourishes, it concentrates the attention on the letter forms. In MS. 75, for instance, where the interlinear space is twice the height of a minim, the ascenders and descenders are barely half that height. Consequently the gap between them is at least a minim's height. In fact, in this manuscript the distance is further increased because the letters are written often somewhat above the ruled line so that the tail of a 'p' or 'q' hardly extends below the line. Pl. 4*a*

1 MSS. 51, 59, 72, 75, 76, 77, 86(2), 90, 101, 107.

2 Paris, Bib. Nat., Lat. 2055, 2088 and 2639. Rouen, Bib. Mun., MS. A.143(427). For these manuscripts see below and Appx. IV.

*Abbreviation and Punctuation.* There is little change from the transitional group. Abbreviation by contraction – e.g.'scdm̄','ds̄', etc. is commoner. The point, and the point and tick are still the regular punctuation marks.

## *The late group*

Pls. 5-6*b* Seventeen manuscripts or fragments of manuscripts still at Avranches belong to this group.[1] These include the first parts of MS. 35 and the last of MSS. 61 and 86 which have been bound in with earlier manuscripts. The fragments are in MS. 10 (Deuteronomy), MS. 88 (Paulus Diaconus), and MS. 86 and 73 (votive masses from a Sacramentary). To these can be added the Dudo of St Quentin, now Berlin, Deutsche Staatsbibliothek, Phillipps 1854, probably made for Fécamp; a Statius, *Thebais*, Paris, Bibliothèque Nationale, Latin 8070, pp. 1–140; part of a manuscript of Lives of Saints, also in Paris, Latin 5290; and the St Athanasius, *de Trinitate*, written by Hilduinus, now at Rouen, Bibliothèque Municipale, MS. A. 178 (425). There are also the two most richly decorated of the Mont St Michel books, the Sacramentary now in New York, the Pier-
Pl. 4*c* pont Morgan Library, MS. 641, and the two-volume Bible which probable belonged already in the twelfth century to the abbey of S. Sauveur de Redon and is now at Bordeaux, Bibliothèque Municipale, MS. 1. Also to be connected with this group are several manuscripts which were either sent as gifts to St Augustine's, Canterbury, or written there by Mont St
Pl. 5*d* Michel monks after the Conquest. These are now in the British Museum, and the Library of Corpus Christi College, Cambridge.[2]

[1] MSS. 9, 10 (fragments), 35(1), 47, 57, 58, 61(1), 73, 73 and 86(1) (fragments), 82, 86(3), 88 and 94 (fragments), 89, 102, 103, 146, 163. In MS. 103, if a word or two overlaps from the last line of the page an animal head is sometimes inserted in front. This is rather an unusual feature but is found later in the Eadwi Psalter and the Dover Bible from Christ Church, Canterbury. Dodwell, *Canterbury School*, pls. 29 d–g.

[2] London, Brit. Mus., Royal MS.13.A.XXII and 13.A.XXIII. Cambridge, Corpus Christi College, MS. 276. The latter has one English hand in it which indicates that it was written at Canterbury. See T. A. M. Bishop, 'Canterbury scribe's work', *Durham Philobiblon*, II pt. 1 (Dec. 1955), 1–3. Fols. 70 line 10 – 71 of Royal 13 A.XXII and fols. 61 line 14 – 94v. of 13 A.XXIII appear to be written by Mauritius who signed part of Avranches 58. A feature of his script is the large final round 's'. Another of the hands of MS. 58 added a copy of the *Trevia dei* of 1080 to Berlin, Phillipps 1854. This suggests Mauritius was still at Mont St Michel about 1080 to contribute to MS. 58 and that the two London manuscripts were presents to St Augustine's.

*Letter forms.* The script is generally written larger and heavier on the page in a good black ink. The attention is focused on the medial part of the letter. That is to say that ascenders and descenders reach an extreme point of abbreviation. At the same time the bowls of 'd' and 'p', 'q' and 'b' are generous and the 'o' and 'u' wide. Similarly the ampersand as it were keels over with a tiny cross stroke and loop but a big bow. This gives a general ponderous stateliness. Round 'd' is found in MSS. 103 and 163 and in MS. 103 a tailed 'e' occurs – ę . The Carolingian minuscule 'a' is almost standard now.[1] The end of the cross stroke tends to protrude – & – as does the minim of 't' which is not upright but curves into the headstroke quite sharply – t . The lower part of the loop of 'g' tends more towards the horizontal. The 'st' ligature continues to be used regularly but the 'ct' ligature, though found in MSS. 35 and 146 for instance, is not regularly used. MS. 35 uses the biting 'ae' – æ . Seriphs tend to be square – the pen is either being held much straighter or is being cut to a slanting nib – and in some manuscripts they are noticeably split (e.g. MSS. 58 and 146). In the latest manuscripts of this group the script is becoming more angular and pointed. Pl. 6*b* Pl. 5*a* Pl. 6*b* Pl. 6*b*

*Spacing.* As has been said ascenders and descenders are even further reduced. In the first hand of MS. 103 they are barely one-third the height of a minim at times. Nevertheless since the interlinear space is also reduced to one and a half to one times the height of a minim the lines do not appear as widely spaced as in the middle group. The weight of the script on the page also makes it look less widely spaced.

*Abbreviation and Punctuation.* For punctuation the point, and the point and tick are usually written rather high. The 'semi-colon' at the end of a sentence is not found. A new mark of punctuation, the 'seven and point' – 7 – mark, is beginning to be quite frequent.[2] Abbreviation both by suspension but more noticeably by contraction is increasing. But it is still not used on any scale. On the first folio of MS. 35, for instance, 'spūalem', 'scdm̄' and 'dn̄s' occur but the verb termination '-ur' is not abbreviated nor are *quod, quae, vel* or *etiam.* Pls. 5*a*, 6*a*

[1] Open 'a' – ɑ – still occurs in MS. 35 fol. 107.

[2] This is found as early as MS. 91, e.g. fol. 36. It is used by the scribe Antonius. For its use see N. R. Ker, *English Manuscripts in the century after the Norman Conquest* (1960), 47.

From the above sketch of the development it can be seen that the scriptorium starts with a script which is still close to ninth-century Carolingian minuscule as seen in the Tours and Franco-Saxon school manuscripts. New influences appear in the transitional group and by the middle group we have a script which is very close to the form of Caroline minuscule found in Anglo-Saxon manuscripts. By the end of the eleventh century the round forms of this script are becoming more angular and progressing towards the sharper more compressed style of the early twelfth century.

## B: SCRIBAL PRACTICES

Pls. *5a*, *1b* If a page from Avranches 103 is compared with one from Avranches 97 the change in the script made in at the most a hundred years seems astonishing. Differences in scribal practice are not so striking. It is rather a standardisation of the early practice than any great change which is apparent over the period.[1]

### *Size*

In comparing sizes, of course, it has to be remembered that the pages may have been cut down by later binders. This difficulty may be partly avoided by taking the measurements of the script on the page, though it is a tiresome fact that they are not always constant, since prickings can vary slightly in width, and scribes often alter the number of lines on a page throughout a book. The amount of margin allowed is in itself interesting and important. Some of the Mont St Michel manuscripts have been cut down almost to the script where, as in MSS. 35, 61 and 86, texts not originally connected have been bound together later. But in others where the gathering and pricking marks remain, the margins can never have been much wider.

The size of the folios of a book depended in the first place on the length of text to be copied, in the second on the size and spacing of the script and the amount of abbreviation used, and thirdly on the number of folios

[1] In the figures given below only manuscripts still at Avranches are considered. Their provenance is assured. Also a few of the outside manuscripts attributed to the scriptorium I have not seen or only been able to examine hurriedly.

of any particular size which it was considered desirable to bind together. With the exception of MS. 240 none of the scripts at Mont St Michel at this date are very small, they are widely spaced, and, as has been seen, abbreviation was not practised to any great extent. A long text therefore like St Gregory's *Moralia in Job* had to be written in a large format and bound in two volumes (MSS. 97 and 98). There also seems to have been an unwillingness to bind more than a certain number of leaves of any particular size together. The result is that the spine is narrow in proportion to its height.[1]

No attempt seems to have been made to evolve books of a standard height and breadth for texts of similar length in any of the four groups at Mont St Michel. This might have been expected for the standard patristic texts of the library, the works of St Augustine or St Ambrose for instance. But even the two volumes of the *Moralia in Job* in the early group (MSS. 97 and 98), or the first and third parts of St Augustine's Commentary on the Psalms of the middle group (MSS. 76 and 77) are not identical in size either of script or of full-page measurements.

Very generally it could be said that the earlier books are squarer in format and smaller. The middle group contains more books of a larger size than any other. The late group in this and other respects seems to return to earlier practice. Thus in the early group there are five out of eleven books under 210 mm. in script height,[2] in the transitional four out of eleven, in the middle two out of ten and in the late eight out of sixteen. The early, middle and late groups have each one or two large books, over 270 mm. tall. In the early group these are the two volumes of St Gregory's *Moralia in Job* (MSS. 97 and 98), 280 × 209 mm. and 292 × 216 mm. respectively. The largest of the transitional group, MS. 68, St Jerome on Genesis, 238 × 174 mm., MS. 115, Haimo on St Paul, 248 × 173 mm., and the two Homiliaries, MSS. 128 and 129, 239 × 171 mm.,

1 In contrast to the typical French thirteenth-century one-volume Bible for instance. Exceptions at first sight, MSS. 35 or 61, turn out to be separate manuscripts of normal proportions bound together later.

2 All the measurements given below are of the script, being the height and width of the rectangle formed by the inner vertical bounding lines and the first and last horizontal ruled lines. The first line in all the manuscripts is written above (not, as from the thirteenth century, below) the top ruled line.

are bulky but not really large books. In the middle group there are MSS. 76 and 77, Parts I and III of St Augustine on the Psalms, 272 × 196 mm. and 279 × 194 mm. respectively, and MS. 107, Bede on St Mark and St Luke, 273 × 191 mm. In the late group the Bible, Bordeaux I, towers over the others, but MS. 89, St Augustine's *Civitas Dei*, is also large, 298 × 201 mm., and so are MS. 82, St Augustine, Homilies, 261 × 184 mm. and MS. 146, Isidore, Decretals, 263 × 178 mm. But in each group books range regularly up the scale between the largest and smallest.

## *The folios and their gatherings. Bindings*

I am not able to say much about the material used and in particular whether the leaves are of vellum (calf-skin), or parchment (sheep-skin). I shall use the word parchment to mean animal skin prepared as a material for writing on.[1]

The quality of the parchment certainly improves. In the earlier manuscripts – e.g. MS. 98 – the ink is often blurred on the page, and flaws resulting in holes are frequent. They are written round by the scribe. The thickness varies with no particular trend to thicker or thinner leaves observable. The sheets of parchment are laid flat one on another alternatively hair and flesh side uppermost and then folded in half. There are generally four sheets which form a gathering of eight folios so that hair side faces hair and flesh side flesh. Gatherings are sometimes of six, ten, or twelve folios particularly at the beginning or end of a book. At Mont St Michel the gatherings are often marked, either with letters of the alphabet or with roman numerals, though it is usually difficult to be certain that the marks are contemporary with the writing. In MS. 72 they are clearly written by the scribe, Frotmundus. The marks come usually at the foot of the last verso of a quire, but occasionally at the beginning of the quire, either as well as, or instead of, the other mark.

Pl. 3*c*

The book was no doubt written first and then the quires bound. The inner margins would have had to be very wide for a book to be written

[1] Paper, of course, is not used for manuscripts at this date. For the difficulty of distinguishing vellum from parchment see G. S. Ivy, 'The Bibliography of the Manuscript Book', *The English Library before 1700*, ed. F. Wormald and C. E. Wright (1958), 34.

after it was bound and the scribe would have had to calculate very exactly the number of pages he would need.[1] Moreover the numbering of the quires would have been unnecessary in a bound book. Occasionally some folios of the last gathering have been cut out. All the manuscripts have been rebound.

## *Pricking and ruling*

Ruling in all the manuscripts is done with a hard point though in the late MSS. 103 and 163 a pencil has been used to re-rule one or two pages, presumably because the parchment is very thick and the point had not come through. In the early group the five larger manuscripts are written in two columns.[2] MS. 211, though only 208 × 145 mm., is ruled in double column. This, the Chronicle, has clearly been written with special care, but the columns are so narrow that often only two or three words go to a line. The remaining manuscripts are in single column.

The same rule of two columns for the larger books and one for smaller (under 220 mm. tall) holds for most of the transitional group.[3] Of the middle group manuscripts only one, MS. 86 (2), 229 × 123 mm., is written in single column. MS. 72, which is smaller than MS. 86 (2), 204 × 143 mm., is in double column and so is MS. 51, 200 × 140 mm. In the late group a return is made to single-column script except for the four largest books and MSS. 9, 61 (1) and 73.[4] Of the nine single-column books two are over 220 mm. tall.[5]

The standard vertical ruling of a page is two bounding lines for a column, so that in a single-column book four lines, and in a double-column book eight lines, run vertically. Exceptions to this are in the early group MS. 35 (2), MS. 78 and MS. 240, single-column books with single

[1] Early mediaeval scribes in the great majority of cases are shown writing in books already bound – Avranches MS. 76, fol. 1 is interesting as an exception. But this does not mean that they actually did so. The codex was shown as completed because that was its significant form. See G. S. Ivy, op. cit., 48-51. See Pl. 20.

[2] MSS. 69, 95, 97, 98, and 109(1).

[3] MS. 61(2) is 204 × 148 mm., but has two columns.

[4] Avranches MSS. 82, 89, 102, and 146. MS. 61 is only 193 × 145, MS. 9, 215 × 166, MS. 73, 202 × 142.

[5] Avranches MSS. 58, 86(1).

bounding lines, and in the transitional group, MS. 128, a double-column book with only six vertical lines (i.e. single inner bounding lines), and MS. 129 with seven vertical lines (i.e. three between the columns).

Standard horizontal ruling as seen in the transitional and middle manuscripts continues the first two lines right across the page and the last two. In a double-column book these lines run across the space between the two columns as the rest do not. In the early group, however, MSS. 35(2), 78, 229(1) and 240 have the first and last lines only ruled right across. MS. 50 is irregular. In the transitional manuscripts MSS. 61 and 129 rule the last three lines across and in MS. 61 sometimes the first three across. In the late group the practice changes to ruling the first and third, the last and the propenultimate right across.[1] MSS. 35(1), 51, 77, 102 and 146 rule sometimes in the old, sometimes in the new way, and sometimes by a combination of the two.

The margins left are still generous in many manuscripts. They vary from a third to a quarter of the height of the page divided over top and bottom, and about a third of its width over the sides. Prickings, where they have not been cut off, are always on the outer margins, which means the sheets were ruled before folding. They vary from 5 mm. intervals at the smallest to 10 mm. at the largest, the latter only being found in the *de luxe* books, the Chronicle, MS. 211 and the Sacramentary, Morgan 641. As would be expected they are more regular in size in the later manuscripts. In MS. 98 for instance they vary from 7-9 mm. By far the commonest interval is 6-7 mm.

## C: THE TEXTS AND THE SCRIBES

Before turning to problems of dating, a word should be said about the texts and the scribes who wrote them. The energy with which the Norman bishops and abbots set out to provide their houses with patristic texts after the Conquest has been demonstrated by N. R. Ker.[2] At Mont

1 Avranches MSS. 9, 57, 58, 82, 88, 89, 103, 163. It would be interesting to know if a similar change was made in other scriptoria.

2 N. R. Ker, *English Manuscripts in the Century after the Norman Conquest* (1960), particularly pp. 7-8.

St Michel it is possible to some extent, caution being necessary, since we do not know how much is lost, to see how the Norman monasteries had first built up their own libraries. It would also, of course, be extremely interesting to know in detail where they got their exemplars, but this is beyond the scope of the present enquiry.[1] The earlier manuscripts from other scriptoria now surviving at Avranches do not contain the kinds of text which were copied in the eleventh century.

Interesting evidence on this point is provided by a copy of Persius now in Paris in which an initial from the late eighth-century Corbie Psalter is copied literally.[2] This suggests strongly that the Mont St Michel scribe who is one of the leading scribes of the early group, went to Corbie to copy texts. It cannot have been possible always to borrow the exemplars.

The early manuscripts begin with four standard texts: Cassian's Collations, MS. 95, which the rule of St Benedict prescribed for reading in the refectory; St Gregory's *Moralia in Job*, MSS. 97 and 98; St Augustine's Commentary on the Psalms, only one part surviving, MS. 78; and St Augustine's *Civitas Dei*, Bayeux 56. In addition to these there is the *Revelatio*, the account of the foundation of the abbey in MS. 211, which was obviously a first priority[3] and the St Clement, *Recognitiones*, MS.50, which like the Cassian was no doubt a book often read in the refectory. It is interesting to find classical texts, the Persius mentioned above, and a fragmentary copy of Juvenal also in Paris.[4] There is also a Macrobius *Saturnalia* and a copy of the Chronicle of Ado of Vienne.[5] Other early manuscripts contain various works of Alcuin, MS. 109, Martianus

[1] See the remarks of Ker, op. cit., pp. 10–11, on the correction of exemplars. It would be profitable to see how the Norman copies of the *Contra Julianum* of Augustine, for instance, including the transitional MS. 91, connect with the results obtained by Ker in his Appx. I.

[2] Paris, Bib. Nat., Latin 8055. See my 'A Romanesque copy from Mont Saint-Michel of an initial in the Corbie Psalter', *Millénaire* (2), 239–45. Possibly the mysterious colophon of MS. 98 saying that it was written in 'loco sancti Juliani' also indicates copying in another library (at Le Mans?).

[3] The text dates from before the introduction of the Benedictine monks with an appendix added. See J. Hourlier, *Millénaire* (2), 124–8.

[4] Paris, Bib. Nat., Latin 8070.

[5] Vatican, Reg. Lat. 2043. Paris, Bib. Nat., Latin 5920 with Leiden, Univ. Bibl., Voss. lat. fol. 39. This manuscript was no doubt the exemplar of the St. Augustine's Canterbury copy.

Capella with Remigius of Auxerre's commentary on him, MS. 240,[1] and various works of Boethius, MS. 229, texts which can be described as 'old favourites' as opposed to many of the patristic works which begin to come in with the transitional manuscripts.

The library is now provided with a series of Commentaries on the Bible, by Jerome, Gregory and Haimo on books of the Old Testament, MSS. 99, 68, 69, 70 and by Augustine and Haimo on books of the New Testament, MSS. 115, 70. There are various treatises of Augustine, MS. 105, and also the somewhat rare *Contra Julianum*, MS. 91. MS. 61 contains Ambrose on Psalm 118 and the Homilies of St John Chrysostom. MSS. 128 and 129 are Homiliaries, and Amalarius, *de officiis ecclesiasticis* is copied, MS. 38.

St Gregory's Dialogues surprisingly only appear with the middle group, MS. 101. Further Commentaries, by Bede on St Mark and St Luke, MS. 107, by Augustine on the Psalms, MS. 76, *de genesi ad litteram*, MS. 75, on St. Paul's Epistles, MS. 79, and by Ambrose on St Luke, MS. 59, follow. There are a whole series of treatises by Augustine and also by Jerome and Ambrose, MSS. 73, 86(2), 51, containing particularly the disputes against heretics whose illustration in full-page frontispieces is a speciality of the Mont St Michel scriptorium, MSS. 72 and 90.

More patristic works are copied in the late manuscripts, including St Augustine, fragments of the *de patientia*, MS. 163, and a second copy of the *Civitas Dei*,[2] MS. 89, and also the *Excerptiones* from Augustine by Eugyppius, MS. 61(1). MS. 163 contains Heraclides, *Vitae patrum*, and MS. 58 Hilary of Poitiers on St Matthew and other works, including the *de vitae ordine* of Abbot John of Fécamp, which cannot have been written very long, if at all, after his death in 1079. There is also Boethius' *de Trinitate* with commentary, MS. 86(3), and Scot Erigena's translation of Dionysius Areopagita, MS. 47. MS. 146 contains Isidore's Decretals.

[1] In view of what is said above, it is significant that J. Préaux, 'Le Manuscrit d'Avranches 240 et l'oeuvre de Martianus Capella', *Horae Eruditae ad codices Sancti Michaelis de periculo maris*, ed. J. Laporte (Steenbrugge, 1966), 135-49, notes textual connections with a Corbie tradition for the Martianus (as well as with Auxerre for the commentary of Remigius). The manuscript was certainly produced in the Mont St Michel scriptorium since of the four scribes one is identifiable as Hervardus, one is close to Martinus of MS. 98, and one is the second hand of MS. 78.

[2] Paris, Bib. Nat., Latin 2088 is a third copy made probably for Fécamp.

Lastly there is a classical text, Statius' *Thebais*, Latin 8055, and also evidence of an interest in historical writing in the fragments of Paulus Diaconus' *Historia Langobardorum* in MS. 88 (the same text is in the St Augustine's manuscript, Royal 13.A.XXII), and the Dudo of St Quentin, Phillipps 1854. Another St Augustine's manuscript, Royal 13.A.XXIII, copies an earlier Mont St Michel manuscript.[1] It contains the Chronicle of Ado of Vienne and Eutropius' *Historia Romae*. There is only one collection of Saints' Lives beside the Heraclides, and it is fragmentary, Latin 5290.

As for losses, there must have been at least one Gospel book and one Psalter. These would probably be more highly illuminated and, therefore, more vulnerable than the other texts. The Sacramentary probably left the library early, before the arrival of the Maurists. How much else the eleventh-century library might have contained, it is impossible to know. The losses seem to have come in the later fifteenth and the sixteenth century, before the Maurists arrived, and perhaps, since the normal texts were patristic and not highly illuminated, they were not so great a temptation to thieves. There are some mutilations, for example the beginning of MS. 72 has been torn out. Books may have decayed through neglect, been destroyed when the buildings collapsed or by fires, or been discarded as unintelligible or useless. The manuscripts which are frequently mentioned by visitors, and which have now disappeared, are mostly classical texts such as the Pliny, the Ovid and the copies of Cicero. Whether or not the eleventh-century library was ever substantially larger, what remains is probably representative of the abbey's production as far as calligraphy and illumination are concerned.

Mont St Michel is somewhat unusual in the number of scribes whose names are known from their colophons. There are fifteen of them. In the early group there are Hervardus who signed Leiden, Voss. lat. fol. 39,
and Gaulterius and Martinus who wrote MS. 98. Uvarinus, Rannulfus Pls. 1–2
and Giraldus wrote the transitional MS. 91. Frotmundus wrote MS. 72 Pl. 2*c*
of the middle group, and Gyraldus wrote MS. 90 of the middle group Pls. 3*c*, 4*a*, *b*
and MS. 77 of the late group. In the late group there are Mauritius who

[1] Paris, Bib. Nat., Latin 5920 with Leiden, Voss. lat. fol. 39.

Pl. *6b* wrote part of MS. 58, and finally the six scribes of MS. 103, the three
Pl. *6a* Bretons, Osbernus (who also signed MS. 163), Esmeraldus and Nicholaus, and (presumably) the three Normans, Scollandus, Hilduinus (who also signed Rouen MS. A.178(425), and Gaulterius. The hands of several of these scribes can be detected in other manuscripts which they did not sign. Thus Frotmundus wrote part of MS. 128 and Osbernus the whole of MS. 146.

It is very difficult to estimate the number of scribes at work on the manuscripts of the four groups. As has been said, variations in the early hands and similarities in the late have no doubt led to errors in identifying different hands. Moreover, there is no knowing what proportion of the manuscripts copied survive. Nevertheless, for the existing manuscripts in each group there seem to be between a dozen and two dozen scribes, and this suggests that a good proportion, perhaps a third, of the monks worked in the scriptorium at one point or another.[1] This shows both how important the work of copying and the possession of texts was considered in the abbey, and also that the ability and patience necessary for this work was not confined to a few specialists.[2]

The work was done, as the colophons say, to provide spiritual food for the reader (MSS. 77 and 103, Rouen MS. A.178(425)), for love of St Michael (MS. 91), in hope of eternal reward (MSS. 72, 77, 103 and 163), and with pride in its achievement (MSS. 72 and 90). The complaints of the hardship of the work voiced in many mediaeval colophons are not heard at Mont St Michel.[3]

## D: DATING THE SCRIPTS

Having examined the development of the scripts it is necessary to consider what evidence there is to date them. For the early group there is one particularly important piece. This is contained in an Anglo-Saxon late

[1] In the Winchcombe Sacramentary list there are the names of fifty living monks. Robert de Torigni increased the numbers from forty to sixty monks, Th. Le Roy, 'Les Curieuses Recherches', op. cit., 332.

[2] Passages in e.g. MS. 128 look as if they were written a page or two at a time for practice by different scribes.

[3] An exception perhaps is the remark at the beginning of Bk. VI of Bayeux 56: 'Quinque superioribus libris satis mihi'!

tenth-century manuscript now at Orléans, Bibliothèque Municipale, MS. 105, a Sacramentary probably made for Winchcombe, which came to Fleury probably under Abbot Abbo (988-1004). At the end of this book is a list of fifty monks of Mont St Michel who are alive and this is Pl. 1*c*
followed by the obits of another thirty-eight monks.[1] The living abbot who heads the list is Mainardus and since among the obits there is also a 'Mainardus Abbot' this must be Mainard II, nephew and successor of the first abbot, who held office from 991 to 1009. The list is in a distinctive hand and the same scribe wrote a number of manuscripts of the early group, particularly Avranches MSS. 97, 211, Latin 8055 and 8070, and Pl. 1*b*
Bayeux 56. A recent discovery by M. F. Avril has even revealed his name since a manuscript now divided between Paris and Leiden and written Pl. 1*a*
by him, has a colophon: 'Fratris Hervardi post longum penna laborem optatam guadens hic tenuit requiem'.[2] Several other names of scribes who are known from their colophons also occur in the list. Of these three can hardly be the same men. Among the living in the list are Osbernus and Frotmundus, and among the dead Uvarinus. An Osbernus wrote MS. 163 and collaborated in MS. 103, manuscripts of the late group; he can hardly be the same man. Nor is the Frotmundus of the list likely to be the scribe of Avranches 72 which belongs, probably early, in the middle group. An Uvarinus who wrote part of MS. 91 of the transitional group is also unlikely to be the Uvarinus of the list, for neither of his collaborators, Rannulfus and Giraldus, appear in the list as either living or dead. However, the two scribes of MS. 98 of the early group, Gaulterius and Martinus are probably the same monks as those named in the list of the living.

Of the other entries none can be used to date the writing of the list more closely. A 'Hildebertus' is second on the list after Mainardus and must be his successor as abbot from 1009 to 1017. He was said to be young when he was appointed. Another Hildebertus lower down would then be Hildebert II, the nephew of the first and abbot 1017-1023. Also

1 See above p. 8, n.5 and *Millénaire* (1), pl. xiv. See also Ch. Niver, 'The Psalter in the British Museum, Harley 2904', *Medieval Studies in Memory of A. Kingsley Porter*, ed.W. R. Köhler (1939), 678–9, and Leroquais, *Sacramentaires*, i, 89 for the Winchcombe Sacramentary.

2 Paris, Bib. Nat., Latin 5920 and Leiden, Univ. Bibl., Voss. lat. fol. 139. Hervardus' name is included in the Orléans Sacramentary among the living monks. Avril, *Millénaire* (2), 204.

an Almodus occurs who may be the next abbot, 1023–1032. These entries would suggest that the list was composed later rather than earlier in Mainard II's time. Among the *obits* that of Heriwardus who succeeded his brother as abbot of Gembloux in 986 or 987 and died in 991 or 989 does not help to narrow the dating.[1]

For the late manuscripts there are two important pieces of evidence. First the departure of Scollandus of Mont St Michel to become abbot of St Augustine's, Canterbury, in 1072 provides a *terminus ante quem*. For MS. 103 was written, according to its colophon, by six scribes, including a Scollandus 'praefulgens dogmate cuncto'. There can be little doubt that these two are the same man, both because the name is uncommon, and also since three manuscripts, with very similar initials and script to those of the Mont St Michel late manuscripts survive from St Augustine's in the British Museum, Royal MSS. 13.A.XXII and 13.A.XXIII, and at Cambridge, Corpus Christi College, MS. 276.

Secondly in the Berlin Dudo, Phillipps 1854, the text of the Council of Lillebonne of 1080 is copied by a hand which can with probability be identified as that of one of the scribes of MS. 58, fols. 28-82$^{v}$. The scribe
Pl. 6*b* Mauritius who wrote fols. 87-127 of MS. 58 also, it seems, wrote parts of the two St Augustine's Canterbury manuscripts, Royal 13.A.XXII-XXIII. This suggests that Mauritius had remained at the Mont when Abbot Scollandus left for England in 1072, and that the manuscripts were sent to England as presents. All four manuscripts were probably, therefore, produced about 1075-85, Phillipps 1854 probably before 1080, MS. 58 perhaps after.

Of the other pieces of evidence for dating the script first must come the middle group manuscript mentioned earlier, now Rouen, Bibliothèque Municipale, MS. A.143(427), containing various works of St Ambrose. This manuscript was written by the scribe Antonius for Fécamp as the second part of the colophon on folio 151$^{v}$ shows, 'editus iste liber Sanctae Trinitatis honore . . . '.[2]

[1] Laporte, *Millénaire* (1), 65–66.

[2] Antonius and the relations of Mont St Michel with Fécamp are further discussed in Appx. IV. Rouen A.143 has also on fol. 151$^{v}$ a copy of the Fécamp foundation charter in a late eleventh- or early twelfth-century hand.

The first part of the colophon runs as follows:—

Codicis istius paginas quicumque legendo
Percurris, memor esto mei, memor esto jubentis
Patris . . . . scribenti cuncta ferentis.
Antonii nomen mihi noveris esse miselli.

The second word of the third line has been partly erased but is still clearly legible in the original. It is 'Supponis'. Suppo ruled at Mont St Michel from 1033-48, and his connections with Fécamp, as has been seen, were particularly close. Rouen A.143 must therefore have been written for Fécamp at Mont St Michel before 1048, and after his disgrace Suppo's name was erased.[1] This, then, gives an approximate date for the middle manuscripts.

Of the charters of the Abbey only two still survive for the eleventh century but photographs have been published of a number of others. For the early period there are reproductions of three charters recording various gifts of land in Maine by Hugo, count of Maine, to Mont St Michel,[2] and of two other charters of gifts by Ivo and Guy of land in the same area.[3] These are variously dated by de Broussillon between 955 and 1015 and were all formerly in the Archives de la Manche. De Broussillon's photographs are all reduced and are not always very clear. Still, if as seems likely, these charters were written at Mont St Michel they confirm dates of about 995-1015 for the early manuscripts. The tall ascenders and descenders, the long tailed 'g's with small bowls, the open 'a' – *ɑ* – are all found in the charters as they are in Hervardus' script, for example.

Somewhat later is a grant of land in Guernsey to Mont St Michel by Robert I, dated between 1028 and 1034, of which Hunger published a

[1] Antonius does not use his characteristic 'g' with long stem and loop in the colophon. The final 's' written round, the 'st' ligature, the 't' and the point written low are all found in his script, however. A scribe might copy a colophon from his exemplar, of course, but it seems to me impossible that he would have copied the word 'Supponis' and then erased it. Nor can this be a later attempt to disguise the provenance since the words 'Sanctae Trinitatis' and the Fécamp foundation charter have been left.

[2] B. de Broussillon, *Cartulaire de Saint-Victeur au Mans, Prieuré de l'Abbaye du Mont-Saint-Michel 994-1400* (1895), pls. i-iii.

[3] B. de Broussillon, 'Cartulaire de l'Abbayette (997-1421)', *Bulletin de la Commission historique et archéologique de la Mayenne*, ix (1894), pls. i and ii. The gift of 997, pl. i, is particularly close to the script of Hervardus.

photograph.[1] This is written in a thin script with tall twirled ascenders and descenders, large trailing-headed 'a's and long-tailed 'r's. It does not fit easily into the Mont St Michel scripts and with the interpolation of a grant by Duke William in the middle, it is suspect.[2] The script can be compared, however, with that of Frotmundus (clearly influenced by charter hands) which has similar flourishes though it is more pointed than the charter. It might suggest, therefore, a date of 1030–5 for the late transitional to early middle manuscripts, but in view of the doubts of its authenticity this cannot be pressed.

The charter by which Raginaldus and Hersinde gave the priory of St Victeur at Le Mans to Mont St Michel in 1040, also now destroyed, but reproduced by de Broussillon,[3] shows already at this date a rounder, statelier hand less widely spaced vertically and with shorter ascenders and descenders in proportion to the minim. There is an uncertainty in the irregular way the letters slope. The script can be compared with the rounder scripts of Avranches MSS. 128 and 76 and would support a date in the 1040's for the earlier middle manuscripts.

Duke William's charter of 1054 confirming William Pichenoht's gift of Perelle in Guernsey still survives.[4] In it the height of the ascenders and descenders is further reduced which was noticed as a feature of the middle to late manuscripts. The script is curiously inept and can be compared with a similarly irregular hand in a charter of *c.*1060, reproduced by de Broussillon, in which Beatrix, wife of Hugo 'Coctus' made gifts to the Priory of St Victeur.[5] But it bears little similarity to the skilful scripts of the middle manuscripts.

Lastly comes the second surviving charter of the abbey, Duke Robert Curthose's grant of a market at Ardevon in 1088, which was published by Léopold Delisle.[6] This is in a magnificent script in which the split seriphs,

1 V. Hunger, *Histoire de Verson* (1908), no. 5. See also M. Fauroux, op. cit., no. 73.

2 It is however accepted by Mme. Fauroux.

3 B. de Broussillon, 'Cartulaire de Saint-Victeur', op. cit., pl. iv.

4 St Lô, Archives de la Manche, H, fonds du Mont St Michel. M. Fauroux, op. cit., no. 133. I owe a photograph to the kindness of Mr. P. Chaplais.

5 B. de Broussillon, 'Cartulaire de Saint Victeur', op. cit. pl. v.

6 Now Paris, Bib. Nat., nouv. acq. latin 1674, fol. 4. Published with facsimile by L. Delisle, 'Charte Normande de 1088', *Société de l'Histoire de France* (1886). Exh., *Millénaire*, no. 123.

the pointed tops of the 'n's and the minim of the 't' projecting above the cross stroke are all details which can be compared with the late manuscripts, for example Avranches MSS. 58 and 89, though the charter goes further in an almost mannered exaggeration.

To sum up, between the terminal dates of the refoundation of the abbey in 966 and the appointment of Scollandus who wrote part of Avranches 103, as abbot of St Augustine's in 1072, a script belonging to the early group and probably identifiable as that of Hervardus is datable between 991 and 1009; a manuscript of the middle group, Rouen, Bibliothèque Municipale, MS. A.143 was written before 1048; and the charters, though their scripts are not close to the book hands, give general support to the following approximate dates which may be suggested for the four groups: Early group, 980-1015; Transitional group, 1015-1045; Middle group, 1040-1070; Late group, 1065-1100.[1] In turning now to an examination of the decoration of the manuscripts it will be possible to check the sketch given of the development of the scripts, and to mention one or two points serving to corroborate the dating suggested.

1 See Appx. I for chronology.

# III

## THE INITIALS OF THE MANUSCRIPTS OF MONT ST MICHEL

### *Part I - The early manuscripts*

OF the sixteen manuscripts assigned to the early group on palaeographical grounds, seven have decorated initials. These are Avranches MSS. 50, 78, 97, 98 and 211, Bayeux 56 and Paris Latin 8055. The initials are very heterogeneous. They differ not only from manuscript to manuscript, but often in the same manuscript. This, of course, is only to be expected as a result of the refounding of the monastery in 966. This is an experimental stage in which the scriptorium has not yet developed its own style.

It will be convenient to consider the early initials under three main headings. The first type will include those initials which are decorated either by patterns inside the letter shape, or by animal-head, leaf or interlace adjuncts to it. To the second type will belong those initials in which the shape of the letter is composed of geometrical, animal or leaf forms, as opposed to being decorated with them. The leaves used in these two groups are still predominantly flat. Initials of the third type are differentiated from the second type by their forms becoming three-dimensional and more organic. At the same time these more organic forms are usually adjuncts to, rather than components of, the letter shape.

#### A: TYPE I INITIALS WHOSE LETTER SHAPE ACTS AS A FRAME FOR DECORATIVE PATTERNS OR ADJUNCTS

They are found in Avranches MSS. 50, 211, 97 and Bayeux 56. Before considering them in detail, a general point may be made. Their most obvious quality is their clarity. They have none of the ambiguity of Insular initials of the eighth century where the letters either become smothered with their ornament or are twisted into decorative shapes; nor of those later Anglo-Saxon initials of the tenth century which tend to fragment into interlaces or animal heads. Nor have they any close connection with eighth-century Merovingian initials where the shape of the letter suggests to the illuminator a conglomeration of animal, bird or fish forms which end by distorting the letter. Many of them are derived from Roman capitals and they are all always easily recognizable. In this they show an ultimate dependence on the initials of the various ninth-century Carolingian schools, especially the two with their centres nearest to Normandy, that of Tours to the south, and the so-called Franco-Saxon school of manuscripts produced in north France at such centres as St Vaast, Arras.[1] This emphasis on the clarity of the letter forms remains a characteristic of the Mont St Michel initials throughout.[2]

## *Interlace initials in MS.50*

The type I initials contain two groups whose main decoration is interlace. The first group is of initials in MS. 50.[3] The interlaces occur at the extremities of the initial but also as part of its articulation, in the bow of
Pl. 7*c* the 'E' for example. In a 'P', fol. 74, an interlace also fills the shaft. There are various other patterns as shaft fillings, and some leaf terminals.

Pls. 6*c*, *e* The symmetrical pointed interlace with its protruding bird head of an 'I', and the whole design of a 'T', proclaim their Franco-Saxon origin.[4]
Pl. 7*a* Ornamental hatching as in the bow of a 'P', fol. 112ᵛ, is also found in manuscripts of that school and is insular in origin. On the other hand the

[1] For a short description of Carolingian illumination with further bibliography see C. Nordenfalk, 'Carolingian illumination', *Early Medieval Painting* (1957), 136–58.

[2] See Avril, *Millénaire* (2), 211. For the history of decorated initials see Schardt, *Das Initial*, van Moé, *Illuminated initials*, J. Gutbrod, *Die Initiale in Handschriften des* 8. *bis* 13. *Jahrhunderts* (1965).

[3] For the provenance of this manuscript, not certainly made in the scriptorium, see above page 45 and the catalogue of manuscripts, Appx II.

[4] For the Franco-Saxon school and survivals of Franco-Saxon types of initial see C. Nordenfalk, 'Ein karolingisches Sakramentar aus Echternach und seine Vorläufer', *Acta Archaelogica*, ii (1931), 207–44. Already in the late ninth century leaf forms foreign to the pure Franco-Saxon style are being combined with the interlace initials at Echternach.

patterns of the leaf scroll in the stem of the 'I' and the alternating palmette of the 'T' are not found in Franco-Saxon manuscripts. Nor are leaf terminals used commonly in that school. Moreover, the squat shapes of the letters and the way they are squeezed, for instance the 'T', into the script point rather to the Tours school.

In fact, both the patterns mentioned, the leaf scroll and the alternating palmette, occur in Tours manuscripts from the Grandval Bible of *c.* 840 onward. There are also terminal leaf forms found in Tours manuscripts and later at St Gall.[1] These initials of MS. 50, therefore, are debased copies of Carolingian initials conflating features of different schools. No doubt numerous examples could be given of similar initials from the late tenth century. To the north interlace decoration is common. In the south animal and leaf forms are more important. Two manuscripts from St Aubin, Angers, a Life of St Gregory[2] and a St Augustine on the Psalms[3] (the former not dissimilar from MS. 50 in script), have initials which are squat in shape and use animal and leaf forms with white reserve alternating vine-leaf and scroll patterns.[4] Pls. 7*a*, *b*

MS. 50 has two other initials, however, which are quite different in style to those so far considered, and, though interlace is a very subsidiary component of these letters, they can best be considered here. They are the 'S', fol. 85ᵛ, and the 'E', fol. 3. The bar of the 'E' is formed by interlacing stems making a palmette shape. The basic components are a stem with a node leaf and a pointed trilobe leaf. In the 'S' the terminals, the lower protruding from an animal head, interlace through the central part of the letter. Pl. 7*c*

The design and form of leaves of these two initials find their closest

1 The alternating palmette occurs for instance in the Bamberg Bible, Köhler (1), Taf.58h. The veined leaf as a terminal occurs in an 'I' in the Gospel Book, London, Brit. Mus., Add. MS. 11848, fol. 75, Köhler (1), Taf.26a, and in the St Gall *Psalterium aureum*, Stiftsbibl. Cod. 22, p. 125, Schardt, *Das Initial*, 94. At Mont St Michel the leaves are yet more stylized than in the Carolingian examples.

2 Angers, Bib. Mun., MS. 819, fol. 1 and fol. 2ᵛ. The abbey's obituaries contain an entry for 27 July of a Hunbertus who is probably the abbot of St Aubin who died *c.* 1020. See J. Laporte, 'Les obituaires du Mont Saint-Michel', *Millénaire* (1), 735.

3 Angers, Bib. Mun., MS. 1320, fol. 1.

4 Similar squat letters and relief patterns are found in late tenth-century Limoges manuscripts which will be considered later for their different type of leaf.

forerunners in the Folchard Psalter, made at St Gall, *c.* 870.[1] The ornamental fillings of the initials of this manuscript and in others of the same school, are a hybrid between interlace and plant scroll. The stems interlace more and the leaves and nodes are more pointed than in the later St Gall and Ottonian school golden rinceaux initials.

Pl. 7*d* In an 'L' on page 332 of the Folchard Psalter an interlace breaks from the centre of the letter and ends in palmette leaves. The 'E' of Avranches 50 is slightly different, since the 'leaf interlace' is the cross bar of the letter, not an ornamental filling. The actual scroll, however, is very similar. The 'S' of MS. 50, also has node leaves and pointed trilobes similar to those in the Folchard Psalter. The way in which a triangular shape fills the corners of a letter form is also typical of St Gall initials – the Folchard 'M', page 305, can be compared with the Mont St Michel 'S'. Furthermore, these initials and others in the manuscript have purple backgrounds, and it is at St Gall that such grounds are first used with the function of throwing up into relief the golden rinceaux scrolls and providing a static setting for their movement.[2] Further similarities between Mont St Michel and St Gall initials in other leaf forms will be mentioned later.

## *Interlace initials in MSS. 97, 98, 211 and Bayeux 56*

The second group of interlace initials is found in Avranches MSS. 97,
Pl. 7*e* 98, 211 and Bayeux 56. The letter forms are mostly tall and they are also very thin which increases the impression of lightness and grace. They are decorated in the shafts and bows with cable, knot and interlace patterns strongly silhouetted white on orange or black. Most of them have leaf terminals which are of a particular form. The leaf has three or four lobes but these are broken up into smaller crenellations by a dark infilling; they are also dotted and striated.

Tall and narrow, these letters form a strong contrast to the squat letters of Avranches 50. They resemble in their proportions Franco-

[1] St Gall, Stiftsbibl., MS. 23, F. Landsberger, *Der St. Galler Folchart-Psalter* (1912). See also Schardt, *Das Initial*, 79–89.

[2] Landsberger, op. cit., 2. Such purple grounds are found later in Ottonian manuscripts and from the late tenth century also in Aquitaine and particularly at St Martial, Limoges.

Saxon initials, and the interlaces reserved white on orange point to the same source. However, leaf terminals are rare, as has been said above, in Franco-Saxon manuscripts. This type of leaf is to be found in Tours school manuscripts, beginning to appear in Köhler's second group of manuscripts assigned to the abbacy of Fridugisus, 807–34. Examples close to the Mont St Michel leaves are in a Bible from Berne,[1] or in the leaves at the corners of frame pages of the Vivian Bible.[2]

Moreover, letters of slenderer proportions using reserve white cables and knot patterns on orange can be found in Tours manuscripts, for example in an 'M', fol. 13 of a Gospel book also of Köhler's second group.[3] The same patterns reserved on orange occur in the Canon Table pillars in a slightly later Gospels.[4] Tours influence particularly in these veined leaf forms may have been transmitted partly via late ninth-century Breton manuscripts which were strongly influenced by Tours style.[5] Mont St Michel had numerous connections with Brittany and its dukes, and later there were Breton scribes in the scriptorium.[6]

Pl. *7f*

Pl. *7g, h*

## B: TYPE II INITIALS COMPOSED OF GEOMETRICAL, VEGETABLE OR ANIMAL FORMS

The most important initials of this type are in MSS. 97, 211 and Paris, Latin 8055. They are much bolder and more skilful than the earlier letters. They are distinguished by a new type of leaf which is predominantly a scroll leaf, but often forms a palmette. It is streaked but only very sparingly dotted where a leaf breaks away from the stem. It never turns over, but occasionally the stems interlace. Where a scroll splits to turn each way a flat fan leaf forms and an inverted palmette appears. The leaves grow out of the stem of the initial as well as forming terminal scrolls.

Pl. *7i*

1 Bern, Stadtbibl. no. 4, fol. 111$^{v}$. Köhler (1), Taf.18e.

2 Paris, Bib. Nat., Latin 1, fol. 1$^{v}$. Köhler (1), Taf.77a.

3 London, Brit. Mus., Add. MS. 11848.

4 London, Brit. Mus., Add. MS. 11849, fol. 18.

5 See C. R. Morey, 'The Gospel-Book of Landevennec (the Harkness Gospels) in the New York Public Library', *Art Studies*, viii. 2 (1931), 225–86.

6 See the colophon of MS. 103. The symmetrical centralized design of two 'Q's anda 'd', fols. 1, 143$^{v}$ and 218 of MS. 98, in particular suggest Breton sources. See Pl. *7g*.

This scrolling, striated type of leaf does not appear in Tours manuscripts. Something approaching it begins to appear in manuscripts of the Palace school of Charles the Bald (823–77), for instance on the *incipit* page of St Luke's Gospel, fol. 66, in the *codex aureus* from St Emmeram, or the initial 'B' of St Jerome's Preface, fol. 2.[1] There one sees the way one leaf as it were emerges out of another. They are large, fleshy and striated, but with very crenellated edges. It is in the St Gall Folchard Psalter in a 'D'[2] that our type of leaf first appears (the leaves on the columns of the litany pages are somewhat similar to those of the St Emmeram *codex aureus*). These leaves in the 'D' are very close indeed to the Mont St Michel type, except that the tip of the leaf does not turn back. However, in other leaves, in the same Psalter, simpler in form and not striated, the tip does curl back.[3] The development after the Folchard Psalter, in for instance the St Gall *Psalterium aureum*, is in the direction of smaller leaves, trilobes and nodes sprouting from the golden rinceaux. The similarity, however, is so great here that some connection between the two must exist.[4]

Pl. 8*a*

It was noted above that purple backgrounds similar to those in the initials in MS. 50 were found in manuscripts in central west France and particularly at Limoges. An examination of the leaf forms in the first Bible of St Martial, Limoges[5] and in the Lectionary,[6] the former perhaps

1 Munich, Bayr, Staatsbibl., Clm. 14000. Schardt, *Das Initial*, 69, 70.

2 St Gall, Stiftsbibl. Cod. 23, p. 304. Landsberger, op. cit., Abb. 13. This is the only example in Landsberger's plates.

3 As it does too in the slightly later *Psalterium aureum*, also from St Gall, in an 'M' and a 'd', pp. 119 and 125. St Gall, Stiftsbibl., Cod. 22. Schardt, *Das Initial*, 94, 95.

4 I know of no direct contact between St Gall and Mont St Michel at this period. For Normandy as a whole, though again I know of no later contact, it is worth mentioning the famous monk of Jumièges who fled from the Norman invaders with his Antiphonary to St Gall. See J. Duft, 'Le "Presbyter de Gimedia" apporte son Antiphonaire à Saint-Gall', *Jumièges, Congrès Scientique du XIIIe Centenaire* (1955), 925–36. Curious resemblances between Fécamp manuscripts and those of St Gall may also be mentioned, for example in the Bible, Rouen, Bib. Mun., MS. 1, fol. 199$^{v}$, the standing figure labelled 'Job' is very like the figure with an initial 'F' in the *Psalterium aureum* St Gall, Stiftsbibl. Cod. 22. A. Merton, *Die Buchmalerei in St. Gallen* (1912), Taf. xxx. 2.

5 Paris, Bib. Nat., Latin 5. Exh., *MSS. à peintures*, no. 319. D. Gaborit-Chopin, 'La décoration des manuscrits à Saint-Martial de Limoges et en Limousin (IX$^{e}$-XII$^{e}$ siecle)', *École des Chartes, position des thèses* (1967).

6 Paris, Bib. Nat., Latin 5301. *Exh., MSS. à peintures*, no. 320.

of the first half, the latter of the end of the tenth century, reveals this same leaf form again. In the Bible the leaves are more luxuriant.[1] In the Lectionary the leaves resemble more the neater, dryer leaves of the 'M'
and the 'Q', fol. 201$^{v}$ and 240$^{v}$. An 'R' from the Lectionary, fol. 145$^{v}$, Pls. 8*d*, *e*
has the reversed palmette exactly as in the 'S', fol. 223$^{v}$.[2] Pls. 7*i*, 8*g*

In connection with these leaves it is also worth noting their similarities
with certain of the capitals in the choir at Bernay.[3] These, dated by Pl. 8*b*
Grodecki 1020–28, have very veined leaves turning in scrolls and one often growing out of another. Grodecki, significantly, notes their resemblance to leaves on a consular diptych recut at St Gall *c.* 900, and now at Monza.[4] He also points to similarities with capitals at St Bénigne at Dijon, though this type of leaf does not appear to have been used there in manuscripts.[5] It is interesting that at Bernay, as at Mont St Michel, this type of leaf is abandoned. The succeeding carving at Bernay though less technically skilful, has, as Grodecki says, more promise for the future development of the romanesque capital. Similarly at Mont St Michel, though these initials are extremely skilful, the type of initial which is finally adopted is different.

The four finest initials of this group require further comment. These
are the 'M' and the 'Q', fol. 201$^{v}$ and fol. 240$^{v}$ of MS. 97, the 'M' of Pls. 8*d*, *e*, 9*a*
MS. 211 and the 'N' of Latin 8055. The central shaft of the 'M' of Pl. 53*d*
MS. 97 is formed by a spread-eagled lion and the two bows of the letter spring from its mask. They are ornamented with bold white reserve acanthus patterns and end in plant scolls. The colours are blue and yellow.

1 Cf. fol. 136, 'L', Micheli, *L'Enluminure*, pl. 280, with MS. 97, fol. 173 'Q'. The Limoges St Gall connection is further shown by the pattern found on one of the Folchard Psalter Litany columns, p. 10, Landsberger, op. cit., Abb. 25, and also in the 'D' already mentioned, p. 304, which recurs in an 'A' on fol. 84 of the St Martial Bible, Paris, Bib. Nat., Latin 5, Lauer, *Enluminures Romanes*, pl. xxxv, and also in the Canon Tables there.

2 Paris, Bib. Nat., Latin 5301.

3 L. Grodecki, 'Les débuts de la sculpture romane en Normandie. Bernay', *Bulletin Monumental*, cviii (1950), 7–67, espec. pp. 26–47. G. Zarnecki, '1066 and architectural sculpture', *Proceedings of the British Academy*, lii (1966), 92–3, pl. vi.

4 Goldschmidt, *Elfenbeinskulpturen* (1), no. 168, Taf. lxxix. An ivory book cover now in Würzburg, Univ. Bibl., MS. theol. fol. 67 should also be compared. *Elfenbeinskulpturen* (1), no. 169, Taf. lxxx.

5 See Appx. III for manuscripts from S. Bénigne.

The 'Q' is drawn in brown pen and is made up of two birds. From their beaks come the two hind legs of another spread-eagled lion and from its mask sprouts a leaf scroll which, intertwining with the birds' tails, goes on to form the tail of the 'Q'.

These initials, it should be emphasized, do not belong to the Carolingian tradition. The 'Q' is more like those Merovingian letters which are made up of birds, animals and fish.[1] This arrangement of flanking beasts grasping a central figure is of Eastern origin. Symmetrical birds forming 'O's, 'S's, or 'Q's with snakes or plants in their beaks are found in Merovingian manuscripts. They survive in the early Tours school manuscripts and are copied in the tenth-century Bible from St Aubin at Angers.[2]

On the other hand, the shapes of the Mont St Michel letters are metamorphosed into plant form[3] which turns again into an animal form. This way in which one form turns into another with a sort of dynamic life engendered by its own movement, is reminiscent of Insular Art, and is as foreign to Merovingian as it is to Carolingian initials.

In looking for the source of such a letter, therefore, one might turn to a point where the two traditions, the Insular and the Merovingian, meet. The nearest precursors of the Mont St Michel initials are, in fact, in a book which fulfils these conditions, being made in north France at the end of the eighth century, the Corbie Psalter.[4] Both the symmetrical arrangement about a central motif, and the principle of the metamorphosis of forms, are found in this manuscript. The Carolingian revival ended further developments in this direction, and the Corbie initials are very exceptional.[5]

1 e.g. the Sacramentarium Gelasianum, Nordenfalk, *Early Medieval Painting*, 128, pl. Avril, *Millénaire* (2), 208, draws attention to an 'e' made up of three birds in the Gellone Sacramentary (reproduced Van Moé, *Illuminated Initials*).

2 Angers, Bib. Mun., MS. 3 and 4. Another famous example of this symmetrical arrangement is on the Sutton Hoo purse lid in the British Museum.

3 The earliest example of such an initial at Mont St Michel is probably the 'B', MS. 78, fol. 1. See *Millénaire* (2), pl. xvii, fig. 40.

4 Amiens, Bib. Mun., MS. 18. Exh., *Karl der Grosse*, no. 436. J. Porcher, 'La Peinture provinciale', *Karolingische Kunst*, ed. W. Braunfels, H. Schnitzler (1965), 59–61, figs. 6–10.

5 At St Gall with its Insular tradition something similar survives. E.g. 'd' Gospels, St Gall, Stiftsbibl., Cod. 367, fol. 104. Schardt, *Das Initial*, 75.

About A.D. 1000 the principle is taken up again and the Mont St Michel scriptorium is one among many experimenting along the same lines which lead towards the Romanesque style of initial. Thus the Mont St Michel 'Q' is in a sense taking up where the Corbie Psalter left off.[1]

The Corbie Psalter, however, is so exceptional in its initials that its influence on early Romanesque initials might reasonably have been doubted. The discovery of a Mont St Michel manuscript of Persius' Satires in Paris, Latin 8055, however, makes it possible to show that the influence of the Corbie Psalter was direct.[2] On page 141 of the Paris manuscript there is an initial 'N' which is a literal copy of the 'N' on Pls. 53*c*, *d*
fol. 31ᵛ of the Psalter. The scribe of the Paris manuscript is Hervardus, the main scribe of the early group. Possibly he was also the artist and copied both initial and text on a visit to the Corbie library. The copy is in any case a remarkable tribute to the stimulus provided by the Psalter's exceptional decoration. There are, however, certain differences between the Psalter initials and the Mont St Michel initials. In the first place in most of the Mont St Michel letters there is a tension between the autonomy of the constituent forms and the letter shape which controls them. But neither is distorted, both are clear and unambiguous. In the Corbie Psalter the artist's fantasy tends to run away with him, and the result is that the letter becomes difficult to recognize. In the second place the principle of dynamic change is carried further at Mont St Michel. The leaves turn and renew themselves out of their own movement with a greater richness; but also in the spread-eagled lion in the 'Q' and the 'M' a new factor is introduced. The form itself as it were changes direction in mid course. Thus the body of the lion starts as a profile view. The Pl. 8*e*
legs extend to each side so that the body is seen as if from the side. The two profiles are then conflated and so become one, seen, as it were, from

[1] See the remarks of O. Homburger, 'Ein vernichtetes Denkmal merovingischer Buchkunst aus frühkarolingischer Zeit, der "Rachio-Kodex" der Bongarsiana', *Festschrift Hans R. Hahnloser*, ed. E. J. Beer, P. Hofer, L. Mojou (1961), 200. Also J. Porcher, 'L'Evangélaire de Charlemagne et le psautier d'Amiens', *La Revue des Arts*, vii (1957), 51–8, and O. Pächt, 'The Pre-Carolingian Roots of Early Romanesque Art', *Studies in Western Art, I. Romanesque and Gothic*, ed. M. Meiss (1963), 67ff.

[2] See my 'A Romanesque copy from Mont Saint-Michel of an initial in the Corbie Psalter', *Millénaire* (2), 239–45. That this was not the only copy from the Psalter is indicated by some initials in the Mont St Michel Bible. See below, p. 194, 207–8 and pls. 55*b*, *d*,*f*.

above. Then the head is added in fully frontal view. This gives three changes of direction, the last particularly abrupt.

In looking more specifically for the origin of this motif of the spread-eagled lion, it may be noted first that something rather similar occurs even in the late Carolingian period at St Gall. In St Gall Stiftsbibliothek MS. 367, a Gospel book, an uncial 'd' is made up of a bird whose neck and head form the tail of the letter whilst the body fills the bowl.[1] In the same manuscript in another 'd' the bird has been as it were turned, so that its wings and feet are spread-eagled, but its head is still in profile.[2]

This same type of initial 'd' is found just over a hundred years later at St Bertin in the Otbert Psalter.[3] And in the St Bertin manuscript there are examples of the profile body combining into a frontal head – in e.g. the 'M', fol. 136, or the 'E's, fol. 67v and fol. 52. The fat fleshy bodies of the St Bertin animals are dependent on Anglo-Saxon models and in the English Salisbury Psalter,[4] 969–78, for instance, some of the dragons are seen as it were from above with their characteristic back-bone ridge, whilst their heads are in profile. However, both in the Anglo-Saxon and the St Bertin manuscripts the letters are less architectonic and the letter form suffers distortion. The Mont St Michel leaves are moreover quite different from anything found at St Bertin or in Anglo-Saxon manuscripts.

In central west France where, as we have already seen, similar scrolling leaves occur at Limoges, similar experiments with animal formed initials were taking place also. The St Gall type of uncial 'd' made out of a bird was known at St Aubin, Angers, for instance, where it occurs in the late tenth-century Bible.[5] The Bible's initials copy early Tours school initials. Another manuscript from St Aubin, a copy of St Augustine on the Psalms, later in date but to judge from the script still early in the eleventh Pl. 8*f* century, has an initial 'M' whose central shaft is formed by a spread-

[1] Fol. 104. Schardt, *Das Initial*, 75.

[2] Fol. 197. Micheli, *L'Enluminure*, pl. 182.

[3] Boulogne, Bib. Mun., MS. 20, fol. 15, fol. 70.

[4] Salisbury Cathedral, Chapter Library, MS. 150. Wormald, *Decorated Initials*, 121, pl. vd.

[5] Angers, Bib. Mun., MS. 3 and 4. MS. 4, fol. 12. In the same manuscript another uncial 'd' is made up of two birds with a central palmette (fol. 21v), whilst a roman 'D' has a bird forming the bowl carrying a leaf in its beak.

eagled lion.[1] This is the earliest example of this motif which I have come across to compare with the Mont St Michel initials. The palmette sprouting from the lion's mouth is comparable to that on fol. 201v, but the leaves are flatter and more fan-shaped. Also to the south, at Limoges, another 'M' in the Lectionary from St Martial, referred to above,[2] is made up of two profile lions for the bows, who share a frontal head. And in Limoges manuscripts from the late eleventh century the spread-eagled beasts become common.[3] Another example from the first half of the eleventh century is in a manuscript of St Jerome's Sermons on the Virgin and various Lives of Saints, which comes from St Germain-des-Prés. The manuscript belongs to the group illuminated by Ingelardus,[4] and has an initial 'U' whose upright is a spread-eagled hairy lion.[5] Pl. 8*c*

Where the motif was invented is not certain therefore. The area Angers/Limoges has a strong claim and from there it may have passed to Mont St Michel and to St Germain-des-Prés. Such ideas are often 'in the air' at a particular period and do not necessarily mean direct contact. But they do suggest some sort of concerted movement in the different abbeys in experimenting with new forms of initials. A later Mont St Michel version of this initial occurs in MS. 47, fol. 181 and is perhaps closer to the Angers initial than are the MS. 97 examples.

One other possible source for the motif is the use of lions for capitals or pedestals of the columns of Canon Tables. The earliest spread-eagled lion known to me is, in fact, in one of the arches of the Canon Tables of the Book of Kells.[6] In the Vivian Bible lion masks with their paws resting on each side support the columns of the Canon Tables.[7] Then in the Folchard Psalter the capitals of a Litany Table are lion masks and feet, but the feet also appear below at the base of the column.[8] In an Anglo-Saxon

1 Angers, Bib. Mun., 169, fol. 218v. Note also the 'U', fol. 6.

2 Paris, Bib. Nat., Latin 5301, fol. 62v.

3 e.g. the Sacramentary, Paris, Bib. Nat., Latin 9438. Van Moé, *Illuminated initials*.

4 Y. Deslandres, 'Les Manuscrits decorés au XIe siècle à St. Germain-des-Prés par Ingelard', *Scriptorium*, ix (1955), 3–16.

5 Paris, Bib. Nat., Latin 11750, fol. 25v.

6 Trinity College, Dublin, fol. 4. E. H. Alton, P. Meyer, *Codex Cenannensis* (Bern, 1950, complete facsimile).

7 Paris, Bib. Nat., Latin 1, fols. 327v and 383v. Köhler (1), Taf. 84 and 85.

8 St Gall, Stiftsbibl., Cod. 23, p. 11. See Landsberger, op. cit., Taf. vi.

Psalter the lion masks above are omitted, but the feet remain below.[1] Finally in a Gospels in Paris in the Bibliothèque de l'Arsenal, a complete lion spread-eagled but with head facing as it were backwards, is found as a capital.[2] This eleventh-century manuscript with Franco-Saxon frames to its miniatures must come from northern France. The leaves sprouting on either side of the capital suggest the form of an 'M' and can be compared with MS. 97, fol. 201v.[2]

The motif has a wide popularity once invented. It is found in two other
Pl. 15*a* later Mont St Michel manuscripts,[3] in manuscripts from other Norman abbeys (Jumièges, Fécamp, and St Ouen), in England after the Conquest, at St Maur-des-Fossés, Paris, and in later examples at Angers and at Limoges, in Italy at Lucca, and as far south as Monte Cassino.[4]

Finally, the 'M' which introduces the account of the founding of the
Pl. 9*a* abbey in the Chronicle, MS. 211, with the word 'Memoria' is a very important initial. The decoration of the manuscript is here integrated with and concentrates on the text rather than being an addition to or an insertion in it. Its design is meant to recall the shape of the 'Vere Dignum' monogram of the Preface to the Mass, in order to emphasize the solemnity of the summons to remember the miracles of the foundation.[5] With its rich colouring, including gold always uncommon at Mont St Michel, it is symptomatic of the new importance the initial will assume in the decoration of the abbey's manuscripts.[6]

1 Salisbury Cathedral 150, fol. 122. See Kendrick, *Late Saxon*, pl. xxix.

2 MS. 592, fol. 16. Exh., *MSS. à peintures*, no. 74. It seems unlikely that at this date the influence of actual carved capitals need be considered.

3 MSS. 47 and 86.

4 See E. B. Garrison, *Studies in the History of Mediaeval Italian Painting*, i no. 4 (1954), 189 for a collection of examples including MS. 97, fol. 201v.

5 Cf. for instance the Raganaldus Sacramentary, Köhler (1), Taf. 64a.

6 C. Nordenfalk, 'Miniature ottonienne et ateliers capétiens', *Art de France*, iv (1964), 47–55, draws attention to the contrast between the imperial patronage in Germany resulting in *codices de luxe* with a profusion of gold, and the situation in France. Nordenfalk, in fact, even raises the possibility that MSS. 97 and 211 might have been imports from the Loire area in connection with his discussion of the Lombard artist Nivardus, illuminator of a Gospels for Fleury, Bib. Nat., Latin 1126. Not only the evidence of the script but also the dissimilarity of the initial scroll seem to be against this. Though a Mont St Michel scribe may have visited Fleury to inscribe the Winchcombe Sacramentary, as we have seen, with a necrology, this was before 1009, and Nordenfalk dates the Nivardus Gospels very plausibly *c.* 1013.

## C: TYPE III INITIALS WITH THREE-DIMENSIONAL LEAVES

In the initials of this group a third dimension is added. The leaves curl and grip the letter frame, sometimes they are hollow cups, and clasps, as it were to rivet the forms, are used regularly. The Type III initials in the early manuscripts, are all in MS. 98 except for a 'B' in MS. 97, fol. 37. There are three prominent leaf forms in these initials which are quite different from anything so far met with. They can all be seen in the 'Q' on fol. 117 of MS. 98. The first is a leaf folded with a crenellated outer Pl. 9*b*
edge. The second is the cup leaf, and the third is the long tubular leaf with a round top which curls over. These three types all occur in Anglo-Saxon initials and their sources and development from the Cuthbert stole (909–16) onwards have been traced by Dr Freyhan.[1] They can be seen for instance in the Bodleian Caedmon manuscript or a Boethius also at Oxford.[2]

The sources of these initials are certainly ultimately Anglo-Saxon. However, since initials of this Type III also occur in the transitional manuscripts, the question of whether this influence was direct or not must be deferred to a discussion of the group as a whole.

## D: SUMMARY

The early initials at Mont St Michel have two main sources. The first, the Carolingian, stands for the principle of clarity of the Roman capital letter form. The manuscripts use initials derived from the Tours and Franco-Saxon schools. At the same time there is evidence of St Gall influence from manuscripts of the period *c.* 870–900. This probably came indirectly, perhaps via north-east French sources on the fringes of Ottonian art, perhaps from the area of Angers and Limoges. Also with St Gall connections but opposed to the Carolingian indissolubility of the Roman capital letter form are the 'scrolling leaf' initials of MS. 97, the

1 R. Freyhan, 'The place of the stole and maniples in Anglo-Saxon art of the tenth century', *The Relics of St. Cuthbert*, ed. C. F. Battiscombe (1956), 409–32.

2 Oxford, Bodleian Library, MS. Junius 11, p. 71, and MS. Auct. F.1.15, fol. 48v. Wormald, *Decorated Initials*, pl. vc and vib.

most important and the finest in quality of all the early group initials. The features of these initials, in particular the principle of dynamic change and the tension between the controlling letter form and the decorative components, have been mentioned. They are features which are typical of the Romanesque style and which are already found in pre-Carolingian sources. They give the artist of MS. 97 the status of a pioneer and his initials were sufficiently admired to be copied in later manuscripts. However, these initials were abandoned at Mont St Michel in favour of a return to the Carolingian Roman capitals but now combined with a new Anglo-Saxon leaf. The reason for the abandonment of the scrolling leaf initials probably was that this pre-Carolingian type of letter made up of animal forms was not felt to be sufficiently strongly architectonic. As a result the tension between letter form and decoration failed. The new Anglo-Saxon leaf with its turning three-dimensionality produced a tension and a contrast which emphasized rather than dissolved the letter form. We must now turn to this new development as seen in the transitional manuscripts.

## *Part II - The transitional manuscripts*

Of the twelve manuscripts distinguished as transitional on grounds of script, MSS. 68, 79 and 129 have only minor initials. MS. 61 with one series of isolated initials and others looking forward to the middle manuscripts will be considered last. The remaining initials fall into two groups. The first consists of Type III initials, those with turning three-dimensional leaf forms which first occur in the early manuscripts in MS. 98. The second group occurring in MSS. 115 and 99, have rather similar types of leaves, but differ in their design.

### A: TYPE III INITIALS IN THE TRANSITIONAL MANUSCRIPTS

These initials of the first group occur in MSS. 38, 70, 91, 105, 115, 128 and Vatican, Lat. 9668. They are very close to the initials of MS. 98 and those of MSS. 91 and 105 seem to be by the same hand. The 'P' of

MS. 98, fol. 132v, may be compared with the 'R' of MS. 91, fol. 137v, Pls. *9c, d*
particularly the almost identical lion mask. An open slack interlace is characteristic of these initials and commonly it forms a pyramid, sometimes with a flat base – e.g. the 'B', MS. 91, fol. 1. Some new kinds of leaf, Pl. *9f*
or really fruit, are introduced, and several initials have white reserve panels of acanthus on orange or black, for instance the 'B' in MS. 91. Initials in MSS. 70, 115 and 128, and Vatican Lat. 9668 are similar in their leaves which, however, are more striated and intertwined, and also in their designs with acanthus panels, and interlace.[1] The development of the initials of these three manuscripts shows that they are later than MSS. 98, 91 and 105.

The scrolls in all these initials are, it was pointed out, ultimately derived from Anglo-Saxon manuscripts since the type of leaves used, Eastern in origin, are not found elsewhere in the tenth century. The question, therefore, arises as to whether the scriptorium had direct or indirect knowledge of Anglo-Saxon manuscripts at this date, the first third of the eleventh century.

Discussion of this question must start from a single Anglo-Saxon initial. This is the great 'B' on fol. 4 of the Harley Psalter of the last quarter of Pl. *9e*
the tenth century.[2] This letter is fundamental to the development of the initial at Mont St Michel and indeed to one current of the development of the Romanesque initial as a whole. Professor Wormald has pointed out the Franco-Saxon origin of the letter form,[3] but it is most important also to emphasize that this is a completely new conjunction. For the Franco-Saxon letter, conspicuous for the clarity and boldness of its design but depending for its effect on its setting on the open parchment, had only used leaf ornament very sparingly, if at all. The contrast was between compressed, clearly silhouetted interlaces and open space.

Carolingian artists of other schools, particularly the Metz School and the palace school of Charles the Bald, had used plant forms and scrolls in

[1] The design of the 'C', MS. 128, fol. 53, may be compared, for instance, with that of MS. 91, fol. 2.

[2] London, British Museum, Harley MS. 2904.

[3] Wormald, *Decorated initials*, 108–9, pl. 1. Idem, *English Drawings*, 71, no. 36. The manuscript may have been made at Ramsey Abbey, Huntingdonshire.

their letters. But they festooned the Roman capitals so that they were almost submerged. Only at St Gall did the artists use a scroll inside the letter form to create a tension between its movement and the solidity of the letter itself. From this point of view the 'D' of the Folchard Psalter[1] or
Pl. 9*h* the 'Q' of the *Psalterium aureum* are important letters.[2] But this leaf scroll developed into the stylized golden *rinceaux* which were taken up in the Ottonian schools from the later tenth century onwards, and which are very different from the Anglo-Saxon scroll.

Nevertheless the Anglo-Saxon artist of Harley 2904 was aiming at a similar effect of stability in the letter form versus movement in the leaf scroll to produce a tension. By using the turning Anglo-Saxon leaf he was able to introduce a new dimension. At the same time the leaf curving forward and back to pass over or grip the letter form, emphasizes its structure. Thus, however great the complexity and richness of the Anglo-Saxon scroll, it does not undermine the clarity of the letter. In the Ottonian *rinceaux* scroll increased complexity leads on the one hand to monotony and on the other tends to obscure the letter form, as in the earlier Carolingian initials. Moreover, the Anglo-Saxon scroll can be varied both by introducing new leaf forms and by inserting beasts and humans in the scroll.

The puzzling thing about the Harley 'B' is its isolation. Not only do there seem to be no preliminary experiments towards it, it stands already perfect as a fully-fledged example of its type, but Anglo-Saxon artists do not seem to have realized the possibilities for development inherent in it. The majority of Anglo-Saxon initials which might be expected to follow it, sumptuous letters in Gospel books and Psalters[3] either use almost pure Franco-Saxon forms,[4] or continue, as in the Tiberius Psalter, to use

[1] St Gall, Stiftsbibl., Cod. 23, p. 230. Schardt, *Das Initial*, 86.

[2] St Gall, Stiftsbibl., Cod. 22, p. 99. Schardt, *Das Initial*, 91.

[3] One would not expect, perhaps, the new type of letter to replace the established initials of Wormald's Type I and II in the less important non-liturgical manuscripts. The principle of tension between scroll and letter form is difficult to apply, admittedly, to the initials 'I' and 'L' of Sts Matthew, Mark and John's Gospels. The 'Q' of St Luke is however perfectly suitable.

[4] e.g. Grimbald Gospels, London, Brit. Mus., Add. MS. 34890; Gospels, Brit. Mus., Royal MS. I.D.IX; Gospels, St Lô, Bib. Mun., MS. I. Talbot Rice, pls. 56*b*), 58. Dodwell, *Canterbury School*, pl. 6*d*.

Wormald's Type II letter, as in the 'Q' made up of three dragons on fol. 72.[1]

Rather it was in northern France and above all in Normandy that this new type of initial was copied. This leads back to the question of whether Anglo-Saxon influence was direct or indirect in the Mont St Michel transitional manuscripts. One argument against its being direct is that there is hardly any hint in any of the manuscripts of the typical late tenth to early eleventh-century Anglo-Saxon initials which are made up of either animal heads or whole animal bodies, as divided by Wormald into his Types I and II initials. Whether the Harley 'B' was an isolated achievement or not, these other initials are so common that direct contact would have acquainted the Mont St Michel artists with them.[2] But there are very few examples of the Mont St Michel letters disintegrating into animal heads or bodies and interlaces in this typical Anglo-Saxon way. Where as in the 'Q' of MS. 98, fol. 117, dragons make up the letter they are most unlike the scaly-ridged-backed Anglo-Saxon Pl. 9*b* dragon.[3]

If Anglo-Saxon influence was not direct, the most obvious source would be the monasteries of northern France which were in contact with and strongly influenced by Anglo-Saxon art, particularly St Bertin and St Vaast. Since the reformed monasticism in Normandy came from the north it is likely that methods of book decoration there would be known and copied. Moreover, houses in this area were ideally suited to appreciate one current which went to make up the new Harley 'B'. St Vaast at Arras, for instance, still possessed Franco-Saxon manuscripts and many of the letters in the great Bible of this house are still purely Franco-Saxon.

The manuscripts from St Bertin associated with Abbot Otbert and

[1] London, Brit. Mus., Cotton Tiberius C.VI. In the Gospels, Cambridge, Trinity College, MS. B.10.4, the initial 'I's are inhabited, thus going one stage further than the Harley artist. The initial 'B's in the Psalters, Rome, Vatican, Reg. Lat. 12, London, Brit. Mus., Arundel 155, and Cambridge, Univ. Lib., MS. Ff.1.23 also follow the Harley principle. All these are manuscripts of the second quarter of the eleventh century.

[2] Wormald notes that the Type II initials are especially common in non-liturgical manuscripts, *Decorated initials*, 122.

[3] Except for their heads, in fact, they are more like birds and recall the great 'Q' of MS. 97, fol. 240v.

therefore datable to the period of his rule (*c*. 986–1004),[1] do not contain initials of the Harley type. There are on the other hand a number of initials closely dependent on Anglo-Saxon models particularly of Wormald's Type I. In spite of their close similarities, the St Bertin initials seem to have a greater sense of the value of blank space in a design, which results in an impression of greater crispness of outline and clarity of form. What matters in an Anglo-Saxon initial is the overall movement and complexity. At St Bertin the beginning and the end of every form is
Pl. 10*d* made perfectly clear[2] and similarly at Mont St Michel in a 'P', MS. 98, fol. 9, for instance, every motif has a clear beginning and end.

This general similarity does nothing to prove Mont St Michel dependence on St Bertin. Some other comparisons can be made. An 'I' from
Pl. 10*c* MS. 98, fol. 101, can be connected for instance with an 'I' in the Otbert
Pl. 10*b* Psalter[3] which has symmetrical leaves twining round the bars of the letter and also a lion mask, though at the top of the letter. The resemblance is general, but what is important is that it shows the Anglo-Saxon influence as fainter at Mont St Michel. In the St Bertin Psalter 'I' the leaves clearly grip the frame of the letter, as would an Anglo-Saxon leaf, whereas at Mont St Michel this motif is uncertain and ambiguous. The conclusion is surely that the Mont St Michel letter is a copy of a copy, in which the Anglo-Saxon ingredient is diluted.

At St Vaast where the Harley 'B' principle begins to be accepted, though still very tentatively, there are similarities to Mont St Michel in technique, in specific motifs and to some extent in style.[4]

The majority of the St Vaast initials, in the Bible for instance,[5] are still at the Folchard Psalter stage. There is a tension between the controlling letter form, at St Vaast emphasized by the relief interlace patterns, and the

1 Porcher, *French Miniatures*, 17–18.

2 Compare the initials in Boulogne, Bib. Mun., MS. 82 and Oxford, Bodleian Library, MS. Junius 11, reproduced Wormald, *Decorated Initials*, pls. v*b* and *c*.

3 Boulogne, Bib. Mun., MS. 20, fol. 40.

4 The key manuscripts of the St Vaast scriptorium in the eleventh century have been studied and a chronology proposed by S. Schulten, 'Die Buchmalerei des 11. Jahrhunderts im Kloster St Vaast in Arras', *Münchner Jahrbuch der bildenden Kunst*, vii (1956), 49–90. The Mont St Michel obituary contains a Leduinus who is probably to be identified with the abbot of St Vaast who died after 1041. See J. Laporte, 'Les obituaires du Mont Saint-Michel', *Millénaire* (1), 730 (2 January).

5 Arras, Bib. Mun., MS. 559(435).

scroll which, however, is still kept strictly within bounds. The three-dimensional leaf using the letter form as a trellis is not common but it does occur for instance in an 'O', on fol. 98$^{v}$ of Volume III of the Bible. Pl. 10*a*
This letter is almost an Anglo-Saxon corner rosette lifted out of place.

The Mont St Michel initials thus show a more ready acceptance of the Harley 'B' principle than the Arras initials. This is not whole-hearted even at Mont St Michel, for the 'B' of MS. 91, fol. 1 has an acanthus Pl. 9*f*
pattern in the bow which, rather than curl out as the similar pattern does in the Harley 'B', emphasizes the bow as a boundary for the scroll.

The most obvious way in which the Mont St Michel initials resemble the Arras letters rather than the Harley 'B', is that they are not painted. They may in a few cases be colour washed, but always thinly, and not with the kind of modelling which produces in the Harley 'B' and other Anglo-Saxon painted leaves in, for example, the border of the Benedictional of St Ethelwold, a thick succulent type of leaf. In the Arras initial the leaves are veined which either shows through the light colour wash, or more commonly the scroll is left reserved white on the colour ground. This results in a wiry appearance which is shared by the Mont St Michel Pls. 10*a*, 11*b*
leaves, and which is quite different from painted Anglo-Saxon leaves.[1]

There are also a number of detailed resemblances to Arras manuscripts. First, the acanthus panels in the Mont St Michel letters are close to Arras panels – the shaft of the 'B' MS. 91, fol. 1, can be compared with the Pl. 9*f*
frame in the Bible, Volume II, fol. 52$^{v}$. Secondly, very similar types of scaly birds and dragons are found, which are very un-Anglo-Saxon looking because lacking the round fleshy appearance. Thirdly, a furled leaf with curving lines which occurs in MS. 115 is found, though not commonly, at Arras. An example where it is doubled is in the scroll of the 'P' of the Bible, Volume II, fol. 123$^{v}$. This type of leaf with the curved lines, which does not seem to occur in Anglo-Saxon manuscripts,

[1] Unpainted leaves in Anglo-Saxon initials of Wormald's Type II, in e.g. the Arator at Oxford, Bodleian Library, MS. Rawlinson C.570 are similar in their wiry appearance and this is no doubt where this type of leaf comes from. See most recently F. Wormald, 'Anglo-Saxon initials in a Paris Boethius manuscript', *Gazette des Beaux-Arts*, lxii (1963), 63–70. But in these Anglo-Saxon initials the leaves are of subsidiary importance, not as at Arras and Mont St Michel the main decorative motif. An exception is the Cambridge Psalter, University Library, MS. Ff.1.23 to be discussed in a moment. This is of the second quarter of the eleventh century.

becomes very common in the north French area, being found in the Life of St Amand from St Amand,[1] and we shall have occasion to mention it
Pl. 10*f* later. Finally, MS. 115, fol. 1$^{v}$, has a framed *incipit* page (unfortunately very faint and damaged) with a medallion at the top with a half figure blessing Christ and three other medallions with dragons, scrolls and birds. The frame is pink, and there are touches of blue on the Christ. A com-
Pl. 10*e* parison of the medallions with those of the Bible, Volume II, fol. 52$^{v}$ is very striking, and again seems to be without Anglo-Saxon parallel.

The combined evidence therefore for St Vaast influence is strong. It does, however, raise a chronological problem. If the earliest initials of the Arras Bible are correctly dated *c.* 1025 by Schulten, this is probably too late for them to have been copied at Mont St Michel in MS. 98. The basis of Schulten's dating is a comparison with the Cambridge Psalter, University Library MS. Ff. 1.23, which cannot be put earlier than the second quarter of the eleventh century. There may of course have been other and earlier Anglo-Saxon manuscripts which have not survived with similar initials following the Harley 'B' principle, less extreme in their elongated foliage but still with the 'wiry' appearance and of the first quarter of the eleventh century. But even were this agreed, it would be difficult to push the date of the St Vaast manuscripts much further back. Moreover, the most striking similarities quoted are in MS. 91 and MS. 115 which, on grounds of script, come later than MS. 98.

It may be, then, that in the early stages it is a question of a parallel development at Mont St Michel and at St Vaast. The Mont St Michel scriptorium would then have got its knowledge of the Anglo-Saxon leaf from centres like St Bertin and St Peter, Ghent,[2] where it was common enough but in a very subsidiary position. The newly adopted three-dimensional leaf continued to hold the same predominant position in the letter as had the scrolling leaf in MS. 97, which it replaced, and as had the leaf scroll in many of the Carolingian initials. St Vaast influence would supervene in MSS. 91 and 115.

1 Valenciennes, Bib. Mun., MS. 502, fol. 10$^{v}$. Swarzenski, *Monuments*, fig. 178.

2 Cf. the Lives of Saints from St Peter (later St Bavon) now Ghent, Bibl. de la Ville et de l'Université, MS. 308. There appear to be no illuminated manuscripts surviving from Mont Blandin, Ghent, of this date.

A number of points in which the Mont St Michel initials markedly differ from those of St Vaast initials should also be mentioned. First, the white relief chain and interlace patterns, so common in the St Vaast manuscripts in the shafts of the letters, are not found at Mont St Michel. In general interlace is sparingly used in the transitional manuscripts. Secondly, the Mont St Michel leaves are broader and less crenellated than those of St Vaast. In many of the St Vaast scrolls the emphasis is on the twining tendril with its prominent stem nodes and the dots where the Pl. 10*a*
nodes break from the scroll. In these features the St Vaast scroll copies a style common in eleventh-century German initials. In the Mont St Michel letters the emphasis is much more on the leaf forms which are distinguished clearly from the scroll. Thirdly, there are two leaf forms which do not seem to occur at St Vaast. One is a kind of fruit form around which leaves curl which may be called a 'pomegranate' leaf. It is seen in the centre of the 'G' on fol. 255 of MS. 91. The second is a trilobe leaf with Pl. 10*i*
serrated edges which can be seen towards the bottom of the lower panel in the stem of the 'R' on fol. $137^{v}$ of MS. 91. These leaves do not seem Pl. 9*d*
to appear in Anglo-Saxon manuscripts of the tenth century or the early eleventh century either.

It looks as if the immediate source of these two particular leaves is St Germain-des-Prés. Both the 'pomegranate' leaf and the trilobe leaf are found in manuscripts of the Ingelardus Group.[1] Ingelardus' name is known from his colophon to a Lectionary in which the abbacy of Adelard (1030–60) is also specified as the date of the execution of the book.[2] But other manuscripts with related initial decoration, for instance a 'Lives of Saints' may perhaps be a little earlier.[3]

The 'pomegranate' leaf of eastern origin may well have come to St Germain via Ottonian illumination. Similar leaves are used for instance in the Sacramentary of Henry II made at Regensburg 1002–14. They

[1] These manuscripts have been studies by Y. Deslandres, 'Les MSS. decorés au XIe siècle à S. Germain-des-Prés par Ingelard', *Scriptorium*, ix (1955), 3–16. For the 'pomegranate' leaf cf. Paris, Bib. Nat., Latin 11550, fol. 169, a 'd' and for the trilobe leaf Paris, Bib. Nat., Latin 12610, fol. 75.

[2] Paris, Bib. Nat., Latin 11751.

[3] Paris, Bib. Nat., Latin 11749. A manuscript attributable to St Germain for its identical initial style, is Alençon, Bib. Mun., MS. 18, which belonged formerly to St Evroul.

occur in the border and without stalks.[1] The trilobe leaf does not appear to occur in Ottonian manuscripts. Further points of similarity with St Pls. *9f, g* Germain can be noted. For instance the Mont St Michel 'B', MS. 91, fol. 1 resembles a 'B' in a Psalter from St Germain in that the bows are not broken up into panels as in the Harley 'B' and its Franco-Saxon models.[2] There is also the same 'containment' of the scroll commented on earlier, and the St Germain 'B' similarly lacks the typical Anglo-Saxon lion mask.

## B: INITIALS IN MSS. 99 AND 115

A second group of initials in MS. 115 and one of the initials in MS. 99 are distinguished by squat thick letter shapes, a tendency of the letter to turn into leaf or animal forms, and by a cruder style of drawing. In general these initials recall Type II initials of the early manuscripts. The frilly voluminousness of the leaves, particularly those in the centre of a 'P' MS. 115, fol. 165, points again to a north French origin, and recalls the Life of St Amand from St Amand.[3]

Another feature of these initials, the animal heads, in the shaft of the Pls. 10*g, h* 'P', MS. 99, fol. 111$^{v}$, for instance, links them closely with a manuscript from Notre-Dame d'Arras, now at Boulogne.[4] In origin these heads are Anglo-Saxon, occurring in Wormald's Type II initials. Similar heads are found in the St Vaast Bible. In the Boulogne manuscript they are very much cruder than in the Bible. In fact the style of the Boulogne initials is almost identical with that of the Mont St Michel ones.

## C: MS. 61

MS. 61 contains a group of letters which are unique at Mont St Michel. They are formed of a tubular plant stem twisted to form the letter but Pl. 3*a* always remaining the same thickness. There are a number of small animal heads. The leaves have crenellated edges and are, except for the

1 Munich, Bayr. Staatsbibl., Cod. 4456. Schardt, *Das Initial*, 160, pl. They perhaps reach Ottonian illumination from St Gall ivories (Tuotilo group) and initials of *c.* 900.

2 Paris, Bib. Nat., Latin 11550, fol. 8. Van Moé, *Illuminated initials.*

3 Valenciennes, Bib. Mun., MS. 502, fol. 10$^{v}$. Swarzenski, *Monuments*, fig. 178.

4 Boulogne, Bib. Mun., MS. 16.

'U', fol. 331, veined and hatched. Some grow from the stem and fan out over it. There are also dotted clasps.

The woody scrolls with little hatching where a leaf breaks from the stem are typical of eleventh-century German manuscripts. But the immediate source is again St Germain-des-Prés where very similar initials are found in the earliest manuscripts of the Ingelardus group, e.g. a 'P' in the Annals.[1] Pl. 11*a*

## D: SUMMARY

It is not certain whether the Abbey received any direct influence from Anglo-Saxon illumination at this period, but it seems unlikely. Many of the motifs particularly the leaves are of Anglo-Saxon origin. But there is no sign of direct copies of the two common types of minor Anglo-Saxon initial. Influence from St Vaast at Arras is recognizable particularly in the later transitional MSS. 91 and 115. There are also links with St Germain illumination which may be explained by William of Volpiano's abbacy of St Germain at the same time as he was 'custos' of Mont St Michel. But whatever the direct sources, the most important step of the scriptorium is the adoption of the new type of initial exemplified in the 'B' of the Harley Psalter. The invention of this type of letter was an Anglo-Saxon achievement and so certainly the ultimate source for the initials was Anglo-Saxon. In the initials of the middle manuscripts, Anglo-Saxon art clearly influences the scriptorium directly, and for the first time a homogeneous initial style based on the Harley 'B' principle and developing it further appears. To this development we may now turn.

# *Part III - The middle and late manuscripts*

Before tracing the development of the main current of middle manuscript initials, directly influenced by Anglo-Saxon illumination, two manuscripts which, standing apart, are the culmination of the transitional Arras-influenced manuscripts, should be mentioned. These are Avranches MSS. 59 and 101.

[1] Paris, Bib. Nat., Latin 12117, fol. $49^v$.

## A: MSS. 59 AND 101[1]

The initials in these manuscripts are linked closely with those of the transitional manuscripts. Initials in MS. 59 are particularly close to those in MS. 128. Features of the transitional manuscripts such as the white reserve acanthus patterns, the interlaces, the pomegranate leaf, the lion with heart-shaped tail and the scaly bird all occur.

Pls. 11*f*, *g* The initials of MS. 59 and 101 are very precisely drawn. The leaf scrolls which are continuously veined, are mostly reserved white on colour grounds which are painted in plain washes of lighter and darker blue or orange. The whole effect is very similar to that of initials of the Arras Bible of St Vaast.[2] The veined scroll at Mont St Michel is more
Pl. 10*a* extreme than in the Bible but it may be compared with the 'O' of Volume III, fol. 98v, for example. On fol. 97v of the first volume of the
Pls. 11*b*, *g* Bible a bird and a beast are enmeshed in the scroll which can be compared with those of the 'P', fol. 77v, of MS. 101. The Mont St Michel scrolls, though not so complex as the Arras scrolls, are more carefully balanced. This and their even veining gives them the appearance of a design engraved in metal. MS. 59 also has two letters of pure Franco-Saxon
Pl. 11*c* design, the two 'Et's, fols. 31v and 53v. These initial 'E's with the 'T' interlaced can be paralleled in a ninth-century Franco-Saxon manuscript from St Bertin now at Boulogne,[3] in the Bible of Charles the Bald,[4] and in a tenth-eleventh-century manuscript from St Bertin, also at Boulogne.[5] However, as Avril has pointed out, it seems likely that these initials are derived from Anglo-Saxon copies of Franco-Saxon letters as well as directly.[6] He points to the acanthus leaf friezes incorporated into the stems

[1] In MS. 101 there are also two initials, a 'Q', fol. 2 and 'F', fol. 23 which are in the late group initial style.

[2] Arras, Bib. Mun., MS. 559(435).

[3] Boulogne, Bibl. Mun., MS. 35, fol. 36.

[4] Paris, Bib. Nat., Latin 2. *Peintures et initiales de la seconde Bible de Charles le Chauve*, Bibliothèque Nationale, Paris, n.d., pls. 11–12.

[5] Boulogne, Bib. Mun., MS. 126, fol. 32.

[6] F. Avril, 'L'influence du style franco-saxon au Mont Saint-Michel', *Art de Basse Normandie*, xl (1966), 35–9 and *Millénaire* (2), 211. For Franco-Saxon initials copied in England, see F. Wormald, 'A fragment of a tenth-century English Gospel Lectionary', *Calligraphy and Palaeography. Essays presented to Alfred Fairbank*, ed. A. S. Osley (1965), 43–6; and A. Boutemy, 'L'Enluminure anglaise de l'époque saxonne (Xe–XIe siècle) et la Flandre française', *Bulletin de la Société nationale des antiquaires de France* (1956), 42–50.

of the letters. Another feature found in the Anglo-Saxon but not in the Franco-Saxon initials is the clasp which is used, for example, in the 'E' on fol. 31v of MS. 59, to join parts of the letter to each other.[1] The lion head terminals found in English manuscripts, for instance the late tenth-century York Gospels are also very close to Mont St Michel examples. Pls. 11*c*, 16*d*

## B: MAIN CURRENT MIDDLE MANUSCRIPT INITIALS

The 'B', fol. 113 of MS. 61 of the transitional manuscripts, is one of the earliest of the new style initials which become standard at Mont St Michel in the middle manuscripts. But there is a difference. It is made up of two dragons and two scrolls. They do not fill a letter form, they make up one. In this respect therefore the letter resembles Wormald's Type II Anglo-Saxon initials in e.g. the Salisbury Psalter.[2] In MS. 61 the two currents which go to make up the Mont St Michel middle initials are seen separate, therefore. For it also contains on fol. 112 a plain initial 'L' with interlace animal head terminals and panels in the Franco-Saxon tradition.[3] Pl. 11*d*

The manuscripts assigned on grounds of script to the middle group, besides MSS. 59 and 101 already considered, are MSS. 51, 72, 75, 76, 77, 86, 90, and 107. There are also the four manuscripts written by Antonius, Paris, Bibliothèque Nationale, Latin 2055, Latin 2088, and Latin 2639, and Rouen, Bibliothèque Municipale, MS. A.143(427). Some initials of the Redon Bible, Bordeaux, Bibliothèque Municipale, MS. 1, which will be discussed as a whole later, also fall into this group, as do those of the Sacramentary, New York, Morgan Library, MS. 641. Pls. 12–14

One of the earliest of these books to judge by its script, is MS. 72 signed by Frotmundus. His hand is also recognizable in the transitional MS. 128. Its initials do not contradict this impression. One of them, the 'S', fol. 44, is very similar indeed to initials in the transitional manuscripts and to the 'S', fol. 2 of MS. 59. In the other initials in MS. 72 the scrolls Pl. 11*h* Pl. 11*f*

[1] An 'L', MS. 61, fol. 110, is straight not curved as in Anglo-Saxon manuscripts, however.

[2] Salisbury Cathedral, MS. 150. Kendrick, *Late Saxon*, pl. xxix. In the Mont St Michel initial the plant scroll has a bigger role to play.

[3] *Millénaire* (2), pl. xxxv, fig. 89.

Pls. 12*a*, 13*b* are relatively open and simple. They are bounded by the letter and only occasionally curl over or under it.

The obvious difference between the 'S' on fol. 44 and the other initials of MS. 72 is that they are painted whereas it is not. Of the earlier initials very few were coloured,[1] and those only with plain washes. In MS. 72, on the other hand, not only is the range of colour very much wider, but here the letters are painted to give a three-dimensional effect. Shading and particularly white highlights are used. The result is that instead of the
Pl. 11*h* veined hard leaves of the transitional initials or the 'S', fol. 44, the leaves are fleshy and rounded, and the stalks tubular. At the same time their
Pls. 12*a*, 13*b* forms are more emphasized and they do not intertwine so much. The whole effect is more organic and less stylized. This is seen in other closely related initials in MSS. 107 and 76, even though they are not painted.

The introduction of the new medium in these painted initials makes it certain that the scriptorium must now have had direct access to Anglo-
Pls. 9*e*, 11*e* Saxon manuscripts. The scrolls are very similar to those of the Harley 'B' or of the Trinity Gospels with the same shadings and white outlines.[2]
Pls. 11*e*, 13*b*, 28 The scroll above the arch of fol. 12 of the latter manuscript can be compared to that of the 'C', fol. 150 or the 'Q', fol. 182ᵛ of MS. 72 for instance. These Anglo-Saxon manuscripts are not, it should be noticed, contemporary, but of the late tenth to early eleventh century. The trend of Anglo-Saxon manuscripts in the second quarter of the eleventh century was to more elongated stringy foliage as Wormald had shown in his comparison of the Cambridge Psalter 'B' with that of Harley 2904.[3] Thus the foliage scrolls at Mont St Michel are becoming more three-dimensional and organic with a new appearance of volume, at the same time as the Anglo-Saxon scroll, developing in the opposite direction, is becoming more linear and stylized.

The Mont St Michel initials differ from the Harley 'B' or the Trinity Gospels page in two respects. First there are leaf forms not used in the

[1] An 'M' in MS. 211, an 'M' in MS. 97, a 'P' in MS. 115, and a 'P' in MS. 128 and some of the initials of MSS. 59 and 101. The colouring of the 'P' in MS. 115 recalls that of the Anglo-Saxon mid tenth-century Psalter, Oxford, Bodleian Library, MS. Junius 27.

[2] London, Brit. Mus., Harley 2904, fol. 4. Cambridge, Trinity College, MS. B.10.4, Dodwell, *Canterbury School*, pls. 7*b* and *c*, pl. 11*a*.

[3] See Wormald, *Decorated initials*, pl. i.

Anglo-Saxon manuscripts. These significantly enough do not occur in the painted initials of MS. 72 but in the pen initials of MS. 76 and MS. 107. They have already been seen in the transitional manuscripts where something was said about their origins. Pls. 12*b*, *c*

Secondly, as opposed to the Harley 'B', the scrolls in these initials are inhabited. The 'P' of MS. 72, fol. 151 even has, perhaps for the first time at Mont St Michel, a human figure in the scroll with raised axe in his right hand attacking a lion. (Pl. 12*a*) Another figure occurs in the 'B' of MS. 76, fol. 1, and in the 'S' of MS. 107, fol. 112, besides another lion fight above, (Pls. 12*b*, *c*) below a man with shield and sword fights a horned satyr. MS. 75, fol. 1, an 'O', also has a combat scene between two men. (Pl. 12*e*)

This introduces the subject of the inhabited scroll at Mont St Michel. The plant scroll inhabited by birds, beasts and humans is of course a common classical motif. This in the late seventh and eighth centuries was transformed by Insular artists.[1] The classical scroll provided a frame for its inhabitants and a spatial setting in which they perched or climbed. In Insular art the whole is made into an interlacing pattern in which the inhabitants and the scroll become equally important ingredients of the design. The spatial setting disappears and instead there is a vigorous counterpoint.

The earliest surviving examples of the inhabited scroll used to decorate the initial are found in the Corbie Psalter of the late eighth century, whose importance for the history of the Romanesque initial has already been emphasized.[2] In the slightly earlier Barberini Gospels (made probably in southern England) an inhabited scroll echoes the fall of the 'X' at the beginning of St Matthew's Gospel.[3] But in the Corbie Psalter, fol. 95, the scroll is enclosed in the top bow of the 'B' and moreover (Pl. 13*a*) related to the letter since it grows out of the chalice which acts as clasp

[1] In the stone carved crosses, for instance that at Croft, Yorkshire. T. D. Kendrick, *Anglo-Saxon Art to A.D.* 900 (1938), pl. lxi. For a discussion of some of their models suggesting Eastern, particularly Palestinian and Syrian, origins for some of the vine scrolls, see E. Kitzinger, 'Anglo-Saxon Vine Scroll Ornament', *Antiquity*, x (1936), 61–71. For the classical inhabited scroll see also J. B. Ward Perkins, J. M. C. Toynbee, 'Peopled scrolls: a Hellenistic motif in imperial art', *Papers of the British School in Rome*, xviii (1950), 1–43, pls. 1–26.

[2] Amiens, Bib. Mun., MS. 18. See above p. 52.

[3] Rome, Vatican, Barberini Lat. 570. Schardt, *Das Initial*, 38.

for the two bows. The next important examples of the inhabited scroll in an initial for our enquiry, occur in the Anglo-Saxon Junius Psalter of
Pl. 13*f* the second quarter of the tenth century.[1] In the period between this and the Corbie Psalter of the late eighth century one or two inhabited initials are found at St Gall, e.g. in the 'C' of the Folchard Psalter.[2] The bird there perches, however, as in the classical scroll and there is no hint of interlacing. Other examples of a later date in Ottonian manuscripts are similar in this respect, for instance the 'D' of a Fulda Sacramentary.[3]

It is the Insular current with its interlacing stems which is important for the later Romanesque style. However, three points need to be made
Pl. 13*f* about the Junius Psalter initials. First, the leaf scroll is of the new type developed from Eastern sources appearing earliest in the embroidered stoles at Durham, *c.* 909–16. Secondly, the animals are separate entities in the scroll. They are not metamorphosed into interlace or leaves, and thus resemble the classical, not the Insular scroll. Thirdly, these Junius initials are not Carolingian letters. They are formed of the scroll simply twisted into the required shape – for example the 'd', fol. 121v. They do not decorate the Roman capital. When the Anglo-Saxon scroll is first
Pl. 9*e* applied to the Carolingian Franco-Saxon letter form in the Harley 'B', the scroll is no longer inhabited.

As was pointed out above, the new principle of the Harley 'B' is not taken up widely in Anglo-Saxon manuscripts. The Trinity Gospels of the late tenth century, however, has initials decorated with animals, two

1 Oxford, Bodleian Library, MS. Junius 27. Wormald, *Decorated initials*, 117, pl. iv*c*, *d*.

2 St Gall, Stiftsbibl., Cod. 23, p. 230. Schardt, *Das Initial*, 86. In a Psalter at Stift Göttweig in a 'B' there is a symmetrical pair of birds. A. Merton, *Die Buchmalerei in St. Gallen*, 1912, Taf. xx, no. 2. Another exceptional Carolingian example is the Abbeville Gospels, Bib. Mun., MS. 4, fol. 1, a 'P' with a lion in the scroll. Köhler (2), Taf. 33a. See also a 'B' in an early ninth century manuscript from St Denis, Oxford, Bodleian, MS. Laud Misc. 464, fol. 1. O. Pächt, J. J. G. Alexander, *Illuminated manuscripts in the Bodleian Library*, i (1966), no. 414, pl. xxxiv.

3 Göttingen, Univ. Bibl., Cod. 231, fol. 16v. Exceptional are two initials in Paris, Bib. Nat., Latin 8915, a Paschasius Radbertus, fol. 77 and 86. This book was in part written and decorated by Leofsinus, an Englishman and given to Echternach after 993. See C. Nordenfalk, 'Abbas Leofsinus', *Acta Archaeologica*, iv (1933), 49–83. Nordenfalk compares these initials to the scrolls of the Jedburgh Cross, but concludes that it is not plausible to infer the existence of Insular manuscripts with similar initials, which have disappeared.

'I's and a 'Q'.[1] In the 'I's the letter acts as a frame, and the animals clamber [Pl. 13*d*] up inside. In some a tail turns into a scroll and they begin to look like inhabited scrolls. The 'Q' is decorated with animals with no hint of a [Pl. 15*e*] scroll, a letter which will be referred to later in connection with the late Mont St Michel initials.[2]

It seems possible, therefore, that it was an Anglo-Saxon artist who first applied the inhabited scroll to the Franco-Saxon letters. As with other new developments different indications of the same trend seem to appear at the same moment in different areas. Thus, as was mentioned, even in Ottonian scrolls isolated examples occur late in the tenth century. In any case, as with the Harley 'B', the new form of decoration is taken up in northern France in the second quarter of the eleventh century, at St Vaast and in Normandy, with more enthusiasm than in England. In England in the second quarter of the eleventh century the scroll of the Cambridge Psalter 'B' is still not inhabited, for instance.

At Mont St Michel the earliest example is probably the 'P' of the early manuscript, MS. 98, fol. 132$^{v}$. Here the two lions are only very [Pl. 9*c*] slightly woven into the scroll. They stand firmly on it and the lower one is enclosed as in a roundel. In the 'R' of the transitional MS. 91, fol. 137$^{v}$, a bird is included in the letter which is also in part made up of a bird and a [Pl. 9*d*] dragon. The initials of MSS. 59 and 101 have animals either poised on, or [Pl. 11*f*, 11*g*] interlaced in, the scroll. Similarities have been pointed to between these manuscripts and the initials of the St Vaast Bible. But in the Bible inhabited initials are still not at all common and where the scroll is inhabited it is more likely to be found springing from an arch – e.g. Volume II, fol. 117, than in a letter.

In the initials in Frotmundus' book, MS. 72, though the inhabitants are few in number and rather small, they have become far more active. They provide both movement, a counterplay to the static initial form, and a new interest. The combat in the scroll of the 'P', fol. 151 is, there- [Pl. 12*a*]

[1] Cambridge, Trinity College, MS. B.10.4, fol. 133, fol. 60, fol. 90. Dodwell, *Canterbury School*, pls. 7*b*, *c*, 11*a*.

[2] These 'clambering initials' are discussed by Dodwell, *Canterbury School*, 11ff.

fore, very important as an early example of an immensely common theme throughout the ascendancy of the romanesque initial.[1]

For the sources from which the artists derived their decorative themes in these scrolls, particularly the combat scenes and hunting scenes, two suggestions may be made. In the first place there is a tradition in Anglo-Saxon manuscripts of framing borders to miniatures in which inhabited scrolls are used. The earliest example of this is the copy of Bede's Life of
Pl. 17*c* Cuthbert presented to Durham by Aethelstan, datable 937–42.[2] There the scroll is rather open and leisurely; there are only lions and birds in it. A later example of *c.* 1000 is in the Aldhelm now at Lambeth where again there are only birds and lions, but the scroll is more involved and the animals much more active.[3] The inhabited scroll passes also to St Bertin, under Abbot Otbert, but again not in initials but only in framing pages. In a Gospel Book, for instance, humans now appear and a hunt is in
Pl. 13*g* progress through the scroll.[4]

A second source for these motifs was probably in metal work or ivory carvings. Besides contemporary or slightly earlier Anglo-Saxon carvings which could have been used as sources,[5] one ivory of importance, though of uncertain date, should be mentioned. This, now in the Cluny Museum,
Pl. 13*e* Paris, was at Beauvais in 1803 and was attributed to northern France by Goldschmidt who dated it ninth-tenth century.[6] It is a diptych recut and

1 Combats are found very much earlier in Anglo-Saxon manuscripts of the tenth century – e.g. Oxford, Bodleian Library, MS. Tanner 10, but not in the scroll.

2 Cambridge, Corpus Christi College, MS. 183, fol. $1^{v}$. Wormald, *Decorated Initials*, 116, pl. iv *b*. Some Ottonian examples should also be noted though it seems less likely that they acted as models since both scroll and inhabitants are more static and less entwined than the Anglo-Saxon examples. Gospels of Otto III, Munich, Bayr. Staatsbibl., Clm. 4453, G. Leidinger, *Miniaturen aus Handschriften der Kgl. Hof-und Staatsbibliothek in Munchen*, Heft I (n.d.), Taf. 34, 44; Bâle, Golden Altar; Sheath of the Essen sword. Swarzenski, *Monuments*, figs. 99, 100.

3 London, Lambeth Palace Library, MS. 200, fol. 69. Kendrick, *Late Saxon*, pl. 33*b*. See also the inhabited scroll in the margin of the Bury Psalter, Rome, Vatican, MS. Reg. Lat. 12, taken, it seems, from a Bestiary.

4 New York, Morgan Library, MS. 333. See also St Omer, Bib. Mun., MS. 56, fol. 36. Swarzenski, *Monuments*, fig. 161.

5 e.g. the ivory penner or the bronze cruet both now in the British Museum. Kendrick, *Late Saxon*, pl. xxxvi, 1, 3.

6 Goldschmidt, *Elfenbeinskulpturen* (2), no. 156–7, Taf. lxix. Neither the date nor the origin of this ivory are, however, yet agreed. Exh. *Byzantine Art* (9th Council of Europe exhibition), Athens (1964), no. 98.

used as a book cover. On one side in the centre a scroll winds in which are various figures and animals. In particular one man fights a lion with a spear, above a satyr picks grapes, and another man clad in skins threatens him with a thyrsis. Very similar combat scenes occur in some middle group initials even with classical mythological figures involved – the 'S', MS. 107, fol. 112, a satyr, and the 'E' of the Redon Bible, fol. 70v, a centaur. The other part of the diptych has four roundels in the centre of which are, as Goldschmidt has pointed out, Sagittarius and Capricorn, the Zodiac signs for November and December. The centaur in the 'E' of the Bible has no bow and arrow but some similar ivory may well have been known at Mont St Michel. It should be noted that these combats have no meaning to connect them with the text but are purely decorative.[1]

Pls. 12*c*, *d*

Pl. 12*d*

The elements of which the typical middle group initials were composed, have been examined. Before looking at the development which takes place in their style, one other point should be made. This concerns the way the initials are used and how they are incorporated into the text.

The texts in these manuscripts are mostly commentaries or treatises and therefore there is no need, and hardly any excuse, for illustration. It is natural, therefore, that the ornament should concentrate on the initial.

The ornamented initial was developed particularly in northern book illumination and reached its most exaggerated form in the insular Gospel books of the seventh and eighth centuries, where the Word of God becomes something mystical or magic to be contemplated not simply read. It has already been emphasized that at Mont St Michel in contrast the letter forms are always clear, and that the Roman capitals are not smothered or disintegrated. Initials occupying a full page are very rare. Of course these full page initials are more naturally found in liturgical manuscripts or the Lives of Saints. But even in the Mont St Michel Sacramentary where such letters do occur, they are usually accompanied by the text they introduce, not just a few letters of the opening word.[2]

Pls. 13*c*, 36, 38

[1] For a wider discussion of the sources of Romanesque decoration see Dodwell, *Canterbury School*, ch. vi.

[2] Morgan MS. 641, fol. 61v, Preface of the Mass, fol. 152v, Collect of Nativity of the Virgin, fol. 66v, Collect Easter Sunday, fol. 156, Collect Exaltation of Cross (the words written in gold are hardly visible in the photograph). Fol. 170, All Saints is exceptional, as it is an illustrated page and there is only room for a few opening words.

For the other works, commentaries and treatises, the scriptorium evolved its own hierarchy of initials whose purpose is to facilitate the reading of the text by marking its divisions. At the beginning of a work a large ornamented initial is to be found and a heading often in mixed capitals. Each book opens with a similar ornamented initial usually in green or in orange,[1] or the two colours combined, with simple foliage terminals or arabesques. Lastly, for the capital letter of each sentence, for the table of contents, for the *explicit* and *incipit* still smaller capitals are used, usually quite plain and in ink, but sometimes with small flourishes and perhaps in orange or green.

The result of all this is that the book has a unity and rhythm about it without its decoration being at all overweighted in any one direction. It is easy to read and the divisions are clearly marked. For the latter the careful contemporary tables of contents usually on the verso of the flyleaf are notable. These manuscripts are not sumptuous or extravagant. They are perfectly adapted to their purpose and their ornament is sufficient to enliven their pages without distracting the attention. St Bernard himself could hardly have disapproved.[2]

MS. 72, the manuscript of which the scribe Frotmundus was so proud, may be taken to illustrate this system working. It contains various treatises by Jerome, Augustine and Ambrose. On fol. 1 is a list of the contents of the later eleventh century. The opening initial of the first work, St Jerome *contra Jovinianum* in two books, is missing with the opening pages. On folio 44, however, is the *explicit* of Book I and an
Pl. 11*h* initial 'S' introduces Book II. This ends on fol. 72$^{v}$ and on fol. 73, a minor work, a letter of Rufinus to Pope Laurentius edited by St Jerome, is introduced by a second grade initial of the type usually used for a chapter opening. The next work is St Augustine's treatise *contra Felicianum*. This
Pl. 22 has a full page miniature as frontispiece (a similar page of St Jerome disputing with Jovinianus is probably lost from the beginning of the manuscript) and then an 'E', a first grade painted initial on fol. 97$^{v}$. The dispute is continued by the *altercatio* between Luciferus and Orthodoxus which begins with a second grade letter in orange, a 'P' fol. 112, inci-

1 In the later manuscripts the orange minium changes to red. It is an important indication of date.

2 His famous denunciation, *Apologia ad Guillelmum*, *P.L.* clxxxii, col. 916.

dentally very typical with its thin 'hairy' scroll and also harking back in
its proportions to early group initials.[1] The next work is introduced by
a preface with a painted initial 'C', fol. 150 and for the text, St Au- Pl. 13*b*
gustine's commentary on Galatians, a rather larger 'P', fol. 151. Finally, Pl. 12*a*
for St Ambrose's treatise *de bono mortis* there is a small picture of the
saint writing and a painted initial 'Q', fol. 182v. Pl. 28

This illustrates perfectly the system of organizing the book. The
relation of heading, initial and text is also important and is well seen on
fol. 150 for example. The letter is set in the column ruled for the script Pl. 13*b*
not separately in the margin. The heading in mixed capitals and the following capitals (C) AUSA PROPTER QUAM serve to bridge the gap
between the script of the text and the initial which is thus easily absorbed
into the page.

It would be interesting to know how far this organization of page, initial and book is an original Norman achievement. It does not seem to be practised in Anglo-Saxon manuscripts – the Psalter divisions would be an exception of course. A similar system is evolving in the Arras Bible and other St Vaast manuscripts.

## C: DEVELOPMENT OF MIDDLE GROUP INITIALS

Close to the initials of MS. 72 are those of MSS. 75, 76, and 107. These
are not painted except for the 'O' of MS. 75, fol. 1. The initial 'S' of Pl. 12*e*
MS. 107, is already a more complex letter in its decoration which is more Pl. 12*c*
closely knit. Very similar to it in style is the 'E' with the centaur from the
Bordeaux Bible, fol. 70v. A whole group of the Bible initials, few of them Pl. 12*d*
painted, are related to these middle group initials. Slightly more developed are the initials of MS. 90 and to be connected with these are the Pl. 14*a*
initials of Paris, Bib. Nat., Latin 2639 and of the Sacramentary, Morgan
MS. 641. Other initials in the Bordeaux Bible can be compared with Pl. 13*c*
these. The leaves tend to be more rounded, larger and fleshier.

Lastly, the 'R' of Rouen A.143 (427) shows a further complication of Pl. 14*b*
its scroll, whilst the leaves are more clearly veined than in the earlier
manuscripts of the group. The other Antonius manuscripts, Latin 2055

[1] Avril, *Notes* (1), 502, pl.

Pl. 14*c* and 2088, are also later. So is a 'C' in MS. 51[1] as is shown by the veined leaves, and the initials of MS. $86_2$. The Rouen 'R' is exceptional in using a dragon to form part of the letter. The only other letters using animal components are 'Q' where the tail is commonly a dragon or a lion (MS. $86_2$, fol. 27,[2] Morgan MS. 641, fol. 38$^v$) and 'S' where a dragon may be bent to form the letter. Animals used to form letters are commoner in the late manuscripts initials, as we shall see. Another unusual feature of the Rouen 'R' is the acanthus pattern in the shaft. A pattern is also
Pls. 14*b*, *d* found in the 'I', fol. 1 of Latin 2055 and in the 'E' of MS. 77, fol. 2, a letter which is very close to the late manuscripts initials. This acanthus pattern is already found in the early initials, e.g. the 'M' in MS. 97, fol.
Pl. 8*d* 201$^v$. The unornamented panels of the letters elsewhere help to preserve the separate entity of the letter from its decoration. In Latin 2088, fol.1$^v$,
Pl. 14*c* another unusual feature is the use of gold[3] and also the bust medallion of a tonsured saint.

## D: INITIALS IN THE LATE GROUP MANUSCRIPTS

The manuscripts having initials, which were assigned to the late group on grounds of script, are MSS. 9, $35_1$, 47, 57, 58, $61_1$, 82, 86, 89, 102, 103, 146, 163 and also the Bible, Bordeaux, Bibliothèque Municipale MS. 1, the Dudo of St Quentin in Berlin, Phillipps 1854, the Lives of Saints, and the Statius in Paris, Latin 5290 and 8055, pp. 1–140, and the two manuscripts from St Augustine's, Canterbury, now in London, Royal MSS. 13.A.XXII and 13.A.XXIII.

The scrolls in these manuscripts continue to grow more complicated and dense, and to fill the spaces of the letters more fully. There even seems to be less room for the inhabiting birds and beasts. There are four particular points in which a development is discernible. First the scrolls
Pl. 16*a* tend to greater symmetry. A good example is the 'Q', fol. 180, of MS. 89. This is divided into four quarters in which the scrolls, though not identical, do balance each other. Round the rim of the letter leaves curl out at regular intervals so that it resembles an Anglo-Saxon corner rosette.

1 *Millénaire* (2), pl. xiv, fig. 33.
2 *Millénaire* (2), pl. xvi, fig. 39.
3 See above p. 56.

Another new feature is the veined leaf. An example of this is the foliage terminals of the 'X' in MS. 86, fol. $138^{v}$. This initial shows also Pl. 15*b* the leaf rolled into the centre which occurs frequently. A greater variety of leaf and fruit forms is used now, and several types are particularly prominent. One is a trilobe leaf curled like a seed pod, a second is the Pl. 55*a* flower leaf which developing from the 'pomegranate leaf' of the transitional manuscripts appears in various forms. Both are seen in an 'E', Pl. 14*d* MS. 77, fol. 2.

It was remarked in the chapter on script that the late manuscripts return to some extent to earlier practice. There seems to be evidence of a similar trend in the initials. Having accepted the Anglo-Saxon leaf style at first hand and having absorbed it, the artists felt free to introduce alien elements from elsewhere or from the scriptorium's past products. At the same time the veined leaf becomes more stylized – less organic – and is further from the Anglo-Saxon models of the middle manuscripts. Where the leaves are painted they are usually only colour-washed, not modelled.

A third feature of the late initials is a greater use of animal and plant forms to make up the letter. This is also a return to earlier practice and was remarked already in the Antonius manuscripts and MS. $86_{2}$. It is a sign that they are late amongst the middle manuscripts. In MS. 86, fol. 32, two dragons form a 'Q' with a spread-eagled lion between them copying Pl. 15*a* the MS. 97 initial 'Q'. On fol. $191^{v}$ of MS. 89 a dragon is twisted to form Pl. 8*e* an 'S',[1] a development of the 'S' of MSS. 59 and 72, and this letter occurs again in Royal 13.A.XXII, fol. $2^{v}$. Dragons or lions are used as the tails Pl. 5*d* of 'Q's in MSS. 86, 89, and 101. In MS. 146 an 'A', fol. 37,[2] and an 'L', Pl. 55*f* fol. 65, are made up of animals. Other examples in the Bible are referred to later and they may copy earlier initials now lost. Related to this trend is the increased use of animal head terminals particularly to interlace, with leaves sprouting from their mouths. In the middle manuscripts the animal head terminal with leaf scroll was only found in the more advanced manuscripts, MS. 90, the Sacramentary, Morgan 641, the An- Pl. 14*a* tonius group and the Bible. In the late manuscripts the heads are seen in

1 *Millénaire* (2), pl. xxxviii, fig. 97.
2 *Millénaire* (2), pl. xxi, fig. 57.

Pl. 15*a* three-quarter view, not straight profile so that both eyes appear, for example MS. 86, fol. 32.

Pls. 15*c*, *d* Fourthly, some of the late initials begin to have animals entwined in their panels or placed one on top of another. Examples are in MS. 89,
Pl. 50*a* MS. 146, and in the 'I', one of the second group of initials in the Bordeaux
Pl. 15*d* Bible, fol. 5. A good example is the 'D' of MS. 89, fol. 103. The animals or birds are frequently symmetrical, often, as the two birds at the top of the shaft of this letter and the two lions at the bottom, adorsed, and they are curled round or bite at the panels which enclose them.

It is important to note that they are not placed in any kind of scroll. Nor do they really climb up the initials as up a ladder. They are static, and in this respect they resemble the decoration of certain Canon Tables. Porcher has pointed out that animals perched on each other are found in Canon Tables in early Tours School manuscripts.[1] Originally an eastern motif (it may, Porcher suggests, have reached Tours via Insular art[2]) it recurs at Limoges in the first Bible of St Martial in the tenth century.[3]

Pl. 46*c* The same motif occurs, too, at the end of the tenth century amongst the Otbert manuscripts from St Bertin in a Lives of Saints.[4] The animals and birds in the capitals and pillars of an arch are more symmetrical there and often adorsed. They also twist round their framing medallions. The St Bertin manuscripts are closely dependent on Anglo-Saxon manuscripts, and there are Anglo-Saxon examples of a related type of decoration in initials even. Dodwell has called the initials of this kind of which the most developed type are in the Trinity Gospels (but which also occur in an eleventh-century copy of Bede's History and in the tenth-century Salisbury Psalter) 'clambering' initials.[5]

[1] Porcher, *French Miniatures*, 27.

[2] Cf. the Cutbrecht Gospels, Vienna, Nat. Library, Cod. 1224, fol. 21$^{v}$, Canon Tables. Zimmermann, Taf. 308.

[3] Paris, Bib. Nat., Latin 5. Volume ii, fol. 131. Porcher, *French Miniatures*, fig. 25. Porcher also draws attention to a similar pyramid of animals on a Byzantine marble slab, now in the Louvre, from Greece of the eleventh century.

[4] Boulogne, Bib. Mun., MS. 107, fol. 6$^{v}$. Porcher, *French Miniatures*, pl. vi.

[5] Dodwell, *The Canterbury School*, 11ff. Cambridge, Trinity College, MS. B.10.4, fol. 133, fol. 60, and fol. 90; Salisbury, Cathedral Chapter Library, MS. 150, fol. 122 'A'; Cambridge, Corpus Christi College MS. 41, fol. 266$^{v}$ and 285. Kendrick, *Late Saxon*, pl. xxix.

There are very close similarities in the Trinity Gospels, for instance, particularly in the way the animals and birds twist round or bite the panels of the letter, to the Mont St Michel initials. But the term 'clambering' draws attention to a characteristic which is absent at Mont St Michel. If the 'I', fol. 2ᵛ of Ms. 146 is compared with the Trinity Gospels, Pl. 15*c*
'I', fol. 60, it is clear that in the latter there is a continuous movement Pl. 13*d*
upwards. Since the tail of one of the animals turns into a scroll leaf, this is almost an inhabited scroll. At Mont St Michel, even where as in the 'I', fol. 2ᵛ of MS. 146, there are no panels to break the continuity, the Pl. 15*c*
animals are placed statically one above another. Thus, in spite of the very close similarities, it is clear that there is another current in the Mont St Michel letters.[1] Probably this comes from the South where such superimposed animals are found again in the second Bible from St Martial, Limoges, and at the end of the eleventh century begin to appear also in sculpture in the Languedoc. They do not, however, twist round their frames. Very typically, therefore, the Mont St Michel artist seems to have made his own synthesis here, using a contemporary and also an earlier source.

These initials of MSS. 89, 146 and the Bordeaux Bible show the latest development of the Mont St Michel initial style, with which we are here concerned. With those of MS. 86, and of MS. 82 which is written and probably decorated by the same hand as MS. 89 (its initials are in red and green ink), they follow after the group of manuscripts associated with Scollandus, one of the scribes of MS. 103, who became abbot of St Augustine's, Canterbury, in 1072. These are MSS. $35_1$, 58, 103, the Paris Lives of Saints, Latin 5290, and in England the two British Museum manuscripts, Royal 13.A.XXII and 13.A.XXIII. The 'B' of MS. Royal 13.A.XXIII, fol. 1ᵛ, drawn in green and brown may be compared with the Pl. 16*c*
'P' in Latin 5290 in very similar colours. Latin 5290 also has a 'T', which Pl. 16*b*
is close to the initials of MSS. $86_3$, 89 and the Bordeaux Bible, and an 'R' which is a typical initial of the second grade which has developed from the 'P', fol. 112 of MS. 72, and is drawn in pen in different colours.

[1] The 'Q', fol. 90 of the Trinity Gospels is divided into panels and the animals do not climb. But even there they are not placed one above another but the top two turned upside down to give a centripetal movement. See pl. 15*e*.

Similar initials are found in other late manuscripts and the finest examples are in the Redon Bible.[1] The latest group of initials in the Bordeaux Bible will be studied separately, as will the rather different initials of MS. 58, fol. 3ᵛ and MS. 103, fol. 5. At the end of the century, or perhaps now early in the twelfth century, the quality of the initials declines. The drawing in MSS. 47 and 57 becomes feeble and lifeless.[2] In MS. 102 there are also indications of new influences, in the rubbery Ottonian style node scroll of a 'P', fol. 59.[3]

### E: SUMMARY

In the middle and late manuscripts a unified initial style is achieved at Mont St Michel. MSS. 59 and 101 showed the final development of the Arras influenced initial. But direct access to Anglo-Saxon manuscripts, not contemporary but of the late tenth and early eleventh century, had the curious effect of at first reversing the development which had taken place in England. The Mont St Michel scriptorium goes from more linear, less organic leaf forms in the transitional manuscripts to modelled and painted foliage scrolls in the middle manuscripts.

At the same time the Franco-Saxon initial design was kept as a frame for this new scroll, and there are few indications of Wormald's Type I initial at Mont St Michel. The scrolls are inhabited and they grow steadily in complexity, but except for the latest initials of the Bible and those of MSS. 58 and 103, there is a continuous development rather than a marked divergence of style. In the middle and late manuscripts the scriptorium also evolves a characteristic method of laying out its books and an hierarchy of initials.

## *Part IV - Chronology*

It is now possible to see how far the development of the initial style fits in with the chronology suggested in the chapter on script and what

1 They anticipate similar fine coloured pen initials of the twelfth century in the Winchester Bible, for example.

2 *Millénaire* (2), pls. xvii, fig. 43, xxi, fig. 55, xxxv, fig. 88.

3 *Millénaire* (2), pl. xl, fig. 107.

additional evidence to support that chronology can be adduced. That chronology was: Early group, 980–1015; Transitional group, 1015–45; Middle group, 1040–70; Late group, 1065–1100.

## A: THE EARLY GROUP

The least developed initials were in MSS. 50 and 78. The fine scrolling leaf initials of MSS. 97 and 211 were connected with manuscripts from St Martial, Limoges such as the Lectionary in Paris, Latin 5301, dated to the late tenth century by Porcher. Capitals at Bernay dated to 1020–8 by Grodecki were also mentioned though the development of sculpture does not necessarily run parallel in time. Similarities with St Germain manuscripts of the Ingelardus Group, 1030–60, were noted with reference to initials of MS. 98 and to the main group of transitional manuscripts. William of Volpiano, who was summoned to Normandy in 1001 by Richard II and who died in 1031, was also abbot of St Germain.

## B: THE TRANSITIONAL GROUP

The main influence in the initials of this group was shown to be Anglo-Saxon art but received indirectly and already transmuted by centres like St Bertin and St Vaast. The great Bible of St Vaast is dated *c.* 1025 by Schulten. Some of the earlier transitional initials look less developed than those of the Bible and the closest similarities to St Vaast manuscripts are in MSS. 91 and 115.

## C: THE MIDDLE GROUP

A date of *c.* 1035–45 for MSS. 59 and 101 whose initials are the culmination of the Arras influenced manuscripts would fit very well. It is at this stage that direct Anglo-Saxon influence is felt at Mont St Michel. Edward the Confessor was crowned in 1043 and it is possible that the abbey received St Michael's Mount in Cornwall as a gift from him. At any rate connections between Normandy and England were for the moment close. The middle group manuscripts would fit well into the 1040's and 50's during the abbacies of Suppo and Radulfus. Robert of Jumièges gave his abbey the Sacramentary, now Rouen, Bibliothèque

Municipale Y.6, during his holding of the see of London 1044–50.[1] This may well have been the immediate stimulus to produce the Sacramentary, now Morgan 641, at Mont St Michel. Manuscripts of this group have often been dated to the second half of the eleventh century on the grounds that Anglo-Saxon influence would have been greatest after the Conquest.[2] However, after the Conquest the Norman Abbeys would have had access to later, nearly contemporary Anglo-Saxon manuscripts which are quite different from the earlier models whose style the Mont St Michel scriptorium has been shown to have copied. The Conquest counts in other words as an argument against a late date for these manuscripts.

## D: THE LATE GROUP

The similar initial style of books which belonged formerly to St Augustine's (now in the British Museum) to Mont St Michel initials connects them with Scollandus' abbacy of St Augustine's, 1072–87. The manuscripts linked in initial style to these, MSS. 35, 58, 163 and Latin 5290 must date from about the time of the Conquest onwards. A parallel development of plant scrolls with large veined leaves can be observed at Jumièges and in the manuscripts of the Hugo Pictor group.[3] This style was already fully developed in the manuscripts given to Durham by Bishop William of St Carilef after his exile in Normandy from 1088–91. The more developed late manuscripts, especially MSS. $86_3$, 89 and 146 may therefore be placed about 1075–95.

[1] See Appx. V for Anglo-Saxon manuscripts in Normandy before the Conquest.

[2] See especially Dodwell, *The Canterbury School*, 14–15.

[3] O. Pächt, 'Hugo Pictor', *Bodleian Library Record*, iii (1950), 96–103.

# IV

## FULL-PAGE ILLUMINATION AT MONT ST MICHEL

THOUGH most of the manuscripts of Mont-Saint-Michel are only decorated with initials, five manuscripts have miniatures as frontispieces. Their iconography and style may now be examined.[1] There are also two unfinished frame pages which were intended to contain miniatures.

## *Part I - The Iconography*

Three major iconographical questions present themselves in these manuscripts. The first concerns the image of St Michael combating the devil or the dragon, the second the two pictures of a dispute between a saint and a heretic, and the third the series of half-length figures of Christ in lunettes or medallions. Some other points of less importance and the general significance of the miniatures will be treated last.

### A: ICONOGRAPHY OF ST MICHAEL

The first full-page miniature in the Mont St Michel manuscripts surviving is that of Avranches 50, fol. 1, dateable on palaeographical grounds and initial style to the earliest period of the scriptorium's production. The subject is the presentation of the book, St Clement's *Recognitiones*, to the Pl. 17*b*

[1] The most extensively illustrated of the Mont St Michel manuscripts, the Sacramentary, New York, Morgan Library, MS. 641 and the Bible, Bordeaux, Bib. Mun., MS. 1, will be discussed in separate chapters.

Archangel Michael. An inscription on the miniature reads 'Gelduinus monachus sci . . . (mani?)'. No Gelduinus is found in the obituary lists of Orléans 105, and whatever the illegible word following 'sancti' it is not 'Michaelis'.[1] The manuscript may have been a present from another monastery, therefore, (the script is not decisive on this point), or alternatively the miniature may be the work of a visiting monk. In either case it can reasonably be treated as a point of departure, since the miniature of St Michael makes its provenance certain.

The scene of the presentation of the book to the protecting saint of a community by its abbot or a benefactor is a common one in early medieval art.[2] The person receiving the book is more usually seated than standing,[3] and often the figure presenting the book is shown on a smaller scale than the saint.[3] Here, however, since St Michael is shown with a special iconography, the artist has had to unite two unrelated scenes in a single composition.

Several details of the iconography of the miniature point to Byzantine sources. First the devil is of human form. His hair is tangled and his features grotesque but he has no wings, tail, hooves or horns.[4] Secondly, St Michael stands on a *scabellum* or footstool which though distorted is still recognisable. In this he resembles numerous Byzantine single standing figures particularly in ivories. Thirdly, the double-headed eagle above the

1 I am grateful to M. F. Avril for checking this inscription under the ultra-violet lamp in Paris for me. That the figure is described as 'monachus' makes a *terminus post* of 966 certain. Dom Laporte, *Millénaire* (1), 76, observes that the name occurs in the family of Rivalo of Dol with whom Abbot Suppo had dealings. From what little is known of Breton manuscripts of the late tenth century, a Breton origin seems to me very unlikely.

2 See J. Prochno, *Das Schreiber-und Dedikationsbild in der deutschen Buchmalerei, 1 Teil 800–1100* (1929). Also P. Bloch, 'Zum Dedikationsbild im Lob des Kreuzes des Hrabanus Maurus', *Das erste Jahrtausend*, ed. V. H. Elbern, i (Textband) (1962), 471–494 (mentioning MS. 50, p. 487).

3 Examples of standing presentations are Cambridge, Corpus Christi College, MS. 183, fol. 1v, King Athelstan and St Cuthbert, and Darmstadt, Hessische Landesbibl., Cod. 1640, Hitda Gospels, where St Walburga stands on a *scabellum* to receive the book from Abbess Hitda, *Das erste Jahrtausend*, Tafelband, ed. V. H. Elbern (1962), no. 352. See Pl. 17c.

4 See O. A. Erich, *Die Darstellung des Teufels in der Christlichen Kunst* (1931). His raised arm is compared by F. Avril, *Millénaire* (2), 217 to the classical gesture of a barbarian asking mercy of the Emperor.

central pillar is very probably derived from a Byzantine or Eastern textile.[1]

The theme of St Michael fighting the dragon or the devil, on the other hand, is unknown in Byzantine art up to this date. It has, of course, a very special importance for the abbey and it will be necessary to trace its development in the West in some detail to decide whether, and if so how, Mont St Michel contributed to the iconography.

The Biblical sources for the iconography of the Archangel Michael are Daniel, X, vv.13 and 21, and XII, v.1, Jude V, v.9, and Revelation XII, vv.7–8, and these give the themes of the two main types of representation. In Daniel he is 'one of the chief princes', 'unus de Principibus primis'. In Jude and Revelation he is the contender against the devil or the dragon.

The early Christian representations and the Byzantine tradition represent the Archangel according to Daniel as a prince.[2] He holds, usually in

[1] See O. von Falke, *Decorative Silks* (1936), particularly fig. 187, a silk of the eleventh century from Vich, now Kunstgewerbe Museum, Berlin. The double eagle does not occur on coins so early in East or West and the earliest examples carved in stone in France are of the twelfth century, e.g. at Moissac, capital of cloister, and capital from Moutiers-St-Jean now Fogg Museum. See D. Jalabert, 'De l'art oriental antique à l'art roman. III. L'aigle,' *Bulletin Monumental*, xcvii (1938), 173–94. They do not generally have the little vases in their beaks. This is a detail which makes it unlikely that the source was a Byzantine ivory carving, but the vases are found on the textiles. There appears to be no significance in the placing of the eagle in this position. Eagles shown frontally, though never it seems double, are common on South Italian pulpits, e.g. at Monte Gargano (1041) and Bari. See A. Petrucci, *Cattedrali di Puglia* (1964), pls. 7 and 130. They occur there also in the illustrations of the Exultet Rolls.

[2] Much has been written about the cult of St Michael, particularly concerning its relation to earlier cults – e.g. in the East Aesculapius, in the West Mercury and Wotan, and its distribution in Germany and North Italy. The iconography has not been so adequately treated. See: F. Weigand, *Der Erzengel Michael in der bildenden Kunst* (1886). A. Renner, *Der Erzengel Michael in der Geistes- und Kunstgeschichte* (1927). O. Dobiash Rojdestvensky, *Le Culte de Saint Michel et le moyen-âge latin* (1927). E. Mâle, *L'Art religieux du XIIe siècle en France* (1928), 257–62. M. de Fraipont, 'Les origines occidentales du type de Saint Michel debout sur le dragon', *Revue Belge d'Archéologie et d'Histoire de l'Art*, vii (1927), 289–301. M. Laurent, 'Le Bas-relief de Saint Michel à l'abbaye de Maredsous', *Revue Belge d'Archéologie et d'Histoire de l'Art*, viii (1938), 337–44. P. G. de Jerphanion, 'L'Origine copte du type de Saint Michel debout sur le dragon', *Académie des Inscriptions et Belles-lettres, Comptes Rendues* (1938), 367–81. *D.A.C.L.* xi (1933), col. 903, 'Michel (Culte de Saint)'. *R.D.K.*, s.v. 'Engelsturz', especially iii.E. *Der Engelsturz als Bestandteil der Michaelslegende* and iv. *Ikonographische Abgrenzung*. B. Brenk, 'Tradition und Neuerung in der christlichen Kunst des ersten Jahrtausends', *Wiener Byzantinische Studien*, III (1966), 189-91, 209-10. F. Avril, *Millénaire* (2), 216.

his right hand, a staff, sceptre, or *labarum*, this often with the 'Trisagion' inscribed on it, and in his other hand the globe often surmounted by or marked with a cross.[1] He appears thus on a fifth-century ivory in the British Museum,[2] and this is the constant Byzantine type. It is found also in the West for instance in the eighth-century Gospels from Echternach,[3] in the Ottonian Golden Altar from Bâle,[4] and at St Angelo in Formis, near Naples, of the eleventh century.

The other pictorial tradition, that of St Michael fighting the devil, occurs only in the west, however: 'and there was war in heaven: Michael and his angels fought against the Dragon (Revelation XII, v.7)'.[5] This militant aspect is emphasized in the Carolingian hymns, for instance Wandalbert of Prüm's Martyrologion:

> Aetherea virtute potens princepsque supernae
> Militiae Michahel terno sibi templa sacravit.[6]

The earliest representative of this type surviving is a Carolingian ivory
Pl. 16*e* plaque, now in Leipzig,[7] of the early ninth century and related to the style of the court school of the Emperor Charlemagne. The question arises, therefore, as to whether this was a new type created by the Carolingian artists, or whether the subject had been represented earlier. The Archangel is a tall thin figure squeezed into a long narrow panel. He has wings and a halo and wears a cloak over his undergarment. He plunges his spear into the jaws of a small dragon which seems to have emerged from a hole in the right-hand corner. In his left hand he carries a diminutive shield which is pointed down at the dragon. He looks up and to the right, not at the dragon.

1 e.g. in the now destroyed mosaics in the Church of the Assumption, Nicaea. D. Talbot Rice, *The Art of Byzantium* (1959), pl. 76.

2 Volbach, *Elfenbeinarbeiten*, no. 109.

3 Trier, Domschatz, MS. 61. Zimmermann, Taf. 269.

4 Paris, Cluny Museum. Swarzenski, *Monuments*, fig. 95.

5 The Apocalypse was not a canonical text in the East, of course. The triumph of St Michael is occasionally represented, but this illustrates the fall of the Rebel Angels rather than any individual combat. See *R.D.K.*, s.v. 'Engelsturz'. Examples are in the Menologion of Basil II, Rome, Vatican, Gr. 1613 p. 168 and on the bronze doors made at Constantinople in 1076 for the church of Monte Gargano, *R.D.K.*, fig. 3. See pl. 16*f*.

6 E. Dümmler, *Poetae Latini Aevi Carolini* (Monumenta Germaniae Historica), ii (1884), 595.

7 Goldschmidt, *Elfenbeinskulpturen* (2), no. 11a, Taf. vi.

Since the text for the fighting Archangel is Revelation, one might expect Apocalypse illustrations to have created the type. However, though the Leipzig ivory shows the Archangel fighting, it is not a descriptive illustration of a particular episode. The dragon is small and subordinate, and it is a general triumph of good over evil of which the issue is not in doubt. St Michael spears the beast disdainfully, rather than actively fights it, and there is no suggestion of the fall described in Revelation. Moreover the text speaks of Michael and his angels, but we have only the one Archangel here. The Leipzig ivory does not seem to be, then, an illustration of the Revelation text, even an abbreviated one, though Revelation is its ultimate source. A comparison with the illustration of the scene in the ninth-century Trier Apocalypse[1] supports this conclusion. For there, first, the angels are shown as a group and not even with one in particular as their leader: and secondly, though the dragon, here a huge beast, and his angels are in flight, the angels of heaven do not triumph but are still intent, for all their puppet-like attitudes, on the fray.

The Leipzig ivory must derive, therefore, from some other pictorial tradition. This would seem to be that of Christ's triumph over the beasts, the 'Christus super aspidem' of Psalm 90 v.13. For the pose of the legs and feet in an ivory of this subject, which also belongs to the Charlemagne 'Court School' group and is now in Oxford,[2] is identical and also Pl. 16g
the right arms are the same. This would be an example of the common medieval process of creation by analogy. The artist faced with the task of representing St Michael as warrior triumphing over the dragon took the Christian subject nearest to this theme, and adapted it by replacing the book with the shield and the cross with the spear.[3] The Leipzig ivory in

1 Trier, Stadtbibl., MS. 31, fol. 38. Exh., *Karl der Grosse*, no. 492.

2 Oxford, Bodleian Library, MS. Douce 176. Goldschmidt, *Elfenbeinskulpturen* (1), no. 5, Taf. iii. Goldschmidt suggests that the Leipzig Ivory may even have been the reverse of a book cover similar to the Bodleian ivory which shows the 'Christus super aspidem'. As evidence that the two subjects could be connected he draws attention to a twelfth century Belgian(?) ivory now in the Bargello. Goldschmidt, *Elfenbeinskulpturen* (3), no. 25–26, Taf. vii. For the 'Christus super aspidem' iconography see below, p. 148.

3 See Laurent op. cit. emphasizing that the St Michael is a type of the victory of Good over Evil and as such has a long iconographical ancestry. The 'Christus super aspidem' is not the only example of this triumph in early medieval art. See for instance the arch of Einhard with riders spearing dragons. Exh., *Karl der Grosse*, no. 9.

that case would be close to the source of the new type and could even be the earliest example of it, not merely the earliest surviving example[1].

If Apocalypse illustrations did not contribute to the creation of the Leipzig type, in the next stage of the development they do become important. In a relief of the Archangel on the early eleventh-century Golden
Pl. 16*h* Antependium at Aachen, St Michael, moving to the left in three-quarter view, tramples a now much larger dragon underfoot. This is a real and dramatic contest. He pushes his spear held in his right hand into the dragon's jaws which twist up to the left spouting flames.[2] And an almost identical angel leaning forward well covered by his shield appears in the
Pl. 18*a* early eleventh-century Bamberg Apocalypse of the Reichenau school.[3] There the scene has been doubled and another angel reversed is on the left. Below a pair of dragons twist back as in the Leipzig ivory.[4] Since the angels in the Carolingian Trier and Cambrai Apocalypses do not carry shields, it would seem that the Aachen altar and the Bamberg Apocalypse develop the Leipzig type.[5] But the greater emphasis on the combat is only attributable to the use of the type in the Apocalypse context.

The other important feature of the Bamberg Apocalypse for our enquiry is that the reversal of the angel on the left produces the arrangement

[1] It might be argued that the 'Christus super aspidem' is a figure already triumphant and therefore stationary, so that the warrior Michael in movement would have been more likely to influence the Bodleian Christus than vice versa. However, an examination of the 'Christus super aspidem' types shows that this bending of the figure's left leg is found in the Genoels Eldern Ivory, Volbach *Elfenbeinarbeiten*, no. 217, and the stucco figure of the Orthodox Baptistery in Ravenna. These significantly are both, as is the Bodleian Ivory, of the 'Christus Miles' type. See F. Saxl, 'The Ruthwell Cross', *Journal of the Warburg and Courtauld Institutes*, vi (1943), 1–19. The pose of the Leipzig St Michael has an awkwardness which suggests that it is an adaptation of another scene.

[2] H. Schnitzler, 'Fulda oder Reichenau?', *Wallraf-Richartz Jahrbuch*, xix (1957), 39 ff., pl.

[3] Bamberg, Staatl. Bib., Bibl. 140 (A.II.42), fol. 30. H. Wölfflin, *Die Bamberger Apokalypse* (1921), Taf. 30.

[4] Was this twisting serpent also an innovation of the Carolingian artist? It would be based on triumphant warriors of late antique ivories such as the Bellerophon Ivory in the British Museum, Volbach, *Elfenbeinarbeiten*, no. 67, or the ivory of the Aachen pulpit, ibid, no. 77, where the beasts twist back their necks. The motif does not seem to appear in the 'Christus super aspidem' type before this date even where Christ holds a staff. Its earliest appearances there are in the Utrecht Psalter and in the Stuttgart Psalter. See discussion of the 'Christus super Aspidem', below, Chapter V, p. 148.

[5] That the Bamberg dragons lack the ten horns and seven crowned heads of the Beast, also supports their connection with the Leipzig ivory type, rather than an older Apocalypse type.

of Avranches 50, though the spear passes, due to the reversal, behind the shield. A number of Ottonian examples of this can be quoted, and that it was a new introduction, not yet generally adopted, in the late tenth century, is indicated by the miniature inserted in an Ottonian Gospels of unknown provenance.[1] For there the Archangel still spears the dragon to the left as in the Leipzig ivory and the Aachen antependium. In a Gradual from Prüm, on the other hand, St Michael attacks the dragon to the right with his spear across his body, though he bends his right knee as if advancing still towards the left.[2] Pl. 18*b* Pl. 18*e*

The cross lance type is seen later in the south of Germany,[3] and a variation of it (St Michael is not fighting the dragon) occurs in the Last Judgment scene at Burgfelden of the mid-eleventh century.[4] There is thus good reason to believe it was invented in Germany. However, there is one important example from England which suggests that it might have been known there also in the late tenth century. This is the Cotton Psalter, in the British Museum.[5] Wormald has suggested that its illuminations are copies of a manuscript in the style of the Psalter, British Museum, Harley MS. 2904. If this is a faithful copy, then St Michael combating the Pl. 18*d*

1 Munich, Bayr. Staatsbibl., Clm. 23630. See D. H. Turner, 'The "Ŏdalricus Peccator" Manuscript in the British Museum', *British Museum Quarterly*, xxv (1962), 11–16. The British Museum MS. is Harley 2970. The most probable origin of the two manuscripts appears to be Lorsch. But the St Michael is on an inserted bifolium. The St Michael on the eleventh-century bronze doors at San Zeno, Verona, also spears to the left. F. Winzinger, *Das Tor von San Zeno in Verona* (Munich, 1958), Taf. 5, and so does the St Michael on the portable altar of Gertrude now at Cleveland, O. von Falke *et al.*, *The Guelph Treasure* (1930), no. 5, pl. 13.

2 Paris, Bib. Nat., Latin 9448, fol. 71. Late tenth century. Goldschmidt, *German illumination* (2), pl. 67–8. In the Prüm Gospels from Manchester, Rylands Library, MS. 7, early eleventh century, St Michael moves unequivocally to the right to spear the dragon. He is accompanied also by a group of angels and the scene is clearly adapted from an Apocalypse miniature. R. Schilling, 'Das Ruotpertus-Evangelistar aus Prüm', *Studien zur Buchmalerei und Goldschmiedekunst des Mittelalters. Festschrift für K. H. Usener* (1967), 143–54, Abb. 5.

3 In a Psalter from Tegernsee later at Lyre, now Évreux, Bib. Mun., MS. 78, fol. 66$^{v}$, late eleventh century. Also Munich, Bayr. Staatsbibl., Clm. 27054 from Freising, early twelfth century. See A. Boeckler, 'Zur Freisinger Buchmalerei des 12. Jahrhunderts', *Zeitschrift des deutschen Vereins für Kunstwissenschaft*, viii (1941), 6, Taf. 3. In these examples the Archangel has become an armed soldier.

4 P. Weber, *Das Wandgemälde zu Burgfelden*, Taf. 1.

5 MS. Cotton Tiberius C.VI. See F. Wormald, 'An English eleventh-century Psalter with Pictures', *Walpole Society*, xxxviii (1960–62), 1–13. St. Michael moves towards the dragon.

dragon to the right with shield and cross lance would have been current in the last quarter of the tenth century in England.[1]

Pl. 17*b* A comparison of the Avranches 50 miniature shows at once that it belongs to this series. The essentials of the lance held across the body with the back of the right hand visible, the bent elbow, the pose of the feet pointing in one direction whilst the body turns back from the waist, are
Pl. 18*e* all in the Prüm Gradual. Points which differ are the helmet, a detail indicating the more realistic conception of the Archangel as an armed warrior, which is found later in a twelfth-century South German Psalter, the *scabellum*, the devil instead of the dragon, and the grasp of the shield (this last found in the Tegernsee Psalter).[2]

The iconography of Avranches 50 suggests a connection, then, with Ottonian art. Some of the Byzantine features noticed above may have been received indirectly, therefore, and it is notable that the devil of the Burgfelden frescoes resembles that of Avranches 50. Another parallel is the Missal of Worms,[3] where Christ has his feet on a clothed devil, 'Mors', who is human and has similar hair.[4] It is interesting that one of the few examples of the twelfth century of St Michael triumphing over a

[1] Wormald also points out that a miniature of St Michael is missing from the Benedictional of St Ethelwold. An Anglo-Saxon Psalter decorated with pictures was in Normandy before 1037 (See Appx. V). Diagonal staffs across the body occur in other Anglo-Saxon manuscripts of the late tenth century, e.g. Sherborne Pontifical. There are also a number of similar combat scenes in the Anglo-Saxon Prudentius manuscripts which might have been the model. A carved slab which may belong to the eleventh century showing a St Michael spearing the dragon with a vertical spear to the left is at Seaford, Sussex. A. Gardner, *English Medieval Sculpture* (1951), fig. 66.

[2] This has its origin, perhaps, in the type of triumphant warrior seen on the Probus and Stilicho Diptychs, Volbach, *Elfenbeinarbeiten*, nos. 1 and 63, where the shield is only kept upright on the ground not impossibly lifted. A Carolingian ivory in the Bargello, Goldschmidt, *Elfenbeinskulpturen* (1), no. 10, Taf. v, shows two men, probably virtues, triumphing over vices in whose mouth one thrusts his spear. Similar triumphing figures occur in Prudentius manuscripts, and Stettiner in fact labels one, Paris, Bib. Nat., Latin 8318, fol. 57$^{v}$, St Michael. R. Stettiner, *Die illustrierten Prudentius Handschriften* (1905), Taf. 16 no. 3. The figure stands on a snake and spears it vertically. He has a similarly held shield by his side but neither wings nor halo, so there is no reason to think him St Michael.

[3] Paris, Bibliothèque de l'Arsenal, Latin 610, tenth century. H. Martin, Ph. Lauer, *Les principaux manuscrits à peintures de la Bibliothèque de l'Arsenal* (1929), 10–12, pl. ii.

[4] Other similar devils are in the Bamberg Apocalypse, fol. 46 and 47. The MS. 50 devil's hands are not bound as in the Harrowing of Hell scenes. In Anglo-Saxon art the emphasis was on the fantastic and grotesque in the representation of the devil, as in the Tiberius Psalter, or 'Mors' in the 'Leofric Missal'. Cf. A. Heimann, *Journal of the Warburg and Courtauld Institutes*, xxix (1966), 39ff.

devil as opposed to a dragon should be an ivory probably from the area of modern Belgium.[1] This is the area from which the reformed community Pl. 18*c* at Mont St Michel came and may be the source of the iconography, too.

The second representation of St Michael in the Mont St Michel manu- Pl. 20 scripts is in Avranches 76. Here the upper part of the Archangel with symmetrical flanking wings is severely frontal. The legs, however, on the back of a dragon seem to stride to the right. The shield is small.

It would seem that this is a combination of disparate elements. The shield and the striding to the right belong to the Northern tradition. The Pl. 18*d* striding pose is fairly close to that of the Tiberius Psalter and the shields also have a common feature in the little scalloped boss from which the centre spike appears.

For the frontal pose, however, we must look elsewhere, and as it does not occur in the Ottonian examples, and since it is similar to the frontal early Christian and Byzantine 'Princeps inter principes' type, it is natural to look to southern Italy, the other most likely source of Byzantine influence.

It is at this stage, in fact, that Monte Gargano may be introduced into the argument. The church there was founded in the cave in the mountain where the Angel appeared on the 8th May 492, and was dedicated in 494. It became with St Nicholas of Bari the most celebrated place of pilgrimage in southern Italy. St Autbert naturally sought relics there for his new foundation at Mont St Michel. And towards the end of the ninth century there is the account of the monk Bernard who made a pilgrimage to the various shrines of St Michael. He saw there an 'imaginem' of the Archangel. Unfortunately he neither specifies whether this work was a painting or a carving, nor says how the figure was represented. Mâle thought that this became the accepted pattern for the representation of the Archangel spreading from there throughout the west, and that it was a figure triumphing over the dragon.[2] The new type therefore would have been created at Monte Gargano.

1 Now in the Bargello, Goldschmidt, *Elfenbeinskulpturen* (3), no. 26, Taf. vii. Another devil in this scene is on a capital at Anzy-le-Duc, first half twelfth century. A. Kingsley Porter, *Romanesque Sculpture of the Pilgrimage Roads*, (1923), pl. 20 (St. Michael has a sword).

2 E. Mâle, *L'Art religeux du XIIe siècle en France* (1928), 257 ff.

There survive three early figures of St Michael at Monte Gargano. The
Pl. 19*b* first (for convenience M.G.1) is a small copper pilgrim's offering of the Archangel carrying a globe in his left hand and with his right hand raised. Petrucci dates this to the late fifth to early sixth century.[1] The
Pl. 19*a* second work (M.G.2) is a stone carving of St Michael with wings and halo and both arms raised.[2] In his right hand he holds a spear which falls vertically into the mouth of the dragon. This Petrucci dates before 1000.
Pl. 19*c* Thirdly, there is the stone carved throne of the Bishops of Siponto (M.G.3), which Petrucci on the basis of the inscription dates shortly after 1023 and certainly before 1050, the year of Bishop Leon of Siponto's death.[3] Here St Michael, severely frontal, holds his spear diagonally across his body with both hands, its point in the dragon's mouth to the right.

The first of these three, then, is the usual Byzantine and Early Christian type though with a short tunic, whilst the second introduces the dragon and the third the cross lance. Both M.G.2 and M.G.3 differ from the northern type in having no shield. This is a more important difference than the mere omission of an attribute. For in the northern examples from the late tenth century the shield is an essential part of a real battle
Pl. 16*h* in which, for instance in the Aachen antependium, St Michael uses it to protect himself from the dragon's belching fire. The Monte Gargano representations on the other hand, resemble rather the Byzantine types, in that they are an angel already triumphant.

But if these Monte Gargano representations are so different from the northern type in spirit, are they nevertheless influenced by it, or why is the dragon introduced at all and where does it come from?[4] An interesting suggestion has been put forward by Jerphanion.[5] He proposes a Coptic origin for the type at Monte Gargano. Accepting wrongly, as I believe, Mâle's view that the Monte Gargano representation was at the
Pl. 19*e* root of the whole western iconography, he draws attention to three Coptic

[1] A. Petrucci, *Cattedrali di Puglia* (1964), colour frontispiece, 11, and 'Note alle illustrazioni', 549. It may well be later, ninth century (?).

[2] Petrucci, op. cit., pl. 14.

[3] Petrucci, op. cit., pl. 8.

[4] There is no evidence that Monte Gargano was itself a centre of artistic production. The new bronze doors of the church commissioned in 1076 were made at Byzantium for instance.

[5] See article op. cit. (p. 87 n. 2).

textiles of the sixth century, one in the Victoria and Albert Museum, London;[1] one, the best preserved, in the Museum of Decorative Art in Athens; and one in the Benaki Museum, Athens.

These show a frontal figure with feet turned towards the right standing on a dragon whose head twists up to receive the lance in its jaws. The left hand is raised and holds a cross. There are no wings and no halo. The figure is balanced by one exactly similar except that it is reversed – that is the lance is in the left hand, etc.

It hardly seems possible in view of the gesture of the left hand to doubt Jerphanion's conclusion that the Monte Gargano representations[2] which he dates to the twelfth century (as he does, following Mâle, Avranches 76), and the textiles are somehow connected. But it is very difficult to go further than this. First, it is not at all clear who the figure on the textiles is. Lacking as it does both the cross halo of Christ and the wings and halo of St Michael, it must remain highly problematic, as Jerphanion readily admits, whether this triumphing figure was ever identified specifically, was not rather a general symbol of the triumph of good over evil, as the eagle and the quadruped above it are. If so, it is not necessary to suppose that there was some recognized eastern, or specifically Coptic, iconography of St Michael, to which only these textiles witness and which would have been adopted at Monte Gargano at some early date. The gesture of the hand raised in triumph could have been adopted in the sculpture from a different model elsewhere, and so have a common ancestry in textile and sculpture.

Pls. 19*a*, *e*

Certainly the horizontal dragon with coiling tail and twisted up head on which the Archangel tramples on the Aachen antependium, in the Munich Gospels and Avranches 76 for instance, is very similar to the textile dragon. But it must be emphasized again that the earlier Ottonian examples have none of the frontality of the textile figures and in several of them the lance is not held across the body.[3] The dragon could come

Pls. 16*h*, 18*b*
Pls. 20, 19*e*

[1] A. F. Kendrick, *Catalogue of Textiles from burying-grounds in Egypt. Vol. iii. Coptic period* (1922) 81, no. 819, pl. xxv.

[2] He reproduces M.G.3. It is not clear if the second sculpture he refers to is M.G.2 or not.

[3] The Gertrudis altar is an exception, von Falke, op. cit. By the mid-eleventh century the frontal iconography has evidently penetrated Germany too.

from other sources.[1] It is, therefore, equally possible to argue that the Coptic textile figure was only seen as a St Michael (if it was so seen) because there *already* existed a similar iconography in the west, as that it inspired that iconography.

If the textiles are to be connected with the Monte Gargano representation it remains quite uncertain at what date the cross-lance type was adopted there and it is rash to assume that the ninth-century 'imago' seen by Bernard was of any particular type. To me it seems that this new frontal cross-lance type may well have been adopted at Monte Gargano precisely at the time when the cross-lance profile combatting St Michael begins to appear in the north, that is, in the second half of the tenth century. It was at this date that Monte Gargano seems to have achieved a new importance with the visit, for instance, of the Emperor Otto III in 999 to the shrine.[2]

It may be said, therefore, with due caution, since between the Leipzig ivory and the late tenth century we have no surviving evidence, that the theme of the fighting Archangel distinguished by his shield, is a Carolingian invention. In the Leipzig ivory, however, the dragon is insignificant and the Archangel is triumphant, as is the 'Christus super aspidem' on which it is modelled. The militant side was developed in connection with Apocalypse illustration, probably in Germany, in the tenth century. At the same time an alteration was made in the iconography in that St Michael, as well as fighting the dragon as in the Apocalypse illustrations, now tramples it in triumph as in the ivory. A similar arrangement is found on a Coptic textile, and might perhaps have been adopted from this or a similar source at Monte Gargano at an unknown date but very possibly also in the tenth century. Various combinations were tried, some representations retaining the independent dragon of the Apocalypse and

[1] e.g. the representations of the constellation Cetus in Aratus manuscripts. The Munich Gospels dragon is very much of this type. The motif of the twisting up head has a much older ancestry which could easily be common to both representations. See discussion of the 'Christus super Aspidem' in Chapter V, p. 148.

[2] This would have been an occasion for the meeting of the two types, the frontal and the cross-lance. For instance in the same year Otto III gave the church of S. Bonifasio e Alessio in Rome a cope on which the whole Apocalypse was embroidered in gold. E. Sackur, *Die Cluniacenser*, i (1892), (1892), 339–40.

using the cross lance, for example in the Tiberius Psalter, others showing St Michael trampling the dragon but spearing it with the vertical lance, for example the Aachen antependium and M.G.2. It is these variations, even between M.G.2 and M.G.3, that suggest, contrary to Mâle, that the iconography was not already an established type at Monte Gargano.

Pl. 18*d*

Pls. 16*h*, 19*a*

Pls. 19*a*, *c*

None of the miniatures so far quoted adopts the frontal pose of the textiles or the Monte Gargano sculptures except Avranches 76. Does this prove that the monks of Mont St Michel knew of the Monte Gargano iconography directly? Though this is perfectly possible, for the devotion of Norman soldiers to the shrine of St Michael at Monte Gargano is attested, and at least one Norman cleric, Ivo, bishop of Sées, journeyed down to southern Italy to collect money to rebuild his burnt cathedral,[1] it is not certain. For there exists another miniature, that of the Ivrea Sacramentary, dateable to 1002,[2] in which the angel, moving to the right tramples the dragon[3] spearing it with the cross lance, but is strictly frontal in the upper part of his body. Here the left arm is raised again in the gesture of M.G.2 and the textile, but without the cross. The gesture of triumph also occurs on the bronze doors of Monte Gargano made in 1076 at Constantinople.[4]

Pl. 19*d*

Pls. 19*a*, *e*

Pl. 16*f*

The presence of this miniature in the Ivrea Sacramentary is particularly interesting, for it is precisely the part of Italy from which William of Volpiano came. His foundation of Fruttuaria on his own lands was in the diocese of Ivrea. It is known that William visited Monte Gargano,[5] and in his church at St Bénigne, Dijon, he dedicated a chapel to St Michael.[6] It may well be through him or through his disciple Suppo,

[1] William of Jumièges, ed. J. Marx (1914), Bk. VII ch. xv.

[2] Ivrea, Bib. Cap., Cod. LXXXVI, fol. 108v. L. Magnani, *Le Miniature del Sacramentario d'Ivrea* (1934), tav. xxv.

[3] This is the Apocalyptic beast with the ten horns and seven crowned heads. Another north Italian manuscript close in style also has an Apocalpytic reference in the cross lance St Michael rescuing the naked child, Rev. XII, vv. 4–5. This is now British Museum, Egerton 3763, fol. 104v, formerly Dyson Perrins MS. 48, G. Warner, *A Descriptive catalogue of illuminated manuscripts in the library of C. W. Dyson Perrins* (1920), 130–35, pl. 51. See also D. H. Turner, 'The prayer-book of Archbishop Arnulf II of Milan', *Revue Bénédictine*, lxx (1960), 360–392.

[4] *R.D.K.*, s.v. *Engelsturz*, fig. 3.

[5] *Vita Sci Guillelmi*, Migne, *P.L.* cxli, 855. Probably in 995.

[6] *Vita Sci Guillelmi*, Migne, *P.L.* cxli, 858.

abbot of Fruttuaria before coming to Mont St Michel, that the new iconography arrived at the abbey. It had already been adapted even in the
Pls. 19*d*, 20 Ivrea Sacramentary by the introduction of the feet striding to the right. The Mont St Michel artist replaces the raised left arm with a shield which has no function as protection and is no more than an attribute.

The later developments in the iconography of St Michael are not relevant here, but as a further argument against Mâle's view it should be pointed out that the Avranches 76 type of St Michael remains uncommon. One example is the fresco at Le Puy, where the Archangel with cross lance is frontal with no shield and wears the Byzantine loros, in this respect being very similar to the Monte Gargano bronze doors. Another is on the capital in the Narthex of S Benoît-sur-Loire, which is interesting since a Lombard is known to have worked at Fleury.[1] This shows St Michael exactly as in M.G.3 but reversed. In Italy there are certain examples of the frontal archangel of the M.G.2 type.[2] But the majority of instances in the eleventh and twelfth centuries show a profile St Michael combatting the dragon either to the left with vertical lance[3] or more commonly to the right with cross lance.[4]

[1] See C. Nordenfalk, 'A travelling Milanese artist in France at the beginning of the eleventh century', *Arte del Primo Millennio* (Congress at Pavia, 1950) ed. E. Arslan (1954), 374–80. C. Nordenfalk, 'Miniature ottonienne et ateliers capétiens', *Art de France*, iv (1964), 47–55. Turner, op. cit., suggests that Nivardus may have executed the initials of the Prayerbook of Arnulph of Milan, London, Brit. Mus., Egerton 3763.

[2] e.g. a relief from San Michele, Pavia (the fighting Archangel also occurs in a struggle for a just man's soul). See E. Arslan, 'Note sulla scultura Romanica Pavese', *Bollettino d'Arte*, xl (1955), 103–118, figs. 16 and 33. Also Oratorio San Giuseppe, Pistoia, and relief from Sant' Appiano, Pieve. See M. Salmi, *Romanesque Sculpture in Tuscany* (1928), figs. 230 and 103.

[3] e.g. relief Sant Angelo in Campo, Mazzarosa Collection, Lucca, Salmi, op. cit., fig. 175; a Belgian(?) ivory, mid-twelfth century, Goldschmidt, *Elfenbeinskulpturen* (3), no. 26; and the tympanum of St Michel d'Entraigues, Charente, Kingsley Porter, op. cit., pl. 1006. See pl. 18c.

[4] Examples are: a) *Eleventh century*. Initial 'N', Paris, Bib. Nat., Latin 11685, fol. 40, St Germain-des-Prés, by Ingelardus, Deslandres, op cit., pl. 4d., a type later found at Canterbury, London, Brit. Mus., Arundel MS. 91 and Royal MS. 1.B.xi, Dodwell, *Canterbury School*, pl. 21 a, b; Gospels from Jumièges, Brit. Mus., Add. MS. 17739; Homiliary, Le Cateau, Cambrai, Bibl. Mun., MS. 528, fol. 198v; Rouen, Bib. Mun., MS. U.20 (1404), Dodwell, *Canterbury School*, pl. 5c (no devil); London, Brit. Mus., Egerton 3763, Prayer Book of Arnulf II of Milan, Warner, op. cit., pl. 51; engraved metal cross, Copenhagen, National Museum, Ch. Oman, 'An eleventh-century English Cross', *Burlington Magazine*, xcvi (1954), 383–4, figs. 17–18. See pls. 19 f, g.
b) *Twelfth century*. Ivory Tau Cross, Victoria and Albert Museum, Goldschmidt *Elfenbeinskulpturen*

Two other Mont St Michel representations of St Michael should briefly be considered.[1] The first is in a full-page miniature of Robert de Torigni's cartulary Avranches MS. 210.[2] Robert was abbot from 1154 to 1186. On fol. 25v there are two registers and in each an altar with the Archangel standing on it. Do these reflect actual statues? They are slightly different in the position of the dragon but in both the Angel carries a little spear point in his left hand which is thrust into the dragon's mouth. Could this be a representation of the famous relic, the sword of St Michael?[3] The second is the seal of Robert de Torigni. There the Archangel stands on the dragon which faces to the right. His right arm is raised in blessing but the right side of the seal is damaged.[4] If it carried a similar short spear, the cartulary and the seal would be evidence of yet another type. Pl. 19*h*

Unfortunately there seems to be no reference to a cult statue or painting of St Michael in the church to this date. Though Mabillon notes[5] that among Abbot Suppo's gifts to the church were two silver angels, there is no indication that they represented St Michael, or that, if they did, they

[1] The Sacramentary, New York, Morgan Library, MS. 641 originally had a miniature of St Michael, now missing. See Appx. VI.

[2] A. Boinet, 'L'illustration du Cartulaire du Mont-Saint-Michel', *Bibliothèque de l'école des chartes*, lxx (1909), 335–343. The cartulary dates from the early years of Robert's abbacy, 1154–1186.

[3] Described as 'une petite dague ou poignard,' *Millénaire* (1), 569, it was at Mont St Michel from the twelfth century. See above p. 98 n. 4.

[4] E. Mâle, *L'Art religieux du XIIe siècle en France* (1928), fig. 172; Exh., *Millénaire*, no. 126.

[5] *Annales Ordinis Sancti Benedicti*, iv (1706), 496.

(4), no. 12, Taf. iii; fresco at Civate illustrating Revelation XII, vv. 4–5; Cîteaux Legendary, Dijon, Bib. Mun., 641, fol. 22v, C. Oursel, *La Miniature du XIIe siècle à l'abbaye de Cîteaux* (1926), pl. xxxv; Ratman Missal, Hildesheim, Domschatz, MS. 37; relief at St Gilles, etc. A series of examples in England are in carved church tympana. See Ch. Keyser, *Norman Tympana* (1927), fig. 140, 141. The iconography of St Michael with a sword which seems to have been common in England in the twelfth century (see Keyser, op. cit.), does not concern us here. A sword and shield as relics of St Michael are attested at Mont St Michel from, it seems, the twelfth century. See J. Laporte, 'L'épée et le bouclier dits "de Saint-Michel",' *Millénaire* (2), 397–410. St Gregory the Great in 590 saw the Archangel standing on the Castel Sant' Angelo sheath his sword to signify the end of the plague. But it does not appear that there was an image of the Archangel there in the eleventh century. E. Rodocanachi, *Le Château Saint-Ange* (1909). I am indebted to Miss Rosalie Green of the Princeton Iconographic Index for a list of representations of St Michael and the dragon.

can be connected either with the Avranches 76 iconography or alternatively with the cartulary drawings. To the end of the twelfth century there appear to be only two instances of the spear held vertically in the left hand, one at Sant 'Appiano a Pieve,[1] the other at Flax Bourton Church in Somerset, a carved tympanum.[2] It would seem probable that if the cartulary drawings really are trustworthy, this is a further variation of late date.

## B: THE TWO 'DISPUTE' PICTURES

Pls. 22, 24*a* On fol. 97 of MS. 72 and fol. 1v of MS. 90 there are full-page miniatures in which St Augustine is shown disputing with a heretic. In MS. 72 the scene is probably based on a book presentation, since Felicianus the Manichaean approaches the enthroned St Augustine and is smaller in scale. The miniature in MS. 50 may well have been adapted for the
Pl. 17*b* scene.[3] In MS. 90, however, the contestants are both enthroned and there is also an equality of scale.

Since the texts are dialogues, the miniatures are a kind of double author portrait. As with the book presentation, there is an older tradition behind the double author portrait. In the tenth-century *Herbarium* of Apuleius and Antonius Musa,[4] the two disputing authors, sit each under separate arches and face each other on fol. 1v and fol. 2. The manuscript was possibly made at Fulda where it was later preserved, but it certainly

[1] Salmi, op. cit., fig. 103. A left-handed St Michael with a cross lance is in Cambridge, Trinity College, MS. o.9.22, fol. 5v, an early twelfth-century St Augustine Enchiridion, M. R. James, *The Western Manuscripts in the Library of Trinity College, Cambridge*, iii (1902), 461, pl. xii, and in Rouen, Bib. Mun., MS. A.85 (467), from Jumièges.

[2] Ch. Keyser, op. cit., pl. 142B.

[3] See below, p. 110. This at least seems more probable than that the Mont St Michel artist knew of such as dialogue as is found in the copy of the Carolingian *Notitia Dignitatum* manuscript, then in Speyer, made for Pietro Donato, bishop of Padua, in 1436 now Bodleian Library, MS. Canon. Misc.378. See my 'Manuscrits enluminés du XIe siècle provenant du Mont Saint Michel', *Art de Basse-Normandie*, xl (1966), 27–33, pl. 7. For the scene of the book presentation, see above, p. 86.

[4] On the left is 'Constantinus mag(ister)', on the right the inscription is torn off. Cassel, Landesbibl., MS. Phys. fol. 10. Goldschmidt, *German Illumination* (1), pl. 19–20. It is closely connected with Leiden Voss.Q.9, seventh century, and the prototype may have been of Lower Italian origin. Also in the Rabbula Gospels some of the Apostles are arranged in pairs on the Canon Tables as if conversing. C. Cecchelli, J. Furlani, M. Salmi, *The Rabbula Gospels* (facsimile edition, 1959), espec. fol. 9v. See also H. Swarzenski, 'The Xanten purple leaf and the Carolingian Renaissance', *Art Bulletin*, xxii (1940), 13–15 for a discussion of this iconography.

depends on earlier prototypes. The iconography is also connected with the Dialogue scene which Saxl considered an invention of Early Christian Art.[1] A close parallel with MS. 90 is in fact a dialogue scene not a dispute.[2] This is the Gospel Book from St Vaast, now in Boulogne, where the letter from St Jerome to Pope Damasus is prefaced by a miniature of the two in conversation.[3] Behind are looped curtains and two figures watch. The arrangement is very similar to that of MS. 90, but the Mont St Michel artist has made his miniature a more dramatic scene with the gesticulating hands and intense expressions of the disputants and the figures behind who take sides. Another St Vaast example of a dispute, in the Bible, initial 'F' to Maccabees,[4] has this excitement (no doubt reflecting an Anglo-Saxon model) which also recalls the Bayeux tapestry in such scenes as the conversations between Harold and Edward the Confessor or Duke William.[5] Pl. 25*a*

The only earlier representation of a saint and a heretic together known to me is in a copy of Jerome, *Contra Jovinianum* from Einsiedeln.[6] St Pl. 25*b*

[1] F. Saxl, 'Frühes Christentum und spätes Heidentum in ihren Kunstlerischen Ausdrucksformen. 1. Der Dialog als Thema der Christlichen Kunst', *Wiener Jahrbuch für Kunstgeschichte*, xvi (1923), 64–77. The most common dialogue is between Sts Peter and Paul (cf. Bernward Gospels, Hildesheim). Compare also Fides and Caritas on the Tribunal with an audience in Prudentius manuscripts, Stettiner, op. cit., Taf. 73 and 74.

[2] P. Bloch, 'Eine Dialogdarstellung des frühen 12. Jahrhunderts', *Festschrift Dr E. Trautscholdt* (1965), has studied a German miniature showing a dialogue between Anselm of Bec and Boso which may well derive from a Norman exemplar. Representations of disputes also occur in illustrations of the Gospel narrative in the scene of the naming of St John the Baptist (Benedictional of St Ethelwold, London, Brit. Mus., Add. 49598, fol. 22v) and that of Christ and the Doctors in the Temple (Gospels of Henry III, Escorial Cod. Vetr. 17 and Echternach Golden Gospels, Nuremberg, Germanisches National Museum, MS. 156142, of which the latter has some of MS. 90's dramatic excitement, P. Metz, *The Golden Gospels of Echternach* (1957), pl. 31).

[3] Boulogne, Bib. Mun., MS. 9, fol. 1v. Schulten, op. cit., Taf. 17.

[4] Schulten, op. cit., Taf. 14.

[5] *The Bayeux Tapestry*, ed. F. M. Stenton (2nd edn., 1965), figs. 1 and 18. Anglo-Saxon manuscripts with dialogue scenes are Durham MS. B.III.32 and London, Brit. Mus., Cotton MS. Tiberius A.III. Wormald, *English Drawings*, pls. 23, 29.

[6] MS. 135. A. Bruckner, *Scriptoria Medii Aevi Helvetica, V, Stift Einsiedeln*, (1943), 174, Taf. XVI. Vercelli, Bib. Cap., MS. 165, Italian, ninth century, and Rome, Biblioteca Vaticana, Lat. 1339, Italian, early eleventh century, contain drawings illustrating councils at which heretics were condemned and their writings burnt. A. von Euw, 'Studien zu den Elfenarbeiten der Hofschule Karls des Grossen', *Aachener Kunstblätter*, xxxiv (1967), 36–38, Abb. 1–5. Much closer to the Norman iconography are some important drawings of triumphant figures in London, Brit. Mus., Harley MS. 2886, Canons, 9th century.

Jerome sits to the left and on the right the Devil whispers in the ear of Jovinianus. Though the idea of painting a frontispiece miniature to the dialogue text is similar, this is not a confrontation in which the saint is confounding the heretic as in the Mont-Saint-Michel miniatures. It seems unlikely that knowledge of this or a similar frontispiece had reached the abbey from the east, therefore.

The sudden appearance of these pictures of Disputes against heretics for which there seems to be only this one parallel elsewhere, raises the question of whether these were occasioned by outbreaks of heresy in Normandy at the time.[1] Most of the texts are disputes against Manicheans. There seem to be no instances of Manicheanism in Normandy itself but a form of it did occur in two places with which the abbey had connections, Arras in 1025, and Orléans in 1022.[2] The disputing figures may also be connected with the new importance of dialectic, for instance in the Lanfranc *versus* Berengar of Tours controversy.[3] They may even be intended as an allusion to that dispute.

## C: THE HALF-LENGTH CHRISTS

The third major iconographical point concerns the half-length Christs
Pls. 22, 26*a* in the lunettes of MS. 72, fol. 97 and Latin 2639, fol. 31v. There are two

1 Two other examples of miniatures depicting the defeat of heretics come from Fécamp, Paris, Bib. Nat., Latin 2079, fol. 1v, and Paris, Bib. Nat., Latin 1684, fol. 1. *Manuscrits à peintures*, nos. 193, 206. In these St Augustine and St Athanasius spear the heretics Faustinus and Arius with their croziers and trample them down. A Byzantine example of St Peter of Alexandria trampling on Arius may be noted, Paris, Bib. Nat., Gr. 580. Exh., *Byzance et la France médiévale*, Paris, Bibliothèque Nationale, 1958, no. 26. The figures are too damaged for this identification to be certain, however. One may speculate on the effect on the Norman illuminators of Augustine's rebuke to Faustinus concerning the sumptuous books the Manicheans used for propaganada – 'Conspuuntur tam multi et tam grandes et tam preciosi codices vestri', Bk. xiii ch. 6, *P.L.* xlii, 285. Did the monks mean to provide the orthodox side with manuscripts as fine?

2 S. Runciman, *The Medieval Manichee*, 1947, 117 with references. For anti-Arrian propaganda at Cîteaux in the early twelfth century see W. Cahn, 'A defence of the Trinity in the Cîteaux Bible', *Marsyas*, xi (1962–4), 58–62.

3 See R. W. Southern, 'Lanfranc of Bec and Berengar of Tours', *Studies in Medieval History presented to F. M. Powicke* (1948), 27–48. Avranches MS. 107 contains a late eleventh-century copy of Berengar's retraction. For later examples of St Augustine disputing see J. Courcelle, P. Courcelle, *Iconographie de Saint Augustin. Les cycles du XIV*e *siècle* (1965).

other half-length Christs in the Sacramentary, Morgan 641, which must be discussed in conjunction with these.

The most abbreviated figure is that above the stoning of St Stephen in
an initial 'D' on fol. $3^{v}$ of Morgan 641. Only Christ's shoulders appear Pl. 31*d*
and His hand is held across His chest with two fingers raised in blessing.[1]
He is bearded and has a cross halo. The roundel is surrounded by a glory
of bands of colour. On fol. $122^{v}$ of the same manuscript, this time a full- Pl. 43
page miniature showing the crucifixion of St Peter, Christ with still only His head and shoulders visible holds up a closed book in His veiled left hand and blesses with His right hand held with palm towards the spectator, His thumb, index and third finger extended. He is bearded and has a cross halo.

In Avranches 72 the figure of Christ is nearly half-length. He holds up Pl. 22
His right hand in blessing as on fol. $122^{v}$ of Morgan 641 and in His left hand holds out a closed book but this time His hand is not veiled. He is again bearded and has a cross halo. His clothing is more noticeable now and consists of a cloak which falls over His right shoulder in a small loop and over His left in complicated folds, also billowing out to the right as if blown by the wind. On His tunic underneath this are bands of material arranged in a pattern of bars and studded with jewels. Finally in Latin
2639 the pose is similar, but Christ has not got a crossed halo, there is no Pl. 26*a*
flying fold to the right, the jewelled *clavi* are less noticeable, and in His veiled left hand He carries a crown.

All these figures are well fitted into the spaces they occupy. None of them seem crowded, nor, on the other hand, is there any effect of emptiness in the lunettes. But there is a difference in the way they occupy their
niches. On fol. $122^{v}$ of Morgan 641 the figure is strictly confined inside Pl. 43
the roundel.[2] The frame medallion almost overlaps the halo. The Avranches 72 figure is also confined to its space except for the flying fold Pl. 22
which slightly overlaps the curtain rod. But on fol. $3^{v}$ of Morgan 641
the halo overlaps the bar of the 'D' and thus gives an illusion that the Pl. 31*d*
Christ is leaning forward slightly towards the scene below. In Latin 2639

[1] A roundel with a blessing Christ occurs on the frame of MS. 115 fol. $1^{v}$, a transitional manuscript. The Christ is not bearded. See Pl. 10 f.

[2] As in MS. 115 fol. $1^{v}$. See Pl. 10 f.

Pl. 26*a* this same impression is given by the halo overlapping the arch and enforced by the drapery veiling the hand, which falls across the architrave. At the same time there is a downward pull, for the space in MS. 72 below the right arm is here eliminated.

The style of these figures is different from that of the other figures in the miniatures. Their faces in particular are oval, not rounded, and their shape is emphasized by the dark pointed beards. They have, in fact, a decidedly Byzantine appearance which is increased by the arrangement of the hair symmetrically on each side of the face with a blob on the middle of the forehead, by the Greek form of blessing, and by the pattern of drapery folds, the curve on the right shoulder and the falling zig-zags over the left. Above all, this Byzantine appearance is registered in the position of these half-length figures, for they recall the half-length 'Pantocrators' filling the upper parts of the apses in Norman Sicily, at Cefalù, in the
Pl. 27*a* Capella Palatina at Palermo, and at Monreale. The earliest of these is at Cefalù, and the mosaics of the apse there were completed in 1148.[1] What, if any, connection can there be, then, between these mosaics and the Mont St Michel manuscripts of nearly a century earlier?

Two questions must be investigated here, in fact. First what evidence is there for the early use of a half-length figure Christ in a lunette or apse? Secondly, what parallels are there in manuscript illumination for a half-length figure similarly placed with a scene below?

To begin with the first question, in spite of their similarities the four Mont St Michel miniatures differ very radically from the Sicilian mosaics. First, three of them show widely extended right hands. Even where the right hand is held in front of the chest in Morgan 641, fol. 43$^{v}$ it is not as in the mosaics held in the fold of the cloak. Secondly, the two Christs with books in the miniatures show them closed not open as in the mosaics.[2] The books are held well clear of the body, moreover, and only

1 O. Demus, *The Mosaics of Norman Sicily* (1949), 9.

2 Christ as a half-length figure with a closed book in Byzantine iconography occurs only in the centre of cupolas and closed vaults, never in apses or lunettes, according to Demus. This is because He is thought of there as Lord of the Angelic Host in the Heaven of the cupola. He is adored by the figures around Him. The open book on the other hand denotes His function as Redeemer, Judge or Ruler and as such occurs in the apses. In the two Mont St Michel scenes, therefore, in which Christ appears with a book to strengthen His saints, an open book might be expected.

the latest of the mosaics, Monreale, can compare in this.[1] Other less important points are that the mosaic Pantocrators show no tendency to overlap the apse – the shape of the apse itself projects them to the spectator below, of course – and that there is no trace of the *clavi* found in the miniatures.

The Sicilian examples are all later than those at Mont St Michel. There are, however, one or two earlier examples of half-length Christs in apses.[2] One is in a mosaic in the chapel of St Venanzio in the Lateran, dating from 642–650.[3] Though it has been restored, the iconography has been preserved. Christ half-length with blessing hand in front of the body but no left arm shown, is flanked by half-length angels. Below stands the Virgin in the *orans* position flanked by Sts Peter and Paul and other saints. Ihm remarks that this is an abbreviated Ascension of the Eastern type with a half-length instead of the enthroned Christ, and saints substituted for the Apostles.

Another instance is the apse fresco formerly in the oratorium of St Felicitas in the Baths of Titus.[4] St Felicitas stands centrally in the *orans* position and above a half-length Christ holds a wreath to crown her. This seems to be a special separate type developed in martyr shrines and in the earlier instances, only the hand of God with the wreath appears.[5] Since two of the four Mont St Michel examples are martyrdoms it has a special interest.

These examples, then, show that half-figure Christs in apses did exist

[1] Demus sees a progression from the Pantocrator at Cefalù which is still contained in the cupola medallion of a centralized Byzantine church, to the Pantocrator at Monreale which with the more expansive gestures is better adapted to fill the apse.

[2] Demus, op. cit., p. 220, says 'the decorators of Cefalù had no need to invent a new solution; they could adopt the established Byzantine prototype'. He gives, however, no example of a half-length Pantocrator in an apse, Byzantine or otherwise. And the examples which can be cited are not strictly Byzantine.

[3] See Ch. Ihm, *Die Programme der Christlichen Apsismalerei vom vierten Jahrhundert bis zur Mitte des achten Jahrhunderts* (1960), 144, Kat. x, Taf. xxiii.2.

[4] Ihm, op. cit., Kat xii, Taf. xxvi.3 after a nineteenth-century drawing. See also Taf. xxvii.1 and p. 208, Kat. liii k) and n) frescoes from Sakkara in Egypt of the sixth to seventh centuries.

[5] St Agnese and St Euphemia, Rome, Ihm, Kat. viii and xviii, Taf. xxvi. 1 and 2. See also A. Grabar, *Martyrium, Recherches sur le culte des reliques et l'art chrétien antique*, ii (1946), 105 ff. Compare the hand of God only in MS. 72, fol. 182v, showing St Ambrose writing. See pl. 28.

before the twelfth century. The St Felicitas Christ moreover has the flying fold to the right. None of them, however, have the closed book in outstretched hand or the *clavi* on Christ's tunic.

One other example should be quoted. This is a fresco in the crypt at
Pl. 27*b* Minuto in southern Italy.[1] There the Christ holds out a closed book in
an unveiled left hand with a flying fold below and blesses with out-
Pl. 22 stretched right hand. The whole is remarkably close to the Avranches 72
miniature, in the flying fold, the jewelled cross to the halo, the facial type, though this is simplified at Mont St Michel, even in the presence of a vertical *clavus*. According to Wettstein it dates to the late twelfth century. Nevertheless, in view of the isolation of the Mont St Michel representations both in style and iconography in the north at this date, and also as far as iconography goes in Byzantine or Sicilo-Byzantine art even in the twelfth century, and in view of the contacts between Normandy and South Italy from early in the eleventh century, it is hard to resist the conclusion that the Minuto fresco and the Mont St Michel miniatures are somehow connected.[2] Can there have been earlier instances in South Italy now lost?

As regards the second question, the use of half-figures in lunettes in manuscript illumination, particularly a half-figure Christ, it should first be noted that one iconography of the Evangelist portrait places the symbol half-length in the lunette of the arch above. The earliest surviving example is in the Gospels of St Augustine of the sixth century, where the arrangement goes back to still earlier models.[3] In the Book of Cerne the position is reversed and the Evangelist is shown half-length in a medallion at the crown of the arch with the symbol below.[4] Figures also appear in

1 See J. Wettstein, *Sant'Angelo in Formis et la peinture médiévale en Campanie* (1960), 97 with bibliography, and pl. 19b.

2 Half-length Christs occur in south Italian Exultet Rolls in medallions and even unattached (e.g. Bari 2, Fratres Karissimi), but never in lunettes. None is earlier than the second half of the eleventh century. See M. Avery, *The Exultet Rolls of South Italy* (1936). In the twelfth century there are a number of examples on Mosan reliquary shrines.

3 Cambridge, Corpus Christi College, MS. 286. See F. Wormald, *The Miniatures in the Gospels of St Augustine* (1954) for plates and discussion of the iconography which is found as early as the Philocalus Calendar of 354.

4 Cambridge, University Library, MS. Ll.1.10. See Wormald, op. cit., pls. xvii–xix.

the arches of Canon Tables in Insular, in Carolingian and in Anglo-Saxon manuscripts.[1]

However, closer to our manuscripts, and the more interesting because it is not a Gospel book but a Lectionary of Sermons by the Fathers, is the Egino Codex made probably at Verona and dating from the last quarter of the eighth century.[2] This has four miniatures of St Augustine, St Ambrose, St Gregory and St Leo the Great(?), enthroned under arches. In the lunettes are conches and in the centre of these, medallions of which two have been cut out, one contains the Dove, and the fourth, fol. 24, St Ambrose, has a bust of a beardless Christ in it. Though the Christ is a contained figure, the general arrangement is similar to the Mont St Michel miniatures. Another similar example though later, is a Byzantine manuscript containing the Homilies of St Gregory Nazianzus, of the second half of the tenth century, which shows St Gregory preaching to the people under an arch. In the lunette a bearded figure, presumably Christ though without the cross halo, is enclosed in a medallion. He blesses with the right hand held before the chest, the left holds a closed book, and two half rosettes fill the space of the lunette on either side.[3] Pl. 27*c* Pl. 27*d*

Two other iconographical types in which a half-length Christ is involved with the figures below Him should be mentioned. The first is in book presentation or dedication scenes, and it was remarked earlier that in MS. 72 Felicianus approaches St Augustine as if to present his book to him. In a Byzantine manuscript of the second half of the tenth century a

1 e.g. Cutbrecht Gospels, Wien, Nat. Bibl., Cod. 1224, fol. 18, eighth century, Apostles, Zimmermann, Taf. 301; 'Soissons Gospels', full-length Christ, and 'Lorsch Gospels', Maiestas Christ, ninth century, Köhler (2), Taf. 76 and 104. For Anglo-Saxon manuscripts, see especially Gospels, Cambridge, Trinity College B.10.4, Bury Gospels, London, Brit. Mus., Harley 76, and Arenberg Gospels, now New York, Morgan Library, a half-length Christ. In ivories also medallion Christs supported by angels with scenes below occur – e.g. Lorsch Book Cover, early ninth century, and Barberini Ivory, early sixth century, where the Christ is independent of the medallion held by angels behind and His blessing hand seems to come forward over the architrave. Volbach, *Elfenbeinarbeiten*, 224 and 48. For the iconography of figures in the Canon tables see C. Nordenfalk, 'The Apostolic Canon Tables' in 'Essais en l'honneur de Jean Porcher', ed. O. Pächt, *Gazette des Beaux-Arts*, lxii (July-August 1963), 17–34.

2 Berlin, Deutsche Staatsbibl., Phillipps MS. 1676. J. Kirchner, *Beschreibende Verzeichnisse der Miniaturen – Handschriften der Preussischen Staatsbibliothek zur Berlin* (1926), 6–9, Taf. i in colour.

3 Milan, Ambrosiana E. 50 inf. Prochno, *Das Schreiber und Dedikationsbild* (1929), Taf. vi.

small kneeling figure presents a book to the standing Virgin who in turn points to a small half-length Christ in a glory in the right-hand corner.[1] The Christ extends His right hand in blessing to signify His acceptance of the gift.[2]

For early Western examples there is the Folchard Psalter[3] where in the Litany Tables a book presentation takes place with a half-length Christ in the centre with both arms raised. Secondly a miniature added *c.*940–970 to a ninth-century north French Gospels[4] has a half-length Majestas Christ in an oval mandorla above two kneeling figures and the standing saint who intercedes for them. Later examples are from Freising, 1060–1080,[5] and an eleventh-century manuscript, probably Bohemian.[6] These miniatures show a progressively greater connection between the figures below and the Christ above and the last two go further than the Mont St Michel miniatures. But in the majority of them a standing saint acts as a bridge, as it were, between heaven and earth.

The second iconographic tradition is that of the crowning of an Emperor by Christ.[7] This is combined, though it is there the crowning of a saint, with the donor portrait in the Bohemian manuscript from Wolfenbüttel mentioned above. In Latin 2639 it is perhaps the crown of eternal life that is held out for St Ambrose's contemplation, since the treatise is the *de bono Mortis*.

Pl. 26a

The crowning motif is certainly of Byzantine origin and there is at

1 Rome, Vatican, Reginensis Gr. I. Prochno, op. cit. Taf. v.

2 Two other examples of a similar iconography, suggesting again Italian intermediaries for a Byzantine type, are in Oxford, Bodleian Library, MS. Add.D.104, fol. 2 dated 1067 and Rome, Vatican, Lat. 1274, late eleventh century, both Roman manuscripts. E. B. Garrison, *Studies in the History of Mediaeval Italian Painting*, ii no. 2 (1955), figs. 81 and 82.

3 Prochno, op. cit., p. 18 and pl.

4 Now Hague, Kgl. Bibl., HS. 76 F.1. Prochno, op. cit., p. 64 and pl.

5 Munich, Bayr. Staatsbibl., Clm. 6831. Prochno, op. cit., p. 100 and pl. Christ in a medallion at the crown of the arch blesses with His right hand and holds a book in His left hand but at the same time lets fall a scroll on which is written, 'Ne dubites in me retinet te pagina vitae'. Below Bishop Ellenhard offers the book to St Andrew.

6 Wolfenbüttel Braunschweigische Landesbibl., MS. 11. 2. Aug. 4°. Prochno, op. cit., p. 102 and pl. Christ is in a half medallion with closed book in His extended left hand and with His right hand reaches out to crown the sainted King Wenceslas at whose feet the donor kneels.

7 A. Grabar, *L'Empereur dans l'art byzantin* (1936), 112–22 and 176–77.

least one example of a half-length Christ. This is the Psalter of Basil II, 976–1025.[1] There the Christ is in a half-medallion with the book in His left hand. He holds out the crown over the head of the standing Emperor below.

To sum up, certain precedents for half-length figures of Christ in manuscripts can be found and these show Him linked with scenes below, particularly in book presentations and the crowning of the Emperor. The second is a theme specifically of Byzantine iconography which connects with the style of the figures, but Byzantine instances of the book presentation occur, too. For the position of the Christ in the lunette of the arch however, only the Egino Codex and the St Gregory Nazianzus in the Ambrosian Library provide a parallel, and there the expansive gestures of the Mont St Michel miniatures are missing. The expansive gestures occur in monumental examples only, and of a later date.

It may not be unreasonable, therefore, to compare the placing of the half-length figures in the lunette and the adaptation of the gestures to the space to be filled, to the process of adapting monumental sculpture to architecture which was one of the Romanesque period's great achievements. The progression would be from the roundels already seen in the transitional MS. 115 and the Sacramentary, to the lunette figures. What Pl. 10*f*
precisely was the model for the Byzantine type of Christ and what is the relationship of the miniatures to it, remain, however, puzzling. This is the more so since Latin 2639 undoubtedly shows the best understanding of the Pl. 26*a*
possible Byzantine model, particularly of the motif of the veiled hand. On these grounds Latin 2639 should precede MS. 72 which would copy it Pl. 22
and so deviate further from the original model. But on grounds of initial style and script Latin 2639 must be the later of the two. The progressive adaptation of the figure to the lunette is also in favour of the later date of Latin 2639. This rather suggests that the model was still in the abbey for the later artist to copy and was, therefore, a portable object. If it was not a manuscript, it might perhaps have been an ivory, an enamel or even some type of icon.

[1] Venice, Bib. Marciana, Cod. Gr. z. 17 (421). D. Talbot Rice, *The Art of Byzantium*, (1959), pl. xi.

## D: FURTHER ICONOGRAPHIC POINTS

Pl. 20 St Michael is not the only figure represented on fol. $A^{v}$ of MS. 76. The three miniatures on this page are, in fact, the equivalent of a title and an *ex libris*. St Michael is shown because he is patron of the abbey to which the book belongs. The seated saint is Augustine, the author of the commentary, and King David appears as the author of the text commented, the Psalms.

Besides the St Augustine of MS. 76, there are two other comparable
Pl. 29*a* miniatures. One, a whole page miniature on fol. $C^{v}$ of MS. 75, St Augustine *de Genesi ad Literam*, shows the saint seated frontally under an arch and looking up at an angel who carries a book in veiled hands. The
Pl. 28 second, in MS. 72, fol. $182^{v}$, is of St Ambrose seated sideways and writing the *de bono Mortis* with the hand of God above in the arch.

These three author portraits are modelled on the portraits of Evangelists in Gospel books.[1] The abbey must have had at least one Gospel book though none is known to survive, and the portraits may afford evidence, therefore, as to its appearance. It was always the scriptorium's practice to adapt and combine from different sources, however, and this makes an attempt at a reconstruction hazardous. Moreover, there are stylistic discrepancies between the portraits, a point which will be returned to below.

Pl. 28 There are two profile figures of different types, the St Ambrose, MS. 72
Pls. 20, 24*a* and the St Augustine of MS. 76 (who is repeated in MS. 90), and one
Pl. 29*a* frontal figure, the St Augustine, MS. 75. A comparison of these with re-
Pl. 27*e* spectively the St Luke of the York Gospels (profile),[2] the St Luke of the
Pl. 37*c* Trinity Gospels (profile with crossed legs), and the St Matthew of the Trinity Gospels (frontal)[3] suggests that the scriptorium may either itself have possessed an Anglo-Saxon Gospels, or else knew of one and had copied it. As for a possible fourth portrait, the dispute miniature in MS.
Pl. 22 72, it has been suggested, may well have been an adaptation of the book

1 Though of course author portraits are not confined to Gospel books, it seems unlikely that these miniatures go back by any form of direct descent to prototypes designed to portray St Augustine or St Ambrose. For the rarity, in fact, of author portraits prefacing patristic texts see below. The Egino Codex, an exception quoted above, was probably at Metz at this date.

2 York Cathedral Chapter Library. *New Paleographical Society*, 2nd ser. (1913–20), pls. 163–5.

3 Cambridge, Trinity College, MS. B.10.4, fols. 19 and $89^{v}$. Talbot Rice, pl. 60a.

presentation in MS. 50. If so, the standing St Michael in MS. 50 may have been replaced in MS. 72 by a frontal seated figure taken from a Gospels portrait differing slightly from the frontal type seen already in MS. 75. Pl. 29*a*

The Anglo-Saxon Gospels, if it existed, would have been a late tenth- or early eleventh-century manuscript. Perhaps like the York Gospels it Pl. 27*e*
had no Evangelist symbols, but only the hand of God as in MS. 72, Pl. 28
fol. 182ᵛ. This seems a possibility since the Matthew symbols in Anglo-Saxon Gospels, if they are shown flying down, carry a scroll, an iconography deriving from the Carolingian Rheims school. In MSS. 75 and Pls. 29*a*, 20
76, on the other hand, the angel carries a book with veiled hands. Since the same angel with book and veiled hands occurs in the Morgan Sacra- Pl. 45*d*
mentary in the All Saints miniature, all three angels probably derive from the same source. The iconography in the Sacramentary derives originally from a Tours school Majestas from a Bible or Gospel Book. The angel in the Vivian Bible, for instance, has veiled hands.[1]

Except for the St Matthew in the Trinity Gospels, the portraits in the York and Trinity Gospels are not shown under arches. Arches do occur Pls. 27*e*, 37*c*
in later Anglo-Saxon Gospels. The similarities, noted below, of the plant scroll and bird ornament on the arches to Carolingian rather than Anglo-Saxon sources, however, suggests that the Mont St Michel artists might themselves have placed the portraits under arches which were copied perhaps from Carolingian Canon Tables. This would be in accord with the Romanesque need to place the figure in a setting, as opposed to the Anglo-Saxon blank space.

The above remarks, however, are to be taken as no more than very tentative suggestions. It is not possible from the evidence to be certain that the scriptorium knew of or owned an Anglo-Saxon Gospel book.[2]

[1] Kohler (I), Taf. 73. Since no surviving Anglo-Saxon Gospels has a Majestas page, the use of a Tours school derived model for the Sacramentary remains most probable. But the existence of such a page in an hypothetical Anglo-Saxon model cannot be ruled out since its ingredients, including an angel with veiled hands, are found incorporated in the Canon Tables of the Trinity Gospels. In MS. 86, a late manuscript, there is a Majestas combined with an initial 'X'. This, however, had a different model from the Sacramentary, since the Eagle carries a book not a scroll and the Angel's hands are not veiled. The contained forms of the symbols suggest that the model was an ivory carving rather than a miniature, perhaps from North France or Flanders. See Pl. 15 b.

[2] For Anglo-Saxon manuscripts in Normandy before the Conquest see Appendix V.

The miniature of King David harping on fol. A$^{v}$ of MS. 76, again the profile cross-legged type, is also a kind of author protrait, found most commonly in Psalters.[1] More usually the king sits frontally. The left hand appears through the strings as it plucks them. This must go back originally to a much earlier prototype painted in the Late Antique illusionistic style, and is a detail which is preserved in particular by the Insular tradition, for example the Vespasian Psalter.[2]

Pl. 20

It is known that an Anglo-Saxon Psalter with miniatures was in Normandy at an early date. It belonged to Archbishop Robert of Normandy who died in 1037, and it was later at St Evroul where it was described by Ordericus Vitalis.[3] A late eleventh-century copy of St Augustine's Commentary on the Psalms from St Evroul incorporates King David harping in an initial 'B'.[4] A comparison of this figure with the Mont St Michel David, especially the details of the crown and of the lion head with the hanging peg on the harp, can leave no doubt that the two representations are closely related. That they go back to a common model, the archbishop's psalter, is proved by an authentic detail preserved in the later St Evroul manuscript, but not at Mont St Michel, the row of pegs at the top of the harp. Other evidence that the scriptorium knew the archbishop's Psalter will be mentioned later in connection with the Sacramentary and the Bible.

Pl. 46*f*

Lastly in Latin 2639 the kneeling St Ambrose is remarkably close to the miniature of St Omer praying for his monks before his death in an illustrated life of the saint from St Bertin.[5] This type of kneeling figure may

Pls. 26*a*, *b*

1 See H. Steger, *David Rex et Propheta* (1961). A von Euw, 'Studien zu den Elfenarbeiten der Hofschule Karls des Grossen', *Aachener Kunstblätter*, xxxiv (1967), 36–60.

2 London, British Museum, MS. Cotton Vespasian A.1. Rickert, pl. 10b. An Anglo-Saxon, probably post-Conquest, example very close to MS. 76 in iconography is now at Cambridge, Corpus Christi College, MS. 391. Wormald, *English Drawings*, no. 11, pl. 39, dated '1064-1093'.

3 See Appendix V.

4 Rouen, Bib. Mun., MS. A.19(456), fol. 1. See Avril, *Notes* (2), 241, pl., publishing a copy of the initial made at S. Père de Chartres. Another Norman version of the 'B' is from Lyre, Évreux, Bib. Mun., MS. 131, *Manuscrits à peintures*, no. 198. *St Alban's Psalter*, pl. 146a.

5 St Omer, Bib. Mun., MS. 698, fol. 25v. Dated by M. Schott, *Zwei Lütticher Sakramentare in Bamberg und Paris und ihre Verwandten* (1931), to the late eleventh century. Another similar St Bertin example is the poet Milo, fol. 26$^{v}$ of Leiden, Univ. Bibl., MS. B.P.L.190, dated early in the eleventh century by Swarzenski, *Monuments*, fig. 163.

go back ultimately to a Byzantine source.[1] Before leaving the iconography of the miniatures in MSS. 72, 75, 76, 90 and Latin 2639, it should be observed that such frontispieces are unusual in patristic manuscripts. Of early examples a portrait of St Jerome *c.*700 comes from Corbie. We have seen that a monk of Mont St Michel copied Persius at Corbie, and it is quite possible that the idea of patristic author portraits comes from this area.[2] A contemporary example is from St Vaast, a manuscript of St Augustine's Confessions.[3] The portraits are an indication of the importance attached to these texts at the abbey. For by inserting an author portrait, in three cases clearly modelled on an Evangelist portrait, the artist suggests a comparable status for the patristic texts to that of the Gospels. The presence of the Angels, the hand of God, and even Christ Himself, suggests similar inspiration and authority.

## E: FRAME PAGES

Two Mont St Michel manuscripts with no form of frontispieces have however unfinished frame pages. These are MS. 59, fol. 1v, St Ambrose Pl. 30*b*
on St Luke and MS. 163, fol. 2v, Heraclides, *Vitae Patrum*. In MS. 59 a Pl. 30*a*
seated frontal figure of the saint has been drawn with a point but was never finished.[4] The frame consists of six squares and two quatrefoils set on widely spaced bars. The plant scroll is thin and twists in complicated but largely symmetrical patterns. The leaf forms are very similar to those Pl. 12
of MSS. 76 or 107 of the middle group. There is some colouring of the

1 Compare the penance of King David in the Paris Psalter, Bib. Nat., Gr. 139, fol. 136v, pl. viii of H. Omont, *Facsimiles des plus anciens MSS. Grecs* (1902), with the St Gall miniature of David before Nathan in a Psalter, ninth century, Zürich, Stadtbibl., MS. CXII, fol. 53, Goldschmidt, *German illumination* (1), fig. 77.

2 Also a portrait of St Isidore comes from north-east France, *c.*800, Exh., *Karl der Grosse*, nos. 405, 408. Oxford, Bodleian Library, MS. Tanner 3, Gregory the Great, Dialogues, is the only Anglo-Saxon example known. The miniature has been retouched but seems to be pre-Conquest.

3 Arras, Bib. Mun., MS. 548(616) fol. 1v. Porcher, *French Miniatures*, pl. viii. Somewhat later is Brussels, Bib. Roy., MS. 10791, fol. 1, St Augustine *de Genesi*, where the Saint is inspired by an angel. C. Caspar and F. Lyna, *Les Principaux MSS. à peintures de la Bibliothèque Royale de Belgique* (1937), no. 18. For twelfth-century examples from the area of northern France see Dodwell, *Canterbury School*, 58 and pl. 32. St Jerome and St Gregory are sometimes shown in author portraits in Sacramentaries, Gospel books or Bibles. See below p. 173.

4 M. F. Avril kindly drew my attention to this figure which had escaped my notice.

frame bars, the squares and the quatrefoils, in blue and yellow. In MS. 163 there are four corner roundels and rectangles in the midst of each side. These are not so strongly emphasized as 'stops' as are those of MS. 59. The plant scroll is larger and fleshier, less entwined and less crenellated and without the clusters of fruit of MS. 59. Many of the leaves are veined and there is no colour.

Plant scroll frames of this type are certainly a sign of Anglo-Saxon influence. The more involved frame of MS. 59 with its scrolls developing from the rosettes and dependent on the frame bars to climb on, but with the rosettes and squares emphasized, resembles the late tenth-century
Pls. 30*b*, 37*c*, 13*d* Anglo-Saxon frames in the Trinity Gospels.[1] The leaves, partly because
they are not painted, are less fleshy and in their crenellation resemble to
Pl. 30*d* some extent a rosette from the St Vaast Bible.[2] The larger, thicker, leaves
of MS. 163 recall the frames of the Sacramentary of Robert of Jumièges of
the early eleventh century. The design is close to that of the frame for the
miniature of St Peter, though not close enough to prove it a direct copy
Pl. 30*c* of it.[3] The two most Anglo-Saxon-looking of the Mont St Michel
frames are in the Sacramentary and will be discussed later.

## *Part II: Style*

This consideration of the frames leads on to questions of style. Of the full page miniatures that of MS. 50 is quite separate in style and since it is the earliest, will be treated first.

### A: AVRANCHES MS. 50, fol. 1

Pl. 17*b* It has already been remarked that the normal presentation of the book to
a seated figure has here had to be adapted to the standing St Michael. To link the two figures the artist has moved the devil to the centre of the page and thus formed a triangular composition. There is no attempt to

1 Cambridge, Trinity College, MS. B.10.4
2 Arras, Bib. Mun., MS. 559(435), vol. iii, fol. 77.
3 Rouen, Bib. Mun., MS. Y.6, fol. 132v.

place these figures in an illusionistic spatial relationship to each other or to the portico which is flattened and elongated so that, with its columns decorated with cable patterns, it resembles rather the arches of a Canon Table. Space is suggested, rather, by two layers superimposed but also interpenetrating. Thus St Michael's wing extends behind, and the monk's left leg and shoulder extend in front of, the pillars.

The figures themselves on the other hand do give a certain illusion of depth. None of them is shown either as strictly frontal or in straight profile. St Michael's pose half turning to the right suggests a movement of the torso, the monk advances at an angle to the picture plane, and the devil is turned at the hips to show the upper part of the body in three-quarter view. On the monk's right arm and over the Archangel's right thigh the material forms in rolls, and the monk's cowl curls up in front. Where the head or the arms emerge, the drapery stands stiff as if starched. Pleats at the hem are shown by a stereotyped convention, as it were an arrow pointing down to meet a 'T'. The drawing of the features is very summary, a system of simple linear conventions. The faces are long and set on long tubular necks and the figures are altogether elongated.

The colours used are restricted. The space between the arches and below extending to the left is painted a red-brown, sometimes almost purple, which runs over the devil's right leg and part of his body.[1] The Archangel's shield and the architecture are variously coloured in green, orange, yellow and the off-white of the parchment left bare. St Michael and the monk have touches of green on the hems of their garments and St Michael has a red spot on his right cheek and a green spot on his left. Otherwise the figures are left unpainted.

The initials of Avranches 50 were connected with Franco-Saxon decoration but also with certain manuscripts from St Gall. The iconography considered above suggested a knowledge of Ottonian art. What are the stylistic connections of this miniature? For certain features the nearest parallels are in Anglo-Saxon manuscripts. The Sherborne Pontifical, for instance, should be compared for the elongated figures with Pl. 17*a*

[1] See Porcher, *French Miniatures*, pl. ix for a coloured plate. The purple also obscures the inscription and is perhaps, therefore, a later addition. It is used also, however, on the initials where it is integral to their design.

small heads and a sense of the articulation of the body under the drapery.[1] The Anglo-Saxon draperies are moving towards the more agitated patterns of the style derived from the Carolingian Utrecht Psalter. Nevertheless the Mont St Michel miniature can be seen as a copy of such a model probably somewhat earlier in date and more in Wormald's Style I. In some respects, particularly in the drapery, the model was simplified. Other features such as the purple ground and the portico may derive distantly from Ottonian works. The conflation of the book presentation and the St Michael suggests there may have been more than one model. If so, the model for the Archangel might well have been an ivory rather than a miniature. For the book presentation the Anglo-Saxon miniature of King Athelstan giving Bede's Life of St Cuthbert to St Cuthbert at
Pl. 17*c* Durham should be mentioned, for besides being a presentation to a standing figure, it has an architectural background with a similar uneven division of the archways of the buildings.[2]

It is possible that at St Peter's, Ghent, where St Dunstan had spent his exile in 956, there would have been the knowledge of both Ottonian and Anglo-Saxon art which the Avranches miniature reveals. If so the frontispiece could have been painted by a monk who had come from the community to Mont St Michel or even have been sent as a present.[3] In either case what is most significant about it is that it has already some of the qualities of Romanesque art. Illusionistic space is rejected in favour of an abstract counterpoint of forms.

## B: THE MIDDLE GROUP MANUSCRIPTS

The five manuscripts with miniatures amongst the middle manuscripts, Avranches 72, 75, 76, and 90 and Paris, Latin 2639, are closely linked stylistically as well as palaeographically.

All the scenes take place under arches. These architectural frameworks
Pl. 28 are mostly coloured plainly or in vertical stripes of colour, but in MS. 72

1 Paris, Bib. Nat., Latin 943. Wormald, *English Drawings*, 26–30, pls. 4a, b, 5a.

2 Cambridge, Corpus Christi College, MS. 183, fol. 1$^{v}$. This also has rather sombre colour in browns and greens. Talbot Rice, pl. 47.

3 See above, p. 6 and catalogue of manuscripts, Appx. II. See, however, above p. 6 n.4, for the possibility of connections with St Bavon rather than St Peter's.

on fol. 182$^{v}$ the pillars are marbled. In MS. 90, fol. I$^{v}$ and MS. 75, fol. c$^{v}$ Pls. 24*a*, 29*a*
they have a white zig-zag ascending and on fol. 97 of MS. 72[1] the arch is Pl. 22
ornamented with an acanthus pattern. The capitals are cut to make a straight rectangular frame. Some of the arches have acroteria, birds in MS. 90 and MS. 75, leaf or tree ornament in MS. 72. The backgrounds Pl. 28
are in all the manuscripts either quite plain or coloured uniformly in pale green, mauve or brick-red. In the arch of MS. 72, fol. 182$^{v}$ there is the effect of waving clouds in a slightly darker shade of pink. The range of colour is wide but the colours are mostly pale and often chalky in appearance, as if white had been mixed with them. White is also used in blobs for highlights and as an hatching, on St Augustine's right sleeve for Pl. 22
instance, MS. 72, fol. 97. It is also common in loops inside a darker line to show the folds on a tunic or in a curtain.

The figures themselves sit uncertainly on their thrones, particularly where they are in three-quarter view. In this side-saddle pose the left leg is commonly drawn up behind the right, as the figure faces towards the right. Where the figure is placed frontally, both the knees and the feet are set wide apart. The dress is sometimes drawn tight over the body, and the ribs, chest and stomach are indicated in lines which tend to run away into pattern, e.g. MS. 75, fol. C$^{v}$ and MS. 90, fol. I$^{v}$. Pls. 29*a*, 24*a*

The heads of the younger unbearded men are round and their necks are long and tubular. The hands are narrow at the wrists and broad in span with large long fingers which in some pictures dominate the composition.[2] Faces are painted a pale pink and shaded in white and green. The ears are commonly shown as a bracket, for instance Felicianus, MS. 72, fol. 97. Pl. 22

The drapery of the figures is more complicated than in the St Clement miniature and different in style. The figures are firmly outlined in black and, in the painted miniatures, particularly, this heavy black line also defines the limbs and the hems of a garment and even the folds in it.The way it turns into a loop at the round of the shoulder or at the knee is characteristic. In this way the figure as a whole and the drapery can be divided into sections.

1 Colour plate in Porcher, *French Miniatures*, pl. x.

2 Particularly in the Ascension in Morgan 641, fol. 75$^{v}$. See Pl. 39c.

So far as the design goes several of these miniatures are so similar that
Pls. 20, 24*a* they are probably the work of one artist. If we compare MS. 90, fol. $1^{v}$
and MS. 76, fol. $A^{v}$, the similarities of the pose of the two St Augustines
and of King David, of the round faces of Faustinus and the spectators in
MS. 90 to those of the Angel and St Augustine in MS. 76, of the drapery
zig-zags below St Augustine's right leg in MS. 90 to St Michael's over-
Pl. 29*a* mantle in MS. 76, are clear. Similarly Avranches 75 is linked closely in its
Pl. 20 Angel to MS. 76, whilst MS. 72 is close to MS. 76 again in such details as
Pl. 22 hands, ears and the leggings of the two heretics. Paris, Latin 2639 is dif-
Pl. 26*a* ferent in design and must be by a different hand.

An examination of the painting of the miniatures, however, shows
noticeable differences between them. First there is the style of MS. 75,
Pls. 29*a*, 20 fol. $C^{v}$ and MS. 76, fol. $A^{v}$, though the latter miniature is unfinished.[1]
Here the paint is used thinly, the colours are light and the lines of the
drapery are painted in delicately. White is used to second these lines which
are always very rounded. The material looks soft and thin, almost trans-
Pl. 28 parent. St Ambrose in MS. 72, fol. $182^{v}$ is treated somewhat similarly
though the colours are not here so pale and the lines thicker and firmer.
Pl. 22 The other miniature of MS. 72 on fol. 97 has altogether thicker lines
for the drapery folds and the use of white highlights is exaggerated – for
example on Felicianus' tunic and the folds of the curtain. The general
impression is hard and brilliant and the jewelled books and the *clavi* add
Pls. 24*a*, 26*a* to this. Thirdly in MS. 90, fol. 1 and Latin 2639 the highlights are large
blobs of paler colour and the silhouette of the figure or the sections of
drapery are outlined in bands of colour, on St Augustine's thigh in MS. 90
for instance.[2]

The initials of the middle manuscripts were directly influenced by Anglo-Saxon art and evidence that the scriptorium knew the Anglo-Saxon Psalter of Archbishop Robert of Rouen and perhaps knew, or even owned, an Anglo-Saxon Gospel book, has been discussed. The main

[1] A small detail also links these two miniatures. The little bead necklace round St. Augustine's neck in MS. 75 is found as a bracelet on St Michael's right wrist in MS. 76.

[2] In both these miniatures and in the St Augustine of MS. 72, fol. 97 a dark line outlined in white runs across the chest from where the neck joins the left shoulder. This is a drapery fold in origin which can be seen already reduced to pattern in a Carolingian MS., the Gospels of St. Médard, Soissons, in the Canon Tables, Köhler (2), Taf. 78.

stylistic source of these miniatures is also certainly Anglo-Saxon. This influence is modified by recollections of Carolingian art but, more important, by a new stylistic impetus which may be at least partly attributed to contact with Ottonian art, mainly via north French and Belgian intermediaries. We have already seen evidence of this contact in the iconography.

First concerning the Carolingian influence, the whole arrangement under the simple porticoes recalls the Evangelist portraits of the Court School of Charlemagne rather than the Anglo-Saxon miniatures in which the twining acanthus invades the architecture. The empty grounds, as opposed to the architectural backgrounds of the Court School, are a significant alteration which will be commented on later. Details also point to Carolingian sources. For instance, birds appear in the spandrels above the arch in the Abbeville Gospels as in MS. 75.[1] Plants appear there too, Pl. 29*a*
and the kind of tree which is found on fol. 92 of Avranches MS. 72 with Pl. 22
its lopped branches and trilobe leaves occurs in the Canon Tables of the St Médard-de-Soissons Gospels and somewhat later in the Bamberg Bible of the Tours school[2] where the branches interlace as in our manuscript. Where birds appear in Anglo-Saxon manuscripts as in the Hereford Troper they are further from such Carolingian originals than in the Norman manuscripts, though in the Mont St Michel manuscripts, too, the birds have been adapted. Typically they are moulded to fit the architecture. Another Carolingian feature is the thrones with their rows of portholes and windows which recall Court School Evangelist portraits, as do the book covers with their lozenge-shaped jewels arranged at corners and centre.[3]

For Anglo-Saxon influence, since outline drawing was an Anglo-Saxon speciality, the St Michael of MS. 76, which remains uncoloured, Pl. 20

1 Abbeville, Bib. Mun., MS. 4, fol. 17v. Köhler (2), Taf. 38.

2 Paris, Bib. Nat., Latin 8850. Köhler (2), Taf. 74, 75, 77, and Bamberg, Staatl. Bibl., Msc. Bib. 1 (in the Genesis scenes), Köhler (1), Taf. 56. Anglo-Saxon leaves in a similar position in e.g. the Monte Cassino Gospels are three-dimensional.

3 It is not so improbable as it might first appear that the Mont St Michel artists knew a Court School Gospels. One was copied at St Germain-des-Prés in the mid-eleventh century, Leningrad, Lat.Q.v.I, Nr. 31. Exh., *Karl der Grosse*, no. 477. The pen drawings with heightening of green and orange can be compared with MS. 76.

may be considered first. The resemblances both in general appearance and in detail are with Anglo-Saxon manuscript drawings of Wormald's 'Style I,' that is of the mid or second half of the tenth century. There is little of the shivering, jagged line which appears in the later Anglo-Saxon drawing style. A good example of the latter, and strictly comparable as it is of the same subject, is the St Michael in the Tiberius Psalter.[1] The
Pl. 18*d* dramatic way in which St Michael strides forward to spear the dragon using his shield to protect himself is increased by the shivering line of the drawing. As an example of 'Style I' we may take the miniature in which
Pl. 21 St Dunstan prostrates himself before Christ.[2] The outline of the form is strong and continuous and in particular never punctured by those little corrugations which appear so constantly wherever the drapery is pulled tight to the body in later Anglo-Saxon manuscripts.[3] The drawing of the Mont St Michel artist is more definite than these early Anglo-Saxon drawings. The lower hem of the Angel's overmantle to the left does not altogether escape the tendency seen in some of the north French houses,[4] and noticeable also in Anglo-Saxon manuscripts of the eleventh century, to hard corrugated folds. Nor does the artist manage the articulation of the body beneath the dress so skilfully. The uncertainty about the right foot and leg is noticeable. But the source is clear, and the drawing is more than an incompetent hardening of the fine, fluttering mature Anglo-Saxon line. As with the initials, the artist copied an earlier model, not a contemporary one.

Of the three different painting techniques, if we look again to Anglo-Saxon manuscripts for models, two of the styles find close parallels. First MS. 72, fol. 97 is close to the painted miniatures of the Benedictional of
Pl. 22 St Ethelwold and related manuscripts. There, too, for instance in the miniature of the three Maries at the Grave, the folds form a complex

[1] London, Brit. Mus., Cotton MS. Tiberius C.VI, fol. 16. Wormald, *Walpole Society* op. cit., pl. 20.

[2] Oxford, Bodleian Library, MS. Auct. F.4.32, fol. 1. R. W. Hunt, *St Dunstan's Classbook from Glastonbury* (Umbrae Codicum Occidentalium) (1961).

[3] e.g. Bury Psalter, Rome, Vatican, Reg. Lat. 12, fol. 74. Wormald, *English Drawings*, pl. 27b.

[4] e.g. later St Omer, Bib. Mun., MS. 698, 'Life and Miracles of St Omer', *MSS. à peintures*, no. 118, cover pl.

surface pattern and white is used to outline a fold and to highlight Pl. 23
hands or faces.[1]

MS. 90 and Latin 2639, however, in their further emphasis on a kind of Pls. 24*a*, 26*a*
striped shading, recall rather later Anglo-Saxon manuscripts. The tendency to this type of painting is already apparent in the Sacramentary of Pls. 30*c*, 37*d*
Robert of Jumièges,[2] but is far more evident in manuscripts of the second
quarter of the eleventh century, such as the St Margaret Gospels in Pl. 24*b*
Oxford.[3] Yet in these examples though the manner of the painting is technically similar, it is used for a different effect. The aim is still an all-over pattern of movement in which the bands of dark colour produce a fluorescent appearance. The Mont St Michel artist on the contrary uses his colour stripes as definitions of outline and parts and even to model his forms.

Thirdly come the more restrained delicate colours of MSS. 75 and 76.
The pale lilac of St Augustine's mantle in MS. 75 and the less exaggerated Pls. 20, 29*a*
and softer lines do not occur in Anglo-Saxon painted miniatures. They are, on the other hand, more than coloured washes. They recall rather Ottonian miniatures in their colour schemes, particularly those of the Master of the Registrum Gregorii and those of later Echternach books of the reign of Henry III. The linear patterns, for instance in the drapery of St Augustine of MS 75, are more extreme than in such works, but the
figures have something of the upholstered look which has been noticed as Pl. 29*b*
characteristic of the figures of the Master of the Registrum Gregorii.[4]

It is not impossible that the artists should have seen some work from the Master's school. It has been suggested that the meeting of the Emperor

[1] London, Brit. Mus., Add. MS. 49598, fol. 51$^{v}$. G. F. Warner and H. A. Wilson, *The Benedictional of St Aethelwold* (1910) (complete facsimile for the Roxburghe Club).

[2] Rouen, Bib. Mun., MS. Y.6. Talbot Rice, pl. 53–5. Given to Jumièges *c.*1044–50.

[3] Oxford, Bodleian Library, MS. Lat. liturg. f.5. Other examples are in the Psalter, Oxford, Bodleian Library, Douce 296, and in the Weingarten Gospels, New York, Morgan Library, MS. 709. Talbot Rice, pls. 63, 75a, 76b. Later, stripes became an exaggerated mannerism in examples from Liège and Corbie. The corrugated folds of the Life of St Omer, St Omer, Bib. Mun., MS. 698 from St Bertin, are close to Latin 2639. This manuscript has already been compared to Latin 2639 for its iconography. See Pl. 26.

[4] C. Nordenfalk, 'Der Meister des Registrum Gregorii', *Münchner Jahrbuch der bildenden Kunst*, iii Folge, Bd. i (1950), 61–77. B. Nitschke, *Die Handschriftengruppe um den Meister des Registrum Gregorii* (1966), 35ff., Taf. i.

Henry II with Robert the Pious in 1023 may have been the occasion on which the Gospels of the Ste Chapelle arrived in France.[1] The fact that the type of portrait exemplified in MS. 75 does not occur in the series deriving from the Master of the Registrum Gregorii suggests caution. But if the model for the iconography was, as has been tentatively suggested above, an Anglo-Saxon Gospel book, then the stylistic alteration would be all the more striking. In any case what needs emphasizing is that the figures in the Mont St Michel miniatures, especially in MS. 75, are more contained and static than Anglo-Saxon figures, and these are essential qualities of the Trier Ottonian miniatures.

There are one or two other pointers to Ottonian sources. One is the widely spaced legs and feet of the figures which make, with the drapery stretched between them, almost a square. Anglo-Saxon seated figures shown frontally seem always to have their feet close together where their knees are wide apart, which results in a triangular shape. St Augustine in
Pl. 22 MS. 72, fol. 97 may be compared, though the pose is reversed, to the Master of the Registrum Gregorii's representation of the Emperor Otto II.[2] Another feature not common in Anglo-Saxon miniatures[3] is the way the inside hem of the garment behind the legs is shown. This is found in Ottonian works. The dotted line of hair, tonsure and beard of St Augustine MS. 72, fol. 92, also recalls Ottonian manuscripts. Finally the bejewelled splendour of the books and *clavi* of the Mont St Michel figures is also uncharacteristic of Anglo-Saxon manuscripts, and could come from Carolingian sources indirectly through Ottonian copies.[4]

In the analysis of the drapery the similarities with Anglo-Saxon styles have been emphasized. However, the main difference remains as important and striking. As was pointed out at the beginning of the discussion, in the Norman miniatures the figure is articulated and the parts of the body and the drapery separated. This is seen in the drawing of the Archangel,
Pl. 20 MS. 76, fol. A$^v$. The bands of drapery across the waist make one division.

1 Nitschke, op. cit., 27.

2 Nitschke, op. cit., Taf. 2. The pose gives weight and stability to the figure and has, therefore, a stylistic rather than an iconographic motivation.

3 The Bury Psalter in the Vatican is an exception. Wormald, *English Drawings*, pl. 27b.

4 Perhaps via St Germain-des-Prés MSS in which they are very common.

The cloak over the left shoulder and falling behind and out to the left of the right thigh is also quite distinct. In Anglo-Saxon miniatures, on the other hand, the artist used the drapery to give his figure a unity over which the eye plays without obstacle, led on by the line.

The Norman artist also uses colour to underline the separate parts which he links by a system of alternations. This can be very clearly seen in Avranches 76, fol. A$^{v}$, where the colouring has perhaps not been Pl. 20
completed. In the two top arches, on the left the capitals and plinths are orange and the columns are green, on the right the capitals and plinths are green and the arch is orange, whilst the columns are left blank. Similarly with the two seated figures, St Augustine's throne is green and his mantle is lilac, whilst King David's throne is lilac and his mantle green.

It remains to consider the composition of the miniatures. The change here is easily seen from a comparison of fol. A$^{v}$ of MS. 76, St Augustine Pl. 20
on the Psalms, with the Presentation page of MS. 50, the *Recognitiones*. The Pl. 17*b*
object of both pages is to proclaim the book's origin and contents and neither have any narrative purpose dependent on the text. But the way the artist of MS. 76 organizes his page is quite different. First, the two arches which are the same size and carefully aligned, are sharply defined by black outlines and the capitals cut off on the outside without any projection.[1] Pl. 20
King David is moved slightly towards the centre and balanced by the fine lettering of the 'Incipit' so that this and the three miniatures form a whole. In the St Clement picture all three pillars start from different Pl. 17*b*
levels and the left arch is larger than the right. The purple ground extends arbitrarily to the left and the miniature is not set in the centre of the page.

Moreover, the relationship of the figures to the architecture is different. In MS. 50 St Michael and the monk are related to the portico by a system of overlapping. In MS. 76 the archways are a setting which constricts the figures' movements. Thus St Michael's wings are kept within the arch and the dragon's head and tail are bent to fit into it. And though St

[1] Engaged pillars are common on the composite supporting piles of Norman churches and occur with this 'cut off' appearance at Mont St Michel itself.

Augustine's sheet of parchment and his foot extend behind and in front of the pillar, they do not trespass beyond it. In MS. 76 the main impression is of a single plane and St Michael is already to some extent an 'homme arcade',[1] and as such has moved from a Carolingian derived sense of space towards a Romanesque one. The miniature of MS. 50, like the early initials, is in a preliminary stage where the style of the models is in process of transformation. In the middle group manuscripts a new style has crystallized.

The subordination to the architectural frame occurs also in the other miniatures of the group. In these none of the figures are crowded together and the space left above them is always noticeable particularly in
Pls. *29a*, *24a* Avranches 75 and 90. There is no trace of the settings of Evangelist portraits of Carolingian manuscripts, neither the architectural survivals of the classical stage front in the 'Court School', nor the landscape conventions of the Rheims school. All that remain are a few stage properties, reading desks and foot stools. Behind is the uniformly painted ground.

In this blank background the miniatures do resemble superficially Anglo-Saxon manuscripts, where either the parchment is left bare as the only setting besides the frame,[2] or, as in the Benedictional of St Ethelwold, for example on fol. 56ᵛ, the doubting St Thomas, similar colour grounds are used, often with the 'wavy cloud' effect of which there is a
Pl. 28 trace in Avranches 72, fol. 182ᵛ. But in another respect the Norman miniatures differ radically. In them there is a proper sense of weight, which sets the scenes firmly on the base line with the blank space above.

The Anglo-Saxon miniatures, particularly well illustrated in the Benedictional, have an extraordinary centripetal tendency. In fact the pillars and arches in them are not so much a setting – their architectural character is anyway more or less submerged by their decoration – as a frame, and one that has to be filled. Thus if the scene cannot be shifted to the middle of the frame to fill it from the centre outwards, so that any parchment left bare balances above and below, then good care is taken to fill the whole page. An example of the first tendency is seen in the Maries at

[1] H. Focillon, *L'Art des sculpteurs romans* (1964), 72.

[2] For example the Gospels, Cambridge, Trinity College, MS. B.10.4.

the Sepulchre of fol. 51$^{v}$, and of the second in the scene of St Peter and two Apostles, fol. 4.[1] Pl. 23

In the Mont St Michel miniatures, in spite of the lack of any background represented within the arches, the architecture remains a setting not a frame, and the simplicity of the few patterns found on the columns and arches emphasizes this. This leads to a second point, however. The figures do not in any way recede into space within the architectural setting as they still do in the Benedictional of St Ethelwold. Antique illusionism has been entirely discarded and instead the figures are as it were pressed flat into planes.

It is in Ottonian manuscripts of the late tenth to eleventh century that a similar way of showing figures as in a frieze before a plain background is found. Nordenfalk has shown how the Master of the Registrum Gregorii in Trier introduced in the late tenth century a new system of space composition.[2] This was a legacy which was taken over particularly in the Reichenau and Echternach Schools[3] where, however, the Master's extraordinarily subtle system was soon simplified. In particular the figures are flattened as if between invisible panes of glass and the use of plain grounds is developed, against which the figures are silhouetted.

In the Mont St Michel miniatures there is undoubtedly a similar emphasis on the plane parallel to the picture surface. Thus the thrones' square fronts are shown, but little of the tops, St Michael's spear passes across his body parallel to the front plane and heads are aligned to emphasize the horizontal line of the base. The frontal figure of Felicianus in MS. 72 may be compared with the oblique approach of the monk of Pl. 22
MS. 50.[4] Pl. 17*b*

It is difficult to say how far the Norman illuminators were directly aware of developments in Ottonian art. Some possible reminiscences have

1 F. Wormald, *The Benedictional of St Ethelwold* (1959), pl. 2.

2 Nordenfalk, *Münchner Jahrbuch*, op. cit.

3 Nitschke, op. cit., espec. 38–54. For convenience the term 'Reichenau school' will continue to be used in this book in spite of the doubts raised particularly as regards the early manuscripts by C. R. Dodwell, D. H. Turner, *Reichenau reconsidered* (Warburg Institute Surveys, ii) (1965).

4 This illustrates the interdependence of style and iconography. The frontal St Michael it was suggested earlier comes from Italy. And yet at the same time quite apart from iconographical considerations there is a stylistic tendency towards frontal figures observable in these manuscripts.

already been mentioned. Iconographical connections in the Sacramentary will be mentioned later. On the other hand there is only one insignificant instance of influence and that indirect, on the initial style.[1] Probably again there were intermediaries in the north French monasteries. Some of these houses show their figures arranged on plain colour backgrounds, though in the earlier manuscripts from St Bertin there is still a strong Pl. 46*c* tendency to symmetrical arrangement from the centre as in Anglo-Saxon art.[2] Later manuscripts from north France have plain colour grounds.[3] In style they are dependent on Liège manuscripts such as the Sacramentary made at St Laurent in the second quarter of the eleventh century and Pl. 48*c* adapted for use at St Bertin.[4] This also has plain colour grounds. The head Pls. 26*a*, 26*b* of St Ambrose in Latin 2639 is very close to the St Bertin type (the iconographical similarity was commented on earlier), and this indicates the kind of route by which Ottonian influences reached Normandy.

To conclude, the Mont St Michel artists were still as in the initials of the early books, eclectic pupils. Their debt to Anglo-Saxon art was undoubtedly considerable, but besides using different styles within that school of the late tenth and first half of the eleventh centuries, they incorporated Carolingian survivals, and made their own contribution in the direction of compositional stability and the architectural values of balance and articulation of parts. In this they seem to have been helped by Ottonian achievements. It is probable that the Belgian and northern French monasteries contributed as intermediaries and transformers both of Anglo-Saxon and Ottonian styles. What is, in any case, significant is the tendency, as in the early initials, towards the new style of the Romanesque period. From this standpoint the artists are pioneers at the start of a new movement, not feeble copiers in the decadence of an old one.

1 In Avranches 61, via St Germain-des-Prés. See above p. 66.

2 Boulogne, Bib. Mun., MS. 107. Lives of St Bertin, etc. St Omer, Bib. Mun., MS. 342 bis. Gospels. Porcher, *French Miniatures*, pl. vi, vii.

3 e.g. Gospels now Brussels, Bib. Roy., MS. II 175. See below, Ch. VI.

4 Paris, Bib. Nat., Latin 819. *MSS. à peintures*, no. 121.

# V

# THE SACRAMENTARY - NEW YORK, PIERPONT MORGAN LIBRARY MS. 641

THE Sacramentary now in the Pierpont Morgan Library, New York, is the most highly illuminated product of the Mont St Michel scriptorium of the eleventh century to survive.[1] Its importance is increased by the fact that there is no other eleventh-century Norman manuscript illustrated either similarly or on such a scale. The Calendar and the Proper for the season of Advent are missing and also three leaves from other parts of the book, one for the Nativity, one from the Canon, and the third for the feast of St Michael on 29th September. Some of the missing parts of the manuscript survive at Rouen.[2]

The illumination remaining consists of, besides a number of foliage or inhabited scroll initials, some in full-page frames, others smaller, fourteen historiated initials and eleven framed full- or half-page scenes. The subjects illustrated are as follows: Pls. 31–46

| | |
|---|---|
| fol. 2ᵛ | The Annunication to the Shepherds. Half-page. |
| fol. 3ᵛ | The Martyrdom of St Stephen. Initial 'D'. |
| fol. 5 | St John Evangelist. Initial 'E'. |
| fol. 6 | The Holy Innocents. Initial 'D'. |
| fol. 9 | Epiphany. The Adoration of the Magi. Initial 'D'. |

1 The grounds for assigning this manuscript to Mont St Michel are stylistic, as it has no indication of its original provenance. For the question of whether it was made for use at Fécamp, a view held by some scholars, see Appendix VI. A bibliography of the manuscript is given in the Catalogue. I should like to thank Mr John Plummer of the Morgan Library for answering a number of questions about the manuscript before I was able finally to see it myself in October, 1967.

2 Bibl. Mun., MS.Mm. 15, Suppl. MS. 116. See Leroquais, *Sacramentaires*, i, 75, no. 29. Reasons for believing the fragment to be part of Morgan MS. 641 are given in Appendix VI. The translation of St Autbert entered on fol. 22 of the fragment means that the Sacramentary must certainly have been used at Mont St Michel in the twelfth century.

| | |
|---|---|
| fol. $14^{v}$ | St Agnes. Initial 'O'. |
| fol. 16 | St Paul. Initial 'D'. |
| fol. 18 | The Purification and the Presentation of Christ in the Temple. Three-quarter page. |
| fol. $20^{v}$ | St Peter. Initial 'D'. |
| fol. $22^{v}$ | St Gregory. Initial 'D'. |
| fol. $23^{v}$ | St Benedict. Initial 'D'. |
| fol. 24 | The Annunciation. Initial 'D'. |
| fol. $52^{v}$ | The Last Supper. Three-quarter page. |
| fol. $61^{v}$ | 'Vere dignum'. Preface to Canon. VD monogram with full-page frame. |
| fol. $66^{v}$ | 'Christus super aspidem'. Initial 'D' with full-page frame. |
| fol. $75^{v}$ | The Ascension. Full page. |
| fol. $80^{v}$ | Pentecost. Full page. |
| fol. $119^{v}$–120 | The Nativity of St John Baptist. Full page and initial 'D'. |
| fol. $122^{v}$ | The Martyrdom of St Peter. Full page. |
| fol. 127 | St Benedict. Initial 'O' |
| fol. $142^{v}$ | The Assumption of the Virgin. Full page. |
| fol. $155^{v}$ | The Exaltation of the Cross. Full page. |
| fol. 170 | All Saints. Initial 'O'. Full page. |
| fol. 173 | St. Martin. Initial 'D'. |

## *Part I: The Iconography*

### A: SYSTEM OF ILLUMINATION

As has been said, the manuscript is both decorated with ornamental
Pls. 13*c*, 46*e* initials and illustrated with narrative scenes.[1] The decorative initials are typical of the Mont St Michel manuscripts of the middle group and do not require further treatment. They are reserved for the less important feasts, or, where a feast is illustrated by a full- or half-page miniature as opposed to an historical initial, they introduce the text. Here our concern

[1] For a discussion of the style and iconography see Avril, *Millénaire* (2), 218–24.

is with the illustrations, whether full- or half-page miniatures, or historiated initials. The two systems used in fact give an indication of the ultimate sources of the manuscript's illustrations.

The one, of full-page pictures or framed pictures separated from the text, is found in the second half of the tenth century in the Ottonian schools, particularly those of Reichenau, Echternach and Fulda. Using late classical models they began to produce illustrated books, especially Gospel and Pericope books, of a kind almost unknown in Carolingian art. There are also some Anglo-Saxon manuscripts illustrated in this way, which survive, notably the Benedictional of St Ethelwold.[1]

The other system, whenever and wherever the historiated initial originated – the earliest surviving examples in the Leningrad Bede and the British Museum Cotton Vespasian Psalter being Insular,[2] of the early eighth century – was used by Carolingian artists not only in the Corbie Psalter[3] whose unparalleled initial decoration is not so important for our purposes, but also in certain of the Court School of Charlemagne Gospels,[4] and more consistently in the Drogo Sacramentary.[5] There are certain iconographic similarities between the Mont St Michel manuscripts and the Drogo Sacramentary. However, the artists were not necessarily dependent on the Drogo Sacramentary or a similar Metz School manuscript for the idea of the historiated initial. For it was used in a number of Anglo-Saxon manuscripts, for instance the Junius Psalter, and also at St Pl. 17*d*
Bertin about 1000 by Abbot Otbert notably in his Psalter.[6]

There is thus no problem in tracing the sources of the illustrative systems. What is peculiar about our manuscript, however, is that it uses both together. In this it would seem to be unique amongst Sacramentaries to this date, and that the artist or artists combined the two is symptomatic of their general eclecticism.

1 London, Brit. Mus., Add. MS. 49598. Warner and Wilson, op. cit.

2 See M. Schapiro, 'The Decoration of the Leningrad manuscript of Bede,' *Scriptorium*, *xii* (1958), 191–207.

3 Amiens, Bib. Mun., MS. 18. See above, espec. p. 52–3.

4 Especially Brit. Mus., Harley MS. 2788, fol. 109, 'Q'. Köhler (2), Taf. 59.

5 Paris, Bib. Nat., Latin 9428. Köhler (3), 2, 143–62, Taf. 76–91.

6 Oxford, Bodleian Library, MS. Junius 27. Boulogne, Bib. Mun., MS. 20. Leroquais, *Psautiers*, 94–101, pl. xix-xxi.

## B: ILLUSTRATED SACRAMENTARIES

A second question concerns the tradition of illustrated Sacramentaries. Mr E. C. Hohler referring to the Sacramentary of Robert of Jumièges has pointed out that the practice of marking the formulary of each of the main feasts in a Sacramentary with an elaborate miniature is uncommon at this date.[1] Besides this early eleventh-century Anglo-Saxon manuscript now at Rouen[2] he lists eleven other examples of the late tenth or early eleventh century. These comprise four from Fulda, one from Cologne, three from Liège, and one each from Ivrea, Trier(?) and St Denis.[3] The Jumièges Sacramentary, Hohler also points out, is the only example of a book of this kind (besides the St Denis Sacramentary which is of clear Ottonian inspiration) not produced within the borders of the Empire. The Morgan Sacramentary, since it is, of course, later than any of these examples, is not mentioned by Hohler.

Of the Sacramentaries surviving from the ninth century or earlier only one which is illustrated on any scale needs to be added to this list for our purposes. This is the Drogo Sacramentary, and has already been mentioned. It is, therefore, not surprising that the system of illustration and the iconography show Ottonian influence.[4]

For the actual scenes chosen for representation, the Annunciation to the Shepherds, Martyrdom of St Stephen, Adoration of the Magi, Presentation in the Temple, Annunication, Last Supper, Ascension, Pentecost and Martyrdom of St Peter are all found in the majority of the thirteen Sacramentaries. The feast of St John Baptist is illustrated with a full page

1 'Les Saints insulaires dans le missel de l'Archevêque Robert', *Jumièges, Congrès Scientifique du XIIIe Centenaire*, i (1955), 293–303.

2 Bib. Mun., MS.Y.6(274). H. A. Wilson, 'The Missal of Robert of Jumièges,' *Henry Bradshaw Society*, xi (1896). Leroquais, *Sacramentaires*, i, 99.

3 Fulda: Göttingen, Universitätsbibl., Cod. theol. 231; Rome, Vatican, Latin 3548; Udine, Bib. Cap., Cod.76v.; Bamberg, Staatl. Bibl., Lit.1 (A.II.52). Cologne: Paris, Bib. Nat., Latin 817. Liège: Paris, Bib. Nat., Latin 819; Bamberg, Staatl. Bibl., Lit. 3 (Ed.V.4); Munich, Bayr. Staatsbibl., Clm. 23261. Ivrea: Bib. Cap., Cod. LXXXVI. Trier (?): Paris, Bib. Nat., Latin 18005. St Denis: Paris, Bib. Nat., Latin 9436 (made at St Vaast, Arras?).

4 For the subject of Sacramentary illustration see Leroquais, op. cit. and A. Ebner, *Quellen und Forschungen zur Geschichte und Kunstgeschichte des Missale Romanum. Iter Italicum*, reprinted Graz (1957). The earliest surviving illustrated Sacramentary is of the late eighth century from Gellone, now Paris, Bib. Nat., Latin 12048. It contains a number of historiated initials.

miniature and an historiated initial as well.[1] The Death of the Virgin or Assumption is found only in the Trier, St Denis, Ivrea and one of the Liège Sacramentaries. The All Saints is also a less common subject and differs from the other versions. The Holy Innocents initial which does not show the slaughter appears to be unique, as does that of St Benedict. Two other subjects not found in any of the other Sacramentaries are the 'Christus super aspidem' and the Heraclius legend illustration for the feast of the Exaltation of the Cross. As for omissions, a miniature of St Michael has been removed, folios 160–1. The 'Te igitur' page has also been removed between folios 61–2 leaving an offprint, on folio 61$^{v}$, of a frame. Since only eleven words are missing from the Canon which continues on folio 62, the Canon initial 'T' was probably on the verso of the missing leaf. The recto may, therefore, have had a miniature of the Crucifixion.[2] Alternatively the scene of the three Maries at the Sepulchre might have been represented. Probably a miniature of the Nativity which is not shown, came between the Rouen fragment and the beginning of the Morgan text where they join, since a folio is missing here also. Other subjects which are fairly common but not shown here, are the Baptism (usually combined with the Miracle at Cana), and the Entry into Jerusalem for Palm Sunday. In the three Fulda and the Ivrea manuscripts episodes from the life of St Martin were shown. Here there is only the Saint in an initial 'D' flanked by monks.[3] Similarly there is no full-page miniature or initial for St Laurence whose martyrdom is illustrated in the Fulda, Ivrea and Drogo Sacramentaries, or for St Andrew whose martyrdom is illustrated in these manuscripts and who is shown enthroned in the Jumièges Sacramentary. As far as the choice of subjects goes, therefore, no one source can be detected.

Before examining the iconography in detail, one further point may be

1 The mass in commemoration of the Saints whose relics are preserved in the church, Rouen, Bib. Mun., Suppl. MS. 116, fol. 25$^{v}$, perhaps implies that Mont St Michel possessed relics of St John but he is not specified as the Baptist. See Leroquais, op. cit., p.75. I do not know the evidence for Leroquais' assertion that there was a chapel dedicated to the Baptist in the church. The abbey certainly possessed relics later, see J. Dubois, *Millénaire* (1), 533, 539, 546, 565–6, 590, but the omission of the Baptism from the miniatures is surprising if they were already there at this date.

2 I am grateful to Dr R. W. Pfaff, Chapel Hill, for this information.

3 The south crypt chapel was dedicated to St Martin.

made. For the illustration of the Sacramentary there were two obvious choices. The first, as has been seen above, was to portray the events celebrated by the different Feasts of the Calendar as they are narrated in the sacred texts. Such illustrations were likely to resemble those of Gospel and Pericope books. The second, often found, for instance in the Drogo and Fulda Sacramentaries, in conjunction with the first, but not at Mont St Michel, was to show the liturgical actions of the Mass and of administering the Sacraments.

In the Mont St Michel Sacramentary, however, one initial altogether ignores the literal representation of the event whether in the Mass or of
Pl. 31*e* the feast it celebrates. The 'D' introducing the Feast of the Holy Innocents shows that Sacramentary illustration could differ radically from that of Gospel books. It therefore raises the question (which cannot be answered here, or without much further enquiry) of whether there was ever a separate illustrative tradition for the different Feasts created specifically for the Sacramentary and separate from Gospel book illustration.

## C: THE MINIATURES

The main sources as before are in Anglo-Saxon and Ottonian art, and for the latter particularly the Reichenau, Echternach and Fulda schools. Certain Ottonian innovations like the 'Long Table' Last Supper and the new style of Assumption of the Virgin can be traced via such intermediaries as St Germain-des-Prés, St Maur-des-Fossés, St Laurent, Liège, and St Vaast, Arras. Various other motifs, Anna the prophetess with both arms raised for example, were probably similarly transmitted. Anglo-Saxon influence is shown by similarities with three surviving liturgical books, in particular the Benedictional of St Ethelwold and the Benedictional of Archbishop Robert, and to a lesser extent the Sacramentary of Robert of Jumièges given to his old abbey whilst bishop of London, 1044–50. The rare iconography of the Pentecost with the rays entering the Apostles' mouths is found in the two Benedictionals, for instance. The actual impetus to produce an illustrated Sacramentary at Mont St Michel may have come from Robert of Jumièges' gift to his old monastery. As we shall see some stylistic but not very many iconographic similarities with the Rouen Sacramentary can be cited to support this suggestion. In the main, as with the style, the Anglo-Saxon iconography is that of earlier not contemporary manuscripts. This is indicated by the All Saints miniature's connection with the Athelstan Psalter for instance and by the absence of the Anglo-Saxon introduction of the 'disappearing Christ' in the Ascension miniature. The 'Christus super aspidem' initial, also, which does not resemble the eleventh-century Anglo-Saxon versions may copy an earlier Anglo-Saxon model. Since it is a very unusual subject belonging properly in a Psalter it may be that this is another borrowing from the Anglo-Saxon Psalter known to have belonged to Archbishop Robert of Rouen.[1]

Anglo-Saxon art continues to use Carolingian iconography to such an extent that it is generally difficult to be sure at Mont St Michel that a motif was transmitted by Carolingian sources and not by an Anglo-Saxon model for which there may be no other evidence. The Sacramentary appears, however, to agree with Carolingian iconography of the Metz school, as against surviving Anglo-Saxon examples of the scene, in the Annunciation to the Shepherds and the Martyrdom of St Stephen.[2] The St Benedict initial has a more distant source, probably, in Monte Cassino itself, but it is not possible to say whether this was known directly or, as is more likely, via an intermediary. The *VD* monogram of the Preface with the cross bar supported by angels is the only iconographic innovation in the illustrations, it seems, and, as with the 'Christus super aspidem', this is rather the adaptation of an ancient motif to a new

1 See Appendix V. and above, p. 112. Did the Psalter, described by Ordericus as 'variis picturis decoratum' have a prefatory cycle of miniatures as did London, Brit. Mus., Cotton MS. Tiberius C.VI? The main difficulty in answering this question is that we have no christological scenes from St Evroul (where the Archbishop's Psalter was later) to compare. This is in itself some indication, though an argument from a negative since we do not know what manuscripts from St Evroul may be lost, that there was no such cycle. Only two of the scenes in the Tiberius Psalter, Ascension and Pentecost, are found in the Mont St Michel Sacramentary and these both differ in various respects. Norman evidence is unlikely, therefore, to contribute to the problem of when the first cycle of prefatory miniatures to a Psalter occurred in England.

2 Anglo-Saxon indebtedness in iconography to the Metz School, particularly in the Benedictional of St Ethelwold, is well known. O. Homburger, *Die Anfänge der Malschule von Winchester im X. Jahrhundert* (1912), idem, 'L'Art Carolingien de Metz et l'école de Winchester', *Gazette des Beaux-Arts*, lxii (July-August 1963), 35–46.

context. It gives further proof of the close connections between St Germain-des-Prés and Mont St Michel and this time shows St Germain to be the borrower. The source of the unique Heraclius illustrations for the Exaltation of the Cross remains so far undiscovered.

The interest of the iconography which will now be treated miniature by miniature, centres, therefore, in the combination of various traditions rather than in any innovations.

## Pl. 31*a* *Fol. $2^{v}$. 25th December, Christmas Day. The Annunciation to the Shepherds*

The division between the one angel and the heavenly choir, according to St Luke, II, vv. 8–15, is shown in Carolingian, Anglo-Saxon and Ottonian examples by the one angel standing on the ground to deliver his message whilst the choir appear
Pl. 31*c* above in a glory.[1] In all the Carolingian examples the division is not made, however. In both the Drogo[2] and the Raganaldus[3] Sacramentary an angel appears from the sky to the shepherds below, and this is also so in the Ivrea Sacramentary[4] and the Otbert Psalter,[5] both of the early eleventh century. The arrangement of the Drogo Sacramentary where the angel appears from the left in an initial 'D' to the shepherds crowded together below on the right, not spread out symmetrically in the centre, is closest to our miniature.

## Pl. 31*d* *Fol. $3^{v}$. 26th December. The Martyrdom of St Stephen*[6]

St Stephen kneels in accordance with Acts, VII, v. 60. Of the three main arrangements of the scene found up to this time, the Mont St Michel initial is again closest
Pl. 31*b* to that of the Drogo Sacramentary.[7] There the Saint is on the left in the bar of an

1 See *St Albans Psalter*, p. 82, for examples.

2 Paris, Bib. Nat., Latin 9428, fol. 23v. Köhler (3), Taf. 80c.

3 Autun, Bib. Mun., MS. 19, fol. 8. Köhler (1), Taf. 63b.

4 Ivrea, Bib. Cap., Cod. LXXXVI, fol. 20. L. Magnani, *Le Miniature del Sacramentario d'Ivrea* (1934), tav. vi.

5 Boulogne, Bib. Mun., MS. 20, fol. 58v. The choir also is shown here above. Leroquais, *Psautiers*, pl. xix.

6 Edward S. King, 'The Carolingian frescoes of the Abbey of Saint Germain d'Auxerre', *Art Bulletin*, xi (1929), 359–375.

7 Paris, Bib. Nat., Latin 9428, fol. 27. Köhler (3), Taf. 81b.

initial 'D' and is stoned by a group of four men to the right. Above appears both the hand of God in the bow of the initial with two Angels and a standing Christ in the bar.

A second group of representations, including the Carolingian frescoes at St Germain d'Auxerre and the Bury Psalter,[1] place the executioners all behind St Stephen, whilst the third, seen for instance in a mid-ninth century copy of St Paul's Epistles,[2] in the Benedictional of St Ethelwold[3] and the Ivrea Sacramentary,[4] turns St Stephen who is on the right, to face his executioners.

The Mont St Michel artist has abbreviated the scene omitting both St Paul presiding and the tower of the City gates,[5] both found in the Menologion of Basil II,[6] for instance, and in some of the other representations. As in the Benedictional, St Stephen does not wear the Deacon's dalmatic.

## *Fol. 6. 28th December. The Holy Innocents* Pl. 31*e*

There is no trace here of the usual scene of the slaying of the Innocents by Herod's order.[7] This is not therefore an abbreviated narrative scene. The emphasis is rather on the idea of martyrdom and its rewards. The female figure is the Church who holds the palm of martyrdom and the crown of everlasting life. And the busts with their long hair and their tunics do not specifically represent the babes of Bethlehem so much as the first of the Church's martyrs. For this reason the iconography has something in common with pictures of the Saints in heaven and to some extent resembles the All Saints miniature on fol. 170. Pl. 45*d*

There are a number of parallels for the use of the bust figure where lack of space made representation of the whole figure impossible; an ivory liturgical bucket in the Morgan Collection[8] of the late tenth century gives some good examples in the Ascension and Last Supper scenes. An initial in an early twelfth century collection of Saints' Lives from St Evroul[9] must also be mentioned as its subject is related. Pl. 31*f*

1 Rome, Vatican, MS. Reg. Lat. 12.

2 Munich, Bayr. Staatsbibl., Clm. 14345, fol. 1ᵛ. Exh, *Karl der Grosse*, no. 472. Cf. also the Prüm Gradual, Paris, Bib. Nat., Latin 9448, fol. 10, late tenth century.

3 London, Brit. Mus., Add. MS. 49598, fol. 17ᵛ.

4 Ivrea, Bib. Cap., Cod. LXXXVI, fol. 21. Magnani, op. cit., tav. vii.

5 '. . . They cast him out of the city', Acts, VII, v. 58.

6 Rome, Vatican, Cod. Gr. 1613, fol. 275. *Il Menologio di Basilio II* (complete facsimile), Turin (1907).

7 St Matthew, II, vv. 16–18.

8 Goldschmidt, *Elfenbeinskulpturen* (2), no. 71, Taf. xxiii.

9 Alençon, Bib. Mun., MS. 14, fol. 85. *MSS. à peintures*, no. 199.

There a 'T' introduces the Passion of St Christina who was imprisoned by her father with twelve other virgins in a tower. The initial is turned into a tower and out of its windows look the twelve virgins with St Christina at the top accompanied by Christ Himself.

Nevertheless, though superficially resembling our miniature, it is an illustration of an episode in St Christina's life and as such a narrative scene, as the Holy Innocents 'D' is not. The Morgan bucket panels are similarly abbreviated and even the All Saints representation has the narrative tradition of the Ascension Majestas and the Apocalyptic visions behind it.

It is difficult to know how far there had been a tradition evolved of representations seeking to emphasize the general significance of one of the Church's Feasts, rather than to narrate the events which the Feast commemorates. There is a hint of such a tradition in the late eighth century Gellone Sacramentary.[1] There in an initial 'O' three bust heads with a hand above them represent the Feast of Pentecost, not as a specific event which occurred in the upper room in Jerusalem after the Ascension of Christ and affected only the Apostles, but more generally as the gift of the Holy Spirit which comes by the laying on of hands and affects the whole Church. A related type of initial is to be found in the Corbie Psalter,[2] another pre-Carolingian revival work. There, illustrating the Magnificat, two female figures with haloes bow before an angel with outstretched arms, to form the initial 'M'. It is not perhaps simply a wish for symmetry which has here doubled the Virgin before the Archangel Gabriel. It is as much this same phenomenon of generalizing a specific event to bring out its universal significance. Not only the soul of Mary but the soul of each Christian magnifies the Lord. It is at least possible, therefore, that the Mont St Michel 'D' is descended from a comparable pre-Carolingian initial.

## Pl. 32*a* *Fol. 9. 6th January. Epiphany—the Adoration of the Magi*[3]

The scene is shown according to what Vezin has called 'la formule hellenistique'. That is to say it is an Adoration in which the Virgin is enthroned with the Christ Child on her knees, not a Nativity with the Christ in a crib, at which the Magi, the Shepherds and St Joseph are also present.

The architectural frame is a background to the whole scene, so that there is no division, as there is in Carolingian examples, between the Virgin and Child inside

1 Paris, Bib. Nat., Latin 12048, fol. 82. Leroquais, *Sacramentaires* i, 1, pl. ii–iv.

2 Amiens, Bib. Mun., MS. 18, fol. 136v. Pächt, 'Precarolingian roots', op. cit., pl. v.

3 Gilbert Vezin, *L'Adoration et le cycle des Mages dans l'art chrétien primitif* (1950).

the building, and the Magi entering it from outside.[1] This division of indoors from outdoors is beginning to disappear in Anglo-Saxon versions where the architecture becomes a throne background for the Virgin. The Norman artist by enclosing the whole scene in an architectural canopy makes his own further modification.

The almost frontal Virgin and the Child with outstretched blessing hand and fully clothed are very similar to the figures in the Benedictional of St Ethelwold.[2] Pl. 32*b* The Magi have lost the Phrygian caps which survive in the Sacramentary of Robert of Jumièges, but the caps have not been replaced by crowns as in the Benedictional.[3] Examples of bare-headed Kings are found in Ottonian miniatures.[4] The Virgin places both hands on the Child's shoulders, which is unusual.[5]

## *Fol. 18. 2nd February. The Purification and the Presentation of Christ in the Temple*[6]

Pl. 33*a*

The source for the Presentation in the Temple is St Luke's account, II, vv. 22–39. There the Purification of the Virgin and the Presentation of the Christ Child are described as if, contrary to Jewish practice, they took place at the same time.

The Mont St Michel miniature belongs to the Western tradition, for the scene is shown within the Temple, not at its gate as in the Byzantine 'Hypapante'. Of the variations distinguished by Dorothy Schorr this belongs to the second where both the Virgin and Simeon hold the Child over the altar. The initial of the Drogo Sacramentary,[7] though it is a 'hypapante', shows a similar arrangement of the

1 See *St Albans Psalter*, p. 83.

2 London, Brit. Mus., Add. MS. 49598, fol. 24$^{v}$.

3 Rouen, Bib. Mun., MS. Y.6(274), fol. 36$^{v}$. *St Albans Psalter*, pl. 105b.

4 In a Gospel Book from Lower Saxony, tenth century, now Wolfenbüttel, Herzog-August-Bibl. Cod. 16. 1 Aug. fol., fol. 18$^{v}$, Goldschmidt, *German illumination* (1), pl. 86, and in the 'Hitda' Codex from Cologne, first quarter eleventh century, Darmstadt, Hessische Landesbibl. Cod. 1640.

5 A famous later example is 'La Belle Verrière' window at Chartres. In the Codex Egberti, Trier, Stadtbibl. MS. 24 and the Sacramentary from Fulda, Rome, Vatican Lat. 3548, fol. 14, the Virgin has one hand on the Child's shoulder. H. Schiel *Codex Egberti* (complete facsimile) (1960).

6 Dorothy Schorr, 'The Iconographic Development of the Presentation in the Temple,' *Art Bulletin*, xxviii (1946), 17–32.

7 Paris, Bib. Nat., Latin 9428, fol. 38. Köhler (3), Taf. 82d. Another Carolingian version is in the Utrecht Psalter, fol. 89v, illustrating the 'Nunc dimittis'. E. T. Dewald, *The illustrations of the Utrecht Psalter* (1932), pl. cxli. It takes place outside the Temple. Anna raises her left hand. St Joseph carries four doves. There is no maid. The distinction, however, between the scene shown inside or outside the Temple is not always easy to draw in Western mediaeval art where the artist is often not concerned with spatial relationships of figure and setting.

figures except that Anna is not shown there. She is present in the Benedictional of St Ethelwold,[1] however, where the same number of figures are similarly disposed
Pl. 33*b* but more congested.

The artist's dramatic sense is again noticeable in the use he makes of the Prophetess' gesture of the upraised arms with the wide sleeves falling down. Anna appears seldom in Northern art and the pose suggests a Byzantine source preserving an originally classical motif of inspired prophecy. In the Menologion of Basil II, for instance, the Prophetess has her right arm raised with a scroll in her left hand and her head thrown back.[2] She is similarly shown in the Salerno Antependium.[3] But the original motif is distorted when she appears with both arms raised
Pl. 32*c* as she does in the three Sacramentaries from Fulda,[4] and also in a manuscript from
Pl. 32*d* St Germain-des-Prés illuminated by Ingelardus.[5] This then is a clear instance of a Byzantine motif transmitted indirectly to Normandy via Ottonian art. In the St Germain manuscript Anna turns to address the crowd, and only Simeon holds the Child, whilst in the Fulda manuscripts it is the Virgin who alone holds Christ. The Mont St Michel artist has given the maid carrying the doves behind St Joseph a halo.

## Pl. 34*a* *Fol. 23^v. 21st March. St Benedict*

The scene represents the soul of St Benedict taken up into Heaven as is clear from the collect:—'Deus qui hodierna die carnis eductum ergastulo beatissimum confessorem tuum benedictum sublevasti ad caelum . . . '.

The representation of the soul as a small naked figure is found in classical art though there it is usually winged, and is taken over in Early Christian art.[6] It occurs in the Carolingian period in the Stuttgart Psalter,[7] and in Ottonian miniatures it appears in the story of Dives and Lazarus in the Escorial Gospels.[1] In the Ivrea

1 London, Brit. Mus., Add. MS. 49598, fol. 34^v.

2 Rome, Vatican, Cod. Gr. 1613, fol. 365.

3 Goldschmidt, *Elfenbeinskulpturen* (4), no. 126, Taf. xlv.

4 Göttingen, Universitätsbibl., Cod. theol. 231, fol. 24^v. E. H. Zimmermann, *Die Fuldaer Buchmalerei in Karolingischer und ottonischer Zeit* (1910), Taf. 6. Udine, Bib. Cap. 76^v, fol. 24^v. Bamberg, Staatl. Bibl., Lit. 1, fol. 35. In the Bamberg MS. Anna holds her hands less closely to her body than in the others.

5 Paris, Bib. Nat., Latin 12,117, fol. 107. Deslandres, op. cit., pl. 5.

6 K. Weitzmann, 'Die Illustration der Septuaginta', *Münchner Jahrbuch der bildenden Kunst*, iii/iv (1952–3), 96–120, Taf. 18, 20, 22, 23. Creation scenes from mosaics of San Marco, Venice, etc.

7 Stuttgart, Landesbibl., MS. Bibl. Fol. 23, fol. 70^v. E. T. Dewald, *The Stuttgart Psalter* (1930).

8 Escorial, Cod. Vetr. 17. A. Boeckler, *Das goldene Evangelienbuch Heinrichs III* (1933), pl. p. 123. Also Echternach Codex Aureus, Nürnberg Germanisches National Museum, Hs. 156142. P. Metz, *The Golden Gospels of Echternach* (1957), pl. 70.

Sacramentary the soul of the dying man is similarly shown escaping from his mouth,[1] and a miniature in a Psalter of the same area, written probably for Arnulph of Milan (998–1018)[2] shows St Michael rescuing a small naked sexless child from a dragon.[3] The naked soul is not, however, common before the twelfth century.[4]

For the composition of the initial another tradition is important. This is associated particularly with martyrdoms and the death of saints. On a sixth-century ivory pyxis probably from Egypt, an angel hovers with a cloth above a saint about to be beheaded.[5] The cloth must be to receive the soul of the martyr and actually so used it is found in a ninth-century manuscript of Prudentius' Peristephanon.[6] Another ninth-century example is the scene of the death of St Ambrose on the Golden Altar in St Ambrogio, Milan; and the single angel carrying a soul occurs also in the Anglo-Saxon Bury Psalter.[7]

The soul held by two angels does not seem to appear before the late tenth and the eleventh century. The earliest surviving examples are in the scenes of the death and Assumption of the Virgin.[8] In the Life of St Amand of the mid-eleventh century Pl. 42*a*
in the scene of the death of the Saint, two angels carry a half-length clothed figure in a napkin.[9] Other early instances are in the Anglo-Saxon Grimbald Gospels Pl. 34*c*

[1] Ivrea, Bib. Cap., Cod. LXXXVI, fol. 195v. Magnani, op. cit., tav. xxxvi.

[2] Formerly Dyson Perrins Collection MS. 48. Warner, *Descriptive Catalogue*, pl. li. Now London, Brit. Mus., Egerton 3763, fol. 104v.

[3] The inscription reads: [In]trat nunc cerebrum Michaelis lancea dirum / Serpentis puerum ne sorbeat impius istum. This refers to Revelation, XII, vv. 4–6. But from the accompanying prayer it is clear that St Michael is also the psychopomp to whom the owner of the Psalter prays to rescue his soul from the devil '. . . ut in novissimo die benigne suscipias animam meam in sinu tuo . . . '. For pointing out the importance of this miniature and for help over the iconography of the soul and other matters I am indebted to Dr R. Harris of Smith University, U.S.A.

[4] See several initials showing the naked soul of the Psalmist in the St Albans Psalter at Hildesheim. *St Albans Psalter*, pls. 49, 59.

[5] O. M. Dalton, *Catalogue of the Ivory Carvings of the Christian era in the British Museum* (1909), no. 12, pl. vii. For the angel as psychopomp see *D.A.C.L.*, s.v. 'Ange', i (1905), 2121, and note the prayers at the burial of the dead in the Gelasian Sacramentary: '. . . Suscipe, domine, animam servi tui illius revertentem ad te. Adsit ei angelus testamenti tui Michael . . . ' and ' . . . Te supplices deprecamur ut suscipi jubeas animam famuli tui illius per manus sanctorum angelorum deducendam in sinum Abrahae'. L. A. Muratori, *Liturgia Romana Vetus*, i (1748), col. 750 and 752. These prayers would justify the inclusion of either one angel or two, therefore.

[6] Bern, Stadtbibl., MS. 264 fols. 61 and 75, the martyrdom of Sts Romanus and Cassianus. O. Homburger, *Die illustrierten Handschriften der Burgerbibliothek Bern* (1962), Taf. lii.

[7] Rome, Vatican, MS. Reg. lat. 12, fol. 72. Wormald, *English Drawings*, pl. 26b. On another page two devils seize a full-length naked soul. See R. M. Harris, op. cit. (p. 239 n. 2 below), 246 ff.

[8] See the discussion below of the 'Assumption' miniature on fol. 142v, note 4. This iconography in turn is connected with the Ascension in which symmetrical angels flank the mandorla.

[9] Valenciennes, Bib. Mun., MS. 502, fol. 30. *MSS. à peintures*, no. 159.

where two angels carry nine souls[1] and in the Life of St Severinus in a St Germain-des-Prés manuscript, an initial 'B'.[2] None of these show the souls as naked except the Grimbald Gospels where they are only head and shoulders.[3]

Apart from this iconographical tradition, the Mont St Michel initial can be connected with an episode in St Benedict's life as narrated by St Gregory the Great in the Dialogues, Bk. II, ch. xxxv. The saint noticed one night a very brilliant light over earth and sky, and looking out of his window he saw the soul of Germanus, bishop of Capua, carried up by angels into heaven in a fiery sphere.[4] The background of the mandorla in the initial is a bright red, and so clearly the description has been transferred to St Benedict himself.

St Benedict's vision is in fact illustrated in the late eleventh-century Monte Cassino
Pl. 34*b* copy of his life.[5] Germanus' soul is there represented as a small frontal bust medallion with the sun and moon to signify the bright light in the middle of the night. The symmetrical angels supporting a roundel in this and the other examples recall the classical 'imago clipeata' taken over in Christian ivories,[6] and this suggests the possibility of a much earlier prototype which has been suspected for other reasons.[7] It may be, therefore, that this scene with its specific textual basis for the inclusion of more than one angel, is the source of the type of the two symmetrical flanking angels which is used in the Assumption and the miniatures from Saints' Lives cited above, even though no example with the two angels, which is earlier than the second half of the tenth century, has yet come to light.[8]

1 London, Brit. Mus., Add. MS. 34890. Talbot Rice, pl. 56a.

2 Paris, Bib. Nat., Latin 11751, fol. 140. Deslandres, op. cit., pl. 1.

3 Other examples of the eleventh and early twelfth centuries are:– Ivory, Frankish, eleventh century, showing the martyrdom of St Kylian and two companions. Goldschmidt, *Elfenbeinskulpturen* (2), no. 148, Taf. xlii; carved capitals from St Hilaire-le-grand, Poitiers, eleventh century, the death of a saint in which the soul is carried full length and apparently naked by two angels; Boulogne, Bib. Mun., MS. 46, fol. 1v, the soul of Lambert, abbot of St Bertin, carried by two angels half-length naked, early twelfth century. Porcher, *French Miniatures*, pl. xxvii.

4 'Vidit Germani Capuani episcopi animam in sphaera ignea ab angelis in coelum ferri', *P.L.* lxvi, 198.

5 Rome, Vatican Lat. 1202, fol. 79v. D. M. Inguanez, M. Avery, *I miniature Cassinesi del secolo xi illustranti la vita di S. Benedetto* (1934), tav. xviii.

6 e.g. the Barberini ivory in the Louvre, Paris. Volbach, *Elfenbeinarbeiten*, no. 48. The mid-fifth-century ivory in the British Museum showing an apotheosis with two winged figures carrying the Divus up to Heaven is also important as a possible late classical source. Volbach op. cit. no. 56.

7 See O. Pächt, *The Rise of Pictorial Narrative in twelfth-century England* (1962), 13 ff., especially pp. 17–18.

8 A twelfth-century stone relief in the Minster at Basel is important as evidence for the existence earlier of the type of the two angels carrying the soul. It shows scenes from the Life of St Vincent including the two angels carrying the soul from the aedicula in which the body is buried. It must go back to earlier models which may be connected with Prudentius' 'Peristephanon' which contains the Life of St Vincent.

Two other miniatures closely connected with the Cassino life should be mentioned. One is in the late eleventh-century Life of St Maur from St Maur-des-Fossés.[1] The scene is very similar but the soul of St Benedict is shown half-length with hands held in prayer similarly to our initial. The other is in the Durham Life of St Cuthbert of the early twelfth century where St Cuthbert's vision of the soul of St Aidan is illustrated and there the half-length soul is naked.[2] Pl. 34*f* Pl. 34*d*

Professor Pächt has already drawn attention to the connections of the illustrative system of the Cuthbert life with the Cassino Life.[3] Perhaps a model for the Cuthbert life passed to Durham via Normandy. What was the Mont St Michel artist's source? One possibility, already suggested by Pächt as a source for the Cuthbert life, is Fleury, with which Mont St Michel certainly had connections in the early eleventh century.[4] Another possibility is north Italy where the rather rare representation of the naked soul, not used at St Maur-des-Fossés for instance, was known. If so, Abbot Suppo's earlier abbacy of Fruttuaria could have been the link.

A third possibility is that an illustrated copy of St Gregory's *Dialogues* was the immediate source. In a manuscript, now in Rouen, which belonged, early in the twelfth century, and perhaps before, to Jumièges, Book III of the *Dialogues* is introduced by an historiated initial showing an episode in the Life of St Paulinus of Nola.[5] This initial is by an Anglo-Saxon artist and is probably of the first

[1] Troyes, Bib. Mun., MS. 2273, fol. 57v. L. Morel-Payen, *Les Plus beaux manuscrits et les plus belles reliures de la bibliothèque de Troyes* (1935), 52 ff, pl. iii. The miniature shows St Maur telling St Romanus of St Benedict's approaching death and then St Maur's vision whilst praying in the Church, of St Benedict ascending into Heaven. It does not fit the account in the text: 'conspexitque viam palliis stratam ac innumeris coruscam lampadibus, recto Orientis tramite, ab ejus [sc. St Benedict] cellam in caelum usque tendentem', *Acta Sanctorum*, January i (1640), 1044 § 30 ff. In the Monte Cassino life a similar account of a vision at the time of St Benedict's death seen by two of the brothers who were elsewhere, is given, and is illustrated on folio 80 with the inscription 'Sic Pater astra petit. Hi spectant. Angelus aedit'.

[2] Oxford, University College, MS. 165, p. 18. In the late twelfth-century copy of the Life also made at Durham, London, Brit. Mus., Add. MS. 39943, fol. 73v, St Cuthbert's Vision is omitted. Instead the angels convey similarly St Cuthbert's own soul in the scene of his death. W. Forbes-Leith, *The Life of St Cuthbert*, Edinburgh (1888), pl. xxxix.

[3] See Pächt, op. cit., 16.

[4] On a capital in the small Norman church of Rucqueville two angels support a profile whole length naked figure. See L. Musset, 'Pour réabiliter la sculpture romane normande, I. Les chapiteaux de Rucqueville', *Art de Basse Normandie*, no. 13 (Spring 1959), 12–15, pl. He compares the style of these capitals which belong to no known Norman school, with those of the Narthex of St Benoît-sur-Loire. G. Zarnecki, '1066 and architectural sculpture', *Proceedings of the British Academy*, lii (1966), 95, pls. x-xi also (independently it seems) draws attention to the stylistic similarity with Fleury, but shows that the capital represents the soul of Lazarus taken up to heaven and is a copy of a capital in Saint Sernin, Toulouse.

[5] Rouen, Bib. Mun., MS. A.337(506). It contains a Jumièges *ex libris* of the twelfth century.

quarter of the eleventh century. The early part of the manuscript including the beginning of Book II is missing but it is possible that an historiated initial with St Benedict's vision has been lost.[1]

## Pl. 34*e* *Fol. 24. 25th March. The Annunciation*[2]

The standing Virgin Annunciate is an Eastern type found for instance on the Monza and Bobbio Ampullae[3] where she is shown engaged in spinning the wool for the veil of the Temple. In one of the Ampullae[4] her chair from which she has started up is behind her. In Western examples the Virgin is generally seated. However, in a number of Ottonian manuscripts the scene is shown as taking place in the Temple which is represented by an arch and a hanging crown, and in these the Virgin stands with hands raised and without wool or spindle.[5] There is no indication of the Temple in the Mont St Michel initial.

Pl. 34*h* Gabriel's pose, as he moves towards the Virgin has a rhythm about it which is closer to the Benedictional of St Ethelwold,[6] however, than to the more static Ottonian figures. This denotes an ultimately classical source, no doubt via a Carolingian intermediary similar in style to the Bodleian Court School ivory book cover.[7] He carries a short staff in his left hand. A staff is carried in the Monza Ampulla where, however, it is longer, and in Ottonian manuscripts where it often has a cross at the top. The Virgin slightly inclines her head as in the Codex Egberti[8]
Pl. 34*g* and other Ottonian manuscripts.

In its combination of the standing Virgin of the Ottonian type, only shown more frontally, with the more articulated pose of the Angel of the Anglo-Saxon miniature, a north French Gospel book with a stylistic affinity to St Vaast minia-
Pl. 35*a* tures is closest to our initial.[9]

1 The initial 'F' of Book II is not, it must be admitted, easily historiated.

2 W. Braunfels, *Die Verkündigung* (1949).

3 A. Grabar, *Les Ampoules de Terre Sainte* (1958).

4 Grabar, op. cit., pl. 5. Monza no. 2.

5 e.g. Gotha, Landesbibl., Cod.I.19; Paris, Bib. Nat., Latin 10438; Aachen, Domschatz, Gospels of Otto III, fol. 11, Braunfels, op. cit., Taf. I.

6 London, Brit. Mus., Add. MS. 49598, fol. 5v.

7 Oxford, Bodleian Library, MS. Douce 176, Goldschmidt, *Elfenbeinskulpturen* (1), no. 5, Taf. 111.

8 Trier, Stadtbibl., MS. 24, fol. 9v.

9 Paris, Bibl. de l'Arsenal, MS. 592, fol. 18v. H. Martin, Ph. Lauer, *Les Principaux manuscrits à peintures de la Bibliothèque de l'Arsenal à Paris* (1929), 13. None of the Annunciations cited show the Archangel's head in strict profile as does the Mont St Michel initial. This is found in a manuscript illuminated by Ingelardus of St Germain-des-Prés, Paris, Bibl. Nat., Latin 11550, fol. 275v, Deslandres, op. cit., pl. 9b, where, however, the Virgin is seated. Also later in the St Albans Psalter.

## *Fol. 52v. Maundy Thursday. The Last Supper* Pl. 35c

The subject is the announcement by Christ to His disciples of His coming Betrayal. The iconography follows St John's Gospel, XIII, vv. 21–30, in which Christ signalizes the betrayer, 'He it is to whom I shall give a sop when I have dipped it' (v. 26). The Byzantine versions at least from the tenth century follow St Matthew's account, XXVI, v. 23, 'He that dippeth his hand with Me in the dish, the same shall betray Me'. They show Christ and the Apostles reclining at the 'sigma' table and Christ in consequence in the position of honour at the left. Judas is not physically separated from the other Apostles though he may be the end figure on the right. The older Western Last Suppers take place at a small round table for instance in the St Augustine's Gospels, the Drogo Sacramentary or the Raganaldus Sacramentary.[2]

The Mont St Michel artist in following neither of these types adopts a scheme which had fairly recently been introduced, almost certainly by Ottonian artists. The innovations are two. First the introduction of the long straight table, secondly the isolation of Judas on the near side of the table.

Amongst the various examples of the straight table from the tenth and eleventh centuries collected by L. H. Loomis none combines all the features of our miniature. Some of the earliest 'long table' Last Suppers still show Christ at the left as if at the 'sigma' table, for example the Bernward Gospels.[3] Another early example, the ivory liturgical bucket from the Morgan Collection[4] dated by Goldschmidt *c.*1000 and connected with the Metz school, has a central Christ. As Judas is not distinguished, however – the twelve Apostles appear as two rows of heads, six each side of Christ – this is rather an 'Institution of the Eucharist'. For that scene, hierarchical in nature, the symmetrical arrangement is clearly more suited. Thus

[1] A. Dobbert, 'Das Abendmahl Christi in der Bildenden Kunst bis gegen den Schluss des 14. Jahrhunderts', *Repertorium für Kunstwissenschaft*, xiii (1890), xiv (1891), xv (1892) and xviii (1895); G. Millet, *Recherches sur l'iconographie de l'Evangile* (1916), 286–309; R. H. Loomis, 'The Table of the Last Supper', *Art Studies*, v (1927), 71–88; *St Albans Psalter*, 58, 89.

[2] Cambridge, Corpus Christi College, MS. 286, fol. 125, F. Wormald, *The miniatures in the Gospels of St Augustine* (1954), pl.IV.2; Paris, Bib. Nat., Latin 9428, fol. 44v; Autun, Bib. Mun., MS. 19, fol. 8. Köhler (3), Taf. 83d and (1), Taf. 63b.

[3] Hildesheim, Domschatz, MS. 18. S. Beissel, *Des hl. Bernward Evangelienbuch im Dom zu Hildesheim* (1891), Taf. xviii.

[4] Goldschmidt, *Elfenbeinskulpturen* (2), no. 71, Taf. xxiii. A silver plaque, now in the church at Susteren, of the tenth century, has a long table with Christ central flanked by an apostle on each side. Christ holds up the Host so this is also an Institution scene. See *Art Mosan*, introduction et notes archéologiques de J. de Borchgrave d'Altena (Paris, 1951), pl. 4, and for the date *Das erste Jahrtausend*, Tafelband, ed. V. Elbern (1962), 344–5.

the St Augustine's Gospels and the Raganaldus Sacramentary where Christ is at the centre of the round table are 'Institution' not 'Betrayal' scenes.[1]

This indicates that it was not only a desire for symmetry that placed Christ in the middle of the table in this new version. And in the Mont St Michael miniature at least, the hierarchical character of the scene is emphasized by the strictly frontal pose of Christ who looks not at Judas but straight before Him, and is larger in scale than the Apostles.

It is in another Ottonian Gospel Book that the nearest precursor of our miniature is found. The Golden Gospels of Henry III, made at Echternach in 1045–6, has, in fact, two 'long table' Last Supper scenes.[2] On fol. 52 there is an 'Institution of the Eucharist' illustrating St Matthew, in which Christ is central and larger in scale
Pl. 35*b* than His Apostles who flank him on either side. On fol. 153 illustrating St John, Christ, again central, hands the sop to Judas who sits, however, at the second place on His left. Other early examples of the central Christ looking straight in front of
Pl. 35*d* Him, are in the Sacramentary of St Maur-des-Fossés[3] and the Vysihrad Gospels[4] of the second half of the eleventh century, and on the bronze doors of San Zeno at Verona of *c.*1030.[5]

Judas's position isolating him from the Apostles in front of the table and placing him opposite Christ in a dramatic confrontation seems also to be a Western innovation. It is found in various Ottonian manuscripts in which Christ sits at the left of the table still.[6] Judas naturally approaches from the right, therefore. He still approaches from the right on the San Zeno doors as if Christ were at the left end of the table not in the centre. In the Prague Gospels where again Christ is central, Judas sits somewhat to the right. This is rather a development of the 'sigma' table tradition where Judas is shown at the end on the right.[7]

Pl. 35*d* In the St Maur and our manuscript, however, Judas approaches from the left where it is possible for Christ to give him the sop with His right hand and where he balances the leaning figure of St John. Thus the Mont St Michel artist is amongst

1 A Norman Institution of the Eucharist is to be found in Rouen, Bib. Mun., MS. A.85(467), St Augustine on St John, second half eleventh century. It has the same peculiarity of only Christ's feet appearing below the table. See Pl. 35*e*.

2 Escorial, Cod. Vetr. 17 (not mentioned by Loomis). A. Boeckler, *Das goldene Evangelienbuch Heinrichs III* (1933), Taf. 61 and 150.

3 Paris, Bib. Nat., Latin 12054, fol. 79. Swarzenski, *Monuments*, pl. 71.

4 Prague, Univ. Library, MS. XIV A.13, fol. 38v. *St Albans Psalter*, pl. 111 f.

5 F. Winzinger, *Das Tor von San Zeno in Verona* (1958), Taf. 9.

6 The earliest example of this confrontation is in the Stuttgart Psalter but there is no table. See *St Albans Psalter*, p. 58 ff. Ottonian examples with tables (some of which are round) separating the two figures, are in the Bernward Gospels, the Aachen Golden altar, the Sacramentary, Bamberg, Staatl. Bibl., Lit. 1, Munich, Bayr. Staatsbibl., Clm.4452 etc.

7 As in Byzantine examples, e.g. the Chludoff Psalter, Moscow, Hist. Mus., Cod. Gr. 129, fol. 40.

the first to weld the central Christ at the long table and the isolated Judas into a coherent scene.

The figure of St John leaning on Christ's breast, illustrating St John XIII, v. 23 also only begins to appear in the eleventh century in Ottonian examples.[1] The Pl. 35*b* pose of St John in the Mont St Michel miniature, with his head resting on his right hand and his left hand on the table, is very close to the San Zeno and St Maur representations, though in the latter the eyes are open. Pl. 35*d*

Lastly two odd features of the Mont St Michel picture may be commented on, of which the first is the roll of material on the far side of the table as it were on the Apostles' knees. This would appear to be a survival from earlier representations of 'sigma' or round table types. Such a 'bolster' object appears in the San Vitale mosaics for instance.[2]

Secondly only Christ's feet appear beneath the table, though the Apostles are upright and thus sitting not lying. This connects the miniature closely with the Escorial Gospels, fol. 52, where there is a footstool below Christ but neither His nor the Apostles' feet are shown. In the St. Maur-des-Fossés manuscript which closely resembles the Morgan page in other respects the feet are shown of the Pl. 35*d* Apostles on the right but not on the left.

## *Fol. 61v. Preface to the Canon. 'Vere Dignum' monogram* Pl. 36

The scheme of the angels supporting the cross bar of the *ω* monogram appears to be unique to this date, and I know only one later example, whose provenance is uncertain.[3] Late in the tenth century and in the 11th century the *ω* monogram begins to be as it were historiated with the 'Majestas' Christ or sometimes the

[1] e.g. Bernward Gospels; Pericope Book given to Echternach in 1046 by Henry III, Bremen, Staatsbibl., MS. B.21; Escorial Gospels; Vysihrad Gospels. Dobbert thought this an Eastern introduction and quoted Ferentillo as the earliest example of it. However, these frescoes are of the twelfth, not the ninth century as Dobbert thought. See A. Grabar, *Romanesque Painting* (1958), 51. The significance of the Gospel text is of course lost when the Apostles sit upright at the table rather than recline at the triclinium and it is possible, therefore, that there is an earlier Eastern prototype behind the Ottonian examples.

[2] See also the fresco of Vibia on the Appian Way, illustrated by Loomis, where the figures lie on the ground. A kind of cloth draped over the knees appears in the St Gall antiphonary, Stiftsbibl., Cod. 390, 986–1017, in the Codex Egberti, Trier Stadtbibl. MS. 24, fol. 100v, and in the Otbert Psalter, Boulogne, Bib. Mun., MS. 20, fol. 103. The cable pattern in the St Maur-des-Fossés miniature is probably a schematization of this feature.

[3] This is a single leaf from a Missal of the second half of the twelfth century made perhaps in eastern France or western Germany. See Martin Breslauer, 2 Weymouth Street, London, W.1, *Catalogue no. 94* (1961), no. 37 (illustrated on the cover). I am grateful to Mr Breslauer for finding me a copy of this catalogue. The leaf is now in a private collection.

the Lamb flanked by angels. Such representations illustrated the actual words of the Preface: '. . . majestatem tuam laudant angeli'.[1]

The emphasis, however, here is on the Cross. And a twelfth-century list of relics received from Apulia, added to Avranches MS. 163, includes a relic of the True Cross. Though there is no indication of when the abbey received this, in view of the present miniature and the equally unique miniature of Heraclius on folio 155$^v$ it is hard to resist the conclusion that the relic was at Mont St Michel already in the eleventh century.[2]

It is therefore interesting to find that the adoring angels flanking (but not necessarily supporting) the cross is a theme specifically connected with the cult of the True Cross, the *Crux gemmata* set up by Constantine on Golgotha. This is seen for instance on two of the surviving sixth-century pilgrim flasks which were filled with Holy oil at the site, and which are now preserved at Bobbio.[3] Another example occurs on a late sixth-century glass cup which has been shown by Professor Elbern actually to be a chalice.[4]

1 For the symbolism of the monogram, the divine and human nature of Christ joined by the Cross, see A. Ebner, *Quellen und Forschungen zur Geschichte und Kunstgeschichte des Missale Romanum. Iter Italicum* (reprinted 1957) 432 ff. A late tenth-eleventh century example of the Majestas combined with the monogram is Monte Cassino MS. 426, fol. 31 from Monte Cassino. An early eleventh-century instance from north Italy is now Novara, Bib. Cap., Cod. LIV. Two Northern examples are Cambridge, Corpus Christi College MS. 422, Wormald, *English Drawings*, no. 14, mid-eleventh century, Anglo-Saxon; and Paris, Bib. Nat., Latin 819, fol. 9$^v$, Sacramentary of St Bertin made at Liège, second quarter eleventh century, *MSS. à peintures*, no. 121. A large collection of monograms has been made by R. E. Kaske, 'Dante's "DXV" and "Veltro",' *Traditio*, XVII (1961), 185–254. I am indebted to Miss Rosalie Green of the Princeton Iconographic Index for this reference.

2 The abbey later possessed a number of relics of the cross. See J. Dubois, *Millénaire* (1), 507, 526, 528. Dom Dubois does not discuss the list in MS. 163. The other relics listed are of Sts Sebastian, Marcus, Marcellianus, Felix Papa, Eremes (sic), Cosmas and Damian, Chrisanthus and Darias, ashes of St Laurence, Sepulchrum Domini.

3 A. Grabar, *Les Ampoules de Terre Sainte* (1958), Bobbio 1 and 2. Two angels flank a cross on a sixth-century silver dish, Stroganov collection, Hermitage, Leningrad. On the throne of St Mark in Venice two figures flank the Cross who are probably Evangelists. A. Grabar, 'La Sedia di San Marco a Venise', *Cahiers Archéologiques*, vii (1954), 19 ff. for a discussion of these and other examples. For the twelfth century True Cross reliquaries with flanking angels, see H. Swarzenski, 'The Kneeling "Acolyte" in the Morgan Library', *Studies in Art and Literature for Belle da Costa Greene*, ed. D. Miner (1954), 179.

4 V. H. Elbern, 'Ein christliches Kultgefäss aus Glas in der Dumbarton Oaks Collection', *Jahrbuch der Berliner Museen*, Neue Folge, iv (1962), 17 ff., with other examples of angels flanking the cross. See also *R.D.K.* s.v. 'Engel', IV D., 'Engel als himmlische Liturgen' and V, 'Engel als Subdiakone und Diakone' for the liturgy on earth as a reflection of the Heavenly liturgy performed by the Angels in Heaven. St Gregory says in the Dialogues, IV, 58 that no-one can doubt '. . . in ipsa immolationis hora ad sacerdotis vocem coelos aperiri, in illo Jesu Christi mysterio angelorum choros adesse'.

The angels, therefore, could be incorporated in the ω monogram, not only as a reference to the abbey's relic, but also in a liturgical context to demonstrate, as they do on the chalice, the inseparable connection between Passion and Resurrection by recalling the topography of Golgotha where the *Crux gemmata* stood close by the Holy Sepulchre.[1]

A connection with these representations is by no means impossible, for pilgrimages from Normandy to the Holy Land were frequent enough. Duke Robert went out in 1035 and Radulfus, abbot of Mont St Michel, died on his return or on his way back in 1058.[2] However, a very close parallel much nearer to Normandy complicates the issue. This is an historiated initial 'M' which introduces the third *figura* of Rhabanus Maurus' treatise *de laudibus Sanctae Crucis*, in a manuscript Pl. 37*b*
written at St Germain-des-Prés and decorated by Ingelardus.[3] Rhabanus says that the orders of holy angels rightly correspond in name and number to the Holy Cross, since not only were they present at the Nativity and the Temptation, '... cum ... verum etiam in tempore passionis et resurrectionis ejus, debito ei officio ipsos affuisse manifeste narret (*sc.* sacer Evangelii textus)'.[4]

Here then the representation has a close connection with the text which might suggest that it was first used at St Germain and adapted at Mont St Michel subsequently. A treatise on the Cross of which his abbey preserved a relic, and which mentions the orders of Angels and St Michael to whom his abbey was dedicated, must have been read with attention by any monk of Mont St Michel. That a St Germain monk would have made the opposite transference would appear less likely.

Nevertheless the scheme makes a very unconvincing 'M' which indicates that the adaptation was from, rather than to, the ω monogram. And this is made almost certain by the interlacing of the upright and vertical shafts of the St Germain 'M'. For this detail cannot come from any Eastern model such as the pilgrim flasks, but must copy the ω monogram where the interlacing is explained because the initial is taken from a model in an illuminated manuscript in which interlace was a major stylistic component.[5]

[1] For the place of the Cross on Mount Golgotha see V. H. Elbern, 'Das Relief der Gekreuzigten in der Mellebaudis-Memorie zu Poitiers', *Jahrbuch der Berliner Museen*, Neue Folge ii (1961), 164 ff., with further literature. There may also be some reference to the controversy between Berengar and Lanfranc concerning the Real Presence. The Crucifixion on the rood screen in Lanfranc's cathedral at Canterbury was flanked by two Cherubim. See P. Brieger, 'England's Contribution to the Origin and Development of the Triumphal Cross', *Mediaeval Studies*, iv (1942), 85–96, with a further discussion of Angels appearing with the cross.

[2] Herveus, archdeacon of Ste Croix, Orléans, brought back relics of the *sepulchrum domini*, *c.*1033. See 'Un pelèrinage à Jérusalem', *Bibliothèque de l'école de Chartes*, li (1890), 206.

[3] Paris, Bib. Nat., Latin 11685, fol. 11.

[4] *P.L.* cvii, 161.

[5] See below p. 164.

At Mont St Michel a reference to the abbey's relic of the Cross was no doubt intended, and it seems likely that the artist was aware of the origin of the representation of the Cross adored by Angels in the veneration of the True Cross at Jerusalem.[1]

## Pl. 38 *Fol. 66*$^{v}$*. Easter Sunday. Christus super aspidem*[2]

The 'Christus super aspidem' representation illustrates verse 13 of Psalm 90 (Vulgate): 'thou shalt tread upon the lion and the adder', 'super aspidem et basiliscum ambulabis et conculcabis leonem et draconem'. This type probably originated in Egypt being based on the representations of the god Horus. A number of early examples show the Christ flanked by angels, but an abbreviated version has no angels and only two beasts. A third division is the type of *Christus Miles*
Pl. 16g where the Christ carries the cross over His shoulder or even fights the dragon in armour.

The Mont St Michel representation is the abbreviated form with no angels and only two beasts. There are a series of Anglo-Saxon Psalters with miniatures of this type.[3] In all of them, however, Christ thrusts His staff into the mouth of the beast on the left, which twists its neck upward. This is a detail which seems to be taken from the ninth-century Utrecht Psalter where, moreover, the Christ is in movement as in most of the Anglo-Saxon manuscripts.[4]

The Mont St Michel Christ in its more static position is close to certain other of the Carolingian examples and particularly to the Lorsch ivory.[5] There the beasts' heads do not twist up but their tails to left and right extend as in our miniature. The beasts without twisting up heads and a more static pose for the Christ, remain

[1] Angels carrying the Cross also appear in Last Judgment scenes. See A. Boeckler, *Die Regensburg-Prüfeniger Buchmalerei des XII. und XIII. Jahrhunderts* (1924), 48 and n.2. Examples of symmetrical angels carrying the Cross are in the Burgfelden frescoes; on an Anglo-Saxon ivory, second half of the tenth century, Talbot Rice, pl. 32; and on the twelfth-century capitals from La Daurade, P. Mesplé, *Toulouse, Musée des Augustins. Les sculptures romanes* (Inventaire des collections publiques françaises, v) (1961), no. 119.

[2] F. Saxl, 'The Ruthwell Cross', *Journal of the Warburg and Courtauld Institutes*, vi (1943), 1–19.

[3] Bury Psalter, Rome, Vatican, MS. Reginensis Lat. 12; Oxford, Bodleian Library, MS. Douce 296, fol. 40$^{v}$; Cambridge, University Library, MS. Ff. 1.23, fol. 195; New York, Morgan Library, Arenberg Gospels, MS. 869, fol. 13$^{v}$; London, Brit. Mus., Cotton MS. Tiberius C.VI, fol. 114$^{v}$. These are all of the eleventh century. See F. Saxl and R. Wittkower, *British Art and the Mediterranean* (1948), for reproductions.

[4] Utrecht, University Library, fol. 53$^{v}$. Dewald, op. cit., pl. lxxxiv.

[5] Rome, Vatican, Museo Sacro. Exh., *Karl der Grosse*, no. 521, Abb. 96.

the characteristics of the continental type.[1] Perhaps the closest example is in the Werden Psalter of the second half of the eleventh century.[2] However, an earlier Anglo-Saxon model cannot be ruled out, since some of the earliest continental examples without the twisting beasts, probably go back to Insular prototypes, for which the Ruthwell and Bewcastle crosses, which also have a static Christ, are a witness.[3] In that case again the artists could be using earlier rather than contemporary Anglo-Saxon sources and the typical Anglo-Saxon border to be discussed below, supports this conclusion. Pl. 39*a*

Some further evidence can be brought forward. The Latin commentators on the Psalms connected this verse 13 of Psalm 90 with the Temptation in the Wilderness. Eusebius in his commentary on this Psalm goes further and links the Easter

[1] e.g. metal cover of the Poussay Gospels, Paris, Bib. Nat., Latin 10514, F. Steenbock, *Der Kirchliche Prachteinband im frühen Mittelalter* (1965), no. 54, Abb. 76; Shrine of St Hadelin of Celles, now at Visé, Liège work, Swarzenski, *Monuments*, fig. 226; Paris, Bib. Nat., Latin 11685, fol. 9, by Ingelardus of St Germain (the Christ is in movement), see Pl. 39*b*; Boulogne, Bib. Mun., MS. 20, fol. 101, St Bertin Psalter; Rheims, Bib. Mun., MS. 295, fol. 30, Homiliary, initial to Augustine, de Symbolo (referred to by Saxl as MS. 245 and as a Sacramentary). These are all of the eleventh century. Of the tenth century is Einsiedeln, Stadtbibl., HS. 176, p. 102, Bede on Apocalypse. A. Bruckner, *Scriptoria Medii Aevi Helvetica*, v (1943), Taf xi. Inserted in the wall of the church of Notre Dame at Maastricht is a stone slab with a 'Christus super aspidem' in which Christ thrusts his cross into the mouth of an *upturned* beast's head. See A. Baird, 'The shrine of St Hadelin, Visé', *Burlington Magazine*, xxxi (1917), 20, pl. iig. I do not know the date of this relief but it may have at least an early model.

[2] Berlin, Staatsbibl., Preuss. Kulturbeste, MS. theol. lat. fol. 358. *Das erste Jahrtausend*, Tafelband (1962) Taf. 389.

[3] For instance the Genoels Eldern Ivory, exh., *Karl der Grosse*, no. 534, Abb. 104. A drawing on the end leaf of the Trier Apocalypse, Trier Stadtbibl. 31, fol. 75, Goldschmidt, *Elfenbeinsskulpturen* (1), Abb. 5. Rome, Vatican, Pal. Lat. 220, fol. iv, St Augustine's Sermons. The border in Morgan 641 is very Anglo-Saxon in style and one Anglo-Saxon example without twisting-up beasts can be quoted – the Alchester ivory tau cross in the British Museum, of the early eleventh century. See also M. Schapiro, 'The religious meaning of the Ruthwell Cross', *Art Bulletin*, xxvi (1944), 232–245, for the Beasts not as conquered but as worshipping Christ in the desert. As such they would not, of course, have twisted-up heads, but our miniature must contain the idea of the Conquest of Death and the Devil by the Saviour. See also the observations of T. Buddensieg, 'Die Basler Altertafel Heinrichs II', *Wallraf-Richartz Jahrbuch*, xix (1957) 140 ff. He sees the later eleventh-century examples (including the Morgan 641 'Christus super aspidem', which he reproduces Abb. 83, and the other examples cited above in notes) as reflections of an earlier model. This he also suggests may be the model behind the Christ of the Basel golden altar now in the Cluny Museum, Paris. He also adds the following eleventh-century examples of the 'Christus super aspidem' of the static type: Paris, Bib. Nat., Latin 12197, fol. 66, St Augustine sermons from St Maur-des-Fossés and Latin 13392, St. Gregory's Sermons, from Corbie; Karlsruhe, Bad. Landesbibl. Cod. CLXI, eleventh century Bavarian, his Abb. 84; ivory carving at Dresden from the Belgian or Rhineland area, *c.*1100, Goldschmidt, *Elfenbeinskulpturen* (2), no. 168, Taf. xlviii. Cambridge, Trinity College, MS. B. 1. 16, contains another Norman example, probably by Hugo Pictor.

victory with the Temptation when he says that Christ 'shows that by His Passion He had accomplished what He began in the Temptation'.[1] Later Honorius Augustodunensis interpreted the four beasts as Sin, Death, Antichrist and the Devil.[2] The type was therefore not inappropriate for the Easter victory.

Eusebius' commentary (which was, of course, in Greek), is not so likely, however, to have been known at Mont St Michel as the Commentary on the Psalms of St Augustine. Now in at least one surviving Anglo-Saxon Psalter a full-page miniature of the 'Christus super aspidem' precedes Psalm 51[3] and St Augustine commenting on Psalm 51 speaks of Christ's victory over death.[4] The Norman artist, it may be suggested, put together a 'Christus super aspidem' from a Psalter – we have seen other evidence that an Anglo-Saxon Psalter belonging to Archbishop Robert was known at Mont St Michel – and his knowledge of St Augustine's commentary, in order to justify the use of this subject in the initial of the Easter collect.

## Pl. 39*c* *Fol. 75*ᵛ*. The Ascension*[5]

This miniature follows the Western tradition of representing the scene by which Christ mounts into Heaven as if climbing the slope of the Mount of Olives. At the bottom of the mandorla there is only a faint suggestion of the mountain on
Pl. 39*d* which Christ walks in the Munich ivory of *c*.400[6] or the Drogo Sacramentary.[7] The reference, therefore, to the specific place where the rock with Christ's footprint was shown to the pilgrims, has almost vanished.

The mandorla does not appear in this type in the West until the second half of the tenth century. In the Eastern[8] and Byzantine representations it surrounds the frontal enthroned Christ and it occurs thus in the West in the Athelstan Psalter of the early tenth century.[9] Combined with the profile mounting Christ it appears

1 Migne, *P.G.* xxiii, 1166.

2 *P.L.* clxxii, 913 ff.

3 Oxford, Bodleian Library, MS. Douce 296, fol. 40ᵛ. Talbot Rice, pl. 75a.

4 *P. L.* xxxvi, 600.

5 E. T. Dewald, 'The Iconography of the Ascension', *American Journal of Archaeology*, xix (1915), 277–319; M. Schapiro, 'The Image of the disappearing Christ', *Gazette des Beaux Arts*, 6e ser. xxiii (1943), 135–152.

6 Munich, Bayr. Nat. Museum. Volbach, *Elfenbeinarbeiten*, no. 110.

7 Paris, Bib. Nat., Latin 9428, fol. 71ᵛ. Köhler (3), Taf. 88b.

8 e.g. the Rabbula Gospels, Florence, Bibl. Laurenziana, MS. Plut.1.56, Cecchelli et. al., op. cit., fol. 13ᵛ and on the Monza Ampullae. Grabar, op. cit., Monza nos. 1, 2, 10, 11, etc.

9 London, Brit. Mus., Cotton MS. Galba A.XVIII, fol. 120ᵛ. E. G. Millar, *English illuminated manuscripts from the Xth to the XIIIth centuries* (1926), pl. 2c.

both in the Benedictional of St Ethelwold[1] and the Codex Egberti.[2] Pl. 39*e*

The Virgin though not specifically mentioned as present either in St Luke, XXIV, vv. 50–53 or in Acts, I, vv. 9–12 is shown here as was common. Her position is again closer to that of the Benedictional of St Ethelwold, than to the central and frontal *orans* Virgin of the earlier Eastern tradition, or the profile figure of the later Byzantine versions.[3]

The angels in the Rabbula Gospels, in the Drogo Sacramentary, and in several Ottonian versions[4] are on the ground in the midst of the Apostles. Here, however, the heavenly sphere is clearly marked off from the earthly, and both Christ and Angels lifted above the latter, again as in the Benedictional.[5] Their pointing gestures, upwards with one hand, downwards with the other, are very similar. Pl. 39*e*

It can be seen from this that in the formal evolution of the scene from the Munich ivory onwards, Christ, the Mount of Olives and the hand of God become increasingly separated. The suggestion that Christ was either lifted up to heaven by the angels or as it were pulled up by the Hand of God had been already attacked by St Gregory the Great who insisted that Christ rose 'sua virtute'. But as late as the Codex Egberti, Christ still grips the hand of God. In the Mont St Michel miniature it only blesses from above.

## *Fol. 80*$^{v}$*. Pentecost*[6] Pl. 40*a*

The account of the coming of the Holy Spirit is found in Acts, II, vv. 1–41. Here again the artist combines various iconographic features from Anglo-Saxon and Ottonian sources, some of them very rare.

1 London, Brit. Mus., Add. MS. 49598, fol. 64$^{v}$. It is significant for the Mont St Michel's artist's use of earlier rather than contemporary Anglo-Saxon sources, that the type of the 'disappearing Christ' introduced in England in the late tenth century is not found here. See M. Schapiro op. cit. and also O. Pächt, *The Rise of Pictorial Narrative in twelfth-century England*, (1962), 8n.1.

2 Trier, Stadtbibl. MS. 24, fol. 101. Cf. also the three Fulda Sacramentaries mentioned earlier.

3 See *St Albans Psalter*, 95.

4 e.g. Sacramentary from St Gereon, Paris, Bib. Nat., Latin 817, fol. 72. P. Bloch, *Das Sakramentar von St Gereon* (1963), Taf, 13.

5 The Gospels, Paris, Bibl. de l'Arsenal, MS. 592, fol. 157$^{v}$ is similar in composition but Christ has no mandorla and turns somewhat frontally. Boinet, pl. cxii. The Prüm Gradual, Paris, Bib. Nat., Latin 9448, fol. 45$^{v}$ is also similar in the grouping of the Apostles below with the Virgin, and Christ above in a mandorla. There are no angels. The separation of the two spheres begins already in the Carolingian Bible of San Paolo, Rome, *St Albans Psalter*, pl. 119*d*.

6 A. Grabar, 'La schéma iconographique de la Pentecôte', *Seminarium Kondakovianum*, ii (1928), 223–39; S. Seeliger, *Pfingsten* (1958).

First the Holy Spirit, reaching the Apostles from the Dove as a thin ray, enters their mouths presumably to signify the gift of tongues. This is found only, it seems, in the two Anglo-Saxon Benedictionals, of St Ethelwold, and of Arch-
Pl. 40*d* bishop Robert now at Rouen.[1] The rays in these manuscripts are, however, more like tongues of flame. The thin rays are also uncommon in the West, but are found in the Poussay Gospels[2] of the late tenth century and are probably Byzantine in origin.[3]

There is no other reference to the gift of tongues and the preaching to the peoples, though the way the figures are raised from the level of the lower frame making a diamond shape with the architecture above is perhaps a last relic of the city wall which in the Carolingian San Paolo Bible[4] separates the Apostles from the crowds outside.

In formal arrangement the miniature resembles Ottonian examples of the tenth and eleventh century, for instance a Reichenau school Pericope book[5] or the St
Pl. 40*b* Gereon Sacramentary[6], which show the Apostles seated in a row not a circle. This
Pl. 40*c* is also the arrangement in the Cotton Tiberius Anglo-Saxon Psalter[7] of *c*.1050, in the Sacramentary of Robert of Jumièges,[8] and in the Hereford Troper,[9] but not in the two earlier Benedictionals, of Archbishop Robert and of St Ethelwold. The St Gereon miniature has an architectural canopy which the Anglo-Saxon examples lack and it is even similar in arrangement, with the pediment in the centre. The way the Apostles turn their heads upwards and are crowded at the sides, on the other hand, resembles rather the Tiberius Psalter and the Hereford Troper.

In most Ottonian examples and in the Anglo-Saxon miniatures, either St Peter alone or regardless of the text of Acts, St Peter and St Paul are at the centre of the scene. The Mont St Michel artist has followed this division into two groups, but

1 Rouen, Bib. Mun., MS. Y.7(369), fol. 29v. V. Leroquais, *Les Pontificaux manuscrits des bibliothèques publiques de France*, ii (1937), no. 189, pl. v. London, Brit. Mus., Add. MS. 49598, fol. 67v. There is no reference to the Gift of Tongues in the Benedictions.

2 Paris, Bib. Nat., Latin 10514, fol. 69v. They do not enter the Apostles mouths. H. V. Sauerland, A. Haseloff, *Der Psalter Erzbischof Egberts von Trier* (1901), Taf. 56.1.

3 For example they appear in the Chludoff Psalter, Moscow, Hist. Museum, Cod. Gr.129 and in many later works.

4 Rome, San Paolo fuori le mure, fol. 292v. See *St Albans Psalter*, pl. 119 for comparisons.

5 Augsburg, Diözesan Museum, MS. 15.

6 Paris, Bib. Nat., Latin 817, fol. 77. Bloch, op. cit., Taf. 15. Cf. also two Fulda Sacramentaries, Göttingen, Universitätsbibl., Cod. theol. 231, fol. 82 and Bamberg, Staatl. Bibl., Lit. 1, fol. 84v.

7 London, Brit. Mus., Cotton M.S. Tiberius C.VI, fol. 15v. F. Wormald, *Walpole Society*, xxxviii (1960–2), pl. 19.

8 Rouen, Bib. Mun., MS. Y.6(274), fol. 84v. Talbot Rice, pl. 54*b*.

9 London, Brit. Mus., Cotton MS. Caligula A.XIV, fol. 31. Talbot Rice, pl. 67*b*.

set the Virgin who, though not specifically mentioned in Acts, is first shown in this position in the Rabbula Gospels and later in the San Paolo Bible, in the place of St Paul. Here it seems that he has adopted an Ottonian innovation for the Virgin similarly placed occurs in an Antiphonary and a Gospel Book both from Prüm.[1]

## *Fol. 119ᵛ and Fol. 120. 24th June. The Nativity of St John the Baptist*[2]

Pls. 40*e*, 41*a*

The account of the birth of the Baptist is found in St Luke I, vv. 5–25 and vv. 57–80. It was illustrated by a cycle of at least four scenes which were known in the West in the ninth century. These were the Annunication by the Archangel Gabriel to Zacharias in the Temple at the hour of incense, Zacharias' appearance to the people praying outside after he had been struck dumb, the Nativity of the Baptist, and the naming of the child eight days later.[3] Three of these episodes are represented here.

First the appearance of Gabriel to Zacharias. The only surviving Western representation of this which is pre-Carolingian, in the St Augustine's Gospels,[4] shows the angel on the left. Of the Carolingian versions three preserve this arrangement[5] but already in the Corbie Psalter[6] the angel is on the right as he is also in the Drogo Sacramentary.[7] This becomes the normal arrangement in the tenth and eleventh

[1] Paris, Bib. Nat., Latin 9448, fol. 49, and Manchester, Rylands Library, MS. 7, fol. 85. See *St Albans Psalter*, 67 ff. (pl. 119*c* is of Morgan 641). R. Schilling, 'Das Ruotpertus-Evangelistar aus Prüm', *Studien zur Buchmalerei und Goldschmiedekunst des Mittelalters. Festschrift für K. H. Usener*, Marburg (1967), 143–54, Abb. 16.

[2] W. Köhler, 'An illustrated Evangelistary of the Ada School and its model', *Journal of the Warburg and Courtauld Institutes*, xv (1952), 48–66; M. Schapiro, review of W. Köhler, *Die Karolingischen Miniaturen II: Die Hofschule Karls des Grossen*, 1958, in *Art Bulletin*, xlii (1960), 301–2.

[3] The whole cycle of four scenes is found in the Pericope book of Henry II from Bamberg, Munich, Bayr. Staatsbibl., Clm.4452, fol. 149ᵛ–150. G. Leidinger, *Miniaturen aus Handschriften der Kgl. Hof. – und Staatsbibliothek in München. 5. Das Perikopenbuch Kaiser Heinrichs II* (1914), Taf. 28–29.

[4] Cambridge, Corpus Christi College, MS. 286, fol. 129ᵛ. F. Wormald, *The Miniatures in the Gospels of St Augustine* (1954), pl. viii.

[5] A fragment pasted in London, Brit. Mus., Cotton MS. Claudius B.V. See Köhler, op. cit. Also Soissons and Harley Gospels. Schapiro, op. cit., also refers to a lost miniature from London, Brit. Mus., MS. Royal I.E.VI, an eighth-century Insular manuscript. The earlier arrangement would be explicable by analogy with the Annunication. But why the change was made is so far unexplained.

[6] Amiens, Bib. Mun., MS. 18, fol. 136. Köhler, op. cit., pl. 14*b*.

[7] Paris, Bibl. Nat., Latin 9428, fol. 83. Köhler (3), Taf. 89*b*. On fol. 84 is another initial with the birth and the naming of the Baptist, Köhler (3), Taf. 89c.

centuries.[1] The angel in our miniature does not carry a staff as he does in the Carolingian versions, nor do the buildings of the Temple survive or the details of the Priest's dress. In the fragment in Cotton manuscript Claudius B.V and the Drogo initial the crowds waiting outside are included. They are not shown in our miniature.

The Nativity is shown very similarly to the birth of Christ except that the ox and ass are missing. It is close to the miniature in the Benedictional of St Ethel-
Pl. 41*b* wold,[2] but there the Nativity is at the top and below Zacharias writes on a tablet
the name of the infant watched by the group of three who lift their hands signify-
Pl. 40*e* ing their question to him as to the child's name. This last episode has been moved to the initial 'D' on fol. 120 where, however, it is abbreviated since only Zacharias is shown. He is frontally enthroned instead of sitting in profile.

The object in his hand is a stylus. To see this it is necessary to compare it with the Benedictional miniature where Zacharias writes with a still clearly recognizable stylus on a wax tablet. This was becoming incomprehensible to the artists of the time as is shown by the Ivrea Sacramentary[3] where the wax tablet with its handle is carefully copied but the stylus has become a quill pen. The Mont St Michel artist has distorted both objects.

## Pl. 43 *Fol. 122$^{v}$. 29th June. St Peter and St Paul. The martyrdom of St Peter*[4]

The account of the Martyrdom of St Peter is told in Ch. 33 ff. of the Acts of Peter written probably by a resident in Asia Minor not later than A.D. 200 and in various later Acts.[5] These accounts tell of St Peter's request to be crucified upside-down but they are ambiguous as to whether he was nailed or tied to the cross.

1 Of the sixteen examples quoted by Köhler (not including Morgan 641) only two preserve the old arrangement. The examples mostly occur in Ottonian manuscripts, with one from Monte Cassino, one from Stavelot, and three from St Bertin. The earlier Eastern examples have the angel on the left.

2 London, Brit. Mus., Add. MS. 49598, fol. 92$^{v}$. Elizabeth in Morgan 641 is on a bed more resembling that of the Benedictional Nativity, fol. 15$^{v}$, where, however, the Virgin faces the opposite way, and also the bed recedes diagonally as in the Metz tradition. The bed is shown as if placed parallel to the picture plane in the Sacramentary of Robert of Jumièges, fol. 32$^{v}$.

3 Ivrea, Bib. Cap., Cod. LXXXVI, fol. 88. Magnani, op. cit., tav. xxii. The Mont St Michel stylus resembles the Drogo Sacramentary one.

4 T. Sauvel, 'Le Crucifiement de Saint Pierre', *Bulletin Monumental*, xcvii (1938), 337–52.

5 *The Apocryphal New Testament*, translated M. R. James (1953 corr. edn.), p. 300 ff., especially ch. 36–39.

In two early representations he is, as here, nailed to the cross, the Paris St Gregory Nazianzus[1] and the Drogo Sacramentary.[2] In both Nero (or Agrippa?) is present to superintend the execution. The Mont St Michel artist had adapted the Drogo scheme keeping only the one bending executioner and adding a crowd of mourners. These presumably represent 'the whole multitude of the brethren . . . both of rich and poor, orphans and widows, weak and strong' who ran together 'desirous to see and to rescue St Peter' when they heard of his condemnation by Agrippa. Mourners are not common, but they do occur in the Fulda Sacramentaries,[3] which, however, also show the beheading of St Paul.[4] The Göttingen and Udine manuscripts also contain the episode of Simon Magus, and in them the executioners are absent. St Peter is fully clothed as at Mont St Michel. Again therefore the Mont St Michel artist seems to be combining features of different schemes. Pl. 42c Pl. 42e

## *Fol. 142$^v$. 15th August. The Assumption of the Blessed Virgin Mary*[5] Pl. 42a

The earliest surviving representation in the West of the Assumption is the Sens Cathedral brocade of the eighth century.[6] Above a row of figures carrying crosses the Virgin in the *orans* position is flanked by two angels, whilst two other angels prostrate themselves below her feet. There is no mandorla. The inscription, without which this might well be thought an Ascension, runs 'Cum transisset Maria Mater Domina de Apostolis'.

Another early representation is that on the ivory book cover carved at St Gall

[1] Paris, Bib. Nat., Cod. Gr. 510, fol. 32$^v$. H. Omont, *Facsimiles des miniatures des plus anciens manuscrits grecs de la Bibliothèque Nationale* (1902), pl. xxii.

[2] Paris, Bib. Nat., Latin 9428, fol. 86. Köhler (3), Taf. 89d. Cf. also St Peter nailed to the cross in the Utrecht Psalter, fol. 19, Dewald, op. cit., pl. xxxi.

[3] Göttingen, Universitätsbibl., Cod. theol. fol. 231, fol. 93. Udine, Bib. Cap., Cod. 76$^v$, fol. 48$^v$. Bamberg, Staatl. Bibl., Lit. 1, fol. 135. Mourners were present in the scene painted in the Church of Sta Maria in Barbara in Rome of which there is a drawing by Ciampini, *Vetera Monumenta* (1690), pl. xxv, and which dated according to him to the fifth or sixth century. But in this painting St Peter is tied to the cross as he is in the Benedictional of St Ethelwold, fol. 45,$^v$ and in the Prüm Gradual, Paris, Bibl. Nat., Latin 9448, fol. 56, for instance. In both these manuscripts, the martyrdom of St Paul is also shown. Goldschmidt, *German illumination* (2), pl. 68.

[4] Since St Paul was martyred on the same day as St Peter the two scenes are commonly combined.

[5] H. Feldbusch, *Die Himmelfahrt Mariae* (1951); O. Sinding, *Mariae Tod und Himmelfahrt* (1903); E. Staedel, *Ikonographie der Himmelfahrt Mariens* (1935); T. S. R. Boase, *The York Psalter* (1962).

[6] See Staedel, op. cit., Abb. 2. For the literary sources see bibliography under 'Assumption' in F. L. Cross, *The Oxford Dictionary of the Christian Church* (1957).

by Tuotilo about 900.[1] The Virgin in the *orans* position and with a mandorla stands in Paradise, and is flanked by two angels on each side. Ottonian versions combine the Byzantine iconography of the 'Koimesis' where Christ is present at the deathbed to receive the soul[2] with this tradition of the *orans* Virgin in various ways.[3]

Pl 42*d* A precursor of the Mont St Michel type is in a Sacramentary from Augsburg.[4] There the Virgin is in the *orans* position in a mandorla supported by two angels below and another two above. She has no palm and no crown, and the blessing hand of God is absent. Two other miniatures of the first half of the eleventh century are close, one in the Sacramentary of St Denis,[5] where the Virgin carries a
Pl. 42*b* palm, the other in a manuscript from Arras[6] where the hand of God appears above. The crown is found in none of these examples. It resembles the crown which descends from Heaven to the dying Virgin in the Benedictional of St Ethelwold.[7]

Since the death of the Virgin is not shown here, the miniature remains ambiguous as to the question of her bodily Assumption. For this is really a Virgin

1 Goldschmidt, *Elfenbeinskulpturen* (1), no. 163, Taf. lxxvi. Another ivory dated by Goldschmidt to *c.* 800 and assigned to Tours, has a female figure orans flanked by candlesticks, then four medallions of the Evangelist symbols and then to each side six half-length Apostles. This seems to be the lower part of an Ascension, but it could also be an Assumption. Clearly the iconography of the two is connected. Goldschmidt, *Elfenbeinskulpturen* (1), no. 180, now in Munich.

2 e.g. an ivory in the Hessisches Landesmuseum, Darmstadt of the late tenth century, reproduced by Feldbusch, op. cit., Taf. ii; the Prüm Gradual, Paris, Bib. Nat., Latin 9448, fol. $60^{v}$ is an adaptation of this iconography, adding a coronation. Goldschmidt, *German Illumination* (2), pl. 67.

3 e.g. Pericope book of Henry II, Munich, Bayr. Staatsbibl., Clm. 4452, a half-length Virgin orans in a medallion with the deathbed scene below, Leidinger, op. cit., Taf. 33; St Bernulf's Gospels, Utrecht, Archbishop's Museum. A. W. Byvanck, 'Les Principaux manuscrits à peintures conservés dans les collections publiques du royaume des Pays-Bas' (*Bull. Soc. francaise de repr. de manuscrits à peintures*) (1939), pl. xxxvii; Hildesheim Orationale, Domschatz 688, Staedel, op. cit., Abb. 10, now destroyed. A manuscript in the Cologne Dombibliothek, fol. 218 shows the half-length Virgin in a medallion supported by two angels with the hand of God above but no Koimesis below. The Prüm Gradual, Paris, Bib. Nat., Latin 9448 besides the Byzantine 'Koimesis' on fol. $60^{v}$ has also on fol. $62^{v}$ a seated *orans* Virgin in a globe mandorla but without crown or supporting angels.

4 London, Brit. Mus., Harley MS. 2908, fol. $123^{v}$, eleventh century.

5 Paris, Bib. Nat., Latin 9436, fol. 129. Probably made at St Vaast, Arras. Swarzenski, *Monuments*, fig. 175.

6 Arras, Bib. Mun., MS. 684(732), fol. $2^{v}$. Swarzenski, *Monuments*, fig. 173. There is also an example in the Sacramentary of St Maur-des-Fossés, Paris, Bib. Nat., Latin 12054, fol. $218^{v}$, an initial 'V'. *MSS. à peintures*, no. 241.

7 London, Brit. Mus., Add. MS. 49598, fol. $102^{v}$. For the crowned Virgin see G. Zarnecki, 'The Coronation of the Virgin on a capital from Reading Abbey', *Journal of the Warburg and Courtauld Institutes*, xiii (1950), 1–12. A seated crowned Virgin with flanking angels is in the Le Cateau Homiliary, Cambrai, Bib. Mun., MS. 528, fol. 169 and this iconography is not necessarily of Anglo-Saxon origin as the crowning of a seated Virgin by angels is found in the Bernward Gospels at Hildesheim, Domschatz, MS. 18. *Das erste Jahrtausend*, Tafelband ed. V. H. Elbern (1962), no. 417.

in Glory, as is the St Gall ivory, and in a sense the question does not arise. Nevertheless, the palm which was brought by the Angel announcing to the Virgin her approaching death, and the way the angels seem to lift the mandorla, refer to the Assumption. The miniature is therefore in a transitional stage, for it is in the twelfth century that certain representations of the bodily Assumption begin to be common, for instance that in a window at Angers,[1], or on a bas-relief from Autun.[2] There are two other Norman Assumptions of the eleventh century showing resemblances with our manuscript, one from the Jumièges Gospel Book, the other by Hugo Pictor.[3] Pl. 41*c*

## *Fol. 155*[v]*. 14th September. The Exaltation of the Holy Cross* Pl. 44

The Feast of the Exaltation of the Holy Cross celebrated originally the dedication of the Constantinian basilica of the Holy Sepulchre at Jerusalem where the Cross was placed after its Invention. Later it was connected with the Emperor Heraclius' return of the relic which had been captured by Chosroes, King of the Persians, to Jerusalem in 630.[4] It was introduced at Rome before the end of the seventh century when it is first mentioned by the biographer of Pope Sergius the Syrian, 687–701.

The source for the return of the Cross in the West was an homily by Rhabanus Maurus.[5] This adds to the Greek seventh-century sources[6] an account of how, when Heraclius approached the Golden Gate of Jerusalem on horseback and in his full regalia, a wall of stone fell miraculously. Terrified, he and his followers looked up and saw the sign of the Cross in flames in the sky and an angel standing above the gateway, who told Heraclius that he should approach meekly and on foot as Christ had entered the same gateway to His Passion. This is the scene in the miniature above, while below the emperor obeys the angel's command.

1 The Angers Virgin is crowned. R. de Fleury, *La Sainte Vierge* (1878), pl. 67. The Mont St Michel type survives in the twelfth century in one of a series of scenes of the death of the Virgin from S. Pierre-le-Puellier now in the Museum at Bourges. A miniature, not mentioned in the literature, from the Sacramentary of St Bertin, Paris, Bib. Nat., Latin 819, fol. 97[v] of the second quarter of the eleventh century, appears to show a bodily Assumption. *MSS. à peintures*, no. 121.

2 Autun, Musée Rolin, from the Cathedral.

3 London, Brit. Mus., Add. MS. 17739, fol. 17[v], crown but no sceptre, and Rouen, Bib. Mun., MS. Y.109(1408), fol. 4, both of the later eleventh century. For the latter see O. Pächt, 'Hugo Pictor', *Bodleian Library Record*, iii (1950), 96–103.

4 A. Frolow, 'La Vraie Croix et les expéditions d'Héraclius en Perse', *Revue des Études Byzantines*, xi (1953), 88–105.

5 'Reversio sanctae et gloriosissimae crucis domini nostri Jesu Christi', *P.L.* cx, 131.

6 Theophanes Nicephorus and George of Pisidia are the principal sources. For the latter see A. Pertusi, 'Giorgio di Pisidia Poemi. I. Panegirici Epici', *Studia Patristica et Byzantina*, vii (1960), 235–239, especially p. 237. I am grateful to Miss R. Barbour, Oxford, for these references.

Something will be said later of the style but one feature of the miniature which suggests an early prototype must be mentioned. In the lower section the figure of Heraclius is duplicated being shown both prostrate and walking and this indicates that in the original model at least the continuous system of narration was used – compare the encounter of Joshua and the Angel in the Joshua Rotulus.[1] Since the Rhabanus version appears to be the earliest text including the legend of the Angel's appearance, this presents a difficulty. Either there was an earlier version of the Emperor's vision current somewhere where the continuous system of narration was not yet abandoned, presumably in the East (this could not, of course, be before 630), or the miniature has been adapted by analogy with some other episode so illustrated. It is somewhat hard to believe that the system of continuous narrative was still sufficiently understood to be used in a new context at Fulda in the ninth century, when Rhabanus wrote his homily.

The subject is a very rare one and the few instances known to me to the end of the twelfth century (none of which antedate the Mont St Michel miniature) seem to give little help with this problem. Closest in date is an initial 'T', made up of the cross as it is carried by Heraclius in an Homiliary from Le Cateau of the
Pl. 45*c* second half of the eleventh century.[2] Two examples of the twelfth century are in the Stuttgart Passionale[3] and in an Homiliary Passionary probably from the region
Pl. 45*a* of Ravenna.[4] These three examples all introduce the Rhabanus Maurus homily. Two other twelfth-century examples are in the Salzburg Pericope book from St Erentrud of *c.*1140[5] and a Premonstratensian Missal of the second half of the twelfth
Pl. 45*b* century where the scene is woven into an 'M'.[6] All these twelfth-century scenes show Heraclius mounted but the angel is sometimes omitted.[7]. The Italian homiliary illustration is the closest to our miniature since the angel carries the cross

[1] Rome, Vatican, Cod. Palat. gr. 431. K. Weitzman, *The Joshua Roll. A work of the Macedonian Renaissance* (*Princeton Studies in Manuscript Illumination*, no. 3) (1948), fig. 13.

[2] Cambrai, Bib. Mun., MS. 528, fol. 195. *MSS. à peintures*, no. 176.

[3] Stuttgart, Landesbibl. Fol. 57, fol. 90v, 1120–1130. A. Boeckler, *Das Stuttgarter Passionale* (1923), Abb. 87. I am grateful to Miss Rosalie B. Green of the Princeton index for a list of representations of Heraclius.

[4] Rome, Vatican, Latin 1269, fol. 117. E. B. Garrison, 'An Emilio-Romagnole Homiliary-Passionary', *Studies in the History of Mediaeval Italian Painting*, iv. no. 4 (1962), 396–406, fig. 338.

[5] Munich, Bayr. Staatsbibl., Clm. 15903. G. Swarzenski, *Die Salzburger Malerei*, i (1913), 87, ii (1908), Abb. 195.

[6] Paris, Bib. Nat., Latin 833, fol. 223. Leroquais, *Sacramentaires*, i, 307.

[7] Other examples are: an enamel plaque formerly in the Grivault Collection, twelfth century(?), N.-X. Willemin, *Monuments Francais inédits*, 2e Livraison, 1814; the so-called Psalter of St Elisabeth, Cividale, Museo Archeologico Nazionale, Cod Sacri 7, twelfth-thirteenth century, *Mostra storica nazionale della miniatura*, Rome (1954), no. 152; a cycle of murals in Brunswick Cathedral referred to by Swarzenski, op. cit., 87 n.1, *c.* 1200(?).

there.[1] This is a detail contrary to Rhabanus' text, where the Cross appears in the sky. It may be an indication that there was another text describing the miracle, possibly an eastern one illustrated at an early date. Of the examples quoted only the Le Cateau homiliary hints at the two scenes of the Mont St Michel Sacramentary. It conflates them, since the angel addresses the Emperor who is already walking submissively with the cross.

One other Heraclius scene not shown at Mont St Michel is his beheading of Chosroes in his palace, a quite unhistorical addition narrated by Rhabanus. This occurs on a Liège reliquary triptych of *c.*1170 which is now preserved in the church of St Mary, Tongern[2] and in the Berthold Missal of *c.*1225.[3]

If the source of the miniature remains obscure the reason for its inclusion in the Sacramentary, it can be again suggested, was the Abbey's possession of a relic of the True Cross.[4]

## *Fol. 170. 1st November. All Saints*[5] Pl. 45*d*

The Feast of All Saints, Eastern in origin, was brought to the West in 610 when Pope Boniface IV dedicated the Pantheon to all the Martyrs to whom the Confessors were later added. In 835 Pope Gregory IV transferred the Feast from 13th May to 1st November and made it a universal Feast which now spread throughout the West where before it had been only Roman.

1 This made Celine Filipowicz-Osieczkowska who first published this manuscript, 'Notes sur la décoration des MSS. Vat. Lat. 1267–70', *Dawna Sztuka*, i, no. 2 (1938/9) suggest that the subject was the angel announcing his coming victory to Constantine. Garrison follows her in this. I am grateful to Dr A. Weigel who is studying the iconography of the Invention of the Cross for giving me his views on this problem. He thinks that the angel holding the Cross may result from a misunderstanding of Rhabanus' text or from an incorrect transmission involving the words 'aspiciens' and 'accipiens'. A connection with the angels in the initial, fol. 61$^{v}$, is perhaps also a possibility. A miniature in the English twelfth-century Psalter now in Copenhagen, Kgl. Bibl., Thott 143, 2°, fol. 13$^{v}$ suggests that our miniature, or one like it, was known in England. It shows an angel carrying a cross flying above the scene of Christ's entry to Jerusalem. A group of men in the city look up as in our miniature. M. Mackeprang et al., *Greek and Latin illuminated manuscripts in Danish Collections* (1921), 32.

2 Swarzenski, *Monuments*, fig. 424.

3 New York, Morgan Library, MS. 710, fol. 114. H. Swarzenski, *The Berthold Missal* (1943), pl. xxxiv.

4 See above, p. 146. Special provision for the Feast of the Exaltation was made in the Mont St Michel Ceremonial of the fourteenth-fifteenth century. See J. Lemarié, *Millénaire* (1), 344.

5 W. S. Cook, 'The earliest painted panels of Catalonia (II)', *Art Bulletin*, vi (1923–24), 38 ff.; F. Van der Meer, *Majestas Domini. Theophanies de l'Apocalypse dans l'art chrétien* (Studi di antichità christiana, xiii) (1938).

The iconography is therefore comparatively late. One tradition is based on Apocalypse scenes. Thus in two Sacramentaries from Fulda and a lectionary either rows of saints, or the figure of 'Ecclesia', adore the Lamb,[1] and in the Anglo-Saxon Sacramentary of Robert of Jumièges the saints stand in two rows below with the Lamb above in a round mandorla supported by two angels. To each side there is a frame medallion with bust figures.[2]

The Mont St Michel miniature differs from these. It is a Majestas picture of Christ enthroned to which the Saints are added in the frame medallions and actually inside the mandorla. This relates it to another representation that of the Athel-
Pl. 45*e* stan Psalter,[3] where Christ is enthroned in an oval mandorla and holds a cross in His left hand. He also shows His wounds and the Apocalyptic nature of the scene is stressed by the letters Alpha and Omega.[4] Christ is surrounded by three divisions distinguished by inscriptions, at the top the Martyrs, in the middle the Confessors, and, below, the Virgins. These three divisions also are seen in the Mont St Michel miniature, the Virgins at the top, the Confessors to the right, and the Martyrs in the remaining two medallions.

The Mont St Michel Christ is not enthroned as in the Athelstan Psalter,[5] but sits in the 'globe mandorla' whose origins, a conflation of the Eastern mandorla with the Western globe of the Heavens, have been examined by Cook.[6] Variations of this, using also the Eastern 'rainbow arch' as here, are not rare at this date. Christ rests His feet on the ball of the world, another feature found already in Carolingian models,[7] and the types of Evangelist symbols, spreading outwards but turning back, and the Eagle with a scroll are originally a Tours school invention.[8]

1 Göttingen, Universitätsbibl., Cod. theol. fol. 231, fol. 111; Udine, Bib. Cap., Cod. 76, fol. 67v; Aschaffenburg, Hofbibl. MS. 2. Zimmermann, op. cit., fig. 19.

2 Rouen, Bib. Mun., MS. Y.6(274), fol. 84v. Leroquais, *Sacramentaires*, pl. xxiii.

3 London, Brit. Mus., Cotton MS. Galba A.XVIII, fol. 21. See also fol. 2v. Millar, op. cit., pl. 2*a*, *b*. The elements of an All Saints miniature are contained in the frame roundels of the miniature of St John in the Grimbald Gospels, London, Brit. Mus., MS. Add. 34890. Talbot Rice, pl. 56*a*.

4 This also connects with the Eastern type of enthroned Ascension an example of which is found on fol. 120v. A Carolingian version of the Saints worshipping the Majestas is in a fragment of a Sacramentary, Paris, Bib. Nat., Latin 1141, Boinet, pl. cxxxi-iv. Wormald points to similarities between this manuscript and the Benedictional of St Ethelwold, see below, 161 n.1.

5 The St Germain-des-Prés version also has an enthroned Christ, Paris, Bib. Nat., Latin 11751, fol. 59v. Deslandres, op. cit., pl. 2. See Pl. 45*f*.

6 W. S. Cook, op. cit. A Cologne ivory of *c*. 1000 shows St Gereon and St Victor crowned by Christ enthroned in a globe mandorla, other saints are below. H. Schnitzler, *Das Schnütgen Museum*, Cologne (1961), no. 8.

7 The earliest Western example is the book cover of the Codex Aureus of St Emmeram, Munich, Bayr. Staatsbibl., Clm. 14000.

8 See F. Van der Meer, op. cit., and also M. Schapiro, 'Two Romanesque drawings in Auxerre and some iconographic problems', *Studies in Art and Literature for Belle da Costa Greene*, ed. D. Miner (1954), 331–349.

The placing of the Majestas in the initial 'O' of the collect resembles closely the Benedictional of St Ethelwold initial for Trinity Sunday.[1]

*Historiated initials with figures of Saints*

| | | | |
|---|---|---|---|
| fol. 5 | 27th December | St John the Evangelist | |
| fol. $14^v$ | 21st January | St Agnes | |
| fol. 16 | 25th January | Conversion of St Paul | |
| fol. $20^v$ | 22nd February | Cathedra of St Peter | |
| fol. $22^v$ | 12th March | St Gregory the Great | |
| fol. 129 | 11th July | Translation of St Benedict | |
| fol. 173 | 11th November | St Martin | Pl. 46*a* |

Except for St John the Evangelist who is seated on the bar of an 'E', and St Martin flanked by two bowing monks in a 'D', the remaining saints are shown as head and shoulder busts in the initials 'O' or 'D'. A bust figure in a medallion, the *imago clipeata*, being a widespread classical motif, appears commonly, in ivories or in the well-known Terence author portrait, for instance.[2] This could be easily transformed into an historiated initial with the letter form acting as frame, and one of the earliest historiated initial surviving, the 'H' from the Leningrad Bede, after 731, a half-figure of Pope Gregory the Great, is of this type.[3] Later examples are in the Corbie Psalter,[4] late eighth century, the Junius Psalter, first half of the tenth century,[5] and in Limoges manuscripts of the second half of the tenth century.[6]

The Lectionary from St Martial, Limoges, also provides a parallel to the 'E' with the enthroned St John in a St Jerome seated on an 'H'.[7] An 'M' with a Saint enthroned on it in the St Vaast Gospels of the first half of the eleventh century shows a similar arrangement.[8]

The 'D' with St Martin resembles certain dedication or book presentation scenes. Thus in the Codex Egberti Archbishop Egbert is flanked by the bowing

[1] London, Brit. Mus., Add. MS. 49598, fol. 70. There are miniatures missing at the beginning of the manuscript which probably contained a Majestas and various choirs completing the existing leaves. See F. Wormald, *The Benedictional of St Ethelwold* (1959), 12.

[2] L. W. Jones and C. R. Morey, *The Miniatures of the Manuscripts of Terence prior to the thirteenth century* (1931).

[3] M. Schapiro, 'The Decoration of the Leningrad manuscript of Bede', *Scriptorium*, xii (1958), 191–207, pl. 23*a*.

[4] Amiens, Bib. Mun., MS. 18.

[5] Oxford, Bodleian Library, MS. Junius 27.

[6] Paris, Bib. Nat., Latin 740, fol. 186, Lectionary, late tenth century. Latin 5301, Lectionary, late tenth century.

[7] Paris, Bib. Nat., Latin 5301, fol. 216. Van Moé, *Illuminated Initials*, 52. J. Gutbrod, *Die Initiale* (1965), 156 ff.

[8] Boulogne, Bibl. Mun., MS. 9, fol. $13^v$.

monks Keraldus and Heribertus, who are smaller in scale.[1] A miniature from St
Pl. 46*c* Bertin by Abbot Otbert shows St Bertin flanked by two other saints in a similar
arrangement.[2] Examples showing the scene cut down as here by a roundel are a
Pl. 46*b* Tournai ivory of *c.* 900 showing St Nicasius,[3] an initial 'O' from a late tenth century manuscript from St Emmeram, Regensburg,[4] and a St Germain-des-Prés
Pl. 46*d* initial 'O'.[5]

## *Part II: The Style*

### A: THE FIGURE STYLE

In contrast to the great divergence of iconographic sources the style of the majority of the miniatures is the same.[6] This style, particularly in regard to figure types and drapery, has already been commented on, where it was shown that it derives from late tenth-century Anglo-Saxon painting, such as that of the Benedictional of St Ethelwold. The style resembles most closely that of Avranches MS. 72 and is, as Professor C. R. Morey was apparently the first to recognize, almost certainly by the same hand. All the features commented on earlier in MS. 72 reappear – the drapery split up into compartments rather than the Anglo-Saxon all-over pattern, white hatched highlights, loops at the shoulder, gesturing prominent hands, round chins and necks often poked forward. In the compositions the placing of the figures as a flat frieze at the bottom of the picture rather than in the centrifugal compositions of Anglo-Saxon miniatures
Pl. 33*a*, 39*c* is well shown in the Ascension and Presentation pages.

The artist of MS. 72 was not, however, the only one at work in the Sacramentary. The colouring of certain of the historiated initials, those on
Pl. 32*a* fols. 20$^{v}$, St Peter, 22$^{v}$, St Gregory the Great, 24, the Annunciation, and

[1] Trier, Stadtbibl. MS. 24.

[2] Boulogne, Bib. Mun., MS. 107, fol. 6$^{v}$. Porcher, *French Miniatures*, pl. vi.

[3] Goldschmidt, *Elfenbeinskulpturen* (1), no. 160, Taf. lxxi.

[4] Munich, Bayr. Stadtsbibl., Clm. 14272. G. Swarsenski, *Die Regensburger Buchmalerei des x. und xi. Jahrhunderts* (1901), Taf. iii, no. 10.

[5] Paris, Bib. Nat., Latin 11751, fol. 142 St Martin. Cf. also the framed 'O' with St Germain flanked by acolytes on fol. 40$^{v}$ of Latin 12610. Deslandres, op. cit., pl. 3.

[6] On certain of the miniatures there appears to have been later retouching, especially the Heraclius, fol. 155$^{v}$, but also fols. 66$^{v}$, 122$^{v}$.

possibly 173, St Martin, recalls the artist of Avranches 90 whose style has Pl. 46*a* been related to Anglo-Saxon painting of the second quarter of the eleventh century.

Also different in style is the Preface to the Canon, fol. $61^{v}$, in which the cross bar of the *Vere dignum* monogram is supported by two angels. The Pl. 36 figures are large for the space of the letter which they occupy, but they do not fill it completely. For instance their bodies echo the curve of the letter but do not touch it. The impression of size, however, is increased by the fact that the heads are large in proportion to their bodies. The wings overlap the letter and those of the right-hand angel extend behind and in front of it. Since the left wing might more naturally overlap the letter than, as it does, extend behind it, the figure seems to turn out towards the spectator. There is thus the appearance of three-dimensionality without any background space, resulting in the sort of impression achieved by stereoscopy. Similar is the device of making the front arm of each angel very light in tone so that it stands out whilst the other arm is hidden. The front feet, too, overlap the bar of the letter, and the ridges of drapery of the undergarments above the feet and the folds falling from each shoulder are sharply highlighted and shadowed to give the same turning effect.

If the pairs of angels in the Assumption, fol. $142^{v}$, or Ascension, fol. Pls. 39*c*, 42*a* $75^{v}$, miniatures are compared with fol. $61^{v}$ they appear quite flat. Another difference is in the jagged outline of the drapery of the ω angels as opposed to the tighter smoother silhouettes of the figures in the majority of other pages. The shapes of the faces are also different. The ω angels are square-jawed with low foreheads and only a narrow band of hair above, where the round-chinned angels of the Assumption, for instance, have a high mass of hair. Nevertheless the ω angels are related in style. They do not appear utterly alien. The pleat from the shoulder is found for instance in other miniatures, though not with so marked a three-dimensional effect, and the features of the faces as opposed to their shapes are not dissimilar.

Certain characteristics, the jagged outline, the isolation of a part of the body and the high-lighted front arms of the angels recall Anglo-Saxon paintings of the eleventh century. This style can be seen in the Sacra- Pl. 37*d*

mentary of Robert of Jumièges, for instance where the square-jawed faces are also noticeable.[1] But there is not the same flickering effect of the miniatures of that manuscript. The figures are solider and more Romanesque in the initial. In these respects they can be compared with rather later Anglo-Saxon manuscripts, the Troper and Gospel Lectionary from
Pl. 37*a* Hereford.[2] Thus in the miniature of St Peter's release from prison in the former manuscript, fol. 22, the figures fill the space by their size not by a multiplicity of incidental details as in the Rouen Sacramentary. Their heads are large and the faces square with narrow foreheads and bands of stylized hair. There is something of the turning effect and the draperies are similarly high-lighted. But the drapery is also more corrugated and metallic, and the divisions broader.

The Hereford style is clearly derived from the Continent.[3] The Hereford miniatures are particularly distinguished by their use of brown and yellow tones. These are absent in the Mont St Michel figures whose colouring with its pale blue, green and pink resembles that of Avranches 90. It is possible, in fact, that this is again the artist of MS. 90, in spite of certain differences of the drapery which is more fluttering and of the faces which are squarer. The shape of the ω monogram is close to that in the Rouen Sacramentary and the frame to be discussed below also suggests an Anglo-Saxon model of this type, rather than the Hereford manuscripts whose frames are quite different. It is possible, therefore, that we have here a Norman artist's response to the style of the Sacramentary of Robert of Jumièges. We should then have to think in terms of parallel developments towards the Romanesque style rather than of influence of some such manuscript as the Hereford Troper.

Pl. 15*b* Possibly by the same artist as the ω angels is the initial 'X' in MS. $86_3$ of the late group. The square-jawed Matthew symbol may be compared. The iconography as remarked above is different from that of the All

1 Rouen, Bib. Mun., MS. Y.6(274).

2 London, Brit. Mus., Cotton MS. Caligula A. XIV and Cambridge, Pembroke College, MS. 302.

3 The colours, proportions of the figures, and the corrugated drapery, are similar in north French manuscripts such as the Gospels, now Brussels, Bib. Roy., MS. II.175 probably from St Bertin. The comparison is made by H. Swarzenski, 'Der Stil der Bibel Carilefs von Durham' *Form und Inhalt, Kunstgeschichtliche Studien für Otto Schmitt* (1951), 91. See also below p. 175*ff*.

Saints miniature of the Sacramentary, fol. 170. If the artist of the monogram is the same as the artist of the MS. $86_3$ initial he would be of a younger generation than the artist of MS. 72, and this would fit in well with his use of later Anglo-Saxon style.[1]

Another page of the Sacramentary whose style must be discussed is that for the Exaltation of the Cross, fol. 155ᵛ. The two episodes of the recovery of the Cross have already been commented on, and it was pointed out that the duplication of Heraclius in the scene below shows that the prototype used the continuous method of narration. This would suggest an Eastern cycle of illustrations behind the Western representations. Pl. 44

There are certain stylistic features which would support this. The figures and draperies are in the same style as the rest of the miniatures – compare for instance the profile faces of the 'Pentecost' fol. 80ᵛ with those of the city inhabitants. But the way the figures are placed on a thin strip of ground represented by a series of lumps with tufts of grass sprouting from them, and the city shown as a small box of turreted walls, recalls late antique miniatures such as those of the Vienna Genesis.[2] Pl. 40*a*

There are signs that the Mont St Michel miniatures is some way removed from such a model in the late antique style, supposing it to have existed. For instance the row of heads in the lower miniatures are obviously an abbreviation of a fuller scene and probably the original model would have shown figures kneeling rather as they do in the Joshua Rotulus.[3]

As was said in discussing the iconography earlier, the existence of such a model is very problematic since there seems to be no trace of the story as narrated by Rhabanus Maurus in the Eastern sources. If there was an Eastern cycle, then Jerusalem would be the obvious place to find it and Abbot Radulfus might have seen it on his pilgrimage in 1058. As a possible Western intermediary or as an adapter of a cycle to Rhabanus' text, St Gall may be suggested. The St Gall *Psalterium Aureum* illustrations, for

[1] If he were also the artist of MS. 90 and if the artist of MS. 90 was also its scribe, Gyraldus, it might be observed that the initials in MS. 77, also written by Gyraldus, are very close in style to those in MS. $86_3$. See Pls. 14*d*, 15*b*.

[2] Vienna, Nat. Bibl., Theol. Graec. 31. E. Wellesz, *The Vienna Genesis* (1960), pl. 3.

[3] Sheet viii, Weitzmann, op. cit., pl. 23.

instance, show a rather similar use of the small city and the tufted ground strip to that of the Mont St Michel miniature.[1] A number but not all of the scenes are divided into two registers. This division is found also in an illustrated copy of the Maccabees[2] which probably also comes from St Gall. In both these manuscripts, the parchment is left bare as an indeterminate space for the figures. That a St Gall manuscript might have been the intermediary or even the source of the cycle illustrating Rhabanus is not inconceivable.

## B: FRAMES AND ARCHITECTURAL CANOPIES

There are twelve framed pages, which include three enclosing initials not figure scenes. The majority of them are plain frames with corner or side medallions[3]. Three constituents may be examined separately, first the running patterns, secondly the medallions, thirdly the panel divisions.

The Mont St Michel artists use only a simple acanthus leaf filling pattern in which the leaves are for the most part flat. Occasionally, as on the
Pl. 44 Heraclius page, fol. 155$^{v}$, they turn over to form an hollow 'purse' leaf. Such running acanthus patterns are characteristic of Ottonian miniatures, occurring for instance in the Poussay Gospels of the Reichenau School.[4]

The medallions on the Mont St Michel frames divide into those which are decorated with rosettes and those in which there are heads or head and shoulder figures, five of each. The leaf medallions are derived from Franco-Saxon types and similar examples appear in eleventh-century north French manuscripts particularly from St Vaast at Arras, for instance in the Bible.[5]

Figure medallions occur in both Ottonian and Anglo-Saxon miniatures.[6]

1 J. R. Rahn, *Das Psalterium Aureum von Sanct Gallen* (1878), especially Taf. viii–x and xv.

2 Leiden, Univ. Bibl., Cod. Perizoni 17. A. Merton, *Die Buchmalerei in St Gallen* (1912), Taf. lv and lvii.

3 On folios 75$^{v}$, 80$^{v}$, 119$^{v}$, 122$^{v}$, 142$^{v}$, 143, 152$^{v}$, 155$^{v}$, 156, 170.

4 Paris, Bib. Nat., Latin 10514, fol. 69$^{v}$. Sauerland, Haseloff, op. cit., Taf. 53–56.

5 Arras, Bib. Mun., MS. 559(435). Schulten, op. cit., Taf. 14. See also the Gospel Book, Paris, Bibl. de l'Arsenal, MS. 592, and the St Denis Sacramentary probably made at St Vaast, Paris, Bib. Nat., Latin 9436.

6 Deriving probably from 'Ada school' examples such as London, Brit. Mus., Harley MS. 2788, fol. 109, 'Q' with Annunciation to Zacharias and medallions of Mary and Elisabeth. Köhler (2), Taf. 59.

In Ottonian examples they always seem to have some connection with the miniature framed.

At Mont St Michel, though the artists go even further than Ottonian examples by enclosing some of the actors in the scene (as opposed to attributes or allegorical figures), for example the Dove in the Pentecost, Pl. 40*a*
or some of Saints in the All Saints miniatures, heads are also used as Pl. 45*d*
decoration, as they are in Anglo-Saxon examples, in the Ascension for Pl. 39*c*
instance.[1]

Another point of difference from Ottonian frames is in the way frame and medallion are combined. In an Ottonian frame it is the continuity of the bounding line which is emphasized, and the patterns are often very simple, for example the running chain taken from late Antique models, used in the Codex Egberti.[2] A medallion breaking this continuity is more likely to be combined with a plain gold band than with running acanthus patterns.[3] Where the two are combined, in a Sacramentary from Trier for example,[4] the medallions are superimposed on the acanthus pattern so that it is thought of as still running continuously underneath.

At Mont St Michel, on the other hand, the acanthus pattern is enclosed in panels which are closed where they meet a medallion. Frames composed of panels of pattern appear in Insular illumination, and from there are adopted by the most Insular-influenced of the Carolingian Schools, the Court School and the Franco-Saxon School. In the later tenth and eleventh century they are found both in Anglo-Saxon and in north French illumination.[5] The Mont St Michel panel frames therefore are a synthesis of the Ottonian continuous frame and the Insular-derived panel frame. The closest similarities are with north French manuscripts making

[1] A frame with a head medallion occurs already in the transitional MS. 115. See Pl. 10f. There are fine examples in the Fécamp Bible, Rouen, Bib. Mun., MS. A.4(1), fol. 1 etc., and also at St Germain-des- Prés, Paris, Bib. Nat., Latin 12610, fol. 1$^{v}$. Anglo-Saxon examples include the Trinity Gospels and the Sacramentary of Robert of Jumièges.

[2] Trier, Stadtbibl., MS. 24.

[3] e.g. Escorial, Cod. Vetrinas 17, Gospels from Echternach. Boeckler, op. cit., Taf. 6–7.

[4] Paris, Bib. Nat., Latin 10501, fol. 9, Goldschmidt, *German illustration* (2), pl. 15, and also in the Escorial Gospels.

[5] e.g. Benedictional of St Ethelwold and St Vaast Bible.

a similar combination, though the Franco-Saxon tradition there results in a frequent use of interlace which is never found at Mont St Michel.[1]

Not only in the use of components, but in the whole relation of frame to the scene which it contains, the Mont St Michel miniatures stand in an intermediate position between Ottonian and Anglo-Saxon practice. In Anglo-Saxon manuscripts the frame is so all-engulfing that it is in Pl. 37*d* danger of losing its function of separating miniature from page. Frame and picture become inseparable, a single decorative pattern. At Mont St Michel on the other hand the frame is used with restraint, to separate miniature from page but also to complete it as an integral part of the composition, for instance in the Assumption (emphasizing the diagonals) Pls. 42*a*, 45*d* or All Saints pictures. This is why the medallions are more often placed in the middle of the sides of the frame, which serves to lead the eye inwards to the central scene.[2] The frame is being used in a much more architectural way, and again this is a sign of the emerging Romanesque.

There remain two frames, on folios 61ᵛ and 66ᵛ, which are of a quite different type. In that of folio 66ᵛ, the 'Christus super aspidem' page, the Pl. 38 leaves curl outwards from the central medallion of each side, intertwining with the bars of the frame which thus becomes as it were a trellis for natural growth. At the corners the leaves are stopped by the roundels and twist back, again as if a living plant.

In the organization of the frame from the medallions outwards and the exuberance of the leaf forms, folio 66ᵛ comes very close to Anglo-Saxon frames.[3] It may be compared, for instance, to the miniature of the Maries

[1] For a discussion of the problem of frames in medieval manuscripts, particularly Franco-Saxon manuscripts, see C. Nordenfalk, 'Ein Karolingisches Sakramentar aus Echternach und seine Vorläufer', *Acta Archaeologica*, ii (1931), espec. 216–18.

[2] Corner rosettes are more common in Anglo-Saxon frames. They only occur twice here and on two other pages there are both side and corner medallions.

[3] R. Freyhan, 'The place of the Stole and Maniples in Anglo-Saxon Art of the tenth century', *The Relics of St Cuthbert*, ed. C. F. Battiscombe (1956), 409–432, derives the Anglo-Saxon frame design from the use of the Eastern Tree of Life which appears in the Cuthbert stoles, laid end to end. Though the leaf forms are no doubt Eastern in origin, he seems to me to play down possible Carolingian influence in the formal arrangement too much. Thus the motif of the trees in the border is found on folio 9 of the San Paolo Bible though they face into the centre not out of it. The motif of leaves extending symmetrically from a bar frame is found, too, in Tours school initials and borders.

at the tomb in the Benedictional of Archbishop Robert[1] particularly for the design of the centre medallions, or with the frame of the enthroned Saint Andrew on folio 164v of the Sacramentary of Robert of Jumièges.[2] Pl. 37*d* It has already been suggested that the 'Christus super aspidem' is modelled on a miniature or initial in Archbishop Robert of Rouen's Psalter and the frame may be, therefore, a close copy of a frame in the Psalter. The Mont St Michel leaf forms are more static than those in many of the pages of the Sacramentary or other later Anglo-Saxon manuscripts. As opposed to their all-over movement there is a strong movement of the scroll outwards from the centre medallions at Mont St Michel. The whole design of the scroll is more coherent than in the Anglo-Saxon examples. The plainness of the corner medallions, which as usual are subordinate to the side medallions, also seems to reveal the Norman hand.

On fol. 61v, the VD page, the frame is a plain gold band from which Pl. 36 leaves sprout only on the outer side. They are arranged symmetrically about a central leaf motif slightly emphasized by its size. Towards the second quarter of the eleventh century there is a tendency for Anglo-Saxon frame decoration to turn outward only.[3] However, the actual form of leaf used, a larger and smaller lobe on a long stalk, is not so common in this group of frames. It is found in a very plain form without the stalks crossing in the Grimbald Gospels.[4] Closer similarities are with the frames of the earlier Trinity Gospels and the Sacramentary of Robert of Pl. 37*c* Jumièges.[5] Pl. 37*d* The formal arrangements and the constituent elements appear, therefore, to come from models of different date. The result is a page which though it could not be mistaken, as could folio 66v, for an Anglo-Saxon work, yet could not have any other source than Anglo-Saxon miniatures.

1 Rouen, Bib. Mun., MS: Y.7, fol. 21v. Talbot Rice, pl. 52*b*.

2 Rouen, Bib. Mun., MS. Y.6, fol. 164v. H. A. Wilson, 'The Missal of Robert of Jumieges,' *Henry Bradshaw Society*, xi (1896), pl. xii.

3 e.g. Oxford, Bodleian Library, MS. Douce 296, fol. 40; New York, Morgan Library MS. 709; London, Brit. Mus., Arundel MS. 155. Talbot Rice, pls. 63, 75*a*. Rickert, pl. 40.

4 London, Brit. Mus., Add. MS. 34890, fol. 73v. Rickert, pl. 36*a*.

5 Cambridge, Trinity College MS. B.10.4. Rouen, Bib. Mun., MS. Y.6(274). They occur even earlier in the New Minster charter frame of after 966, London, Brit. Mus. Cotton MS. Vespasian A.VIII, fol. 2v. Rickert, pls. 25, 28*a*, 31.

Something should be added about what may be called the architectural canopies.[1] There is a settled convention in the Sacramentary with regard to those scenes which take place indoors, of which there are six, the Annunciation to Zacharias, the Birth of St John the Baptist, the Adoration of the Magi, the Presentation, the Last Supper and Pentecost.

During the early Middle Ages the classical methods of representing indoor space were gradually lost. This can be seen in a comparison of the two great ninth-century Tours Bibles, the Moutiers Grandval and the Vivian Bible.[2] Nordenfalk has commented on the transformation of the scene where Moses addresses Aaron and the Israelites.[3] In the earlier of the two Bibles, the Grandval, the coffered ceiling of the palace is still represented as foreshortened but in the Vivian Bible of 846, only a few years later, this is abandoned and 'the illusion of real depth gives place to a system of separate planes echeloned tier on tier.' This 'purely medieval schema' is adopted in Ottonian miniatures and is seen for instance in the page showing
Pl. 29*b* St Gregory writing in the Registrum Gregorii manuscript now at Trier.

However, a comparison of this Trier page with the Last Supper in
Pl. 35*c* Morgan 641, shows a difference almost as great as that between the Trier page and the Grandval illusionistic scene. For the Trier miniature still has a frame enclosing the building. This means that the observer looks at the scene as though through a window, and the building remains an object which is seen from outside. In the Mont St Michel miniature there is no frame, or rather the architecture has itself become the frame.[4] It is this schema which should perhaps be called purely mediaeval, for here the observer cannot imagine himself as inside or outside the building. There is nothing left at all of the classical illusionistic representation of space.

This second stage only emerges gradually in the miniatures. In the
Pl. 40*a*, 41*a* Nativity of St John and the Pentecost the frame is still there. In the
Pl. 33*a* Presentation it has disappeared at top and bottom, and then finally in the Last Supper it is gone altogether.

[1] See F. Wormald, 'The Fitzwarin Psalter and its allies', *Journal of the Warburg and Courtauld Institutes*, vi (1943), 71–72, for a discussion of this subject.

[2] London, Brit. Mus., Add. MS. 10546, fol. 25ᵛ. Paris, Bib. Nat., Latin 1, fol. 27ᵛ. Köhler (1), Taf. 51, 71.

[3] *Early Medieval Painting* (1957), 148.

[4] Cf. C. Nordenfalk, 'Ein karolingisches Sakramentar', op. cit., 217 on architectural frames.

Architectural canopies can be found already in late antique ivories[1] and also occur in Carolingian examples.[2] In the San Paolo Bible, for instance, King David and his musicians play under an archway which is surmounted by architectural canopies on either side.[3] In the late tenth century a group of Ottonian ivories have extremely complicated and remarkable canopies, of which that of a representation of St Gregory writing is outstanding.[4]

Nor is the canopy replacing the frame an original development at Mont St Michel. In the San Paolo Bible miniature the columns frame the scene, though the canopies there are not integrated with the arch. More important, they do not dominate the miniature as they do in the Last Supper and the Pentecost at Mont St Michel. But even this way in which the canopy organises the picture, ambiguous in its function as both frame and setting, can be seen already about the year 1000 at St Bertin under Abbot Otbert, for instance in a miniature of St Bertin and his companions.[5] The twisting Pl. 46*c*
beasts in the roundels and the scroll below, show the influence of Anglo-Saxon frames with their profusion of decoration.[6] But the essentials of the canopy are there, and it is probably from north France that the Norman artists learnt its use. Its further development in Normandy can be seen,

1 e.g. Volbach, *Elfenbeinarbeiten*, no. 52. Middle part of ivory diptych, *c.* 500, showing an enthroned Empress, now in Vienna, Kunsthistorisches Museum.

2 e.g. the Canon Tables of the Grandval Bible, Köhler (1), Taf. 47–49. The high cornices above the Evangelists in the 'Ada' School Harley Gospels, which ultimately derive from the stage architecture of the Asiatic theatre of the Hellenistic period, are also a possible source.

3 Rome, San Paolo fuori le mure, fol. 167$^{v}$. Boinet, pl. cxxiv. See also the Codex Aureus from St Emmeram, Munich, Bayr. Staatsbibl., Clm. 14000, Boinet, pl. cxv.

4 Formerly at Heiligenkreuz, now Vienna, Kunsthistorisches Museum. H. Fillitz, 'Die Wiener Gregor-Platte. Ein Beitrag zum Lothringischen Elfenbeinrelief des 10. Jahrhunderts', *Jahrbuch der Kunsthistorischen Sammlungen in Wien*, N.F. xxii (1962), 7–22, revises Goldschmidt's dating.

5 Boulogne, Bib. Mun., MS. 107, fol. 6$^{v}$. Porcher, *French Miniatures*, pl. vi. The St Maur-des-Fossés Sacramentary also has a tentative canopy frame. See Pl. 35d. Fully developed examples occur in a Gospel book of the eleventh century from St Peter's, Salzburg, Stiftsbibl., Cod. A.X.6. See G. Swarzenski, *Die Salzburger Malerei*, i (1913), 30 ff. and ii (1908), Taf. xvi-xix. Swarzenski suggests these derive from Bavarian illumination and also draws attention to Fulda manuscripts of the Ottonian period, pp. 32 and 37.

6 Canopies are not common in Anglo-Saxon miniatures – examples are in the Psalter, Cambridge University Library, MS. Ff.1.23. The only pre-conquest examples of a canopy frame known to me are in the Arenberg Gospels, now New York, Morgan Library, and in the Evangelist portrait in the Boethius from Fleury, Paris, Bib. Nat., Latin 6401, fol. 13$^{v}$.

for instance, in Hugo Pictor's miniature of St Jerome[1] and it becomes widespread in the later Romanesque period.

## C: CONCLUSION AND DATING

A date of *c.*1050–65 was suggested earlier on grounds of script and initial style. It was also suggested that Robert of Jumièges' gift of his Anglo-Saxon Sacramentary to Jumièges between 1044 and 1050 may have been the stimulus to produce the Sacramentary. Other evidence from the consideration of the iconography above supports this dating. First there is the close connection with the Rhabanus Maurus from St Germain-des-Prés, in which almost certainly the Sacramentary 'UD' was copied. Ingelardus, the artist of the Rhabanus Maurus, states in a colophon of another manuscript that he was working under Abbot Adelard (*c.* 1030–60).[2] Secondly, the earliest example of the new iconography of the Last Supper with a central Christ at the straight table is in the Echternach Escorial Golden Gospels of *c.*1046. This presents an approximate *terminus post*. Thirdly, the unique Heraclius miniature and the UD initial which probably reflects a Palestinian iconography may perhaps be connected with Abbot Radulfus' pilgrimage to Jerusalem of *c.*1058.

Anglo-Saxon influence reaches its culmination at Mont St Michel in the Sacramentary. The general appearance of the miniatures, especially their colouring, the plain green and orange capitals, and the fine round script all proclaim it unmistakably. In many other respects the miniatures stand at a transitional point, looking ahead to a new style and adopting a new iconography. And yet Morgan 641 is an isolated manuscript, a masterpiece seemingly without influence. The huge Bible, which was probably the scriptorium's next great project, abandons the full-page miniature to experiment with historiated and figure initials. No doubt the Conquest re-directed the energies of the religious houses both in Normandy and in England. Faced with the task of stocking the English libraries with the essential patristic texts, it may well have seemed otiose to the Norman monks to produce Sacramentaries and Gospel Books to compete with such superb works as Robert of Jumièges' Sacramentary.

1 Oxford, Bodleian Library, MS. Bodley 717, fol. V$^{v}$. Pächt, 'Hugo Pictor', op. cit., pl. vi*b*.

2 Paris, Bib. Nat., Lat. 11751, Lectionary. *MSS à peintures*, no. 245.

# VI

## THE LATE MANUSCRIPTS

THE predominant influence on the scriptorium of Mont Saint Michel in the first half of the eleventh century was Anglo-Saxon art. In the second half of the century this is no longer so. We see instead evidence, first, of contact with the art of the Franco-Flemish borderland, and secondly, towards the end of the century with the art of the Loire valley to the south of Normandy.

## *Part I: MSS. 103 and 58*

### A: MS. 103, ST GREGORY THE GREAT, HOMILIES

This manuscript was written by the 'renovatores' amongst whom was Scollandus who became Abbot of St Augustine's after the Conquest in 1072. On fol. 4ᵛ a miniature shows St Gregory sitting frontally on a high Pl. 47
throne with his feet on a footstool. He writes on a scroll with a quill, and turns his head slightly to the right as if to listen to the Dove which flies towards him from behind the flanking curtain on the left. The miniature is framed in a series of rectangles. The whole is drawn and shaded in red and the background is painted green.

### *Iconography*

This iconography[1] of St Gregory is based on an incident in his life related by Paulus Diaconus (*c.* 720–*c.* 800). During a long silence in St Gregory's dictation a scribe peeped through a curtain which divided him from the

[1] See R. Eisler, 'Un ivoire sculpté français dans une abbaye Autrichienne', *Gazette des Beaux Arts*, sér. 6, xviii (1937), 297–303. The attribution of the Heiligenkreuz ivory to Marchiennes can be discounted. See Fillitz, op. cit., p. 171 n. 4 above.

Saint and saw the Holy Spirit as a dove sitting on his shoulder and speaking into his ear.[1] This story has a basis in St Gregory's own words in the Homilies on Ezekiel, 'audio quod dico'.

The Mont St Michel miniature omits the scribe and the dividing curtain,[2] and the dove instead of perching on the Saint's shoulder flies towards his ear. A number of examples of the Dove flying can be quoted and amongst these the scribe is not always shown.[3] The pose of the Saint, however, actually writing on the scroll held before him is much rarer. One example is a St Jerome in the Hillinus Codex, a Reichenau school manuscript, where the saint is accompanied by two scribes, one of whom writes on the other end of the same scroll.[4] Scribes with scrolls if they sit frontally usually dip their pens to the left but do not write. If they do write on a scroll they turn to the right.[5] The way St Gregory turns his head slightly to listen to the Dove is similar to the pose of the St Gregory in the St Gereon, Cologne, Sacramentary.[6] Probably, therefore, this is again a case of an Ottonian type being transmitted via Liège or north French manuscripts. That St Gregory should be writing at all is, of course, contrary to the narrative of the original source.

1 An earlier account is by an anonymous monk of Streoneshalch, Northumbria in an eighth-century manuscript at St Gall. *D.A.C.L.* vi (1924), 1771, s.v. 'Gregoire I'.

2 A well-known example of the scene is that by the Master of the Registrum Gregorii, a leaf now in the Stadtbibliothek in Trier. See Pl. 29*b*.

3 Metz Sacramentary, Paris, Bib. Nat., Latin 1141, ninth century with scribes, Boinet, pl. cxxxi; Leipzig, Stadtbibl., Cod. CXC, tenth century, R. Bruch, *Die Malereien in den Handschriften des Königreiches Sachsen* (1906), Abb. 14; Munich, Bayr. Staatsbibl., Clm. 4456, Sacramentary of Henry II from Regensburg, 1002–14, G. Swarzenski, *Die Regensburger Buchmalerei* (1901), Taf. vii; St Gall, Stiftsbibl., Cod. 376, Gradual, eleventh century, Merton, op. cit., Taf. lxxiii.1.; Ivory bookcover, formerly, Berlin, Kgl. Bibl., theol. lat. f.2, 1022–36, Minden, Goldschmidt, *Elfenbeinskulpturen* (2), no. 146, Taf. xli. The Father in the right lower corner (St Ambrose (?) ) writes frontally on a scroll but an angel inspires him. St Gregory with the dove is in the upper left hand corner. For Ottonian types of St Gregory see also H. Schnitzler, 'Hieronymus und Gregor in der Ottonischen Kölner Buchmalerei', *Kunstgeschichtliche Studien für Hans Kauffmann* (1956), 11–18, and B. Nitschke, *Die Handschriftengruppe um den Meister des Registrum Gregorii* (1966), n. 143.

4 Cologne, Domschatz, Hs. 12, fol. 4v. Schnitzler, op. cit., fig. 7. There is no dove.

5 Coronation Gospels of Charlemagne, Vienna, Schatzkammer, for instance. An earlier frontal scribe with a scroll is the Barberini Gospels, Rome, Vatican, Barberini Lat. 570, fol. 50v, Zimmermann, Taf. 313b, southern England, late eighth century. A later example is from Jumièges, Rouen, Bib. Mun., MS. Y.80(1383), fol. 35v.

6 Paris, Bib. Nat., Latin 817, fol. 21. Schnitzler, op. cit., fig. 8.

## *Style*

The feature that first distinguishes this miniature from earlier full-page portraits at Mont St Michel is its shape. It is long and narrow where they are almost square.[1] There is no architectural arch and only the curtains give a setting. St Gregory is an extremely elongated figure with a small head but large hands. The row of little blobs for his beard and the hair over his brow, the ear and the beady eyes are noticeable in the features. The drawing is sharp, clear and angular, for instance at the corner of the right sleeve, or the bottom of the scroll. The drapery encases the Saint, particularly the upper part of his body, like armour. Below there are crinkled folds but again they are metallic. St Gregory wears a tunic which is ornamented with little stars, dots and ovals, and a similar pattern is on the hem of his garment below the knees. The miniature is notable for the absence of any attempt to show recession, and the figure looks as if it had been pressed flat between panes of glass.

The shape of the miniature and the plain rectangular frame point at once to houses in the area of north France and Belgium for the origin of this style. Dr Schilling has suggested that this long, narrow format may be due to the influence of the Echternach school where there are narrow panels confined to one column of a manuscript written in double columns.[2] The miniatures of this shape particularly discussed by Dr Schilling are the two Evangelist portraits added to the Breton Gospels presented to Exeter by Bishop Leofric and known as the Leofric Gospels,[3] Pl. 48*b*
the Sacramentary from St Lambert's, Liège,[4] and the Sacramentary from Pl. 48*c*

[1] An exception is St Ambrose in MS. 72, fol. 182$^{v}$, but there the portrait is fitted to the shape of the column of script in a book written in two columns. In MS. 103 there is no such reason for the shape of the miniature. See Pl. 28.

[2] R. Schilling, 'Two unknown Flemish miniatures of the eleventh century', *Burlington Magazine*, xc (1948), 312–17. I can only find examples of script arranged in these narrow columns, never of miniatures, e.g. in the Nuremberg and Escorial Codices.

[3] Oxford, Bodleian Library, MS. Auct.D.2.16. See also J. J. G. Alexander, 'A little-known Gospel Book of the later eleventh century from Exeter', *Burlington Magazine*, cviii (1966), 6–16, figs. 10–11.

[4] Bamberg, Staatl. Bibl., Lit. 3. K. H. Usener, 'Das Breviar Clm. 23261 der Bayerischen Staatsbibliothek und die Anfänge der romanischen Buchmalerei in Lüttich', *Münchner Jahrbuch d. bildenden Kunst*, i (1950), 78–88.

St Lawrence, Liège, adapted for use at St Bertin.[1]

Of these manuscripts, Dr Schilling considers the St Lawrence manu-
Pl. 48*c* script to be the latest. A comparison between the St Gregory of MS. 103 and the Christ of fol. 8v shows a good many points of resemblance. The frame is rather narrower and longer in proportion in the Sacramentary and it is ornamented with a band of pattern. Also the blessing Christ overlaps the frame on three sides. But the proportions of the body are very similar to those of the St Gregory, only the head being larger. In both miniatures the setting is provided by a pair of curtains. There are general resemblances too in the drapery, such as the wide falling sleeves, the lower hem of the over garment, and especially about the legs where the drawing of the right leg and the drapery to the left of it, with the wide hem behind the legs also shown, is very close.

Nevertheless, in spite of these general resemblances, the style of the two miniatures differs. The drapery of the Christ lacks the metallic incisiveness of the St Gregory. This is seen particularly if the silhouettes of the two figures are compared, for example the drapery in the lower left corner by their right legs which is otherwise so similar in design. The St Gregory also is not squeezed into his frame. He fills but nowhere overlaps it, as does the Christ. Finally, the heads are quite different in proportion and physiognomy.

Pl. 48*b* The two miniatures added to the Leofric Gospels, St Mark, fol. 72$^{v}$, and St John, fol. 146, are dated to the second quarter of the eleventh century by Dr Schilling. In style these two portraits are close to the Sacramentary Christ but are somewhat more schematized. This is noticeable in the painting of the features, for instance, or the lines of the drapery about the feet of the St Mark.[2]

The two portraits bear a number of similarities to the Mont St Michel St Gregory both in the general proportions, type of frame, hanging

[1] Paris, Bib. Nat., Latin 819, M. Schott, *Zwei Lütticher Sakramentare in Bamberg und Paris und ihre Verwandten* (1931), 183.

[2] Dr Schilling places the St Lawrence Sacramentary *after* the Leofric Gospels on the grounds that in it the figure of Christ for example is more strictly confined to its space whereas the Leofric Evangelists still have the 'Ottonian vagueness of space'. I should prefer to put it earlier. The progression is towards a more linear style.

curtains, pose of St Mark (frontal with head turned), and more specifically in the harder, sharper drapery lines, and a feature like the rolls of material over the knees. However, the St Gregory is a more compressed design in which the Saint, central and silhouetted, fills the space without the incidental detail or the patterned background of the Leofric figures. The Mont St Michel miniature also lacks the flow of their draperies in the gold hems coming down over the shoulder in a swinging loop, for instance, or the way the pleats fan out.

Another manuscript connected by Dr Schilling with the Leofric Gospels Evangelists is a Gospel Book from the Franco-Flemish border- *Pl. 48f*
land.[1] This has portraits of St Jerome and St Damasus by one hand and three Evangelist portraits by a second hand. The Evangelists sit under architectural canopies and are squatter in proportion with larger heads. The other two figures by the first hand are longer with smaller heads and have plain frames. All the figures share a more sharply drawn drapery with almost corrugated folds. This style at its most exaggerated is seen in the Life of St Omer from St Bertin, now St Omer, Bibliothèque Munici- *Pl. 26b*
pale, MS. 698. The effect is achieved by juxtaposed bands of different shades of the same colour, and is therefore lacking in the unpainted St Gregory of MS. 103. A point of similarity, however, is the flattened planar appearance of St Jerome in the Brussels Gospel Book. In the St Lawrence Sacramentary in Paris there was still a plasticity about the drapery folds over Christ's shoulder and those falling between the knees which is lacking in MS. II. 175, as it is in the St Gregory.[2]

The Brussels Gospels is dated by Schott to the third quarter of the eleventh century.[3] Another manuscript, a Gospels from Corbie,[4] has *Pl. 49e*
been variously dated to the second half of the eleventh century[5] and to the end of the eleventh century.[6] This contains four Evangelist portraits with a number of stylistic features in common with the MS. 103 St Gregory.

[1] Brussels, Bib. Roy., MS. II. 175. Perhaps from St Bertin. Schott, op. cit., 186–7.

[2] The Gospel book presented to Weingarten by Judith of Flanders, now Fulda, Landesbibl. Aa 21, is an intermediate stage in this respect. Schott, op. cit., 189. The corrugated effect probably comes from Cologne manuscripts.

[3] Schott, op. cit., Ch. iv.

[4] Amiens, Bib. Mun., MS. 24, Schott, op. cit., 78ff.

[5] Swarzenski, *Monuments*, pl. 81.

[6] Porcher, *French Miniatures*, pl. xxii.

On fol. 15 of the Corbie Gospels St Matthew is shown seated frontally under an archway over which a curtain is twisted. At the top to the left a small angel flies down holding a scroll whose other end is grasped by St Matthew in his right hand. He sits on a low square throne with his feet on a stool.

Again there are a number of general points of similarity, in the frontal pose, the proportion of the body and here also in the colour, which is predominantly green and red. St Matthew's head is larger and he sits on a lower throne, but his footstool is a rectangle and as in the St Gregory, the last traces of the illusionistic foreshortened stool have disappeared. St Matthew sits under an arch but the curtain is draped over it. Other detailed points of similarity are in the large hands with their small lines emphasizing the joints of the fingers, and the way the beard and hair is
Pl. 49*e* shown which is closer in the St Luke, fol. 77$^{v}$. In comparing the drapery there are again certain points of similarity. The way St Matthew's right arm emerges from the sleeve bending inorganically at the wrist, and the method of using double curved lines, is very close to the drapery of St Gregory on the upper right arm for instance. Also, St Matthew's left elbow is emphasized under the drapery in the same schematic way by a bulge, as is St Gregory's right elbow. The use of a group of curved lines, one much thicker than the others, for a fold (for example in St Gregory's lap) is also found in the Corbie draperies.

In spite of these similarities, the Corbie drapery has a different appearance from that of the St Gregory. It is soft and swirling, rather than hard and sharp. The treatment of the hem around the legs of the St Matthew shows this difference. And this is apart from the effect of the bands of paint which add to this rhythm and which connect the Corbie Gospels with another Gospel Book from St Lawrence, Liège.[1] This softer style will have to be discussed in a moment in connection with the author portrait of St Hilary in MS. 58. One other Corbie manuscript should be mentioned, though it seems to be later in date, for its figure of a seated St Peter to whom the monk Nevelo offers his book.[2] This again is similar in type to the MS. 103 St Gregory.

[1] Brussels, Bib. Roy., MS. 18383. Swarzenski, *Monuments*, pl. 80.

[2] Paris, Bib. Nat., Latin 17767. Nevelo died under Abbot Robert (1123–42). *MSS. à peintures*, no. 134.

The St Gregory of MS. 103 clearly, then, is modelled either on an Evangelist portrait, or on a portrait of St Jerome or Pope Gregory from a Sacramentary, from the north French or Flemish area. Perhaps the nearest manuscript which could have acted as a model is the Gospels, Brussels II.175, but other manuscripts of the area have other features of our manuscript which are lacking in the Gospels, particularly the colour. This would mean that, if the Brussels Gospels is dated correctly to the third quarter of the eleventh century, the Mont St Michel artist was copying a contemporary or slightly earlier work.

The initial 'd' on fol. 5 does not resemble the type of initial with gold Pl. 48*e*
scrolls on a green or blue background commonly found in these north French manuscripts. Though close to other late Mont St Michel initials in the use of the panelled frame for the letter, in its inhabited scroll and in some of its leaf types, the 'd' is distinguished by the emphasis on the convolutions of the stem of the plant scroll and by a fondness for a curved form at the tip of a leaf for instance. A purse leaf with curving lines where it turns over is also noticeable. These helical veined leaves were commented on when they occurred in the transitional manuscripts and it was pointed out that they are found in certain north French manuscripts. They continue in the second half of the eleventh century particularly at St Vaast, Arras and St Amand and the 'purse' leaf becomes common too.[1] Pl. 48*d*
Here they are in a very schematized form. Very similar leaves occur in borders and initials added about 1080 to the Arundel Psalter which probably comes from Winchester.[2] The open turning scroll with helical leaves is also used in the frames of a Psalter of the second half of the eleventh century from Angers.[3] Nevertheless, in view of the origin of the miniature the leaf scroll probably has also a north French source.

1 e.g. Dijon, Bib. Mun., MS. 30, the Psalter of St Robert made at St Vaast, C. Oursel, *La Miniature du xii^e siècle à l'abbaye de Cîteaux* (1926), pl. ii, and Valenciennes MS. 93, Gospels from St Amand.

2 London, Brit. Mus., Arundel MS. 60, fol. 13, 52^v, 53, 85. See Dodwell, *Canterbury School*, Appx. 2, for evidence that these illuminations were added after the Conquest.

3 Amiens, Bib. Mun., MS. fonds Lescalopier 2. Dodwell op. cit., pl. 72, compares the Crucifixion page in this manuscript to fol. 52^v of the Arundel Psalter and to a St Evroul manuscript, Rouen, Bib. Mun., MS. A.287 (273).

## B: MS. 58, ST HILARY, COMMENTARY ON ST MATTHEW

A rather different style but one whose origins are also to be sought in the
Pl. 49*a* area of north France may be seen in MS. 58. This book containing St Hilary's Commentary on St Matthew and written in part by the scribe Mauritius, also belongs in script to the late manuscripts and reasons have been suggested for dating it about 1080 or somewhat later.

The opening 'G' on fol. 3$^{v}$ contains St Hilary sitting on a stool to write at a lectern. He faces to the right and his feet rest on a twisting scroll in which a small lion can be seen. The initial is drawn in brown ink but certain parts, most obviously the right thigh, have been copied over in a darker ink.

The author portrait is here contained for the first time at Mont St Michel in an initial. This is especially significant in view of the tradition of full-page portraits which precede it. It points to a new development in the initial which becomes the main feature of Norman and Anglo-Norman manuscripts of the last quarter of the eleventh century. The plant scroll in the initial, formerly inhabited by figures with no connection with the text, but used only to enliven the decoration, now absorbs figure scenes illustrating or prefacing the text, which were before the subject of independent, often full-page illumination. The inhabited scroll initial thus becomes the historiated scroll initial.[1]

However, if one compares this initial with an example of the fully fledged late eleventh-century Norman historiated scroll initial, also a
Pl. 49*b* scribe portrait and in general design very close to our 'G', the 'C' from the St Gregory's *Moralia in Job*,[2] it is clear that the Mont St Michel initial does not go very far towards combining the figure and the plant scroll.

In the 'G' there is still a recollection of the blank space which surrounded the earlier author portraits. For the scroll is not allowed to invade the upper part of the initial and the two elements do not fuse. In the Bayeux 'C' the scribe is surrounded and enmeshed, and no division is made between the decorative and historiated elements. Thus the lion is both an inhabitant in the scroll and supports the throne. Similarly the

[1] 'Historiated scroll initial' and 'inhabited scroll initial', therefore, should be used as distinct terms.

[2] Bayeux, Chapter Library, MS. 57, fol. 42. H. Swarzenski, *Form und Inhalt*, op. cit., 89, Taf. 1–5.

isolated terminal head above the Mont St Michel initial is brought in the *Moralia* into direct contact with the figure.

At first sight, therefore, the Mont St Michel 'G' looks like a tentative step in the direction of an historiated initial. In the wider context of illumination at Mont St Michel this is more doubtful. There is only one other historiated scroll initial in the late manuscripts. This is in the Bible where, however, the majority of historiated initials are not scroll initials, Pl. 54*e*
but show a new solution to the problem of combining figure and initial.[1] They use the letter as a stage background to project the figures. Something of this is already to be seen in the way St Hilary's stool leg projects over the letter form, as does a fold of his drapery. It is only a hint admittedly, for his head is made to conform to the shape of the letter in the old way, using the initial as a frame to a scene as in the Sacramentary.

Stylistically the miniature is again different from the Mont St Michel miniatures seen so far. The plant scroll is very close to that of the initial 'd' on fol. 5 of MS. 103, but the figure style has no connection with that Pl. 48*e*
of St Gregory. In particular the drawing is of a very great delicacy. If the hard clumsy lines which have been added are ignored, the drapery has a gossamer quality very different from the angular metallic folds of MS. 103. Again the figure is neither elongated nor pressed flat into planes as in MS. 103. The hard dark line of the thigh obscures the ease of the pose and the skill with which the three-quarter face turn of the body is shown. Behind the Saint there is a flying fold and the folds below the right thigh are a series of more stylized pleats.

There is here, in fact, a body/drapery relationship shown. In the full page miniatures of the middle manuscripts the body was sporadically shown to exist where it dictated the shape of the drapery – i.e. where the drapery was pulled tight over it, in MS. 90, for instance, the torso of Faustinus. But there was an equal interest in drapery patterns for their Pl. 24*a*
own sake, quite unrelated to the body underneath. In MS. 103 the body is inferred under its encasing sheath only because it emerges from it at Pl. 47
feet, head and hands. But in MS. 58 the drapery is loose and the effect is of transparency, for the lines of the body, the left forearm or the right leg for instance, are drawn in in addition to the folds of the drapery.

[1] See below, p. 185 ff.

The model used must have been quite different from that of MS. 103. Ultimately it might go back to an Evangelist portrait of Charlemagne's Court School where a similar sort of transparent drapery is found. The flying fold behind suggests the intervention of an Anglo-Saxon drawing
Pl. 17*a* of the 'First Style' such as the Sherborne Pontifical.[1] But in the MS. 58 figure there is observable both a more rounded, less jagged drawing of the folds, and a more stylized treatment of them – for example the accordion pleats below the right thigh.

That an Anglo-Saxon drawing of the second half of the tenth century was the model seems unlikely, but the model may well have come from an area in which such drawings could have been known. The sensitive
Pl. 49*c* line drawings found in the Gospels from St Lawrence, Liège, fol. 85 and fol. 115, probably unfinished first sketches for the Evangelists, St Luke and St John, who are painted by another hand on fol. $84^{v}$ and fol. $124^{v}$, should be compared with MS. 58.[2] These lack some of the fine inner drawing of the St Hilary, no doubt because they were intended to be painted. They are also more contained in silhouette than the St Hilary. The Corbie Gospels,[3] already referred to as in some respects close to the
Pl. 49*e* St Gregory of MS. 103, connects in others, in the softer drapery for instance, and the agitated folds between the feet, with the St Hilary. The pose of the St Hilary is close to that of the Brussels St Luke, fol. 85, and the Corbie St Luke, fol. $77^{v}$. A copy of St Gregory Nazianzus, perhaps from Stavelot, should also be compared for its extraordinarily sensitive clinging drapery combined with a certain stiffness observable in the St Hilary.[4]

Finally from Normandy itself two drawings of very fine quality in a
Pl. 49*d* manuscript of St Gregory's Dialogues, which comes from Fécamp,[5] are

1 Paris, Bib. Nat., Latin 943. Wormald, *English Drawings*, pls. 4a,b, 5a.

2 Brussels, Bib. Roy., MS. 18383, eleventh century, second half. C. Gaspar, F. Lyna, *Les Principaux manuscrits à peintures de la Bibliothèque Royale de Belgique* (1937), 43ff.

3 Amiens, Bib. Mun., MS. 24.

4 Brussels, Bib. Roy., MS. II. 2570, eleventh century, second half. Gaspar, Lyna, op. cit., 58, pl. xi.

5 Paris, Bib. Nat., Latin 2267. The Fécamp provenance of this MS., formerly in the Bigot collection, indicated by the initials is confirmed by the script and initial figure style which is the same as that of Rouen, Bib. Mun., A.89(445), St Jerome on Ezekiel, from Fécamp. See Avril, *Notes* (2), 220.

also close both to the Gospel book drawings in Brussels and to MS. 58. They have again the soft clinging drapery and to judge by their script belong to the late eleventh or early twelfth century.

## *Summary*

MSS. 58 and 103 use models which come from the area to the north and east of Normandy. This is part of a general wave of influence on the Norman houses which is observable in the second half of the eleventh century and which it is interesting to find penetrating as far south as Mont St Michel. Other Norman examples of it have been cited by Dodwell[1] and it is the more noteworthy since at this time Anglo-Saxon influences might have been expected to be paramount. MS. 103 and MS. 58 show the opposite extremes of styles current in the north French and Flemish area, extremes which sometimes curiously meet in a manuscript like the Corbie Gospels. In turning to the Bordeaux Bible, a different current of influence must be considered, which comes this time from the south.

## *Part II: The Mont St Michel Bible*

The two-volume Bible, now Bordeaux, Bibliothèque Municipale, MS. 1, belonged until the French Revolution to the Abbey of La Sauve Majeure in the diocese of Bordeaux. On fol. 249$^{v}$ and fol. 259$^{v}$, however, are copies of two bulls addressed to the Abbey of S. Sauveur at Redon. One of these, fol. 259$^{v}$, is of Pope Gregory VII dateable 1073–1085, the other of Pope Eugenius III of 24 June 1147, fol. 249$^{v}$. For this reason it has been referred to as the 'Redon' Bible.[2] The grounds for attributing it here to Mont St Michel are solely stylistic being based on the evidence of the script and initials.

1 C. R. Dodwell, 'Un manuscrit enluminé de Jumièges au British Museum', *Jumièges, Congrès scientifique du XIIIe centenaire*, ii (1955), 737–41, discussing London, Brit. Mus., Add. MS. 17739 from Jumièges. Also *St. Albans Psalter*, 202–3.

2 *MSS. à peintures*, no. 227 (as from S. *Pierre* de Redon). Porcher also noted 'certains rappels du Mont St Michel'. Two fragments of the Book of Deuteronomy used as pastedowns in MS. 10 are perhaps reject leaves from the Bible. For a discussion of the initials see Avril, *Millénaire* (2), 226–9.

The contents are the Old and New Testaments omitting the Gospels but including the Psalms. The second volume breaks off in the Epistle to the Hebrews and the Book of Revelation has, therefore, it can be assumed, been lost. The foliation of the two volumes is consecutive, Vol. I, fols. 1–151, Vol. II, fols. 152–404. The leaves measure 455 × 180 mm.

It does not appear that the text has been anywhere studied.[1] The order in which the books are arranged is (Vol. I) Pentateuch, Joshua, Judges Ruth, Kings I–IV, Paralipomenon I and II, (Vol. II) Isaiah, Jeremiah, Lamentations, Ezekiel, Daniel, XII Minor Prophets, Job, Psalms, Wisdom Books, Esdras, Esther, Tobias, Judith, Maccabees I–II, Acts, VII Canonical Epistles, XIV Epistles of St Paul (Romans to Hebrews, not Laodiceans). This does not correspond to that of any of a sample list of ten late tenth- and eleventh-century Bibles.[2] The main difference lies in the placing of Paralipomenon I and II after Kings IV and in the arrangement of the books of Esdras, Esther, Tobias and Judith in that order.[3] The St Vaast Bible places the two books of Paralipomenon after Kings IV as do none of the other eight Bibles (Vol. I of the Carilef Bible is missing), but it has the order Tobias, Judith, Esdras, Esther.[4]

The illumination consists entirely of initials which introduce each book and usually the preface to each book. None of them is particularly
Pl. 50*a* large except for the 'I' to 'Genesis' which runs the whole length of the page. Though there are one or two blank leaves, there is no evidence that there were ever any full page illustrations, or that such were contemplated.

1 It is not mentioned by S. Berger, *Histoire de la Vulgate*, Paris (1893).

2 These are (a) from Normandy. Rouen, Bib. Mun., MS. A.6(8), Jumièges Bible; Rouen, Bib. Mun., MS. A.3–4(1), Fécamp Bible; Rouen, Bib. Mun., MS. A.5 and 20(2–3), Lyre Bible (2 vols.); Durham Chapter Library, A.II.4, Carilef Bible (vol. I missing). All second half eleventh century. (b) From North France. Arras, Bib. Mun., MS. 559, St Vaast Bible (3 vols.), second quarter eleventh century; London, Brit. Mus. Add. MS. 28106–7, Stavelot Bible (2 vols.), 1097–8. (c) From Central France. Paris, Bib. Nat., Latin 5, 'First' Bible of St Martial, Limoges (2 vols.), late tenth century; Paris, Bib. Nat., Latin 8, 'Second' Bible of St Martial Limoges (2 vols.), late eleventh-twelfth century; Angers, Bib. Mun., MS. 3–4, Bible of St Aubin, Angers (2 vols.), late tenth century; Dijon, Bib. Mun., MS. 2, St Bénigne, Dijon Bible, early twelfth century.

3 The scribe was aware of this discrepancy. On fol. 151$^{v}$ he wrote in red and green capitals: 'Alibi aliter ordinati sunt isti libri, scilicet post Paralipomenon Esdras, post Esdram, Hester, Judith, Tobias. Paralipomenon autem post Isaiam Hieremiam, duodecim prophetas, Job quoque et Psalterium, necnon et libros Sapientiae. Verum hic secundum quod ordinati sunt et tituli facti sunt'. Who had arranged the books and written the titles or does this refer to the exemplar?

4 The present Vol. III of the St Vaast Bible should be Vol. II.

The initials fall into three main groups.[1] The first group of seventeen are typical Mont St Michel middle manuscript initials as described in Chapter III. (Pl. 12*d*) They all occur in the first volume of the Bible. Only six of them are painted. Two, fols. 131v and 135, have blue grounds and the remaining nine are drawn in pen. The second group are typical Mont St Michel late manuscript initials. (Pl. 55*a*) They all occur in the scond volume of the Bible except one, the 'C' of fol. 140v. There are sixteen of them altogether of which ten are fully painted, three have coloured grounds which are again blue, fols. 237v, 291v and 295v, and three are drawn in pen only. Thirdly there is a group of fifteen initials which all contain figures. One of these, the Genesis 'I', is in the first volume but it is in a different style from the others and belongs with the second group. The rest of the initials with figures are in the second volume. Eleven of this third group are painted and only four are drawn, fols. 300v, 301, 314v and 322. After this the illumination of the Bible fails. Two initials remain, fols. 314 and 369, of poor quality. For the rest either the spaces are left blank for the initials, or they are filled with plain red letters.

The first two groups are so close to Mont St Michel letters that it is impossible to doubt that the Bible originated in the Mont St Michel scriptorium. The 'e' of fol. 70v may be compared to the 'B' of MS. 76, (Pls. 12*b*, *d*) fol. 1, and the 'F', fol. 1v, to the 'F' of MS. 90, fol. 2, for the first group; and for the second the 'O' of fol. 294 to the 'Q' of MS. 89, fol. 159, or the 'O' of MS. 35, fol. 75v, and the 'V', fol. 243, to the 'L', fol. 65 of MS. 146. (Pls. 55*b*, *f*) The third group will require further discussion.

## A: INITIAL TYPES

First, it will be necessary to analyse the types of initials used. Thirteen of the fifteen initials of the third group are historiated, that is to say they contain or enclose figures who have some connection with the text introduced by the initial. Two, the initial 'd' to the prologue to Daniel,

[1] The script of the Bible is close to that of MS. 103 and it is just as difficult to distinguish the different hands. In volume II, fols. 152–335v appear to be by one hand and fols. 336–75v by another. There are different hands at work on volume I but as in MS. 103 it is difficult to find clear breaks between one scribe and the next. On fol. 356 is the inscription: 'Tandem finitis veteris Instrumenti libris quos ecclesia catholica in canone divinarum recepit scripturarum, ad Evangelia Novumque Testamentum, Christo juvante pervenimus. Amen.' Either then it was decided not to include the Gospels or they have been removed leaving no trace.

fol. 207, and the 'M', fol. 300$^{v}$, prologue to Ecclesiasticus, seem to have no connection with the text.

Historiated initials have been discussed above in Chapter V, since they occur in the Morgan Sacramentary. However, a group of the historiated initials of the Bible differ in important respects from those of the Sacramentary. Again they must be divided up. First in the 'B' introducing Psalm I, fol. 261, the scene of David fighting the lion, takes place in the
Pl. 54*e* midst of an entangling scroll. This leaves little room for the protagonists
who are squeezed away at the bottom of the letter. Moreover, it has even dictated the composition of the scene in a way which distorts the story. For David grasps not the lion but the plant scroll, and the lion also is biting the scroll, as if it, not David, was the attacker. In fact, if no other representation of David fighting the lion had happened to survive, this might have been thought purely a piece of Romanesque decoration. This is not so in the Sacramentary, nor in the other Bible initials. Only in the
Pl. 51*a* 'U', fol. 168$^{v}$, of Jeremiah is there a piece of plant scroll threatening to
Pl. 49*a* invade the letter. As was said above in connection with the 'G' of MS. 58,
the trend of the last quarter of the eleventh century in Norman and Anglo-Norman decoration was decidedly towards historiated scroll
Pl. 46*f* initials. A good example is the 'B' of St Augustine's Commentary on the
Psalms from St Evroul.[1] The 'B', then, and it is interesting that it introduces the Psalter, is the only historiated scroll initial in the Bible.[2]

But if the other figures resemble the Sacramentary initials in not being encumbered by the scroll, they stand in a very different relationship to the letter form. A scene like the Adoration of the Magi in a 'D', fol. 9 of the
Pl. 32*a* Sacramentary, may be compared with the 'A' of Daniel, fol. 207$^{v}$ of the
Pl. 51*e* Bible. In the former the letter is a frame, and, though there is little setting
and no perspective attempted, we see the scene as if through a window.[3]

1 Rouen, Bib. Mun., MS. A.19(456), fol. 1. Avril, *Notes* (2), 241.

2 Illustrated Psalters and their Commentaries are commoner than illustrated Bibles and so are more likely to reflect the type of historiated initial of this period.

3 See M. Schapiro, 'The Decoration of the Leningrad manuscript of Bede', *Scriptorium*, xii (1958), 191. Speaking of the origin of the historiated initial he says 'In its manner of combining the image and the letter the historiated initial of the Anglo-Saxon artists presupposes the classic practice of framed illustration (though classic art could not easily admit the asymmetrical forms of letters, except the 'O' as a proper frame).'

It is very different with the 'A'. There the letter is a backdrop to present the actors who thus come forward with a greater immediacy. This is strikingly so in all the initials except that to Haggai, fol. 244, a bust medallion. Pl. *52e* Note the tail of the fish in the 'E', fol. 240, or the crown and staff of the medallion figure of the 'I' on fol. 314v. The figures, it should be observed, are in this way much more closely related to, and dependent on, the letter. Pls. *50b*, *54a* Though they stand before it, they never trespass beyond it.

Five of the initials are figure initials, fols. 207, 240v, 260, 300v and 322. Pls. *50c*, *52b*, *53b*, *e*, *f* The earliest surviving examples of this use of the human figure to make up a letter are of the eighth century.[1] In particular the Gellone Sacramentary made in the diocese of Meaux, *c*. 780, has a number of figure initials of which the 'I', a female figure standing holding censer and cross and labelled 'Sca Maria', a 'd' in which the bow is held by a flying angel, and another 'd', fol. 76v, in which the bent figure of Judas is shown discovering the cross, may be singled out.[2] In these early examples a figure as an 'I' or as the stem of a 'P', 'Q', or 'T' is common, and also a bent figure as an 'E' or a 'C'.

In the Gellone Sacramentary these letters are in some cases also historiated initials and the 'd', fol. 76v, of the discovery of the cross, is a part of a narrative cycle adapted to an initial.[3] This process is taken even further in the Corbie Psalter of the late eighth century.[4] Perhaps the most remarkable of its initials from this point of view is the 'P', fol. 123v, showing David's fight with Goliath. This is not in fact quite strictly a figure initial since parts of the letter are not formed by the figure, but are drawn in. This is so also with initial 'N' to the 'Nunc dimittis' showing the Presentation, fol. 84v, another striking initial, and is perhaps symptomatic of the Carolingian reforms. For the only figure initial in the Carolingian

[1] Probably the earliest example is a commentary on Job dated to the first half of the eighth century by E. A. Lowe, Cambrai, Bib. Mun., MS. 470. *Codices Latini Antiquiores*, vi (1953), no. 740, Anglo-Saxon half uncial. See also Trier, Domschatz MS. 61(134), *C.L.A.* ix, no. 1364, saec. VIII, Zimmermann, Taf. 279a and St Gall, Stiftsbibl., MS. 731 dated 793, *C.L.A.* vii, no. 950, Zimmermann, Taf. 150–1. J. Gutbrod, *Die Initiale in Handschriften des achten bis dreizehnten Jahrhunderts* (1965), especially 97ff., 129ff.

[2] Paris, Bib. Nat., Latin 12048. *C.L.A.* v, no. 618. Zimmermann, Taf. 153, 159.

[3] Reproduced in *C.L.A.* v, no. 618. The cycle has survived in a ninth-century manuscript of which a facsimile has been edited by C. von Krauss, *Die Handschrift des Wesobrunner Gebets* (1922), Munich, Bayr. Staatsbibl., Clm. 22053, fol. 13.

[4] Amiens, Bib. Mun., MS. 18. See above Ch. III (pp. 52–3) or a bibliography of this manuscript.

manuscripts reproduced by Köhler is the Angel forming the 'L' of St Matthew in the Metz Gospels.[1]

As far as the origin of the figure initial goes it is noticeable that three of these manuscripts have insular connections. At the same time in Italo-Byzantine ninth- and tenth-century manuscripts some remarkably similar figure initials to those of the Gellone Sacramentary occur.[2] In any case the next group of figure initials to be considered have marked Byzantine characteristics. These are in a Psalter from north Italy now in Munich[3] and in the Lectionary from St Martial, Limoges,[4] both manuscripts of the late tenth century. Porcher has noted the resemblance of certain figures in the Lectionary to Byzantine ivories.[5] An ivory cannot, however, be the source for the appearance of figure initials like the 'L',
Pl. 48*a* fol. 252, or the 'M', fol. 196, in this manuscript.

The fact that figure initials appear in two manuscripts in which pronounced Byzantine influence is observable of about the same date, may not be accidental. The stylistic similarities between the figures of the two manuscripts are only of the most general kind, in their contraposto positions and classical dress, with also some minor resemblances of detail like the colour spots on the cheeks, the hair, and the proportions of the figures rather short but with large hands. But in the eleventh century figure initials became fairly common in Byzantine manuscripts and it seems quite probable that an Eastern tradition of figure initials was introduced into the West at this time. Whether the Eastern tradition is ancient and could lie behind the earlier as well as the later Western examples needs further investigation.[6]

1 Paris, Bib. Nat., Latin 9388, fol. 17v. Köhler (3), 139, Taf. 70a. Remarkable figure initials are, however, found in two ninth-century Italian manuscripts, Vercelli, Bib. Cap., MS. CXLVIII, and Rome, Vallicelliana, MS. B.25II. Exh., *Karl der Grosse*, nos. 462, 461.

2 See K. Weitzmann, *Die byzantinische Buchmalerei des 9. und 10. Jahrhunderts* (1935), Taf. xc–xciii, Patmos MS. 33, especially, written 941 in Reggio, Calabria.

3 Munich, Bayr. Staatsbibl., Clm. 343. Schardt, *Das Initial*, 119.

4 Paris, Bib. Nat., Latin 5301. Van Moé, *Illuminated initials*.

5 J. Porcher, 'Les Manuscrits à peintures de Saint-Martial', pp. 44–57 of the Exhibition Catalogue *L'Art roman à Saint-Martial de Limoges*, Musée Municipal, Limoges (1950).

6 For striking late eleventh-century examples see K. Weitzmann, 'The Constantinoplitan Lectionary Morgan 639', *Studies in Art and Literature for Belle da Costa Greene*, ed. D. Miner (1954), 363, figs. 296–7 etc. Weitzmann comments that figure initials of this type fit so well in the system of lectionary illustration that it seems reasonable to assume that they were invented for it.

Whatever their sources, figure initials are fairly widespread in central France already in the eleventh century. Amongst various examples from St Aubin, Angers, a Commentary on St Paul's Epistles has some remarkable initials – for example fol. 204, 'T', and fol. 139, 'R'.[1] From Le Mans a St Augustine may be cited for an 'E', fol. 1,[2] and also of the eleventh century is the St Ambrose from St Bénigne, Dijon.[3] The figure initial is also found already in the tenth century in England in manuscripts now at Salisbury and Oxford.[4] Other Anglo-Saxon examples occur in the second quarter of the eleventh century in the Psalter probably from Winchcombe, and they are also to be found in an Isidore, and in a copy of Bede's Ecclesiastical History.[5] Pl. 50*d*

This survey shows that whether the figure initial was an Insular invention or not, it was common enough in central France by the eleventh century for that area to be the source of the initials in the Bible.[6] This origin will be supported by the stylistic evidence. The late appearance of figure initials at Mont St Michel (with the one notable exception of the 'N' copied from the Corbie Psalter in Latin 8055) is also an argument against their derivation from English manuscripts. Pl. 53*d*

## B: ICONOGRAPHY

The fifteen initials with which we are here concerned are all to books of the Old Testament. Two of them, the 'H', fol. 260, and the 'B', fol. 261, are connected with the Psalter, whilst the Genesis 'I', fol. 5, also has Pls. 53*e*, 54*e* Pl. 50*a*

1 Angers, Bib. Mun., MS. 67. Second half eleventh century.

2 Le Mans, Bib. Mun., MS. 216.

3 Paris, Bib. Nat., Latin 11624. See Appx. III.

4 Salisbury, Chapter Library MS. 150, mid-tenth century. Oxford, Bodleian Library, MS. Tanner 10, tenth century first half. Kendrick, *Late Saxon*, pl. xxviii.2, xxix.

5 Cambridge, Univ. Library, MS. Ff.1.23; London, Brit. Mus., Royal MS. 6.B.viii; Cambridge, Corpus Christi College, MS. 41. Wormald, *Decorated initials*, 125ff, pl. vii b–d.

6 Some figure initials can also be quoted from the eleventh century in north France. The most ambitious examples occur in the Le Cateau Homiliary, Cambrai, Bib. Mun., MS. 528, especially fol. 195, 'T', and fol. 198ᵛ, 'H'. Examples of standing figures forming 'I's are Valenciennes, Bib. Mun., MS. 169, fols. 21 and 81, and MS. 39, fols. 2ᵛ and 36, both St Amand; Douai, Bib. Mun., MS. 867, fol. 53, Marchiennes; and Cambrai, Bib. Mun., MS. 544, fol. 122, the Cathedral. Except for the Homiliary these initials do not show figures in action which is the distinguishing mark of the central French initials. This point should be borne in mind in discussing the origins of the famous Cîteaux initials of the next century. See Pl. 45*c*.

subjects taken not from Genesis but from the Psalter. Here again, it may be suggested, is evidence of a knowledge of the Anglo-Saxon Psalter owned by Archbishop Robert of Rouen.[1] The remaining eleven initials are to various books of the Prophets, Jeremiah, Daniel, Hoseah, Jonah, Micah, Haggai, Esdras, and to Job, Esther and Ecclesiasticus. Before considering each initial separately, a word may be said about the iconography of these in general.

It can be seen that the books for which these initials have been made, are not for the most part those for which picture cycles are well known or common. These would be particularly the books of the Octateuch and to a lesser extent the four books of Kings.[2] In fact there only seem to be two Bibles surviving from the early Middle Ages, which contain cycles of illustration to the books of the Prophets. These are the so-called Farfa Bible from S. Maria, Ripoll, and the Bible from S. Pere de Roda, both studied by Wm. Neuss.[3] I think it is possible to show that two of the
Pls. 51*e*, 52*b* Redon initials, that of Daniel, fol. 207$^{v}$, and of Micah, fol. 240$^{v}$, contain echoes of these cycles. Of the remaining initials, those not connected
Pl. 50*b* with the Psalter, that of Jonah, fol. 240, is the only one which shows an episode narrated in the book it introduces. It may also be connected with the Spanish cycles but this subject is a commoner one so that this cannot be so certain.

Pl. 52*f* As opposed to these 'narrative' initials, those of Job, Esdras and Eccle-
Pl. 54*b* siasticus are all motivated by the opening words of their books rather than illustrative of episodes in them. Thus the 'I' of fol. 314$^{v}$, introducing
Pl. 54*a* Esdras, refers to the opening words 'in anno primo regni Cyri'. It is Cyrus who is shown. This is related to the medieval system of 'Wortillustration', used particularly in the Psalter.

Pl. 51*a* The remaining three initials are author portraits, fol. 168$^{v}$, Jeremiah,

[1] See above, pp. 112, 133, 150.

[2] A number of recent studies have been concerned with the Jewish sources of these cycles. See especially C. O. Nordström, 'Some Jewish legends in Byzantine Art', *Byzantion*, xxvi (1957), 487–508; O. Pächt, 'Ephraim-illustration, Haggadah und Wiener Genesis', *Festschrift für K. M. Swoboda* (1959), 213–21, and K. Weitzmann, 'Die Illustration der Septuaginta', *Münchner Jahrbuch der bildenden Kunst*, 3 Folge, iii–iv (1952/3), 96–120.

[3] Rome, Vatican, Latin 5729; Paris, Bib. Nat., Latin 6. Wm. Neuss, *Die Katalanische Bibelillustration um die Wende des ersten Jahrtausends und die altspanische Buchmalerei* (1922).

fol. 234ᵛ, Hosea, and fol. 244, Haggai, the first two of which are standing figures. Pictures of the prophets as standing figures with scrolls or codices are known from several Eastern examples of the seventh century or earlier. They are not, of course, attached to initials there. The oldest examples are in a copy of an Alexandrian World Chronicle of which papyrus fragments of the fifth century survive.[1] Pictures of the prophets also occur in the Rabbula Gospels of 586 beside the Canon Tables[2] and in a Syriac manuscript probably of the seventh century where they actually introduce their texts.[3] Most of these are simply standing figures with scrolls, but one or two of them are identified, for example, Daniel in Phrygian costume, Zaccharias with the winged sickle, whilst in a few cases, Jonah, Job, Ezekiel for instance, a scene is shown. Figures of the Prophets in Carolingian Bible initials are not common.[4] In the Stavelot Bible of the end of the eleventh century the figures are only half length with scrolls, on those folios where there is not a whole scene depicted, whilst in the Carilef Bible they sit (for example, Hosea, fol. 9) clearly by analogy with an Evangelist portrait. The standing figures of the Bordeaux Bible, therefore, are to be taken as an indication of ultimately Byzantine influence. Later, standing against the background of initials, they are seen in the English Bibles of the twelfth century.[5] Pls. 52*c*, *e*

In general, with regard to the question of the model of the Bible, the fact that only in the later stages of illumination did the scriptorium introduce historiated initials, suggests that when the Bible was planned originally they did not have access to, or knowledge of an illustrated Bible. This militates against the otherwise attractive theory that it was

[1] A. Bauer and J. Strzygowski, 'Eine Alexandrinische Weltchronik. Text und Miniaturen eines griechischen Papyrus der Sammlung W. Goleniščev', *Denkschriften der Kaiserlichen Akademie der Wissenschaften Phil-Hist. Klasse*, li (1906), Abb. 2.

[2] *The Rabbula Gospels*, facsimile edition with commentary by C. Cechelli, G. Furlani and M. Salmi (1959).

[3] Paris, Bib. Nat., MS. Syr.341. H. Omont, 'Peintures de l'Ancien Testament dans un manuscrit syriaque du VIIe ou du VIIIe siècle', *Monuments et Mémoires, Fondation Piot*, xvii (1909), 85–98.

[4] Sapientia in the Grandval Bible, London, Brit. Mus. Add. MS. 10546, fol. 262ᵛ, Köhler (1), Taf. 43c, and Isaiah in the Vivian Bible, Paris, Bib. Nat., Latin 1, fol. 192ᵛ, Köhler (1), Taf. 87b.

[5] Standing prophets also occur early in the twelfth century in Bibles from Salzburg and from Italy. See also D. J. A. Ross, 'A late twelfth-century artist's pattern sheet', *Journal of the Warburg and Courtauld Institutes*, xxv (1962), 119–28.

the St Vaast Bible which acted as a stimulus to Mont St Michel to produce its own Bible.

If models did become available at a later stage, where might they have come from? The stylistic evidence points definitely to the area south of Normandy and particularly to Le Mans, Angers and Limoges. The new style there observable in the second half of the eleventh century is dependent on Byzantine sources and this, as we have seen, is also so of the iconography of the standing prophets. Moreover, knowledge of cycles of which the only earlier surviving representatives come from Spain, must also derive from the south.[1]

At the same time, it should be mentioned that two of the later initials in the St Vaast Bible, the 'D', Vol. III, fol. 106$^{v}$, with a figure of Christ with a sword, the 'ulciscens dominus' of the opening words of Nahum, and the 'O', fol. 108, showing Habbacuc standing with a scroll, both in a quite different style from the earlier figures, are iconographically comparable to the Mont St Michel initials. They are, in fact, an author portrait and an illustration of the opening words of the book, as are the Mont St Michel initials to Hosea and Job.

The style, however, of the St Vaast initials, though again there are signs of Byzantine influence, differs from that of the Mont St Michel figures, lacking in particular their movement. Moreover, the initial is still a window frame not yet a backcloth as at Mont St Michel. Probably, therefore, this is rather a matter of similar sources for both, than of direct contact. The southern influences in the Mont St Michel initials remain undoubted. The historiated initials may now be considered separately.

## Pl. 50*a* *Fol. 5. Genesis. Initial 'I'*

There are two scenes, David and the Lion, and a figure harping. These are both commonly to be found in Psalters. In the twelfth century the episodes of the creation become usual as medallions of the 'I'. David straddles the lion, a variation of the common kneeling (Mithras) position on the

[1] It is tempting to suggest that, as these historiated scenes except for Jonah are taken from Daniel, the artist knew of a Beatus Commentary on the Apocalypse with St Jerome's Commentary on Daniel. If the Book of Revelation was highly illuminated, that would explain its disappearance.

lion's back, which is found for instance on the Cyprus silver dish now in the Morgan Collection.[1] He rescues the lamb with the left hand. The position of David straddling the lion is found also in two Anglo-Saxon Psalters and in the St Evroul Augustine on the Psalms mentioned above. It seems very likely that this again is an echo of the Archbishop of Rouen's Anglo-Saxon Psalter.[2] Pl. 17*d* Pl. 46*f*

The figure harping sits frontally, not as the King David in MS. 76. His head is in profile towards the left and his hands are crossed in front of the instrument.[3] The harp held frontally is seen in the portraits of King David in the Anglo-Saxon Tiberius Psalter of the mid-eleventh century, but probably the Bible figure is one of David's musicians since a similar figure frontal with profile head is used in the St Albans Psalter.[4] The style of this initial is different from that of the other figure initials and it must have been done earlier. The sombre colour, particularly the purple and brown, reinforces the evidence for an Anglo-Saxon model in which the colour was similar to that in the Junius Psalter. Pl. 20

## *Fol. 168ᵛ. Jeremiah. Initial 'V'* Pl. 51*a*

The prophet with a halo stands holding a book in his left hand. He looks up to his right where an angel appears half length with outstretched finger. The hand of God appears in a similar position in the Syrian Bible in Paris.[5] In the twelfth-century Winchester Bible, God Himself appears to Jeremiah and touches him on the lips.[6]

## *Fol. 207. Prologue to Daniel. Initial 'D'* Pl. 50*c*

An archer forms the tail of the initial letter. It does not appear that there

1 For the iconography of David and the Lion see H. M. Roe, 'The "David Cycle" in early Irish art', *Journal of Royal Society of Antiquaries of Ireland*, lxxix (1949), 39–59. Also D. H. Wright, *The Vespasian Psalter* (Early English Manuscripts in facsimile) (1967), 58, 68–78.

2 Oxford, Bodleian Library, MS. Junius 27, fol. 118 and London, Brit. Mus. Cotton Tiberius C. VI, fol. 8. Rouen, Bib. Mun., MS. A.19(456). See above pp. 112, 133, 150.

3 For the iconography of David harping, see H. Steger, *David Rex et Propheta* (1961).

4 London, Brit. Mus., Cotton MS. Tiberius C.VI, fol. 10 and 30ᵛ, Wormald, op. cit. pls. 8, 27. *St. Albans Psalter*, pl. 100.

5 Paris, Bib. Nat., Syr. MS. 341. Omont, op. cit., fig. 9.

6 W. Oakeshott, *The Artists of the Winchester Bible* (1945), pl. vi.

is any connection between this figure and the Book of Daniel.[1] The figure
Pl. 13*a* is very close to that in an initial 'B' in the Corbie Psalter.[2] Perhaps like the 'M' on fol. $300^{v}$ to be considered in a moment, this is a copy of a copy from the Psalter in an early manuscript which has not survived.[3]

## *Fol. 207^v. Daniel. Initial 'A'*

Pl. 51*e* In the centre a naked figure stands with hands by his sides but palms turned to the front. He has no halo. Flanking him are two figures blowing trumpets, and around are a row of dots forming a sort of mandorla. In some of the early Christian representations Daniel is naked in the lion's den, but there are no lions here and the musicians have no place in that episode.

For the explanation of this mysterious scene it is necessary to look at the cycle of scenes illustrating the Book of Daniel in the Roda Bible on
Pl. 51*d* fol. $64^{v}$ of Vol. III.[4] There the statue which Nebucadnesor after his dream put up for the people to worship, is shown as a towering naked figure. To the left, the people bow down, and around the statue musicians blow their trumpets and play other instruments (Daniel, III, v. 5). The Roda statue is not quite frontal. However the scene is also illustrated in some of the manuscripts of Beatus' Commentary on the Apocalypse which contain St Jerome's Commentary on Daniel. An example very close to our figure in pose is in the Beatus from St Sever, though there the figure is draped round the waist, and also the musicians are absent.[5] It is not bearded, as is that of the Roda Bible.

[1] Cain according to an apocryphal source was killed by the blind archer Lamech. This scene is shown on fol. 6, vol. I of the Roda Bible. Neuss, op. cit., fig. 2.

[2] Amiens, Bib. Mun., MS. 18, fol. 95.

[3] The 'B' in MS. 76, fol. 1 also has a figure similar in pose though not an archer. Pl. 12b.

[4] See Neuss, op. cit., fig. 98.

[5] See Neuss, op. cit. fig. 43. The manuscript is Paris, Bib. Nat., Latin 8878, fol. 224; another Beatus finished by Facardus in 1047 now Madrid, Bib. Nac. B.31 has a symmetrical arrangement of worshippers and musicians about the central statue. Wm. Neuss, *Die Apokalypse des Hl. Johannes in der altspanischen und altchristlichen Bibel-illustration* ii (1931), Taf. cxli. Yet another example is in the Beatus Commentary in Gerona Cathedral, fol.$248^{v}$. The dream of Nebucadnesor is also illustrated in an Ottonian manuscript, Bamberg, Staatl. Bibl., MS. A.1.47, but though this may go back originally to the same sources as the Spanish scenes, it cannot have any connection with the Mont St Michel initial since it does not show the worship of the statue. See H. Fischer, *Mittelalterliche Miniaturen aus der Staatlichen Bibliothek Bamberg. I. Reichenauer Schule* (1926) for a coloured plate.

It is doubtful if the illuminator of the Bible knew the significance of the scene he painted. The bowing people are omitted, and the statue is no bigger than the symmetrically flanking trumpeters. The left of these, it is interesting to note, preserves the pose of the classical *tubicinarius* whose trumpet was strapped to his mouth leaving the right arm free to rest on the hip.[1] A similar posed trumpeter plays before the Ark in the Gumpertus Bible.[2] The whole scene of the worship of the image, now a small figure on a pedestal, is found in the twelfth century in England in the Lambeth Bible.[3]

The small dots surrounding the naked figure remain unexplained. They are part of the original decoration, the figure of Daniel having, however, been defaced. They are not found in the Spanish manuscripts. Possibly the artist was influenced by the initial of St Benedict in the Sacramentary where the frontal naked figure is in a mandorla. Pl. 34*a*

## *Fol. 234ᵛ. Hoseah. Initial 'V'* Pl. 52*c*

Hoseah advances to the right with outstretched hand and pointing finger. He seems to hold tablets with rounded tip, rather than a *codex* in his right hand.

## *Fol. 240. Jonah. Initial 'e'* Pl. 50*b*

Above the central bar of the letter is a boat with four men in it. Jonah is being thrown out and at the same time is given a push with a paddle by the man on the right. He falls head first into the open mouth of a fish. The water is a green colour and the boat's hull is seen through it illusionistically.

The story of Jonah is frequently represented in early Christian art. Here the sea monster is a large fish as on fol. 83 of the Roda Bible, rather Pl. 50*e*

1 See O. Pächt, 'A Giottesque episode in English Medieval Art', *Journal of the Warburg and Courtauld Institutes*, vi (1943), 54–5, for a discussion of a later example. This pose is not found in the Roda Bible or the Beatus manuscripts cited.

2 G. Swarzenski, *Die Salzburger Malerei*, ii (1908), Abb. 124. Salzburg, late twelfth century.

3 London, Lambeth Palace MS. 3, fol. 285ᵛ. E. Millar, *Les Principaux manuscrits à peintures du Lambeth Palace à Londres* (Bull. de la Société Française de reproductions de manuscrits à peintures) (1924), pl. viii.

than the scaly tailed monster of earlier examples, for example the Lateran Sarcophagus or the Paris Psalter.[1] The hull of the boat is also seen through the water in the Roda Bible.

Jonah is clothed but seems to be already bald. The Jewish tradition taken over in Christian iconography was that he entered the monster fully clothed and with his hair but emerged naked like a baby.[2] The scene is similarly fitted into an 'E' in the Bible of St Bénigne[3] and the Souvigny Bible.[4]

Pl. 52*b* *Fol. 240ᵛ. Micah. Initial 'V'*

The initial is made up of a dragon and the prophet who holds a round object in his left hand.

In design it resembles one of the earliest surviving figure initials, that in Cambrai, Bib. Mun., MS. 470, fol. 69, though there the beast faces its assailant, and Micah in the Bible has no spear. The initial seems to have no connection with any episode in Micah's life or prophecy. The dragon turning away, however, and the fact that Micah is unarmed give a clue to an interpretation.

Possibly the initial refers to another episode of the Daniel cycle, the slaughter of the Dragon, Daniel, XIV, v, 26, 'Then Daniel took pitch and fat and hair and did seethe them together and made lumps thereof: this he put in the dragon's mouth so the dragon did eat and burst asunder'. This would explain the object in Micah's hand and the dragon turning away
Pl. 52*a* and can be compared with fol. 66ᵛ of the Roda Bible, Vol. III.[5] Daniel's position is remarkably similar, except that for the initial he has been placed to the right, not the left of the dragon.

If this interpretation is accepted it would suggest strongly that these two initials, Daniel and Micah, derive from an illustrative cycle for

[1] Paris, Bib. Nat., Gr. 139, fol. 431ᵛ, early tenth century. H. Buchthal, *The Miniatures of the Paris Psalter* (1938), pl. xii.

[2] See C. O. Nordstrom, 'Some Jewish Legends in Byzantine Art', *Byzantion*, xxvi (1957), 501–8.

[3] Dijon, Bib. Mun., MS. 2, fol. 225. First half twelfth century. *MSS. à peintures*, no. 287.

[4] Moulins, Bib. Mun., MS. 1. Second half twelfth century. *MSS. à peintures*, no. 331.

[5] Neuss, op. cit., fig. 102. This is a fairly common subject in early Christian art, for example on sarcophagi. See B. Brenk, 'Tradition und Neuerung in der christlichen Kunst des ersten Jahrtausends', *Wiener Byzantinische Studien*, iii (1966), 187, Abb. 67 ( a gold glass).

Daniel. Such a model is unlikely to have come from anywhere but southern France or Spain.

### *Fol. 244. Haggai. Initial 'I'* Pl. 52*e*

The prophet is shown half length in a medallion.

### *Fol. 250*$^{v}$*. Job. Initial 'V'* Pl. 52*f*

Job is enthroned with the orb in his left hand, scales in his right and with a crown but no halo.

This may be an abbreviation of a scene like that of Job in prosperity surrounded by his family in the Ripoll Bible, fol. 162$^{v}$.[1] But there the crowned and enthroned Job carries only a sceptre. The scales would be motivated by the opening words 'vir ille simplex et rectus'.

### *Fol. 260. Prologue to Psalms. Initial 'h'* Pl. 53*e*

This shows Sofronius bowing low to receive the book from St Jerome. This is an adaptation of the common scene of the Presentation of the Book, of which an example has already been studied in MS. 50,[2] with the Pl. 17*b*
difference that Sofronius, the bending figure, receives the book from, rather than presents it to the Saint.

### *Fol. 261. Psalm I. Initial 'B' [eatus vir . . .]* Pl. 54*e*

In the lower bow of the letter appear David and the lion. David does not straddle the animal as in the Genesis initial and there is no sign of the lamb.

### *Fol. 300*$^{v}$*. Prologue to Ecclesiasticus. Initial 'M'* Pl. 53*b*

The initial is made up of two men supporting a dragon, one with a spear. It is an adaptation of the design of the initial 'N' in Latin 8055 which, we Pl. 53*d*
have already seen, copies an 'N' in the Corbie Psalter, fol. 31$^{v}$.[3] No more Pl. 53*c*

[1] Rome, Vatican, Latin 5729. Neuss, op. cit., fig. 124.

[2] See J. Prochno, *Das Schreiber und Dedikationsbild* (1929), for examples and Ch. IV above, p. 86.

[3] See above, pp. 52–3. Other copies of initials in the Psalter are found in an eleventh-century manuscript from Corbie itself, Paris, Bib. Nat., Latin 13392.

striking proof of the Romanesque qualities of the Corbie Psalter could be given than this copying by two different artists of the eleventh century of one of its designs. Curiously enough an 'N' in the Roda Bible, fol. 1, vol. III, is also made up of two figures, there naked, with an animal as cross bar.[1]

Pl. 54*b* *Fol. 301. Ecclesiasticus. Initial 'O'*

In the letter sits a crowned female without halo, frontally enthroned. Her cloak falls over her outstretched arms which support a number of objects which must be *codices*, though only two to the left have the lines which indicate their leaves.

The figure must be intended for 'Sapientia' illustrating the opening words of the book.[2] Four frontally enthroned female figures in Bibles
Pl. 54*c* may be quoted for comparison. On fol. 221ᵛ of the Jumièges Bible[3] in an 'O', introducing Ecclesiasticus, a woman sits similarly with outstretched
Pl. 54*f* arms, but with only one book carried in her left hand. In the Limoges Bible a woman seated frontally without crown or halo carries in her right hand seven books and in her left a sceptre.[4] The whole is again in the initial 'O' to Ecclesiasticus, and above the figure's head is a roundel containing seven stars. Another crowned woman frontally enthroned in the Ecclesiasticus 'O', this time with the book held out in her right hand and in her left (also held out) an orb with cross inscribed 'fides', is found in the Winchester Bible. Fourthly holding a scroll in front of her and with a sceptre in the left hand is the figure in the Ecclesiasticus 'O' in the St Bénigne Bible, Dijon MS. 2.[5] This iconography of the sceptre and the

1 Neuss, op. cit., fig. 197. Spanish figure initials are an explored field which could throw light on the problem of origins.

2 For the iconography of 'Sapientia' see M. Th. d'Alverny, 'La Sagesse et ses sept filles', *Mélanges Félix Grat*, i (1946), 245–78, and also 'Le Symbolisme de la Sagesse', *Bodleian Library Record*, v no. 5 (1956), 232–44. I am indebted to Dr K. Hoffmann (Bonn) for help over this iconography.

3 Rouen, Bib. Mun., MS. A.6(8), second half eleventh century.

4 Paris, Bib. Nat., Latin 8, fol. 74ᵛ. *MSS. à peintures*, no. 325. d'Alverny, 'La Sagesse', op. cit., pl. ii.

5 Yet another example is Rheims, Bib. Mun., MS. 21. *MSS. à peintures*, no. 257 (I owe this reference to Dr Walter Cahn). In the Gumpertus Bible illustrating the book of Wisdom, fol. 141, a crowned female holding before her two scrolls sits frontally between scenes of the Crucifixion on the right and the Flagellation on the left. See G. Swarzenski, *Die Salzburger Malerei*, ii (1908), Abb. 138.

books is based on the description of Wisdom in Boethius' *de consolatione philosophiae.*[1] The Limoges miniature includes stars around the figure's head to represent 'Sapientia' sometimes seeming to touch the Heavens as Boethius says.

More usual in the twelfth-century Bibles, however, is an enthroned Majestas Christ in the 'O'.[2] Earlier representations of 'Sapientia' but with no similarity occur in the Tours School.[3] In Ottonian manuscripts there are one or two examples of bust medallions.[4]

A remarkable thing about the Mont St Michel 'Sapientia' is the position of the outstretched arms which is also found in the Jumièges and Winchester Bibles. This gives it a great similarity to representations of the Constellation Cassiopeia, particularly as shown in the copies of Aratus from St Gall, Stiftsbibl. Cod. 90, mid-ninth century, and Cod. 250 mid-tenth century. Only the books and the cloak falling over the shoulders have been added to the figure in the later of these two, in the Mont St Michel representation.[5] Possibly the gesture is meant to signify Wisdom as all embracing.

## *Fol. 314ᵛ. Esdras. Initial 'I'* Pl. 54*a*

The half-length crowned figure in the 'I' is Cyrus motivated by the words of verse 1 'In anno primo regni Cyri regis Persarum'.

1 Bk. I.1, 'Et dextera quidem ejus libellos, sceptrum vero sinistra gestabat'.

2 e.g. St Omer Bible, Paris, Bib. Nat., Latin 16745, fol. 127, Orléans, Bib. Mun., MS. 13, fol. 112, Beaune, Bib. Mun., MS. 1, fol. 110ᵛ, Troyes, Bib. Mun., MS. 458, fol. 42.

3 Grandval Bible, London, Brit. Mus., Add. MS. 10546, fol. 262ᵛ, initial 'D' to Wisdom, a standing female with halo, book and flowering sceptre. Köhler (1), Taf. 43c, and Bamberg Bible, Staatl. Bibl., Misc. Bibl. 1, fol. 260ᵛ, 'O' to Ecclesiasticus, a female seated to the right with open book and inscribed 'SOPHIA SCA'. Köhler (1), Taf. 58c.

4 e.g. Rome, Vatican, Ottob. 74, Gospels of Henry II.

5 A. Merton, *Die Buchmalerei in St. Gallen* (1912), Taf. lxiv no. 2. A Norman example with this seated figure with outstretched left hand (the right is damaged) is on a capital from Bernay, but there is no indication of whom it is meant to represent. In the Stuttgart Psalter, fol. 72ᵛ, the illustration to Psalm 60 shows the Annunciation to a seated frontal Virgin with outstretched hands though no book or scroll. E. T. Dewald, *The Stuttgart Psalter* (1930), 57, pl. The Psalter is now thought to have been made at St Germain-des-Prés, Exh., *Karl der Grosse*, 1965, no. 490. Dewald does not comment on the meaning of the gesture.

Pl. 53*f* *Fol. 322. Esther. Initial 'I'*

Esther crowned and holding a small sceptre stands on a bowed figure who is labelled Aman. This is therefore Esther triumphing over her people's
Pl. 53*e* enemy. Aman is the figure of Sofronius, fol. 260, reversed. The initial is adapted from the pose frequently found in late antique ivories or for instance in Prudentius manuscripts, showing the triumph of a Virtue over a Vice.

## C: STYLE

As a typical example of the figure style of these initials we may take the
Pl. 51*a* initial 'V' of the Book of Jeremiah, fol. 168$^{v}$. In the centre the prophet stands before the letter, whilst above to the left the angel appears. Jeremiah stands in a contraposto attitude with his weight on the left leg and the right leg advanced. The body is turned to the right, but the head turns up to the left to listen to the angel. There is thus a sense of movement in the figure and the gestures of the hand also contribute to this.

The prophet wears an overmantle draped over his shoulder and wrapped round his body to fall over his left arm. The drapery is pulled tight over the left fore-arm and on the right thigh to reveal the body. The folds indicated by darker lines give it a soft appearance and a pliancy. White lines are used to outline the hems and sometimes a blob as a highlight, but never as a network of criss-cross lines. Highlights are more usually in a lighter tone of whatever colour is being used.

The figure is tall. The hands and feet are emphasized but not over-large. The head is slightly craned forward on a long neck. It bulges at brow and cheeks, so that it is of a figure of eight shape. The features are finely drawn, the eyebrows emphasized and the round of the chin and the underlip drawn. The hair and the beards are painted rather than drawn.

The more classical type of dress, the awareness of the body drapery relationship, and the contraposto stances revealed in these initials can only mean one thing – a renewal of contact with classical style through Byzantine art. This is evidently part of a general wave which was travel-

ling northward, and which has been commented on by Porcher.[1] One source of this was probably southern Italy and the murals of a church like St Angelo in Formis. But added to these Byzantine features is what Porcher has called the 'frenzy of the South'.[2] The figures of these initials are more subdued than those of the Josephus quoted by Porcher[3] but Pl. 52*b*
Micah, fol. 240ᵛ, Hoseah, fol. 234ᵛ, and the trumpeters of Daniel, fol. 207ᵛ, Pls. 52*c*, 51*e*
are all raised on tiptoe swaying forward with bent knees.

In fact the closest parallels to these figures are to be found in manuscripts now at Le Mans, particularly MS. 214 and MS. 227 both Lives of saints which come from La Couture. Porcher has suggested that MS. 214 could be by the same hand as the Josephus. Certain details in it, particularly the convention for the hair round the temples, make one doubt this. Nevertheless the manuscripts are certainly stylistically related and do show a progression northwards of the new style.[4] With the Bordeaux Bible this reaches into Normandy.

The figures in the La Couture initials are not as unequivocal in using the letter form as a backcloth as those of the Bible. Some, as in the 'T', fol. 13 of MS. 227, are overlapped by the letter, others, as in the 'Q', Pl. 51*c*
fol. 199 of the same manuscript, are framed by it. But in a 'Q' on fol. 27 of MS. 227, St Mary Magdalen's pointing finger overlaps the letter and in all the initials the figures are of such a size that they dominate the initial and produce the impression of 'immediacy' referred to as characteristic of the Bible figures. There are no figure initials in these Le Mans manuscripts.

[1] Porcher, *French Miniatures*, 25ff. For the succeeding stage of absorbtion of Byzantine influence see W. Köhler, 'Byzantine Art in the West', *Dumbarton Oaks Papers*, i (1941), 63–97.

[2] 'La frénésie meridionale', p. 32.

[3] Paris, Bib. Nat., Latin 5058. Perhaps from S. Sernin, Toulouse. *MSS. à peintures*, no. 313.

[4] Porcher, *French Miniatures*, pl. xix. The Josephus initials are different from those at Le Mans. The La Couture manuscripts have two types of initials. The first are golden scrolls on blue, red or green grounds and the second veined white reserve leaves, fleshy and striated on alternating grounds of red, yellow and green principally. The latter type of leaf is not southern-looking and may well have come from Normandy, where also alternating colour grounds were much used at Lyre and St Evroul for instance, though never at Mont St Michel. A Bible of the twelfth century survives from La Couture but unfortunately the illumination was never finished and there are no historiated or even figure initials. Two entries in the Mont St Michel obituaries may concern abbots of La Couture, one *c.* 1010, the other *c.* 1070. See J. Laporte, 'Les obituaires du Mont Saint-Michel', *Millénaire* (1), 733, 738.

In style the figures are very close to those of the Bible, in their swaying tiptoe postures, the gestures of the hands, the features and shape of face, the drapery, and their pressed forward stomachs. Le Mans 214, fol. 26$^{v}$,
Pls. 51*b*, *e* an 'M' may be compared with the 'A', fol. 207$^{v}$, of the Bible, the 'Q', Le Mans 227, fol. 199, with the 'I', fol. 244, of the Bible, and the 'I',
Pls. 54*b*, *d* fol. 122 of Le Mans 227, with the 'O', fol. 301, of the Bible. The abbey's possession of a priory at Le Mans provides a possible channel by which the new style may have reached Normandy.

Another manuscript which raises a most interesting problem, is an illustrated Life of St Martin from St Martin at Tours.[1] The miniatures which are incorporated in the text and are unpainted, are very close to the Le Mans style. But they can also be compared with figures in the Bible,
Pls. 52*d*, *f* for instance the enthroned figure of a king on fol. 11, with the figure of Job, fol. 250$^{v}$, of the Bible, and the figure about to strike St Martin on
Pls. 53*a*, *b* fol. 13, with the left hand figure of the initial 'M' on fol. 300$^{v}$ of the Bible. Both the general similarity of the pose of these figures (especially the swivelling latter pair) and the detailed resemblances, for instance the double lines in hoops on the torsos or the knot of the cloak at the shoulder of the seated figures, are remarkable. The St Martin life figures differ most notably in their proportions, being stockier and with larger heads.

The majority of the initials in the Life are rather plain letters in red minium and are typical of manuscripts of the central west part of France at this period. On folios 5$^{v}$ and 176$^{v}$, however, there are initials, an 'I' and an 'A', whose similarity to the Mont St Michel late style initials is at once recognizable.

What conclusions are to be drawn from this? These two initials seem not quite expert enough for them to have been either made at Mont St Michel or by a Mont St Michel artist, and the script is not that of a recognizable Mont St Michel scribe. In addition the type of leaf used in the 'I' is the flat fan-shaped leaf, not the curling veined Mont St Michel leaf. Tours, of course, is exactly where this fan-shaped leaf could be expected.

But this evidence suggests some kind of connection between the artist

[1] Tours, Bib. Mun., MS. 1018. E. K. Rand, *A survey of the Manuscripts of Tours*, i (1929), 200, no. 225, ii, pl. cxciii–v. There are some Tours entries in the obituaries too. Laporte, op. cit., 730, 736, 739.

of the Life and Mont St Michel. One explanation of the surviving works would be that we have to do with a single artist working in various centres, but deriving his figure style (and possibly himself coming) from the south. It is significant that it is just at this period that we hear of the professional lay artist Fulk who worked at Angers,[1] and even earlier there had been the Lombard Nivardus executing commissions at Fleury.[2] The use of a single figure in two different contexts, as Sofronius, fol. 260, and Aman, fol. 322, may also suggest a professional artist working with a pattern book. Pls. 53*e*, *f*

This can remain at present no more than a very tentative hypothesis. To support it it should also be emphasized that this is a very expert and sophisticated style. That such a style could have been transmitted and have remained so well understood (there are admittedly a number of divergencies) when executed by monastic painters in different centres, is difficult to believe. Further study of the painting in the Loire valley at this date, however, may show whether this was a regional style practised by numerous different artists and which might have been taken up anywhere, or whether it was rather, at least in the early stages, the creation of one or two distinguishable artists or groups, executing commissions wherever they were available. Other manuscripts are evidence of the same stylistic trends, and there are also the surviving cycles of wall paintings, amongst the most important being those at Vic, St Savin and Poitiers, to be considered.[3] By the late eleventh century the disconnected

[1] Porcher, *French Miniatures*, 30. Fulk was called in by Gerard, abbot of St Aubin, 1082–1108. The manuscripts associated with him by Porcher, the Psalter, Amiens Bib. Mun., MS. Lescalopier 2 and the Life of St Albinus, Paris, Bib. Nat., n. acq. Latin 1390, with their squat figures and encasing sheath of drapery are not like the Mont St Michel Bible figures.

[2] See C. Nordenfalk, 'A travelling Milanese artist', op. cit., p. 98 above.

[3] Among manuscripts there are the second Bible of St Martial Limoges, Paris, Bib. Nat., Latin 8, the Life of St Radegonde, Poitiers, Bib. Mun., MS. 250 and several manuscripts from Angers, e.g. Angers, Bib. Mun., MS. 150, St Jerome on Isaiah, fol. 4, initial 'V', and MS. 25, a Gospel book, fol. 1 and 85$^{v}$, both from St Aubin. Exh., *MSS. à peintures*, nos. 325, 222, 224, 226. Of the paintings at St Savin, the frescoes in the crypt, again a cycle of a Saint's life, are the closest to the Tours manuscript. There is also the illustrated Terence, Rome, Vatican, Latin 3305, which was compared with Tours 1018 by L. W. Jones and C. R. Morey, *The Miniatures of the Manuscripts of Terence*, i (1931), 163–74, see especially page 174 where the authors speak of 'an intrusion into the scriptoria of Tours . . . of a migrant artist from the south'.

styles of individual houses which are so striking earlier, are beginning to merge into a more uniform style, a process which reaches its culmination in the late twelfth century with an international style whose products in England and France are extremely difficult to distinguish.

## D: DATING

These paintings and manuscripts are usually dated to the end of the eleventh century, for example the Le Mans manuscripts, and to the early twelfth century, for example, St Savin. The Bible figures have not got the system of white veining to give highlights on the drapery which is used at St Savin and in the figures of the Baptistery at Poitiers for instance. This probably indicates an earlier date for the Bible initials and they are probably still of the eleventh century.

This touches on the problem as to when the Bible passed from Mont St Michel to Redon and whether in fact these last initials were done at Mont St Michel at all. There seems to be nothing comparable to the figure style surviving in the abbey's production.[1] Nor, however, is there anything similar surviving from Redon, which is of course nearer to the centres from which the style and iconography of these late initials have been seen to derive.

The earlier of the two bulls addressed to Redon and copied in the Bible, that of Gregory VII which has been dated 1073–85,[2] fol. 259ᵛ, is in a different and earlier hand than that of Pope Eugenius III dated 24 June 1147, fol. 249ᵛ.[3] The earlier hand is round with tall ascenders and looks as if it belongs still to the eleventh century. If so, then the Bible could already have been at Redon late in the eleventh century and it is at least possible that the initials were done there.

1 The only exception to this is a sketch on fol. 40ᵛ of MS. 163 which in spite of its poor style shows some resemblances to the Bible figures. If the Bible initials are the work of a visiting artist, as is suggested above, then this difficulty is overcome.

2 Ph. Jaffé G. Wattenbach, *Regesta Pontificum Romanorum*, i (1885), 647, no. 5280.

3 Jaffé, Wattenbach, op. cit., ii, 45, no. 9087. On fol. 259ᵛ after the earlier bull a document apparently referring to the ninth century, records the authorization of Lyosoc, abbot of Redon, to take stones for the building of the abbey by Mala Manus de Sancto Johanne, Armiger. This is in a different hand again and dates probably from the second half of the twelfth century. This grant could surely only have been copied at Redon.

Against this it can be said, first that the two Redon bulls were also copied in the twelfth century into a Mont St Michel manuscript of the eleventh century, which is still at Avranches, MS. 82, and which, therefore, there is no reason to suppose was made anywhere else or ever left Mont St Michel. The monks would have been interested in the bulls because of the permission they give to the community to elect its own Abbot. This was a privilege also claimed by Mont St Michel, though, as was seen earlier, resting on a forgery. Secondly, there appears to be no break in the style of the initial decoration. The foliage scrolls in the figure initials develop clearly out of the middle Mont St Michel manuscripts style. Thirdly, the copying of the initial 'N' in Latin 8055 by our artist Pl. 53*b*, *d*
for his 'M' on fol. 300v is more or less conclusive evidence that he was working at Mont-Saint-Michel. For though the provenance of Latin 8055 before it came into the hands of Jacques de Thou (1553–1617) is unknown, there is certainly no reason to suppose that it was at Redon rather than at Mont-Saint-Michel by *c.* 1100.

What could have been the cause of the later removal of the Bible to Redon is obscure but it may be connected with the dispersals of their number by Abbot Roger I, of which the monks complained to Henry I in 1106. The bulls certainly suggest that there was some relationship between Mont St Michel and St Sauveur which remains to be elucidated.[1]

## E: COLOUR AND INITIAL DEVELOPMENT

Finally something should be said about the ornament of the latest initials of the Bible, first to show that they are continuous with what has gone before and secondly to comment on one or two innovations. Also something must briefly be said about colour.

The second group of the Bible's initials, it was said earlier, are typical of late Mont St Michel manuscripts. However, this was an over-simplification. Of these late initials a number are certainly so close to the initials

[1] An abbot Mainard of St Sauveur is recorded in 1008 but there is no proof that he is identifiable with Mainard II of Mont St Michel. *Gallia Christiana*, xiv (1856), 941. That there was a close connection between the two abbeys is confirmed in the obituaries in which Redon monks figure 41 times, more than any other monastery except Fécamp. See J. Laporte, 'Les obituaires du Mont Saint-Michel', *Millénaire* (1), 727. For another manuscript with Redon connections see the catalogue of manuscripts, p. 231 below, Vat. Lat. 9668.

Pl. 15*a* of MS. 86 that they are probably by the same hand. Others, however,
Pl 55*a* are slightly different. The 'C' of the Bible, fol. 250, is a typical Mont St
Pl. 14*d* Michel late initial and is very close for instance to the 'E' of MS. 77,
Pl. 55*c* fol. 2. However, if it is compared to the 'V', fol. $237^{v}$ of the Bible, certain
differences appear, though the letters are very similar in structure. First
the leaves are rather larger in the 'V' but there are fewer of them and they
are more widely spaced. The effect is simpler. Secondly they are not so
veined as those of the 'C'. Thirdly the animals and birds are less entwined
in the scroll and stand out more clearly.

These differences are not to be exaggerated. The vocabulary of leaf and
animal forms remains the same and the letters are similarly constructed
with their panel frames. It is a different artist working in the same tradition rather than a clear break. It is this second type of ornament which is
found in the third group of Bible initials, those with figures, on fol. $168^{v}$,
Pl. 51*a* the 'V' of Jeremiah, for instance. If this letter is compared with the 'C', fol.
Pl. 55*a* 250, both the similarities and the differences will be demonstrated. It is
this which makes it difficult to believe that these last initials of the Bible
could have been done anywhere but in the scriptorium of Mont St Michel.

One or two other characteristics may be noted. It was pointed out that
symmetrical arrangements were typical of late group initials. This is
noticeable particularly in this last group of the Bible initials. Secondly,
Pl. 51*a* many of the animal or bird head terminals in this group bite at one or
more round objects, a sort of fruit, with their open mouths. Sprigs of
berries are common in the scroll from the middle group initials onwards,
but this is a new use for them for which I have not found a parallel so
early elsewhere.[1]

1 The berries in the animals' mouths do not occur in the Le Mans manuscripts but are found in the Tours MS. 1018. Later they occur in the Gloucester candlestick, in the Victoria and Albert Museum, London. This is significant since Serlo of Mont St Michel, d. 1104, was the first post-Conquest abbot at Gloucester. The parallels noted by A. Harris, 'A Romanesque candlestick in London', *Journal of the Archaeological Association*, xxvii (1964), especially p. 45 n. 5, with manuscripts from St Augustine's, Canterbury whose first post-conquest abbot was Scollandus of Mont St Michel, would thus be due to common ancestry and the reason for attributing the candlestick to St Augustine's disappear. Mrs Harris states that there is no evidence from existing manuscripts that the monks at Gloucester illuminated their manuscripts in this manner. To me, however, it seems extremely probable that they did so. Very few manuscripts survive from Gloucester at all (unlike St Augustine's) and none from the early post-Conquest period.

Thirdly, human heads are used occasionally as terminals. There is an early example of this in MS. 97, fol. 214,[1] and another in the 'D' of Paris, Latin 2088, fol. 1$^{v}$, one of the 'Antonius' group of manuscripts. Then on Pl. 14*c*
fol. 137$^{v}$ of Avranches $86_3$ an 'I' has two horned satyr heads as terminals. These can be compared to an 'F' of fol. 1$^{v}$ of the Bible, a middle group initial. There is a certain awkwardness in the way they join the interlace, as there is in the 'D' of Latin 2088 which is not found in the later MS. $86_3$ 'I'. Another human head in the Bible is on fol. 250$^{v}$, 'V', Job. This has a Pl. 52*f*
pointed cap which makes it very similar to the heads which emerge from leaves of the 'C', fol. 140$^{v}$, with objects protruding from their lips, Pl. 55*e*
perhaps to be thought of as trumpets.

Heads used as terminals in initials occur already in the Corbie Psalter[2] and in the tenth century can be found both in an Anglo-Saxon initial of the Athelstan Psalter and in the St Martial, Limoges Lectionary.[3] The motif of the head emerging from a leaf is a separate theme and is of Eastern origin, being found for instance in textiles.[4] In the West it occurs already in an Ottonian manuscript,[5] but it only becomes a common form of decoration in the twelfth century. A well-known example is the capital from Hyde Abbey.[6] Parallel examples of the terminal head with Phrygian cap in Normandy are to be found in St Evroul manuscripts from Alençon.[7]

Finally, it may be noted that two initials, the 'O', fol. 242, and the 'V', Pls. 55, *b*, *d*, *f*
fol. 236, the former with its entwining birds hinting at oriental motifs, again recall the Corbie Psalter.[8] Since we have already seen that the 'N'

[1] *Millénaire* (2), pl. 56, fig. 132.

[2] Amiens, Bib. Mun., MS. 18.

[3] London, Brit. Mus., Cotton MS. Galba A.XVIII, Paris, Bib. Nat., Latin 5301, fol. 85$^{v}$. Cf. also the Leofric Missal, Oxford, Bodleian Library, MS. Bodley 579, fol. 154$^{v}$.

[4] O. von Falke, *Decorative Silks* (1936), pl. i. Silk from Antinoe in Greco-Egyptian style of the sixth century. See also J. Baltrusaitis, *Le Moyen Age fantastique* (1955), 109–32, for other Eastern examples and particularly the 'talking tree'.

[5] Munich, Bayr. Staatsbibl., Clm. 4453, in a border, fol. 26, and elsewhere in the arches. G. Leidinger, *Miniaturen aus Handschriften der Kgl. Hof.- und Staatsbibl. in München*, i (1912), Taf. 16.

[6] See A. Gardner, *English Medieval Sculpture* (1951), fig. 120. For manuscript examples see *The St. Albans Psalter*, 168 and pl. 156, and C. M. Kauffmann, 'The Bury Bible', *Journal of the Warburg and Courtauld Institutes*, xxix (1966), 79.

[7] e.g. Alençon, Bib. Mun., MS. 26, fol. 62.

[8] Amiens, Bib. Mun., MS. 18. See above, pp. 52, 197.

of the early Persius, which is a literal copy of the Corbie Psalter, was copied in the Bible on fol. $300^{v}$ and that the archer in the 'D' of the prologue to Daniel is remarkably close to another initial in the Corbie Psalter, it looks as if there may have been quite a number of copies of the Psalter initials in the early Mont St Michel initials to serve as inspiration for the artists of the Bible.[1]

Two initials remain, the 'N', fol. 369, and the 'U', fol. 314. The second is a poor version of the Mont St Michel style similar to the 'V' of fol. 152, but lacking its tautness and vigour. It seems to be by the same artist who did another rather feeble initial in MS. 146, fol. 69, a 'd'. The other letter is an 'N', fol. 369, reviving the acanthus panel filling pattern and with veined leaf scroll terminals.

The majority of the initials in the late manuscripts, all those in MS. 89 and MS. $86_3$ for example, are not coloured. Of the Bible initials those that are closest to these manuscripts are not for the most part coloured. One or two have the grounds filled in, and a start has been made on painting
Pl. 55*a* the 'C' of fol. 250. With these initials the design is so complex that they were probably not intended to be painted.

With the other group it is different. Their design is more open and the
Pl. 55*c* leaf forms are bolder. The system used is in general to paint the background either a very brilliant colour, or one that is deeper in tone. The
Pl. 54*e* scrolls and leaves then are painted in much lighter tone, or sometimes left unpainted, so that they stand out. The same procedure is used in the
Pl. 51*a* initials with figures. The result is to increase the effect already referred to of a backcloth which throws the figures or the scroll forward.

With the earlier initials it is quite different. These in the Bible are, as has been said, less often painted. But they tend to rather paler colours and the contrasts are achieved simply by colour, not by tone. Very often, also, the ground is a neutral green or blue and the result is that the scroll is projected back or even merged into the ground.

[1] One might almost have suspected that the Corbie Psalter had actually been brought to Mont St Michel. But Paris, Bib. Nat., Latin 13392, a Gregory the Great, Sermons of the late eleventh to early twelfth century proves the Psalter was still at Corbie at that date, since it contains copies of initials in the Psalter, especially fols. 27 and 43 (the latter the same motif of the man spearing the dragon behind him). These copies were unfortunately not known to me at the time of my paper in *Millénaire* (2), 239–45.

The actual colours used in the earlier and later initials are also different. In the earlier initials the predominant colours are pale green, blue, orange with some yellow and red, and a smudgy mauve. In the later initials a dark brown red, fol. 250$^{v}$ and fol. 168$^{v}$, a dark green, and a mauve pink are used for the backgrounds, whilst these colours and also orange, blue in various shades and pale yellow, are common. The later initials are altogether darker in tone than the earlier, and very much richer in effect. It is noteworthy that these colours are not at all like those used in the Le Mans manuscripts which were so close in their figure style. They and also manuscripts from Limoges, like the second Bible, use almost exclusively a bright green, yellow and orange-red. The subtler and more developed use of colour in the Bible is then one of its most distinguishing features and one which links it to the great illuminated manuscripts of the twelfth century.

# CONCLUSION

In tracing the development of the illumination of the manuscripts of Mont St Michel it has been possible to follow the emergence of a new style. The scriptorium started with the materials of an artistic tradition which was still Carolingian. But with the weakening of that tradition formal tendencies which it had largely obliterated, begin to appear again. The two currents then combined and out of them a new style is formed, the style of the Romanesque period.

This process is seen both in the initials and in the miniatures. To the Carolingian letter forms is joined the inhabited scroll as it had been adapted in Insular art. The principle of the metamorphosis of forms, giving variety and vitality to the initial, also reappears, and some letters are constructed out of animal and bird forms. Merovingian sources are used in these letters as well.

In the miniatures the Anglo-Saxon figure style is combined with a treatment of the problem of spatial relationship on a flat surface, which is no longer derived from late classical practice as it was revived in the Carolingian schools and is still recognizable in Anglo-Saxon manuscripts. Instead, the artists at Mont St Michel adopt the new methods which were developed in the second half of the tenth century in Ottonian art, abandoning any attempt at illusionistic perspective and using a system of overlapping planes. When at the end of the eleventh century or early in the twelfth a new wave of influence ultimately deriving from Byzantine art is transmitted from the south and results in a fresh treatment of the relationship of body to drapery, there is no change in the solution already worked out for the relationship of the figure to its setting. In fact this system is now adapted to the historiated initial and, where the letter form in the Morgan Sacramentary had acted as a frame or window, just as it had in the Carolingian Drogo Sacramentary, it is now a background for the figure, a kind of stage backcloth to project it.

From these points of view it is possible to see Mont St Michel and the other Norman abbeys as pioneers in the emergence of the Romanesque style in book illumination. If the present study has concentrated more on the sources than on the impact of the Norman achievement, that has been necessary to show what the new style owed to the past and how it differed from it. As for the immediate influence of Mont St Michel in England, the disappearance of any highly illuminated manuscripts which may have been made at St Augustine's or St Peter's, Gloucester during the abbacies of Serlo and Scollandus, makes this impossible to judge. But on a wider view, in spite of undoubted stylistic continuity with Anglo-Saxon art after the Conquest, one of the main currents of Anglo-Norman illumination, the inhabited or historiated scroll initial, was a Norman development. Even when English Romanesque book painting returned to the full-page miniature in the twelfth century with various (and predominantly non-Norman) sources, its use of 'planar' space and many of its detailed features, for instance the architectural canopy frames, had already been anticipated in Norman manuscripts.

England quickly reasserted itself as the creative centre in the twelfth century. But if the chronology here proposed is accepted, it is clear that many of the steps towards the new style were taken in Normandy before the Conquest, not in England after it. In this sense behind the great achievement in book illumination in England in the twelfth century, stands in part the Norman achievement of the eleventh century.

# APPENDIX I

## CHRONOLOGY

Taking into account the palaeographical development and the development of the initial style which, as has been seen, is very continuous with no sign of any break between one group and the next, the following schema may be drawn up.

| *Date* | *Manuscripts* | *Contemporary* |
|---|---|---|
| *Early group* | | |
| *c.* 980–1000 | MS. 50, 78 | |
| *c.* 990–1015 | MSS. $35_1$, 69, 95, 97, 99, 109, 211, 229, 240, Paris, Latin 8055, p. 141–78, Latin 8070, Vat. Reg. Lat. 2043 | Limoges manuscripts |
| *c.* 1000–1020 | MSS. 98, Bayeux 56, Leiden, Univ. Bibl., Voss. lat. fol. 39 with Paris, Latin 5920 | |
| *Transitional group* | | |
| *c.* 1015–1035 | MSS. 38, 68, 70, 79, 91, 99, 105, 115, 128, 129, Vat. Lat. 9668 | St Vaast manuscripts |
| *Middle group* | | |
| *c.* 1030–1045 | MSS. $61_2$, 59, 101 | St Germain-des-Prés manuscripts, St Vaast manuscripts |
| *c.* 1040–1055 | MSS. 72, 75, 76, 107 | |
| Written before 1048 | MS. Rouen A.143(427) | |
| *c.* 1050–1065 | MSS. 10 (fragments), 90, Morgan 641, Latin 2639, Bordeaux 1 (first group of initials) | Robert of Jumièges gifts to his old monastery |
| *c.* 1055–1080 | MSS. 51, $86_2$, 77, 73, Latin 2055, Latin 2088 | |
| *Late group* | | |
| *c.* 1065–1080 | MSS. $35_2$, 103 (before 1072), 163, Royal 13. A.XXII, Royal 13. A.XXIII, Cambridge, Corpus MS. 276, Latin 5290, Berlin, Phillipps MS. 1854 (before 1080?) | Scollandus' abbacy of St Augustine's, 1072 |

| | | |
|---|---|---|
| c. 1070–1095 | MSS. 58, $61_1$, 73 and $86_1$ (fragments), 82, $86_3$, 88 and 94 (fragments), 89, 146, Bordeaux 1 (second group of initials), Latin 8055, p. 1–140, Rouen A.178(425) | Carilef manuscripts, Charter of Robert Curthose, 1088 |
| c. 1080–1100 | MSS. 9, 47, 57, 102, Bordeaux 1 (last group of initials) | Le Mans manuscripts |

This grouping presents certain difficulties. The transitional manuscripts may seem to be dated too early in view of the Arras connection, but it must be remembered that MS. 115 with its frontispiece so close to the St Vaast Bible, was partly written by Hervardus who also wrote MS. 97 with its scrolling leaf initials and the obituary in the Wincombe Sacramentary before 1004. The Morgan Sacramentary and earlier Redon Bible initials belong to the middle period but their script placed them in the late group. Men of different generations could work on the same manuscript, of course, but initials deriving immediately from the Frotmundus style of MS. 72, as these do, cannot be much later than *c.* 1050–65. MS $86_2$ and MS. 77 which have late initials but middle script may easily have been written by a scribe of the older generation – in fact MS. 77 is signed by Gyraldus, who is almost certainly the same man as the Gyraldus who signed the earlier MS. 90. The slight difference in script is only to be expected if there is a difference of between ten and twenty years in the writing of the two manuscripts. But also as can be seen in MS. 101, initials were sometimes added later to unfinished manuscripts.

# APPENDIX II

## MANUSCRIPTS SURVIVING FROM MONT ST MICHEL, *c.* 966–1100[1]

Medieval indications of provenance only are given. All the manuscripts still at Avranches are found in Le Michel's catalogue of 1639 a concordance of which is given by G. Nortier, *Revue Mabillon*, xlvii (1957). The bibliography omits works concerned with the text, for the most part. Further reproductions though much reduced are to be found in L. Bossboeuf, *Le Mont-Saint-Michel au peril de la mer. Son histoire et ses merveilles*, Tours (1910), pp. 164 (MSS. 75, 76), 165, 167 (MS. 72), 184 (MS. 75), 194 (MS. 211), 198 (MS. 50), 207 (MS. 76). A number of manuscripts are mentioned incidentally by F. Avril, *Notes* (1) as follows: MS. 35, p. 515, 521, MS. 59, p. 500, MS. 61, p. 520, MS. 75, p. 510, MS. 86, p. 510, 512, MS. 89, p. 510, 512, MS. 90, p. 510, MS. 91, p. 500, MS. 101, p. 510, 512, MS. 103, p. 521, Paris, Latin 2055, pp. 509–10, 514, 520, Latin 2088, p. 509–10, 524, Latin 2639, p. 510, 514, 520, Berlin, Phillipps 1854, p. 521, Rouen A.178, p. 521. The millenary number of *Art de Basse Normandie*, xl (1966), has reproductions of the following manuscripts in addition to those principally discussed (for which full references are given below): MS. 29, p. 21, fig. 2, MS. 9, p. 44, fig., MS. 58, p. 42, fig., MS. 86, p. 39, fig., MS. 89, p. 48–9, figs., MS. 102, p. 46, fig., MS. 103, p. 46, fig., MS. 107, p. 45, fig., MS. 238, p. 21, fig. Finally many of the manuscripts are reproduced and the most important discussed by M. Bourgeois-Lechartier, 'A la recherche du scriptorium de l'abbaye du Mont Saint-Michel', *Millénaire* (2), 171–202 and F. Avril, 'La décoration des manuscrits au Mont Saint-Michel (XI$^{e}$–XII$^{e}$ siècles)', *Millénaire* (2), 203–38. References to these two articles and others in *Millénaire* (*1*) and (*2*) are not generally given below since the volumes are fully indexed.

Avranches, Bibliothèque Municipale, MS. 9 *c.* 1080–1100.
Angelomus Monachus, Comm. on Kings.

Initials drawn in pen in red and green

[1] A fuller catalogue of the manuscripts with palaeographical data can be found in my thesis, Oxford, Bodleian Library, MS. D.Phil. d. 3190 (submitted January, 1964), with an attempt to distinguish hands and a larger selection of plates.

Avranches, Bibliothèque Municipale, MS. 10 *c.* 1050–1070.
Book of Deuteronomy. Fragments used as pastedowns.

Small capitals in orange minium

Avranches, Bibliothèque Municipale MS. 35, fols. 74–193$^{v}$ *c.* 1065–1080.
Eugyppius, Excerpts from Augustine.

Initial, fol. 75$^{v}$, with leaf scroll in pen with green and red. [Pl. 5*c*]

Avranches, Bibliothèque Municipale, MS. 35, fols. 194–316 *c.* 990–1015.
Alcuin, Augustine, *opuscula*.

Minor initials in pen, some with interlace

Avranches, Bibliothèque Municipale, MS. 38 *c.* 1015–1040.
Amalarius, *de officiis ecclesiasticis*.

Initial 'V' with leaf scroll and interlace, fol. 2. Pen-sketch of figure presenting a book, fol. 137$^{v}$, eleventh century (?)

Avranches, Bibliothèque Municipale, MS. 47 *c.* 1080–1100.
Dionysius Areopagita, works.

Numerous initials in green and red pen with leaf scrolls, animals and some figures. Small diagrams
*Bibliography*. J. Chatillon, 'Notes sur quelques manuscrits Dionysiens . . .', *Millénaire* (2), 313–6

Avranches, Bibliothèque Municipale, MS. 50 *c.* 980–1000.
Clement, *Recognitiones*.

Full-page miniature of the Presentation of the Book to St Michael, fol. 1, initials with interlace, animal head and leaf decoration, some with purple grounds. Several initials added later. [Pls. 6*c*, *e*, 7*a*, *c*, 17*b*]
*Prov*. Fol. 1, under the purple ground are visible the words 'SCS MICHAEL' and 'GELDUINUS MONACHUS SCI . . .'. No Gelduinus is mentioned in the Orléans obituary and the word after SCI does not appear to be 'Michaelis'. The manuscript may perhaps have been made in another centre for presentation. The script is not conclusive but the first hand in particular is close to script in MSS. 78 and 240
*Bibliography*. Martin, 557; *MSS. à peintures*, no. 186; Porcher, *French Miniatures*, 20, pl. ix (fol. 1 colour); P. Bloch, 'Zum Dedikationsbild im Lob des Kreuzes des Hrabanus Maurus', *Das erste Jahrtausend*, text ed. V. H. Elbern (1962), 487; Exh., *Millénaire*, no. 178, pl. (fol. 1 colour).

Avranches, Bibliothèque Municipale, MS. 51 *c.* 1055–1080.
Cyprian, Augustine, Orosius.

Initial 'C' fol. 1$^{v}$, veined leaves on green ground. This and certain rubrics appear to be added. They belong to the late group.
*Prov.* Fifteenth-century list of contents, fol. 1$^{v}$.

Avranches, Bibliothèque Municipale, MS. 57, fols. 49–110 *c.* 1080–1100.
John Chrysostom, Homilies (incomplete).

Pen initials with some green and red.

Avranches, Bibliothèque Municipale, MS. 58 *c.* 1070–1090.
Hilary of Poitiers, Comm. on St Matthew. John of Fécamp, *de vitae ordine et morum institutione*. Sentences from Isidore, Ambrose, etc.

Historiated initial 'G' with St Hilary writing, fol. 3$^{v}$. Written in part by Mauritius, colophon, fol. 119$^{v}$. Another hand, fols. 28–82$^{v}$, seems to be the same as that which added the copy of the *Trevia Dei* (after 1080), to Phillipps MS. 1854. Mauritius' script is also recognizable in the two St Augustine's manuscripts, Brit. Mus., Royal 13. A.XXII–XXIII. Rubrication in red, blue and green. Sketch for similar historiated initial on fol. 2$^{v}$. [Pls. 6*b*, 49*a*.]
*Prov.* Fifteenth-century list of contents, fol. i.
*Bibliography.* A. Wilmart, 'Jean L'Homme de Dieu. Auteur d'un traité attribué à S. Bernard', *Revue Mabillon*, xv (1925), 5–29.

Avranches, Bibliothèque Municipale, MS. 59 *c.* 1030–1045.
Ambrose, Comm. on St Luke.

Frame with acanthus foliage scroll and corner medallions painted yellow and blue, fol. 1$^{v}$. Initials with veined leaf scrolls drawn in pen, painted blue, orange, yellow and brown. [Pls. 3*b*, 11*c*, *f*, 30*b*.]
*Prov.* Fifteenth-century list of contents, fol. 2.
*Bibliography.* Martin, 558, fig. 2 (fol. 2 'S'); F. Avril, 'L'Influence du style franco-saxon au Mont Saint-Michel', *Art de Basse Normandie*, xl (1966), 35–9, fig. 4 (fol. 31$^{v}$ 'Et').

Avranches, Bibliothèque Municipale, MS. 61, fols. 1–110 *c.* 1070–1095.
Ambrose, various works. Augustine, *contra Pelagianos*.

Initial with animal heads and leaf scrolls, fol. 2$^{v}$. Script isolated in style. Same contents as Paris, Latin 2639.

Avranches, Bibliothèque Municipale, MS. 61, fols. 112–343 *c.* 1030–1045.
Ambrose, Comm. on Ps. 118. John Chrysostom, Homilies.

Initials, fol. 112, 'L' of Franco-Saxon style, fol. 113, 'B' with dragons and scroll, painted. Initials from fol. 317 in pen close to style of initials from St Germain-des-Prés, Paris. Possibly this last part of the manuscript is slightly earlier in date. Pricking and ruling are the same in both parts, and list of contents, fols. 1 and 111 by the same hand, late eleventh century. [Pls. 3*a*, 11*d*]
*Prov*. Fol. 344ᵛ, *ex libris*, early twelfth century (?).

Avranches, Bibliothèque Municipale, MS. 68, fols. 1–112 *c*. 1015–1035.
Jerome, Comm. on Genesis. Haimo, Comm. on Genesis and Deuteronomy. Homiliary (fragment). Augustine, *de natali Domini*.

Minor initial, fol. 1.
*Bibliography*. R. Etaix, 'Les homiliaires patristiques du Mont Saint-Michel,' *Millénaire* (1), 399–400.

Avranches, Bibliothèque Municipale, MS. 69, fols. 119–302 *c*. 990–1015.
Jerome, Comm. on the Minor Prophets.

Minor initials (fols. 267 and verso with leaf scrolls). Fol. 120 sketch of figure in plummet, second half eleventh century (?) and on fol. 221ᵛ in ink, first half eleventh century (?).

Avranches, Bibliothèque Municipale, MS. 70 *c*. 1015–1035.
Jerome, Comm. on Daniel. Augustine, Homilies on Epistles of St John.

Initials, fols. 1 and 55.

Avranches, Bibliothèque Municipale, MS. 72 *c*. 1040–1055.
Treatises against Heretics by Jerome, Rufinus, Augustine. Ambrose, *de bono mortis*.

Full-page miniature of St Augustine disputing with Felicianus, fol. 97. Miniature of St Ambrose writing, fol. 182ᵛ. Painted initials (except fol. 44ᵛ), with inhabited scrolls. Written by Frotmundus. [Pls. 3*c*, 11*h*, 12*a*, 13*b*, 22, 28]
*Prov*. Colophon, fol. 199ᵛ: Ipsa manus vivat quae tam bene scribere curat.
Si quis sit scriptor quaeris cognoscere, lector,
Hunc studuit totum Frotmundus scribere librum;
Maxima conscripsit, quam plurima sancta peregit,
Felix Frotmundus, per secula, frater amandus.
*Bibliography*. Gout, fig. 51 (fol. 182ᵛ–3); Martin, 559, fig. 5 (fol. 182ᵛ); *MSS. à peintures*, no. 187; Porcher, *French Miniatures*, 20, pl. x (fol. 97); Avril, *Notes* (1), 503, 510, 520, figs. (fols. 112, 128ᵛ); P. Bloch, 'Eine Dialogdarstellung des frühen 12. Jahrhunderts', *Festschrift Dr. E. Trautscholdt* (1965), 59, Abb. 17 (fol. 97); J. J. G. Alexander, 'Manuscrits enluminés du XIe siècle provenant du Mont-Saint-Michel', *Art de Basse Normandie*, xl (1966), 27–33, figs. (fols. 97, 150ᵛ–1).

Avranches, Bibliothèque Municipale, MS. 73, fols. 1–2v, MS. 86, fols. 1–2v (MS. $86_1$) *c.* 1070–1095.

Sacramentary. Votive masses, unfinished fragments.
No decoration.

Avranches, Bibliothèque Municipale, MS. 73 *c.* 1055–1080.
Jerome, *opuscula.*

Penwork initials in red and green with alternating fleurons.
*Prov.* Fol. 3, list of men of the Mont owing service, twelfth century.

Avranches, Bibliothèque Municipale, MS. 75 *c.* 1040–1055.
Augustine, *de Genesi ad litteram.*

Full-page miniature of St Augustine, fol. Cv. Inhabited scroll initial, page 1, painted. Initials on pp. 56 and 236 related to those in MSS. 59 and 101. Written by Gyraldus the scribe who signed MS. 90. [Pls. 12*e*, 29*a*]
*Prov.* Erased colophon, p. 273. List of contents, fifteenth century.
*Bibliography.* Martin, 559; *MSS. à peintures*, no. 190; Exh., *Millénaire*, no. 190.

Avranches, Bibliothèque Municipale, MS. 76 *c.* 1040–1055.
Augustine, Comm. on Ps. 1–50.

Full-page miniature, fol. Av, of St Michael, St Augustine and King David. Inhabited scroll initials in pen, fols. 1 and 9v. Script related to Vat. Lat. 9668. [Pls. 12*b*, 20]
*Bibliography.* Gout, fig. 72 (fol. Av); E. Mâle, *L'Art religieux du XIIe siècle en France* (1928), 262, fig. 173 (fol. Av, detail); M. de Fraipont, 'Les origines occidentales du type de Saint Michel debout sur le dragon', *Revue Belge d'Archéologie et d'Histoire de l'Art*, vii (1937), 292–3, fig. 3 (fol. Av, detail); Martin, 559; Dodwell, *Canterbury School*, 9, pl. 5d (fol Av, detail); *MSS. à peintures*, no. 189; Avril, *Notes* (1), 497, 500, 510, fig. (fol. 1); Exh., *Millénaire*, no. 182.

Avranches, Bibliothèque Municipale, MS. 77 *c.* 1055–80.
Augustine, Comm. on Ps. 101–50.

Initial in green pen with late group veined leaves on blue ground, fol. 2. Written by Gyraldus, the scribe who also signed MS. 90. Rubrics in red, green and blue. [Pls. 4*b*, 14*d*]
*Prov.* Colophon, fol. 238v: Melos Daviticum caelesti melle refertum,
Sed clausum typicis consignatumque figuris
Ut mentes pascas pater Augustine, resignas,
excutiens gratum studiosis hinc alimentum.

Hunc ego premodicus magnus (*corr.* magni)
Michaelis alumnus,
Gyraldus nomen transcripsi dulce volumen,
Ut me caelesti conscribat gratia Christi.

Avranches, Bibliothèque Municipale, MS. 78 *c.* 980–1000.
Augustine, Comm. on Psalms 119–33.

Initial 'B' with animal head and leaf decoration, painted orange and blue, fol. 1. Other minor pen initials in orange.
*Prov.* Fol. 114, 'Liber Sancti Michaelis. Si quis illum abstulerit anathema sit. amen. fiat. fiat. fiat', second half eleventh century.

Avranches, Bibliothèque Municipale, MS. 79 *c.* 1015–1035.
Comm. on Epistles of St Paul, Romans, Galatians, Ephesians, *beg.*: 'Paulus Servus J. C. Multos igitur Hebreorum dionimos' (here attrib. to St Augustine).

Plain initial. Marginal sketch, fol. 55v.

Avranches, Bibliothèque Municipale, MS. 82 *c.* 1070–1095.
Augustine, Homilies *de verbis domini* et *quibusdam sententiis Pauli apostoli* (incomplete). [Fol. 1v, Bulls of Popes Gregory VII and Eugenius III in favour of Redon are copied, early twelfth century.]

Numerous small initials with painted fleurons in red, blue, and green, some with veined leaves. Same style and same scribe as MS. 89.

Avranches, Bibliothèque Municipale, MS. 86, fols. 3v–135 (MS. $86_2$, for $86_1$ cf. MS. 73) *c.* 1055–80.
Augustine, Ambrose, Athanasius.

Painted inhabited scroll initials in late style. Marginal sketches, fol. 3, figure on horseback, fol. 101v, Crucifixion, fol. 134, initial. Script close to Gyraldus who signed MSS. 90 and 77. [Pl. 15*a*]
*Bibliography.* Martin, 559.

Avranches, Bibliothèque Municipale, MS. 86, fols. 136–73 (MS. $86_3$) *c.* 1070–1095.
Boethius, *de Trinitate.*

Penwork initials with veined leaves, that on fol. 138v 'X' with bust of Christ and four evangelist symbols, with gold. [Pl. 15*b*]

Avranches, Bibliothèque Municipale MS. 88, fol. 167 and MS. 94, fols. I and II. *c.* 1075–1095.
Paulus Diaconus, *Historia Langobardorum* (fragments).
No decoration.

Avranches, Bibliothèque Municipale, MS. 89 *c.* 1070–1095.
Augustine, *de civitate Dei.*

Numerous pen-drawn initials, some in red and green. Same style and same scribe as MS. 82. Badly damaged. [Pls. 15*d*, 16*a*]

Avranches, Bibliothèque Municipale, MS. 90 *c.* 1050–1065.
Augustine, *contra Faustum Manichaeum.*

Full-page miniature of Augustine disputing with Faustinus, fol. 1ᵛ. Painted initials, fols. 2, 115ᵛ. Written by Gyraldus who also signs MS. 77. [Pls. 4*a*, 14*a*, 24*a*]
*Prov.* Colophon, fol. 185ᵛ: Ut pater Aurelius Faustinos contudit ausus
Scriptoris, lector, dum legis esto memor.
Quod si scire cupis humilis de nomine fratris
Gyraldi calamus [hoc renovavit opus]'.
[the last 3 words deleted]

*Bibliography.* Martin, 558–9, pl. 3 (fol. 1ᵛ); *MSS. à peintures*, no. 192; *L'Art Roman*, Catalogue of 9th Council of Europe Exhibition, Barcelona (1961), no. 57; Bloch, op. cit. (MS. 72), 62, n. 37; J. J. G. Alexander, 'Manuscrits enluminés', op. cit. (MS. 72), 27–33, figs. (fols. 1ᵛ, 2); F. Avril, 'L'Influence', op. cit. (MS. 59), fig. 3 (fol. 115); Exh., *Millénaire*, no. 181, pl. 10 (fol. 1ᵛ).

Avranches, Bibliothèque Municipale, MS. 91 *c.* 1015–1040.
Augustine, *contra Julianum*, *Retractationes*, Letters.

Numerous initials. Marginal sketches, fols. 153ᵛ, 258. Written by Uvarinus, Rannulfus and Giraldus. [Pls. 2*c*, 9*d*, *f*, 10*i*]
*Prov.* Colophons, fol. 175ᵛ: Uvarinus primam, Rannulfus necne secundam
Postremamque Giraldus in hoc conscribere libro
Particulam voluit, causa regno pociendi,
Militis et Christi summo Michahelis amore.
fol. 234ᵛ: Solibus haud plenis decies haec dicta quaternis,
Patris Augustini per mille volumina fantis,
Seclis, precipue ductus Michaelis amore
Ternis Rannulfus digitis transcripta reliquit.
List of contents, fifteenth century.

Avranches, Bibliothèque Municipale, MS. 95 *c.* 990–1015.
Cassian, *Collationes* (only 17 books. Misbound so that Bks. 1–10 follow 11–17).
Plain initial, fol. 1. Fine title-page in mixed capitals, fol. 78.

Avranches, Bibliothèque Municipale, MS. 97 *c.* 990–1015.
Gregory the Great, *Moralia in Job*, Bks. 1–16 (incomplete).

Initials to each book mostly in pen or orange minium. Fol. 201$^{v}$ 'M' with spread-eagled lion and scrolling leaf painted blue and yellow. Fol. 240$^{v}$ 'Q' with two birds and a spread-eagled lion. The scribe is Hervardus who signed Leiden, Voss. lat. fol. 39. He is the main scribe of the early group. Bk. 16 which ends incomplete was written by the scribe Antonius (see Appendix IV). [Pls. 1*b*, 7*i*, 8*d*, *e*].

*Prov*. Fifteenth-century list of contents, fol. 1.

*Bibliography*. C. Nordenfalk, 'Miniature ottonienne et ateliers capétiens', *Art de France*, iv (1964), 55; A. Grabar, C. Nordenfalk, *Romanesque Painting*, Skira (1958), 142; E. B. Garrison, *Studies in the History of Medieval Italian Painting*, i. 4 (1954), 189, fig. 269 (fol. 201$^{v}$); J. J. G. Alexander, *Millénaire* (2), 239–45, fig. 132 (fol. 217).

Avranches, Bibliothèque Municipale, MS. 98 *c*. 1000–1020.
Gregory, the Great, *Moralia in Job*, Bks. 17–25.

Initials to each book in pen and orange minium. Written by Gualterius and Martinus. [Pls. 2*a*, *b*, 7*g*, 9*b*, *c*, 10*c*, *d*.]

*Prov*. Colophon, fol. 227$^{v}$: 'Hic liber est Sancti Michaelis Archangeli inchoatus a Gualterio venerabili viro, ex maxima autem parte scriptus a Martino monacho in loco Sancti Juliani. Si quis eum abstulerit anathema sit. Amen. Fiat. Fiat. Amen in domino'. The meaning of 'in loco Sancti Juliani' is obscure as there does not appear to be any place connected with St Julian on the Mont. Conceivably it might refer to the priory of St Victeur at Le Mans. On fol. 228$^{v}$ Hymn to St Michael on a separate leaf written by a late group hand. Fifteenth-century list of contents, fol. 1.

*Bibliography*. Abbé Desroches, 'Notice sur les manuscrits de la Bibliothèque d'Avranches', *Mémoires. Société des antiquaires de Normandie*, xi (1840), 91, pl. 3; H. Walther, 'Ein Michaels-Hymnus vom Mont-St.Michel', (with Nachwort by C. Erdmann), *Corona Quernea, Festgabe Karl Strecker*, 1941, 254–65, Tafel iv (fol. 228$^{v}$).

Avranches, Bibliothèque Municipale, MS. 99 *c*. 1015–1035.
Gregory the Great, Comm. on Ezekiel. Life of Sts Aychardus and Hugo, bp. of Rouen.

Initials in ink and orange minium with leaf scrolls. [Pl. 10*g*.]

Avranches, Bibliothèque Municipale, MS. 101 *c*. 1030–1045.
Gregory the Great, Dialogues.

Initials in pen with background washes of blue, green or orange and leaf scrolls, some inhabited. On fols. 2 and 23 initials 'Q' and 'F' added in late group style (rubrication red as opposed to orange minium elsewhere in the manuscript). [Pl. 11*g*.]

*Prov.* Fifteenth-century list of contents, fol. 2.
*Bibliography.* Martin, 559.

Avranches, Bibliothèque Municipale, MS. 102 *c.* 1080–1100.
Gregory the Great, *Registrum Epistolarum.*

Initial with seated figure, fol. 188, other initials, fols. 155, 166. Pen drawn initials (fol. 1 with seated St Gregory) are perhaps additions of mid-twelfth century, also 'Q', fol. 200, painted.

Avranches, Bibliothèque Municipale, MS. 103 Before 1072.
Gregory the Great, Homilies.

Full-page miniature of Pope Gregory, fol. 4ᵛ. Fol. 5, initial 'd', inhabited scroll in red and green. Initials with human and animal head terminals, fols. 134ᵛ, 186ᵛ. Written by six scribes amongst them Scollandus, later abbot of St Augustine's, Canterbury, Osbernus who signed MS. 163, and Hilduinus, perhaps the scribe of Rouen, MS. A.178. [Pls. 5*a*, *b*, 47, 48*e*.]

*Prov.* Colophon, fol. 220ᵛ: Valde patres sancti sunt laude pia venerandi,
Qui donante Deo fulxerunt dogmate sacro.
Post renovatores scripturae mente fideles
Sunt precibus digni quod possideant paradisi
Gaudia, quae cuncti mereantur subtitulati
Principis aetherei sancti Michaelis alumpni.
GUALTERIUS, digno dictus cognomine cantor,
HILDUINUS libros renovavit qui pie multos,
SCOLLANDUSque sacro prefulgens dogmate cuncto,
Hinc ERMENALDUS, post OSBERNUS, NICHOLAUS,
Tres qui Brittones vixerunt mente fideles.
Cuncti divina repleti philosophia
Ac decus aecclesiae fulxerunt atque columpnae.
Qui tibi, militiae celestis signifer alme,
Corde placere pio cupientes tempore cuncto,
Scripserunt librum legis hunc, quem, lector, amandum
Ad decus ecce tuum, Michahel semper venerandum,
Pro mercede sibi quod reddas dindima caeli
Ut precibusque tuis, Gregori sancte, beatis,
Alma laude Dei possint feliciter uti,
Haec tua mente pia renovarunt dogmata sacra,
In quibus attente quisquis legis invenies quae
Sint reddenda Deo cum lucro corde benigno.

*Bibliography. MSS. à peintures*, no. 194.

Avranches, Bibliothèque Municipale, MS. 105, fols. 6–177v *c.* 1000–1035.
Isidore, Augustine, Julianus Toletanus, Gennadius, etc.

Initials in pen or orange minium. Marginal sketches, fols. 160 and 170v. 'U' added, fol. 102.

Avranches, Bibliothèque Municipale, MS. 107 *c.* 1040–1055.
Bede, Comm. on St Mark and St Luke. Fol. 154, Glossary in Hebrew, Greek and Latin, third quarter eleventh century. Fol. 157, Berengar's retraction of 1079, late eleventh century.

Initials in pen with inhabited scrolls. Closely related in style to MS. 76 and the early initials of the Bordeaux Bible. [Pl. 12*c*.]
*Bibliography*. B. Bischoff, 'Das griechische Element in der abendländlischen Bildung des Mittelalters', *Byzantinische Zeitschrift*, xliv (1951), 32 n.2 (on the glossary).

Avranches, Bibliothèque Municipale, MS. 109, fols. 37–73v *c.* 990–1015.
Isidore, comm. on the Song of Songs. Alcuin, *de Trinitate*.

Plain initials.
*Prov*. Hymn to St Michael, fol. 76v, with musical notation, in transitional script 'Liber Sancti Michaelis. Qui furatus fuerit anathema sit, amen, amen', twelfth century, fol. 76.

Avranches, Bibliothèque Municipale, MS. 115 *c.* 1015–1035.
Haimo, Comm. on St Paul's Epistles.

Frame page with medallions that at the top with the head of Christ, fol. 1v. Numerous initials in ink and orange minium, and on fol. 67 'P' painted. Written in part by Hervardus, fols. 67–125. [Pl. 10*f*.]
*Prov*. Fifteenth-century list of contents, fol. 1.

Avranches, Bibliothèque Municipale, MS. 128 *c.* 1015–1035.
Homiliary.

Painted initial 'P', fol. 2. Pen initials with scroll or animals. Fols. 136–143v, 280, 284, written by Frotmundus, cf. MS. 72.
*Prov*. Documents connected with the abbey are copied fol. 279v etc., the earliest of the twelfth century.
*Bibliography*. R. Etaix, 'Les homiliaires patristiques du Mont Saint-Michel', *Millénaire* (1), 400–13.

Avranches, Bibliothèque Municipale, MS. 129 *c.* 1015–1035.
Homiliary.

Plain capitals.
*Prov*. Documents connected with St Malo of the late eleventh century are copied, twelfth century.
*Bibliography*. R. Etaix, 'Les homiliaires patristiques du Mont Saint-Michel', *Millénaire* (1), 400–13.

Avranches, Bibliothèque Municipale, MS. 146 *c*. 1075–1095.
Isidore, Canons.

Initials, drawn in pen, sometimes blue, red or green. Written by the scribe who signed MS. 163, Osbernus, a Breton. He was also one of the six scribes of MS. 103. [Pls. 15*c*, 55*f*.]
*Bibliography*. Exh., *Millénaire*, no. 189.

Avranches, Bibliothèque Municipale, MS. 163 *c*. 1065–1080.
Heraclides, *Vitae Patrum*. Fulbert of Chartres. Augustine.

Unfinished acanthus scroll frame page, fol. 2$^{v}$. Initials with leaves, interlace and animal heads. Marginal sketch, fol. 40$^{v}$. Written by Osbernus, cf. MSS. 103, 146. [Pls. 6*a*, 30*a*.]
*Prov*. Colophon, fol. 77: Quisquis habes visum quo conspicias Paradisum,
Si queris flores qui sunt capientis honores,
Mens presentetur, presens Paradysus habetur.
Elige quod captas, hic sanctis moribus aptas,
Invenies escas, quas mandere nolo quiescas.
Nunc anime pastum, qui te facit undique castum,
Corde tene leto, dicens: Osberne vigeto,
Librum scripsisti, tibi magna dari meruisti,
Optimus annisus (?) tuus hic per quem Paradysus
Scriptus alit mores, Xpisti reparando favores.
Fol. 77, *ex libris* of fifteenth century. Fol. 2, 'Iste liber est monasterii montis de libraria communi', fifteenth century.
*Bibliography*. Martin, 558.

Avranches, Bibliothèque Municipale, MS. 211, fols. 156–210$^{v}$ *c*. 990–1015.
Chronicle of the Abbey (the 'Revelatio').

Initials in minium with white interlace and leaf terminals. Fol. 156, initial 'M' with beast heads, interlace and scrolling leaf painted yellow, pink, blue and gold. Written by Hervardus who signed Leiden, Voss. lat. fol. 39. [Pls. 7*e*, 9*a*.]
*Bibliography*. Th. le Roy, 'Les Curieuses recherches du Mont-Sainct-Michel' ed. E. de Beaurepaire, *Soc. des Antiquaires de Normandie* (1878), Appx. 1. gives a

transcript of the text; Gout, fig. 1 (fol. 156); C. Nordenfalk, 'Miniature ottonienne et ateliers capétiens', *Art de France*, iv (1964), 55.

Avranches, Bibliothèque Municipale, MS. 229, fols. 1–190ᵛ *c.* 990–1015.
Boethius, Logical commentaries.

Minor initials. Fol. 118, 'M' with leaf terminals. Fols. 1–10ᵛ and 99–115ᵛ possibly not Mont St Michel.
*Prov. Ex libris* of fifteenth century, fol. 117.
*Bibliography*. A. van der Vyver, 'Les étapes du développement philosophique du Haut Moyen-Age', *Revue Belge de Philologie et d'Histoire*, viii (1929), 449 and n.1.

Avranches, Bibliothèque Municipale, MS. 240 *c.* 990–1015.
Martianus Capella, Bks. 1–11, commentary of Remigius of Auxerre on Bks. 1–7.

Diagrams, fols. 8 and 8ᵛ. Fol. 87, initial 'C'. Fols. 1–16, 49–86ᵛ can be attributed to the scribe Hervardus. Cf. Leiden, Voss. lat. fol. 39.
*Bibliography*. J. Préaux, 'Le Manuscrit d'Avranches 240 et l'oevre de Martianus Capella', *Horae Eruditae ad codices Sancti Michaelis de periculo maris*, ed. J. Laporte, Steenbrugge (1966), 135–49.

Bayeux, Bibliothèque du Chapitre, MS. 56 *c.* 1000–1020.
Augustine, *de civitate Dei.*

Initials to each book, many close to those in Avranches 97 and 211. Written by different scribes one of which is Hervardus, others close to hands in MSS. 91 and 128.
*Prov*. Bk. XIX after the incipit 'GLORIO[A over erasure]SCE TRINITATIS'. This perhaps implies a connection with Fécamp, as suggested by Dom J. Laporte.

Berlin, Deutsche Staatsbibliothek, Phillipps 1854 *c.* 1075–1085 (probably before 1080).
Dudo of St Quentin, *Historia Normannorum*. Additions: Council of Lillebonne, 1080 (Trevia Dei), fol. 94ᵛ, Poem in praise of Fécamp and Abbot John, late eleventh-twelfth century, fol. 95ᵛ.

Initials in late group style, fols. iv and 32ᵛ. The addition on fol. 94ᵛ is written by one of the hands of MS. 58.
*Prov*. The attribution to Mont St Michel rests on palaeographical and stylistic grounds. The manuscript later belonged to the Jesuit College of Clermont in Paris, MS. 687 (paraphé mark, fol. 1ᵛ), and then passed via the Meermann collection to Sir Thomas Phillipps. The poem on fol. 95ᵛ indicates that it was probably at Fécamp by the late eleventh or early twelfth century. M. Fr. Avril observed that the thirteenth-century glosses, fol. 1ᵛ, are by the same hand as those in Paris,

Latin 2088 from Fécamp. He also solved the problem of how the manuscript might have arrived at the College of Clermont by suggesting that it could have been part of the legacy to the College by François de Joyeuse, who was archbishop of Rouen and abbot of Fécamp at the time when Fécamp books were being sold to Jean Bigot and Mareste d'Alge.

*Bibliography*. Dudo of St Quentin, *De Moribus et actis primorum Normanniae ducum*, ed. J. Lair (1865), 109–10 (then in the Phillipps Collection, Lair's MS. 'M'); V. Rose, *Die Handschriften-Verzeichnisse der Königlichen Bibliothek zu Berlin. XII. Verzeichniss der Lateinische HSS*, i (1893), no. 139; J. Kirchner, *Beschreibende Verzeichnisse der Miniaturen-HSS. der Preussischen Staatsbibliothek zu Berlin, I, Die Phillipps-HSS* (1926), 34, Abb. 39; F. Avril, 'L'Influence', op. cit. (MS. 59). 35–39, fig. 6 (fol. iv).

Bordeaux, Bibliothèque Municipale, MS. 1 *c.* 1050–1100.
Bible in two volumes, without the Gospels and ending incomplete in Hebrews.

Numerous initials for which see Chapter VI. Unfinished. [Pls. 12*d*, 50–55.]

*Provenance*. Attributed to Mont St Michel on palaeographical and stylistic grounds. On fol. 259ᵛ a grant to an early Abbot of Redon in a twelfth-century hand, of no interest elsewhere, suggests it was at least by then at the Abbey of St Sauveur, Redon, if not when the two bulls, Eugenius III, fol. 249ᵛ, and Gregory VII, fol. 259ᵛ, in favour of Redon were copied (cf. Ch. VI). It passed, again at an unknown date, to the Abbey of La Sauve near Bordeaux.

*Bibliography*. Exh., *IIe Centenaire de la Bibliothèque de Bordeaux* (1936), nos. 16 and 17, pl. 1 (fol. 240ᵛ); *MSS. à peintures*, no. 227; Exh. *Millénaire*, no. 183; J. J. G. Alexander, 'A Romanesque copy from Mont Saint-Michel of an initial in the Corbie Psalter', *Millénaire* (2), 239–45, fig. 131 (fol. 300ᵛ), 135 (fol. 168ᵛ); Exh., *Millénaire*, no. 183.

Leiden, Rijksuniv. bibl., MS. Voss. lat. fol. 39 with Paris *c.* 1000–1025.
Bibliothèque Nationale, Latin 5920.
Gregory of Tours, *de gestis Francorum*. Ado of Vienne, Chronicle.

Initials on fols. 25ᵛ, 39ᵛ, 58ᵛ, 77ᵛ of Paris close in style to transitional group manuscripts especially MS. 91. Initials on fols 28ᵛ of Leiden and fol. 11 of Paris added or retouched later in the century. Written by the main scribe of the early group and signed on fol. 135ᵛ of Leiden:

'Fratris Hervardi post longum penna laborem
Optatam gaudens hic tenuit requiem.'

Hervardus also wrote the obituary in Orléans 105, and MSS. 97, 211 and parts of 78, 95, 115, 229 and Bayeux 56. [Pl. 1*a*.]

*Prov*. Leiden contains gatherings 1–10 and 21–27, Paris gatherings 11–20. On fol. 25$^{v}$–26 of Paris across the opening written by the scribe at the top of the page is: 'Liber Sci Michaelis qui fueratus (sic a dot under the e) fuerit anathema sit'. (An *ex libris* similarly written across an opening is in Orléans 105.) Paris belonged to J. A. de Thou and J.-B. Colbert, Leiden to Cl. Fauchet and P. Petau.
B. Krusch, W. Levison, 'Gregorii Episcopi Turonensis, Libri Historiarum X', *Monumenta Germaniae Historica, Script. Mer.* I.1 (1951), xxx (D.3); F. Avril, *Millénaire* (2), 204; J. G. Espiner-Scott, *Claude Fauchet. Sa Vie. Son Oevre* (1938), 296–7, fig. 16.

London, British Museum, MS. Royal 13. A.XXII *c.* 1065–1080.
Paulus Diaconus, *Historia Langobardorum.*

Initial 'S', close to late group Mont St Michel style, fol. 2$^{v}$. Fols. 70 line 10–71 written by Mauritius who signed part of Avranches MS. 58. Sketches on fols. 1* and 73, and diagram in hard point on fol. 1. [Pl. 5*d*.]
*Prov*. Written at Mont St Michel or at St Augustine's, Canterbury, under abbot Scollandus. Cf. Avranches 88 for a fragment of the same text. *Ex libris* of St Augustine's, Canterbury, fol. 1$^{v}$, fifteenth century.
*Bibliography*. M. R. James, *Ancient Libraries of Canterbury and Dover* (1903), 293, no. 893; G. F. Warner, J. P. Gilson, *Catalogue of Western MSS. in the Old Royal and King's Collections, British Museum*, ii (1921), 87–8 with further bibliography on the text and related manuscripts; Wormald, *English Drawings*, 72, no. 40; Dodwell, *Canterbury School*, 55 n.5.

London, British Museum, MS. Royal 13. A.XXIII *c.* 1065–1080.
Ado of Vienne, Chronicle to A.D. 869. List of Emperors to Constantine Copronymus (A.D. 723). Chronology of the Dukes of Normandy from the landing of Rollo to the death of Robert I in 1035. Genealogy of the kings of France.

Initial 'B', fol. 1$^{v}$ in style of late group Mont St Michel manuscripts. Fols. 61 line 14–94$^{v}$ written by Mauritius who signed part of MS. 58. [Pl. 16*c*.]
*Prov*. In the chronology on fol. 96 special emphasis is given to events connected with Mont St Michel (written in green capitals), the foundation, the beginning of the building of the church, and Suppo's abbacy, 1033 (the bull of Pope John XIII forged *c.* 1058 is included and gives a terminus post. Cf. Avril, *Millénaire* (2), 206). *Ex libris* of St Augustine's, Canterbury, fol. 1, fifteenth century. For the same text see Leiden, Voss. lat. fol. 39.
*Bibliography*. M. R. James, *Ancient Libraries of Canterbury and Dover* (1903), 295, no. 912; Dodwell, *Canterbury School*, 122 (as 1090–1120); Warner and Gilson, op. cit., p. 88.

New York, Pierpont Morgan Library, MS. 641 *c.* 1050–1065.
Sacramentary (incomplete, mutilated).

Full-page miniatures, historiated initials. Numerous other initials, those on fols. 143, Assumption, 152$^{v}$ Nativity of the Virgin, 156 Exaltation of the Cross, with whole page frames. A number of initials more open in texture and painted in lighter tones. The figure and initial style are very close to MSS. 72 and 90. [Pls. 13*c*, 31–46.]
*Prov*. See Appendix VI for the grounds of attributing the manuscript to Mont St Michel. It was bought by the 4th Earl of Ashburnham in 1844 from Samuel Woodburn, the picture dealer. It then passed via the H. Yates Thompson Collection (sale of Ashburnham Appendix, 1897) to Mr Pierpont Morgan in 1919.
*Bibliography*. *A descriptive catalogue of the second series of fifty manuscripts in the Collection of Henry Yates Thompson* (1902), 126–130, no. 69 (by W. H. J. Weale); *Illustrations of one hundred Manuscripts in the Library of Henry Yates Thompson*, i (1907), pls. 1–3 (fols. 66$^{v}$, 155$^{v}$, 166$^{v}$); B. da Costa Greene and M. P. Harrsen, *The Pierpont Morgan Library, Exhibition of Illuminated manuscripts held at the New York Public Library, November* 1933–*April* 1934, 13, no. 22, fig. 3 (fol. 142$^{v}$) and pl. 22 (fol. 170); *The Pierpont Morgan Library. Illustrated catalogue of an exhibition held on the occasion of the New York World's Fair*, 1939, no. 31, pl. 1A (fol. 142$^{v}$ in colour); A Strittmatter, 'An unknown "Apology" in Morgan MS. 641', *Traditio*, iv (1946), 179–196; Exh., *Illuminated books of the Middle Ages and Renaissance*, Baltimore, 1949, no. 17, pl. xii (fol. 18); *MSS. à peintures*, no. 188; Swarzenski, *Monuments*, fig. 174 (fol. 142$^{v}$).

Paris, Bibliothèque Nationale, Latin 2055 *c.* 1055–1080.
Augustine, *de civitate Dei*.

Painted initial 'I' in red, blue, green, mauve-pink and gold, fol. 1. Incipit and initial on fol. 1$^{v}$ cut out. Close in style to Avranches MS. 86$_{3}$ and the Bordeaux Bible second group of initials. Written by the scribe Antonius who signed Rouen MS. A.143.
*Prov*. Attribution on grounds of initial style. For Antonius see Appx. IV. Bigot MS. 48. Bigot arms on the binding and book plate. Probably therefore from Fécamp. Above the book-plate the shelf-mark C.1.
*Bibliography*. F. Avril, *Millénaire* (2), 238.

Paris, Bibliothèque Nationale, Latin 2088 *c.* 1055–1080.
Augustine, *de Trinitate*.

Painted initial 'D', fol. 1$^{v}$, with scroll and head in a medallion. Other painted and penwork initials. The first two leaves have been removed but a stub remains

showing an Anglo-Saxon type corner rosette. Written by Antonius the scribe who signed Rouen MS. A.143. [Pls. 4*d*, 14*c*.]
*Prov.* Attribution to Mont St Michel on grounds of initial style. For Antonius see Appx. IV. Bigot MS. 44. Bigot arms on the binding and book-plate. Above the latter C.3 in ink. On fol. 62 an inscription of which the first part is erased '. . . legit Frater Robertus de Plune (?) toto in isto libro tempore domini Willermi de Putot tunc temporis abbatis'. This was noted by M. Fr. Avril and the Abbot identified by him as William of Fécamp (1286–96).
*Bibliography.* F. Avril, *Millénaire* (2), 237.

Paris, Bibliothèque Nationale, Latin 2639 *c.* 1050–1065.
Ambrose, treatises including *de bono mortis*.

Full-page miniature, fol. 31v, of St Ambrose in prayer crowned by Christ. 'Q' with painted scroll close in style to MSS. Morgan 641 and Avranches 90, fol. 32. Written in part by Antonius, the scribe who signed Rouen MS. A.143. [Pl. 26*a*.]
*Prov.* Attribution to Mont St Michel on palaeographical and stylistic grounds. Bigot MS. 358, arms on the binding. Above the bookplate, D.26. There is a rust mark at the top of fol. 1. Probably from Fécamp.
*Bibliography. MSS à peintures*, no. 191; F. Avril, *Millénaire* (2), 237.

Paris, Bibliothèque Municipale, Latin 5290, fols. 1–26 *c.* 1065–1080.
Lives of Saints.

Initials in red and green pen with veined late group style leaves very close to MSS. Bordeaux I, and Royal MSS. 13 A.XXII–XXIII. [Pl. 16*b*.]
*Prov.* The remainder of the manuscript is of different dates and scripts and was probably written at Fécamp. Bigot MS. 175 and book-plate with above it E.37.
*Bibliography.* F. Avril, *Millénaire* (2), 236.

Paris, Bibliothèque Nationale, Latin 5920. *See* Leiden, Rijksuniv. bibl., Voss. lat. fol. 39.

Paris, Bibliothèque Nationale, Latin 8055, p. 1–140 *c.* 1070–1095.
Statius, Thebais.

Initials to each book drawn in pen with veined leaves, very close in style to manuscripts of the Scollandus group, Latin 5290, and Royal MSS. 13 A.XXII and XXIII.
*Prov.* Jacques Auguste de Thou (1553–1617). J.-B. Colbert.
*Bibliography.* J. J. G. Alexander, 'A Romanesque copy from Mont Saint Michel of an initial in the Corbie Psalter', *Millénaire* (2), 239–45.

Paris, Bibliothèque Nationale, Latin 8055, p. 141–78 *c.* 990–1015.
Persius, Satires.

Initial 'N', p. 141, copying 'N', fol. 31$^{v}$ of the Corbie Psalter, Amiens, Bib. Mun., MS. 18. Written by Hervardus who signed Leiden, Voss. lat. fol. 39 and is the main scribe of the early group. [Pl. 53*d*.]
*Prov*. Jacques Auguste de Thou (1553–1617), J.-B. Colbert.
*Bibliography*. É. Chatelain, *Paléographie des classiques latins*, ii (1894–1900), pl. cxxv; J. J. G. Alexander, 'A Romanesque copy from Mont Saint Michel of an initial in the Corbie Psalter', *Millénaire* (2), 239–45, fig. 129 (p. 141).

Paris, Bibliothèque Nationale, Latin 8070, fols. 1–129$^{v}$ *c.* 990–1015.
Juvenal, Satires.

No decorated initials. Script related to that of Hervardus who signed Leiden Voss. lat. fol. 39. I am grateful to M. F. Avril for bringing this manuscript to my attention.
*Prov*. Cl. Fauchet, J.-B. Colbert.
*Bibliography*. É Chatelain, *Paléographie des classiques latins*, ii (1894–1900), pl. cxxxi; U. Knoche, 'Handschriftliche Grundlagen des Juvenaltextes', *Philolologus*, Suppl., xxxiii (1940), 20 (MS. 'D').

Rouen, Bibliothèque Municipale, MS. A.143(427) Before 1048.
Ambrose, *de fide*, *de officiis*, *Hexameron*.

Painted inhabited scroll initials, fols. 1$^{v}$, 65. Written by the scribe Antonius on the order of Abbot Suppo, 1033–48, for Fécamp. [Pls. 6*d*, 14*b*.]
*Prov*. Colophon, fol. 151 and 151$^{v}$:

(fol. 151) Codicis istius paginas quicumque legendo
Percurris, memor esto mei memor esto jubentis
Patris [Supponis, erased] scribenti cuncta ferentis.
Antonii nomen nihi noveris esse miselli.
(fol. 151$^{v}$) Editus iste liber sancti Trinitatis honore,
Divinus inhians et terrea pauca retexens,
Ut solis radius tenebrosa cuncta serenat,
Lumine sic fidei sacre per cuncta nitescit.
Hunc quisquis tulerit maledictus pure peribit,
At benedictus erit salvum qui fecerit omnis.

Bigot MS. A.31, book-plate and arms on the binding. Fol. 151$^{v}$, foundation charter of Fécamp copied, late eleventh–twelfth century.
*Bibliography*. Avril, *Notes* (1), 514, 524; F. Avril, *Millénaire* (2), 237–8; Exh., *Millénaire*, no. 187.

Rouen, Bibliothèque Municipale, MS. A.178(425) *c.* 1070–1095.
and Paris, Bibliothèque Nationale, n. acq. lat. 2389, fol. 19.
Athanasius, various works.

Title page with mixed capitals now a fragment in Paris. Fleuron initials in red, blue and green. Initial 'A', fol. 89, with scroll and lion mask. Written by Hilduinus, probably one of the scribes of MS. 103 of which the fifth hand is closest.
*Prov.* Acrostic colophon, fol. 93: Hoc tibi Michael quidam se munere frater
Inspirante sibi quod scripsit pignore Christi
Laude pia dignum renitet quia nectare plenum
Dogmatis egregie, stet lector mente fideli.
Utile cum fuerit, sis constans murus asili
Illi cum proprium referes ex hoste triumphum,
Ne cum dampnatis, dampnetur ut improba pestis.
Ut nomen fratris lector cognoscere possis.
Signant hunc apices summi de versibus omnes.

Fol. 93ᵛ, another colophon in acrostic also giving the name Hilduinus, and very similar in sense. Comes from Fécamp. Belonged to Mareste d'Alge, d. 1672. I am grateful to M. Fr. Avril for bringing this manuscript to my attention.
*Bibliography.* Avril, *Notes* (1), 521; F. Avril, *Millénaire* (2), 236; Exh., *Millénaire*, no. 188.

Rouen, Bibliothèque Municipale, MS. Mm.15 (Suppl. Cat. 116) *c.* 1050–1065.
Sacramentary. Fragments containing, fols. 1–10, 28 Episcopal Benedictions, 11–14ᵛ, Offices of third Sunday in Advent (starts incomplete) to Vigil of Christmas, 15–21ᵛ, Common of Saints, 22, Translation of St Autbert (added twelfth century), 22ᵛ–45, various votive Masses (twelfth-century additions on fols. 43, 44, 44ᵛ, 45, 45ᵛ).

Painted initials with inhabited scrolls on fols. 14 and 22ᵛ. Same size, style and script as Morgan MS. 641. [Pls. 4*c*, 46*e*.]
*Prov.* J.-C. H. Crosse sale 1899. Attribution to Mont Saint Michel on grounds of translation of St Autbert, fol. 22. Formed part of Morgan 641. See Appendix VI.
*Bibliography.* Leroquais, *Sacramentaires*, i (1924), 75; A. Strittmatter, op. cit. (Morgan MS. 641), 180 n.8; Exh., *Millénaire*, no. 179.

Vatican City, Biblioteca Vaticana, Vat. Lat. 9668, fols. 32–154. *c.* 1030–1050.
Lives of Saints.

Inhabited leaf scroll initials, fols. 32, 78, 81ᵛ, close in style to MSS. 91 and 76. Minor initials with fleurons in orange as in MS. 72. Script close to MSS. 91 and 76.

*Prov*. Bound in with a manuscript from St Sauveur, Redon, fols. 1–32, but perhaps still at Mont St Michel in 1373 (note of a fire). Jesuit College of Clermont, Paris (paraphé mark, fol. 3.) Cardinal Angelo Mai. I am grateful to M. F. Avril for bringing this manuscript to my attention.
*Bibliography*. Avril, *Notes* (1), 492–504, pls. (fols. 54, 78, 81$^{v}$, 145); id., *Notes* (2), 246–7.

Vatican City, Biblioteca Vaticana, Reg. Lat. 2043 *c*. 990–1015.
Macrobius, *Saturnalia*, to Bk. VII, 14, 11.

Plain initials in pen. Written by Hervardus who signed Leiden, Voss. lat. fol. 39. I am grateful to M. F. Avril for bringing this manuscript to my attention.
*Prov*. Florence, Laurentiana, MS. 51. 8, thirteenth century, is a copy of our manuscript according to Willis.
*Bibliography*. J. Willis, *Ambrosii Theodosii Macrobii Saturnalia*, Teubner (1963), viii (MS. 'R').

# APPENDIX III

## MANUSCRIPTS FROM ST BÉNIGNE, DIJON

St William of Volpiano, first abbot of St Bénigne, Dijon, played a central role in the monastic revival in Normandy in the early eleventh century, and he has also been seen as a link in architectural developments between Normandy and Burgundy and possibly also Lombardy. It may naturally be asked, therefore, whether there are any connections between manuscript illumination at St Bénigne and in Normandy.

Of the manuscripts surviving from St Bénigne at Paris and in Dijon three are important in this connection, an Ambrose *Hexameron*,[1] a Clement *Recognitiones*[2] and a manuscript containing Rhabanus Maurus, Jerome, etc.[3] These are related in their initial styles which, however, are very mixed. There are figure initials, historiated initials and leaf scroll initials. The leaf scrolls are of two types, either thin white node scrolls drawn in orange, or veined and dotted leaves which turn and twine to grip the plant stalk or the letter form. Both can be seen together in an 'E' in Latin 9518, fol. 138$^{v}$. The figure initials resemble initials found at Angers and in western France, types which are commented on in Chapter VI.[4] The historiated initials contain figures drawn in flowing linear draperies but also with a certain indication of the articulation of the body beneath.

Fortunately there are two colophons which suggest an explanation of these initials. The first, in a Pontifical for the use of Langres, now at Dijon, says that this manuscript was given by Himbertus, bishop of Paris, in 1036 to abbot Halinardus of St Bénigne who ruled at St Bénigne from 1031 to 1052[5], and who had succeeded Himbertus as archdeacon of Langres in 1030. The second colophon, in Paris, Latin 9518, fol. 252, says that a Halinardus 'devotus famulus' gave the manuscript

1 Paris, Bib. Nat., Latin 11624. M. Schapiro, 'A relief in Rodez and the beginnings of romanesque sculpture in southern France', *Studies in Western Art. Acts of the 20th International Congress of the History of Art*, i (1963), 58, fig. 15. Idem, *The Parma Ildefonsus. A romanesque illuminated manuscript from Cluny and related works* (1964), 27 n. 89, 28n. 99, 55n. 234, fig. 62.

2 Paris, Bib. Nat., Latin 9518. Schapiro, *Parma Ildefonsus*, op. cit., 27n. 89, 55n. 234.

3 Dijon, Bib. Mun. MS. 51.

4 e.g. Latin 11624, fol. 104$^{v}$.

5 Dijon, Bib. Mun., MS. 122. V. Leroquais, *Les Pontificaux Manuscrits des Bibliothèques Publiques de France*, i (1937), 142, no. 48. The decoration of the manuscript is unfinished, spaces being left for initials. On fols. 6 and 62 are St Bénigne style initials.

to St Bénigne. If this is the same man, which seems probable, then the manuscript was written before he became abbot.

The deductions which I would make from these two colophons are these. The abbey did not have a flourishing scriptorium under abbot William of Volpiano. His successor tried to remedy this and may have obtained help from Paris where William had been abbot of St Germain-des-Prés and where he still had connections. This would explain the source of the second type of veined leaf in the manuscripts and also probably the linear figure style. The first type of leaf, the node scroll, may come from north Italy with abbot William as the link, or the abbey may have received Ottonian manuscripts as gifts. William was, it may be remembered, the Emperor Otto III's godson.

This does not suggest, therefore, that in abbot William's time there was an active scriptorium at St Bénigne or that he will have had any direct influence on manuscript production in Normandy. Where similarities do exist (these are more noticeable, as would be expected, at Fécamp[1] than at Mont St Michel) it may be that St Germain-des-Prés was the common source.

1 Cf. the small bunches of grapes pushing out from the tail of the 'Q' in Paris, Bib. Nat., Latin 1684, fol. 13 from Fécamp with the similar tail of an initial 'D' on fol. 6$^{v}$ of Latin 11624 from St Bénigne.

# APPENDIX IV

## MONT ST MICHEL, FÉCAMP AND THE SCRIBE ANTONIUS

The four manuscripts with Mont St Michel type initials and written by the scribe Antonius, three now in Paris and the signed manuscript in Rouen, all belonged to the Norman collector Jean Bigot who formed a library of manuscripts in the late sixteenth and early seventeenth century at Rouen.[1] A large number of his manuscripts were bought from Fécamp and there is every reason to believe that he acquired these manuscripts too from Fécamp. A fifth manuscript containing Lives of Saints and also belonging to Bigot, is made up of various fragments of which folios 1–26 are written and illuminated in the Mont St Michel late style, whilst the rest of the volume was made at Fécamp.[2]

Relations between Mont St Michel and Fécamp will have been close during the abbacies both of Suppo (1033–48) and of Radulfus (1048–58). Suppo was, like abbot John of Fécamp, a disciple of William of Volpiano and like John he came from Italy. Radulfus was originally a monk of Fécamp. It would not be surprising to find manuscripts written at Mont St Michel for Fécamp during either of their rules, therefore. Besides the five manuscripts mentioned already, a copy of Dudo of St Quentin now in Berlin which belongs to the late group, was also probably later at Fécamp and may have been another gift.[3]

A sixth manuscript in the Vatican, discovered by Avril, though from Fécamp and apparently written there, seems to have received additions by Mont St Michel scribes and has a fine initial 'P' in the style of the late group manuscripts.[4]

1 Rouen MS. A.143(427), whose colophon says it was written at Suppo's order for Fécamp, Paris, Latin 2055 and 2088 were all written by Antonius alone. Latin 2639 was written by Antonius and three other scribes. See F. Avril, 'Les rapports artistiques entre Fécamp et le Mont Saint Michel', *Millénaire* (2), 235–8. For Bigot see L. Delisle, *Bibliotheca Bigotiana Manuscripta* (1877) and G. Nortier, 'Les Bibliothèques médiévales des Abbayes bénédictines de Normandie: Fécamp', *Revue Mabillon*, xlvii (1957), 22–4.

2 Paris, Bib. Nat., Latin 5290.

3 Berlin, Deutsche Staatsbibl., Phillipps 1854. This contains a passage in praise of Fécamp and abbot John. M. F. Avril observed that the thirteenth-century hand adding glosses is the same as that in Latin 2088. See also above p. 225, the Catalogue of manuscripts, Appx. II under provenance.

4 Avril, *Notes* (1), 512, suggests that two Mont St Michel scribes worked on the manuscript. His scribe 'D' he identifies with the scribe of MS. 86, fol. 137ff. and his scribe 'E' with the scribe of MS. 77, fols. 1–26.

Avril has suggested that Antonius may have been a monk of Fécamp on the grounds of the Fécamp provenance of these manuscripts and also because he has found his hand in a Fécamp charter.[1] Besides the fact that the four manuscripts mentioned above have initials in the Mont St Michel style, and that his colophon says that he wrote for Suppo, the only other evidence that Antonius was a monk of Mont St Michel are some leaves written by him at the end of the early MS. 97 still at Avranches, which seems to have been left unfinished. It is perfectly possible that monks from one scriptorium should have worked in another. Antonius, indeed, may have started as a monk at Mont St Michel under Suppo and gone to Fécamp after Suppo's disgrace.

However, there is a third possibility which may be put forward. It is difficult to know to what extent a colophon may be interpreted literally, for it may be only a formula adapted for use. But it is noteworthy that whereas most of the other scribes write 'for St. Michael' or call themselves 'frater' or ask the reader to pray for them, Antonius who asks to be remembered though 'misellus', wrote at the order of Suppo 'cuncta ferentis', who provides all things for him. Is this a general phrase or could it mean that Antonius was paid by Suppo, in other words that he was a professional scribe who worked on commissions both at Mont St Michel and at Fécamp?

[1] See his thesis 'La décoration des manuscrits dans les abbayes bénédictines de Normandie aux XIe et XIIe siècles', 1963; idem, *Notes* (1), 509–10, 514, 524. The Fécamp initial style is recognizably different from that of Mont St Michel. See e.g. Avril, *Notes* (2), 217ff., pls.

# APPENDIX V

## ANGLO-SAXON MANUSCRIPTS IN NORMANDY BEFORE THE CONQUEST

The only surviving Anglo-Saxon manuscript known to have been in Normandy before the Conquest is the Sacramentary of Robert of Jumièges given to Jumièges by him whilst he was bishop of London (1044–50).[1] The other richly decorated Anglo-Saxon manuscript, the Benedictional of archbishop Robert, now at Rouen, it has been conjectured on the strength of an eighteenth-century inscription, was given to the Cathedral of Rouen also by Robert of Jumièges, probably after he had been forced to leave England in 1052.[2] Two other Anglo-Saxon manuscripts of the late tenth or early eleventh centuries which may have been in Normandy before the Conquest are a Gospel book now in Paris, formerly in the Bigot collection and possible therefore coming from Fécamp, whose illuminated pages have been torn out leaving a fragment of a corner rosette,[3] and secondly a copy of St Gregory's Dialogues with one historiated initial and one initial of Wormald's type I, which has a twelfth-century *ex libris* of Jumièges in it.[4]

One other Anglo-Saxon manuscript certainly in Normandy before the Conquest

[1] Rouen, Bib. Mun., MS. Y.6(274). This has an inscription on fol. 228 recording the gift which since Robert is said to be Bishop not Archbishop is likely to be contemporary with the gift. H. A. Wilson, 'The Missal of Robert of Jumièges', *Henry Bradshaw Society*, xi (1896), 316 gives the inscription. For Anglo-Saxon manuscripts of the tenth-eleventh centuries on the Continent see E. Lesne, *Histoire de la propriété ecclesiastique en France*, iv (1938), 65ff.

[2] Rouen, Bib. Mun., MS. Y.7(369). V. Leroquais, *Les Pontificaux manuscrits des bibliothèques publiques en France*, ii (1937), 300–5, no. 189. Whether the Benedictional belonged to archbishop Robert of Rouen or to Robert of Jumièges, archbishop of Canterbury, it would still have been in Normandy before the Conquest if the late inscription is to be trusted at all, O. Homburger, *Die Anfänge der Malschule von Winchester im X. Jahrhundert* (1912), 49 n. 2. The 'Egbert Pontifical' now Paris, Bib. Nat., Latin 10575 of the mid-tenth century was at Évreux in the eleventh century but has no illumination. N. R. Ker, *Catalogue of Manuscripts containing Anglo-Saxon* (1957), 441, no. 370.

[3] Paris, Bib. Nat., Latin 272. Mentioned by M. Fr. Avril in his thesis, this manuscript does not appear to have been published anywhere. It has annotations in a Norman hand which does not look late. For Bigot as collector see Appendix IV above.

[4] Rouen, Bib. Mun., MS. A.337(506), fol. 20, historiated initial 'D' and fol. 51 initial 'P'. See F. Avril. 'La décoration', op. cit.

has not survived. This is the Psalter, decorated with pictures, given by Emma, wife of Ethelred, to her brother Robert, archbishop of Rouen (980–1037). It is mentioned by Ordericus Vitalis who knew it later at St Evroul.[1] Evidence that this Psalter was known and copied at Mont St Michel has been mentioned already (pp. 190, etc). None of the other manuscripts still in Normandy or known to have been there formerly are likely to have been brought in before the Conquest. These are the Lanalet Pontifical,[2] a Gospel book now at St Lô,[3] a collection of Lives of Saints including hymns to St Swithun and St Ethelwold probably written at Winchester but later at Jumièges,[4] and a manuscript with various works of Augustine and Alcuin from Mont St Michel itself.[5]

Outside Normandy there are a number of Anglo-Saxon manuscripts which either survive or are known from the literary sources, and which could have been accessible to Norman monks before the Conquest. Thus at Fleury, besides the Winchcombe Sacramentary in which a monk of Mont St Michel wrote the obituary discussed in Chapter I, there was a Benedictional which had been sent to Gauzlin, Abbot from 1020–30,[6] and even probably an Anglo-Saxon artist working

[1] Ed. Prévost, ii, p. 41, 'magnum psalterium variis picturis decoratum'. Quoted by Dodwell, *Canterbury School*, 14. Archbishop Robert was at Mont St Michel in 1032 or 1033 to reconcile Alan of Brittany and Duke Robert. *William of Jumièges*, ed. J. Lair, Bk. VI, ch. 10. A fragment of an Anglo-Saxon liturgical book from St Evroul survives at Alençon, Bib. Mun., MS. 14, fols. 91–114ᵛ, but there is no indication of when it reached the abbey. It is probably eleventh century and contains benedictions for Sts Swithun and Etheldreda. It was evidently missed by the Abbé Leroquais. Another Anglo-Saxon manuscript, apparently now lost, a Psalter, was seen at Jumièges by Montfaucon who dated it to the late tenth century, *Bibliotheca Bibliothecorum*, ii (1739), 1205, no. 15. Lesne, op. cit., 66. (Unless it is Rouen A.44(231) certainly twelfth century.)

[2] Rouen, Bib. Mun., MS. A.27(368). Wormald, *English Drawings*, no. 57.

[3] St Lô, Bibl. Mun., MS. 1. Dodwell, *Canterbury School*, 14–15, pl. 6b and d.

[4] Rouen, Bib. Mun., MS. U.107(1385). L. Delisle, 'Vers et écriture d'Orderic Vital' (review of the publication of the hymns by C. Blume) *Journal des Savants*, n.s. i (1903), 428–40. I am grateful to Miss M. Gibson for this reference. I have not seen the manuscript. N. R. Ker, op. cit., 448 no. 376, dates it 'early eleventh century'. Delisle, op. cit., p. 440 also refers to the story of a Sacramentary written by Wulfruna at Barking which was stolen by a priest after the Conquest but later restored by him after a miraculous escape from shipwreck. This is told in a twelfth-century copy of a Life of St Ethelburga from Barking, formerly belonging to Sir George Wombwell, now in Cardiff, Public Library, MS. 1, 381, fols. 81–146.

[5] Avranches, Bib. Mun., MS. 81. This has only plain colour initials and to judge by its script is of the second half of the eleventh century.

[6] This was identified by L. Delisle, *Mémoire sur d'anciens Sacramentaires* (1886), 217, with the Anglo-Saxon Benedictional, now Paris, Bib. Nat., Latin 987. Dodwell, however, *Canterbury School*, 21, believes this manuscript was begun at Winchester in the second half of the tenth century but was continued at Canterbury *c.* 1030–40 and that it had the drawing on fol. 111 added to it there in the first quarter of the twelfth century.

at the end of the tenth century.[1] The same or another Anglo-Saxon artist travelled to St Bertin to execute a Gospel Book there also at the end of the tenth century.[2] Precious manuscripts also travelled widely as the story of the Sacramentary and Psalter made by Earnwini at Peterborough, which Wulfstan admired as a boy and which finally returned to him when prior of Worcester, after being given to Cologne by Cnut, shows.[3] Cnut also gave an illustrated manuscript of Saints' Lives to the Duke of Aquitaine in connection with the extension of the cult of St Martial of Limoges.[4]

There is no difficulty therefore in supposing that the artists of Mont St Michel had first-hand knowledge of Anglo-Saxon manuscripts before the Conquest. It is significant that the majority of the manuscripts surviving still or known to have been given as presents to houses on the Continent, are sumptuous liturgical manuscripts. It was their decoration which was adapted in Normandy to the patristic and other texts used for everyday reading and study. The decoration of the equivalent Anglo-Saxon manuscripts for private reading was not copied to the same extent. This is a further argument for the transmission of Anglo-Saxon influence to Normandy before, not after the Conquest.

[1] In Orléans, Bib. Mun., MS. 175. Wormald, *English Drawings*, 73, no. 45. See also the Boethius, Paris, Bib. Nat., Lat. 6401, *MSS. à peintures*, no. 122, Swarzenski, *Monuments*, fig. 164.

[2] Boulogne, Bib. Mun., MS. 11. Porcher, *French Miniatures*, 17, pl. v. A. Boutemy, 'Un monument capital de l'enluminure anglo-saxonne: le manuscrit 11 de Boulogne-sur-mer', *Cahiers de civilization médiévale*, i (1958), 179–82. See also R. M. Harris, 'The marginal drawings of the Bury St. Edmunds Psalter' (Princeton University Phil.D., 1960, University Microfilms), 278ff. with other examples of Anglo-Saxon influence on the Continent.

[3] *Vita Wulfstani of William of Malmesbury*, ed. R. R. Darlington, *Camden Society*, xl (1928), 5–16.

[4] Acta concilii Lemovicensis II, *P.L.* cxlii, 1369, 'Codicem litteris aureis scriptum in quo nomina sanctorum distincta cum imaginibus continebantur'.

# APPENDIX VI

## THE PROVENANCE OF THE SACRAMENTARY, NEW YORK, MORGAN LIBRARY, MS. 641

It is not necessary to review in detail the contents of the Sacramentary and the evidence for its origin and use, since it has been thoroughly examined from a liturgical point of view by Chanoine Tardif.[1] It will be useful, however, to repeat the main arguments and to add one or two points.

Unfortunately the provenance of the manuscript is not known before it came into the possession of the 4th Earl of Ashburnham who bought it on 23 April, 1844, from the London picture dealer Samuel Woodburn.[2] It was sold in 1897 as part of the Ashburnham 'Appendix' collection to Mr Henry Yates Thompson at whose sale in 1919 it was bought for £500 by Mr Pierpont Morgan. It seems unlikely that anything further as to its provenance can be discovered. For it appears that at some time the manuscript was mutilated with the express purpose of disguising its origin. Thus the quires were rearranged (the manuscript was put in order and rebound in 1947) and certain parts, notably the calendar, removed.

The Mont St Michel provenance of the manuscript was first recognized (on stylistic grounds, apparently by Professor C. R. Morey) in the catalogue of an exhibition of manuscripts held by the Morgan Library in 1933.[3] It has since then been suggested, however, that the Sacramentary was made for use at Fécamp.[4]

1 H. Tardif, 'La liturgie de la Messe au Mont Saint-Michel aux XI^e, XII^e et XIII^e siècles', *Millénaire* (1), 353–77.

2 I am grateful to Mr A. N. L. Munby for allowing me to quote this unpublished information from his 1963 Lyell lecture at Oxford. This means that the manuscript was not acquired by the Earl of Ashburnham with the 1,923 manuscripts he bought from the notorious Guglielmo Libri in 1847. S. de Ricci, *English Collectors of Books and Manuscripts* 1530–1930 (1930), 131. Further evidence which makes it unlikely that it was Libri who mutilated the manuscript (he is suspected by Tardif, op. cit.) is that the Sacramentary does not appear in the inventory of the abbey's library made in 1795, Avranches MS. 246. It had evidently left before this date. M. M. Delalonde drew attention to the importance of this inventory, 'Petite histoire des manuscrits du Mont-Saint-Michel', *Art de Basse Normandie*, xl (1966), 24 and kindly gave me this information.

3 B. da Costa Greene, M. P. Harrsen, *The Pierpont Morgan Library, Exhibition of illuminated manuscripts held at the New York Public Library, November 1933 – April 1934*, 13 no. 22. W. H. J. Weale's entry in *A descriptive catalogue of the second series of fifty manuscripts in the collection of Henry Yates Thompson* (1902), 126–30, no. 69 attributes the manuscript to the diocese of Langres.

4 As in the typescript catalogue entry kept in the Morgan Library (suggestion by Professor M. Schapiro). I am grateful to Mr John Plummer, Curator of Medieval and Renaissance Manuscripts for sending me a copy of this and for kindly answering various questions on the manuscript. Dr H. Swarzenski also quotes this suggestion, *Monuments*, 51, fig. 184.

The main evidence for the Mont St Michel provenance and use is as follows. First, the dedication of the church at Mont St Michel on 16 October is included, fol. 166v, and emphasized by a large initial in a frame page. The absence of a miniature or initial for the Feast of St Michael on 29 September might at first sight seem to negate this evidence, but in fact the page following the vigil of St Michael between fols. 160–1, is lacking and so almost certainly there was a miniature.[1] Secondly, there is a group of Breton and Norman saints which are also found in the later Missal of Mont St Michel.[2] Thirdly the stylistic similarities of the decoration to that of Mont St Michel manuscripts, particularly Avranches 72, is undoubted and was first noted in the 1933 catalogue. Fourthly, and conclusively a fragment of the Sacramentary survives at Rouen and this contains on fol. 22 an added mass for the Translation of St Autbert. This is in a twelfth-century hand and a translation was made by abbot Robert de Torigni in 1158. On the strength of this the Abbé Leroquais had already assigned the fragment to Mont St Michel.[3]

The Rouen fragment contains a series of Benedictions, fols. 1–10, part of the office for the third Sunday in Advent, fol. 11, which then runs to the first mass of the Christmas vigil, fol. 14v, the Common of the Saints, fol. 15, and finally various votive masses, fols. 22v–45v. The size of the page is 293 × 220 mm. where the Sacramentary is 286 × 216 mm. and in both there are twenty lines to a page ruled at 10 mm. intervals. Moreover, both the script and the style of initial

[1] I was unable to detect any offprint of this miniature when I examined the manuscript.

[2] Especially the Breton saints Melanius, 6 November, and Samson, 28 July, and Philibert, 20 August, the first abbot of Fécamp, who is added in a twelfth century hand on fol. 154v. Tardif, op. cit., 369, noting, however, that Norman saints are strangely lacking. Dijon influence due to William of Volpiano is noticeable and there is a group of Rheims saints whose presence is unexplained.

[3] Leroquais, *Sacramentaires*, i, 75, no. 29. Tardif, op. cit, 353–4, 361–2. A. Strittmatter, 'An unknown "Apology" in Morgan MS. 641', *Traditio*, iv (1946), 179–96, mentions the fragment but seems to deny that it belongs with the Sacramentary. The Apology in the Sacramentary he suggests was composed by Jean d'Alie, abbot of Fécamp 1028–78. The late Wilhelm Köhler was evidently the first to recognize that the fragment might be part of the Sacramentary (letter to the Morgan Library, 1950). I noted the fact in my 'Manuscrits enluminés du XIe siècle provenant du Mont-Saint-Michel', *Art de Basse Normandie*, xl (1966), 32 n. 1. The fragment was acquired by the Bibliothèque municipale, Rouen, from Joseph-Charles Hippolyte Crosse, a distinguished conchologist. His sale held at the Maison Sylvestre, 28 Rue des Bons Enfants by M. Léon Tual, commissaire-priseur, 56 rue de la Victoire, Paris, lasted from 20–30 November, 1899. The fragment was item 23 and there were about twenty other medieval manuscripts in the collection. A copy of the sale catalogue is in Rouen, Bibliothèque Municipale, mm. 1312. There is unfortunately no further indication of the provenance of the fragment. Both the fragment and Morgan 641 have additions in twelfth-century hands but apparently by different scribes.

decoration are identical in the Sacramentary. Any possible further doubt is removed by the fact that the text continues without a break from fol. 14v of the fragment to fol. 1 of the Sacramentary.[1] That the Sacramentary was made for Mont St Michel and at Mont St Michel and that it was in use at Mont St Michel in the twelfth century can, therefore, be regarded as certain.

[1] The collation of the Sacramentary is as follows: $1^8$ (1–6 missing), $2^8$ (1 missing), $3^8$–$8^8$, $9^8$ (5 missing), $10^8$–$21^8$, $22^8$ (1 missing), $23^8$–$24^8$, +1. Of the present first gathering of the Morgan Sacramentary Rouen, suppl. 116, fols. 11–14 (two bifolia) formed leaves 3, 4, 5, 6, Morgan 641, fols. 1–2 were leaves 7 and 8, and the original leaves 1 and 2 are lost. The other missing leaves fall between fols. 2 and 3, 61 and 62 and 160 and 161. The first contained the Mass for Christmas with probably a miniature of the Nativity. The second contained the 'Te igitur' page with a frame page on both recto and verso as can be seen from offprints left by the gold on fol. 61v and 62 (Pl. 36). There was probably a miniature of the Crucifixion and a large initial 'Te'. The loss of this leaf is not mentioned by Ch. Tardif but the first eleven words of the Canon are missing since fol. 62 begins, 'supplices rogamus'. I am very grateful to Dr R. W. Pfaff, Chapel Hill, for this information and for checking various points for me. The last missing leaf contained the Mass for St Michael and again probably contained a miniature.

# BIBLIOGRAPHY

*The works listed on pp. XXV–XXVI are not repeated*


ALEXANDER, J. J. G., 'Manuscrits enluminés du XIe siècle provenant du Mont-Saint-Michel', *Art de Basse Normandie*, xl (1966), 27-33.

ANFRAY, M., *L'architecture Normande* (Paris, 1939).

*The Apocryphal New Testament*, translated by M. R. James (corrected edn. Oxford, 1953).

AVRIL, F., *La décoration des manuscrits dans les abbayes bénédictines de Normandie aux XIe et XIIe siècles.* (Positions des thèses de l'École des Chartes, 1963).

AVRIL, F., 'L'Influence du style franco-saxon au Mont-Saint-Michel' *Art de Basse Normandie*, xl (1966), 35–39.

*The Bayeux Tapestry* (a comprehensive survey by Sir F. Stenton (gen. ed.) and others) (London, 2nd edn., 1965).

BAZIN, G., *Le Mont Saint-Michel* (Paris, 1933).

BLOCH, P., 'Zum Dedikationsbild im Lob des Kreuzes des Hrabanus Maurus', *Das erste Jahrtausend*, textband i, ed. V. H. Elbern (Düsseldorf, 1962), 471–94.

BOASE, T. S. R., *English Art 1100–1216*. Oxford History of English Art, vol. ii (Oxford, 1953).

BOECKLER, A., *Abendländische Miniaturen bis zum Ausgang der romanischen Zeit* (Berlin, 1930).

BOINET, A., 'L'Illustration du Cartulaire du Mont-Saint-Michel', *Bibliothèque de l'école des Chartes*, lxx (1909), 335–343.

DE BOUARD, M., 'Le Duché de Normandie', *Histoire des Institutions Françaises au Moyen Age*, i (Paris, 1957).

DE BOUARD, M., 'L'église Notre-Dame-sous-Terre au Mont Saint-Michel. Essai de Datation', *Journal des Savants* (Janvier-Mars, 1961), 10–27.

DE BROUSSILLON, B., 'Cartulaire de l'Abbayette (997–1421)', *Bulletin de la Commission historique et archéologique de la Mayenne*, ix (1894), suppl.

DE BROUSSILLON, B., *Cartulaire de Saint-Victeur au Mans, Prieuré de l'Abbaye du Mont-Saint-Michel (994–1400)*. Published for the Société d'Agriculture, Sciences et Arts de la Sarthe (Paris, 1895).

'The Cartulary of St Michael's Mount, Hatfield House MS. 315', ed. P. L. Hull, *Devon and Cornwall Record Society*, new series v (1962).

*Catalogue Général des Manuscrits des Bibliothèques Publiques de France* (Paris, 1886– in progress).

CHANTEUX, H., 'L'Abbé Thierry et les églises de Jumièges, du Mont-Saint-Michel et de Bernay', *Bulletin Monumental*, xcviii (1939), 67–72.

*Codices Latini Antiquiores*, ed. E. A. Lowe, *Part VI. France, Abbeville–Valenciennes* (Oxford, 1953).

DELISLE, L., *Le Cabinet des manuscrits de la Bibliothèque Imperiale (Nationale)*, 3 vols. (Paris, 1868–81).

DELISLE, L., *Chronique de Robert de Torigni, Abbé du Mont-Saint-Michel suivie de diverses opuscules historiques* (Société de l'histoire de Normandie, 2 vols., Rouen, 1873).

DELISLE, L., *Bibliotheca Bigotiana Manuscripta* (Société des bibliophiles de Normandie, Rouen, 1877).

DELISLE, L., *Mémoire sur d' anciens Sacramentaires* (Extrait. Mémoires de l'Académie des Inscriptions et Belles-Lettres, t.xxxii, 57–423) (Paris, 1886).

DELISLE, L., 'La Commémoration du Domesday-Book à Londres en 1886. Charte Normande de 1088 communiquée au comité de cette fête', *Société de l'Histoire de France* (1886).

DESLANDRES, Y., 'Les Manuscrits decorés au XIe siècle à Saint Germain-des-Prés par Ingelard', *Scriptorium*, ix (1955), 3–16.

DESROCHES, ABBÉ, 'Notice sur les manuscrits de la Bibliothèque d'Avranches', *Mémoires de la Société des antiquaires de Normandie*, xi (1840), 70–156.

DODWELL, C. R., 'Un manuscrit enluminé de Jumièges au British Museum', *Jumièges. Congrès scientifique du XIIIe centenaire*, ii (Rouen, 1955), 737–41.

DUDO OF ST QUENTIN, *De moribus et actis primorum Normanniae Ducum*, ed. J. Lair (Caen, 1865).

DUPONT, E., 'Les possessions du Mont Saint-Michel en Angleterre', *Revue d'études Normandes*, ii (1908), 341–2.

*The English Library before 1700*, ed. F. Wormald and C. E. Wright (London,1958).

VON FALKE, O., *Decorative Silks* (3rd edn., London, 1936).

FAUROUX, M., *Recueil des actes des ducs de Normandie de 911 à 1066* (Mémoires. Société des antiquaires de Normandie, xxxvi) (Caen, 1961).

FOCILLON, H., *L'An Mil* (Paris, 1952).

FREYHAN, R., 'The place of the stole and maniples in Anglo-Saxon Art of the tenth century', *The Relics of St Cuthbert*, ed. C. F. Battiscombe (Oxford, 1956), 409–432.

*Gallia Christiana*, vol. xi, ed. P. Piolin (Paris, 1874).

GRABAR, A. and NORDENFALK, C., *Early Mediaeval Painting from the fourth to the eleventh century*, translated by S. Gilbert (Skira, 1957).

GRABAR, A. and NORDENFALK, C., *Romanesque Painting from the eleventh to the thirteenth century*, translated by S. Gilbert (Skira, 1958).

GRABAR, A., *Les Ampoules de Terre Sainte* (Paris, 1958).

GRODECKI, L., 'Les débuts de la sculpture romane en Normandie. Bernay', *Bulletin Monumental*, cviii (1950), 7–67.

GUTBROD, J., *Die Initiale in Handschriften des achten bis dreizehnten Jahrhunderts* (Stuttgart, 1965).

HOMBURGER, O., *Die Anfänge der Malschule von Winchester im X. Jahrhundert* (Studien über christliche Denkmäler, N.F. xiii) (Leipzig, 1912).

HOMBURGER, O., 'Ein vernichtetes Denkmal merovingischer Buchkunst aus frühkarolingischer Zeit, der 'Rachio-Kodex' der Bongarsiana', *Festschrift Hans R. Hahnloser*, ed. E. J. Beer, P. Hofer, L. Mojou (Basel, 1961).

HUNGER, V., *Histoire de Verson* (Caen, 1908).

HUYNES, J., *Histoire Générale de l'Abbaye du Mont Saint-Michel*, ed. E. de Beaurepaire (Société de l'histoire de Normandie, 2 vols., Rouen, 1872).

*Inventio et Miracula Sancti Vulfrani*, ed. J. Laporte (Mélanges, Société de l'histoire de Normandie, Rouen and Paris, 1938).

JAMES, M. R., *The Western Manuscripts in the Library of Trinity College, Cambridge. A descriptive catalogue*, 4 vols. (Cambridge, 1900–4).

JAMES, M. R., *A descriptive catalogue of the Manuscripts in the Library of Corpus Christi College, Cambridge*, 2 vols. (Cambridge, 1909–13).

KENDRICK, T. D., *Anglo-Saxon Art to A.D. 900* (London, 1938).

KENDRICK, T. D., *Late Saxon and Viking Art* (London, 1949).

KER, N. R., *Medieval Libraries of Great Britain* (Royal Historical Society, *Guides and Handbooks* no. 3, 2nd edn., London, 1964).

KER, N. R., *Catalogue of Manuscripts containing Anglo-Saxon* (Oxford, 1957).

KER, N. R., *English Manuscripts in the century after the Norman Conquest* (Oxford, 1960).

KIRCHNER, J., *Beschreibende Verzeichnisse der Miniaturen-Handschriften der Preussischen Staatsbibliothek zu Berlin. I. Die Phillipps-Handschriften* (Leipzig, 1926).

KITZINGER, E., 'Anglo-Saxon Vine-scroll Ornament', *Antiquity*, x (1936), 61–71.

KOEHLER, W., 'Byzantine Art in the West', *Dumbarton Oaks Paper no. 1. Inaugural Lectures, 1940* (Cambridge, Massachusetts, 1941), 63–87.

LABBE, P., *Nova Bibliotheca Manuscriptorum Librorum*, 2 vols. (Paris, 1657).

LANDSBERGER, F., *Der St Galler Folchart-Psalter* (St Gall, 1912).

LAPORTE, J., 'Les origines du monachisme dans la province de Rouen', *Revue Mabillon*, xxxi (1941), 22–41, 49–68.

LAPORTE, J., 'Gérard de Brogne à S. Wandrille et à S. Riquier', *Revue Bénédictine*, lxx (1960), 142–66.

LEROQUAIS, V., *Les Pontificaux manuscrits des bibliothèques publiques de France*, 3 vols. (Paris, 1937).

Le Roy, Th., *Les Curieuses Recherches du Mont-Sainct-Michel*, ed. E. de Beaurepaire (Extrait des Mémoires de la Société des antiquaires de Normandie, ix (1877)), 2 vols. (Caen, 1878).

Le Roy-Laduire, M., 'Rôle des abbayes du val de Loire dans la colonization monastique normande', *Revue Historique de Droit Francais et Étranger*, 4e ser. xxxi (1953), 322–3.

Lesne, E., *Les Livres, 'scriptoria' et bibliothèques du commencement du VIIIe à la fin du XIe siècle* (Histoire de la propriété ecclesiastique en France, t. iv, Lille, 1938).

Mabillon, J., *Annales Ordinis Sancti Benedicti*, 5 vols. (Paris, 1703–13).

Magnani, L., *Le Miniature del Sacramentario d'Ivrea e di altri codici Warmondiani* (Vatican, 1934).

Mâle, E., *L'Art religieux du XIIe siècle en France* (3rd edn., Paris, 1928).

Merton, A., *Die Buchmalerei in St Gallen vom neunten bis zum elften Jahrhundert* (Leipzig, 1912).

Musset, L., 'Pour réabiliter la sculpture romane normande. I. Les chapiteaux de Ruqueville', *Art de Basse Normandie*, xiii (Spring, 1959), 12–15.

Mynors, R. A. B., *Durham Cathedral Manuscripts to the end of the twelfth century* (Durham, 1939).

Neuss, Wm., *Die Katalanische Bibelillustration um die Wende des ersten Jahrtausends und die altspanische Buchmalerei* (Veröffentlichungen des romanischen Auslandsinstituts der rheinischen Friedrich Wilhems-Universität, Bonn, Bd. 3, Bonn and Leipzig, 1922).

Neuss, Wm., *Die Apokalypse des Hl. Johannes in der altspanischen und altchristlichen Bibel-illustration* (Spanische Forschungen der Görresgesellschaft), 2 vols. (Münster in Westfalen, 1931).

Nitschke, B., *Die Handschriftengruppe um den Meister des Registrum Gregorii* (Münstersche Studien zur Kunstgeschichte, Bd. 5) (Recklinghausen, 1966).

Nordenfalk, C., 'Der Meister des Registrum Gregorii', *Münchner Jahrbuch der bildenden Kunst*, 3rd ser., i (1950), 61–77.

Nordenfalk, C., 'A travelling Milanese artist in France at the beginning of the eleventh century', *Arte del Primo Millennio*, ed. E. Arslan (Milan, 1954), 374–80.

Nordenfalk, C., 'Miniature ottonienne et ateliers capétiens', *Art de France*, iv (1964), 47–55.

Nortier, G., 'Les Bibliothèques médiévales des abbayes bénédictines de Normandie. La Bibliothèque du Mont Saint-Michel', *Revue Mabillon*, 3e ser. xlvii (1957), 135–72.

Ordericus Vitalis, *Ecclesiasticae Historiae*, ed. A. le Prevost and L. Delisle, *Société de l'histoire de France*, 5 vols. (1838–55).

Pächt, O., 'Hugo Pictor', *Bodleian Library Record*, iii (1950), 96–103.

PÄCHT, O., *The Rise of Pictorial Narrative in twelfth-century England* (Oxford, 1962).

PÄCHT, O., 'The Pre-carolingian roots of early Romanesque Art', *Studies in Western Art. Acts of the 20th Congress of the History of Art*, ed. M. Meiss, i (Princeton 1963), 67–75.

*Paris, Bibliothèque Nationale. Catalogue Général des Manuscrits Latins*, 5 vols. published so far (Paris, 1939–66).

PORCHER, J., 'Les Manuscrits à peintures de Saint-Martial', *L'Art Roman à Saint-Martial à Limoges* (exhibition catalogue) (Limoges, 1950).

PORCHER, J., 'L'Evangéliaire de Charlemagne et le psautier d'Amiens', *La Revue des Arts*, vii (1957), 51–8.

PORCHER, J., 'La peinture provinciale', *Karl der Grosse*, ed. W. Braunfels, iii (Düsseldorf, 1965), 54–73.

PROCHNO, J., *Das Schreiber- und Dedikationsbild in der deutschen Buchmalerei, I Teil. 800–1100* (Leipzig and Berlin, 1929).

*The Rabbula Gospels*, facsimile edition with commentary by C. Cechelli, G. Furlani and M. Salmi (Olten and Lausanne, 1959).

RAND, E. K., *A Survey of the Manuscripts of Tours* (Mediaeval Academy of America. Publication no. 3), 2 vols. (Cambridge, Massachusetts, 1929).

RAVAISSON, F., *Rapports au Ministre de l'Instruction Publique sur les bibliothèques des départements de l'Ouest* (Paris, 1841).

RODULFUS GLABER, *Historiarum Libri Quinque*, ed. M. Prou (Paris, 1886).

RODULFUS GLABER, *Vita Sancti Guillelmi*, ed. J. P. Migne, *Patrologia Latina*, cxlii (Paris, 1853), 703–20.

SACKUR, E., *Die Cluniacenser in ihrer Kirchlichen und allgemeingeschichtlichen Wirksamkeit bis zur Mitte des elften Jahrhunderts*, 2 vols. (Halle, 1892).

SAXL, F. and R. WITTKOWER, *British Art and the Mediterranean* (Oxford, 1948).

SCHAPIRO, M., 'The Decoration of the Leningrad manuscript of Bede', *Scriptorium*, xii (1958), 191–207.

SCHAPIRO, M., *The Parma Ildefonsus, a romanesque illuminated manuscript from Cluny, and related works* (College Art Association of America, 1964).

SCHILLING, R., 'Two unknown Flemish miniatures of the eleventh century', *Burlington Magazine*, xc (1948), 312–17.

SCHOTT, M., *Zwei Lütticher Sakramentare in Bamberg und Paris und ihre Verwandten* (Studien zur Deutschen Kunstgeschichte, Heft 284, Strassburg, 1931).

SCHULTEN, S., 'Die Buchmalerei des 11. Jahrhunderts im Kloster St Vaast in Arras', *Münchner Jahrbuch der bildenden Kunst*, vii (1956), 49–90.

STEGER, H., *David Rex et Propheta* (Erlanger Beiträge zur Sprach- und Kunstwissenschaft, Bd. 6, Nürnberg, 1961).

STETTINER, R., *Die illustrierten Prudentius-Handschriften* (Berlin, 1905).

SWARZENSKI, H., 'Der Stil der Bibel Carilefs von Durham', *Form und Inhalt. Kunstgeschichtliche Studien für Otto Schmitt* (Stuttgart, 1951).

TURNER, D. H. 'The prayer-book of Archbishop Arnulf II of Milan', *Revue Bénédictine*, lxx (1960), 360–92.

TURNER, D. H., 'The Odalricus Peccator Manuscript in the British Museum', *British Museum Quarterly*, xxv.1 (1962), 11–16.

VOEGE, W., *Eine deutsche Malerschule um die Wende des ersten Jahrtausends* (Westdeutsche Zeitschrift für Geschichte und Kunst, Ergänzungsheft 7) (Trier, 1891).

WALTHER, H.,'Ein Michael's Hymnus vom Mont-St. Michel (Cod. Avranches 98)', *Corona Quernea. Festgabe Karl Strecker* (Leipzig, 1941), 254–65.

WARNER, G. F., and H. A. WILSON, *The Benedictional of Saint Aethelwold, bishop of Winchester 963–984* (Roxburghe Club, 1910).

WARNER, G. F., and GILSON, J. P., *Catalogue of Western MSS. in the Old Royal and King's Collections*, 4 vols. (London, British Museum, 1921).

WETTSTEIN, J., *Sant'Angelo in Formis et la peinture médiévale en Campanie* (Geneva, 1960).

WILLIAM OF JUMIÈGES, *Gesta Normannorum Ducum*, ed. J. Marx (Société de l'histoire de Normandie, Rouen and Paris, 1914).

WILMART, A., 'Jean l'Homme de Dieu. Auteur d'un traité attribué à S. Bernard', *Revue Mabillon*, xv (1925), 5–29.

WORMALD, F., 'The development of English illumination in the twelfth century', *Journal of the British Archaeological Association*, 3rd series, viii (1943), 31–49.

WORMALD, F., 'A fragment of a tenth-century English Gospel Lectionary', *Calligraphy and Palaeography. Essays presented to Alfred Fairbank*, ed. A. S. Osley (London, 1965), 43–6.

WORMALD, F., 'The Survival of Anglo-Saxon illumination after the Norman Conquest', *Proceedings of the British Academy*, xxx (1944), 128–145.

WORMALD, F., *The Miniatures in the Gospels of St Augustine* (*Corpus Christi College MS. 286*) (Cambridge, 1954).

WORMALD, F., *The Benedictional of St Ethelwold* (London, 1959).

WORMALD, F., 'An English eleventh-century Psalter with pictures', *Walpole Society*, xxxviii (1960–2), 1–13.

ZARNECKI, G., *English Romanesque Sculpture, 1066–1140* (London, 1951).

ZARNECKI, G., *Later English Romanesque Sculpture 1140–1210* (London, 1953).

ZARNECKI, G., '1066 and architectural sculpture', *Proceedings of the British Academy*, lii (1966), 87–104.

# INDEX OF MANUSCRIPTS

# GENERAL INDEX

# PLATES

## NOTE ON THE PLATES: ACKNOWLEDGEMENTS

In order to accommodate as many objects as possible on the plates it has been necessary to reduce many of the originals. The specimens of script (Pls. 1–6) are reproduced actual size, however.

All objects are reproduced by kind permission of the owners. I am also grateful to the authorities of the various libraries and museums who have given permission to use photographs of which they own the copyright. In addition I am indebted to the following for permission to reproduce photographs:

Barcelona, Ampliaciones Mas. Pl. 35*b*.

Cambrai, Studio Delcroix. Pl. 45*c*.

Cologne, Rheinisches Bildarchiv. Pl. 39*a*.

Florence, Alinari. Pls. 18*c*, 27*a*.

Marburg/Lahn, Bildarchiv Foto Marburg. Pls. 16*f*, *h*, 18*a*, *b*, 26*b*, 27*b*, 29*b*, 34*g*, 40*b*, 42*e*, 46*b*, *c*.

London, Courtauld Institute of Art, Pls. 5*d*, 11*e*, 13*d*, 15*e*, 16*c*, 17*c*, 18*d*, 19*g*, 34*b*, *d*, 37*c*, 40*c*, 45*e*.

London, Warburg Institute. Pls. 16*e*, 23, 27*e*, 32*b*, 33*b*, 34*h*, 39*e*, 41*b*.

Paris, Monuments historiques. Pls. 13*e*, 18*e*, 35*a*, 48*c*, 50*e*, 51*d*, 52*a*.

St Gall, Photohaus Zmbühl. Pls. 9*h*, 25*b*.

Professor C. R. Dodwell. Pls. 11*b*, *f*, *g*, 13*a*, 14*a*, 15*b*, 17*b*, 20, 22, 30*a*, *c*, *d*, 34*c*, 35*e*, 37*d*, 41*c*, 42*b*, 49*e*, 53*c*, 54*c*, 55*d*.

Professor E. B. Garrisson. Pl. 45*a*.

Professor O. Pächt. Pl. 34*f*.

Professor G. Zarnecki. Pl. 8*b*.

*a*. Leiden, Voss. lat. fol. 39, fol. 135$^{v}$. Hervardus

*b*. Avranches 97, fol. 92. Attributed to Hervardus

*c*. Orléans 105, p. 361. Attributed to Hervardus

*a*. Avranches 98, fol. 24^v. Gualterius

*b*. Avranches 98, fol. 173. Martinus

*c*. Avranches 91, fol. 175^v. Giraldus

*a.* Avranches 61, fol. 329

*b.* Avranches 59, fol. 56v

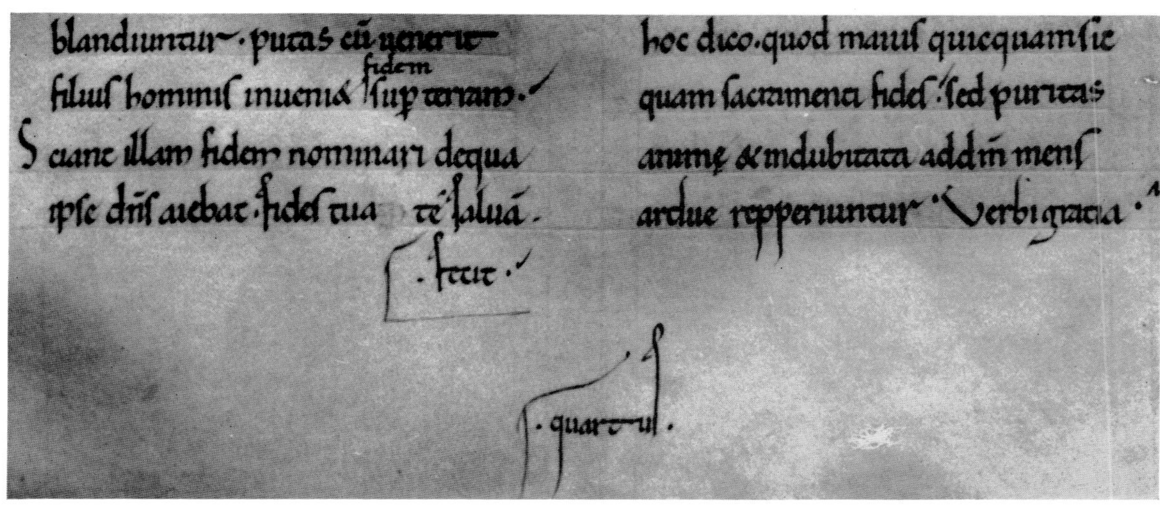

*c.* Avranches 72, fol. 120. Frotmundus

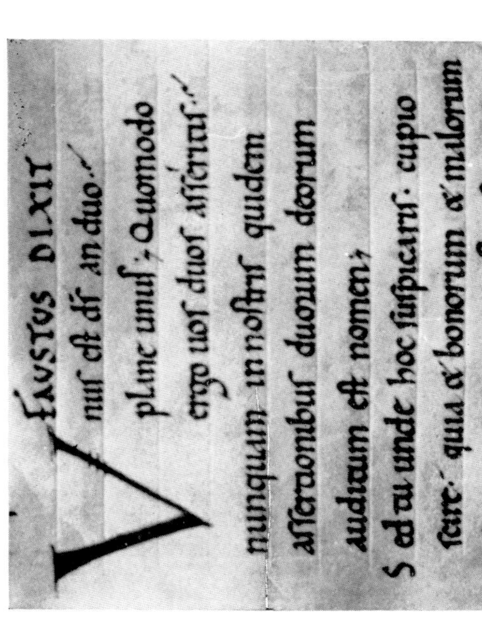
VFAUSTUS DIXIT
nus est ds an duo
pline unus. Quomodo
ergo uos duos asseritis
nunquam in nostris quidem
assertionibus duorum deorum
auditum est nomen.
Sed tu unde hoc suspicaris: cupio
scire: quia et bonorum et malorum

*a*. Avranches 90, fol. $107^{v}$. Gyraldus

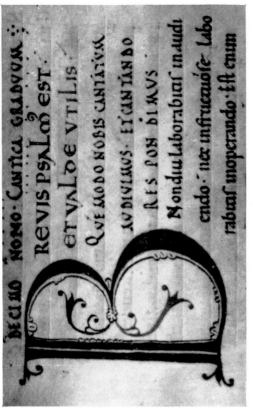

*b*. Avranches 77, fol. $106^{v}$. Gyraldus

*c*. Rouen, Suppl. 116, fol. $43^{v}$

*d*. Paris, Latin 2088, fol. 78

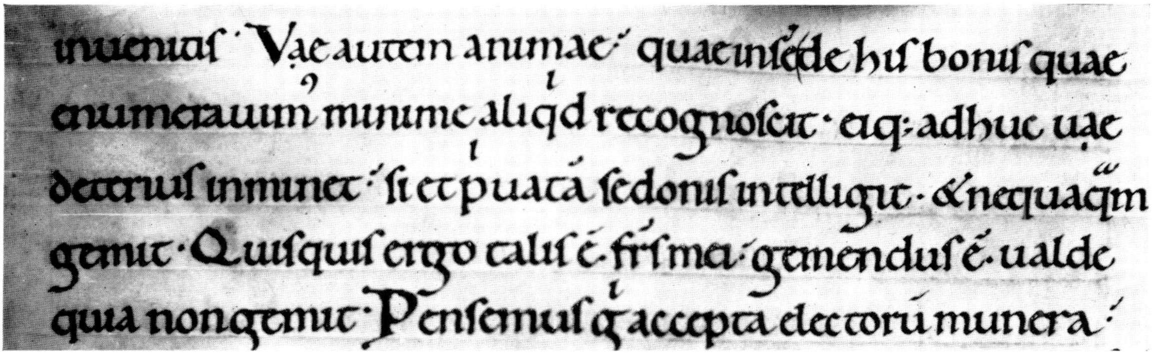

*a*. Avranches 103, fol. 166

*b*. Avranches 103, fol. 89v

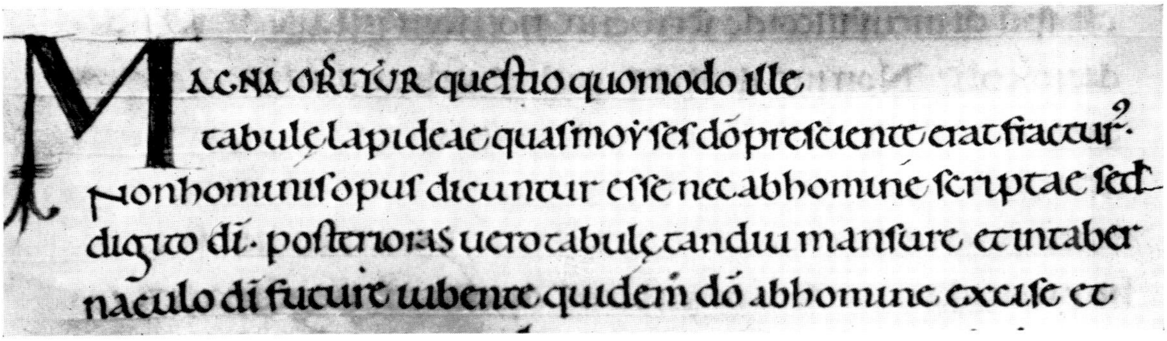

*c*. Avranches 35, fol. 111

*d*. London, Royal 13. A.XXII, fol. 2v

PLATE 6

*a*. Avranches 163, fol. 21. Osbernus

*b*. Avranches 58, fol. 119v. Mauritius

*c*. Avranches 50, fol. 52. 'I'

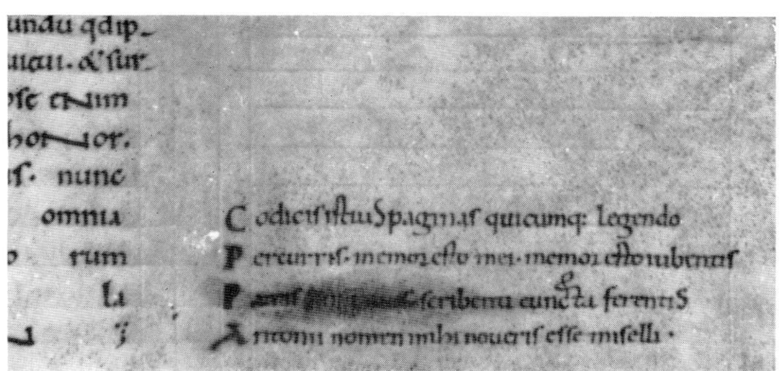

*d*. Rouen A.143, fol. 151. Antonius

*e*. Avranches 50, fol. 1v. 'T'

*a.* Avranches 50, fol. 112$^{v}$. 'P'

*b.* Angers 819, fol. 2$^{v}$. 'G'

*c.* Avranches 50, fol. 3. 'e'

*d.* St Gall 23, p. 332. 'L'

*e.* Avranches 211, fol. 161$^{v}$. 'P'

*f.* London, Add. 11848, fol. 13. 'M'

*g.* Avranches 98, fol. 143$^{v}$. 'd'

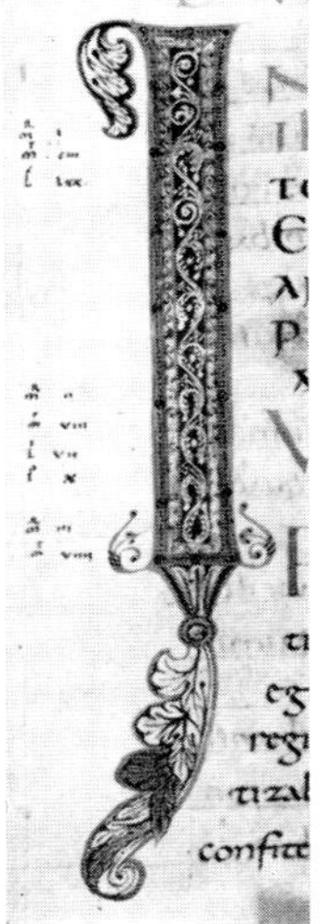

*h.* London, Add. 11848, fol. 75. 'I'

*i.* Avranches 97, fol. 223$^{v}$. 'S'

*a*. St Gall 23, p. 304. 'D'

*b*. Bernay. Capital

*c*. Paris, Latin 11750, fol. 25ᵛ. 'u'

*d*. Avranches 97, fol. 201ᵛ. 'M'

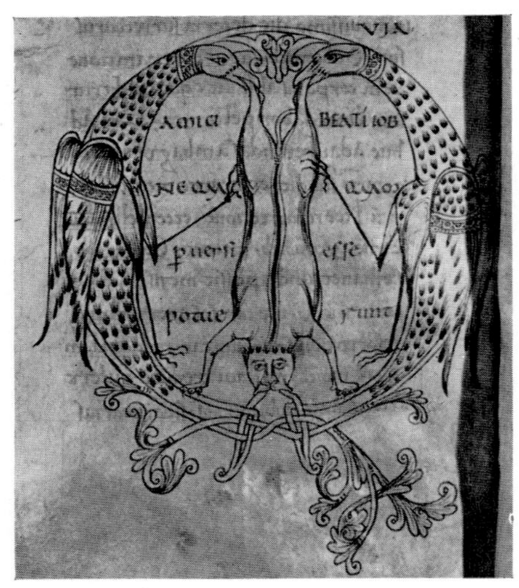

*e*. Avranches 97, fol. 240ᵛ. 'Q'

*f*. Angers 169, fol. 218ᵛ. 'M'

*g*. Paris, Latin 5301, fol. 145ᵛ. 'R'

*a.* Avranches 211, fol. 156. 'M'

*b.* Avranches 98, fol. 117. 'Q'

*c.* Avranches 98, fol. 132v. 'P'

*d.* Avranches 91, fol. 137v. 'R'

*e.* London, Harley 2904, fol. 4. 'B'

*f.* Avranches 91, fol. 1. 'B'

*g.* Paris, Latin 11550, fol. 8. 'B'

*h.* St Gall 22, p. 99. 'q'

*a.* Arras 559, vol. III, fol. 98ᵛ. 'O'

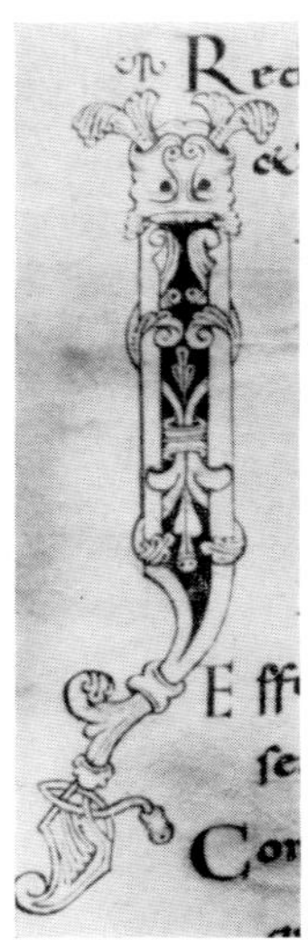

*b.* Boulogne 20, fol. 40. 'I'

*c.* Avranches 98, fol. 101. 'I'

*d.* Avranches 98, fol. 9. 'P'

*e.* Arras 559, vol. II, fol. 52ᵛ. Roundel of frame

*f.* Avranches 115, fol. 1ᵛ. Frame page

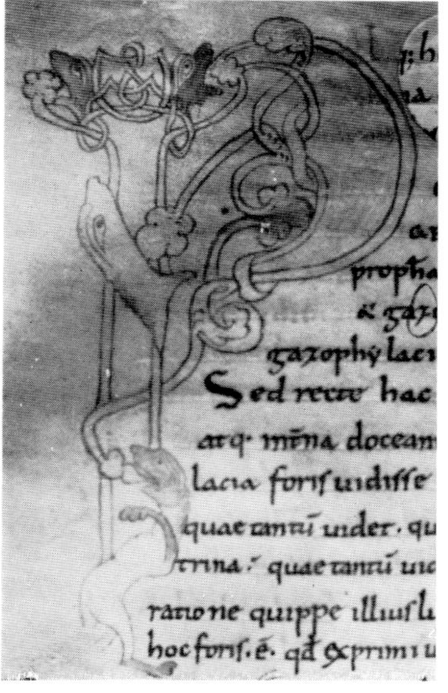

*g.* Avranches 99, fol. 111ᵛ. 'P'

*h.* Boulogne 16, fol. 116ᵛ. 'P'

*i.* Avranches 91, fol. 255. 'G'

*a*. Paris, Latin 12117, fol. 49ᵛ. 'P'

*b*. Arras 559, vol. I, fol. 97ᵛ. 'F' (detail)

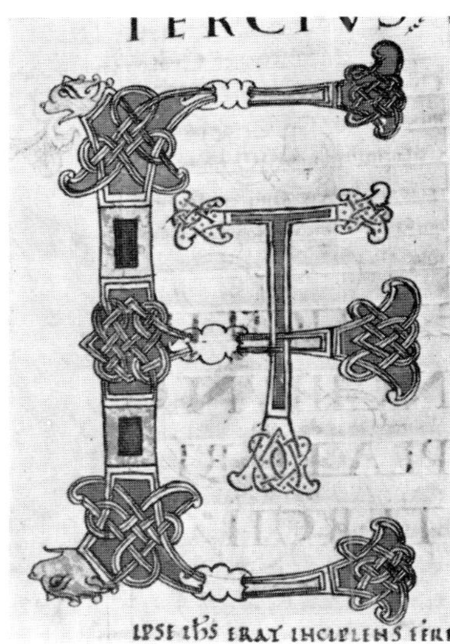

*c*. Avranches 59, fol. 31ᵛ. 'Et'

*d*. Avranches 61, fol. 113. 'B'

*g*. Avranches 101, fol. 77ᵛ. 'P'

*e*. Cambridge, Trinity B.10.4, fol. 12. Detail of Canons

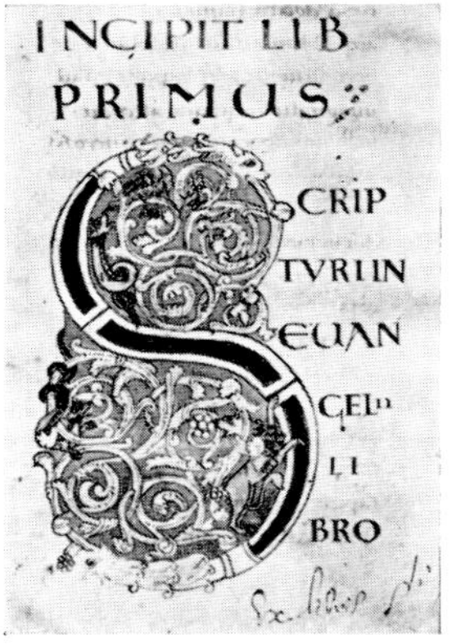


*f*. Avranches 59, fol. 2. 'S'

*h*. Avranches 72, fol. 44. 'S'

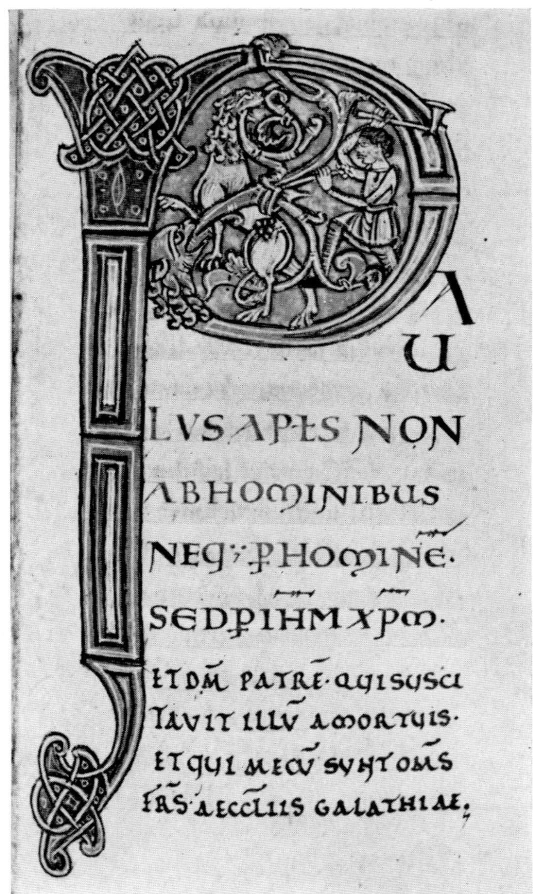


*a*. Avranches 72, fol. 151. 'P'

*b*. Avranches 76, fol. 1. 'B'

*c*. Avranches 107, fol. 112. 'S'

*d*. Bordeaux 1, fol. 70^v^. 'E'

*e*. Avranches 75, p. 1. 'O'

*a*. Amiens 18, fol. 95. 'B'

*b*. Avranches 72, fol. 150. 'C'

*c*. New York, Morgan 641, fol. 156. 'd'

*d*. Cambridge, Trinity B.10.4, fol. 60. 'I'

*e*. Musée de Cluny. Ivory diptych

*f*. Oxford, Junius 27, fol. 121ᵛ. 'd'

*g*. New York, Morgan 333, fol. 1. Detail of frame

*a*. Avranches 90, fol. 2. 'F'

*b*. Rouen A.143, fol. 1ᵛ. 'R'

*c*. Paris, Latin 2088, fol. 1ᵛ. 'D'

*d*. Avranches 77, fol. 2. 'e'

*a*. Avranches 86, fol. 32. 'Q'

*c*. Avranches 146, fol. 2v. 'I'

*b*. Avranches 86, fol. 138v. 'X'

*d*. Avranches 89, fol. 103. 'D'

*e*. Cambridge, Trinity B.10.4, fol. 90. 'Q'

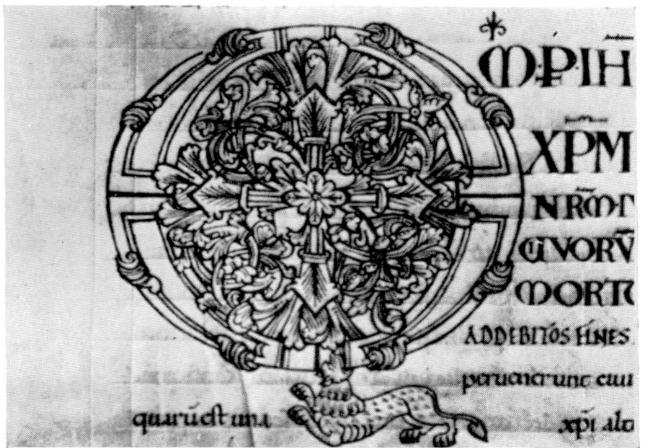

*a*. Avranches 89, fol. 180. 'Q'

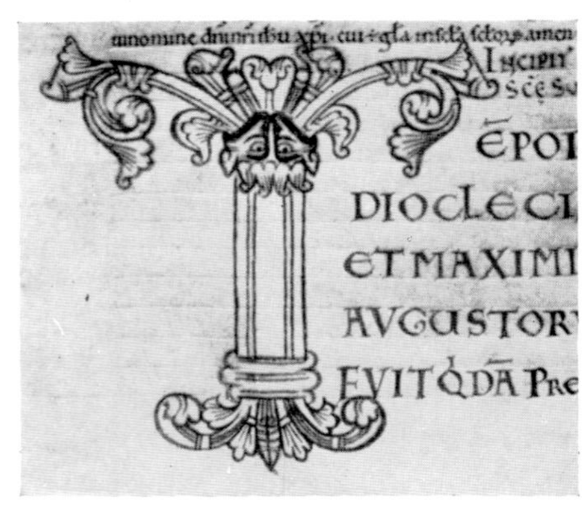

*b*. Paris, Latin 5290, fol. $16^{v}$. 'T'

*c*. London, Royal 13 A.XXIII, fol. $1^{v}$. 'B'

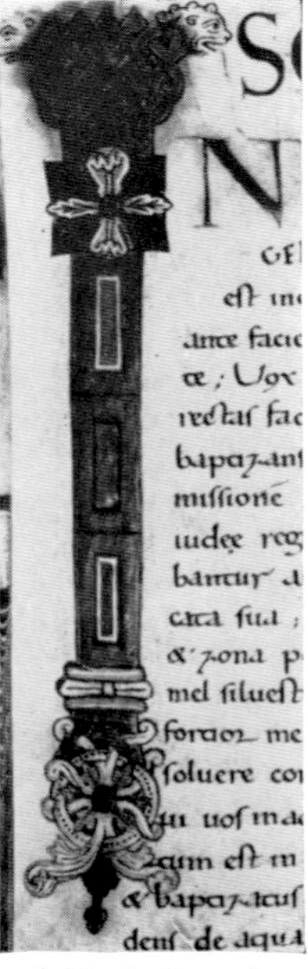

*d*. York Gospels, fol. 61. 'I'

*e*. Leipzig. St Michael

*f*. Monte Gargano. St Michael

*g*. Oxford, MS Douce 176. 'Christus super aspidem'

*h*. Aachen. St Michael

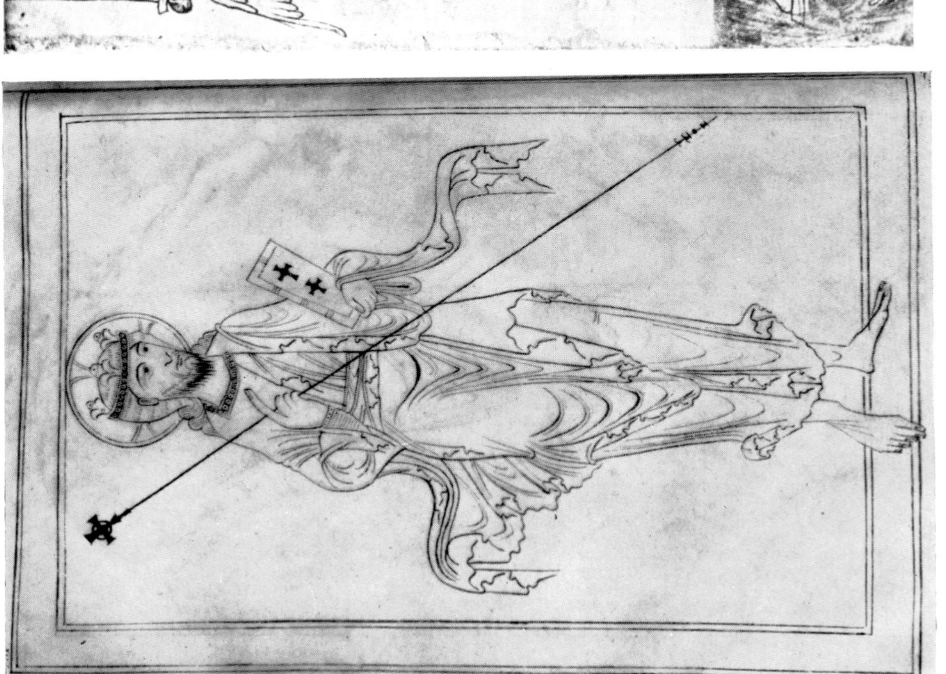

*a*. Paris, Latin 943, fol. 5ᵛ. God the Father

*b*. Avranches 50, fol. 1. St Michael

*c*. Cambridge, Corpus 183, fol. 1ᵛ. King Athelstan and St Cuthbert

*d*. Oxford, Junius 27, fol. 118. 'D'. David and the Lion

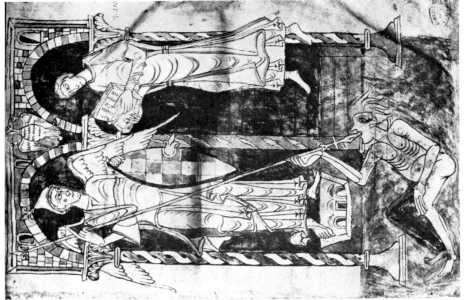

# PLATE 18

*a.* Bamberg A.II.42. Apocalypse

*b.* Munich, Clm 23630. St Michael

*c.* Florence, Bargello. St Michael

*d.* London, Tiberius C.VI, fol. 16. St Michael

*e.* Paris, Latin 9448, fol. 71. St Michael

*a*. Monte Gargano. St Michael

*b*. Monte Gargano. St Michael

*c*. Monte Gargano. St Michael

*d*. Ivrea Cod. LXXXVI, fol. 108v. St Michael

*e*. Coptic textile.

*f*. Paris, Latin 11685, fol. 40. 'N'

*g*. London, Add. 17739, fol. 17. St Michael

*h*. Avranches 210, fol. 25v. Gifts to St Michael

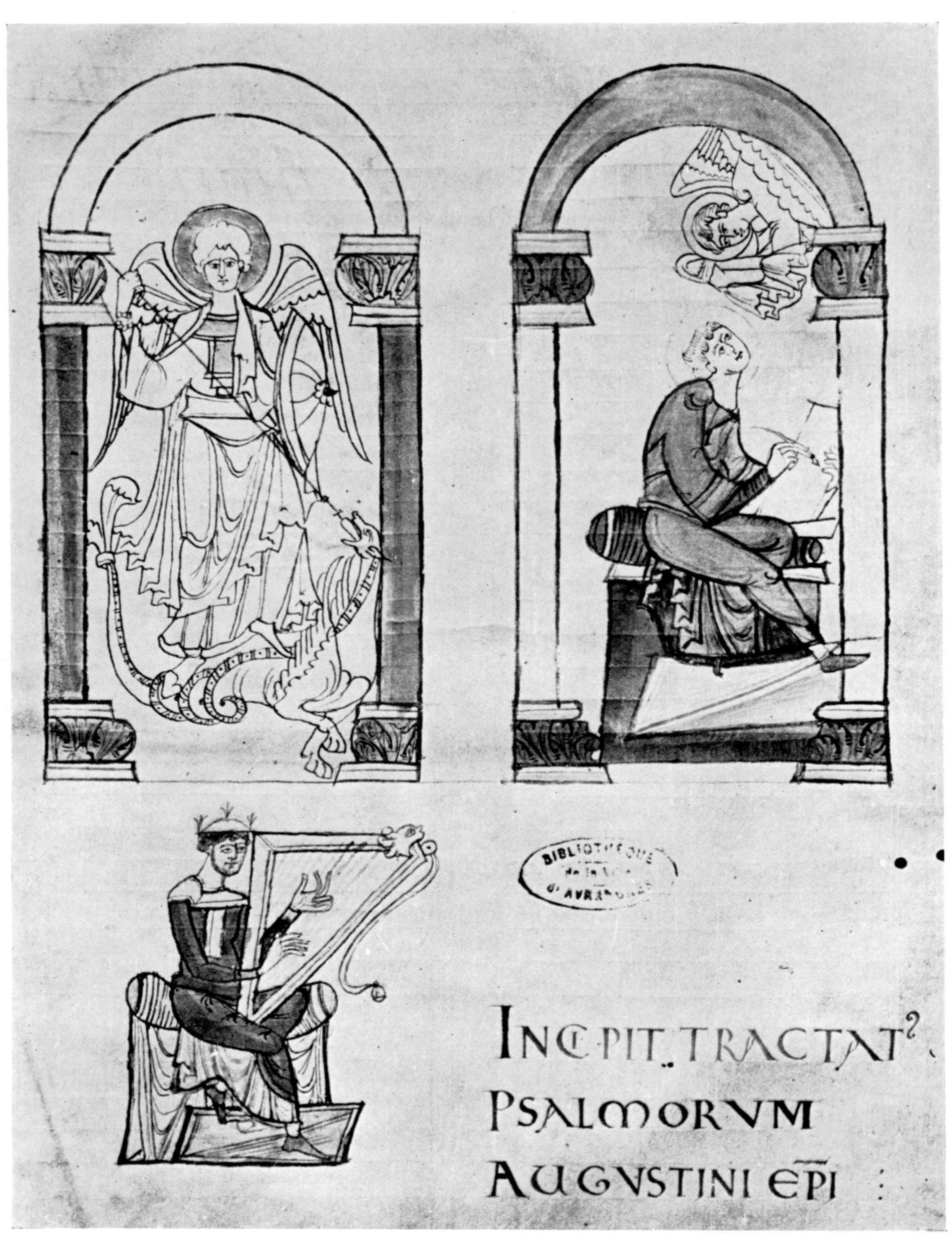


Avranches 76, fol. Av. St Michael, St Augustine and King David

Oxford, Auct.F.4.32, fol. 1. St Dunstan adoring Christ

Avranches 72, fol. 97. St Augustine disputing with Felicianus

London, Add. 49598, fol. 51v. The Maries at the Sepulchre

PLATE 24

*a*. Avranches 90, fol. 1ᵛ. St Augustine disputing with Faustinus

*b*. Oxford, Lat. liturg. f. 5, fol. 21ᵛ. St Luke

*a*. Boulogne 9, fol. 1ᵛ. St Jerome and Pope Damasus

*b*. Einsiedeln 135, p.2. St Jerome and Jovinianus

*a*. Paris, Latin 2639, fol. $31^{v}$. St Ambrose in prayer

*b*. St Omer 698, fol. $25^{v}$. St Omer in prayer

*a*. Monreale. Pantocrator

*b*. Minuto. Pantocrator

*c*. Berlin, Phillipps 1676, fol. 24. St Ambrose

*e*. York Gospels, fol. $85^{v}$. St Luke

*d*. Milan, Ambrosiana, E.49–50 inf.
St Gregory Nazianzus

Avranches 72, fol. 182v. St Ambrose

*a.* Avranches 75, fol. C$^{v}$. St Augustine

*b.* Trier. St Gregory the Great

*a*. Avranches 163, fol. 2$^{v}$. Frame page

*b*. Avranches 59, fol. 1$^{v}$. Frame page

*c*. Rouen Y.6, fol. 132$^{v}$. St Peter

*d*. Arras 559, vol. III, fol. 77. Detail of Frame

*a*. New York, Morgan 641, fol. $2^{v}$.
Annunciation to the shepherds

*b*. Paris, Latin 9428, fol. 27. 'D'.
Martyrdom of St Stephen

*c*. Latin 9428, fol. $23^{v}$. 'D'.
Annunciation to the shepherds

*d*. Morgan 641, fol. $3^{v}$. 'D'. Martyrdom of St Stephen

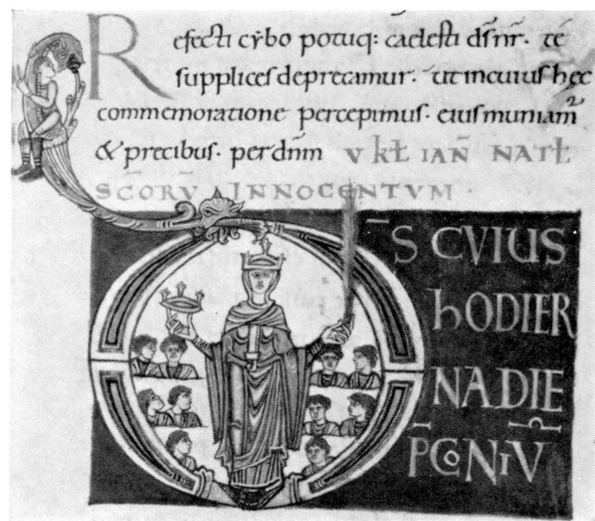

*e*. Morgan 641, fol. 6. 'D'. The Holy Innocents

*f*. Alençon 14, fol. 85. 'T'. St Christina

PLATE 32

*a*. Morgan 641, fol. 9. 'D'. Adoration of the Magi

*b*. London, Add. 49598, fol. 24$^{v}$. Adoration of the Magi

*c*. Göttingen, theol. fol. 231, fol. 24$^{v}$. The Purification

*d*. Paris, Latin 12117, fol. 107. The Purification

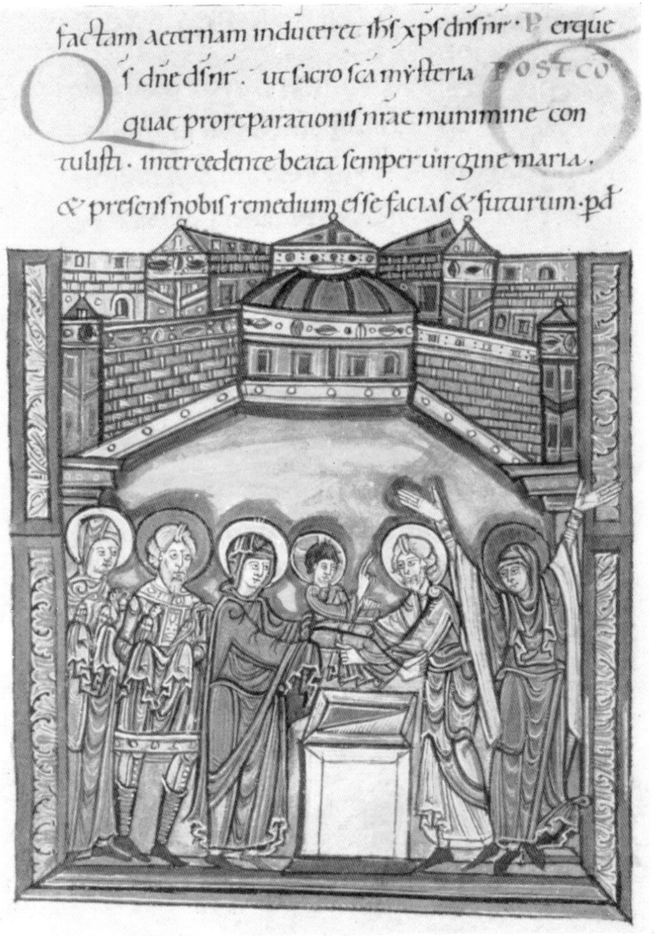


*a*. Morgan 641, fol. 18. The Purification

*b*. London, Add. 49598, fol. 34$^{v}$. The Purification

*a.* Morgan 641, fol. 23ᵛ. 'd'. The soul of St Benedict

*b.* Vat. Lat. 1202, fol. 79ᵛ. Vision of St Benedict

*c.* Valenciennes 502, fol. 30. Death of St Amand

*d.* Oxford, University College 165, p.18. Vision of St Cuthbert

*e.* Morgan 641, fol. 24. 'D'. The Annunciation

*f.* Troyes 2273, fol. 57ᵛ. Death of St Maur

*g.* Trier 24, fol. 9ᵛ. The Annunciation

*h.* London, Add. 49598, fol. 5ᵛ, The Annunciation

*a*. Paris, Arsenal 592, fol. 18v.
The Annunciation

*b*. Escorial 17, fol. 153. The Last Supper

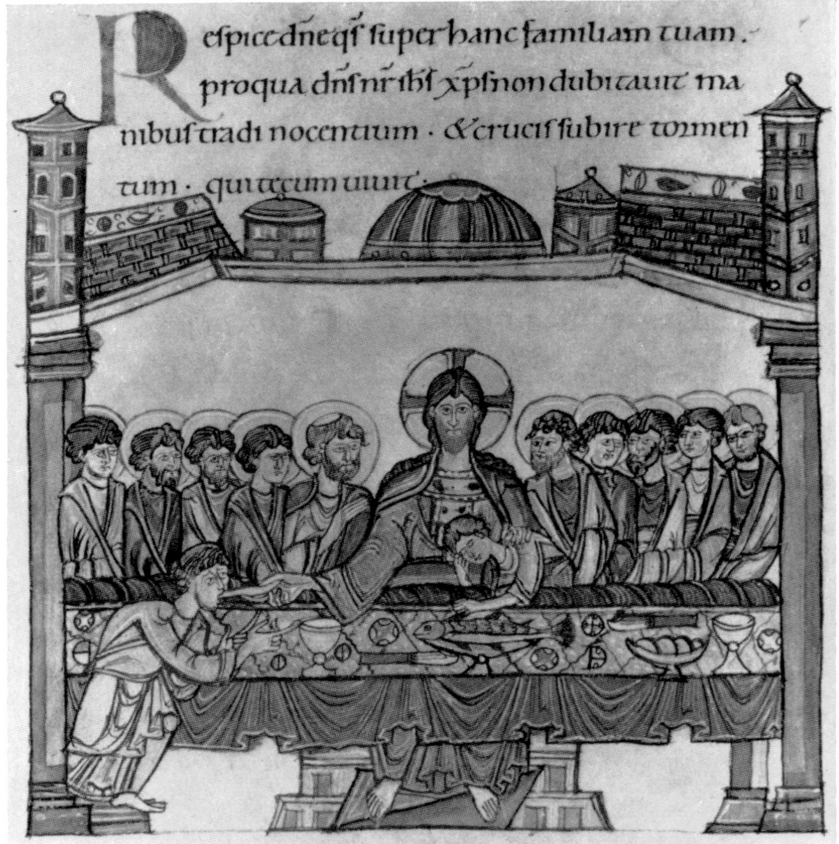


*c*. Morgan 641, fol. 52v. The Last Supper

*d*. Paris, Latin 12054, fol. 79.
The Last Supper

*e*. Rouen A.85, fol. 121.
The Last Supper

E IG
NVM
& IVSTVM EST · AEQVVM
& salutare · Nos tibi semper & ubi
q; gras agere · Dne sce pater ·
omps aeterne ds · per xpm dnm
nrm · Per quem maiestatem tua
laudant angli · Adorant domi
nationes · tremunt potestates ·
Caeli celorumq; uirtutes · ac beata
seraphin socia exultatione conce
lebrant · Cumquib; & nras uoces
ut admitti iubeas deprecamur ·
Supplici confessione dicentes ;
Scs · Scs · Scs dns ds
sabaoth ·

Morgan 641, fol. 61v. The 'Vere Dignum' monogram

*a*. London, Caligula A. XIV, fol. 22. The release of St Peter

*b*. Paris, Latin 11685, fol. 11. 'M'. Two Angels

*c*. Cambridge, Trinity B.10.4, fol. 89ᵛ. St Luke

*d*. Rouen, Y.6, fol. 164ᵛ. St Andrew

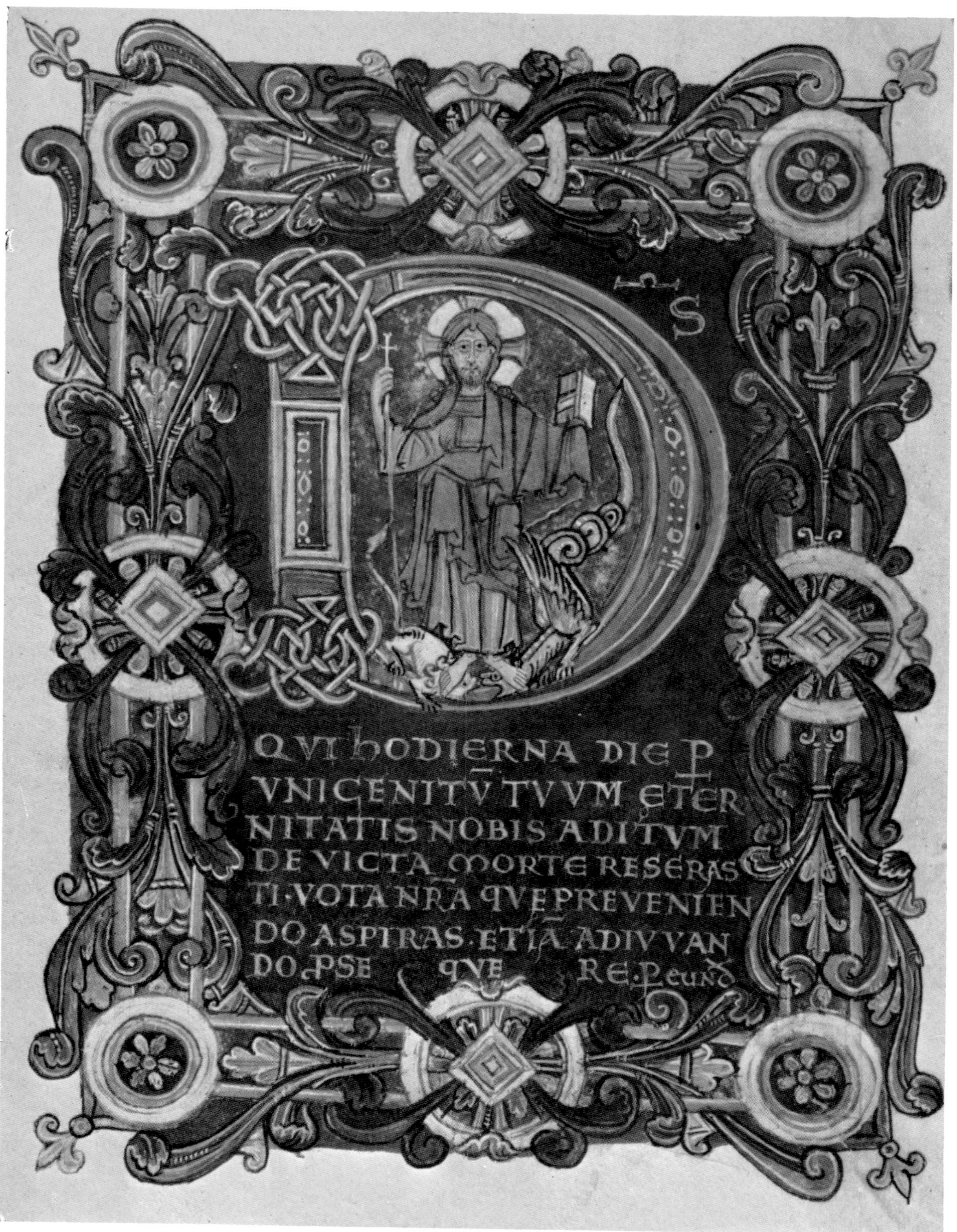


Morgan, 641, fol. 66ᵛ. 'D'. 'Christus super aspidem'

*a*. Berlin, theol. lat. fol. 358. 'Christus super aspidem'

*c*. Morgan 641, fol. $75^{v}$. The Ascension

*b*. Paris, Latin 11685, fol. 9. 'E'. 'Christus super aspidem'

= St Germain-des-Prés.

*d*. Paris, Latin 9428, fol. $71^{v}$. The Ascension

*e*. London, Add. 49598, fol. $64^{v}$. The Ascension

*a*. Morgan 641, fol. 80<sup>v</sup>. Pentecost

*b*. Paris, Latin 817, fol. 77. Pentecost

*c*. London, Tiberius C.VI, fol. 15<sup>v</sup>. Pentecost

*d*. Rouen Y.7, fol. 29<sup>v</sup>. Pentecost

*e*. Morgan 641, fol. 120. 'D'. Zacharias

*a*. Morgan 641, fol. 119$^{v}$. Nativity of St John Baptist

*b*. London, Add. 49598, fol. 92$^{v}$. Nativity of St John Baptist

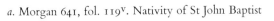

*c*. Rouen Y.109, fol. 4. The Assumption

*b*. Arras 684, fol. 2v.
The Assumption

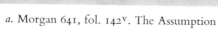

*c*. Paris, Latin 9428, fol. 86.
Martyrdom of St Peter

*a*. Morgan 641, fol. 142v. The Assumption

*d*. London, Harley 2908, fol. 123v.
The Assumption

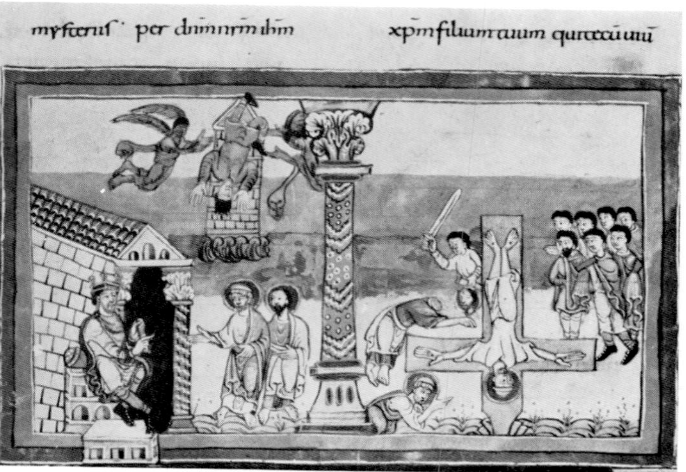

*e*. Göttingen, theol. fol. 231, fol. 93. Martyrdom of St Peter

Morgan 641, fol. 122ᵛ. Martyrdom of St Peter

PLATE 44

Morgan 641, fol. $155^{v}$. The return of the True Cross

*a*. Vat. Lat. 1269, fol. 117. 'T'.
The return of the True Cross

*b*. Paris, Latin 833. 'N'.
The return of the True Cross

*c*. Cambrai 528, fol. 195. 'T'.
The return of the True Cross

*d*. Morgan 641, fol. 170. All Saints

*e*. London, Galba A. XVIII, fol. 21.
All Saints

*f*. Paris, Latin 11751, fol. 59$^{v}$. All Saints

*a*. Morgan 641, fol. 173. 'D'. St Martin

*b*. Tournai. St Nicasius

*c*. Boulogne 107, fol. 6$^{v}$.
St Bertin and his companions

*d*. Paris, Latin 11751, fol. 142. 'O'. St Martin

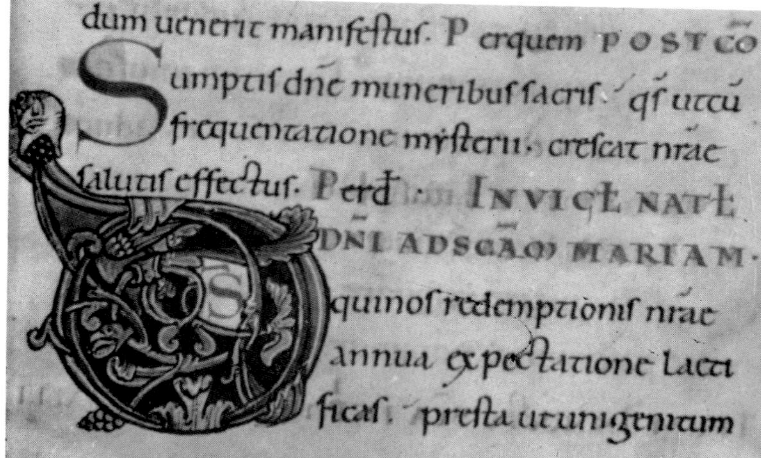


*e*. Rouen, Suppl. 116, fol. 14. Initial 'd'

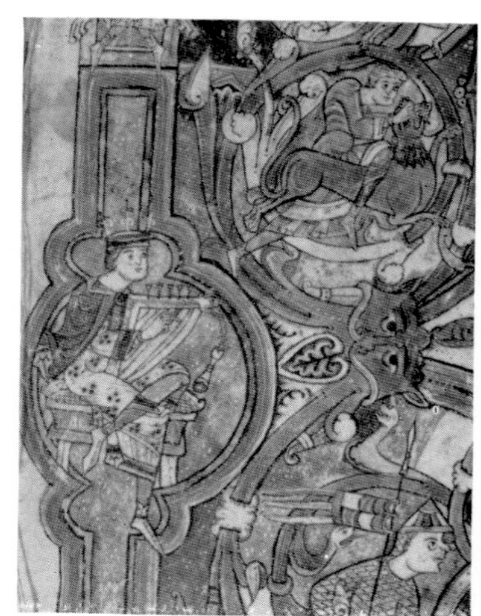

*f*. Rouen A. 19, fol. 1. 'B' (detail).
King David

Avranches 103, fol. 4[v]. St Gregory the Great

PLATE 48

*a.* Paris, Latin 5301, fol. 196. 'M'. Christ flanked by angels

*b.* Oxford, Auct. D.2.16, fol. 72ᵛ. St Mark

*c.* Paris, Latin 819, fol. 8ᵛ. Enthroned Christ

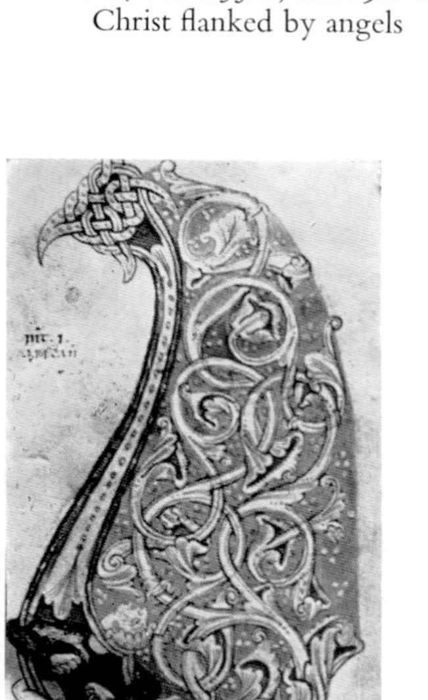


*d.* Valenciennes 93, fol. 10. 'L'

*f.* Brussels II.175, fol. 57ᵛ. St. Mark

*e.* Avranches 103, fol. 5. 'd'

*a.* Avranches 58, fol. $3^{v}$. 'G'. St Hilary of Poitiers

*b.* Bayeux 57, fol. 42. 'C'. A Saint writing

*c.* Brussels 18383, fol. 85. St Luke

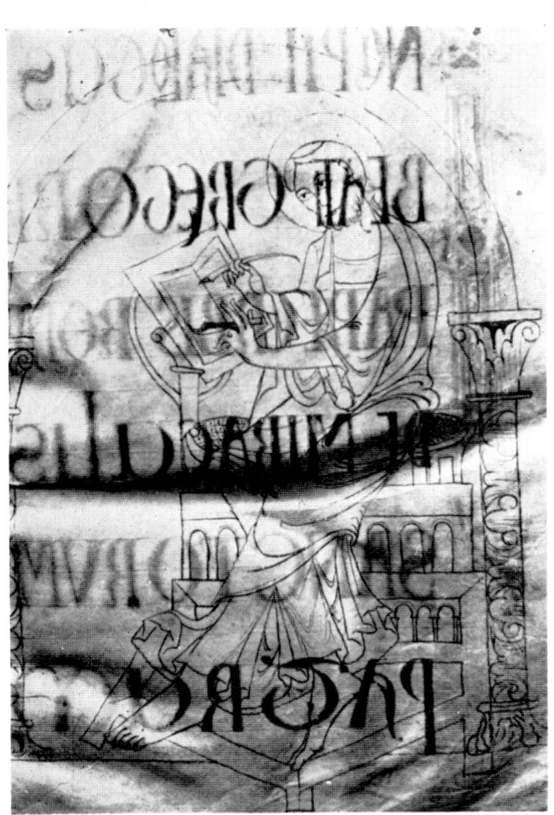

*d.* Paris, Latin 2267, fol. 6. St Gregory the Great

*e.* Amiens 24, fol. $77^{v}$. St Luke

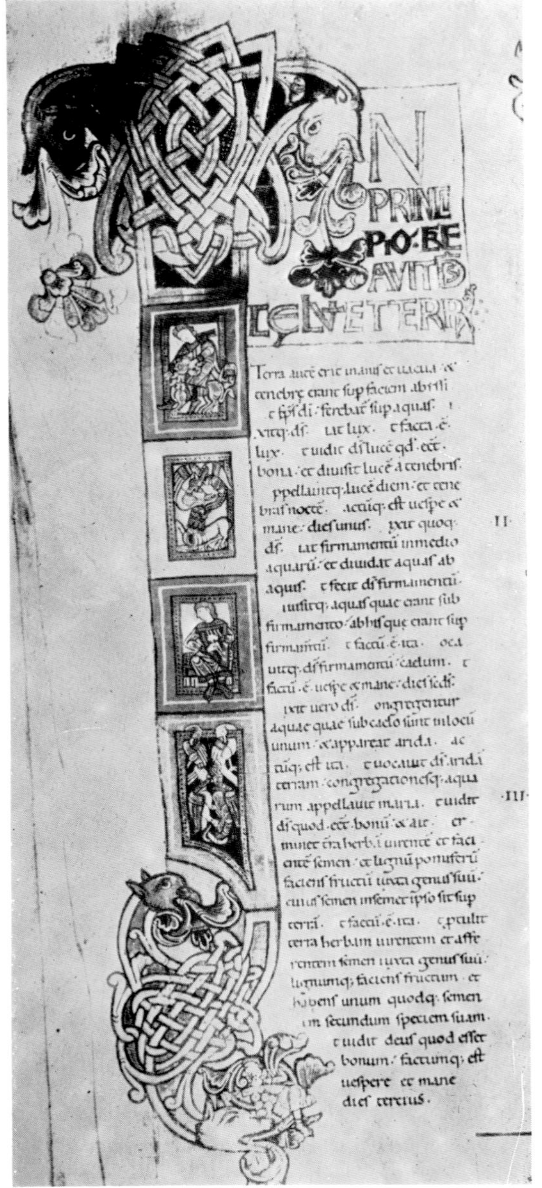

*a*. Bordeaux 1, fol. 5. 'I' with King David and the lion

*b*. Bordeaux 1, fol. 240. 'e'. Jonah and the whale

*c*. Bordeaux 1, fol. 207. 'd'

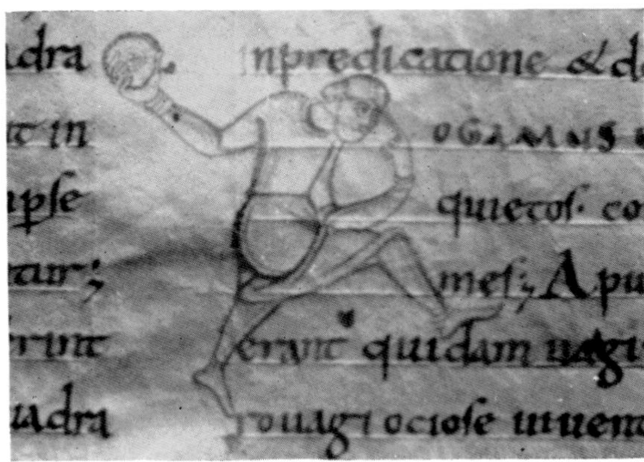

*d*. Angers 67, fol. 139. 'R'

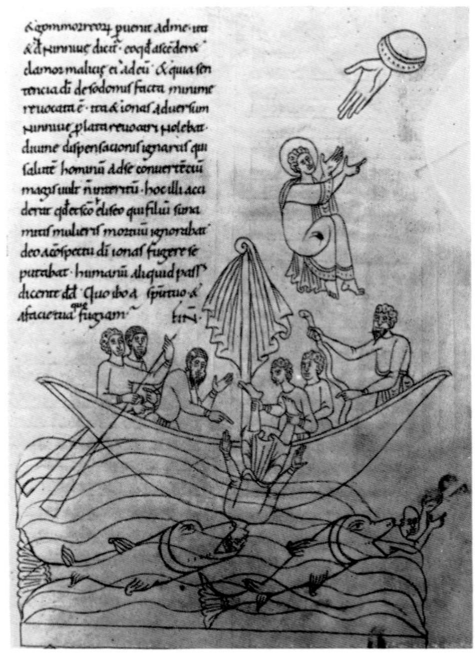

*e*. Paris, Latin 6, vol. III, fol. 83.
Jonah and the whale

*a*. Bordeaux 1, fol. 168ᵛ. 'V'. Jeremiah

*b*. Le Mans 214, fol. 26ᵛ. 'M'

*d*. Paris, Latin 6, vol. III, fol. 64ᵛ.
The statue set up by Nebucadnesor

*c*. Le Mans 227, fol. 13. 'T'

*e*. Bordeaux 1, fol. 207ᵛ. 'A'. Nebucadnesor's statue

*a*. Paris, Latin 6, vol. III, fol. 66$^{v}$.
Daniel and the dragon

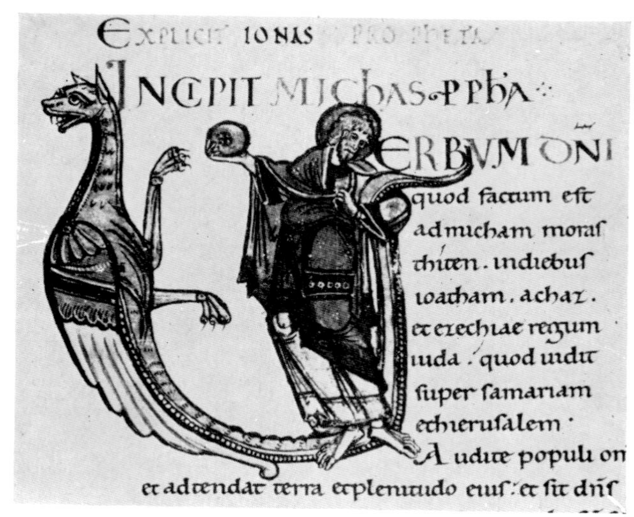


*b*. Bordeaux 1, fol. 240$^{v}$. 'V'. Micah

*c*. Bordeaux 1, fol. 234$^{v}$. 'V'. Hoseah

*d*. Tours 1018, fol. 11.
St Martin before the Emperor Julian

*e*. Bordeaux 1, fol. 244. 'I'. Haggai

*f*. Bordeaux 1, fol. 250$^{v}$. 'V'. Job

*a*. Tours 1018, fol. 13. St Martin and the thieves

*b*. Bordeaux 1, fol. 300^v^. 'M'

*c*. Amiens 18, fol. 31^v^. 'N'

*d*. Paris, Latin 8055, p.141. 'N'

*e*. Bordeaux 1, fol. 260. 'h'

*f*. Bordeaux 1, fol. 322. 'I' Esther and Aman

*a*. Bordeaux 1, fol. $314^{\mathrm{v}}$. 'I'. Esdras

*b*. Bordeaux 1, fol. 301. 'O'. Wisdom

*c*. Rouen A.6, fol. $221^{\mathrm{v}}$. 'O'. Wisdom

*d*. Le Mans 227, fol. 122. 'I' (detail)

*e*. Bordeaux 1, fol. 261. 'B'. David and the lion

*f*. Paris, Latin 8, vol. II, fol. $74^{\mathrm{v}}$. 'O'. Wisdom

*a*. Bordeaux 1, fol. 250. 'C'

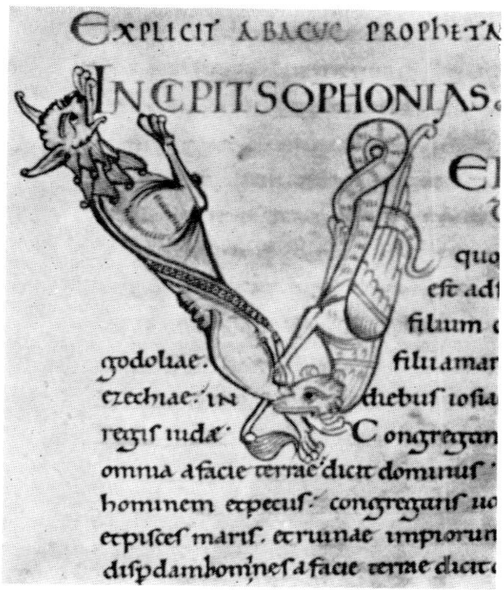


*b*. Bordeaux 1, fol. 243. 'V'

*c*. Bordeaux 1, fol. 237$^{v}$. 'V'

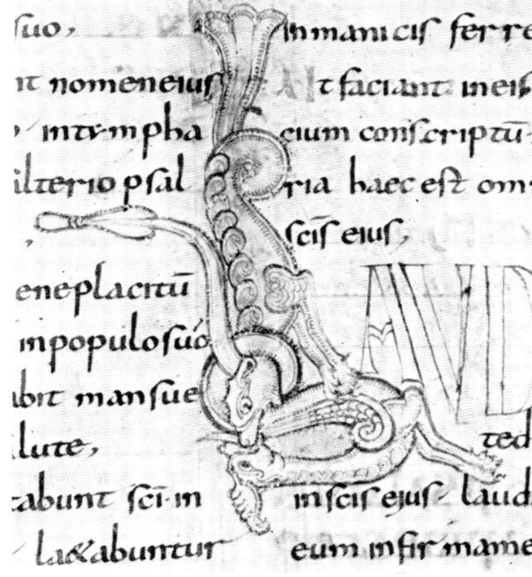

*d*. Amiens 18, fol. 123. 'L'

*e*. Bordeaux 1, fol. 140$^{v}$. 'C'

*f*. Avranches 146, fol. 65. 'L'

THIRD SERIES

# Modern Collector's Dolls

by

Patricia R. Smith

Published by Collector Books
Box 3009
Paducah, Kentucky, 42001

*Distributed by*

Crown Publishers, Inc.

*419 Park Ave. South*
*New York, New York 10016*

# DEDICATION

Series III is dedicated to all my pen pals who have helped me in so many ways. Their friendship, assistance and trust have made this Series much easier to put together.

ALL PHOTOGRAPHS BY DWIGHT. F. SMITH
except those of Maish, Flack & Houston or unless noted.

COVER DOLL; SWEET AMY, School Girl
made by Deluxe

I would like to thank the following for loaning their dolls and many pieces of literature that helped to date and identify them: Jaynn Allen, Louise Alonso, Frances & Mary Anicello, Joan Amundsen, Joan Ashabraner, Sally Biethscheider, Margaret Biggers, Peggy Boudreau, Ruth Brocha, Alice Capps, Bessie Carson, Ruth Clark, Pearl Clasby, Barbara Coker, Edith, DeAngelo, Sibyl DeWein, Helen Draves, Cecelia Eades, Marie Ernst, Thelma & Joleen Flack, Linda Fox, Bev. Gardner, Helen Garrett, Adele Gioscia, Susan Goetz, Edith Goldsworthy, Martha Gonyea, Ellie Haynes, Maxine Heitt, Robbie Heitt, Phyllis Houston, Virginia Jones, Elaine Kaminsky, Kimport Dolls, Tilly Kobe, Angie Landers, Donna Maish, Marge Meisinger, Jay Minter, Barb Mongelluzzi, Grace Ochsner, Pat Raiden, Julia Rogers, Dodi Shapiro, Diana Sorenson, Donna Stanley, Pat Stewart, Mary Partridge, Karen Penner, Carolyn Powers, Mae Tetters, Teri Schall, Shelia Wallace and Kathy Walter.

My very special thanks go to Laura Zwier for the interview of Cushman and Glass and to a very delightful lady Miss Mollye who interviewed herself!

EDITOR: KAREN PENNER

The current values in this book should be used only as a guide. They are not intended to set prices, which vary from one section of the country to another. Auction prices as well as dealer prices vary greatly and are affected by condition as well as demand. Neither the Author nor the Publisher assumes responsibility for any losses that might be incurred as a result of consulting this guide.

Additional copies of this book may be ordered from:

COLLECTOR BOOKS
P.O. Box 3009
Paducah, Kentucky 42001

@$17.95 Add $1.00 for postage and handling.


ISBN: 0-517-52666-2





Printed by IMAGE GRAPHICS, Paducah, Kentucky

# CONTENTS

# New and Revised Information

Series I: Page 140: The 1965-1966 11½" (12") Cinderella by Horsman Dolls came packaged with only one doll body and had an extra head that had the hairdo of Rich Cinderella. The 12" Rich Cinderella was also sold in a package by herself. The same flyer from Horsman Company shows a 16" Mary Poppins doll. The above flyer was sent to me by Mrs. J. C. Houston.

Series I: page 161: Ideal Baby Big Eyes also came with flirty sleep eyes. Marks; (-5/Ideal Doll.

Series I: page 188: 17" "Jolly" of Jolly Toys was also used as "Happy" of the twins, "Happy & Nappy," in 1963. They came with a white/pink wooden swing set.

Series I: page 113: 13" "Junie" of 1968 was also marketed as "Jackie" in 1969.

I find that I made a mistake in saying that the last Gerber Baby was made by the Uneeda Doll Co. I wish to thank Mrs. Frank Wilson for the correct information and will quote a letter, received by Frank Wilson, from Mr. Ralph Merrill of the Gerber Products Company: 'Our records show that we have had three Gerber Baby dolls. The first doll was offered twice. 1. 1956: Sold: 300,000. Made of rubber by Sun Rubber Company. 2. 1965: Sold: 75,000. Made by Arrow Toy Company. 3. 1972: Sold: 58,000 white and 90 black (this was the first time Gerber offered an ethnic doll). Made of vinyl by AMSCO INDUSTRIES.'

Sasha dolls are being made at the Freidland Group in Trenton, England. The firm owner's wife, Mrs. Sara Doggart is the "guardian angel" who watches over the production of the dolls. Mrs. Doggart keeps tract of the quality of the dolls they are producing, to keep the standards high as the designer of the dolls: Sasha Morgenthaler insists upon. These dolls were first "mass-produced" in 1965. The original, hand done ones are still available at $250.00 to $350.00 prices. Fisher of America has taken over the rights to distribute the dolls in the United States. For many years they have been a part of the Creative Playthings line.

Series I: Page 143: The Horsman "Princess" doll caption name was reversed and the doll's name is actually "Gloria Jean."

Series II: Page 178: 29" "Miss Echo" was made by the American Doll & Toy Company 1963.

Kenner's "Baby Alive" was featured by Simplicity Patterns (1974-Dec.) in its counter catalog, Holiday Catalog and Fashion News. It is shown modeling 6 dresses designed by Simplicity especially for her. More than 100,000 catalogs featuring Baby Alive were distributed.

6" "WHIMETTES" by the American Character Co. included: Pixie, Swinger, Granny, Mini Mod, Jump'n and GoGo.

To show how the use of names can be confusing: BABY SUSAN: one made by the Marlin Co., one by Eegee (1958), one by Natural Doll Co. and yet another by the Belle Co.

Lorrie Dolls are made by the Eugene Doll Company.

Princess Grace Dolls Inc. is also the Mego Corp.

There were four different "Blythes" in the Kenner series. Each had a different set of eye color changes.

The Alexander Baby Ellen is the Black version of Sweet Tears.

Mattel's #2 "Barbie" is the same as the #1 except there are no metal cylinders in the feet and legs forming holes for a stand. She does have the white eyes and painted brows. She has a heavy solid torso. MARKS: PATS. PEND. MCMLVIII.

Eege Company also used mold codes of "VS" and a "V" on the lower back.

Susy Smart was made by Deluxe Reading Corp.

The American Character 1963-64 Tressy Series included Cricket, Mary Makeup (Girlfriend), a Bonus Tressy and called "Pre-Teen" Tressy. She is 14" tall, a standard size doll and has the grow hair feature. She is shown in this book.

The little Uneeda dolls shown on page 313 and 314 of Series II were also marketed under the names: Ping & Pong.

The Ralph A. Freundlich, Inc. Company made the 1940 "Baby Sandra" doll (Sandra Henville). The doll was produced in different screen costumes that included: "East Side Of Heaven," "Unexpected Father," "Little Accident" and "Sandy is a Lady."

I have been asked many, many times "Just how is a doll conceived and made?" Wanting to answer the questions, I wrote to 102 different doll companies, mould makers and doll designers. I received "resumes" back from only three, and these three have the fewest dolls to offer than any company in the industry! (Kamar, Tomy & Gabriel).

I did receive a reply from the Perfect Doll Moulds Corp. Mr. Mark M. Schaffer outlined what "made" a doll:

1. The type of doll is conceived.
2. The doll is sculpted.
3. Wax models or plaster models are made according to the method of molding to be used for the various doll parts.
4. The proper molds are made for rotation, blow, or injection molding.
5. The doll parts are produced from the molds and assembled.

## Care

TO CLEAN CLOTH BODIES: Use a paste of cornstarch and water. Add a drop or two of ammonia. The paste should be of the same thickening as you would use for making gravy. Smear the paste over the entire cloth area and let it dry. As it dries it will turn a yellowish color. Use a vegetable brush, gently but also thoroughly, to brush paste from body.

TO CLEAN COMPOSITION: Another of the many suggestions is to use VASELINE INTENSIVE CARE lotion.

TO GET RID OF "STICKY" VINYL: Go over it with nail polish remover. This from Rua Belle Green. It sure works for her.

TO CLEAN HARD PLASTIC: Yet another suggestion: Use Liquid Wrench. Wipe on and off quickly.

Metal plate holders for holding plates upright can be used to hold plastic or composition in a sitting position.

# New and Revised Information

The product "No More Tangles" can be used very successfully to clean old mohair wigs. Remove wig from doll, then spray on the "No More Tangles." Rub wig with soft cloth or pad made of tissues to remove dirt. Also makes the wig easy to comb.

Q tips can be used to clean ears, noses or other hard to clean places. Dip the Q tip in "Jubilee" Kitchen wax cleaner to clean plastic and compo dolls.

Doll shoes can be made out of felt with lace or pearls, etc. for bows.

For Bride dolls: Second hand stores usually have a Bride's dress for sale.

Clean bisque or porcelain with milk and cotton pads.

MAKE RAG DOLLS, stuff with sawdust, paint features with hobby enamels, OMIT HAIR. Dip doll into wax to which 1 teaspoon of powdered alum for each cup of wax has been added. When doll has desired wax look let it cool and harden before gluing hair on or wig. Dolls with stitched joints can be posed while still very warm and let cool for a permanent position. Doll will have a very lovely and different skin tone.

When fragile antique lace needs washing, baste it first to a clean white cotton fabric then wash by hand, dipping gently through warm suds, then rinse well, to remove all soap and dirt. Then lay between layers of a towel and press firmly to nearly dry it.

To put snap fasteners on easily, put all snaps on one side first. Then use a piece of chalk on each fastener and rub against opposite side of material. This will insure your getting the snaps exactly opposite.

For mildew on vinyl use Crisco. It will generally remove it and won't damage the finish.

When gluing wigs on doll heads always use Rubber Cement as it will peel off at a later date without damaging the wig or head.

In combing out old matted doll wigs use a metal dog comb, the kind with the long wire teeth. Divide the hair into small sections by running your fingers through the hair and find the seam circles from the bottom to the top. Then carefully comb out the sections...you will lose some hair...a lot of hair...there is usually too much hair in a wig anyway, proceed until all is combed out. THEN the wig can be washed dipping up and down gently, as not to tangle, in luke warm water suds, use a mild soap. Rinse: recomb when partly dryed and set hair, using curlers and wave lotion. Also Dippety Doo works good. Let dry thoroughly. Comb out and spray with hard hair spray. Put on a net and let dry.

Use Johnson's furniture PASTE WAX and coat composition with it. This not only prevents further cracking or crazing but it also makes your doll sparkle.

Rub a little Johnson's Baby Oil into palms of hands then apply to doll's hair. As you comb or brush the hair will shine.

If you have a glued wig of snythetic shiny type that is sticky to the touch, you can eliminate this by sprinkling Johnson's Baby Powder on it. Then rub the excess out with a towel and brush with a bristle brush. The baby powder acts as a dry shampoo and it will make the doll smell better. After this you can set or style the doll's hair with a slight dampening with water.

# How to Use Price Guide

The prices in this book are the retail prices of the dolls, if bought from a dealer. Prices change by demand and supply and doll prices are no different and once in awhile the prices shoot up due to stimulated interest in a particular doll or doll company.

The CONDITION of the doll is uppermost in pricing. An all original and in excellent condition doll will bring top dollar and sometimes more, where one that is dirty or damaged or without original clothes will bring less. The cost of doll repairs has soared and it is wise to judge the damage and estimate the cost of repair before you buy or sell a damaged doll.

An all original means, original clothes and original wigs/hair. This type of doll is what the prices in this book are based on. The prices shown are top dollar prices for excellent and original dolls. IF YOUR DOLL IS LESS THAN ORIGINAL, DISCOUNT FROM THE PRICES SHOWN TO ALLOW FOR CONDITION.

Another factor in pricing is size. For example a 16" Dionne Quint will be worth more than a 7½" one, or a 11" Shirley Temple may be worth a lot more than a 13" one.

No one knows your collection better than yourself and in the end YOU must decide if a certain doll and asking price is worth it. If you don't think so, then you will pass it by.

A PRICE GUIDE IS JUST THAT    A GUIDE

# Alexander Doll Co.

For complete information about the Alexander Doll Co. refer to Series I, page 11. The following is a list of some of the most desirable dolls by this company.
1925: Blue Boy, Pinkie (rag)
1933: Alice in Wonderland, Little Women
1935: Little Colonel (often mistaken for Shirley Temple), Jane Withers
1936: Dionne Quints, Five Little Peppers (book: Little Genius), Little Lord Fauntleroy, Doris Kranne in "Romance" (Movie), Geraldine Farrar in Carmen, Pitty Pat and Tippy Toes from Eugene Field's Poem and were of cloth and made in three sizes, Susie and Bobby from a comic strip.
1937: Princess Elizabeth in three sizes, Scarlet O'Hara from "Gone With the Wind," Melanie, Margaret O'Brien, Neva Wet, Tweeny Winkle, Princess Alexander, McGuffey Baby, McGuffey Anna (McGuffey Readers), Snow White, Annie Laurie, Little Shaver (cloth from Elsie Shaver painting), Madelaine du Bain in French 1880 costume (exclusive for F.A.O. Schwartz) reissued 1938-39.
1938: Flora McFlimsey (books by Mariana) re-issued in 1952, Dickens character dolls, Mother and Me, Sonja Henie in three sizes. Re-issued in hard plastic/vinyl in 1951.
1939: Madeline, Jennie Walker
1940: Butch McGuffey, Madeline as a blonde
1941: Lov-Le-Tex dolls
1942: Fairy Princess in four sizes
1943: Southern Girl, in four sizes, Kate Greenway in four sizes, Carmen in six sizes, Bride in five sizes, Baby Genius in five sizes with molded hair, also wigged in three sizes, So-Lite-Dolls (cloth, wigs of yarn and in five sizes) Special Girl (soft body and cry Mama voice), Country Cousins.
1949: Mary Martin from "Sound of Music"
1951: Clara Belle (Clown from Howdy Doody Show), Portrait Group (two dolls in formal dress with chairs), Slumber Mate, Maggie in three sizes, Violet a fully jointed plastic doll and made in 1952, 53 and 54, Penny (teenager from comics), Christening Baby in three sizes, Sunbeam a new born infant in three sizes, Bonnie a toddler in three sizes, Bitsey in five sizes, Honey Bun in three sizes, Kathy in three sizes, Littlest Cherub, Nina Ballerina in three sizes, Wendy Bride in three sizes, Rosamund Bridesmaid in three sizes.
1952: Tommy Bangs, Stuffy, Cynthia in three sizes
1953: Mary Muslin (pansy eyes that wink), Sunflower (clown with flower eyes and a pompom nose), Ruffles the Clown, Alexander-kins, Quiz Kids, Benny Walker, Story Princess, Glamor dolls, including Queen Elizabeth, Gody period, Edwardian Period, Victorian Period, Blue Danube, Gardian party dress (opera), Snow Baby, Commodore Peary's daughter (1903 dress), Bride
1954: Flower girl, Mary Ellen in three outfits, Bonnie Baby (rooted hair), Christening Baby, Kathy, Bible Character dolls, Nina Ballerina
1955: Romeo & Juliet, McGuffey Anna-re-issued
1957: Cissy, Cissette, Sleeping Beauty, Mary Belle, Kathy Tear, Sheri Lewis, Elise, Lissy, Dumplin
1960: Betty Walks (flirty eyes), Joanie (Joni) 36" & flirty eyes, Little Genius re-issued, Cissette, Portrait series: Bride, Belle of the Ball, Maid of Honor, Creole Beauty, Queen Elizabeth II, Gody Girl
1961: Baby Genius, Wendy, Kitten, Caroline, Jacqueline, Timmie, Mary Sunshine, Madeline, Little Lady, Betty Talks, Maggie Mix-up, Mimi (30"), Pollyanna
1965: Leslie, Katie (12"), Baby Ellen
1966: Laurie, Sound of Music, Little Orphan Annie (with poem by James Whitcomb Riley), Pussy Cat, Alice in Wonderland re-issued, Sweet Tears, Children around the World, USA, Ballerina Girl, Granny, Bride, Scarlett, Amish Boy & Girl.

Due to the continuing cost rise in making dolls, the Alexander dolls have cut some of the quality from the clothes as well as the dolls themselves and since 1974, the 8" dolls no longer have "bend knees."

Alexander Bi-centennial dolls will be released in 1976. Madame Alexander chose the 6 First Ladies to be issued: Martha Washington, Dolly Madison, Abigail Adams, Martha Randolph, Elizabeth Monroe and Louisa Adams.

Alexander--19" "Betty." All composition. Blue sleep eyes (also came with brown eyes), Eyeshadow. Marks: None. Had paper tag on front of dress: Betty/Madame Alexander. 1935. $75.00. (Courtesy Karen Penner)

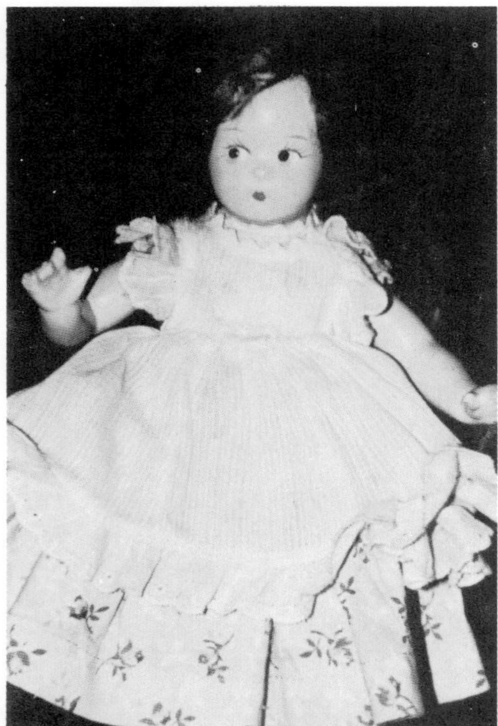

Alexander--7" "Wendy" All composition with dark brown mohair wig. Painted blue eyes. Painted on white socks/black shoes. Bent right arm. Dress is red roses on yellow with white pinafore. Marks: Mme/Alexander, on back. Madame Alexander, etc. on tag. 1936. $35.00. (Courtesy Pat Raiden)

## Dionne Quint Prices

7½" baby with molded hair. $200.00 set. Each $25.00.
7½" baby with wigs. $225.00 set. $28.00 each.
8" Toddler with molded hair. $200.00 set. $25.00 each.
8" Toddler with wigs. $225.00 set. $28.00 each.
11" Baby with molded hair. $75.00.
11" Toddler with wig. $75.00.
14" Toddler, wig and sleep eyes. $85.00.
16" Toddler, wig and sleep eyes. $85.00.
17" Toddler, wig and sleep eyes. $85.00.
17" Toddler, wig and sleep eyes. $85.00.
17" Cloth body, baby legs, with molded hair and sleep eyes. $95.00.
19" Toddler, wig and sleep eyes. $95.00.
20" Toddler, wig and sleep eyes. $95.00.
23" Toddler, wig and sleep eyes. $100.00.
24" All stuffed pink stockinette body and limbs. Molded felt face mask. Painted features. $125.00.

Alexander--Set of all original 8" toddlers. $200.00 set.



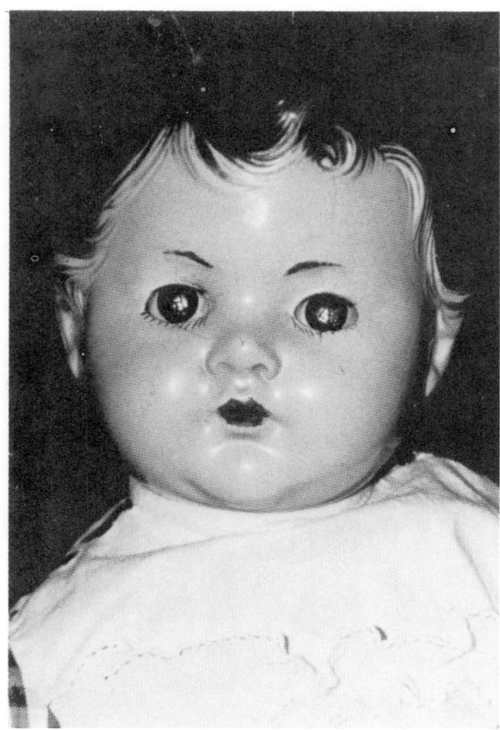

Alexander--17" Dionne Quint. Composition shoulder plate with jointed neck. Cloth body with composition bent baby legs. Original tagged dress. Marks: Alexander, on head. $95.00. (Courtesy Alice Capps)

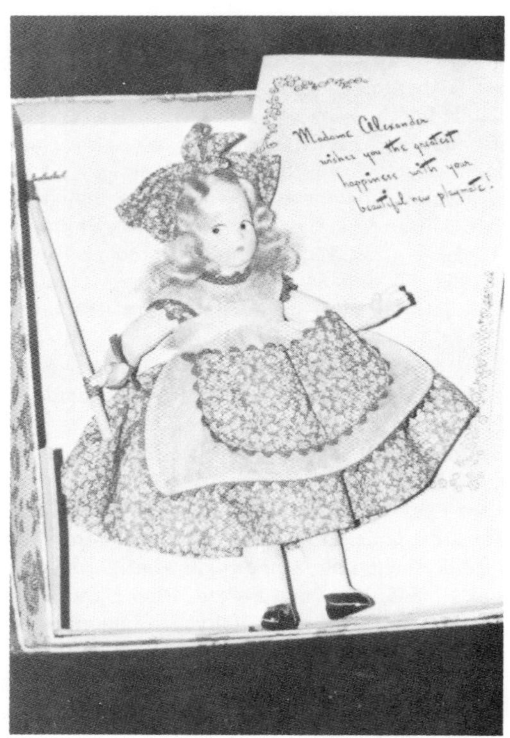


Alexander--8" "Wendy Ann" All composition. All original. 1936. $35.00. (Courtesy Jay Minter)

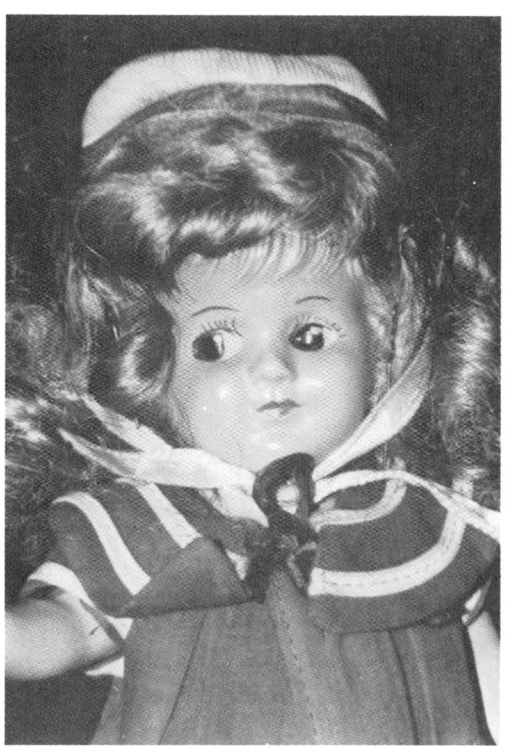

Alexander--8½" "Little Colonel" All composition. Painted brown eyes. Wig over molded hair (hair pushed back to see bangs). Original. Marks: Tag: Picture as on "Little Colonel" Book/Trademark/Little Colonel/Alexander Doll Co./New York. 1936. $55.00. (Courtesy Marge Meisinger)

Alexander--Full view of "Little Colonel" 8½". Original. 1936. (Courtesy Marge Meisinger)

Alexander--21" "Prince Phillip" All composition. Blue sleep eyes. All original. Tagged clothes. $95.00.

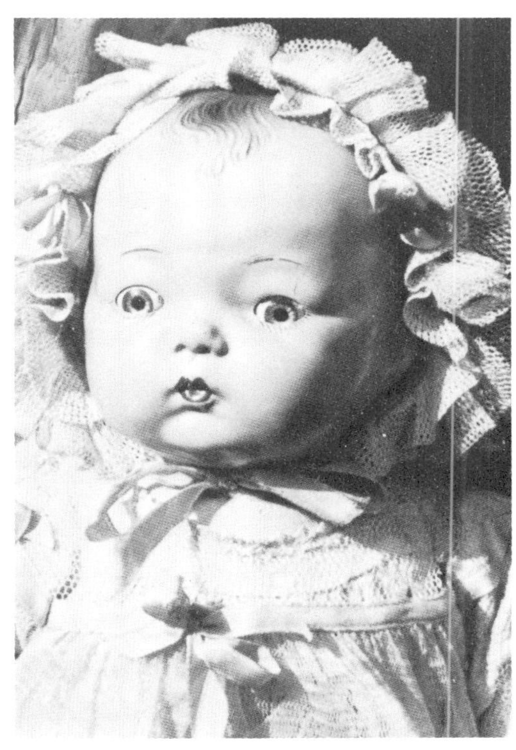

Alexander--23" "Pinkie" Cloth and composition. Blue sleep eyes. All original. 1937. $65.00. (Courtesy Mrs. J.C. Houston)

Alexander--14" "Madelaine" All composition. Brown sleep eyes/lashes. Painted lashes below eyes only. Eyeshadow. Blue skirt with roses. Pink top. Marks: Mme Alexander, on head. Tag: Madelaine/Madame Alexander, etc. 1939. $85.00. (Courtesy Marie Ernst)

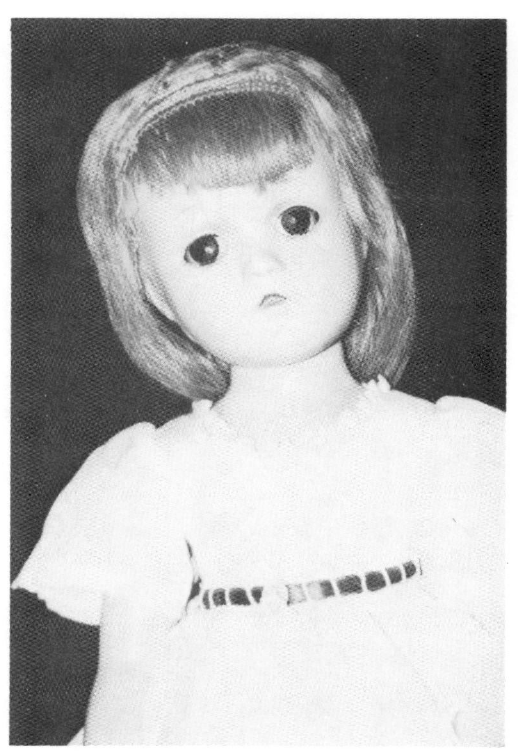

Alexander--17" "Madelaine" All composition. Brown sleep eyes/lashes. Eyeshadow. Blonde human hair wig worn off. Lashes below eyes only. White dress/red ribbon trim. Knee length pantaloons. Hoop skirt. Marks: Mme Alexander, on head. Tag: Madelaine/Madame Alexander. 1940. $75.00. (Courtesy Marie Ernst)

Alexander--21" "Bride" All composition. Tag: Created by/Madame Alexander. 1941. $75.00. (Courtesy Marie Ernst)

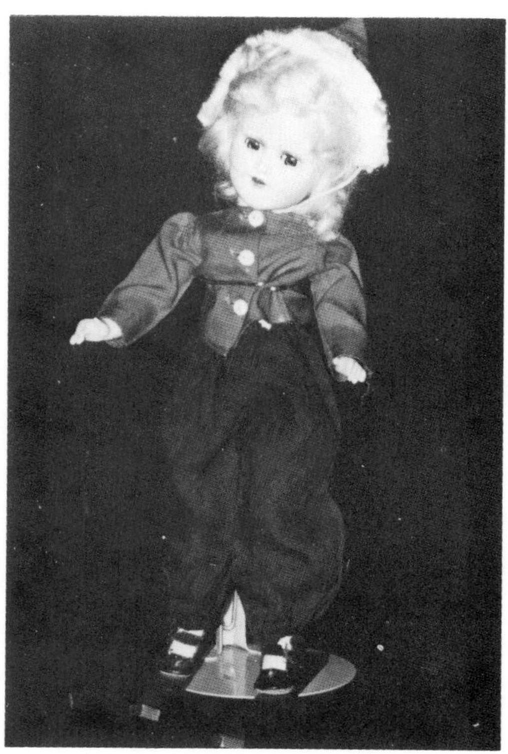

Alexander--14" "Sonja Henie" Shown in original ski clothes. $75.00. (Courtesy Jay Minter)

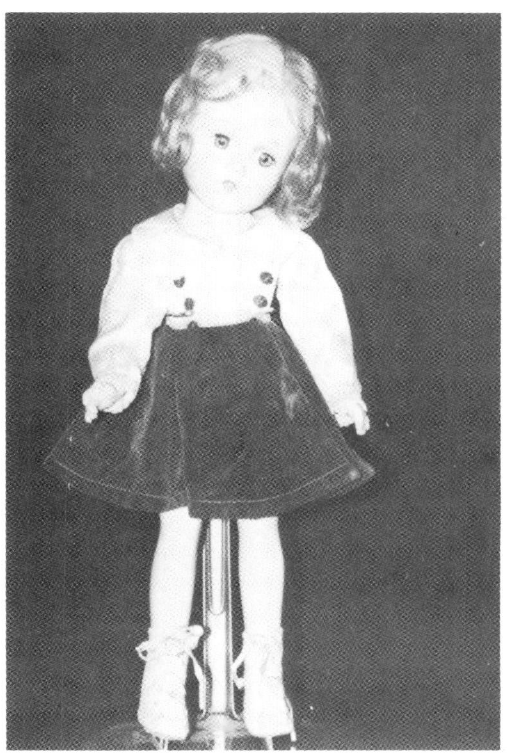

Alexander--14" "Sonja Henie" Closed mouth version. All composition and all original. 1942. $65.00. (Courtesy Jay Minter)

Alexander--14" & 9" "Mother & Me" All composition. Mother: Blue sleep eyes. Me: Brown painted eyes to side. Gowns are blue. Marks: Madame Alexander. 1942-43. $125.00 set. (Courtesy Jay Minter)

Alexander--23" "Special Girl" All composition with cloth body. Blue sleep eyes. Straight long legs. Marks: None. 1942. $85.00. (Courtesy Marie Ernst)

Alexander--23" "Special Girl" to show original clothes. 1942. (Courtesy Marie Ernst)

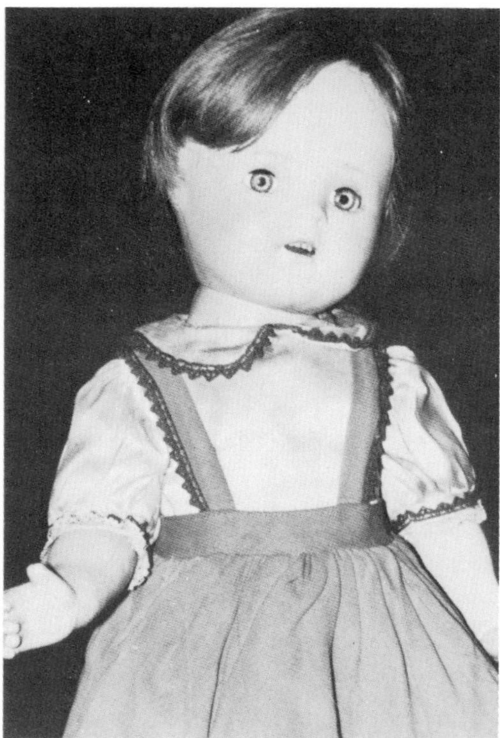

Alexander--20" "Miss Victory" All composition. Blue sleep eyes. Magnets in hands. Red skirt/ white top with blue trim. Marks: Princess Elizabeth/Alexander Doll Co., on head. Tag: Madame Alexander/New York, etc. Replaced wig. 1944. $90.00 (Courtesy Marie Ernst)

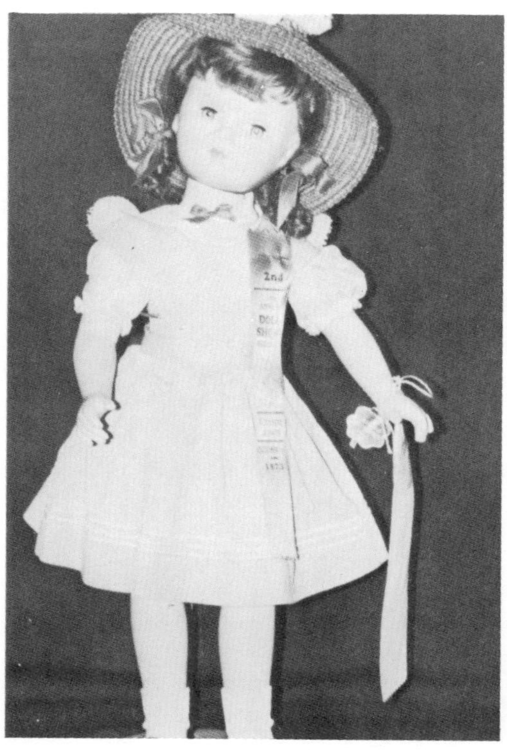

Alexander--21" "Margaret O'Brien" All composition. Original. 1946. $185.00. (Courtesy Barbara Coker)

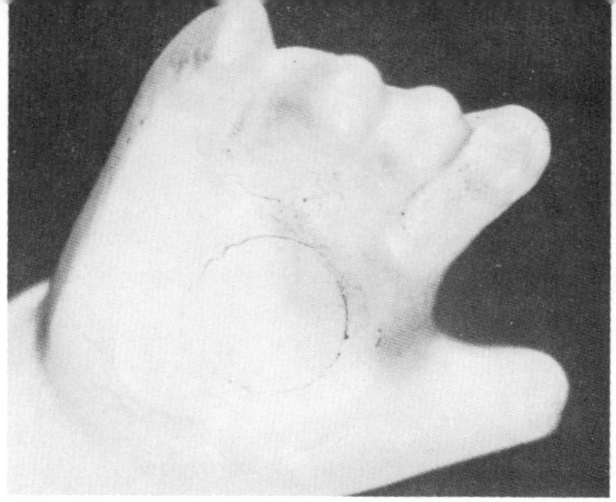

Alexander--Shows magnets placed in hands of the Miss Victory doll by F.O.A. Swartz Co.

Alexander--24" "Maggie Walker" All hard plastic walker, head turns. Blue sleep eyes. Original red satin dress. Shoes not original. Marks: Alexander, on head. Tagged clothes. $45.00.

Alexander--This is a movie still of Hedy Lamarr. Refer to the color photo of the doll made for the 1949 movie Samson & Delilah, although this is an unconfirmed, by Alexander, doll.

Alexander--15" "Amy of Little Women" All hard plastic. Original. 1948. $60.00. Complete set $275.00. (Courtesy Sally Bethscheider)

Alexander--Shows back hair view of the 1948 Amy.

Alexander--17" "Bride" All hard plastic with dark skin tones. Dark red glued on wig. Blue sleep eyes. Original clothes. Marks: Alexander, on head. ca. 1950. $40.00

Alexander--29" "Alice in Wonderland" Stuffed vinyl with blue sleep eyes. Original. Marks: Alexander, on head. Tag: Alice in Wonderland/ By Madame Alexander. 1951. $115.00. (Courtesy Mae Teters)

Alexander--15" "Margot Ballerina" All hard plastic. Blue sleep eyes. Orange hair. 1952. $55.00. (Courtesy Jay Minter)

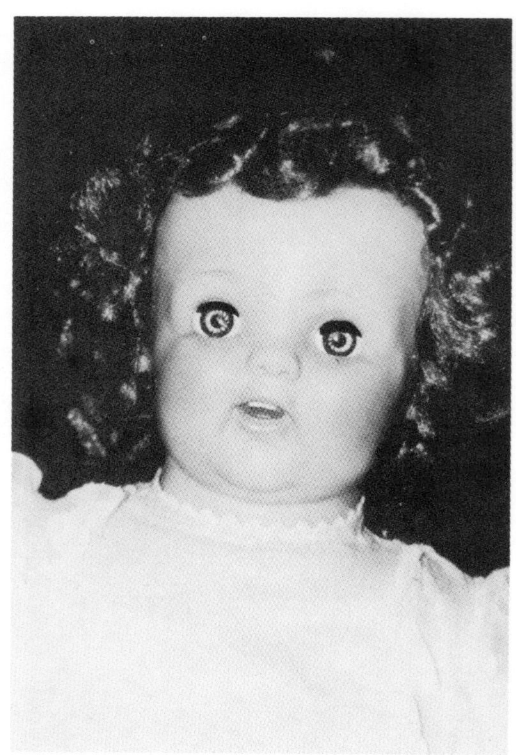

Alexander--18" "Honeybun" Cloth body with vinyl limbs and head. Glued on Saran wig. Open/closed mouth with two inserted upper teeth. Cryer in lower back. Blue sleep eyes. Marks: Tag: Madame Alexander, etc. 1952. $42.00. (Courtesy Bessie Carson)

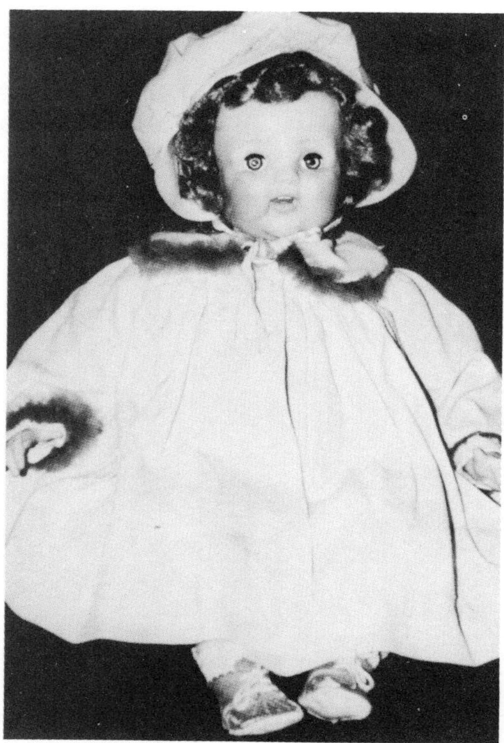

Alexander--18" "Honeybun" Shows original coat/bonnet, both are yellow with real fur trim on collar and cuffs. (Courtesy Bessie Carson)

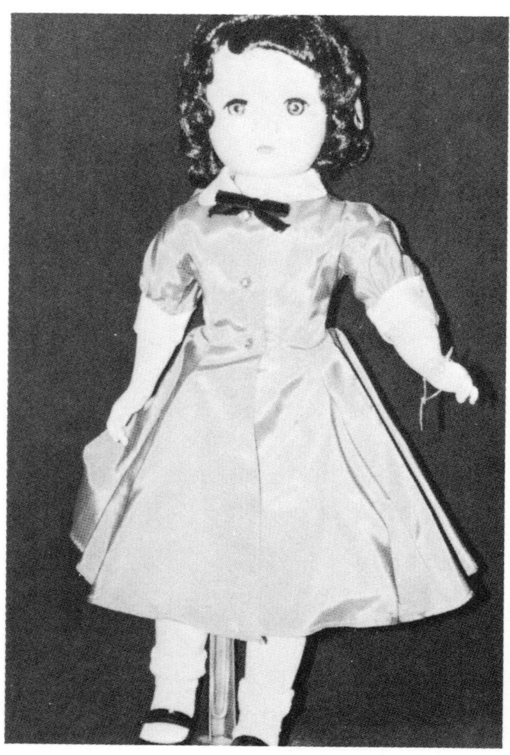

Alexander--17" "Maggie Walker" All hard plastic. Brown sleep eyes. Red dress. Tag: Fashion Academy/Mme/Alexander/Award. 1953. $45.00 (Courtesy Jay Minter)

Alexander--8" "Jo" All hard plastic. One on right is a walker. Left one earlier than other. $45.00. (Courtesy Jay Minter)

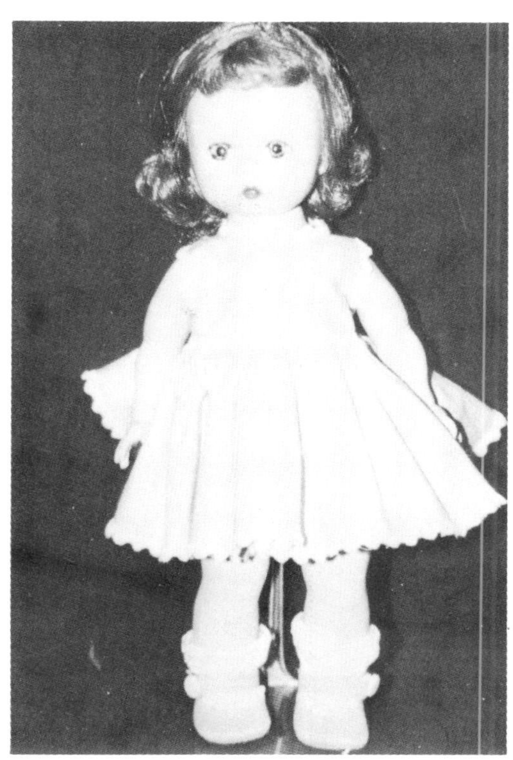

Alexander--8" "Quiz-Kin" All hard plastic. Bend knees. Has knob in back that makes head move. 1954. $55.00. (Courtesy Jay Minter)

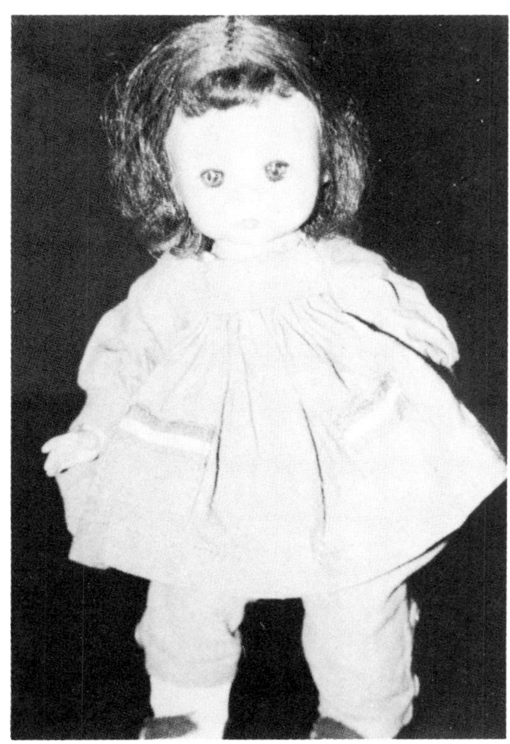

Alexander--8" "Madelaine" All hard plastic. Bend knees. Tag: Madelaine/Madame Alexander, etc. 1954. $35.00. (Courtesy Jay Minter)

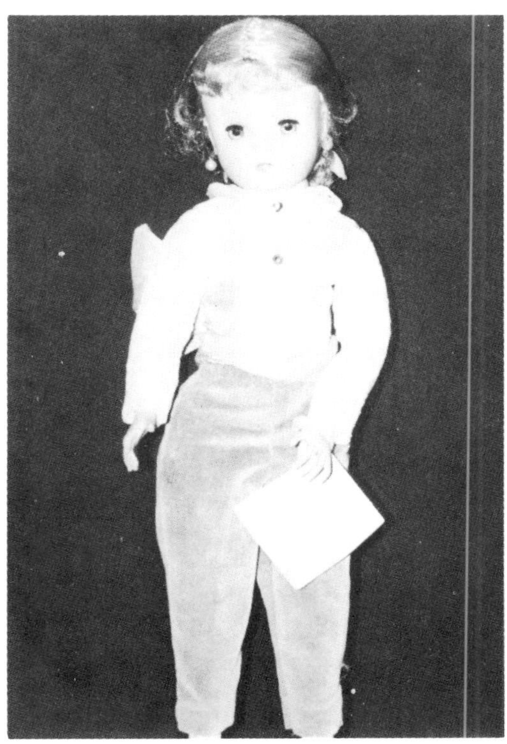

Alexander--16" "Elise" Hard plastic with vinyl oversleeve arms and jointed at the elbows. Original. 1957. $45.00. (Courtesy Jay Minter)

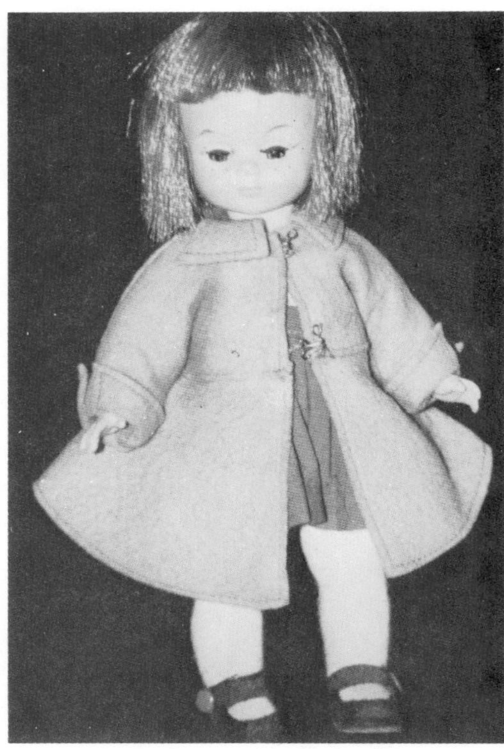

Alexander--8" "Maggie Mix Up" All hard plastic. Blue sleep eyes. Freckles. Usually came with green eyes. 1960. $55.00. (Courtesy Jay Minter)

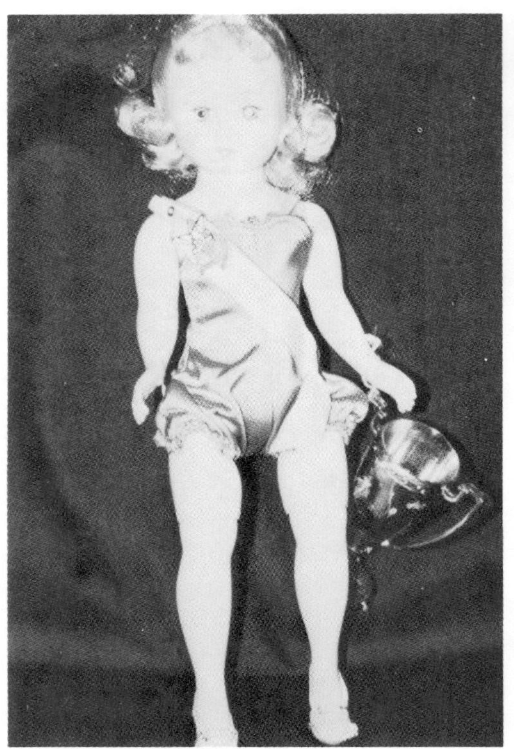

Alexander--9" "Cissette" Beauty Queen. All hard plastic. Jointed knees. Bluish grey outfit. Yellow-gold band with gold eagle emblem. Gold cup. 1961. $40.00 (Courtesy Jay Minter)

Alexander--8" "Scotland" All hard plastic with straight legs. Green sleep eyess. 1961 to date. This one is 1974. Currently available. (Courtesy Marie Ernst)

Alexander--8" "Italian" Bend knees. 1961 to date. $18.00. (Courtesy Marie Ernst)

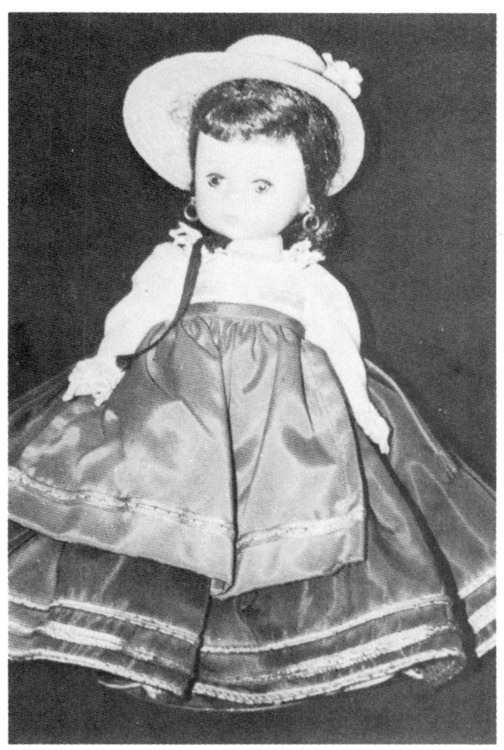

Alexander--8" "Italy" Variation of costume. Bend knees. 1961. $18.00. (courtesy Jay Minter)

Alexander--8" "Tyrolean Girl" Hard plastic. Bend knees. 1962-1973. In 1974 this became "Austria." $18.00. (Courtesy Jay Minter)

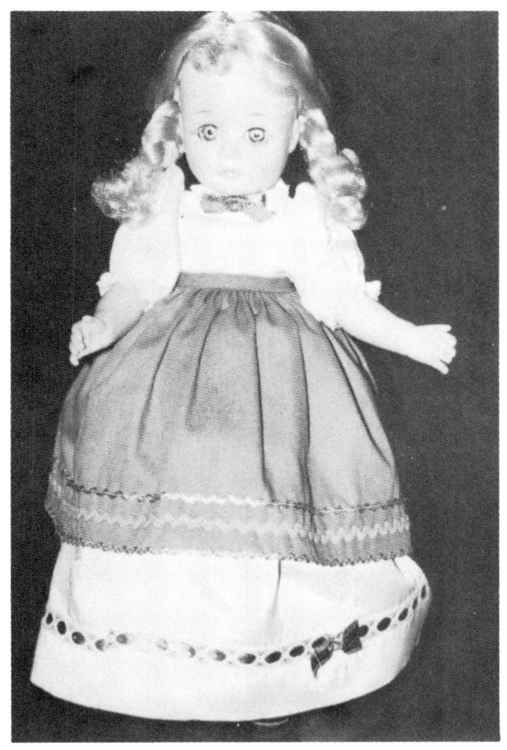

Alexander--12" "Pamela" Plastic and vinyl. Blue sleep eyes. Came with change of wigs that attach with a velour strip. 1962. $60.00 (Courtesy Jay Minter)

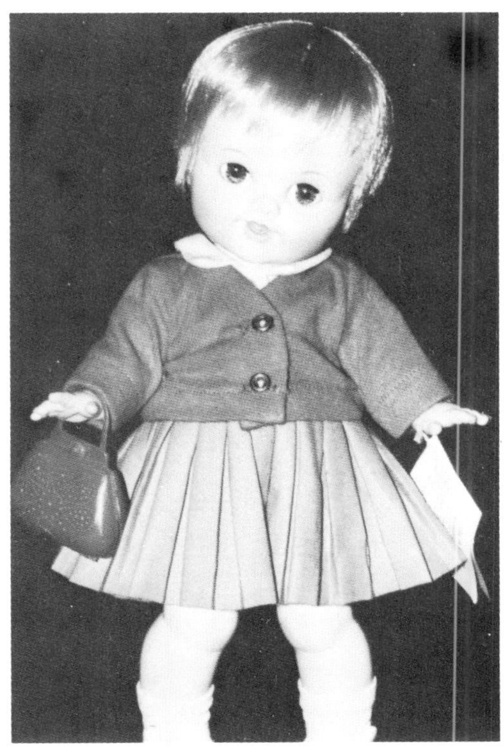

Alexander--12" "Smarty" Orange/red rooted hair. Blue sleep eyes. Open/closed mouth. Marks: Alexander/1962, on head. Tag: Smarty/ Madame Alexander. Original. $35.00.

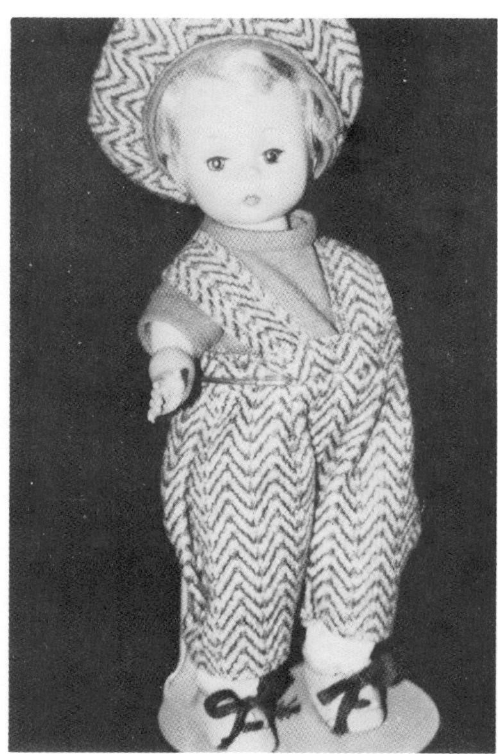

Alexander--8" "Bill" All hard plastic. Bend knees. 1963. $45.00. (Courtesy Jay Minter)

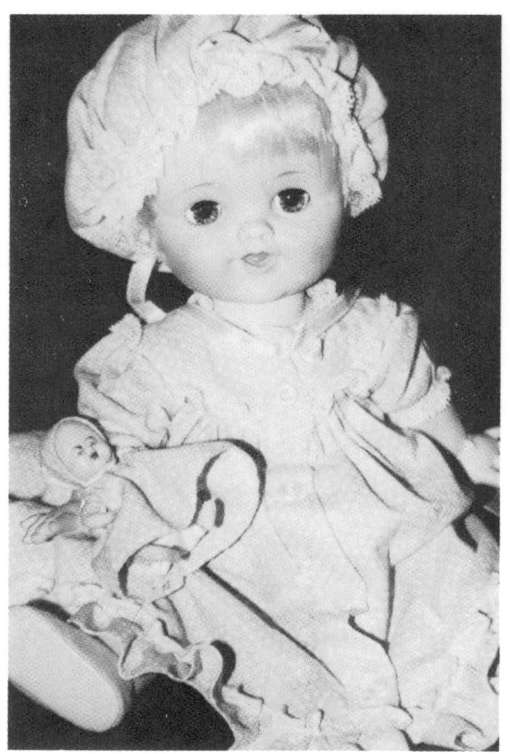

Alexander--11" "Smarty & Baby" All original. Baby is Hong Kong plastic. Blue sleep eyes. 1963. $45.00. (Courtesy Jay Minter)

Alexander--8" "Irish" Bend knees. 1964 to date. $18.00. (Courtesy Marie Ernst)

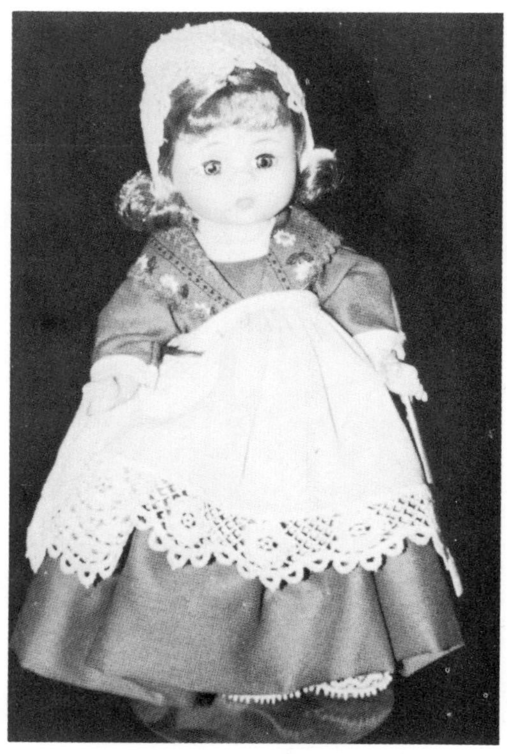

Alexander--8" "Irish" Has different shawl. Bend knees. 1964. $18.00. (Courtesy Jay Minter)

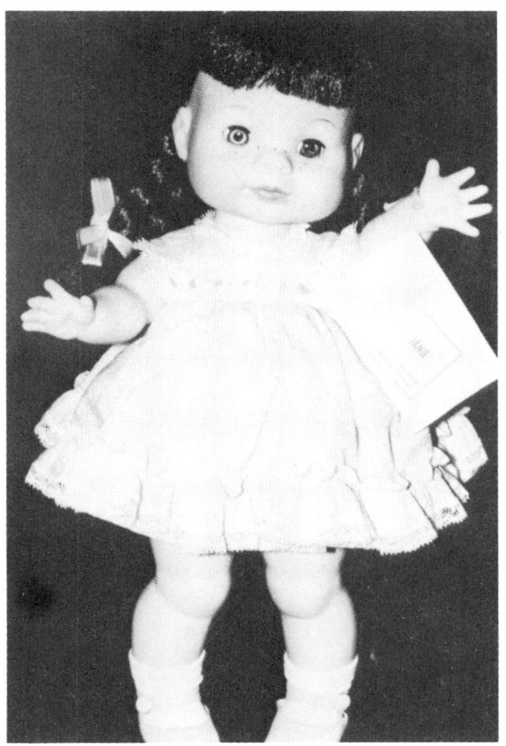

Alexander--12" "Janie" Black rooted hair. Blue sleep eyes. Freckles. Marks: Alexander/1964, on head. Tag: Janie/created by/Madame Alexander. Original. $35.00.

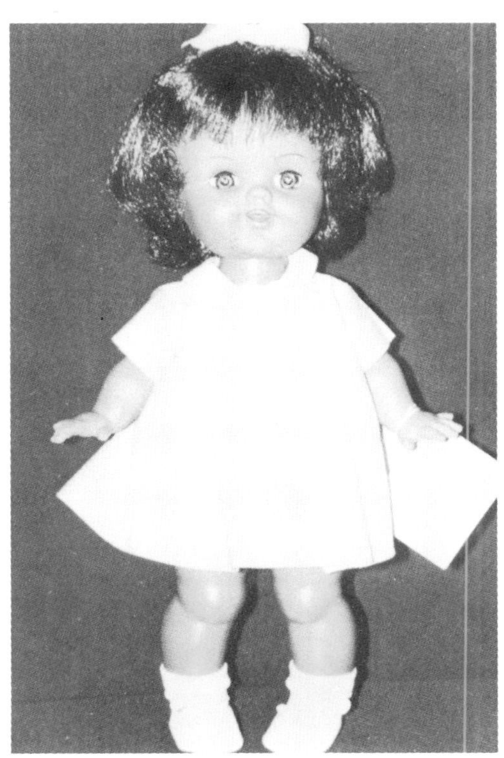

Alexander--11" Plastic and vinyl. Open/closed mouth. Tag: Madame Alexander, etc. 1964. $32.00. (Courtesy Jay Minter)

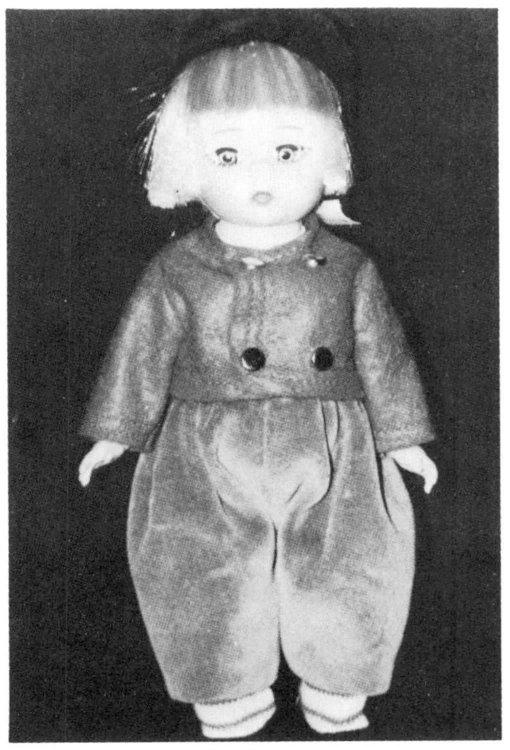

Alexander--8" "Dutch Boy" Hard plastic. Bend knees. 1964. $30.00 (Courtesy Jay Minter)

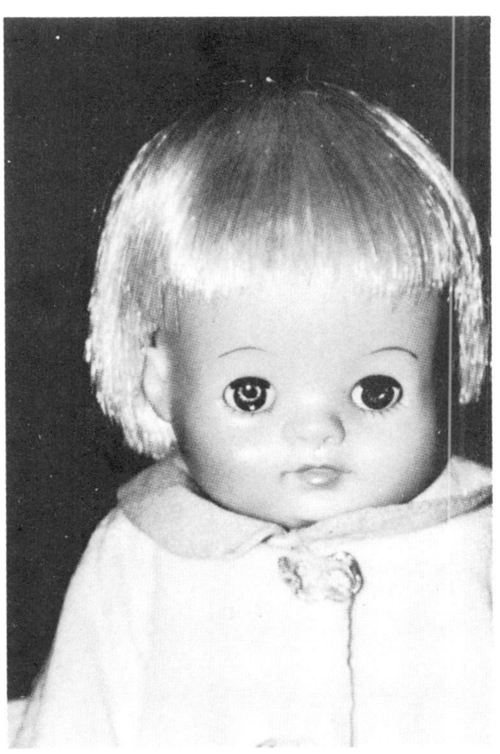

Alexander--7" "Littlest Kitten" All vinyl. Blue sleep eyes. Marks: Alex. Doll Co., on head. 1963-64. $25.00. (Courtesy Alice Capps)

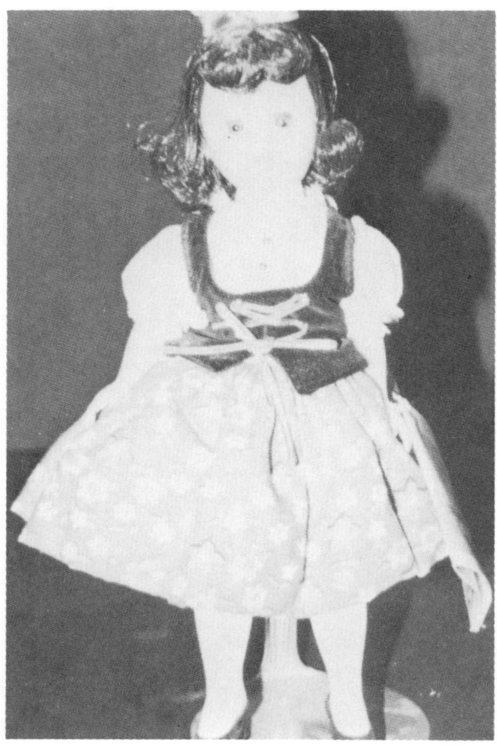

Alexander--9" "Brigetta" Of Sound and Music. 1965. $45.00. (Courtesy Jay Minter)

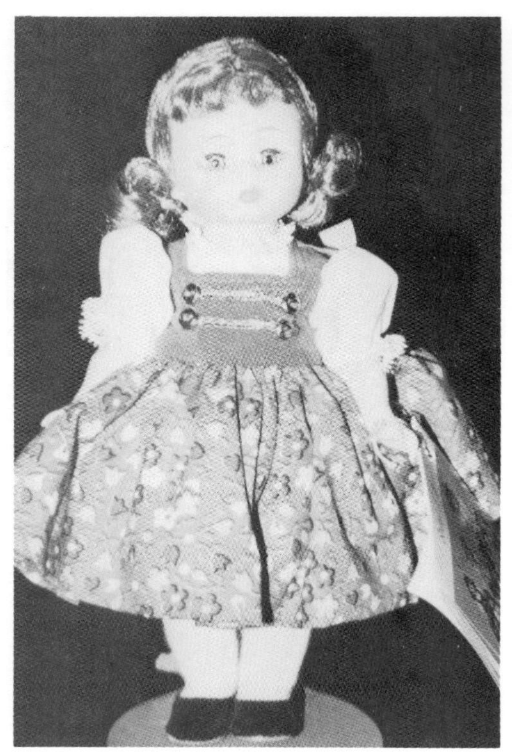

Alexander--8" "Gretl" of Sound of Music. 1965. $35.00. (Courtesy Jay Minter)

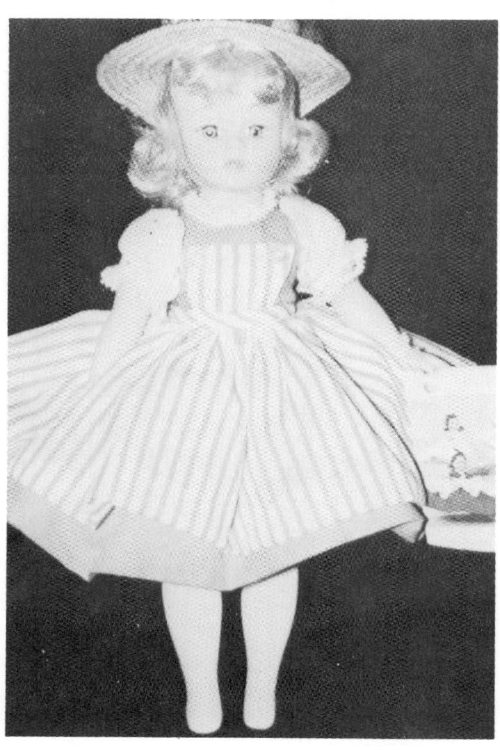

Alexander--9" "Lissl" of Sound of Music. 1965. $35.00. (Courtesy Jay Minter)

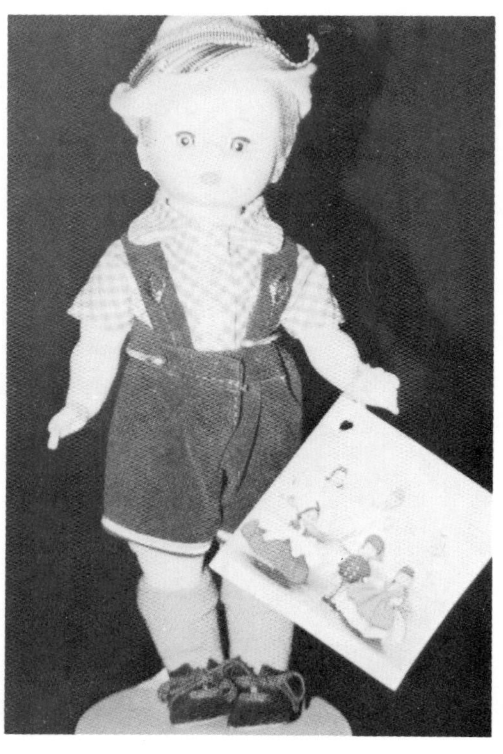

Alexander--8" "Friedrich" of Sound of Music. 1965. $35.00. (Courtesy Jay Minter)

Alexander--8" "Miss Muffet" Hard plastic. Bend knees. 1965. $18.00. (Courtesy Jay Minter)

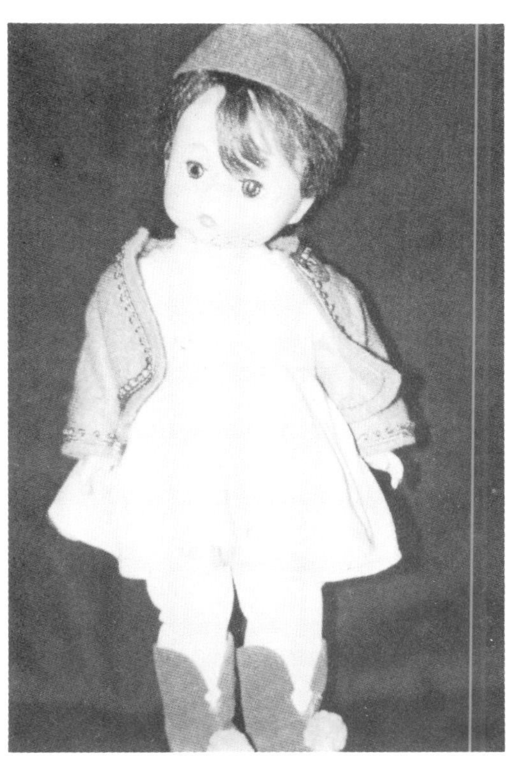

Alexander--8" "Greek Boy" Hard plastic. Bend knees. 1965 to 1968. $50.00. (Courtesy Jay Minter)

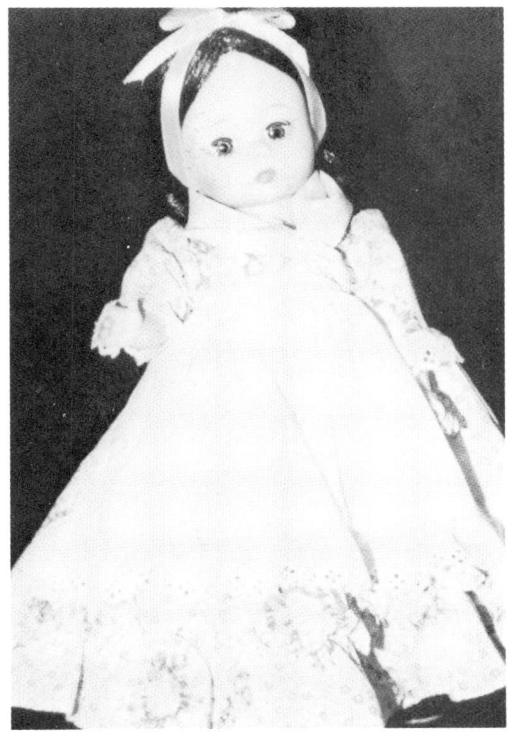

Alexander--8" "Argentine Girl" Hard plastic. Bend knees. 1965. Discontinued 1972. $35.00. (Courtesy Jay Minter)

Alexander--8" "Mary, Mary" Hard plastic. Bend knees. 1965. $18.00. (Courtesy Jay Minter)

Alexander--8" Newer "Mary, Mary" Hard plastic. Bend knees. $18.00. (Courtesy Jay Minter)

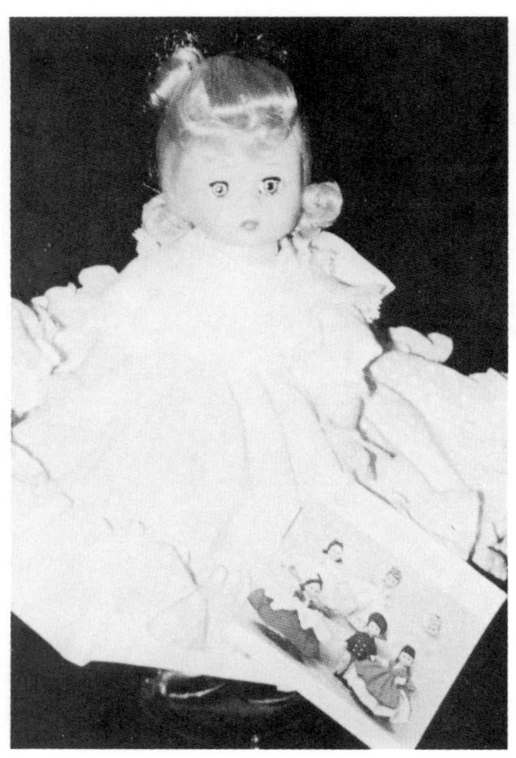

Alexander--8" Newer "Amy" of Little Women. Hard plastic. Bend knees. $18.00. (Courtesy Jay Minter)

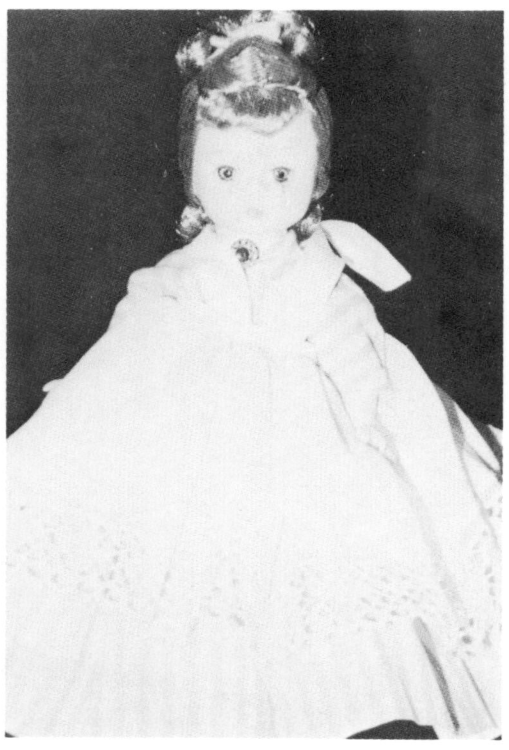

Alexander--8" Older "Meg" of Little Women. Hard plastic. Bend knees. $25.00. (Courtesy Jay Minter)

Alexander--17" "Elise Bride" 1966. $35.00. (Courtesy Marie Ernst)

Alexander--17" "Leslie" Bride. 1966. $50.00. (Courtesy Marie Ernst)

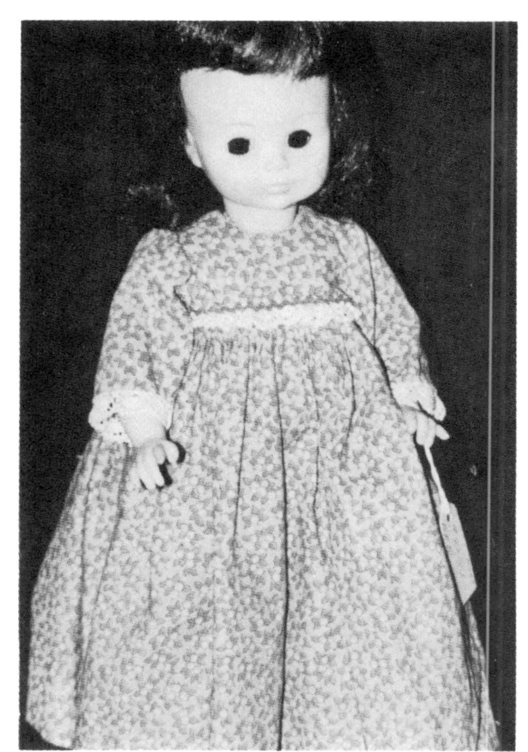

Alexander--14" "Little Granny" This is the first "Granny." Black eyes. Plastic and vinyl. Original. Tag: Little Granny/Madame Alexander. 1966. $45.00. (Courtesy Marie Ernst)

Alexander--8" "German" Bend knees. 1966 to date. $18.00. (Courtesy Marie Ernst)

Alexander--17" "Leslie" In pink formal. 1967. $50.00. (Courtesy Marie Ernst)

Alexander--14" "Renoir Girl" White dress with red trim. 1967. $55.00. (Courtesy Jay Minter)

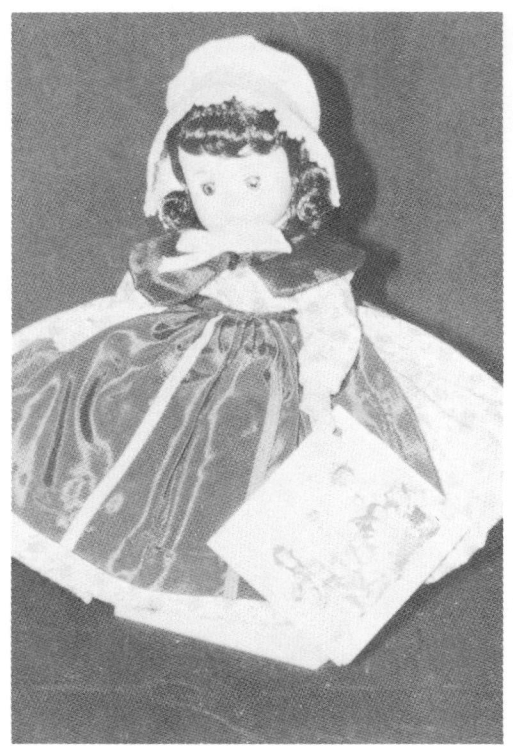

Alexander--8" "Canada" All hard plastic with unjointed knees. 1968 to date. Currently available. (Courtesy Marie Ernst)

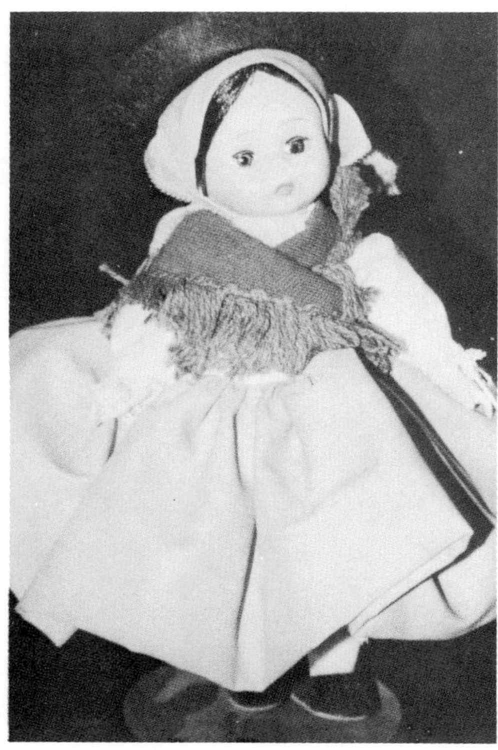

Alexander--8" "Portugal" Bend knees. 1968 to date. $18.00. (Courtesy Marie Ernst)

Alexander--8" "Korea" Bend knees. With "Maggie" face. Eyes are partly closed. 1968. Discontinued 1970. $45.00. (Courtesy Marie Ernst)

Alexander--17" "Leslie" In blue formal. 1968. $50.00. (Courtesy Marie Ernst)

Alexander--14" "McGuffey Ana" 1968. $45.00. (Courtesy Marie Ernst)

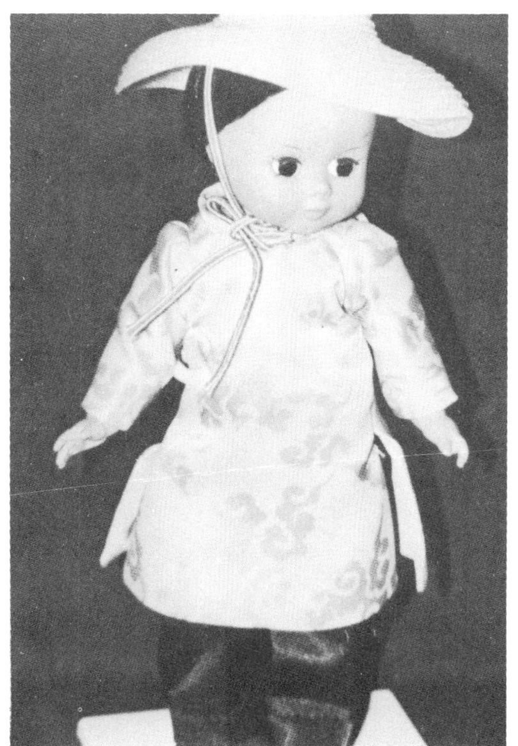

Alexander--8" "Vietnam" Bend knees. 1968. Discontinued 1969. $45.00. (Courtesy Marie Ernst)

Alexander--8" "Turkey" With bend knees. 1968 to date. $18.00. (Courtesy Marie Ernst)

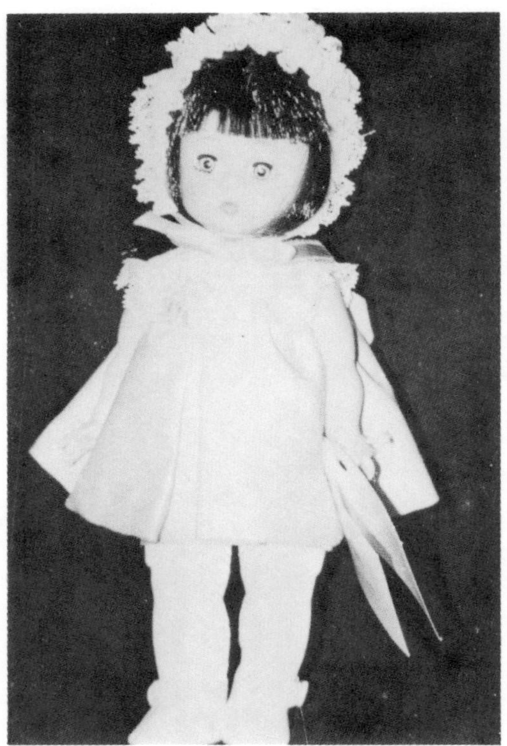

Alexander--8" "Easter" Hard plastic. Bend knees. 1968 only. $60.00. (Courtesy Jay Minter)

Alexander--8" "Greece" All hard plastic. Bend knees. 1968 to date. $18.00. (Courtesy Jay Minter)

Alexander--8" "Morocco" All hard plastic. Bend knees. 1968 to 1970. $45.00. (Courtesy Jay Minter)

Alexander--10" "Melinda" Jointed knees. Bright blue taffeta with white lace and trim. White straw hat with flowers. Tag: Gold paper tag over regular one: Melinda/By Madame Alexander. 1969. $50. (Courtesy Peggy Boudreau)

Alexander--21", 14" and 11" "Jenny Lind" All in pink. 1969. 21" $125.00; 14" $50.00; 11" $65.00. (Courtesy Marie Ernst)

Alexander--8" "Indonesia" Bend knees. 1970 to date. $18.00. (Courtesy Marie Ernst)

Alexander--14" "Sleeping Beauty" Long curly hair. Plastic and vinyl. 1971. $35.00.

Alexander--21" "Melanie" 1971. $125.00. (Courtesy Jay Minter)

Alexander--21" "Cornelia" 1972. $125.00. (Courtesy Jay Minter)

Alexander--21" "Gainsboro" In blue with overlace. 1972. $125.00. (Courtesy Marie Ernst)

Alexander--8" "Czechoslavakia" Hard plastic. Bend knees. 1972. $18.00. (Courtesy Jay Minter)

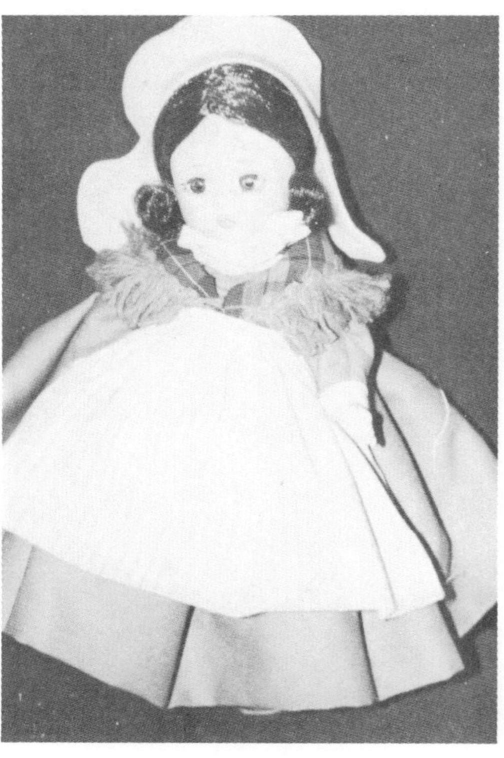

Alexander--8" "Belgium" Hard plastic. Bend knees. 1972. $18.00. (Courtesy Jay Minter)

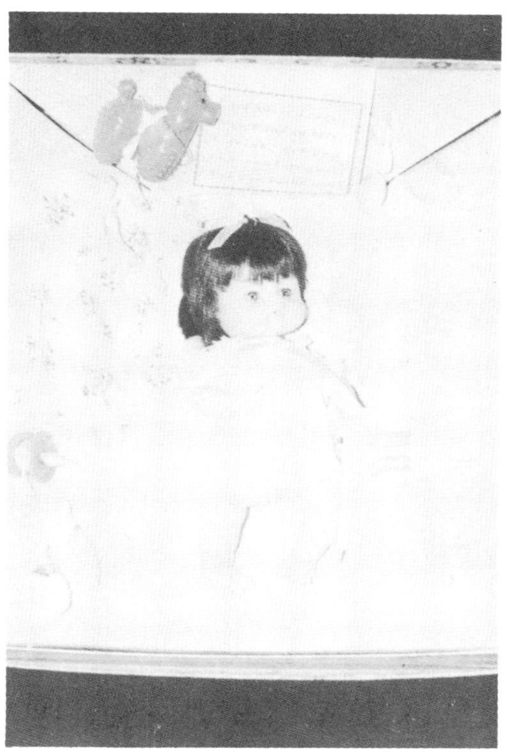

Alexander--9" "Sweet Tears" All vinyl. Open mouth/nurser. Discontinued in 1973. $25.00. (Courtesy Jay Minter)

Alexander--21" "Renoir" 1973. $125.00.

Alexander--8" "United States" Hard plastic. Straight legs. 1974. Some first issues had misspelled tags that read "Untied States." Most were recalled. Currently available. (Courtesy Jay Minter)

Alexander--21" "Melanie" Red and white. 1974. $125.00. (Courtesy Marie Ernst)

Alexander--21" "Cornelia" In blue with black trim. 1974. $125.00. (Courtesy Marie Ernst)

Alexander--14" "Pinky" Plastic and vinyl Blue sleep eyes. 1975. Currently available. (Courtesy Phyllis Houston)

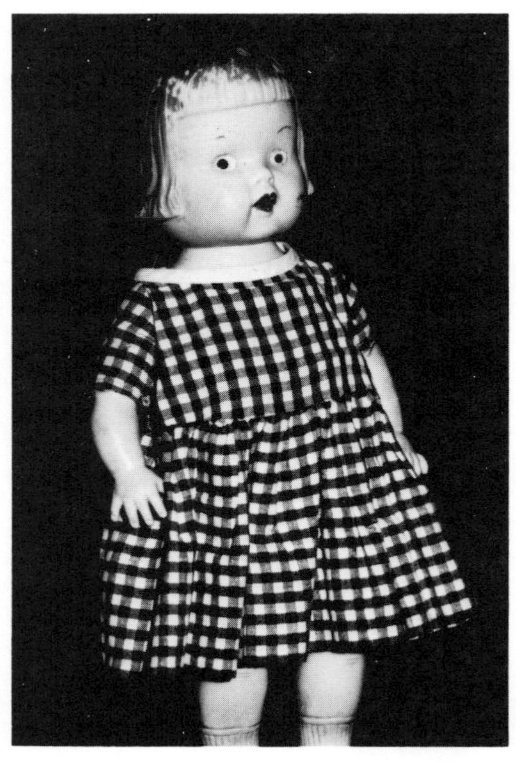

Allied Doll Co.--10" "Wendy" All vinyl with molded hair. Painted features. One piece body, arms and legs. Molded on shoes and socks. Marks: Allied Grand Doll/Mfg. Co. Inc. 1958. $3.00.

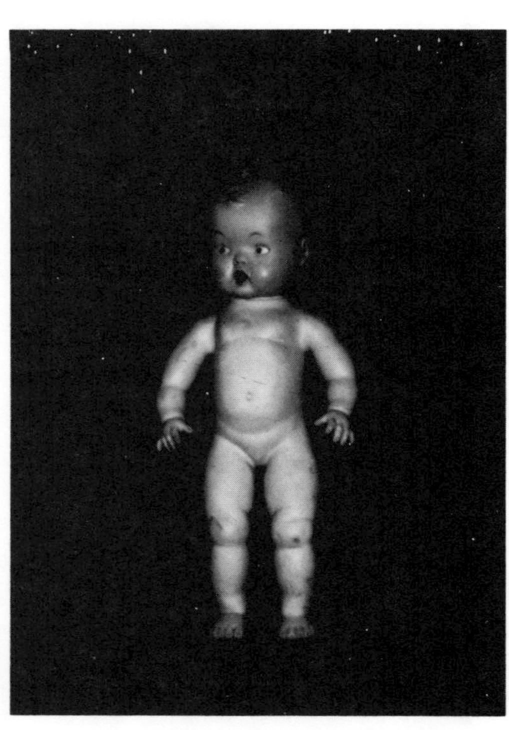

Allied Doll Co.--11" One piece vinyl body. Painted blue to side eyes. Molded hair, topknot with hole for ribbon. Marks: Allied Grand Doll/ Mfg. Inc. 1958. Large "A," on backside. $3.00. (Courtesy Carolyn Powers)

Shows an all original "Little Colonel" Shirley Temple. (Courtesy Marge Meisinger)

14" "Miss Teenage America"--Pageant Doll. Plastic body and legs. Vinyl arms and head. Painted features. High heel feet. Marks: 3426/Kaystan Co./1972/ Hong Kong, on back. Original. Medal says: Miss Teenage America. (Courtesy Marie Ernst)

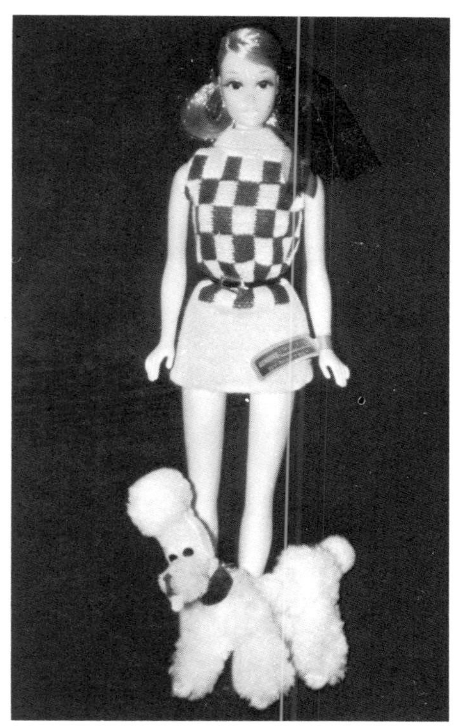

11½" "Walking Jamie"--Brown decal eyes/lashes. Red hair, but came in various colors. Fuzzy, wired poodle. Felt nose and tongue. Plastic eyes. Marks: 1967 Mattel Inc/U.S. Patented/Pat'd Canada 1967/Other Pats. Pend/Japan. Dog is unmarked. (Courtesy Bessie Carson)

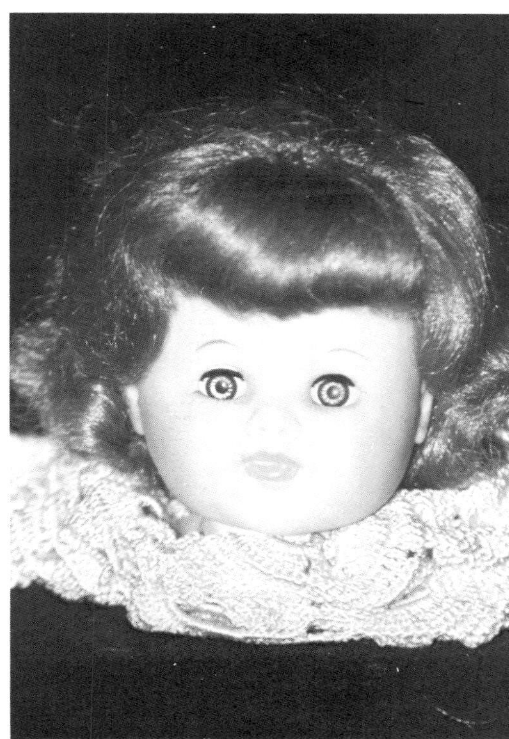

19" "Baby Dawn"--Early vinyl head. Latex one piece body. Brown sleep eyes/lashes. Open/ closed mouth with molded tongue. Beautiful modeled ears. Marks: Uneeda, on head. 1953. (Courtesy Bessie Carson)

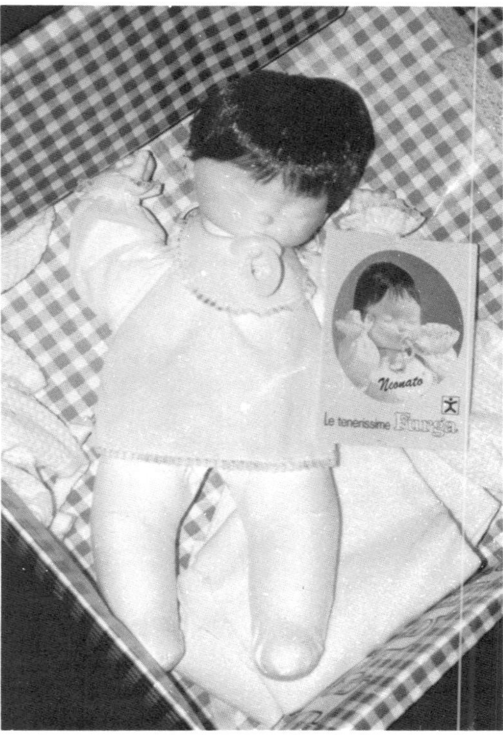


17" "Neonato"--Body is pink cloth over foam. Vinyl gauntlet hands. Vinyl head. Not a nurser but comes with a pacifier. Marks: Furga, in square/122ol. (Courtesy Virginia Jones)

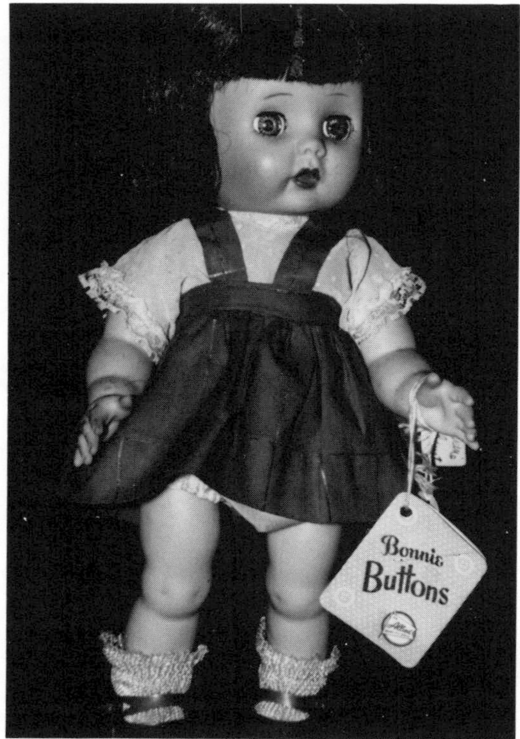


Allied Doll Co.--10½" "Bonnie Buttons" All vinyl with blue sleep eyes. Open/closed mouth. All original. Marks: 39AE 1 A, on head. 1964. $6.00. (Courtesy Marie Ernst)

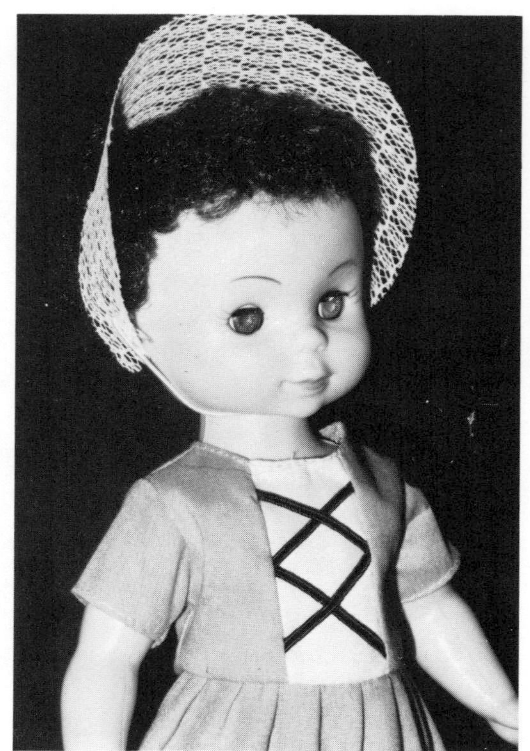

Allied Doll Co.--10" "Susan" Plastic body, arms and legs. Vinyl head with rooted dark brown hair. Blue sleep eyes. Original clothes. Marks: No. 2112, on head. Made in Hong Kong, on back. Box: Susan/1967 Allied Doll & Toy Corp $1.00.

Allied Doll Co.--22½" "Valerie" White version in Name Doll/Mfg. Unknown section of Vol. I, page 230. Also sold as "Meri" in a 19" version in 1970 and came with a 15 pc. "mod" wardrobe. Marks: KT, on head. Made by Allied Doll. Same mold (different marks) used by P&M Sales as "Belinda." See Vol. I, page 237. $7.00.

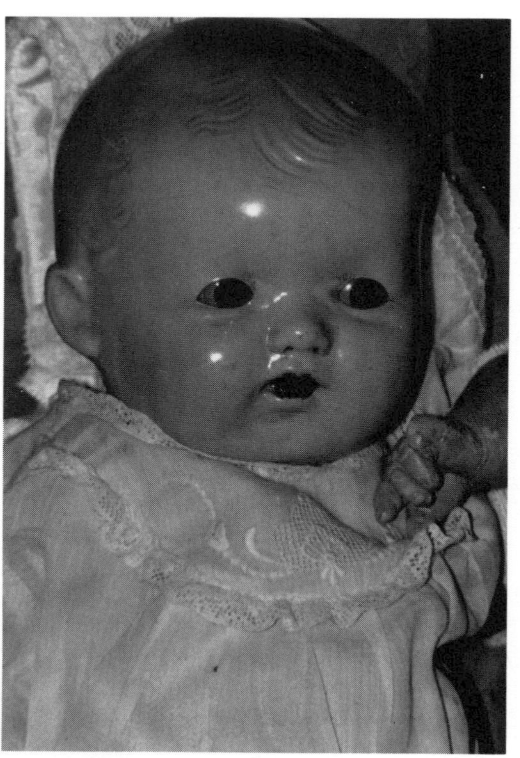

For complete information on the American Character Doll Co. refer to Series I, page 34. American Character--13" "Toddle Petite" Composition head. Rocker sleep eyes. Open/closed mouth. No eyebrows. Molded yellow hair. Rubber body, fully jointed. Tag: Petite/Doll/Toddle. ca. 1936. $38.00. (Courtesy Marie Ernst)

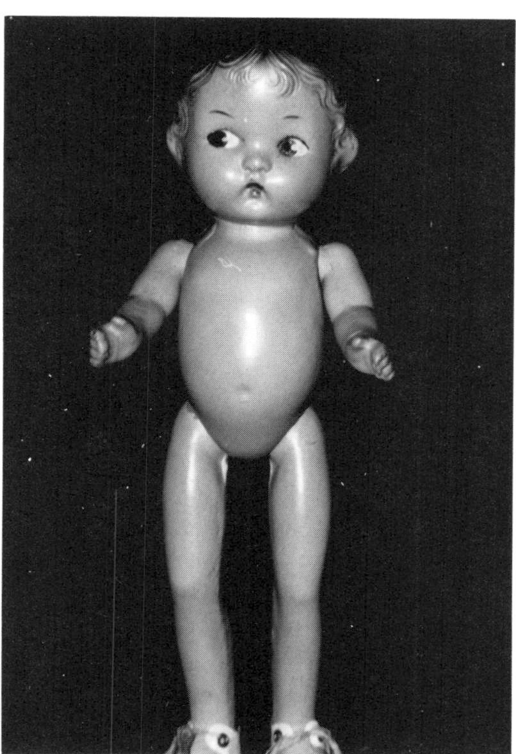

American Character--10" "Wee Girl" All composition. Painted brown eyes. Molded, painted black hair. Marks: Noen. 1940. $20.00. (Courtesy Mary Partridge)

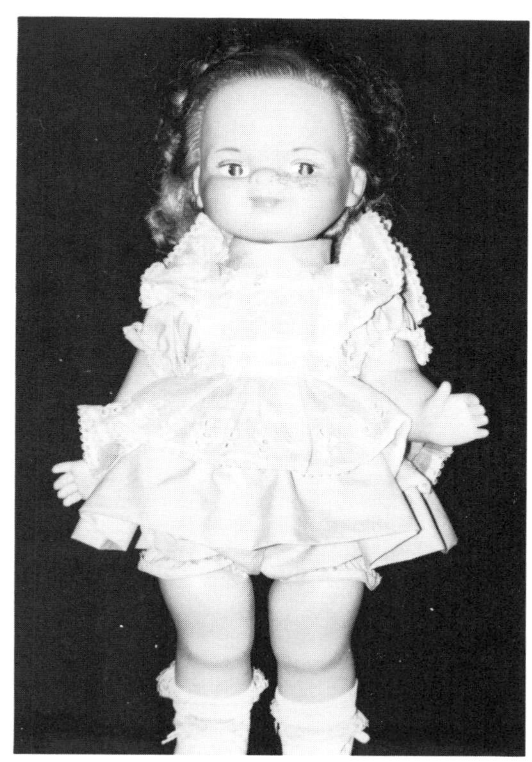

American Character--23" "Chuckles" All vinyl with elastic strung legs. Painted brown eyes with molded lashes and lids. Also came with painted blue eyes. Marks: Amer. Doll & Toy Co/ 1961. $40.00. (Courtesy Barbara Coker)

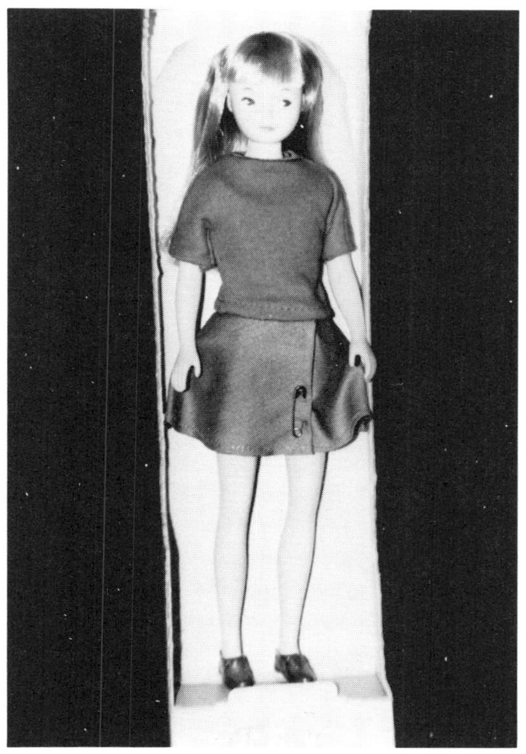

American Character--9" "Cricket" Tressy's little cousin. Sold as a Sears exclusive, later when sold as "little sister," she had the grow hair. Original olive green skirt. Red sweater (snaps on back) with green piping at neck and sleeves. Brown tennis type shoes. Marks: Amer. Char./ Inc/1961, on head. $10.00. (Courtesy Bessie Carson)

American Character--Grow hair Tressy shown in "Miss American Character" outfit. White dress with two large pink flowers. Red roses and silver cup. Pearl tiara. Navy Blue streamer says "Miss American." 1963. $12.00. (Courtesy Bessie Carson)

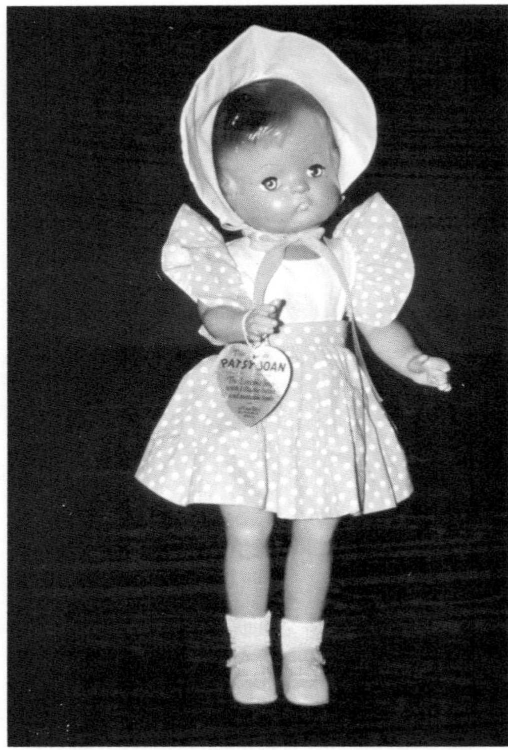


16½" "Patsy Joan"--All composition and all original. 1946. Marks: Effanbee, on back. Tag: This is/Patsy Joan/The Lovable Imp/With Tiltable Head/and Movable Limbs/an Effanbee Durable Doll. (Courtesy Frances & Mary Jane Anicello)

17" "Hedy Lamarr"--All hard plastic. Black Saran hair, curls drop down neck. Not original clothes. Doll was to have been issued with the 1949 movie "Samson & Delilah." Not confirmed by Alexander Doll Co. Refer to the Alexander section for a photo of Hedy Lamarr. (Courtesy Bessie Greeno)

16" "Robbi"--An original doll by artist Judi Kahn. Won a Blue ribbon in competition at Rockford, Ill. in 1973.

9" "School Girl"--All felt with jointed shoulders and hips. Mohair wig. Painted features. Tag: Old Cottage/Doll/Hand Made/In/Great Britain. (Courtesy Marge Meisinger)

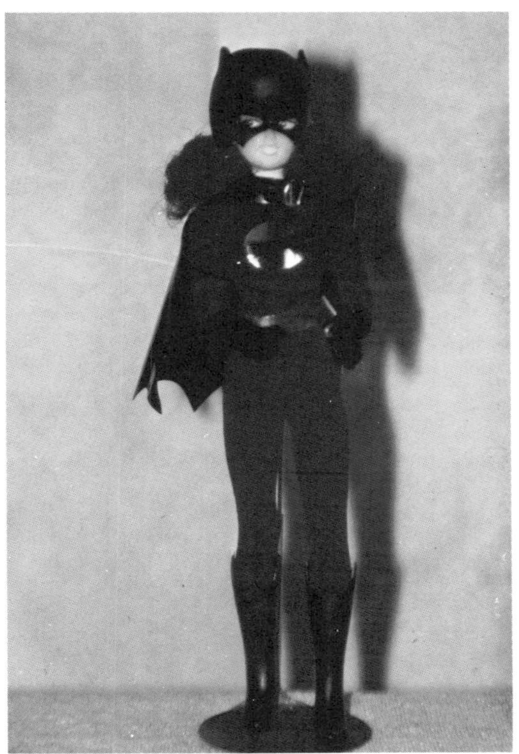

12" "Batgirl"--All vinyl with same body as posable Tammy. Green eyes/shadow. Marks: 1965/ Ideal Toy Corp./W-12-3, on head. 1965/Ideal, in oval/2 M-12, on hip. (Courtesy Lisa Lineberger)

8" "Capt. Kirk" (William Shatner) and "Mr. Spock" (Leonard Nimoy). Action figures by Mego Corp. 1975.

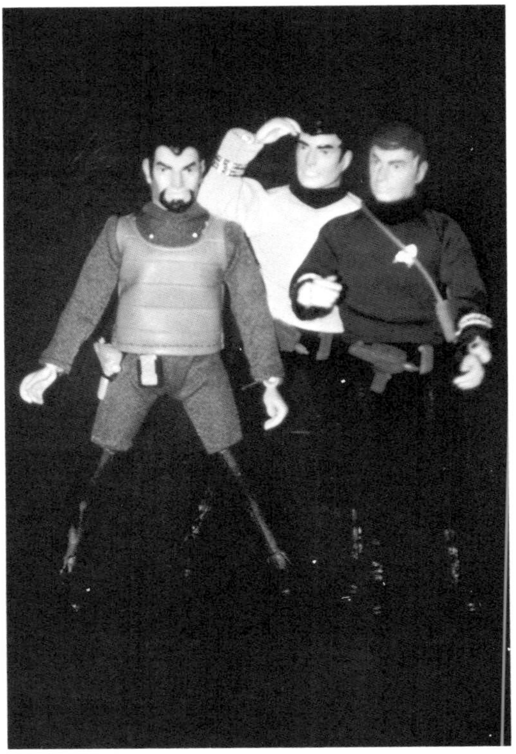

8" "Mr. Scot" (Scotty), "Dr. McCoy (DeForest Kelley) and "Klingon" (Kang* Michael Ansara). Action figures by Mego Corp. 1975. All are marked 1974 Paramount/Pict. Corp. on head and have MCMLXXI on the back.

American Character--13" "Pouty Miss Marie" Plastic body and legs. Vinyl arms and head. Black pupiless sleep eyes to the side in "googly" fashion. Marks: Amer. Char. Inc./1965, on head. $20.00. (Courtesy Bessie Carson)

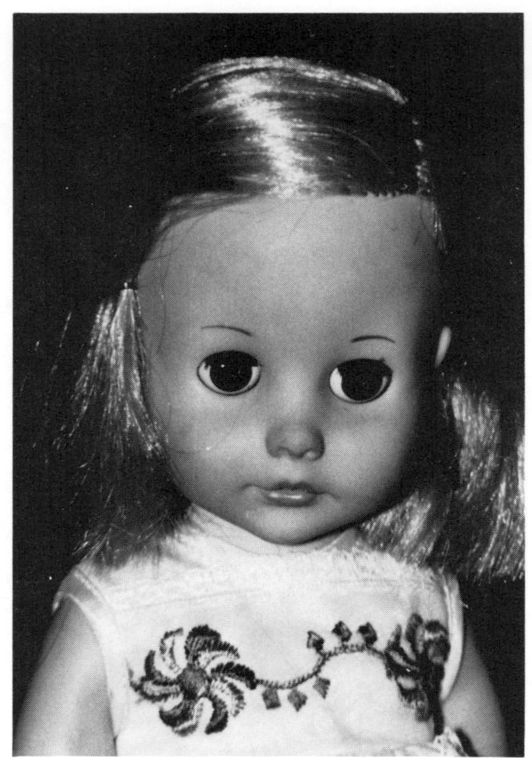

American Character--13" "Marie Lee" Plastic body and legs. Vinyl arms and head. Sleep eyes that change from blue to light brown, depending on light direction. Original. Marks: 3/American Character/1966, on head. $20.00. (Courtesy Jayn Allen)

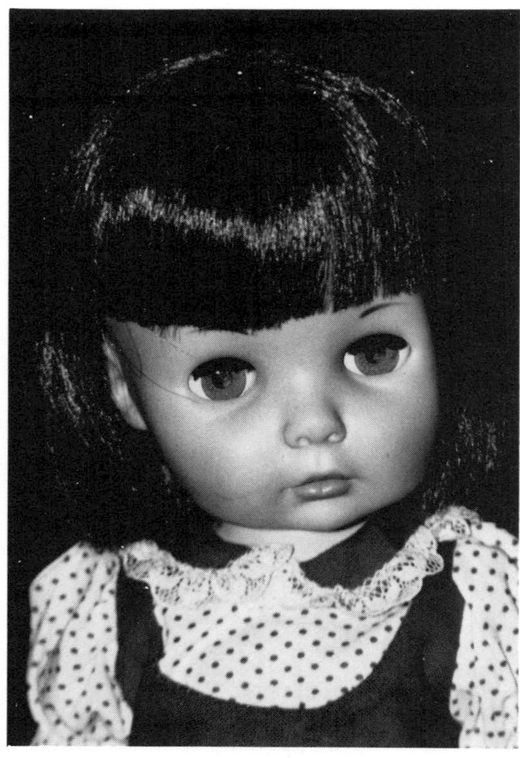

American Character--13" "Marie Ann" Plastic body and legs. Vinyl arms and head. Dark red hair. Blue sleep eyes/lashes. Marks: American Character/1966, on head. $20.00. (Courtesy Jayn Allen)

American Character--8" "Little Joe Cartright" All rigid vinyl with molded clothes. Marks: Portugal, on back. Little Joe was played by Michael Landon. $35.00.

Amsco--12" "Buffy" (T.V. series) Make up and hairdressing head. Marks: 1971/Amsco Ind. Inc. Hopefully "Buffy" will look like this as a young woman, as the head is much too old looking for a child star. $35.00. (Courtesy Phyllis Houston)

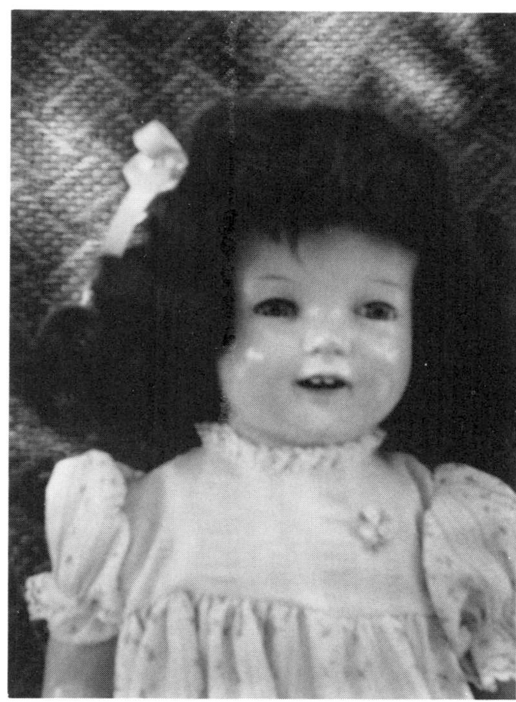

For complete information on the Arranbee Doll Co. refer to Series I, page 43.

Arranbee--23" "Nancy" Cloth with composition shoulderhead. Narrowed blue tin sleep eyes. Molded hair under wig. Open mouth/2 teeth. Marks: Fiberoid, on head. Arranbee, on body. $40.00. (Courtesy Flacks)

Arranbee--12" "Nancy" All composition. Jointed arms and legs. Painted hair and eyes. Original clothes and trunk. Marks: Nancy, on back. 1930-1936. $32.00. (Maish Collection)

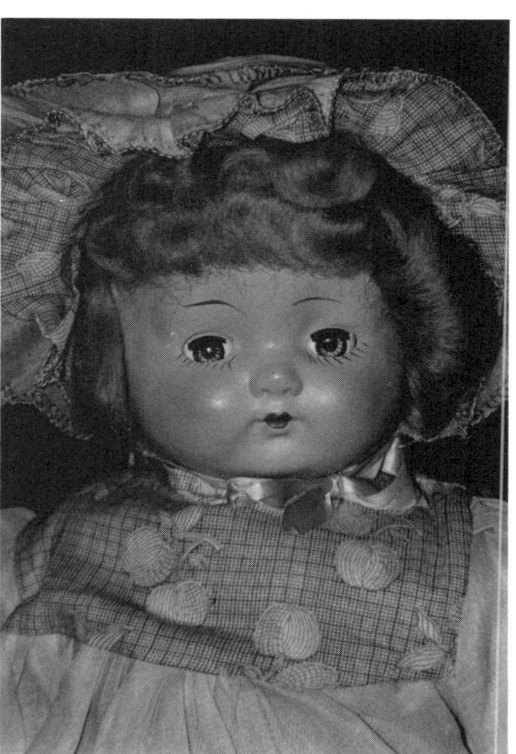

Arranbee--19" Cloth with composition head, arms and legs. Blue sleep eyes. Original. Box marked Salesman Sample. 1937. $30.00 (Courtesy Jay Minter)

14" "Snuffy Smith"--All cloth with nylon pressed face mask. Removable clothes. Painted features. Felt ears and sewn on shoes. Tag: This is an original comic strip doll that all America loves. Copyright King Features Syndicate Inc. By Columbia Toy Products/Kansas City, Missouri. (Courtesy Virginia Jones)

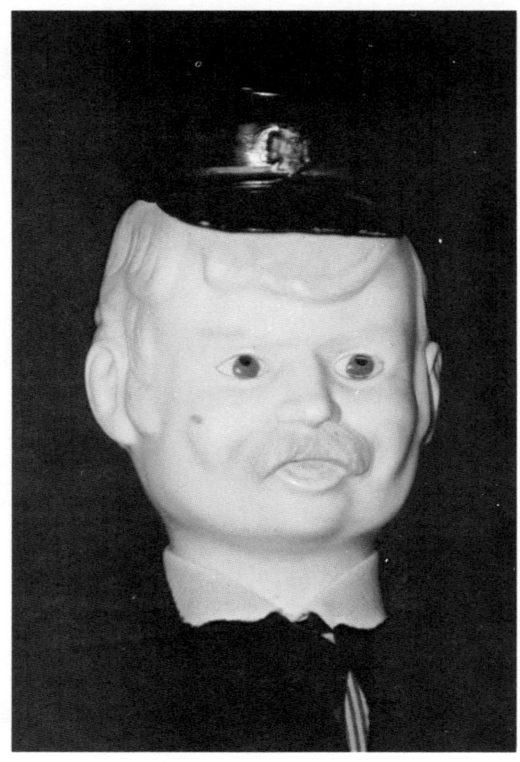

19" "Capt. Kangaroo"--Cloth stuffed with vinyl head and painted features. Marks: 1961 Robt. Keeshan/Assoc. Inc. (Courtesy Shirley Puertzer)

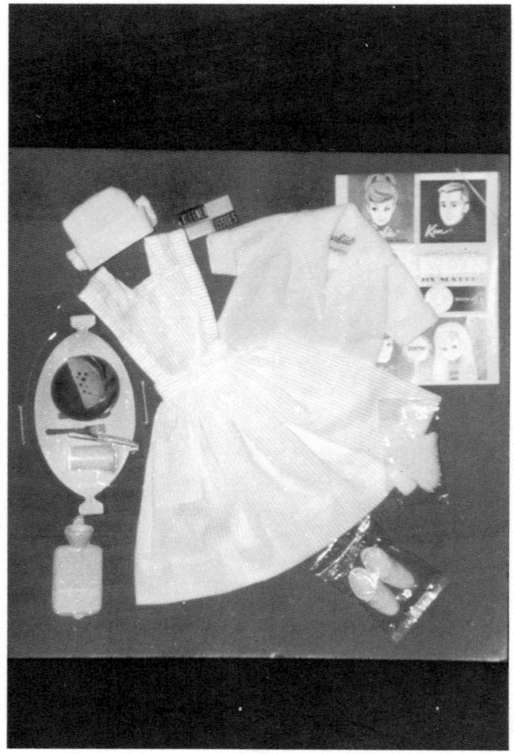

One of the most desirable of the Barbie early clothes. The Candy Striper. (Courtesy Bessie Carson)

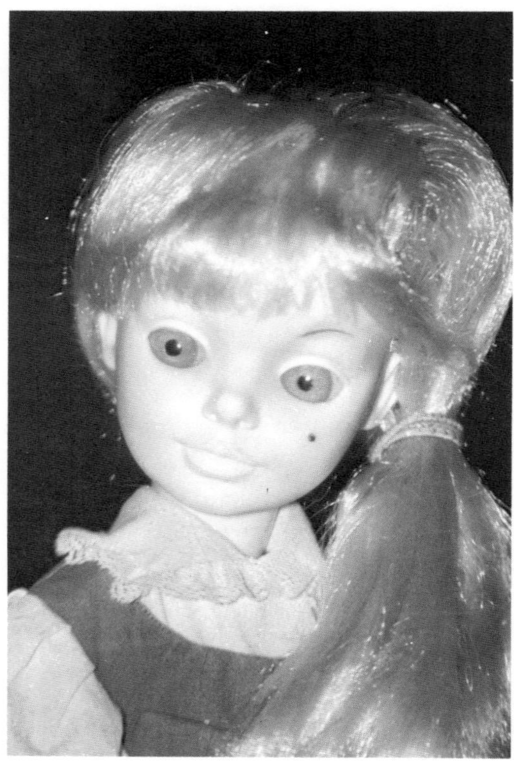

17" "Simona"--All vinyl. Had long inset lashes. Marks: Furga, Italy. 1968. (Courtesy Virginia Jones)

Arranbee--16½" "Miss International" All composition with blue sleep eyes. Open mouth/four upper teeth. Marks: Design/Pat. Pend., on head. Came with four outfits, Swiss, American, Mexican, and Dutch. 1938. $35.00. (Courtesy Mary Partridge)

Arranbee--26" "Baby Nancy" Composition head with 3/4 composition arms and legs. Deep blue-green sleep eyes. Open mouth with two upper and lower teeth. Marks: Arranbee. 1939. $40.00. (Courtesy Flacks)

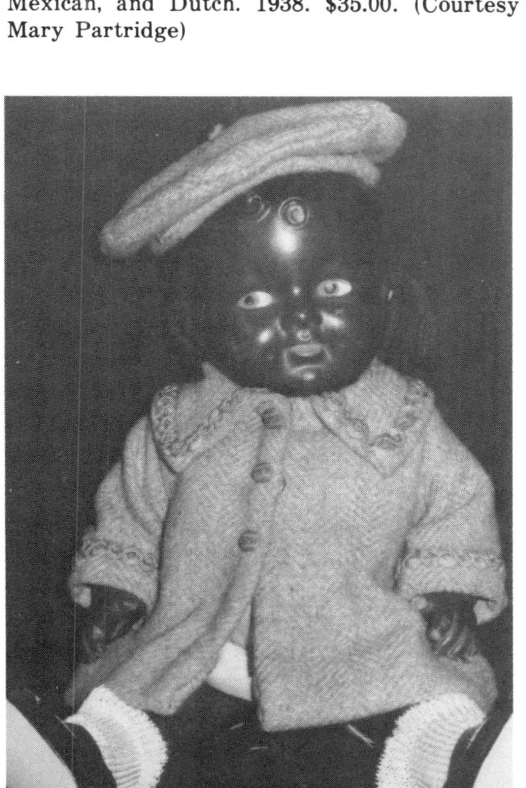

Arranbee--14" "Bessie Toddler" All composition. Fully jointed. Painted side glancing eyes. Closed mouth. Dimpled cheeks. Molded hair with three outfits of silk hair. Marks: R&B on head. 1940. $35.00.

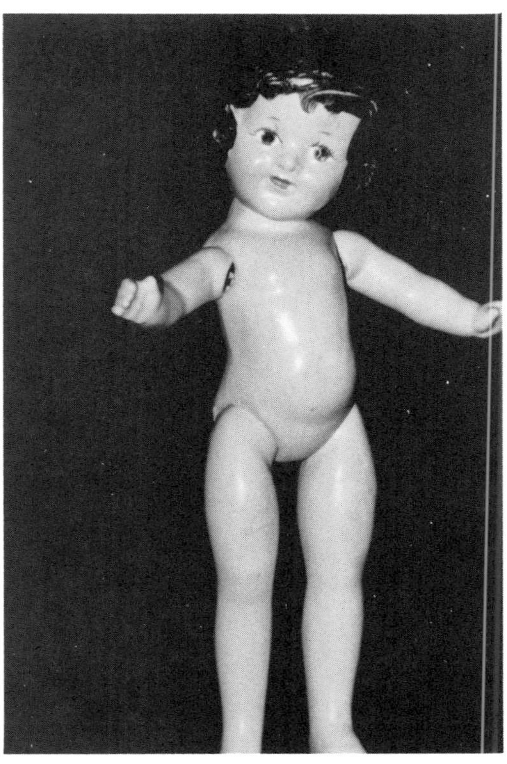

Arranbee--8½" "Carolyn Lee" Black painted molded hair. Smile/closed mouth. 5 year old played in Virginia with Fred McMurray and Madelaine Carroll. 1941. Arranbee also produced sets of five labeled "Quint." Doll also used for "Round World" series. Marks: R&B/Doll Co., on backs. $22.00. (Courtesy Marie Ernst)

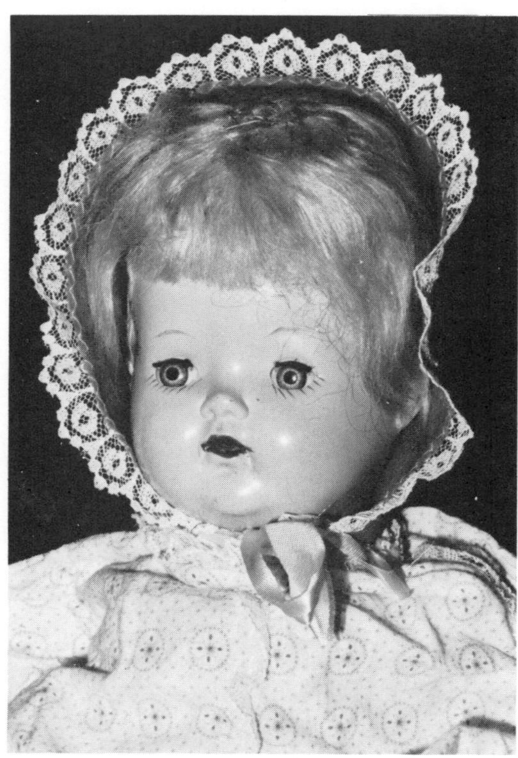

Arranbee--15" "Happy Time" Hard plastic head. Glued on mohair wig over molded hair. Rocker blue sleep tin eyes. Cloth body, composition arms and legs. Marks: R&B/250, on head. ca. late 1940's. $10.00

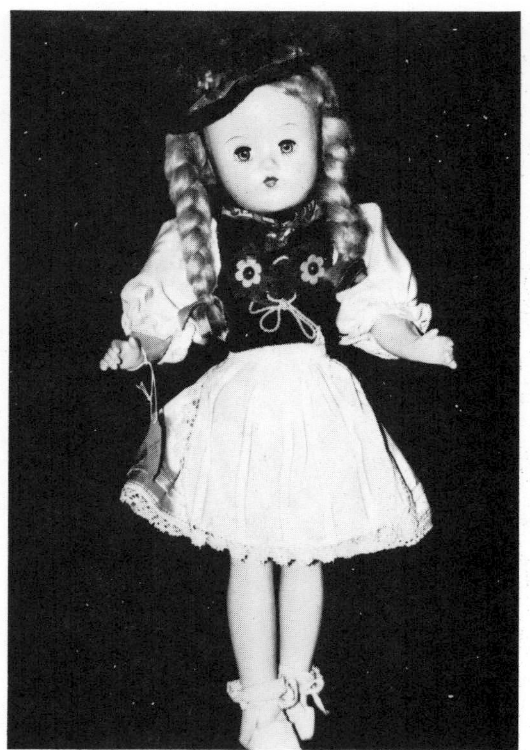

Arranbee--18" "Swiss Girl" All composition. Blue sleep eyes/lashes. Original. Doll by Arranbee. Tag: National Mission/Gift Shop/156 Fifth Ave/N.Y.C. 1946. $38.00. (Courtesy Marie Ernst)

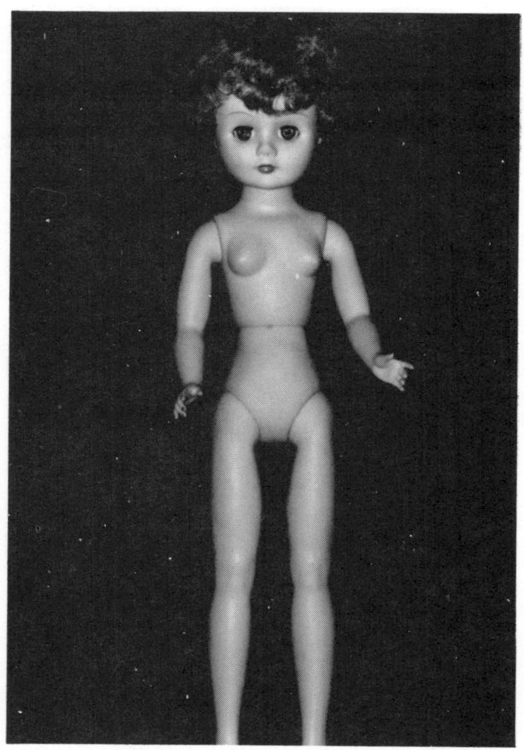

Arrow--24" "Stunning," "Sweet Judy," and "Marlene" Excellent quality rigid vinyl. Jointed waist. Softer vinyl head. Blue sleep eyes. Painted fingernails and toes. Marks: ⟐ 55. Some are marked and some were used by Premium Doll Offer Companies. Refer to Volume I, page 227. $30. (Courtesy Bessie Carson)

Arrow--24" "Marlene" Dress. Also sold in 1957 by Alden's as "Shirtwaist Sally."

Averill--13½" All cloth with pressed face mask. Lashes are set in a slit. Felt coat, cotton dress. ca. 1940's. $65.00. (Courtesy Phyllis Houston)

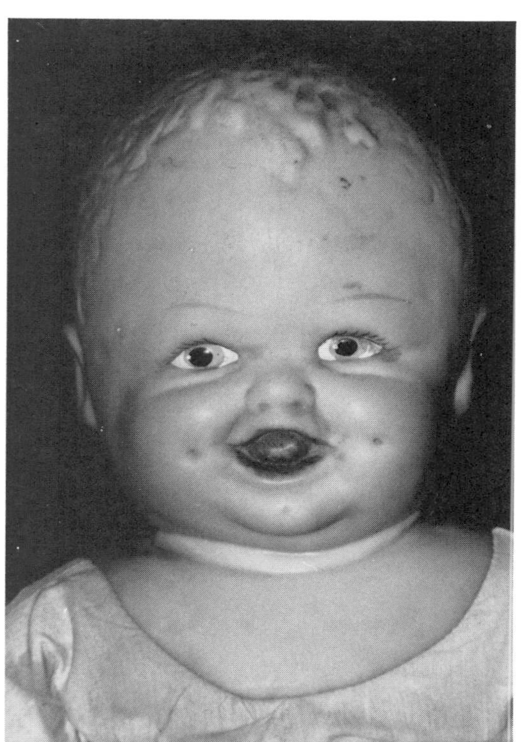

Averill--20" Cloth body and legs. Early vinyl guantlet hands and head with vinyl sew to cloth at neck. Painted blue eyes. Open/closed mouth with molded tongue. Averill. 1945. $55.00. (Courtesy Virginia Jones)

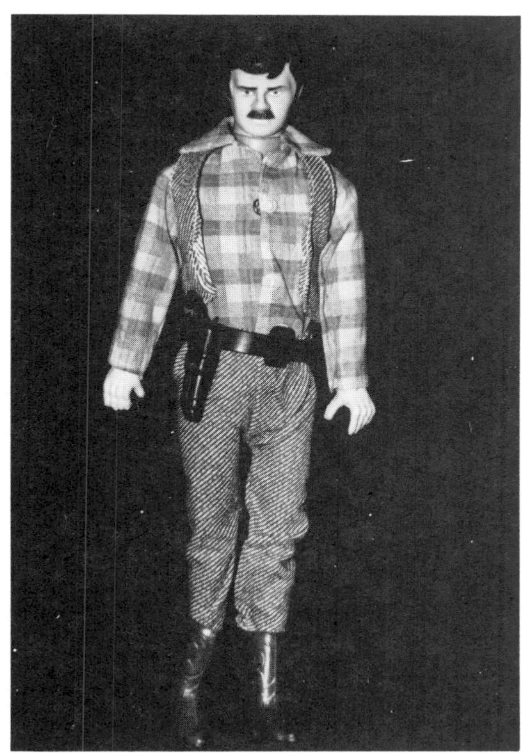

Azark-Hamway--12" "Kit Carson" Plastic body and legs. Vinyl arms and head. Jointed knees and waist. Marks: Hong Kong, on head and back. Made by Azark-Hamway in 1973 for 1974 market. Still available in some areas.

Teen--11½" "Calamity Jane" Jointed waist. Posable hollow legs. Painted blue eyes/lashes. Pink lips. Brown skin tones. Made by Azark-Hamway. 1973. Marks: Hong Kong, on head and body. Still available in some areas.

Baby Berry--18" "Christopher Robin" Stuffed orange cloth body. Pink cloth arms and legs. Vinyl head with molded orange hair. Painted blue eyes. Marks: None. $30.00. (Courtesy Margaret Biggers)

Bauer & Black--21" "Miss Curity" All composition. Blue sleep eyes. Original. 1946. $35.00. (Courtesy Marge Meisinger)

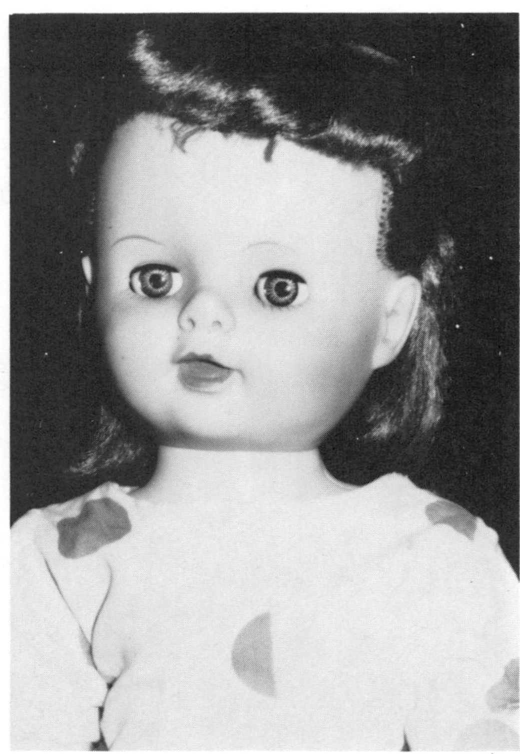

Belle--22" "Perfect Companion" Walker, head turns. Hard plastic with vinyl head. Rooted red hair. Blue sleep eyes. Jointed knees. Arms positioned to go no higher than shoulder. Marks: AE/553. 1953. $7.00.

Belle--19" "Ballerina Belle" Hard plastic arms and legs. Jointed knees and ankles. Walker, head turns. Vinyl head and arms. Rooted blonde hair. Sleep eyes. Marks: AE/200/21. 1956. $8.00.

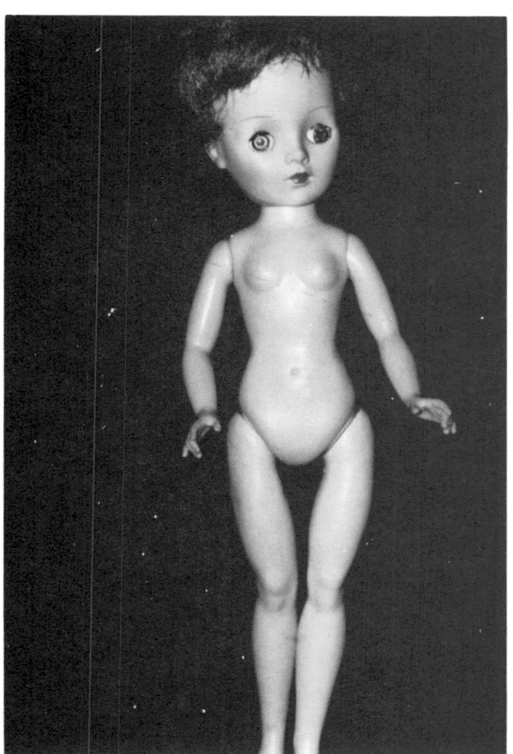

Belle--14" Plastic disc jointed legs. Marks: 15 BAL HH, on lower back. 1957. $4.00.

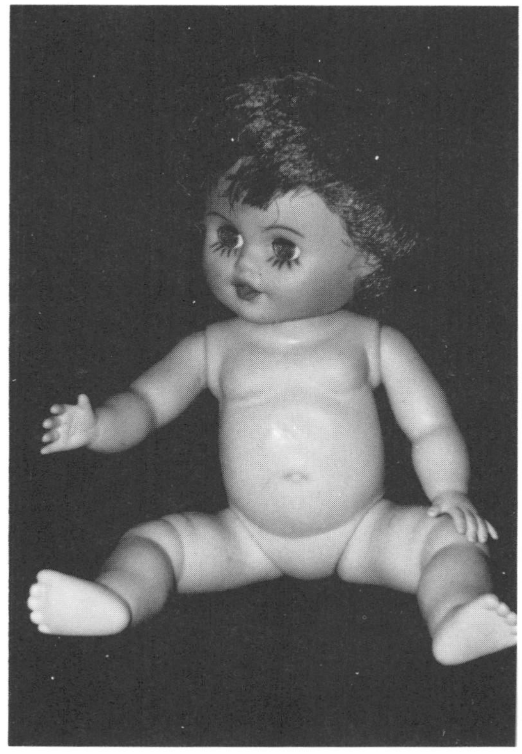

Belle--8" "Baby Gem" All vinyl with blue sleep eyes. Lashes under eyes only. Open mouth/nurser. 1956. Came dressed in baby dress reflecting the birthstones of the year, also had a glass stone of the same color tied to the arm. Marks: None. 1958. $4.00.

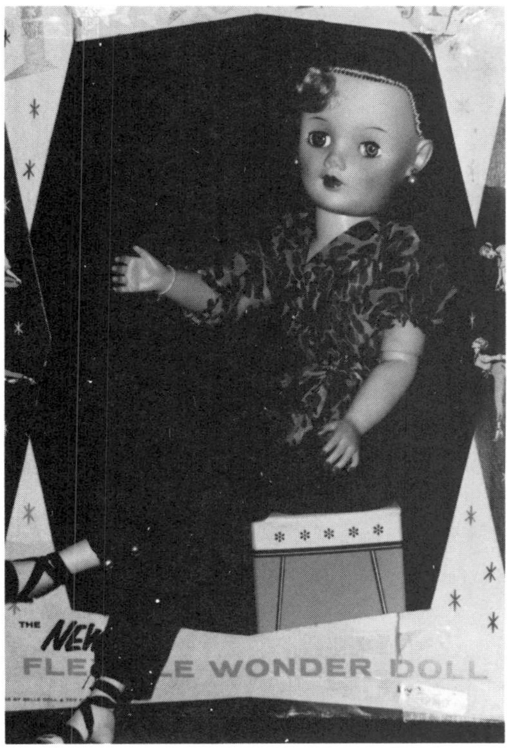


Belle--19" "Twixie, The Twisting Pixie" Hard plastic with vinyl head and vinyl arms that are jointed at the elbow. Jointed waist with series of raised dots all around bottom half. Jointed knees and ankles. High heel feet. Original. Marks: P-16, on head. 1958. $20.00. (Courtesy Edith De-Angelo)

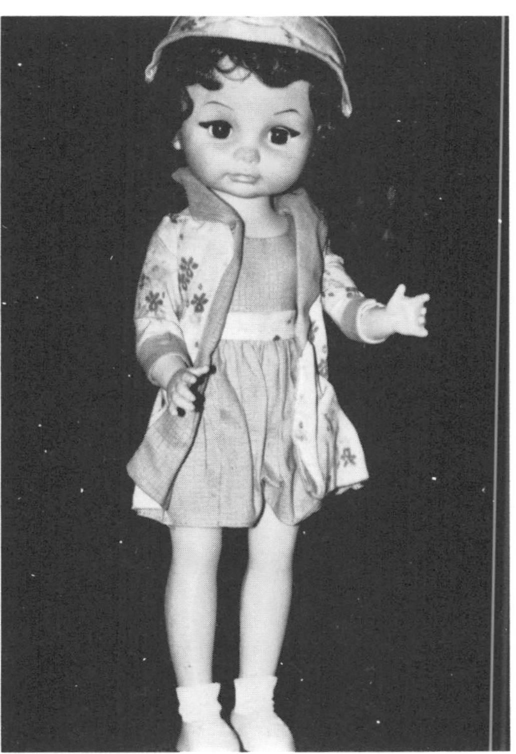

Belle--14" "Melinda" All plastic with vinyl head. Black sleep eyes with black eyeshadow. Rooted brown hair. Staples on hat and removable clothes. All original. 1961. $5.00. (Courtesy Marie Ernst)

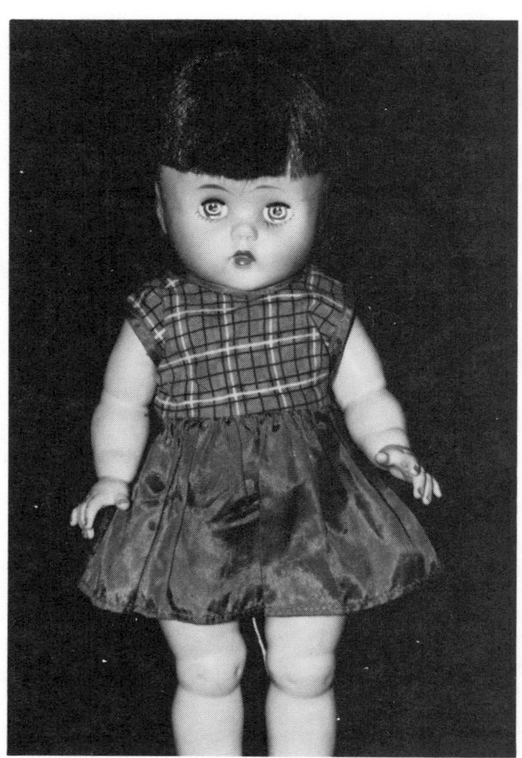

Blumberg--15" "Sally" All vinyl with blue sleep eyes/lashes. Sold with suitcase/clothes. Marks: 26/AE, on head. 1958.

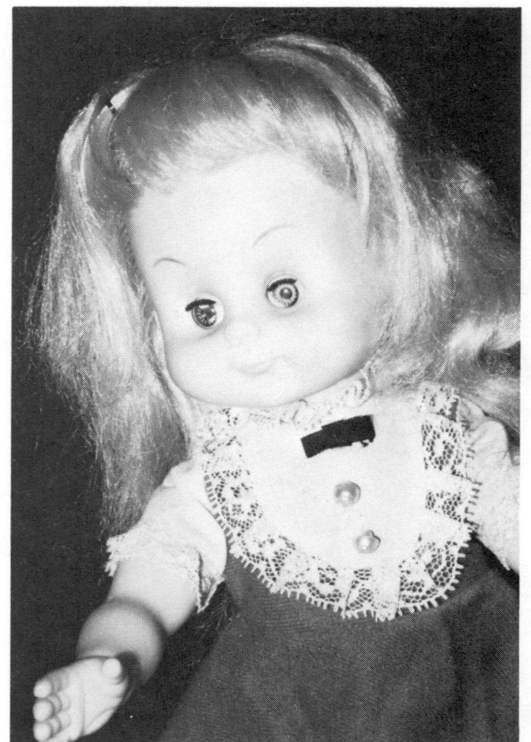

Camay--15" "Trease" All soft polifoam. Rooted blonde hair. Blue sleep eyes. Original dress. Marks: Made in Taiwan, in a circle/15/10, on head. 15/Made In Taiwan, on back. 1969. $4.00.

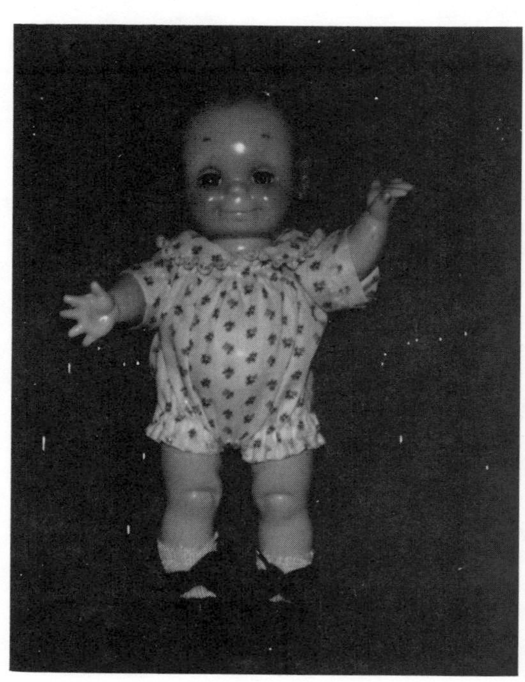

For information on the Cameo Doll Co. refer to Series I, page 57.

Cameo--16" All Hard plastic. Sleep eyes. ca. 1952. $75.00. (Courtesy Adele Gioscia)

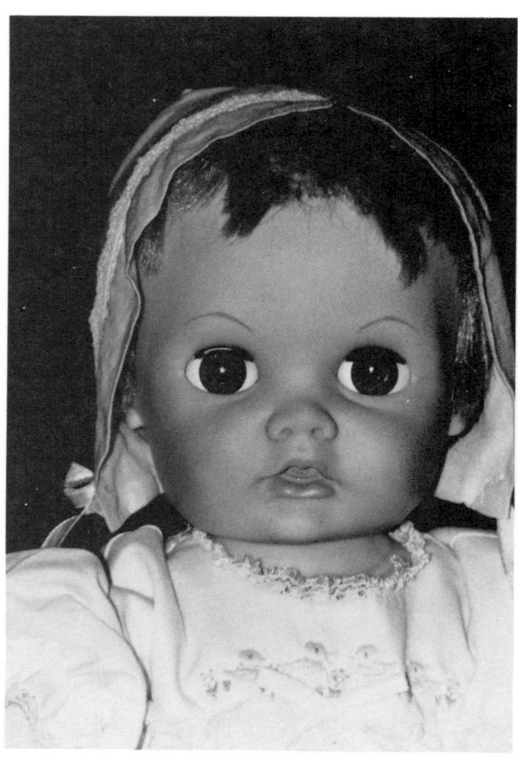

Cameo--20" "Baby Mine" Sleep eyed version. Open/closed mouth. Molded tongue. All vinyl body that is the same as Miss Peeps and jointed the same. Marks: Cameo, on head and back. $50.00. (Courtesy Alice Capps)

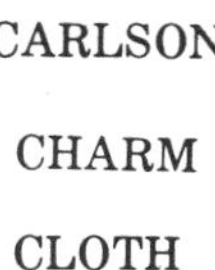


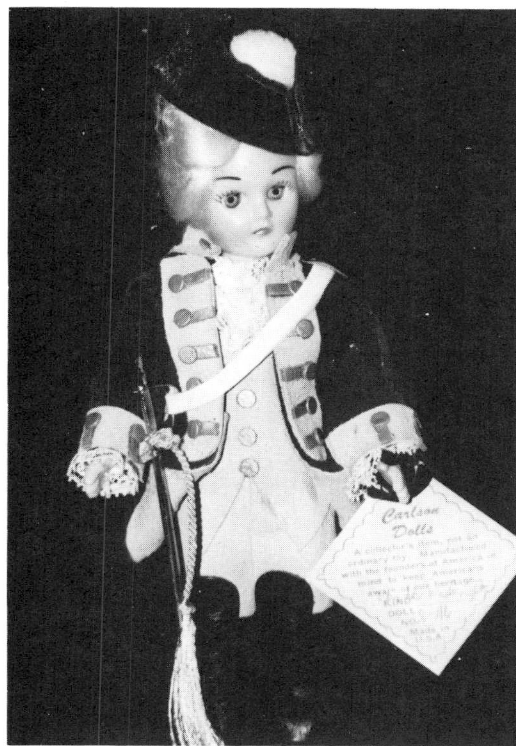


Carlson Dolls--7½" "George Washington" Very good quality hard plastic head. Jointed shoulders and neck. Blue sleep eyes/molded lashes. Excellent clothes. Marks: None. Tag: Carlson/Dolls/A Collector's Item. Not An Ordinary toy. Manufactured/With the Founders of America In/Mind to Keep/Americans Aware of Our Heritage. (Courtesy Edith DeAngelo)

Charm--4" Half doll of hard plastic with blue sleep eyes. Hoop skirt is over a wire frame that is a lamp. Marks: Charm Lamps/Rock Island, Ill. $4.00. (Courtesy Marie Ernst)

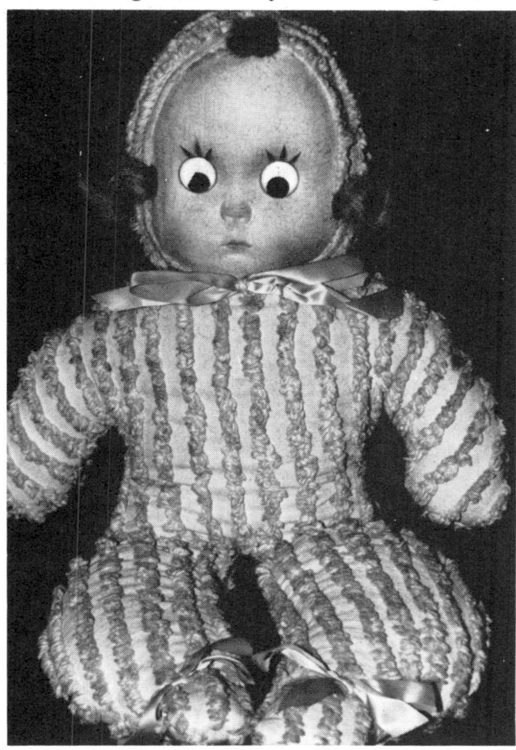

Cloth--18" "Crib Mate" Buckram face mask. Large googly eyes/paper discs. Tuffs of mohair. Chenille body. Tag: Thompkin Co./1939. $5.00.

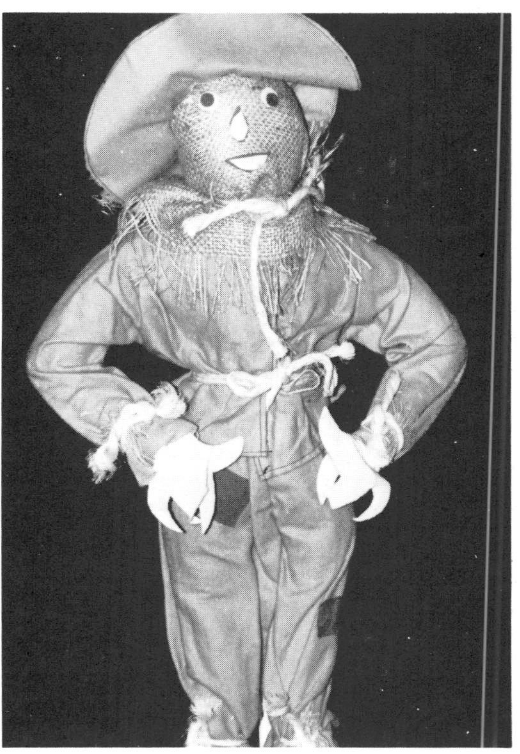

Cloth--23½" "Scarecrow" From the Wizard of Oz. All stuffed cloth/"gunny-sack" face. Tag: Knickerbocher. 1939. $65.00. (Courtesy Donna Stanley)

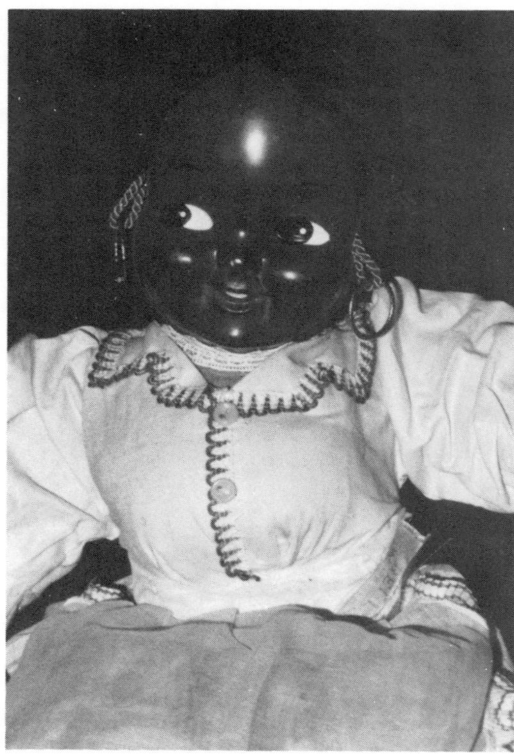

Cloth--18" "Beulah" All cloth with buckram face mask. Painted features. Yarn hair. Bust made of "yarn dust." Dimples. Original. Marks: It's the Beulah/Doll/Mfd by Juro Novelty Co. ca. 1940. $50.00. (Courtesy Virginia Jones)

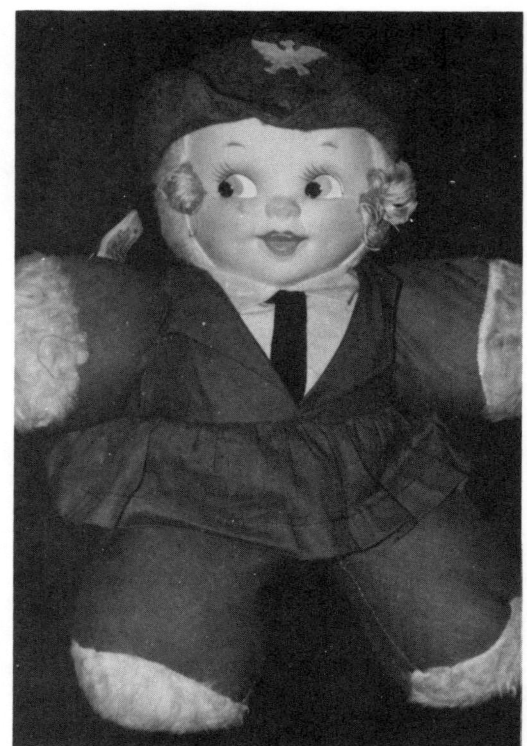

Cloth--16" "Honey Lou, the Airforce Colonel" Cloth with pressed face mask. Dimples. Original. Tag: Honey Lou/A Gund Product. Other side: J. Swedlin, Inc. 1943. $30.00. (Courtesy Marge Meisinger)

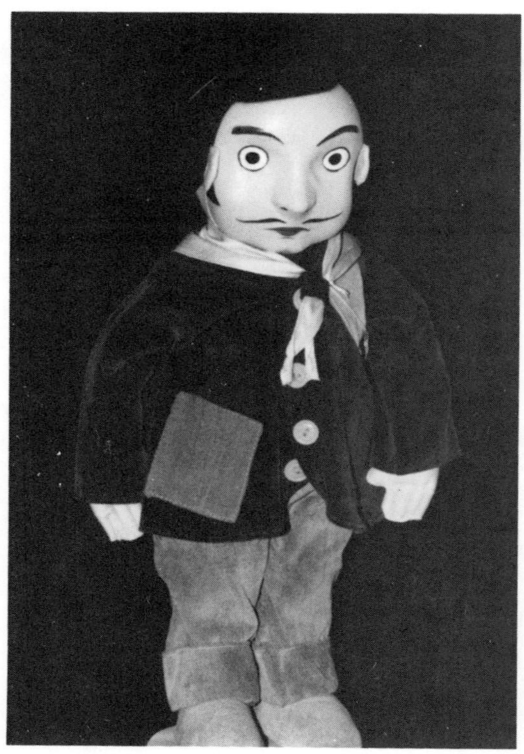

Cloth--16" "Poncho" (Of Cisco Kid, Played by Leo Carrillo). Cloth with highly painted buckram face mask. Hat missing. ca. 1944. $75.00. (Courtesy Kimport Dolls)

Leo Carrillo who was famous for his roles as "Pancho" of the Cisco Kid series of movies. His was a much loved man in Hollywood and Santa Barbara, California.

Cloth--15½" "Little Lulu" Cloth with pressed face and felt clothes. Tag: Georgene Novelties Inc./Corp. 1944/Marjorie H. Buell. $45.00. (Courtesy Marge Meisinger)

Cloth--23" All stuffed cloth with plastic face mask. Marks: None. $3.00.

Cloth--6" Yarn and cloth Indian. From the collection of 5-year old Angie Landers.

Cloth--10½" "Papa Bear," 9" "Mama Bear," 6½" "Baby Bear" & 6½" "Goldilocks" All cloth, printed. Do it yourself kind that are sold in kits. $4.00 set.

Cloth--23" "Desmond" & 20" "Rhoda" (Short for Rhododenron) All cloth with removable top clothes. Tag: Gund. Wrist Tag: An Exclusive Creation/By Gund Mfg. Co. Other side: Gund Mfg. Official Licensee/Al Victor. 1971. $40.00 pair.

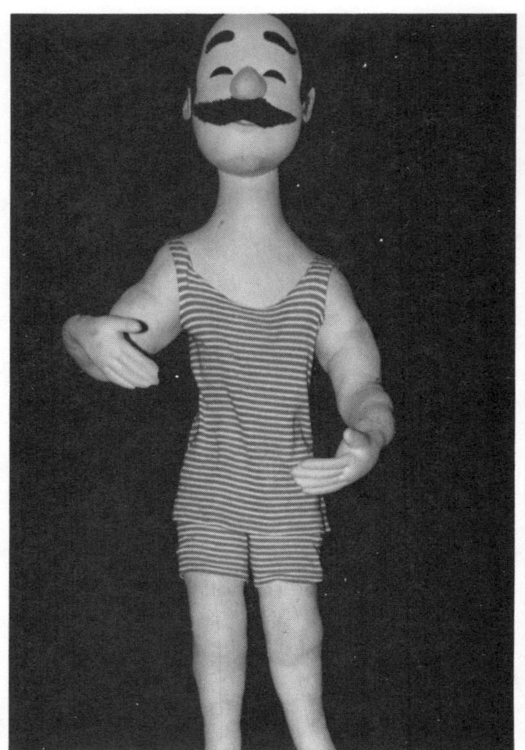

Cloth--38" Display doll. All felt with stitched individual toes and fingers. Separate thumbs and ears. Fur black hair. Plastic eyes. Wired to be posable. $25.00. (Courtesy Elaine Kaminsky)

Cloth--23" "Wednesday" For "Wednesday's child is full of woe." Made by Aboriginals Inc. for Cartoonest Charles Addams. Cartoon called "Addam's Evils." 1962. $50.00. (Courtesy Elaine Kaminsky)

Cloth--18" "Tiny Tim" All cloth with felt features. Body and limbs are wired for posing. Tag: Tiny Tim, on jacket. $18.00.

Cloth--12" "Sister" All printed cloth. Do it yourself kind. 1957. $3.00.

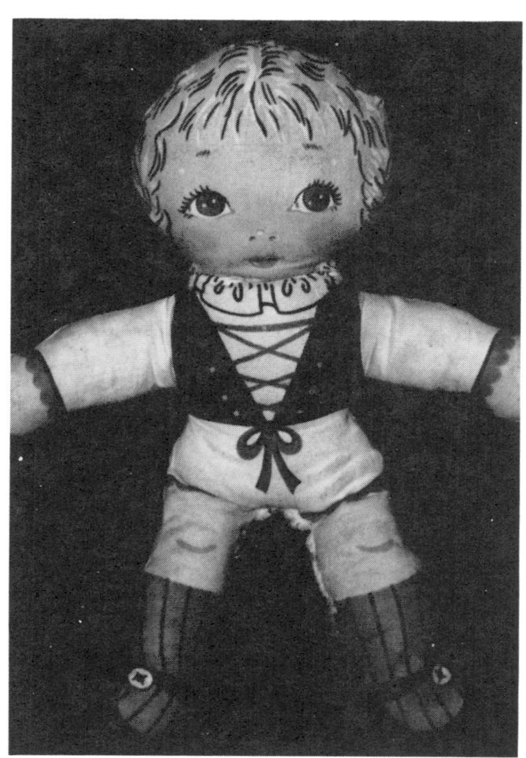

Cloth--12" "Sister" All printed cloth. Do it yourself kind. Without skirt and apron. 1957.

Cloth--15" "Mailman" Printed cloth. Jacket missing. Tag: Toy Innovations, Ltd./Family Friends. $2.00.

Cloth--This uncut boy doll is in 2 tones of green. Came from the "Wee Bit O' Ireland" Store in Seattle. $6.00. (Courtesy Bessie Carson)

Cloth--Uncut linen doll. Colors are blue and green. This girl doll came from a store in Seattle called "Wee Bit O' Ireland." $6.00. (Courtesy Bessie Carson)

Cloth--7½" "Pocket Doll" Stuffed stockinette. Original well detailed removable clothes. Tag: Pocket Doll/Boucher Associates/San Francisco. $9.00.

Cloth--7½" "Brave Cowboy" All cloth stockinette face. Excellent clothes detail. Small eyes only. Marks: Pocket Doll/1962, 1970 Wolfpit Enterprises, Inc. These "pocket" dolls are from Joan Anglund's books. $9.00.

Cloth--16" "Grandpa" All cloth. Tag: Joyce-Miller Original/Copyright/Sears Roebuck & Co./Grandpa. $18.00.

Cloth--26" All cloth and plush. Key wind music box in backs. Sold exlusively with Nemis-Markus. 1965. $35.00 set. (Courtesy Jay Minter)

Cloth--14" "Tom & Becky" "Country Cousins" All cloth with removable clothes. "Bean" filled lower legs. Tag: Amsco Ind. A Milton Bradley Co./Country Cousins. There are four of these, the other two are Jenny (blonde) and Katie (Brunette). Still available in some areas.

Cloth--17" "Spanish" A UNECEF Doll. Tag: Mary, Many Face/Aurora Products/Corp. All cloth with flip up skirts. $12.00.

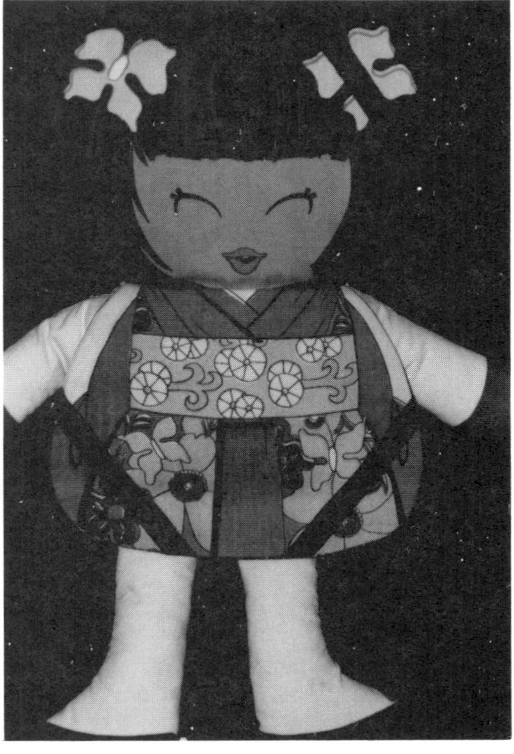

Cloth--17" "Oriental" Mary Many Face.

Cloth--17" "African" Mary, Many Face.

Cloth--17" "Scandinavian" Mary, Many Face.

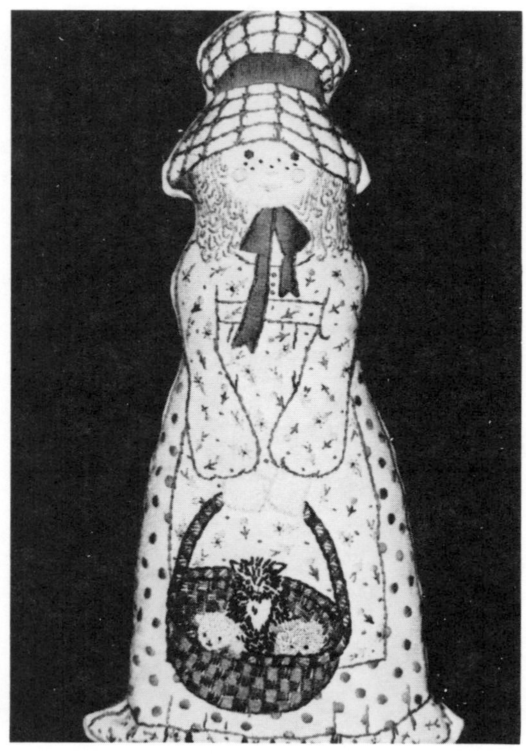

Cloth--17" "Holly Hobbie" Embroidery. Made from Simplicity Pattern #6248. Made by Barbara Baker.

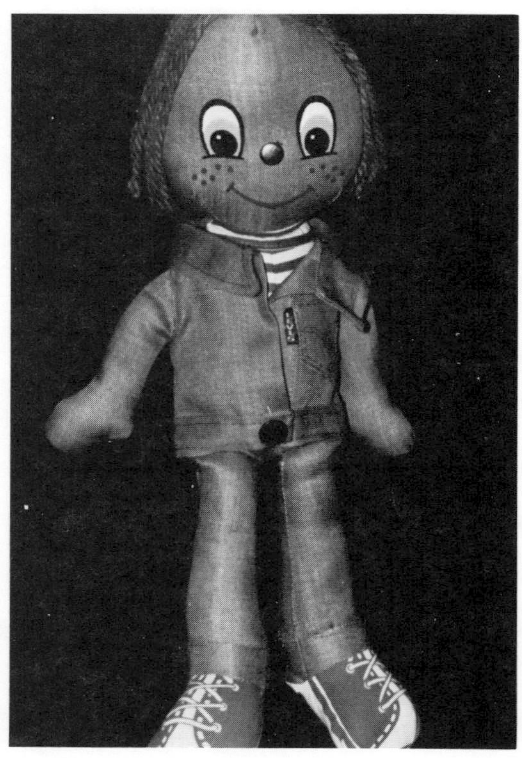

Cloth--16" "Official Levi's Rag Doll" Only the jacket is removable. Glued red yarn hair. Marks: Tag: Levi's Denim/Rag/Doll. Other side: Knickerbocher. Tag on jacket: Levi's. 1974. Still available.

Cloth--12" "Korean" Baby, Many Face/173/ Aurora Products. This UNECEF doll has flip up skirts that changes faces. $16.00.

Cloth--12" "Nigerian" Baby, Many Face.

Cloth--12" "Mexican" Baby Many Face.

Cloth--6¼" "Nancy" Asst. #9223. All printed cloth. Tag: Nancy/Knickerbocher. Box: Copyright United/Feature/Syndicate/Inc. 1973. $4.00.

Cloth--6½" "Sluggo" All printed cloth. Vest removable only. Marks: Tag: Sluggo/Copyright United Feature Syndicate 1973. Other side: Knickerbacher. $6.00.

Cloth--13" "Becky Thatcher" All cloth with embroidery features. One of the "official" Hanibal, Mo. dolls. This one is made commercially by 70 year old Mrs. Quattrocci and she has been making these dolls for over 30 years. $6.00.

Cloth--8" "Floppy Sox" Removable top clothes and scarf. Plastic eyes and felt hands. Tag: Floppy Sox/Knickerbocher. Still available.

Cloth--8" "Floppy Sox" Felt hands. Removable top clothes and bonnet. Plastic eyes. Tag: Floppy Sox/Knickerbocher. Still available.

8" All hard plastic with floss blonde glued on wig. Sleep eyes with long molded lashes. Head fits flush onto neck. Walker. Marks: A Hollywood Doll, around a star. (Courtesy Bessie Carson)

Two originally dressed Ginny dolls by Vogue. (Courtesy Marge Meisinger)

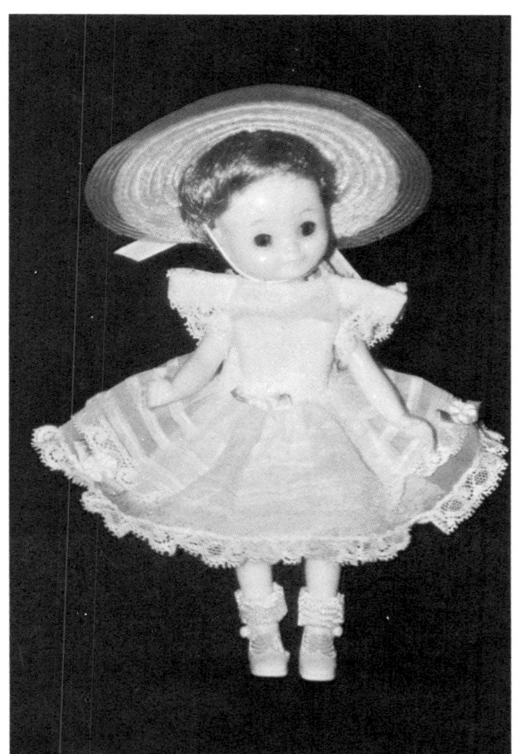

Tiny Betsy McCall dressed in "Sunday Best" (B-41). Made by American Character Doll Co. (Courtesy Jay Minter)

Vogue's Ginny doll dressed in two original outfits. (Courtesy Marge Meisinger)

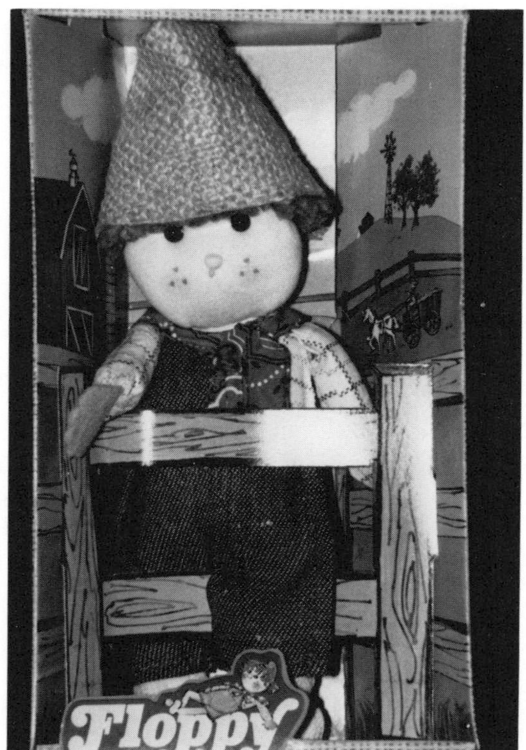


Cloth--8" "Floppy Sox" "Sock" doll with felt hands, plastic eyes. Removable top and bonnet. Tag: Floppy Sox/Knicherbocher. Still available.

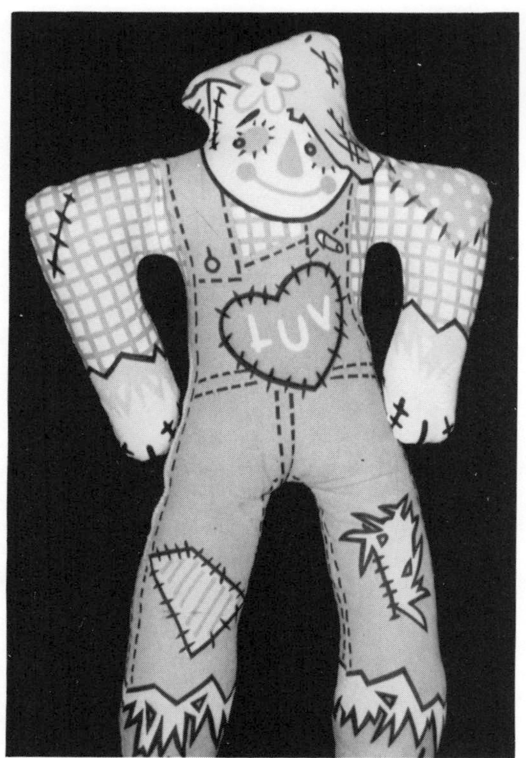


Cloth--17" Brock Candy "Sam The Scarecrow" $10.00. (Courtesy Robbie Heitt)

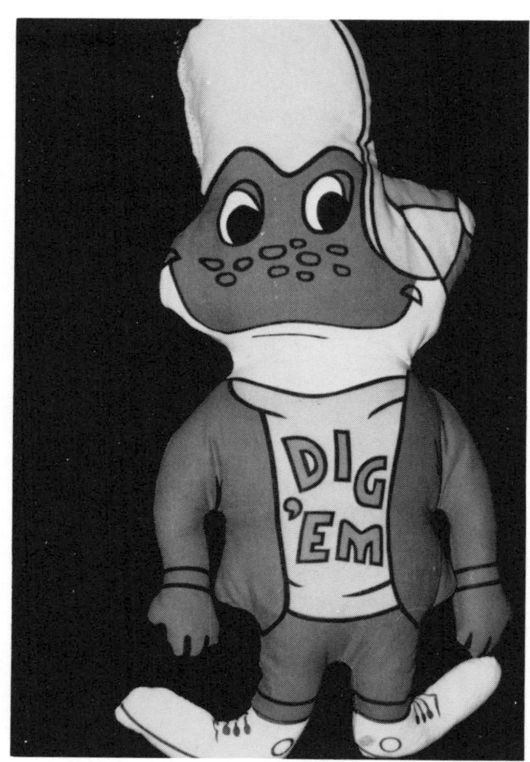


Cloth--17" "Dig 'Em Frog" All printed stuffed cloth. Premium (1973-74) from Kellogg's Corn Flakes. Marks: 1973 Kellogg Co., on back of right foot. $4.00.

Cloth--18" "Jack Frost" Premium Doll. $8.00.

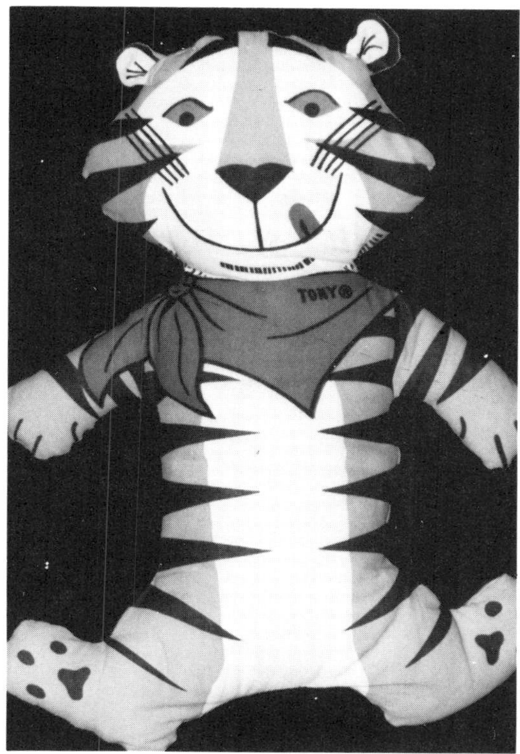


Cloth--18" "Tony, the Tiger" Kellogg Co. 1973. $12.00. (Courtesy Robbie Heitt)

Cloth--14" "Sugar Bear" $9.00. (Courtesy Robbie Heitt)

Cloth--19" "Archie" $12.00. (Courtesy Robbie Heitt)

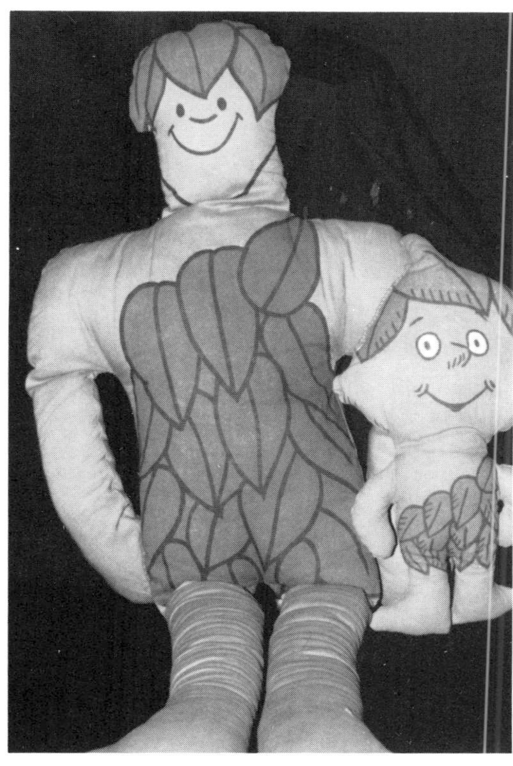

Cloth--27" "Jolly Green Giant" & 10" "Sprout" Giant, $18.00. Sprout, $7.00. (Courtesy Robbie Heitt)

Deluxe--Dawn on her "Floral Stand." Came in pink, yellow, green and blue. Will hold 3 dolls. Doll comes with each stand. Bendable knees. Marks: K11A, on head.

7½" "Muffie"--All hard plastic. Walker head turns. All original. Marks: Storybook/Dolls/California/Muffie. (Courtesy Bessie Carson)

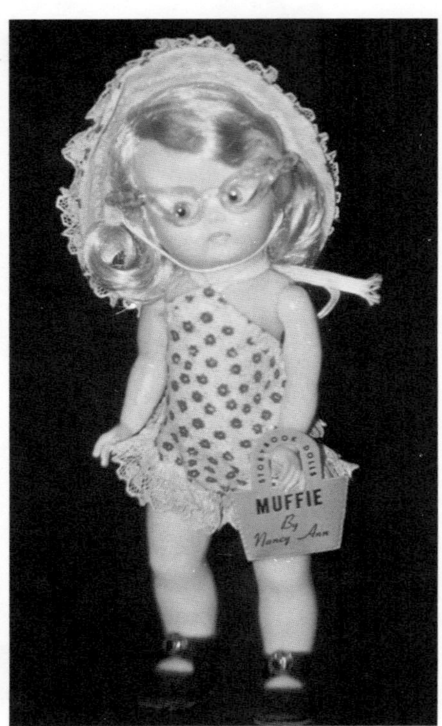

7½" Early brown eyes "Muffie" by Nancy Ann Storybook Dolls. All hard plastic. Not a walker. Brown sleep eyes with no brows or lashes. Painted lashes above eyes. No Muffie name on doll, used purse (paper to identify. Marks: Storybook/Dolls/California. (Courtesy Bessie Carson)

9" "Court Man & Women"--All felt. Jointed at shoulders and hips. Removable clothes. Mohair wigs. Painted features. Marks: Old Cottage/Doll/Hand Made/in/Great Britain. (Courtesy Marge Meisinger)

Hong Kong--7" "Bo Bo" Plastic with vinyl head. Sculptured, painted eyes. Painted clown's face. Rooted hair but bald on top with hole for hat. Posable head. Original. Marks: Made In/Hong Kong, on head and back. (Courtesy Marie Ernst)

11" "Trine"--All rather orange vinyl. Rooted red hair. Painted green eyes. One molded tooth. Marks: The V/bee/W. Goebel/1957/Charlot BYJ/2901/Made in Germany. 10, inside ears. O2, back of left leg. 01, back of right leg. Charlot Byj is the designer. (Courtesy Virginia Jones)

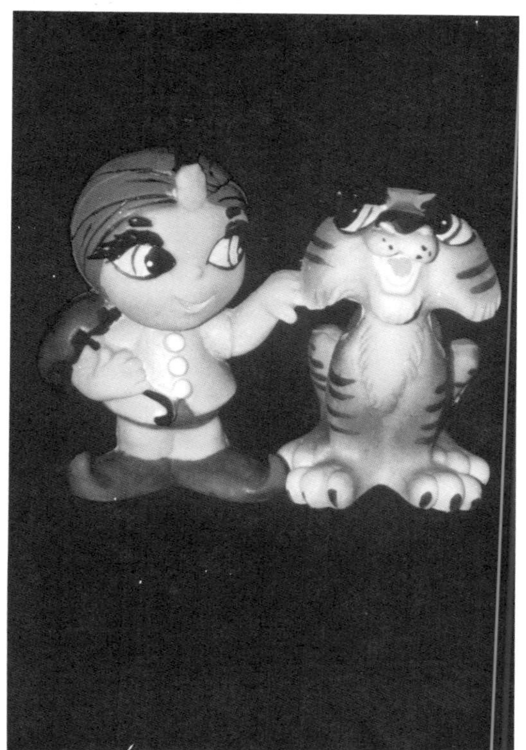

Sambo restaurant advertising dolls. See Squeeze Toy section for marks.

17" "Mary Hoyer"--All hard plastic. Marks: Original/Mary Hoyer/Doll, in circle on back. Dress tag: Handmade/Annie Kilborn. Information on the Mary Hoyer Doll Co. is located in Series II, page 182. (Courtesy Mary Partridge)

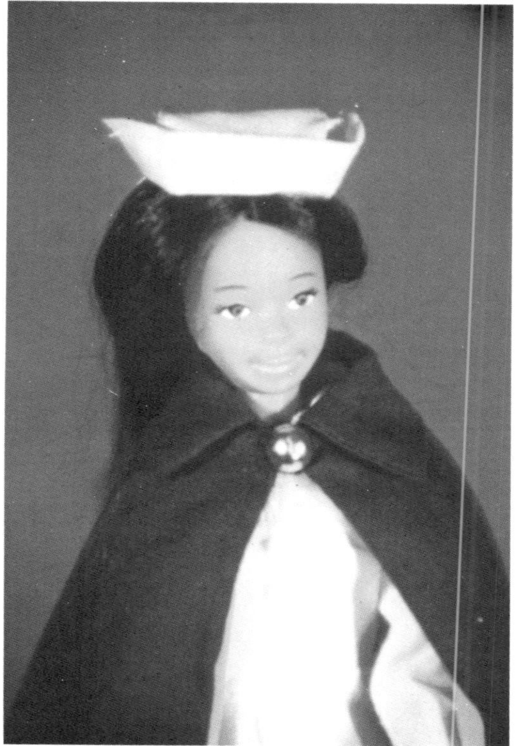

"Police Nurse" See teen section for black/white photo and description.

Cloth--20" "Jack Frost" Premium doll. $5.00.

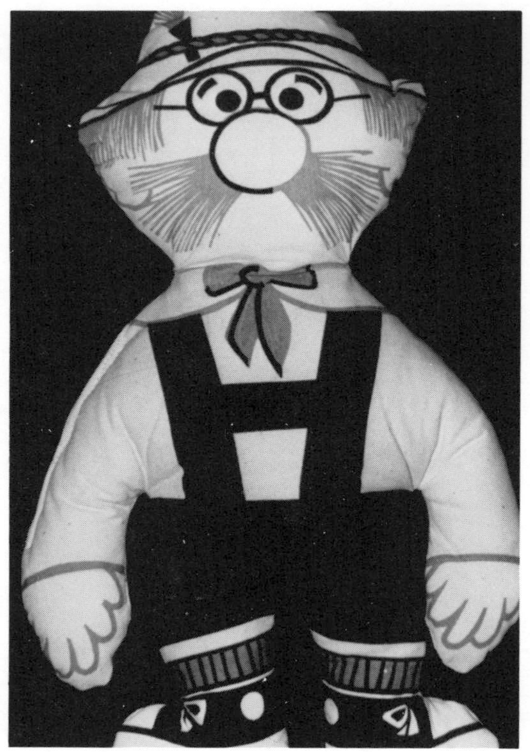

Cloth--12" "Chocolate Man" from Nestles as a premium doll. $5.00.

Cosmopolitan--8" "Ginger" shown in Disneyland dress. Doll: $5.00. Outfit: $5.00. 1955. (Courtesy Marge Meisinger)

Cosmopolitan--8" "Mousketeer" Another version of the outfit shown in Series II. Doll: $5.00. Outfit: $3.00. 1954. (Courtesy Marge Meisinger)

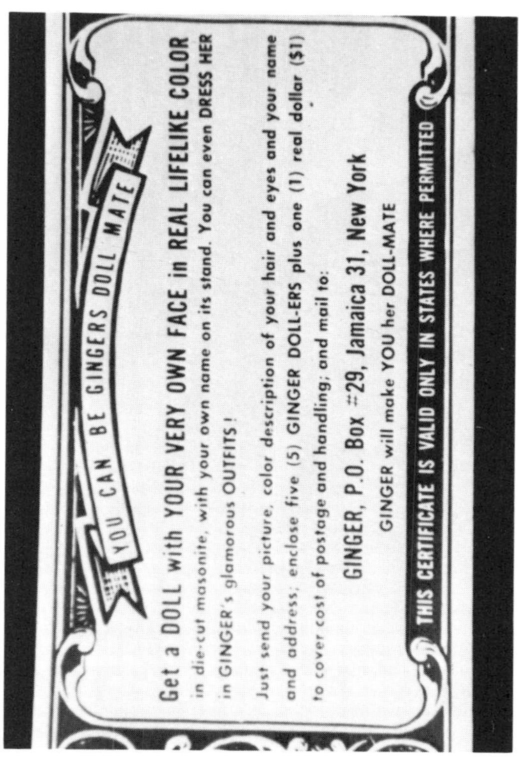

YOU CAN BE GINGERS DOLL MATE

Get a DOLL with YOUR VERY OWN FACE in REAL LIFELIKE COLOR
in die-cut masonite, with your own name on its stand. You can even DRESS HER
in GINGER's glamorous OUTFITS!

Just send your picture, color description of your hair and eyes and your name
and address; enclose five (5) GINGER DOLL-ERS plus one (1) real dollar ($1)
to cover cost of postage and handling; and mail to:

GINGER, P.O. Box #29, Jamaica 31, New York
GINGER will make YOU her DOLL-MATE

THIS CERTIFICATE IS VALID ONLY IN STATES WHERE PERMITTED

Cosmopolitan--Ginger Doll-er. With this certificate, a child could have a die-cut masonite doll with her own face. She had to send a picture, give color of hair and eyes. This "doll" could wear Ginger's clothes. 1956.

Cosmopolitan--Shows a Ginger Doll Mate. 1956.

Cosmopolitan--Shows box top for the 10" "Make-Ur-Own" doll kit.

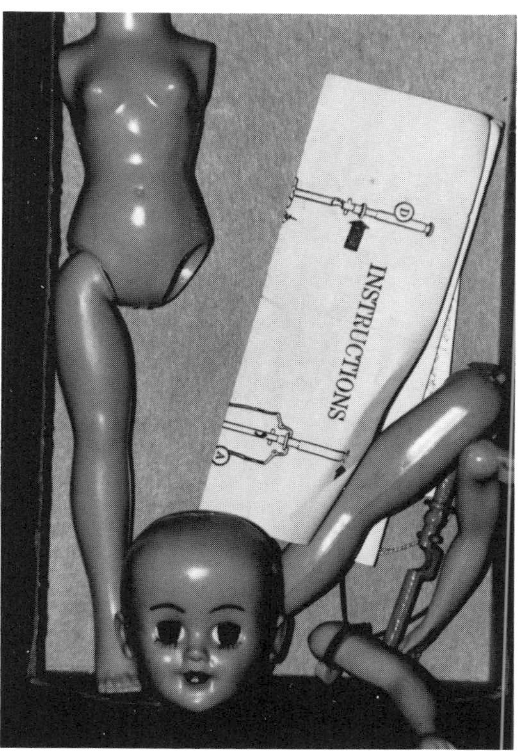


Cosmopolitan--10" "Make-Ur-Own" Complete Walking Doll Kit. All hard plastic. Dark blue sleep eyes/long molded lashes. High heel feet. Came with wig and shoes. 1956. $8.00. (Courtesy Bessie Carson)

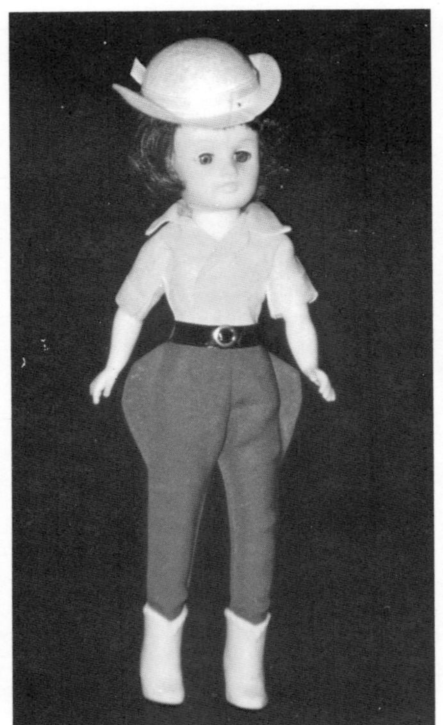

10½" "Miss Nancy Ann"--All vinyl with jointed waist. Blue sleep eyes/molded lashes. Tagged riding habit. Marks: Nancy Ann, on head. (Courtesy Bessie Carson)

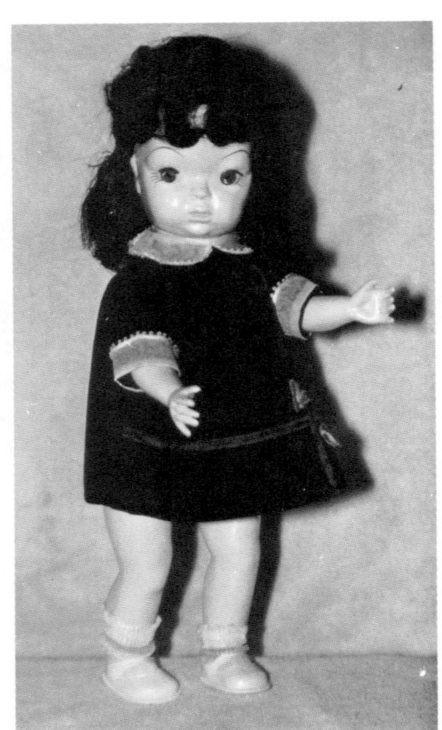

16½" "Mary Jane"--All hard plastic. Walker, head turns. Flirty, sleep eyes/long molded lashes. Marks: None. (Courtesy Margaret Biggers)

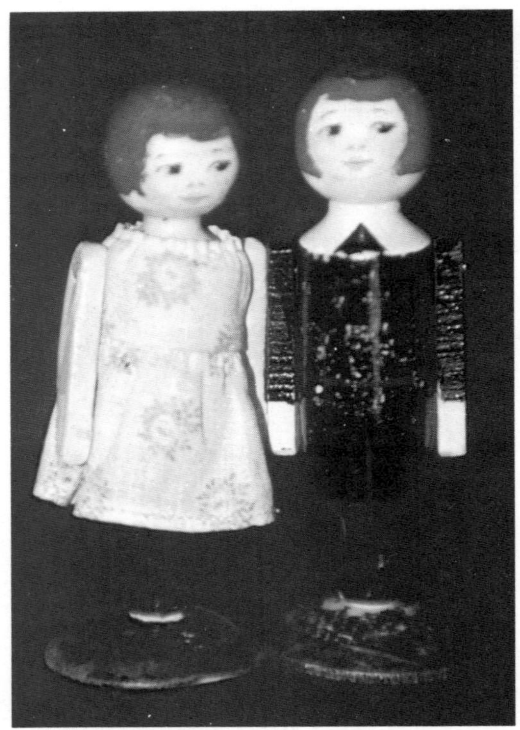

4" All wood. One piece body, legs and head. Jointed shoulders only. Pegged to fit into stand. Nailed on clothes. Oil painted features and hair. Marks: Patent Pending, on bottom of base. (Courtesy Mary Partridge)

11½" "Cleodine"--All vinyl. Sleep eyes. Squeeker in head. Nurser. Marks: Turtle in diamond/Schildkrot/Germany, on back. Turtle mark/63, on head. 1958. (Courtesy Virginia Jones)

Cosmopolitan--Shows "Zip" the monkey, pet for the Ginger doll, in the six outfits he was able to wear. The monkey is all vinyl with jointed shoulders and hips. Has sleep eyes. Marks, if any, would be CBS Television Enterprises, or Columbia Broadcasting System.

Cosmopolitan--Zip of Television fame, shown holding one of his own vinyl images and a Ginger doll. 1956.

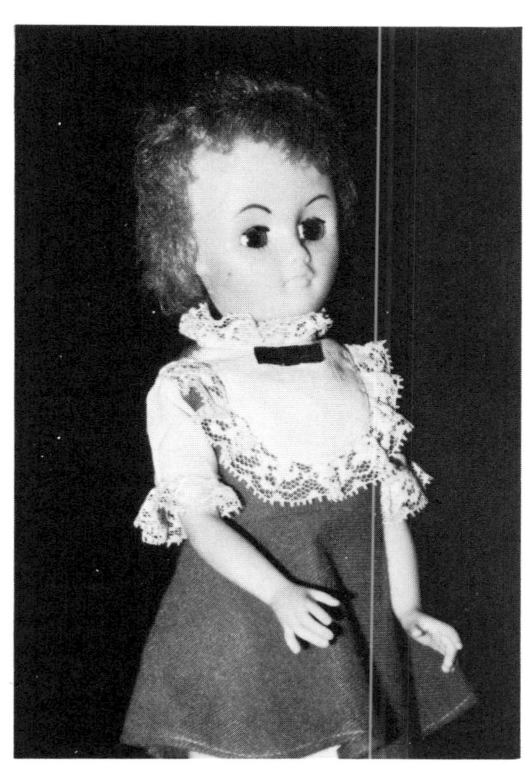

Cosmopolitan--14" "Merry" Plastic and vinyl with rooted blonde hair. Blue sleep eyes. High heel feet. Was originally dressed in red gown with white "fur" trim. Marks: AE 1406/41, on head. Backward AE, lower back. 1960. $3.00.

Dakin, R--15" "Dream Doll, Aloha Alice" All stuffed nylon net. Painted features. Glued on dark blonde wig. Original. Tag: Dream Dolls/R. Dakin & Co. 1956. $6.00. (Courtesy Virginia Jones)

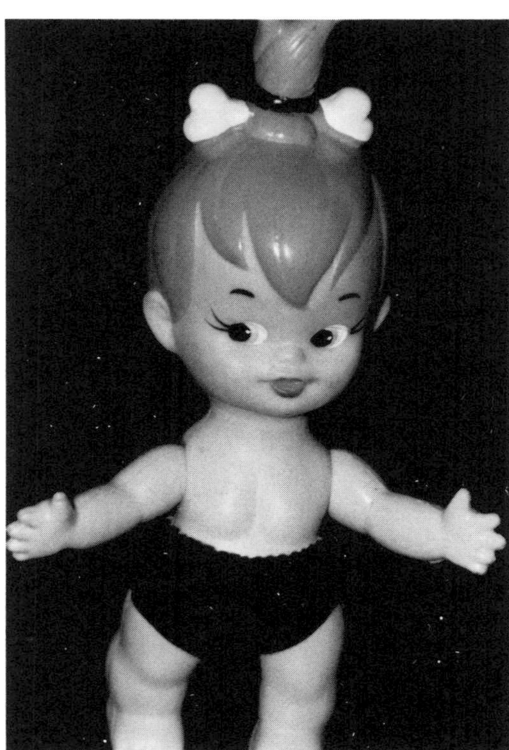

Dakin, R.--8" "Pebbles" Plastic with vinyl head. Marks: R. Dakin Co./Product of Hong Kong, on back. Trademark of Screen Gems/Hanna Barbera Corp./Productions Inc./1970, on head. $3.00. (Courtesy Maxine Heitt)

# DAM TROLLS

Trolls, in Scandanavians language are what leprechauns are to the Irish or genies are to the Persians. In Norse mythology trolls are little creatures and at the same time, in Icelandic literature they are giants who dwell underground. Trolls are very kind to humans but are said to be mischievious and do things like stealing food and in some cases anything that is not nailed down. They are supposed to be able to make themselves invisible, can foretell the future and, if believed in very strongly, they can bestow great wealth and great strength upon people. Because of the nature of beliefs, the trolls are both loved and feared by Scandanavian people.

In 1952, Helena and Martti Kuuskoski of Tampere, Finland, "invented" the modern day version of the troll. Helena was the designer and since they were poor, the Kuuskoskis made two doll-size clowns, stuffed them with sawdust and put them under the Christmas tree for their two children.

Helen Kuushoski made a few more of these clowns and tried to sell them at the local shops and couldn't find anyone who wanted them but one shop keeper gave her an idea, he told her to make them smaller and put a string through the head so they could be hung in an automobile, and that is what she was trying to do when she accidently "put everything together" and up came the troll design. It was an instant success. It was not long before the Kuuskoskis had over 100 people working making these lovable creatures.

It did not take long for the trolls to enter the United States and they were very popular and reached a peak about 1966. Trolls have been used for many advertising ventures and premiums. All trolls are collectable and the most desirable seems to the DAM ones as they are the original design of the Kuuskoskis. Second are the ones that have a horsehoe on the feet; they too are the original design.

Dam Things--Troll shown dressed as "Sappy Claws" Marks: Dam, on back. $3.00.

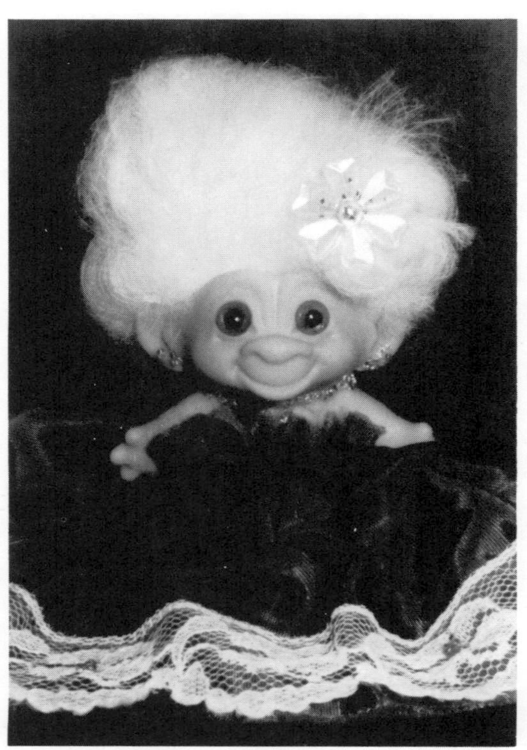

Dam Things--3" "Nite Out Troll" All vinyl with inset, stationary brown eyes. Glued on white mohair wig. Glued on sequins earrings and necklace. Original clothes. Marks: '64/Dam, on back. 1964. Made by Thomas Dam, Denmark, Dist: Scanda House. $3.00.

Dam Things--7½" "Troll Bank" All vinyl. Jointed neck only. Inset stationary green eyes. Green mohair glued on wig. Marks: USA Feeler Co., on head. Wrist Tag: The First National Bank of Odessa. Used as a promotion item. Original. Made for Feeler by Dam, Things, Ind. 1967. $7.00.

Dam Things--Troll shown in outfit called "Lover Boy-Nik. Marks: Dam, on back. $3.00.

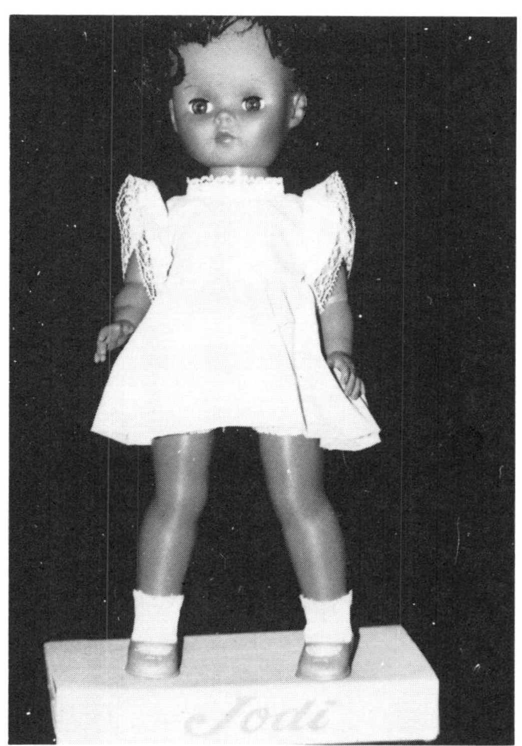


Dee Dee--15" "Jodi" Plastic with vinyl arms and head. Brown sleep eyes/lashes. Original. Marks: AE/7, on head. $3.00.

Deluxe Topper--Deluxe Topper, Deluxe Reading, Topper Corp., Topper Toys & Deluxe Toy Creations are all the same company. Refer to Series I, page 61 for full company information. Complete Dawn series shown in Series II, pages 63 to 69. For the two year production of the Dawn dolls, 56 outfits were made. I have tried to show as many as possible, although I was only able to buy 33 of them.

23" "Sweet Amy" School Girl Doll. One piece body, arms and legs of latex. Vinyl head. Blue sleep eyes. Was $16.98 new. Accessories: Schoolbag, blackboard, eraser, chalk, coloring book, jigsaw puzzle, flag. Marks: A-1, on head. Made by Deluxe Toy Creations, part of Deluxe Reading (out of business). $25.00.

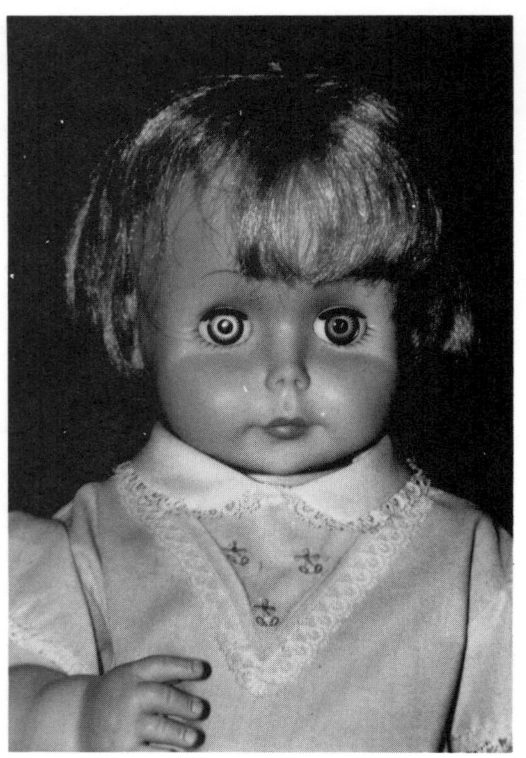

Deluxe Reading--16" "Schoolgirl Writing Doll" Plastic with rigid vinyl arms and head. **Arms move in all direction, fingers especially molded to hold crayon. Came with and without freckles.** Marks: 1963/Deluxe Reading/2. $8.00. (Courtesy Mrs. John Eades)

Deluxe--"Dawn's Sofa Telephone" White and blue. Battery operated conversation between Angie and Dawn. Phone case marked: QEN/ Pat. P. 69528/71647/72768/51406/53452/Made In Japan. Has record that is reversable. $15.00.

"Dawn and Her Fashion Show" The stage, etc. was made by Irwin Toy Limited of Canada. Doll by Topper. Marks on Doll: 586/H11A. Dress is gold top with silver and gold threaded, 2 tier pink skirt. $12.00.

Deluxe Topper--Dawn's "Dress Shop" Lever operated, makes her turn. $12.00. (Courtesy Sibyl DeWein)

Deluxe--Dawn's Beauty Parlor. Pink/lavender/ white chair that swivels and tilts back. Pink/ lavender hair dryer that adjusts. Pink/lavender stool. Pink/lavender/white sink and stand marked: Cat. No. 1031/Made by/Topper Corp./ Elizabethport, N.J. $10.00

Disney, Walt--6" (Size of head only) "Grumpy" All dark brown rubber. Molded beard. Painted features. Marks: Gund/W.D.P. 1938. $12.00.

Disney, Walt--11" "Minnie & Mickey Mouse" All rubber. Marks: 50/Walt Disney Prod./Sun Rubber Co./Barberton, Ohio. ca. 1945. Mickey: $20.00. Minnie: $25.00. (Courtesy Maxine Heitt)

Disney, Walt--26" "Mickey Mouse" Hard plastic walker, head turns. Vinyl face mask with felt ears. Vinyl molded on shoes. Marks: 207, on back of hands. 1954. $65.00. (Courtesy Barbara Coker)

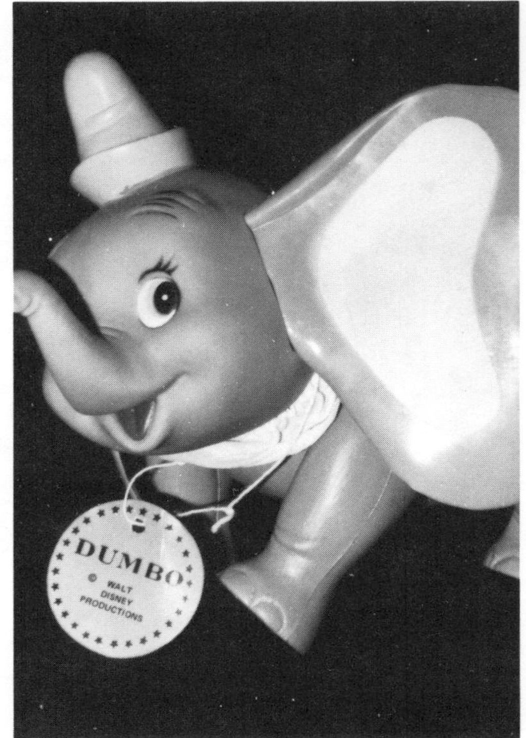


Disney, Walt--7" "Dumbo" Plastic and vinyl. Marks: Walt Disney Productions/R. Dakin Company/Product of Hong Kong. 1973. $2.00.

## SMALL WORLD DOLLS

Boys and girls could take a "boat trip around the world" at the UNICEF exhibit at the New York World's Fair. Walt Disney designed this wonderful exhibit called "It's A Small World" which was dedicated by the Pepsi Cola Company to all the World's children.

The Tower of the Four Winds soared over the UNICEF exhibit that contained the life sized figures that were dressed in native costumes of 12 foreign lands.

By May 1965 8" replicas of the life size figures appeared to be advertised as Ambassadors for peace. Each was dressed in authentic foreign costume. Each doll came with the name and address of a pen pal and each came with an international 15 language dictionary plus pen and stationery. The dolls were made by Pressman-Lipson and extra costumes of any nation were sold at $1.89 each.

The original Pepsi Cola UNICEF exhibit had 12 figures and Pressman released 15 foreign costumed dolls. I have only been able to locate 13 and do not know what the other 2 are: Japan, Switzerland, India, Holland, Africa, France, Chile, Spain, Russia, Ireland, South America, Scotland, Turkey. I would venture a guess that they were England and Germany.

Disney, Walt--8" "Small World Doll-Scotland" Plastic and vinyl. Painted features. 1965. $10.00 (Courtesy Marge Meisinger)

Disney, Walt--8" "Chile" A Small World Doll. Plastic and vinyl. Painted features. 1965. $10.00. (Courtesy Marge Meisinger)

Disney, Walt--8" "Small World Doll" Country unknown. Plastic and vinyl. Painted features. Hat belongs to "Chile" Doll. $10.00. (Courtesy Marge Meisinger)

# Doll Artists

As long as there have been dolls there have been doll artists, even if it were just an uncle making a wood doll for his favorite niece. In modern times that we are interested in (1935-1976) the mass amount of dolls have been designed by many artists and the best known are people such as Bernard Lipfert, Eloise Wilkin and Mollye or the largest and one of the most respected is the Marvin Glass Co. who has over 70 designers working for them. These "type" of artists are referred to as "commercial," I guess because they sell a lot of dolls; but at any rate there is a group of American doll artists that are referred to as just "doll artists" and it is not "acceptable" to refer to them as "commercial" although many sell a pretty gigantic amount of "dolls" and many of their creations are not really dolls but figurines. There seems to be a very thin line between the two. (figurines and dolls).

The difference seems to lay in the fact that the-"commercial" artists are filling the needs of the American public and the magic of childhood where as the American Doll Artist is filling the collector needs of the COLLECTOR. In fact, the most sought after artist dolls, by the collectors, are the ones made by artists who have died, retired, are very ill or getting ready to be ill. This seems to please collectors as they know the prices will increase on the dolls. Second in desirability is the "limited" edition dolls. Here I am referring to original designs.

As in every case there are exceptions and a few of these American Doll artists stand out for their ability to capture what "dolls" are all about. The first on my own list would be any dolls made by Dewees Cockran. They are all delightful children who not only appeal to the child but also to the adult. Dewees has always been accepted as an American Doll Artist even though she certainly was "commercial" during the 1930's when her designs were used by the Effanbee Doll Co.

There are many other of these artists that appeal both to children and adults but there are a great many that in no way can it be said that there is "children" appeal as no adult, in their right mind, would allow a child to play with such dolls, for they are truly display manikins for elaborate clothes.

The name of the American doll artist group is the National Institute of American Doll Artists (N.I.A.D.A.). It was formed in 1963 with 11 Charter members and Helen Bullard was its founder. Prior to its existence, there were a great many artists at work, such as Madame Alexander, Grace Storey Putnam, Bernard Ravca (native of France), Dorothy Hiezer, Dewees Cockran, Gertrude Florian, Emma Clear and Maggie Head, just to name a few. Some of these artists would be denied membership to N.I.A.D.A. on various grounds.

The requirements for artist membership is supposed to be based on high standards, meet the organization's aims, have "genuine" originality and be professional in craftsmanship and the creations should not be "commercial."

New members are presented as candidates through sponsorship of one of the artist members. This artist member familiarizes herself with the work and BACKGROUND of the applicant, provides a completed questionnaire and arranges for the doll examples to be delivered to the artist meeting (held at the National Convention of the United Federation of Doll Clubs as ALL members of

N.I.A.D.A. must be members of the Federation) at which time judging takes place. The dolls and background material of the candidate are carefully considered and vote is taken.

These "accepted," by N.I.A.D.A., artists use many medias to get across their idea of dolls. They work in felt, ceramic, porcelain, composition, papier mache, wax, cloth, latex, wood, stone, clay, bronze, sheet metal, paper, plastics, etc.

It is to be assumed that N.I.A.D.A. artists are the "amateurs" and the commercial artists are the "pros," set up such as Olympic competitors are amateurs and major league members are pros. At any rate let's look at some of the pros: Marvin Glass Co., Eloise Wilkin and Mollye Goldman.

Marvin Glass, the owner and President of Marvin Glass & Associates played a major part in innovating new styles and concepts in the toy industry for over 35 years. He built a company that employs over 75 designers, engineers, scientists, model makers and artists. A complete unit for the design of toys.

The following was taken from a Press Release from the firm of Aaron Cushman and Associates Inc., the Public-Relations firm that handles the Marvin Glass account. The time of this release was at the death of Marvin Glass, in January 1974.

MARVIN GLASS

'Mr. Glass was the outspoken champion of safe toys, the first to openly take a position in opposition to war toys and always upheld the ingenuity, integrity and technological superiority of the American toy manufacturer. In February 1970, Glass was honored at the British International Toy Fair in Brighton, England when he was named Toy Man of the Year.

Credited with being the father of automated toys, Marvin Glass was also known as the originator of proper names for toys and the creator of the first toy to participate with children in play, the first toy with selective sound, the first talking puzzle, the first three dimensional game and the first games based on the use of the electric light.

Mr. Glass's designs have put 500 toys on the market in the past 10 years. During his lifetime he held several hundred patents.

Mr. Glass felt that toys were as much a part of the entertainment world as the theatre. He saw the toy as a catalyst between the child and the world of fantasy. To him the word "toy" had become a misnomer denoting something frivolous, inconsequential and even rudimentary and he felt this image was inaccurate. To Glass, modern toys were important products of highly sophisticated design requiring advanced technologies and were often forerunners of adult tools, appliances and vehicles.

Glass organized his company in 1941 with capital of $80.00. The son of an engineering consultant, he was raised in Evanston, Illinois and he was making toys in his childhood--cardboard animals, a submarine that shot wooden torpedoes and models of pirate ships. He was educated at military prep school in Wisconsin and the University of Chicago.

His pointed and poignant views on dolls, games and toys made him the subject of numerous national magazine articles. Consumer publications, including Time, Newsweek, Business Week, Fortune, Coronet, Playboy, Better Homes & Gardens and similar magazines as well as newspapers nationwide, recognized him in print as the nation's leading designer.'

Since the death of Marvin Glass, the new head of the firm is Anson Isaacson. Mr. Isaacson has been active in the toy industry for over a quarter of a century and it was in 1954 that he became associated with the Ideal Toy Company in the engineering department. From there he rose through the ranks first as manager of the plastics devision and then became vice president of product development. It was in this position that he met Marvin Glass, the independent toy designer.

In 1964 Isaacson left Ideal to become president of the troubled A.C. Gilbert Company. Three years later the company was liquidated and Isaacson started his own marketing consulting business with Marvin Glass as one of his clients.

Isaacson joined the staff of Marvin Glass & Associates in 1971. When Marvin Glass died in 1974, Isaacson was elected managing partner of the firm. In this position, he and eight general partners of the company work closely, continuing the design philosophy and goals that were initiated by the late Marvin Glass.

No single individual is responsible for a completed product from Marvin Glass & Associates. A new concept may be the result of the input of many staff workers, artists, engineers, designers, etc. The General Partners are involved and aware of the progress in all stages of development to final completion of model or proto-type.

Toy manufacturers do not come to Marvin Glass asking for a new toy or doll development. When Marvin Glass comes up with a new concept, a proto-type is made up, and they go to any manufacturer who they think would be interested in it and sell them the manufacturing rights.

It was the personal observation of Laura K. Zwier, who

conducted the interview with Jeffrey Breslow, a General Partner of Marvin Glass & Associates, for me, that Marvin Glass seems to be an 'invention' factory. The manufacturers have their own product development departments, but will also buy new concepts from an outside source if they feel it will be a highly marketable product.

All work is done under closely guarded conditions to prevent possible disclosure of product ideas in stage of development to possible competitors. This is reflected in the new headquarters building of Marvin Glass & Associates at 815 North LaSalle in Chicago as the workshops and design studios are off limits to anyone besides authorized staff members. A unique closed-circuit television system is used to identify arriving visitors.

The exterior of the Marvin Glass & Associates building

The following is a list of some of the dolls designed by Marvin Glass & Associates and does not include them all:
Tiffany Taylor for Ideal Toy Co. (refer this Vol.)
Lazy Dazy for Ideal Toy Co. (refer to Vol. I)
Kissy for Ideal Toy Co. (refer to Vol. I)
Real Live Lucy for Ideal Toy Co. (refer to Vol. II)
Tubsy for Ideal Toy Co. (refer to Vol. I)
April Showers for Ideal Toy Co. (refer to Vol. I)
Dusty for Kenner (refer this Vol.)
Nancy Nonsense for Kenner (refer this Vol.)
Polly Pretend for Amsco (refer to this Vol.)
Baby Peek-A-Boo for Hasbro (refer to Vol. II)
Lainie for Mego (refer to Vol. II)
Peggy Pen-Pal for Horsman (refer to Vol. II)
Pirate Series for Lesney (refer this Vol.)

To sum up the design concepts of the Marvin Glass & Associates would be look at a couple of their doll designs: for example, Tiffany Taylor reflects current real-life interest in changing hair color, and in interest of safety, it is done by non-chemical means; Dusty represents the new athletic freedom of today's women. She can simulate the action of various sports, wears a casual hairdo and make up.

Now let's take a look at an individual American Doll Artist. The following is reprinted with permission. Originally written for United Federation of Doll Clubs publication "Doll News."

# Contemporary Collectables: The Work of Eloise Wilkin

by Pat Stewart

When my first son was about a year old (1950), I bought a little Golden Book entitled "Busy Timmy" to read to him. This I did over and over until the pages were tattered. That book inspired my personal admiration society for Eloise Wilkin, the illustrator of Busy Timmy. Through the years that followed there were 3 more children and many more Little Golden Books bought and read in our house but Busy Timmy remained the favorite, by now really worn to a frazzle! A second favorite came on the scene with my daughter; this was "Baby Dear" and produced in conjunction with it was a doll, the original Baby Dear from Vogue Dolls Inc. In the meantime I had begun to collect dolls and was later invited to join a doll club.

About four years ago at a club meeting someone brought in a current book illustrated by Eloise Wilkin and a number of other ladies expressed their admiration for her work. They had been saving her books as I had. We decided we wanted to know about her, so I wrote many letters to try and contact her. Then one day there was a letter from Mrs. Sidney J. Wilkin with my questions answered and a handwritten list of books she had illustrated. We formed the Eloise Wilkin Fan Club and had our first meeting on February 29, 1968.

Eloise Burns (Wilkin) was born in Rochester, New York. She spent most of her childhood in New York City. At 11 she won a prize in a Wanamaker drawing contest for New York school children; this marked the beginning of her career. After completing the illustration course at the Rochester Institute of Technology, she did free lance work for a year. She went to New York City and obtained a job the very first day. Her first book was "The Shining Hours" for the Century Company. Four years later she married Sidney Wilkin. They had 4 children which kept her busy from doing too much drawing for the next 8 to 10 years. In 1944, she signed a contract with Simon & Schuster of New York which lasted until 1969. She illustrated 47 Little Golden Books for them, while at the same time doing other illustrations, altogether about 81 children's books.

Eloise Wilkin was asked to join the American Artist Group of New York City (Not N.I.A.D.A.) an honor accorded few illustrators. She is listed in Illustrators Of Children's Books-1744-1945, published by the Horn, Inc. Boston and in the Supplement 1946-56.

The book, "Baby Dear" was published in 1961. Vogue Dolls, Inc. produced "original Baby Dear," Eloise Wilkin's first doll, at the same time. It was a sensation! A 14" news article in the New York Times was devoted to it: "Doll Feels and Looks Like Child," the heading proclaimed. It then went on to sing the praises of Baby Dear, saying:

"Unlike most dolls that have a stiff, set personality, this doll called "Baby Dear" is amazing in its seeming ability to change moods and age (counted in months). This circumstance made the doll counter the scene of several controversies as sales clerks tried to convince customers that all the dolls were the same, only the clothing and their posture had been changed."

While I was trying to locate Mrs. Wilkin, one of the many letters I wrote was to Vogue Dolls. I received a very nice reply from the current president which helped me to reach her by mail. At the time Eloise Wilkin took her brown clay model of Baby Dear to the company, Mrs. Jennie Graves, the founder of Vogue, was president. They became close business friends during the years they worked together. In the 1962 Vogue catalog is a letter from Mrs. Graves which says in part, "we were joined a year or so ago, by the adorable Baby Dear, the most real-like infant baby doll in the world." The catalog advertises it as "soft, cuddly, real-live one month old baby, with delicately sculptured chubby features of soft vinyl, downy soft rooted hair, and stuffed to make me feel real. I flop like a real-life new born infant and I fold my way into your arms and heart when you hold me in your arms and love me."

The doll came in 12" and 18" sizes and was priced at $6.00 and $12.00 respectively.

Eloise Wilkin told me that she worked over a 20 year period before she was satisfied with the final design which was produced. I saw a picture of her with a table covered with baby doll heads she had modeled while trying to achieve her goal. Figure 1 shows the doll manufactured by Vogue and produced until 1964. An additional model came out with a moving mechanism and music box in it. There is also a hand puppet with the Baby Dear head.

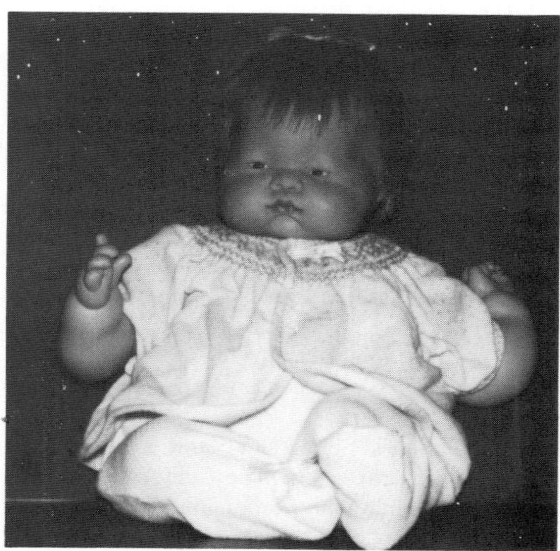

Fig. 1 "Original Baby Dear" Marked on Leg; 1960/E. Wilkin (Courtesy Adele Gioscia)

After this doll, she designed a one year old called "Baby Dear One" for Vogue (see fig. 2). It is described in the 1962 catalog as: "A bouncy, flouncy, 25" one year old darling. The all new Baby Dear One has the same delicately soft, safe, vinyl features of a real live baby, she has sparkling moving eyes and her rooted hair is just like a one year old's, she sits up very well and is so proud of her two front teeth."

She was priced at $15.00. In 1964 Vogue advertised the third Eloise Wilkin design in the series.

Chubby "Two Dear," the cherubic, dimpled, pudgy, toddling 17" two year old likeness of the "Original Baby Dear" made of vinyl, she stands, sits and walks, has sleeping eyes and rooted hair. Too Dear and her twin brother are exquisitely outfitted at from $8.00 to $13.00. (fig. 3)

Once you are familiar with the doll designs of Eloise Wilkin, you will always recognize them. Her detailing is perfect. Each arm, hand and finger has its special little wrinkles and dimples as do the legs, feet and toes. The faces have a quality and individuality unlike that of any other doll.

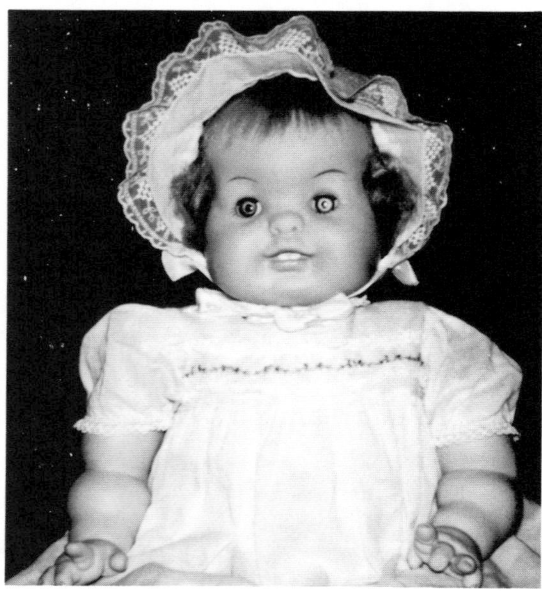

Fig. 2 Baby "Dear One."
Marked on head: 1961/E. Wilkin/Vogue Dolls

Mrs. Wilkins has also designed some dolls for another company which are on the market now but it is not their policy to give credit to any particular artist's work. A few of her dolls are shown in modern doll books. Currently there is an ad on television for Bayer's Asprin which she drew; it shows a little girl looking at a book, turning the pages, ending with a bottle of Children's Bayer Asprin. Many of her books are available now; some are new and some are reprints.

Collecting Eloise Wilkin could be a hobby all in itself; there are individual items which I have not mentioned, while 81 books almost comprise a full library. I feel especially fortunate to have corresponded so much with her from 1968 until the present with the highlight in April 1971. I flew back east and spent two wonderful days as her guest. I met some of her family, including her sister Esther, who has written quite a few of the books I love. I saw places and people she has drawn in her books, sketches she is doing for a coming books AND a partially finished doll sculpture on which she is working. It was a truly thrilling experience to become involved personally in two days in the life of my favorite illustrator of children's books. I shall never forget it."

In addition to the above article by Pat Stewart, I would

Fig. 3 "Too Dear."
Marked on head: 1963/E. Wlkin/Vogue Dolls
(Courtesy Adele Gioscia)

Eloise Wilkin shown in her apartment with the President of her fan club..Pat Stewart. November 1972.

like to point out that not only are the Eloise Wilkin dolls highly collectable, but all her illustrations in books are beautiful additions to a doll collection. Her personality and beauty of spirit are reflected in her drawings which are born to capture the hearts of the children she draws for.

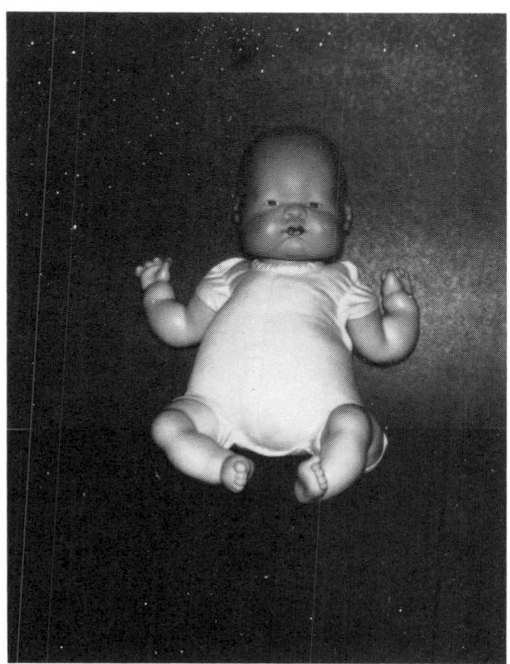

Doll Artist--12" "Baby Dear" Completely bald. Marks: E. Wilkins on left upper leg. (Courtesy Adele Gioscia)

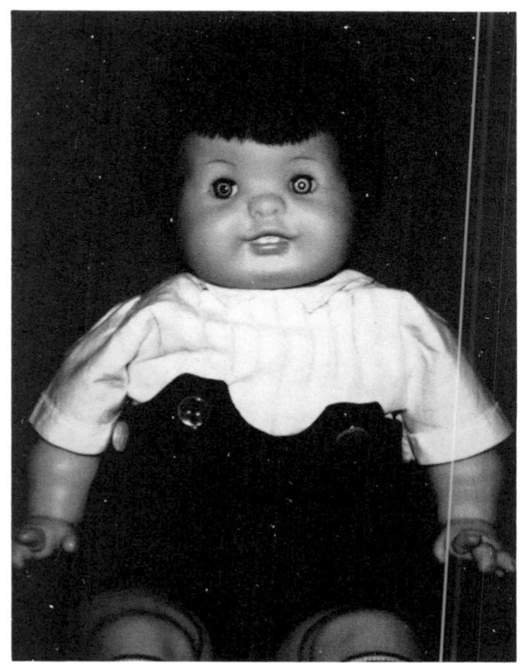

Doll Artist--24" "Bobby Dear One" Boy version of Baby Dear One. Marks: 1961/E. Wilkins/ Vogue Dolls/Incorporated. (Courtesy Adele Gioscia)

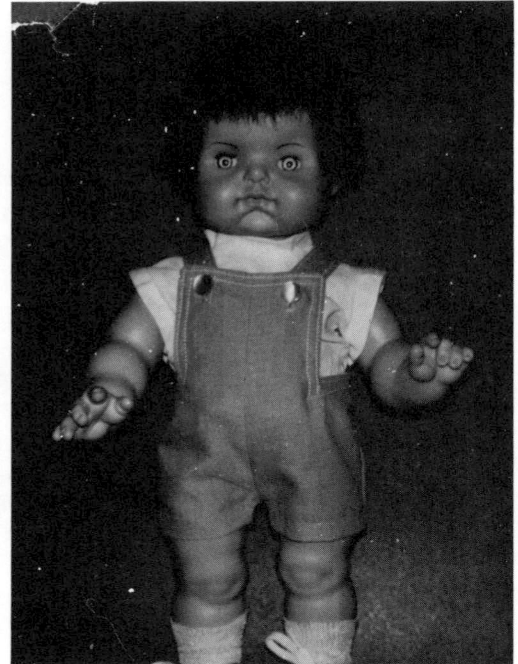

Doll Artist--17" "Too Dear" Dark hair and eyebrows. Vivid blue eyes. Marks: 1963/E. Wilkins/ Vogue Dolls. This is the boy and there was also a matching girl. (Courtesy Adele Gioscia)

Doll Artist--25" "Bobby Dear One & Baby Dear One" Cloth bodies. Vinyl head and limbs. Two lower teeth.

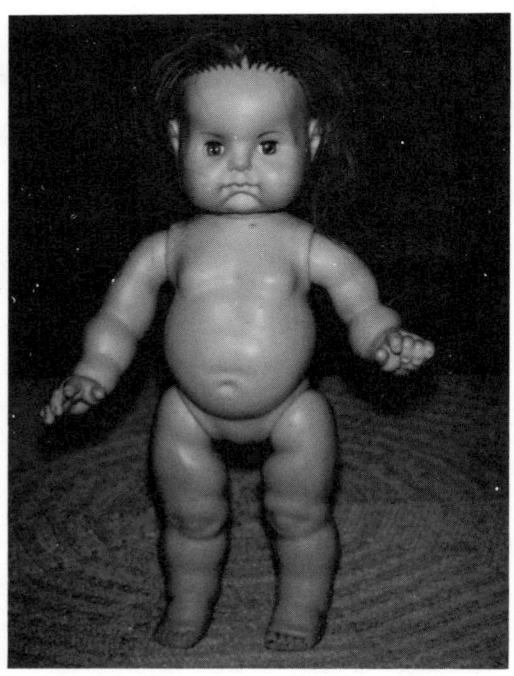

Doll Artist--17" "Baby Dear Too" Shows the body style. Marks: 1963/E. Wilkin/Vogue Doll

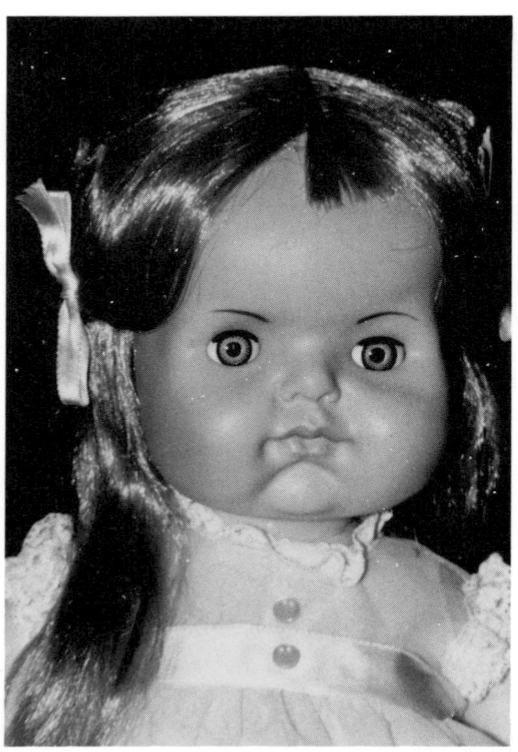

Vogue--17" "Baby Dear Too" Rigid plastic body and legs. Vinyl arms and head. Closed mouth with protruding upper lip. Blue sleep eyes/ slashes. Original clothes. Marks: 1963 E. Wilkin/ Vogue Dolls, on head.

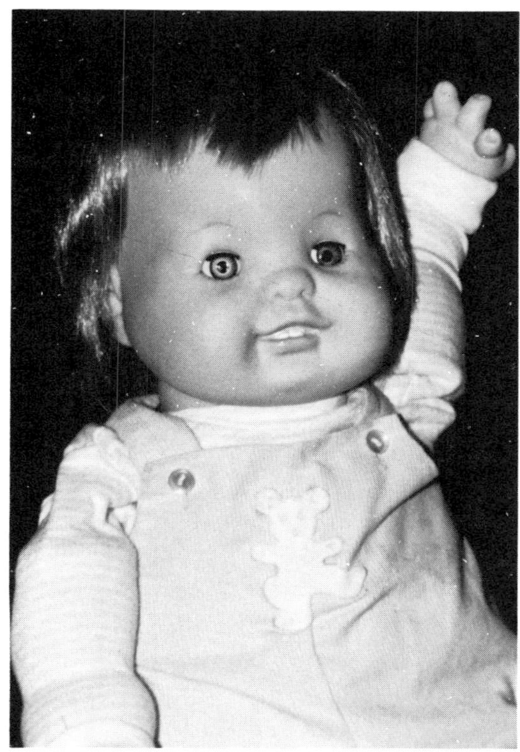

Vogue--23" "Baby Dear One" Cloth body with vinyl arms, legs and head. Blue sleep eyes/lashes. Open/closed mouth with two lower teeth. Marks: E. Wilkin/1961 high on right leg. 1961/E. Wilkin/Vogue Dolls/Incorporated, on head. Original clothes.

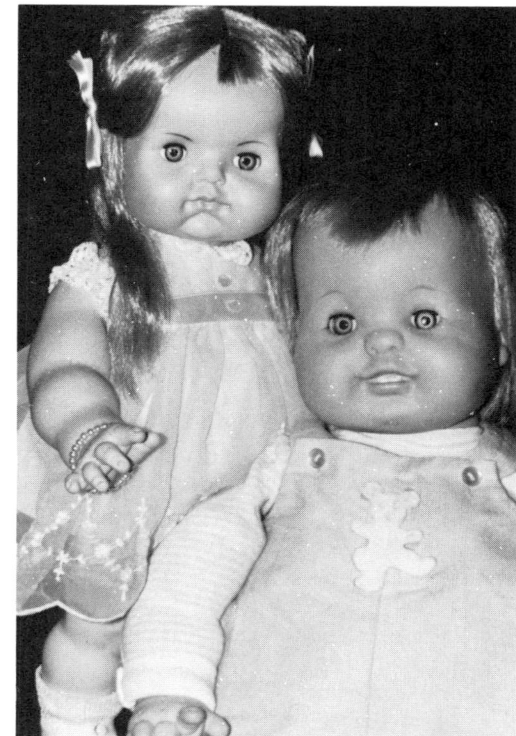

Vogue--Shows Baby Dear One and Baby Dear Too to show the comparative sizes of the heads.

List of Books Illustrated by

## Eloise Wilkin

1927: The Shining Hours
1928: Adventures in Health (Moulton)
1930: The Reckless Seven
1932: The Choosing Book (Dalgliesh)
1936: Robin & Angus (Robinson)
? Robin & Tito (Robinson)
? Rusty Ruston (McNeely)
1938: Mrs. Peregoin & The Yak (Burns)
1939: Mrs. Peregoin at the Fair (Burns)
1939: Going on Nine
1940: A Good House for a Mouse (Eberle)
1941: Sheep Wagon Family
1944: The Great Gold Piece Mystery
1948: Rainbow For Me (Kiser)
1949: Seatmates (Reely)
1949: Apple Tree Cottage
1949: A Baby is Born (Levine & Seligmann)
1949: Sunshine for Merrily (Kiser)
1950: The Tune is in the Tree
1953: Birthday Story (Buntain)
1967: Thank You Book (Zens)
1968: Evening Prayer (Wilkin)
1970: Song of Praise

Illustrated by E. Wilkin 1960

List of "Little Golden Books" Illustrated by Eloise Wilkin

1946: New House in the Forest
1947: Fit It Please
1947: Noises and Mr. Fibberty Jib
1948: Busy Timmy
1948: The New Baby
1948: Come Play House
1949: Good Morning, Good Night
1949: Guess Who Lives Here?
1951: Holiday Book
1951: A Day at the Playground
1952: Prayers For Children
1952: My Toy Box
1952: The Christmas Story
1953: Wiggles
1953: My Kitten
1954: Hi Ho, 3 in a Row
1954: Georgie Finds a Granpa
1954: Linda & Her Little Sister
1954: Hansel & Gretel
1954: The Twins
1954: My Baby Brother
1954: My Puppy
1954: First Bible Stories
1955: The Night Before Christmas
1955: My Snuggly Bunny
1956: My Little Golden Book About God
1956: A Catholic Child's Book About God
1957: The Story of Baby Jesus
1957: Child's Garden of Verses
1957: Lord's Prayer
1958: Baby's Mother Goose
1959: Baby's First Christmas
1959: This World of Ours
1959: We Help Mommy
1960: Baby Looks
1960: Baby Listens
1960: My Dolly & Me
1961: Baby Dear
1962: We Help Daddy
1962: Christmas A B C
1963: My Teddy Bear
1963: Jamie Looks
1965: We Like Kindergarten
1965: Good Little, Bad Little Girl
1967: Play With Me
1969: So Big
1969: The Little Book
1969: Little Boy With a Drum
1970: Eloise Wilkin's Mother Goose
1973: Baby's Birthday

Other Than "Little Golden" Books

1949: Make Believe Parade (Wonder Books)
1950: Busy A B C
1961: The Lord's Prayer
1965: Mother Goose Rhymes (Open Door Book)
1965: Flight Bag Book
1967: Wonders of Nature
1967: Wonders of the Season
1967: Birds
1968: The Golden Calendar
1969: The Golden Treasury
1971: The Baby Book (Golden Shape Book)
1972: I Hear (Heritage Press)
1974: Where Did Baby Go (Little Golden)
1974: Re-release: The New Baby (Little Golden Book)
1975: Book of Prayers

Illustrated by E. Wilkin 1969

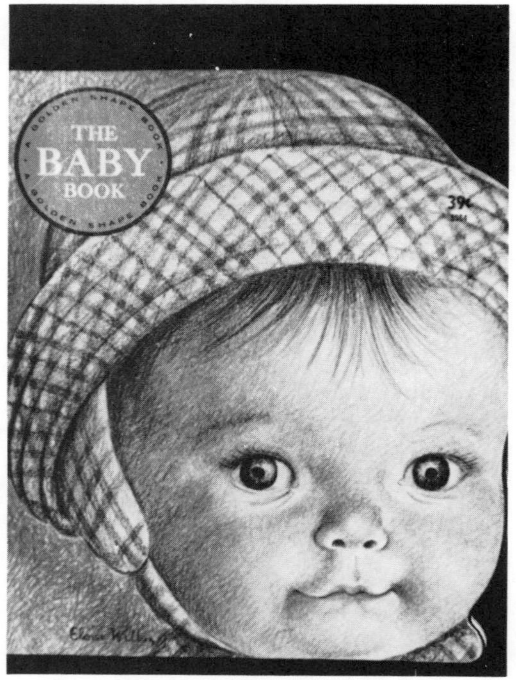


Illustrated by E. Wilkin 1970

# Miss Mollye,
# Americas Leading Doll Designer

Mrs. Mollye Goldman is one of the outstanding women of our times. Her dolls stand out in quality and she was a genius in the clothes design department and not only designed for her own dolls but for other companies also, including Horsman, Effanbee and Ideal. She is the designer/maker of all the Shirley Temple clothes of the 1930's. Her husband is as great of Mollye, in the realm of stuffed animals and his line was called "Golden Fleece," and these animals are as collectable to toy collectors as Mollye dolls are to doll collectors. We will let Miss Mollye tell you about herself in her own words:

"The gentleman who sent you the Mollye history seems to remember more than I do and some day I hope to thank him for the sweet memories. Most of his information is correct and most of it was contained in old Toy magazines, newspaper ads which showed that we had one of the largest factories in the Country, was the largest maker of doll clothes and later had the outstanding line of the 1940 Glamour girls and I recall one ad in the Philadelphia Inquirer, with a model named Charlotta, sitting on Golden Fleece skins wearing the same dress I made for a doll. They did call me America's leading doll designer, at the Chicago Fair, in Toy and Novelties and in many other Trade news items.

I must call my career a stormy one as no women manufacturers showed dolls at the Toy Fairs and it was an uphill climb all the way but to begin my story. I loved dolls as long as I can remember and at the age of 8, I cut up straw hats and made doll clothes and hats out of scraps. I had a beloved Aunt Nettie who saved pieces of material for me to sew with. As I look back now, I see how much my mother was against my sewing for the doll, as she thought I would end up a dressmaker and she did not approve of this and you must remember the times during the turn of the Century, a woman's lot was difficult and many "working women" ended up sewing 16 hours a day for very few dollars. As I loved to sew, I made an apron for my mother and various things for the rest of the children and finally she gave in and agreed to let me continue my sewing.

It was in 1917 that my boyfriend, Meyer Goldman, who is my wonderful husband, enlisted in the Navy and was stationed at the Great Lakes Naval Station in Illinois. It was very cold so he asked me to make sweaters for the boys. I knew nothing about knitting or crocheting but I learned fast enough and night and day I made sweaters.

It was in 1919 that we were married and moved in with his parents as Meyer was still in the Service. One day a call came that he was coming home on a furlough and I wanted to surprise him so I crocheted a multi color wool sweater and hat and in my nervous energy also made an identical outfit and a dressed a 12" celluloid doll. I remember that the sweaters had many ripples.

A short time later Meyer and I were on the Boardwalk of Atlantic City and I had the doll with us when a man approached and asked where I bought the doll and I told him that I had dressed it. He wanted to know if we would sell him a few dozen just like mine and that he would pay very well for them. My answer was "No, I am married."

When we returned to Philadelphia, Meyer returned to his ship and I recalled what the man on the Boardwalk said to me and the very next day I took a trip South where all the wholesale Toy Jobbers were and purchased 6 small 8" celluloid dolls that had movable arms and legs and could stand and sit. My father-in-law laughed at me and said, "You will never stop playing with dolls!" In pink wool, I crocheted short pants, a very full skirt, jacket, muff and booties and when I sat the doll down, she looked like a pancake and that's what I named her.

As I set out to sell my creations, I decided to make my first call to Lit Bros. where a Mrs. McCormac was the buyer and Miss Reba was her assistant. After I showed them my dolls they both smiled as they looked me over. I looked much younger than I was and weighed only 82 pounds. They told me later that they thought I was playing a game but gave me an order for several dozen dolls anyway.

After returning home and working on the orders I had gotten, I recalled an incident of two precious books of yellow trading stamps which netted me a 36" very glamorous bisque head doll with large blue eyes, golden curls, a composition body and marked Germany. What a thrill and joy it was to be surprised by my family, with a gift so desired. In those days it was a great sacrifice to waste two books of stamps for a plaything and after receiving my beautiful doll, I had a guilty conscience but could not part with my doll. My mother and sisters, who were as happy as I was, named her "My Mollye" and after bestowing much love on her and many, many hours of friendship, I thought she looked tired and one day I very carefully had packed her away.

After recalling my childhood gift of love, I went looking for her and I found My Mollye waiting for me. I dressed her in light blue wool knit. A beautiful dress, large hat trimmed in ribbon, a large muff with a rose in the center, gloves and a hand bag. And of course the first one to see her was Miss McCormac as I took her along when I delivered an order for Pancake.

Both Miss Reba and Miss McCormac thought she was very good and I left with several imported dolls and an order for 12 dozen in assorted sizes and colors.

I then called on all the department stores in Philadelphia and all placed orders for this outfit. They brought the dolls to my home and we dressed them. Some of these dolls retailed with prices as high as $25.00. So it was that for two years, I worked with 5 girls in my bedroom and had many women who worked for me, working in their own homes. After two years, we moved to a second floor flat and bought a factory machine.

While at Wanamaker's Department Store, one day, I noticed a beautiful baby doll, 20" long with a composition head, arms and legs and that cried "Mama." I bought her because I thought she was in need of better clothes.

I made that doll a Smoked Pink organy dress and bonnet with fine cotton panties and slip. I trimmed her in bows and took her back to Wanamakers to show her to Mr. McDonald. I remember the doll was marked E.I. Horsman on the back of her head.

With one look at the changed baby doll, Mr. McDonald ordered 12. He took the dolls from stock and they were all Horsman dolls. We undressed the dolls and redressed them in dresses, coats and rompers, all made of good materials. From this I received a staggering order.

It was not very long before we moved to our own home and also rented a large factory flat with 24 sewing machines and still used many "home workers." We made and designed doll clothes for the entire countries Department Stores, for their imported dolls. Price was no object.

A Miss Wheeler was the Toy Buyer for F.A.O. Schwarz and she sent me bisque By-lo babies in all sizes and I designed and made their Christening sets for $85.00 each.

It was in 1923 when Mr. Harold Bowie called to see me at the factory and we agreed to manufacture doll clothes and design exclusively for the Horsman Company and for no other doll manufacturer but that we could continue our business with the stores. Mr. Bowie deposited $10,000.00 to my account for the purchase of materials. It was the most wonderful, trusting business relationship, with the grandest people I have ever met.

Mr. Goldenberger was their designer, Mr. William Eirenfield was the President and Mr. Bowie was in charge of all sales and production. We worked with Horsman until 1932 and both became very successful with all Mollye products. In 1932, Mr. Goldenberger retired, Mr. Eirenfield passed away and Horsman was sold to another doll manufacturer. It was the end of a great era.

We made another contract much on the same basis as the one with Horsman and thinking that they were the same great caliber people as Horsman but how wrong we were! For one entire year we financed them with materials and labor on all the doll clothes they were in need of and we were never compensated at all. They declared themselves bankrupt. It broke us but we paid all their debts and with much determination we stayed in business. It was a time of Depression when the entire country was experiencing sadness and one ray of sunshine, shone during these dark days. Her name was Shirley Temple, a child that made the people forget their own problems for a short time in darkened theatres. I saw the first picture that Shirley Temple played in and fell in love with her. I asked the theater manager where I could reach Shirley Temple so I could use her name and he remarked, "Go ahead and use it, no one knows the kid and you will be doing her a favor." At home, I called on several movie houses and received the same answer, so I set about making a line of doll dresses designed like the ones she wore in the picture and sent them to the Bureau Registration of Design in New York.

It was a few days later that I received a telegram from a gentleman, whom I had always respected, wanting to know about Shirley Temple and wanted me to come to New York to see him.

Arriving in New York, I went directly to his office. He was connected with the Toy Ass'n at the time. He said, "What is this Shirley Temple you made these beautiful dresses for?" I told him about her and that she would make a beautiful doll and that everyone would love her as much as I did. These were his very words, "A child! A doll! You are crazy, no one has ever heard of such a thing." I again told him how wonderful it would be to make a doll of her. He finally agreed and said he would see about tying her up to a contract and if we did, I would make all her doll clothes and, yes, we would make the same arrangements on the same basis as our working arrangement with Mr. Bowie of Horsman's. We shook hands on that and that was our agreement, for he was a gentleman. From 1933 to 1936, I made all of the Shirley Temple clothes they sold for their dolls.

In 1936 this fine gentleman passed away and all promises were broken. I spent many days and nights in New York looking for materials and spent many hours in the factory, advising and designing without any compensation. Making close to 1000 dozen Shirley Temple outfits a week did not keep me from making new creations and in 1935 I had the Lone Ranger, Thief of Bagdad movie tied up, Hollywood Cinema Fashions and designed and made Dolls of all Nations and Beautiful Brides.

We had the most beautiful plant, with all the special pleating machines that we bought for Shirley Temple dresses and in 1940 the Government needed our building for War materials and we turned over our largest floor to them.

Mr. Goldman joined the American Tobacco Co. and became Field Sales Manager and he later joined me in the factory as manager.

Of all the dolls dressed by Mollye Creations, Perky was about the favorite, along with Little Queen and dolls of all Nations. One buyer bought 48,000 Perkys and said she didn't do anything but sell well!

We were entirely wiped out by flood water in 1965 and only stayed long enough to pay all debts and in 1970, we retired to private life." Signed Mollye Goldman (Mrs. Meyer) December 1975.

Following are photographs, stationary cuts and other items that tell the pictorial story of Mollye Creations.

**International Doll Co.** *Manufacturers of DOLLS*

6510-16 Upland Street • Philadelphia 42, Pa. • SAratoga 9-4079

*Design Studio of*

*Mollye Creations*

LOMBARDY AND GARRETT ROADS CLearbrook 9-5131 DREXEL HILL, PENNSYLVANIA 19026

# PLAYTHINGS

381 FOURTH AVENUE, NEW YORK CITY

**Your attention is called to the following item which appeared in the current issue of "PLAYTHINGS"**

Virginia Weidler with Her Dolls

This is a photo of the Winchester's Golden Fleece Teddy Bear that used real Lamb's skins. Mollye Goldman's husband, Meyer Goldman was President of the company. 1939.

### FAMOUS JUVENILE SCREEN STARS PLAY WITH "RAGGEDY ANN" DOLLS

The accompanying photograph shows pretty little Virginia Weidler, the talented Paramount child movie star, surrounded by a bevy of "Raggedy Ann" and "Raggedy Andy" dolls. Mollye, of Molly-'es Doll Outfitters, Inc., who are exclusive manufacturers of "Raggedy Ann" and "Raggedy Andy," says that these dolls are favorites among many of the little screen stars in Hollywood. She has literally dozens of photographs showing the talented youngster playing with their "Raggedy" dolls. Mollye reports that many leading stores from coast-to-coast will feature her Hollywood Cinema Fashions for dolls during the coming Holiday season. Through exclusive arrangement Molly's organization is reproducing in doll costumes the latest screen fashions worn by the little girls in their new pictures. Children can now see their favorite young movie star and, thanks to Molly's Hollywood Cinema Fashions, go home and dress their dolls in like manner. Molly-es' large plant is operating at full capacity, turning out the largest volume of business in the history of the concern.

Mollye--These little Mollye Creations are 8" tall, all cloth with pressed faces made exclusively for her, in England. These dolls are called "Little Angels" and made in the 1920's. $75.00 each.

Mollye--This 12" all cloth doll was made in the late 1920's. $65.00.

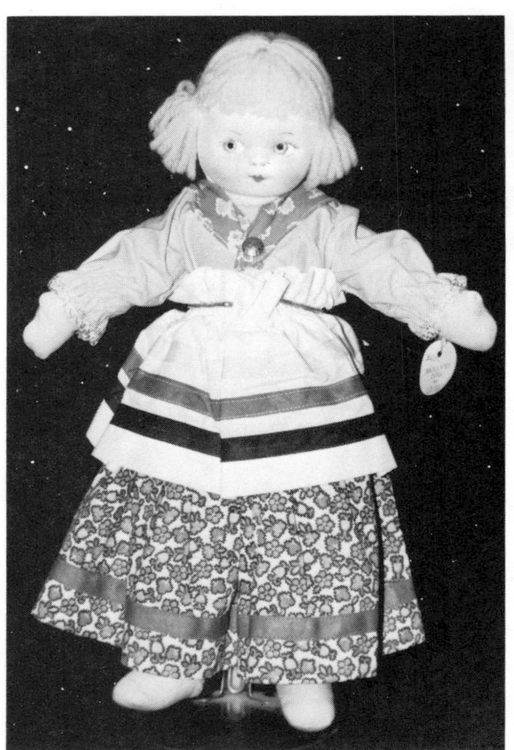

Mollye--15" "Belgium Girl" from International Series. All original. Tag: paper tag on wrist: A Mollye's Doll/T.M.Reg./App. For. Other side: Mfd. By/Mollye's/Doll Outfitters/Inc. $55.00.

Mollye--This is a beautifully dressed all cloth doll made in 1935. $75.00.

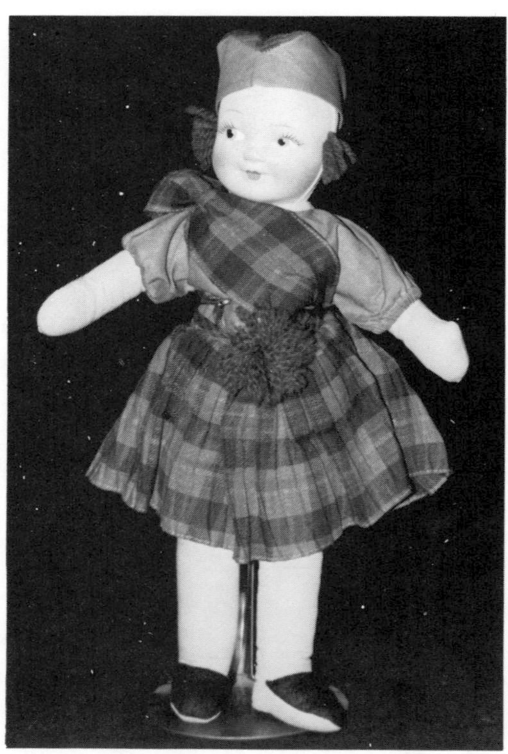

Mollye--15" "Scotland" from International Series. All original. Tag, on left hip: A Mollye's/ American Made. $55.00.

Mollye--15" Cloth Internationals. Came in 12 countries: Irish, Mexican, Swedish, Polish, Gypsy, Czeck, English, Italian, Swiss, French, Romanian, Dutch. $35.00 each.

Mollye--24" "Baby Criss" 1945. $75.00.

Mollye--24" All cloth "Darling" 1937. $65.00.

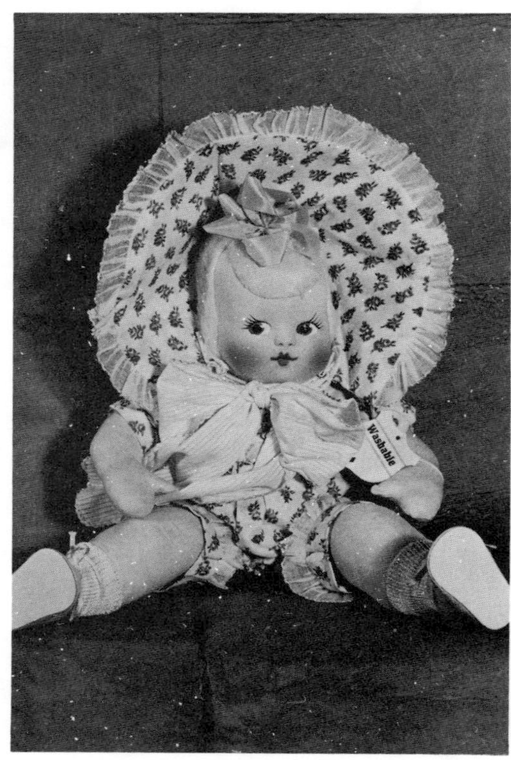


Mollye--24" Cloth with pressed face mask. Fur white hair. All original. Tag: A Mollye Doll. $75.00.

Mollye--21" "Royal Wedding." All composition. Blue sleep eyes with eyeshadow. Closed mouth. Doll unmarked and clothes are tagged. $125.00.

Mollye--27" "Dutch Girl" 1941. These exclusive dolls sold for as high as $80.00 in 1941. $75.00.

Mollye--18" "Debbie Deb" All high grade composition. Closed mouth and sleep eyes/eyeshadow. Stands on revolving music box. Sold for $125.00 during the 1930's.

Mollye--18" All high grade composition "Queen Elizabeth." Doll made by Effanbee and so marked. $125.00.

Mollye--22" "Lone Ranger." $125.00.

Mollye--22" "Hi-Buzzy" All cloth with pressed face mask. All original. Ideal Toy sold two dolls very similar to this as Roy Rogers with smile mouth and painted teeth and Hopalong Cassidy with white fur hair. 1949. $95.00.

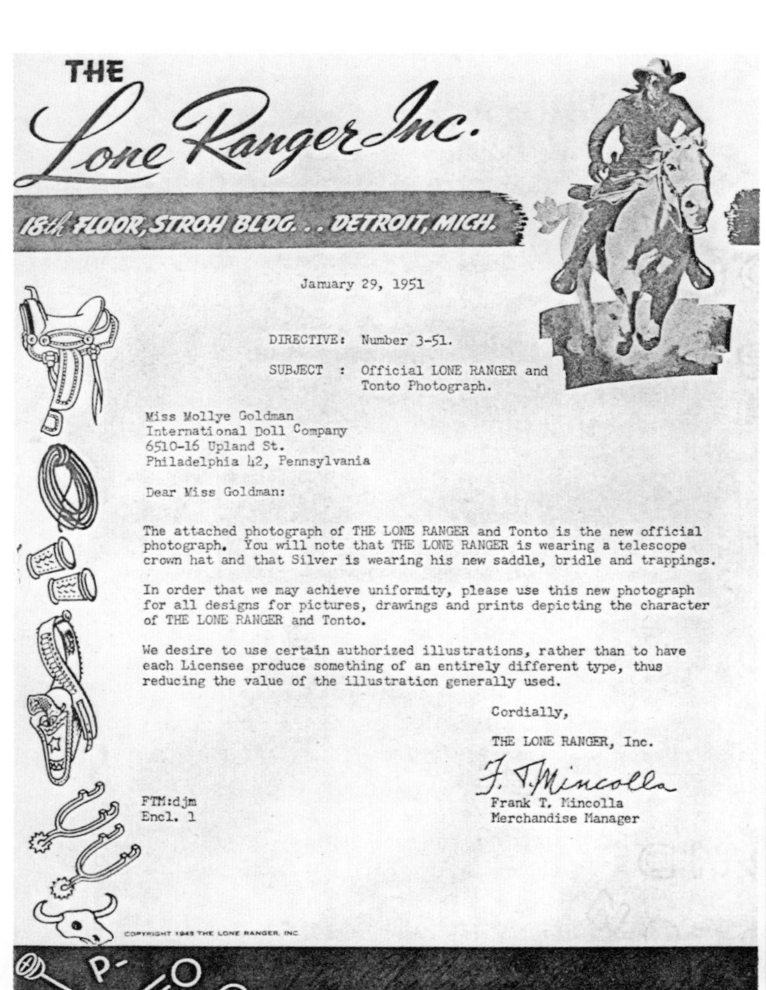

THE
Lone Ranger Inc.

18th FLOOR, STROH BLDG. . . DETROIT, MICH.

January 29, 1951

DIRECTIVE: Number 3-51.

SUBJECT : Official LONE RANGER and Tonto Photograph.

Miss Mollye Goldman
International Doll Company
6510-16 Upland St.
Philadelphia 42, Pennsylvania

Dear Miss Goldman:

The attached photograph of THE LONE RANGER and Tonto is the new official photograph. You will note that THE LONE RANGER is wearing a telescope crown hat and that Silver is wearing his new saddle, bridle and trappings.

In order that we may achieve uniformity, please use this new photograph for all designs for pictures, drawings and prints depicting the character of THE LONE RANGER and Tonto.

We desire to use certain authorized illustrations, rather than to have each Licensee produce something of an entirely different type, thus reducing the value of the illustration generally used.

Cordially,

THE LONE RANGER, Inc.

F. T. Mincolla
Frank T. Mincolla
Merchandise Manager

FTM:djm
Encl. 1

COPYRIGHT 1945 THE LONE RANGER, INC.

Mollye--30" This is the doll used for the Lone Ranger and also Cowboy Joe. All latex body filled with foam rubber. Hard plastic head. Blue sleep eyes. Open mouth/two upper teeth. 1949. Marks: 28, on head. $55.00.

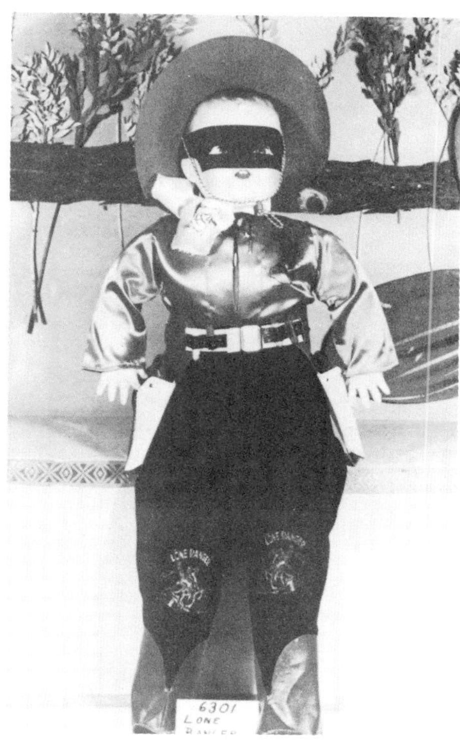


Mollye--Shows Lone Ranger, Tonto, Cowboy Joe and cowgirls. Latex bodies and hard plastic heads. Two dolls center, front are all hard plastic.

Mollye--Shows a display of the exclusive rights Lone Ranger and Tonto dolls. Top row and doll on far right have hard plastic heads and magic skin bodies. Two in center are all composition. The girls were called Rangette and Tonta.

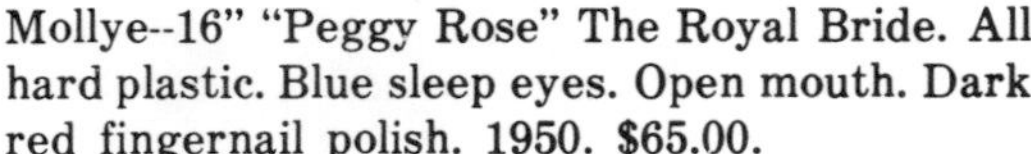

Mollye--16" "Peggy Rose" The Royal Bride. All hard plastic. Blue sleep eyes. Open mouth. Dark red fingernail polish. 1950. $65.00.

Mollye--20" "Embassy Bride" All hard plastic. Revolves on music box with wedding music. Dressed in finest laces and satins. 1949. Clothes are tagged "Mollye Creations." Doll is unmarked. $65.00.

Mollye--20" "Margaret Rose, Bride" All hard plastic. Blue sleep eyes. Open mouth. Clothes tagged "Mollye." Dolls unmarked or with 210 on head or back. $40.00.

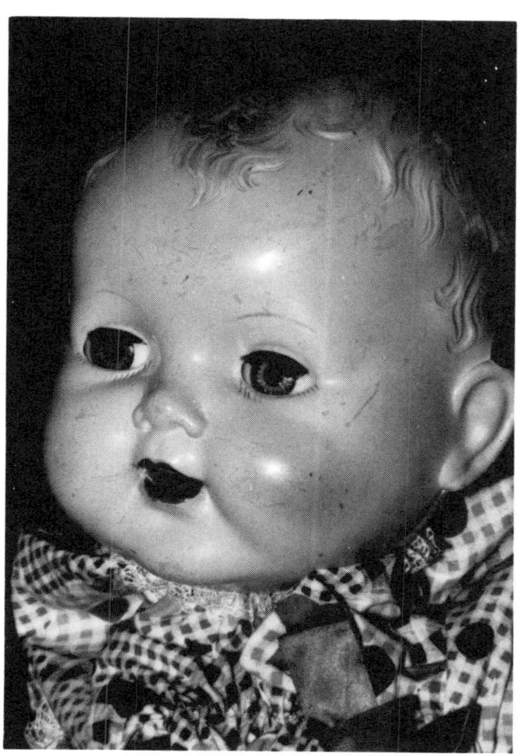

Mollye--24" "Angel Face" 1948. Cloth and composition. Cry box. Sold for $19.95 in 1948. $35.00.

Mollye--23" "Precious" Hard plastic head, cloth body with vinyl arms and legs. Called the wonder doll, she could sleep sitting up, play a tune, play patti cake, etc. without being wound up. $35.00.

Mollye--16" All composition toddlers. Came with molded hair and wigs. Sleep eyes. Top: Penny. Left: Minnie. Right: Rosalee. 1939. $35.00 each.

Mollye--24" "Baby Princess" Cloth body with composition head and limbs. Sold for $35.00 in 1935. $55.00.

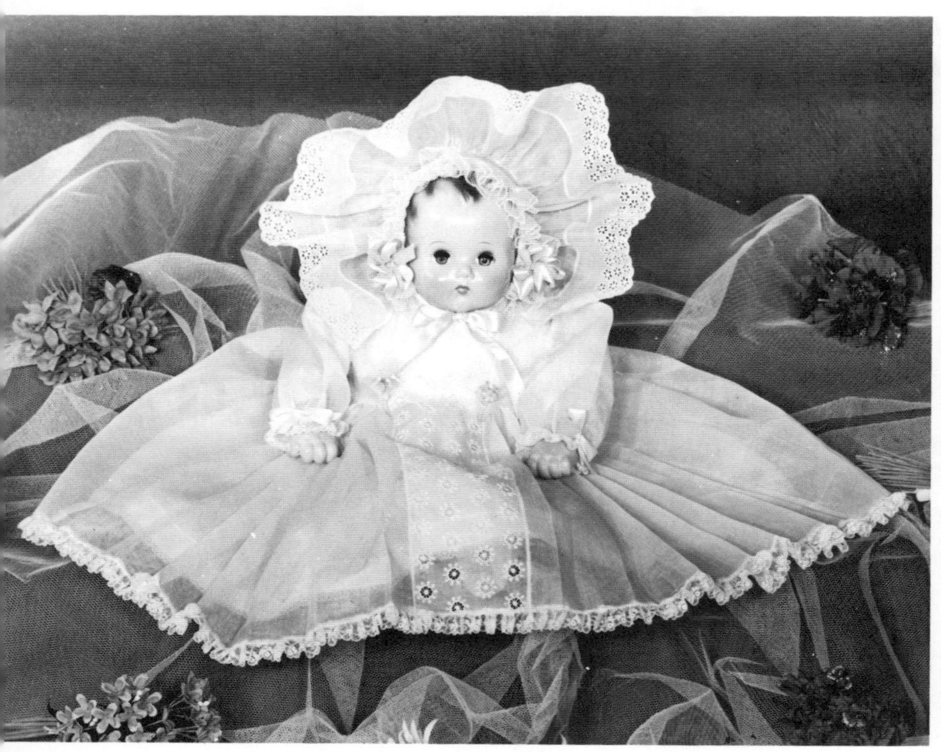

Mollye--20" "Baby Fun" Shown in original outfit. $55.00.

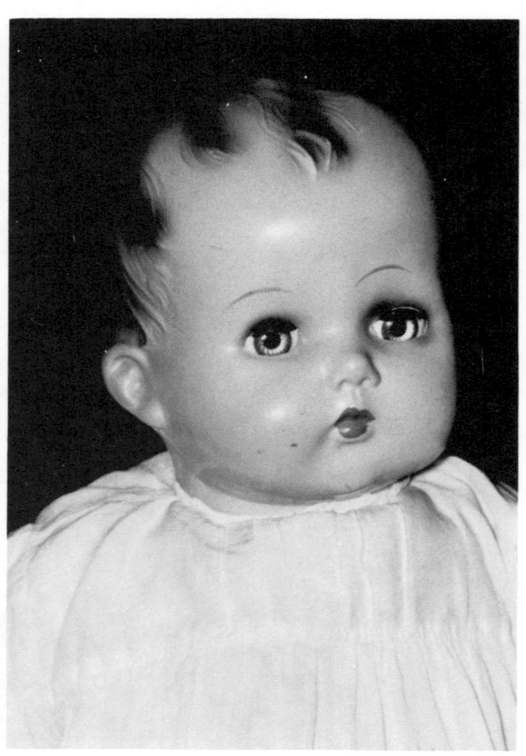

Mollye--20" "Baby Fun" Cloth body with full cloth arms and gauntlet composition hands. Composition legs and head. Blue sleep eyes/ lashes. Marks: None. (Courtesy Joan Amundsen)

Mollye--20" "Baby Fun" All composition toddler. Came with or without wigs over molded hair. $55.00.

Mollye--15" "Little Girls" All old fashioned costumes. Vinyl heads with latex bodies. Cryer. Inset eyes. Dolls not marked. Clothes are tagged. Top row, left to right: Mary Lou, Emma Lou, Sara Lou. Bottom row, left to right: Sally Lou, Pattie Lou. $35.00 each.

Mollye--This is also the "Baby Lov-Lee" (Bundle of Charm doll). $35.00.

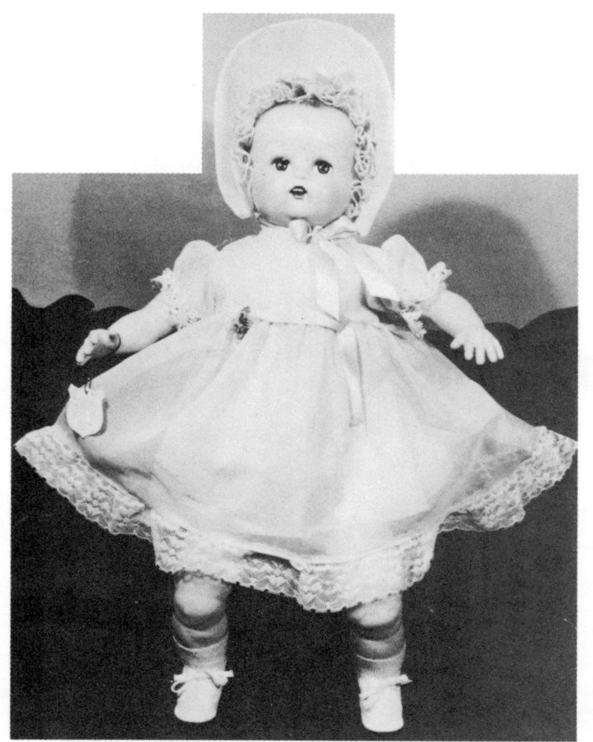

Mollye--24" "Baby Lov-Lee" and advertised as "Bundle of Charm" See page 177, Series II. Marks: A backward 650.

Mollye--This is the wigged version of "Baby Lov-Lee (Bundle of Charm). $35.00.

Mollye--8" "Holiday Girls" All hard plastic with hand painted faces. Top row left is Martha Washington. Second row is Miss Columbus and front row: Valentine Day and St. Patricks. $10.00 each.

Mollye--Shows miniature Bridal party. Bride top row center. Maid of Honor center, second row along with six Bridesmaids. All hard plastic and 8" tall. Each face is hand painted. $10.00 each.

Mollye--9" "Darling Tiny Women" See Series I, page 211 for a photo of doll. Marks: Molly E, on head. Was also used as "Darling Little Women" with mother, Meg, Jo, Beth and Amy. Also used for "Queen of the Month" and came dressed in six different outfits. Was also used for International dolls. $35.00 each.

Mollye--9" "Molly" A cute little girl. 1952. $12.00.

Mollye--9" "Italian Girl" All vinyl with sleep eyes. Dolls were mostly unmarked, some were marked "Mollye." Clothes were tagged. $18.00.

Mollye--20" "Irene Dunn" All composition. Stands on music box. Special human hair wig. All lace dress. This is one of the "Hollywood Cinema Fashions" by Mollye. She also designed stars such as Jeannette McDonald, Joan Crawford, Marilyn Monroe and many others. $125.00.

Mollye--12" "Tyrolean Girl" All vinyl. Blue sleep eyes. Closed mouth. Doll marked "Mollye" and clothes are tagged. $18.00.

Mollye--15" "Sabu" of the "Thief of Bagdad." All composition. Doll and clothes designed by Mollye. $165.00.

Mollye--11" "Perky" Came with and without freckles. Also came with all hair colors. Marks: back left: AE10/33, on head, Large AE/1 lower back. Back right: AE10F, on head. Large AE/1, lower back. Front: AE/9, on head. AE/1, lower back. $15.00. (Courtesy Carolyn Powers)

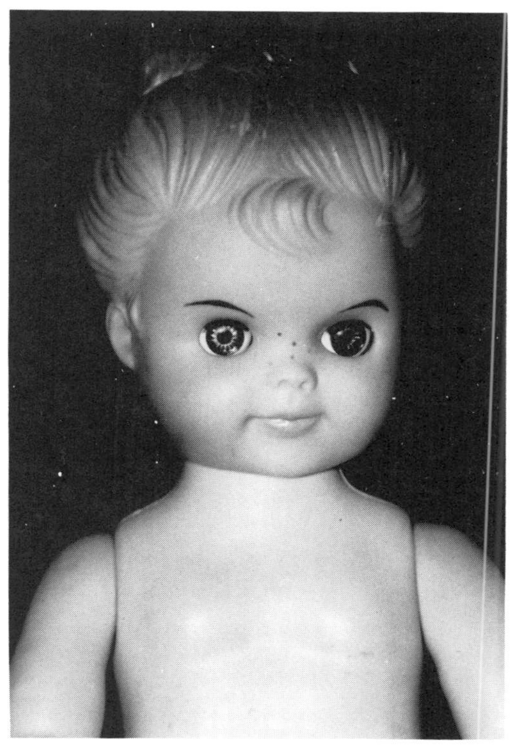

Mollye--11" "Perky" With molded hair. Freckles. Marks: AE/1, on lower back. $17.00. (Courtesy Alice Capps)

Mollye--12" "Perky" All vinyl, black hair and brown eyes. No freckles. $115.00.

Mollye--11" "Ida Bell" Also sold as "Lindy Sue" in different outfit. Came with or without freckles. Also sold as "Perky" and as "Darling Little Women:" Mother, Meg, Jo, Beth and Amy. $20.00.

Mollye--12" "Perky" All vinyl with white hair and blue eyes. Freckles. $15.00.

Mollye--12" "Perky-Pert" All vinyl. Blue sleep eyes. Closed smile mouth. Came with and without freckles. Clothes tagged and some dolls' heads were marked "Mollye." 1958. $15.00.

Doll Artist--19" "Court Man" and 18" "Court Lady" Portraits by Halle Blakely. 1953. Man, $495.00; Lady, $500.00. (Courtesy Kimport Dolls)

Doll Artist--26" "Marie Ann Portrait" by Halle Blakely. 1951. $575.00. (Courtesy Kimport Dolls)

Doll Artist--29" Portrait by Halle Blakely. 1958. $495.00. (Courtesy Kimport Dolls)

Doll Artist--12" "Grandpa & Grandma" by Marie Berger. Pre-1964. $300.00 pair. (Courtesy Kimport Dolls)

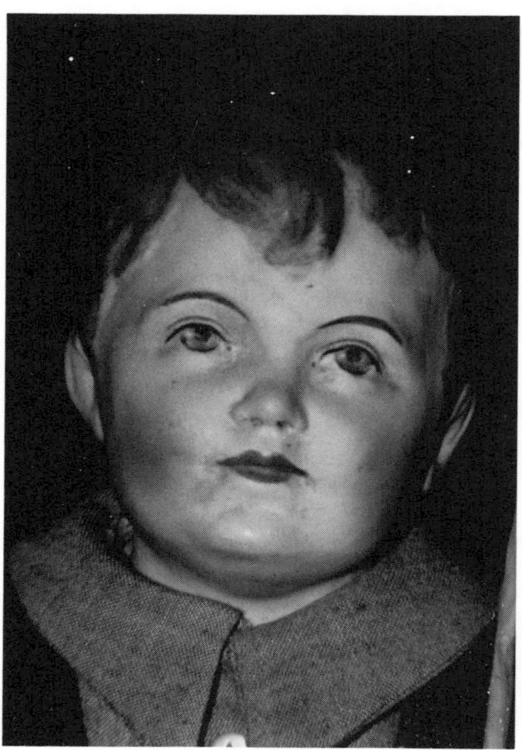

Doll Artist--16" "Danny Boy" Signed Emma Clear 1945. $300.00. (Courtesy Helen Draves)

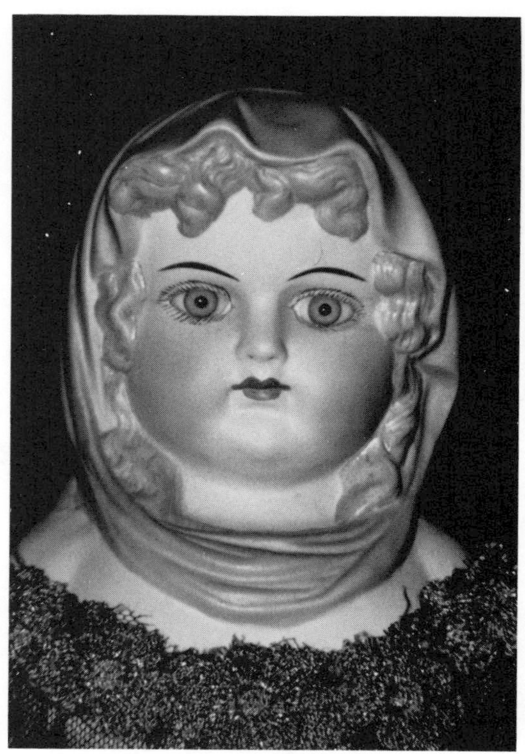

Doll Artist--20" "Blue Scarf" doll by Emma Clear in 1948. $295.00. (Courtesy Helen Draves)

Doll Artist--22" "Parian" signed by Emma Clear in 1949. $125.00. (Courtesy Helen Draves)

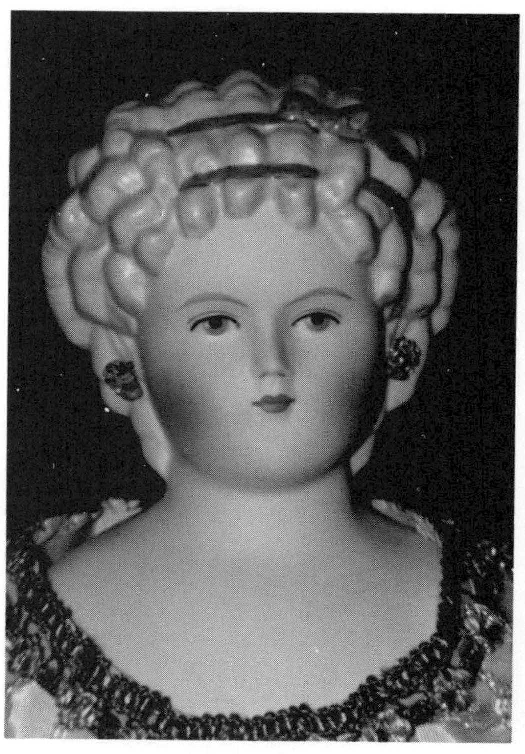

Doll Artist--18" "Parian" by Emma Clear in 1948. $125.00. (Courtesy Helen Draves)

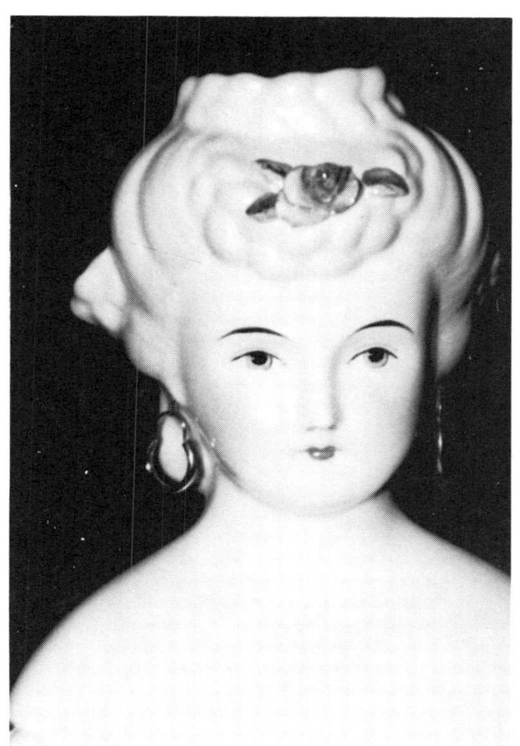

Doll Artist--18" Blonde china finish "Parian" Applied rose and pierced ears. Marks: Clear, 1946. $165.00. (Courtesy Kimport Dolls)

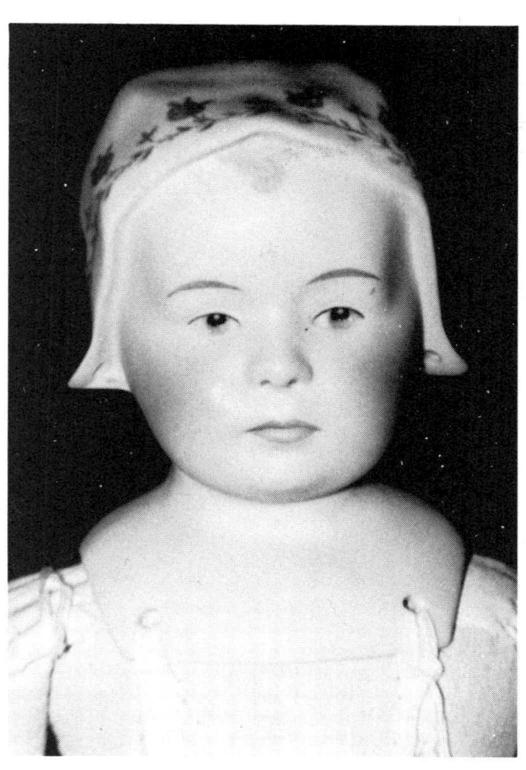

Doll Artist--16" "Baby Stuart" by Emma Clear. Signed 1946. $165.00. (Courtesy Kimport Dolls)

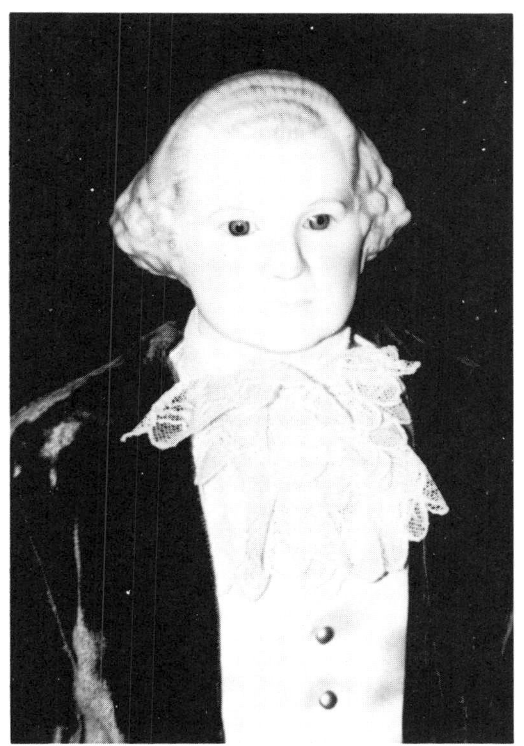

Doll Artist--19½" "George" Inset eyes. 18½" "Martha" Inset eyes, molded bonnet over molded hair. By Emma Clear. $575.00 pair. (Courtesy Kimport Dolls)

Doll Artist--18" Coronation hairdo, applied necklace, feather and earrings. By Emma Clear, signed 1947. $175.00. (Courtesy Kimport Dolls)

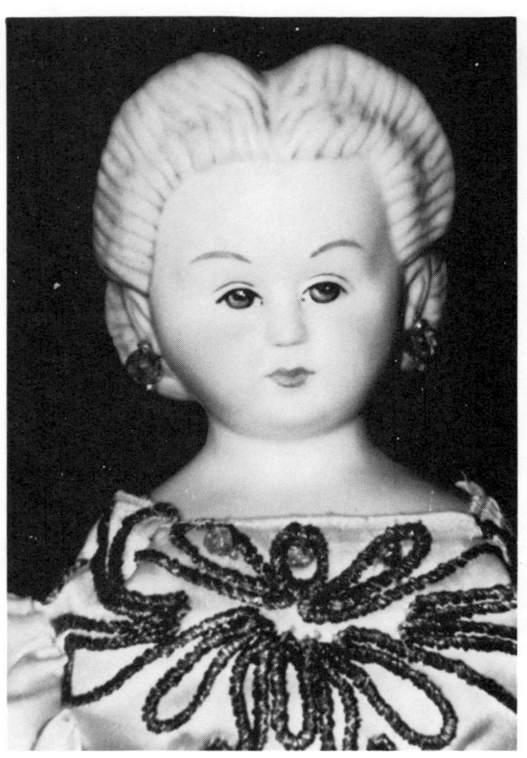

Doll Artist--16" Brown eyed Parian with grey hair. Pierced ears. Signed Anna Mae 1962. $95.00. (Courtesy Kimport Dolls)

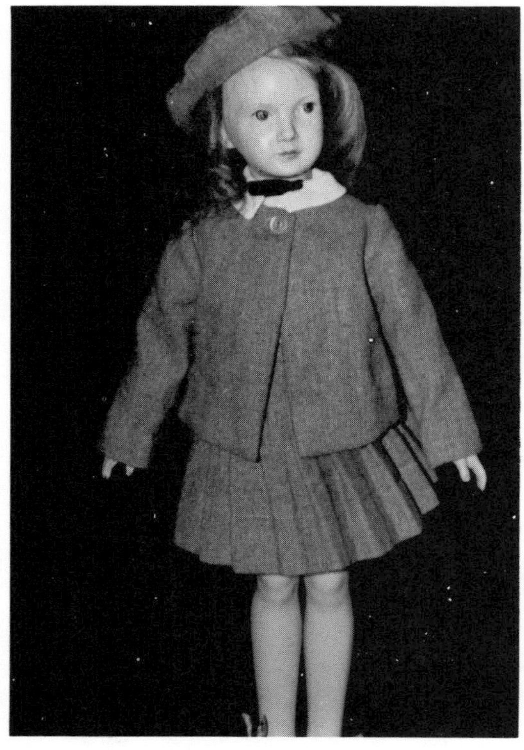

Doll Artist--15" "Look a Like" One of the children by Dewees Cockran. Original. Artist signed under left arm. $250.00. (Courtesy Barbara Coker)

Doll Artist--18" "Gibson Girl" by Emma Clear. $175.00. (Courtesy Kimport Dolls)

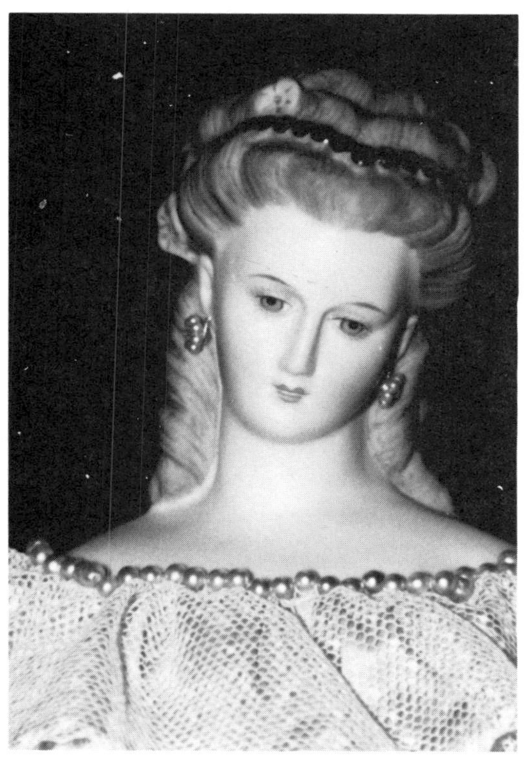

Doll Artist--17" Beautiful Parian with pierced ears, applied flowers and head band. Marks: Patti Jene 1964. $165.00. (Courtesy Kimport Dolls)

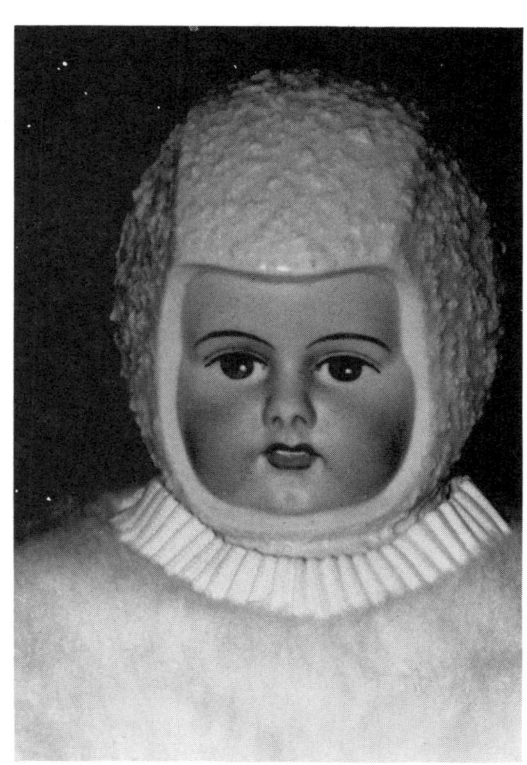

Doll Artist--18" A most beautiful Snow baby made by Gerald La Mott Pacoima. 1964. $185.00. (Courtesy Helen Draves)

Doll Artist--20" "Queen Elizabeth" Signed Rene 1959. $175.00. (Courtesy Kimport Dolls)

Doll Artist--15" Brown eyed Parian with pierced ears. Applied neck scarf. Marks: PJ '64 Patti Jene. $125.00. (Courtesy Kimport Dolls)

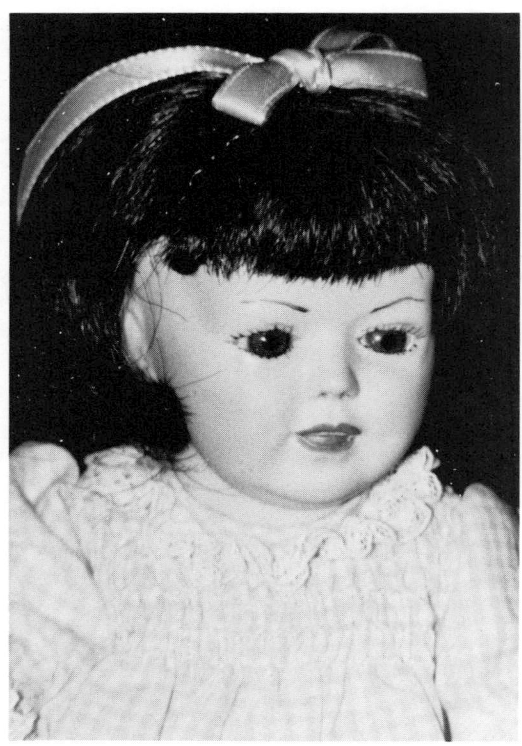

Doll Artist--9½" "Little Girl" An all bisque with open/closed mouth and painted teeth. Inset blue eyes. Dimples. Signed by Edith Gammon. 1975. $60.00. (Courtesy Kimport Dolls)

Doll Artist--23" Portrait in wax by Lewis Sorenson. (Courtesy Kimport Dolls)

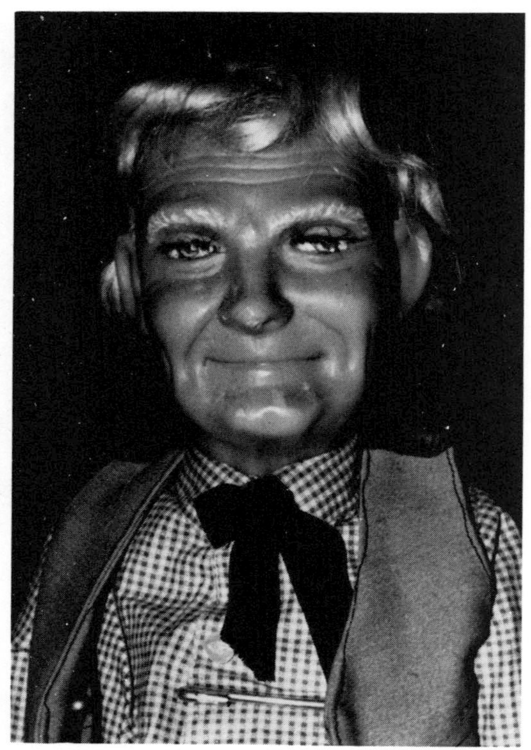

Doll Artist--23" Portrait in wax by Lewis Sorenson. $200.00. (Courtesy Kimport Dolls)

Doll Artist--18" "Paul Laurence Dunbar" (1872-1906). Often known as the poet of the people, he wrote in both Negro dialect and conventional English and also authored many works of prose. Marks: Bertabels Dolls-1965. The doll was designed by Roberta Bell N.I.A.D.A. artist. $265.00. (Courtesy Maxine Heitt)

Doll Artist--This is a picture of a U.S. Postage stamp that is currently available, commemorating Paul Laurence Dunbar. (Courtesy Maxine Heitt)

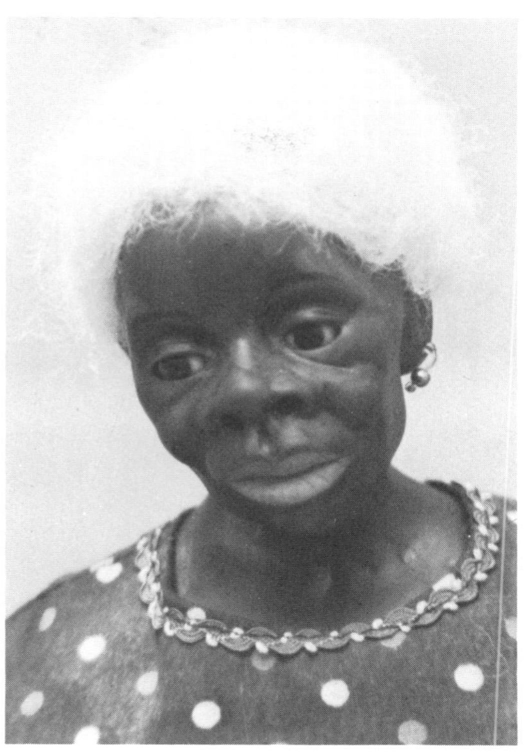

Doll Artist--14" "Caldonia" Glass eyes. 1966 by Maggie Head. First made in 1958. Still being produced. $265.00. (Courtesy Grace Ochsner)

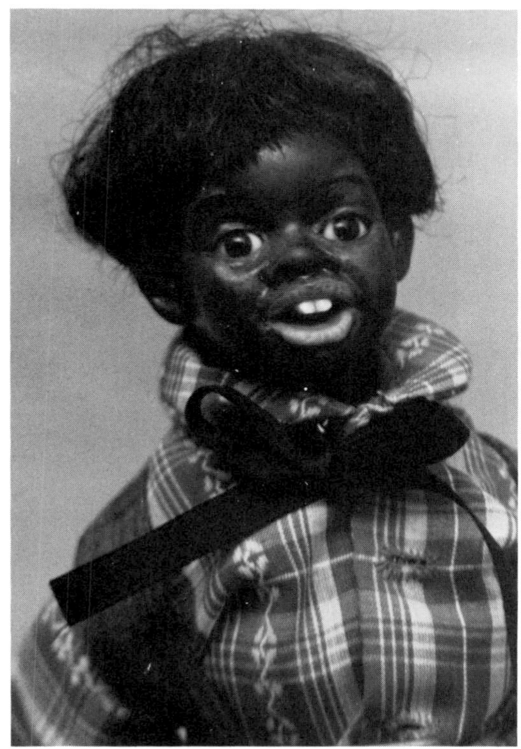

Doll Artist--15" "Nicodemus" Open/closed mouth with two upper teeth. Glass eyes. By Maggie Head. $125.00. (Courtesy Grace Ochsner)

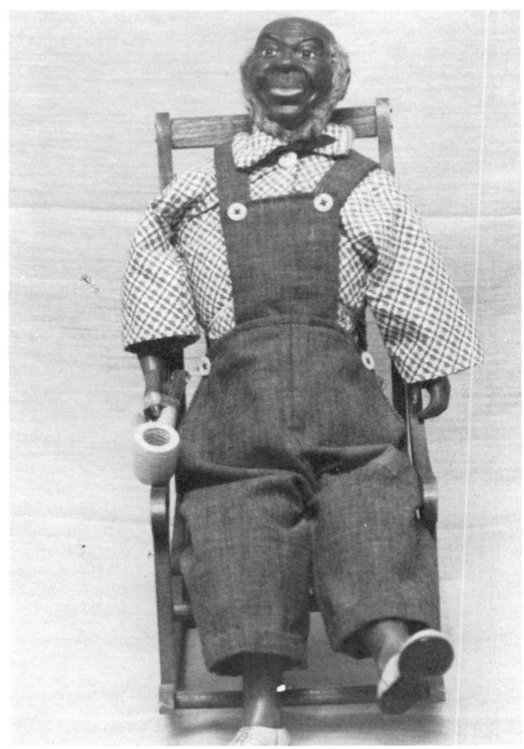

Doll Artist--15" "Uncle Ned" Glass eyes. Maggie Head. 1966. First made in 1958. $265.00. (Courtesy Grace Ochsner)

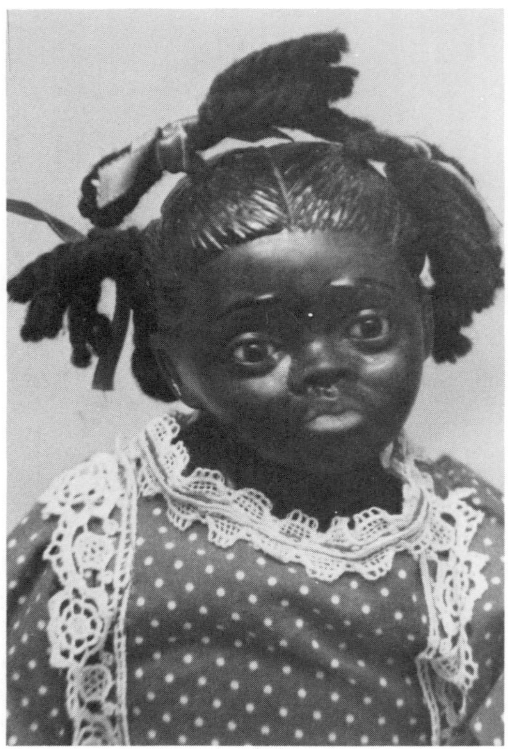

Doll Artist--14" "Peach Blossom" Glass eyes. Holes in head for hair. Signed Pattie Jean 1966. $85.00. (Courtesy Grace Ochsner)

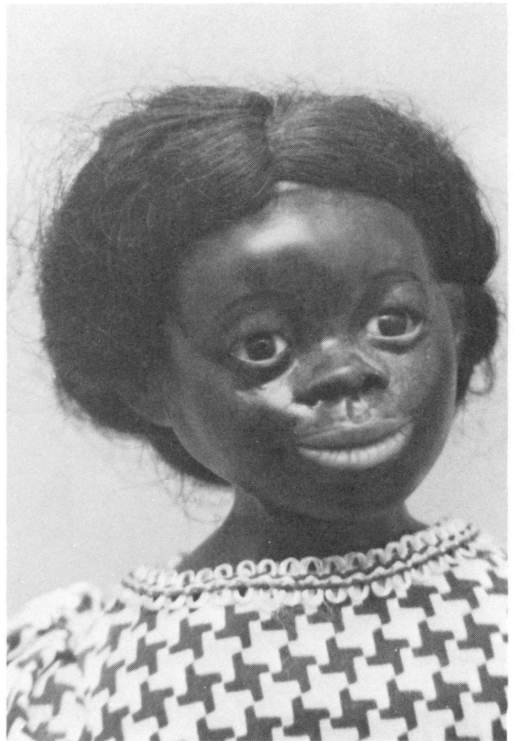

Doll Artist--14" "Marigold" 1966 by Maggie Head. Glass eyes. First made in 1959. Still being produced. $125.00. (Courtesy Grace Ochsner)

Doll Artist--20" Parian Biedermeir type by Grace Lathrop. $225.00. (Courtesy Kimport Dolls)

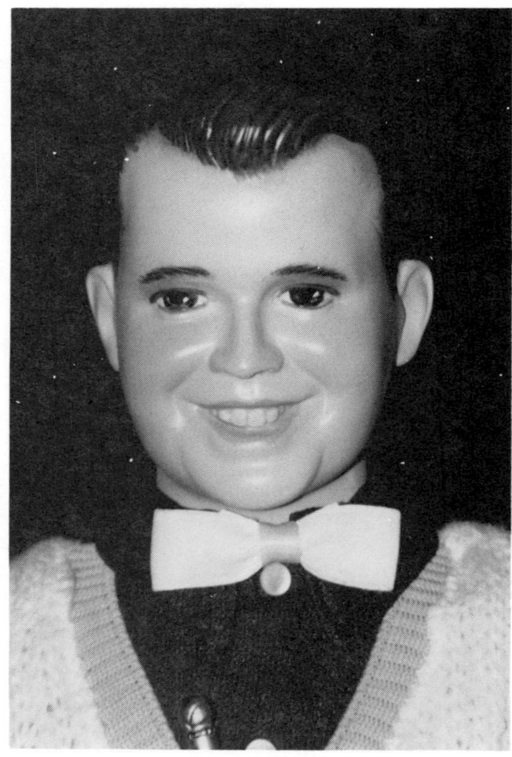

Doll Artist--22" "Dick Clark" Bisque head with cloth body. Composition hands. Marks: None. The workmanship of the doll is outstanding, it is unfortunate we do not know the artist who made him. $165.00. (Courtesy Barbara Coker)

Doll Artist--16½" "Miami Miss" 1961, by Fawn Zeller. $175.00. (Courtesy Kimport Dolls)

Doll Artist--"Little Howie" A modern wax portrait by Eva Bee Hill. $115.00.

Doll Artist--13½ All tanned leather. Painted eyes. Yarn hair. An Oujibbua. Artist: Margaret Chief. $35.00. (Courtesy Maxine Heitt)

Doll Artist--18" Indian by Mildred Helmuth. $60.00. (Courtesy Kimport Dolls)

Doll Artist--16½" "Cinderella" by Lita Wilson. 1966. Made on special order for Mrs. M.A. Resch of Iowa. $200.00. (Courtesy Kimport Dolls)

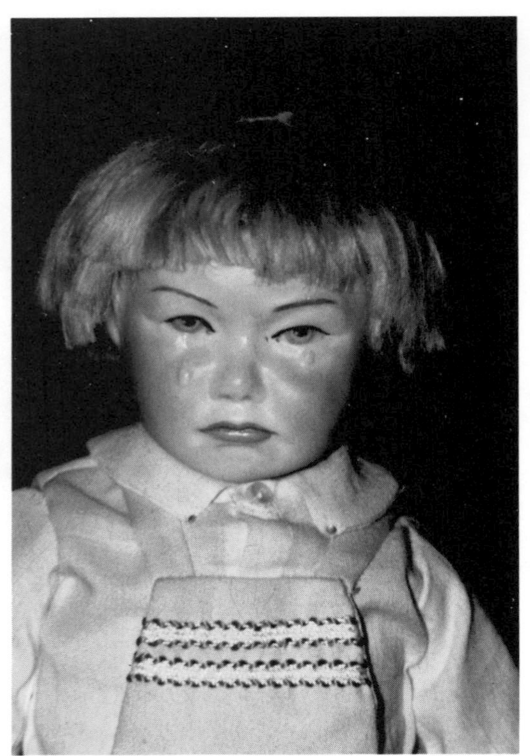

Doll Artist--13" Boy with tears by Ellery Thorpe. 1970. $250.00. (Courtesy Kimport Dolls)

Doll Artist--15½" "Charlotta" Parian with applied crown and necklace. Pierced ears. Made exclusively for Kimport Dolls in 1954 by Polly Mann. $175.00.

Doll Artist--18" Girl with a dimple by Suzanne Gibson. $175.00. (Courtesy Kimport Dolls)

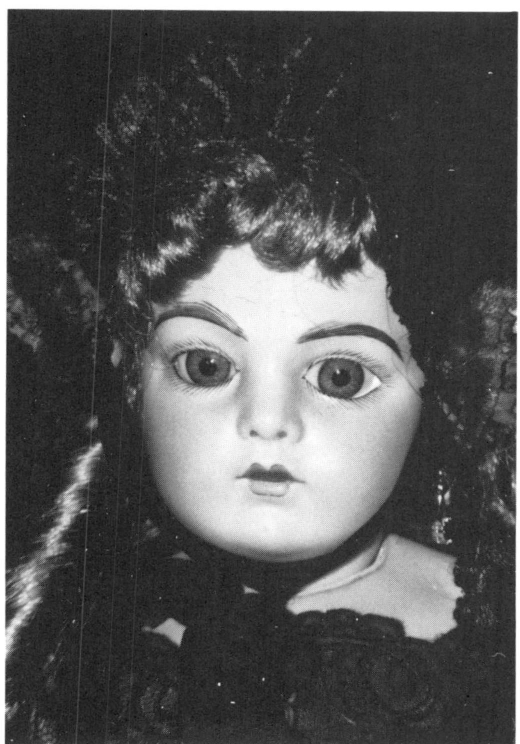

Doll Artist--18" Bisque shoulder head on bisque shoulder plate. Kid/cloth body. Marks: Jackie '71/Bru Jne/10. $85.00. (Courtesy Helen Draves)

Doll Artist--5" "Chocolate & Vanilla Fakco" Designed and made by Julia Rogers. $22.00.

Doll Artist--"Martha Gonyea" designer and originator of many cloth dolls, which are shown in this section. She also runs a doll shop and repair hospital in Roswell, N.M.

Doll Artist--25" "Little Chief" Face and clothes are originals of Martha Gonyea. This doll won a blue ribbon at Fair. $45.00.

Doll Artist--33" "Miss Ping-Pong" Made during the time President Nixon went to Red China. Both face and clothes are original designs of Martha Gonyea. $65.00.

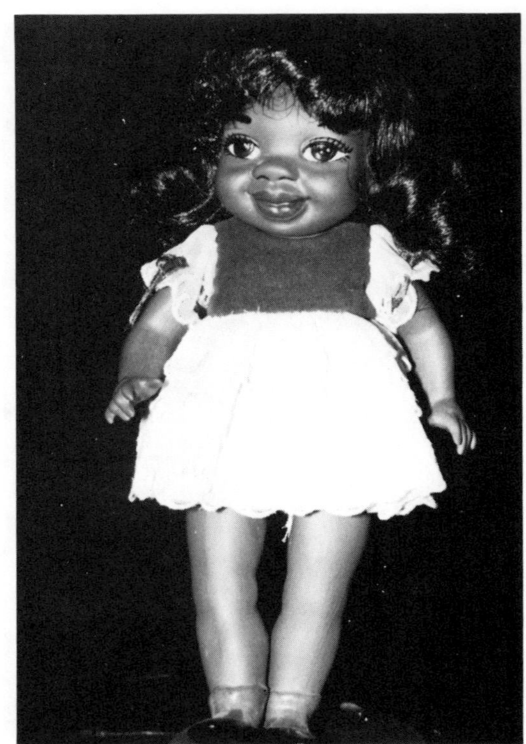

Doll Artist--8" All bisque. By Gertrude Zigler. $65.00. (Courtesy Jay Minter)

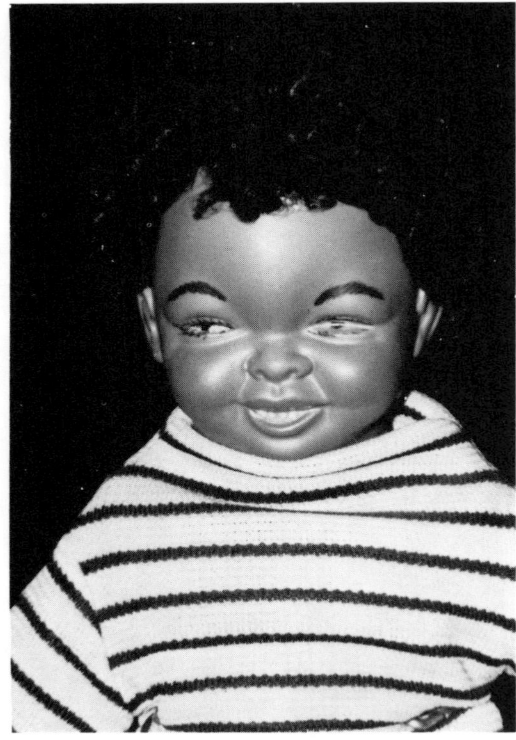

Doll Artist--12" Original by Gertrude Zigler. $65.00. (Courtesy Jay Minter)

Doll Artist--Cloth portraits of Mr. and Mrs. Houston of Richmond, Va. done by Maxine Clasen. They were made from the small photograph. (Courtesy Phyllis Houston)

Doll Artist--Original photo of Mr. and Mrs. J.C. Houston.

Doll Artist--28" "W.C. Fields" By Maxine Clasen. Composition head and hands. Wire armiture, bendable body. $165.00. (Courtesy Phyllis Houston)

Doll Artist--28" "W.C. Fields" with an unlikely friend.

These following Historic Wax Costume Dolls by Sheila Wallace of Grove City, Pa. could be best described as miniature versions of the historic figures seen in the wax museums throughout the world. Although the methods vary, as they are the result of Sheila's own training, experience and research. Sheila's background in the fields of painting, drawing anatomy and sculpture as taught in London art colleges, her visits to the doll and costume museums in Europe and her love of history are all reflected in the beauty of her work.

Each figure is a separately planned and executed project. Each head and pair of hands is individually molded, not cast, thus each is an original work. They are molded from bleached beeswax using a formula based on one used by European wax modelers of the 17th century. They are taken from portraits or death masks of famous people. The hair, eyelashes, eyebrows, beards and hair on the hands of the male characters are all implanted. Sheila's research in the field of the development of cosmetics insures that the hand painting of the faces and the dressing of the hair is correct for each period.

The basic construction of the bodies is cloth filled with polyester fiber over flexible wire armatures so each figure can be suitably posed on its own wooden stand. The lower limbs are composition with appropriate footwear, fitted to the foot and not molded on as part of the limb. Each costume is carefully researched to be as historically correct as possible and appropriately scaled, correct accessories are added to enhance the authenticity. In some cases a doll is also given a "wardrobe" of interchangeable head dresses, bonnets or wigs and a container is provided for storage of these extra accessories.

The dolls made by Sheila Wallace are extremely beautiful to see and would be fantastic to own and display in a fine collection.

Doll Artist--Family group done in wax by Sheila Wallace. This is the family of Louis XVI, Marie Antoinette, children, Maria Theresa and Louie Charles. $1,500.00 set.

Doll Artist--Close up of Marie Antoinette.

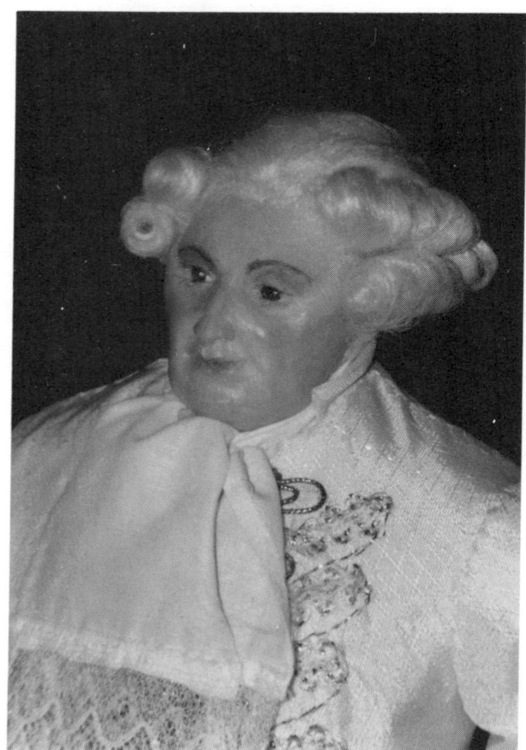

Doll Artist--Close up of Louis XVI.

Doll Artist--Close up of Maria Theresa and Louie Charles.

Doll Artist--Close up of the hand of Marie Antoinette which shows the vein lines and rings.

Doll Artist--Another original by Sheila Wallace. This is Elizabeth I. She is done in wax and has red hair. $695.00.

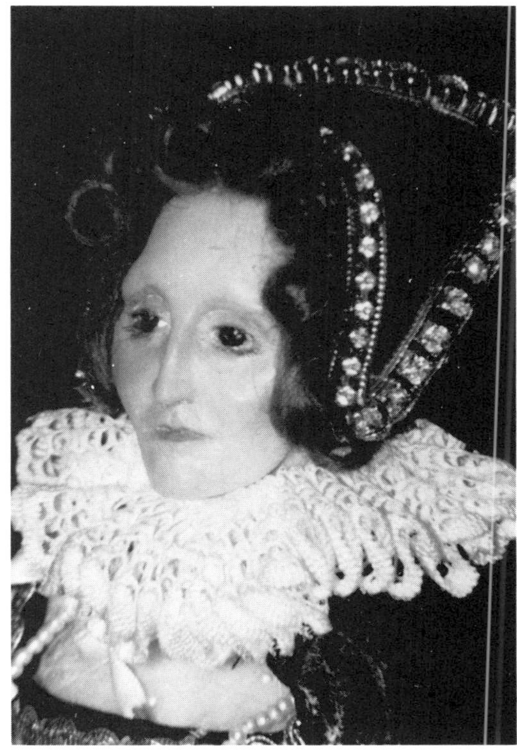

Doll Artist--A close up of Elizabeth I.

Doll Artist--A wax original by Sheila Wallace. This one is Sir Walter Raleigh. $695.00

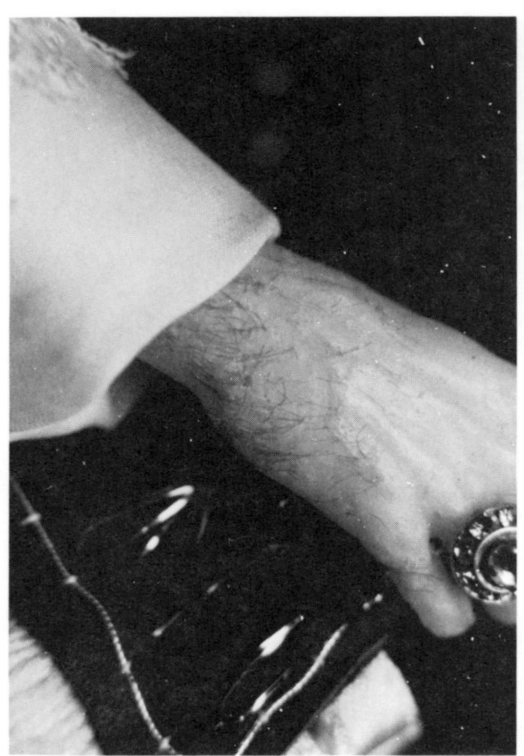

Doll Artist--Close up of the hand of Charles I. Shows embedded hair.

Doll Artist--Sheila Wallace's wax figures of Charles I and Henriette Maria. $695.00 each.

Doll Artist--Close up of Henriette Maria

# The Dolls Collectors Forgot

The following article written by Thelma C. Flack, is reprinted with permission. It appeared in the "Antique Trader" February 26, 1975. Its title is: The Dolls Collectors Forgot; W.P.A. Dolls.

A grayed building designated "Pony Express" stood on Eighth Street in Marysville, Kansas. It was almost passed by this summer, but curiosity is a magnetic leader and who knows what may exist there.

After a deep step upward one stood before a tall glass-doored case full of what appeared to be exciting little dolls about twelve to fourteen inches tall and dressed in what might be American and foreign costumes. They were well constructed and must be of some historical value.

The young lady in charge of the Express station stated that the case of the dolls was gotten for them by a retired public superintendent who had to put up a struggle to keep them from being sent West. She thought they had been made by the Public Works Administration.

There are those that remember the W.P.A. For those too young to recall the Depression, back in 1933 during the first hundred days of Franklin Roosevelt's administration, the joblessness was so bad that "made work" became necessary. Capable committees were set up to work it out. They did a splendid job, but many people considered the road work as all that was being accomplished because this was what they saw being done. Tax payers said that too many workers were just leaning on shovels and demurred at the "new deal." The dolls merit recognition and compliments from people, even today.

I read that San Diego, Cal. had such dolls. They were called "figurines" and used for visual aids in public schools and colleges. The dolls were American and Foreign historical characters.

The Visual aid man from the San Diego public schools gave me much information, but their visual aid building had burned in the Fifties, so I turned to the Kansas Historical Society and received some excellent material.

The construction of these visual aids was brought about by the need of jobs. Back in the first hundred days of Roosevelt's administration there was a haunted look in human eyes and some faces showed fear because of the scarcity of work. The larger families were already in need. Letters such as C.C.C., meaning Civilian Conservation Corps. represented camps where young men could learn to save old trees and attain health from the outdoor life. Their work was valuable to the country because we would need more wood in the future.

Fathers took hard road jobs, engineering, and building state and national buildings, while mothers and older girls met to carry out such projects as sewing for the needy. It was clearly evident that people wanted work and not a dole. W.P.A. jobs were divided into blue collar and white collar sections. Authors explored rivers and wrote historical stories about life on the river and on the shores. Photographers made documentary films of the country which are still shown on T.V. and are valuable to our education. Artists made murals and panoramas for museums and visual aid projects. Writers produced plays. Imagine all of this for approximately twenty dollars per week!

During the first hundred days in office, Roosevelt made ten speeches, sent fifteen messages to Congress, eased some laws to enactment, and talked to the press twice a week. The Federal Emergency Relief Act of May 12th appropriated $500 million and later increased to $5 billion for direct relief to the states, cities and towns. Harry Hopkins headed this, also the Civil Works Administration which grew out of it.

By January 1934, C.W.A. had over four million people on its rolls and at its height, 400,000 separate projects were underway. These included everything Hopkins could think of that would be of public benefit.

Next in importance was the N.R.A. organization. Title I of this law prescribed the drafting and application of "Codes" in every sort of industry. With multiple objectives such as recovery, reform, encouragement of collective organizing, selling, maximum hours, minimum wages and the forbidding of child labor, the N.R.A. got underway.

N.R.A. was administered by Wm. Hugh S. Johnson, a West Pointer who was in charge of the draft in World War I and had occupied a high place in army logistics. With much hard work and the alloting of the dark blue eagle clutching a cog wheel as a symbol to every store firm that adopted the system, Johnson codified about 700 industries. Businessmen in general did not like the N.R.A. They wanted to be free to cut wages and raise prices. As soon as they were "out of the woods," Title I was declared unconstitutional. In 1935, before this happened, some four million unemployed people had been reabsorbed into industry and about twenty-three million workers were under codes.

The second part of the N.R.A. was the Works Progress Administration and the Supreme Court allowed it to stand. Harry Hopkins administered it and spent billions on reforestration, water works, sewage plants, school buildings, slum clearances, and student scholarships. This is where the artists really began their best work.

A feature which caught the public eye and became named "Boondogling" was the setting up of projects to employ artists, musicians, writers and other "white collar" workers. A great many people such as librarians, catalogued the contents of state and municipal library buildings.

The Federal Theater employed over fifteen thousand workers at an average of twenty dollars a week. John Houseman directed authors who wrote and produced plays, often traveling as actor troops about the country. Orson Wells was one of the best.

On the fine arts projects, artist George Biddle, who headed the artists, says they were democratic, humane, and as intelligent as any artists the world over. The dolls seem to bear this out. They had developed through trial and error. The programs were suited to needs and one of the needs in the public schools was for visual aids which the artist could make so excellently. All of these things preceded the development of visual aids.

The foreign costume figurines show the costumes of twenty-four different nationalities. These figurines are similar in construction to the American figures. Orders were by sets made to represent such as Austria, Czechoslovakia, Denmark, Finland, France, Germany, Greece, Holland, Hungary, Ireland, Italy, Rumania, Switzerland, Wales and Yugoslavia. They ran about a dollar a pair or eighty-six cents for cloth. What would I pay to have one today!

Also available were fourteen in figurines of either men or women ready to dress for use in designing and modeling costumes as a class program. A folding wooden exhibit case would open up to exhibit the figurines and which could be made for three dollars.

The historical figurines from our country stand gravely, representing dates, costumes and important Americans. Their faces are paper-mache or hard rubber. They have mache or wooden bodies and stand fastened to a small platform with their identification printed on the base. My favorite wears a jaunty feather, my adored one in pink taffeta ruffled dress. Names one could order from included Jane Adams, Clara Barton, Steven Foster, Benjamin Franklin, Robert Fulton, Sarah Hale, Ann Hutchinson, Abe Lincoln, Paul Revere, Betsy Ross, George Washington, Frances Willard and Will Rogers.

The American figurines show development of costume for both men and women from 1600 to 1900.

The 14" figurines were hard rubber and plaster. They were authentically costumed, in proper materials, and mounted separately in a standing posture. These were dated from 1607 to 1900 and could be ordered in a twenty-four pair set or singly. The buyer ordered by date.

The figurines were offered to help give the students visual understanding of historic and nationalistic costumes that flat pictures could not portray. They were used at all ages and interest levels as teaching aids when they might correlate with learning experiences in classes such as art, music, language, dramatics, literature and social science.

There were rules to govern the visual aid dolls such as:

1. to be made in a durable and practical medium.
2. each to meet the need for which it was planned.
3. to follow specifications.
4. to be capable of being produced in quantities by workers with limited training and well-executed workmanship as an attractive visual aid article.

The object was to aid in the teaching process by supplying material which would give clearer concepts and supplement the most modern and approved classroom methods of presentation. Educators who used the models gave approval. Much research went into the production. Everything was well planned and executed. Some were made at the college in Emporia, Kansas, and some in Wichita.

The little figurines stand solemnly at the Pony Express Station in Marysville. Hundreds of little hands must have held them. Hundreds of young minds must have stored away information for the future and, thanks to an educator who cared, the little dolls were saved to represent an era, looking as attractive and authentic as they did then. Our W.P.A. era did much, much more than lean on a shovel. It helped to give our country a successful forward push. There must be many more "figurines" hidden somewhere in our country. Let us bring them out to our doll collectors and "dibs" on the first in market!

The following pictures are of the Flack collection of W.P.A. dolls and the pictures were taken by Joleen Flack. W.P.A. dolls are selling $65.00 to $85.00 per set.

Doll Artist--W.P.A. Greek

Doll Artist--W.P.A. Czechoslvakia

Doll Artist--W.P.A. Italy

Doll Artist--W.P.A. Mexico

Doll Artist--W.P.A. Switzerland

Doll Artist--W.P.A. Sweden

Doll Artist--W.P.A. Russia

Doll Artist--W.P.A. Poland

Doll Artist--W.P.A. Turkey

Doll Artist--W.P.A. Old Wales

Dream World--11" "Flower Vendor" All composition. Wig over molded hair. Original. Marks: None. Tag: Dream World Dolls/Reg. U.S./Make Dream's Come True. $25.00. (Courtesy Frances Anicello)

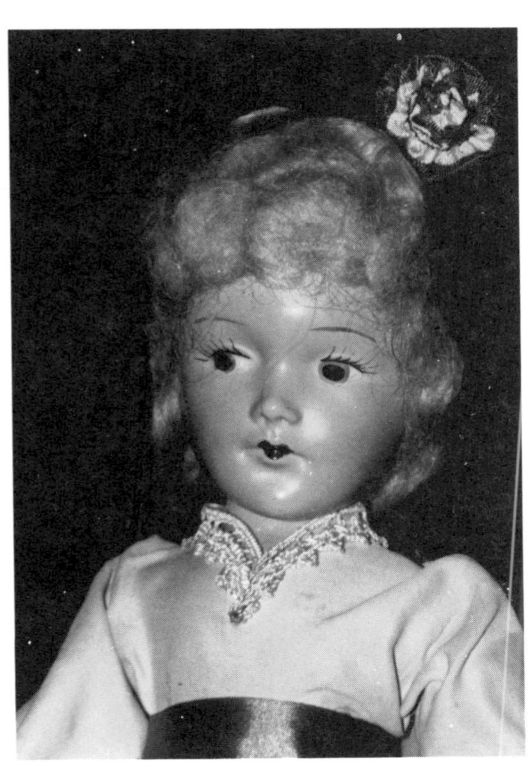

Dream World--11" "Florence Nightengale" All composition. Painted eyes. Original "nurse" uniform. $25.00. (Courtesy Dodie Shapiro)

Dream World--11" "Cuba" All composition. Painted features. $25.00. (Courtesy Mary Partridge)

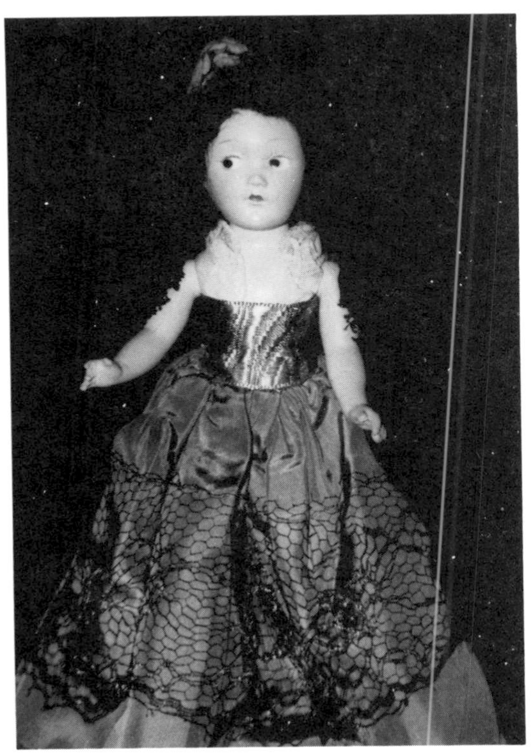

Dream World--11" "Spanish" Molded hair under wig. All composition. Dimple in left cheek. Painted eyes. Marks: None. $25.00. (Courtesy Mary Partridge)

Dream World--11" "Providence" All composition. Molded hair under wig. Original. $25.00. (Courtesy Frances Annicello)

Dreamland--11" "To Market, To Market" All composition. Fully jointed. Stapled on clothes. Painted blue eyes. Original. Marks: None. $25.00. (Courtesy Mary Partridge)

Dream World--11" Close up to see the molded hair under the Dream World doll wigs.

Dream World--11" "Bride" All composition. Original. Shows wooden discs used by manufacturer for "falsies." $25.00. (Courtesy Mrs. J.C. Houston)

Dream World--11" "Bride" All composition with painted features. Molded hair under wig. $25.00. (Courtesy Mary Partridge)

Dream World--11" "Scotch" All composition. Wig over molded hair. Original. Marks: None. $25.00. (Courtesy Frances Anicello)

Dutchess--7½" "Mary Hartline" All hard plastic. Felt clothes. Mohair wig. Blue sleep eyes. Original. $10.00. (Courtesy Phyllis Houston)

Dutchess--7" "Roy Rogers" & "Dale Evans" All hard plastic. Roy: Blue sleep eyes. Dale: Brown sleep eyes. Both original. Marks: Dutchess Doll Corp/Design Copyright/1948, on back. $5.00 each.

A most popular cowboy: Roy Rogers

Roy Rogers' "Leading Lady:" Dale Evans.

Durham--8" "Wyatt Earp" All molded on clothes except hat. Button in back operates right arm to "draw." Marks: Same as Wild Bill Hicock. Still available.

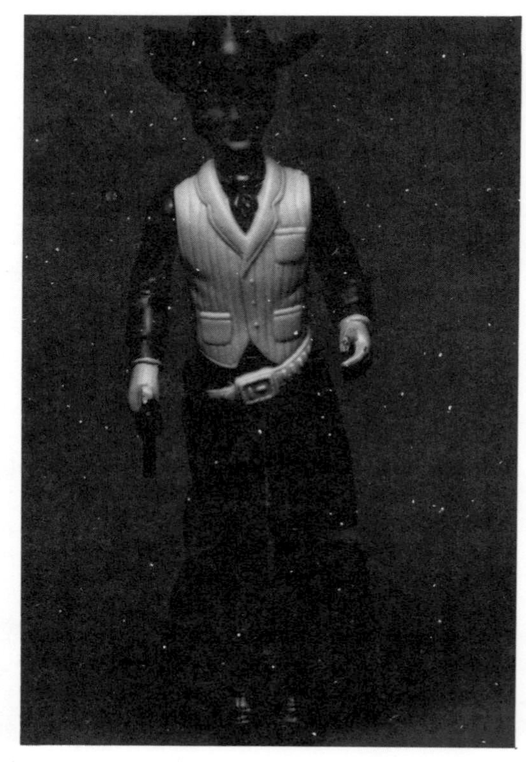

Durham--6" "Young Kung Fu" Plastic with vinyl head. Button in back to make right arm "chop." Painted upper teeth. Original. Marks: Hong Kong, head. Picture of world and "I" inside "D"/ Durham Ind. Inc./New York NY 10010/Made in Hong Kong/Item No. 3010, on back. Still available.

Durham--6" "Fireman" Plastic with vinyl head. Molded ax in hand. Button in back makes ax "swing." Plastic legs are molded on pants and boots. Marks: Same as Young Kung Fu. Still available.

Durham--8" "Billy The Kid" All molded on clothes except hat. Button in back operates arm to "draw." Marks: Same as Wild Bill Hicock. Still available.

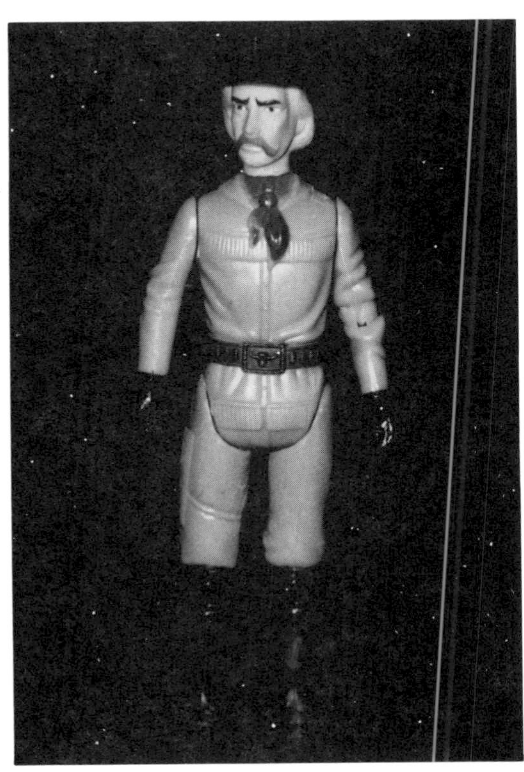

Durham--8" "Wild Bill Hicock" All molded on clothes except hat. Button in back operates right arm to "draw." Marks: D/Durham Ind. Inc./New York N.Y. 10010/Made in Hong Kong/ Item No. 3020/Design Reg. No. 965717/Durham Ind. Inc. 1975. Still available.

Durham--11" "Skinny Jimmy" All flat vinyl. Will fold up. Marks: Picture of world and "I" inside "D"/No 1500/Durham Industries Inc./New York NY 10010/Made in Taiwan. $3.00.

For complete information on the Eegee Doll Co. refer to Series I, page 74.

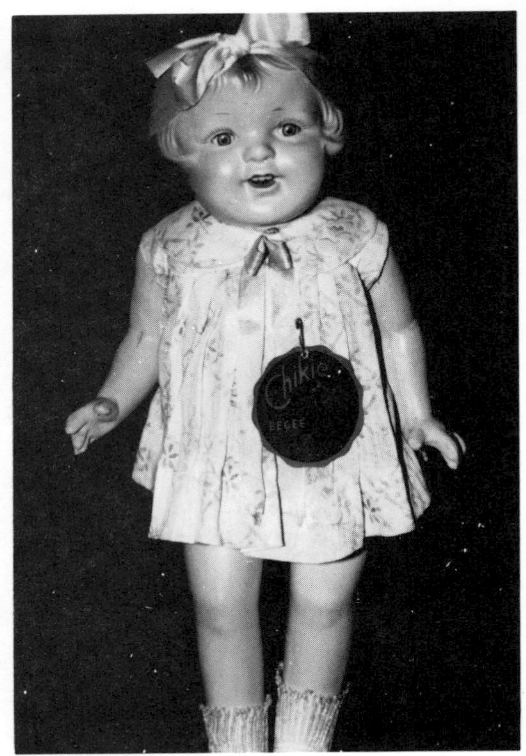


Eegee--16" "Chikie" All composition with small blue tin sleep eyes. Open mouth/3 upper teeth. Molded hair. Bangs are different than the "Patsy" doll. Bent right arm. Original. Marks: None. Tag: Chikie/Another Eegee Doll, with a picture of little girl feeding baby chicks. $60.00. (Courtesy Pat Raiden)

Eegee--18" "Sleepy-Time Girl" Blue sleep eyes. Molded hair. Came on a latex body (unjointed). Vinyl head. Marks: Eegee. $10.00. (Courtesy Marie Ernst)

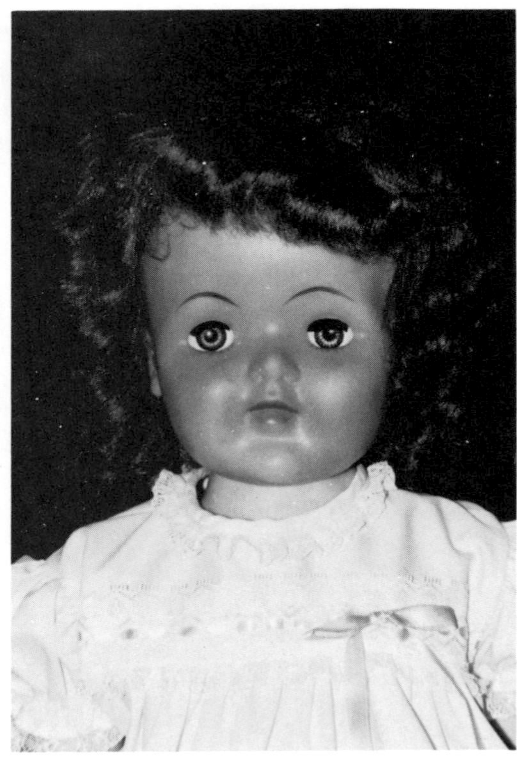

Eegee--29" All early stuffed vinyl. Blue sleep eyes. One piece body and legs. Disc jointed arms. Marks: Eegee, on head and body. $6.00. (Courtesy Elaine Kaminsky)

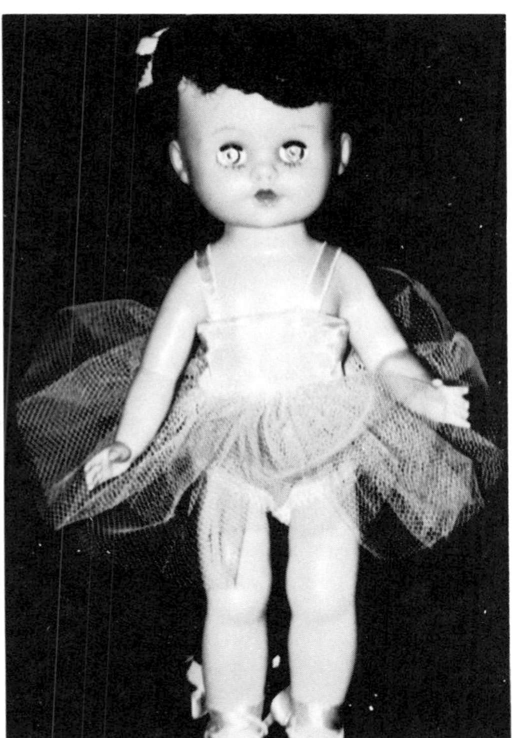

Eegee--8½" "Ballerina Sherry" One piece stuffed vinyl body. Pale blue with white net overskirt. Pink slippers. Blue ribbon/pink flowers to tie ponytail. Marks: Eegee, head. Eegee/8, on body. $5.00. (Courtesy Bessie Carson)

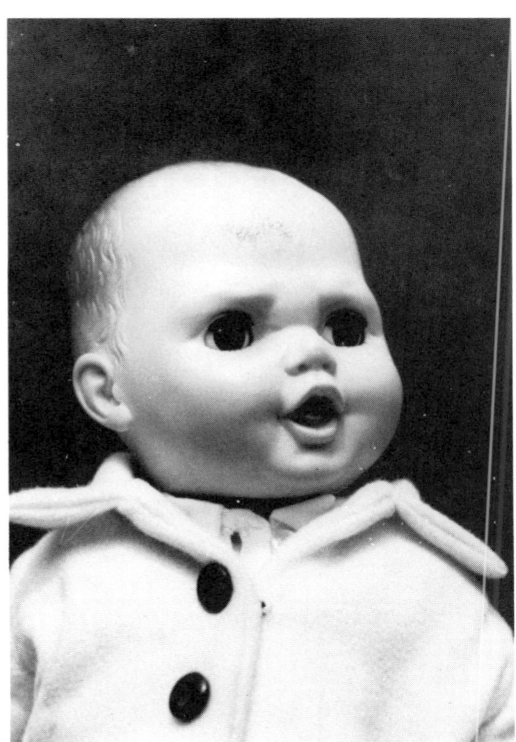

Eegee--17" "Buster" Plastic body and legs. Vinyl arms and head. Open/closed mouth. Marks: 1959/Eegee. Molded hair. Blue sleep eyes. $7.00. (Courtesy Phyliss Houston)

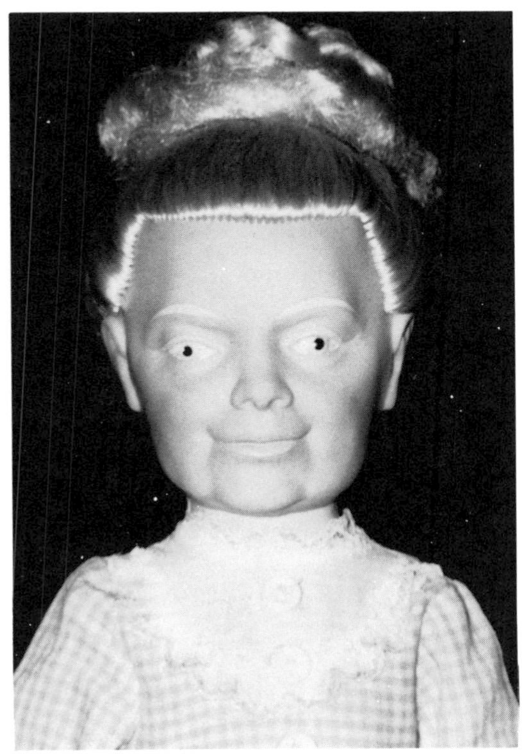

Eegee--14" Granny type. Plastic and vinyl with grey brows and eyes. Long white hair pulled up in a bun. Original. Marks: Eegee/3. $30.00. (Courtesy Linda Fox)

Eegee--15" "Luvable Baby" Also known as "Sherry Lou." All vinyl one piece body, arms and legs. Vinyl head. Blue sleep eyes. Marks: Eegee, on head. Eegee, on body. 1956. $6.00.

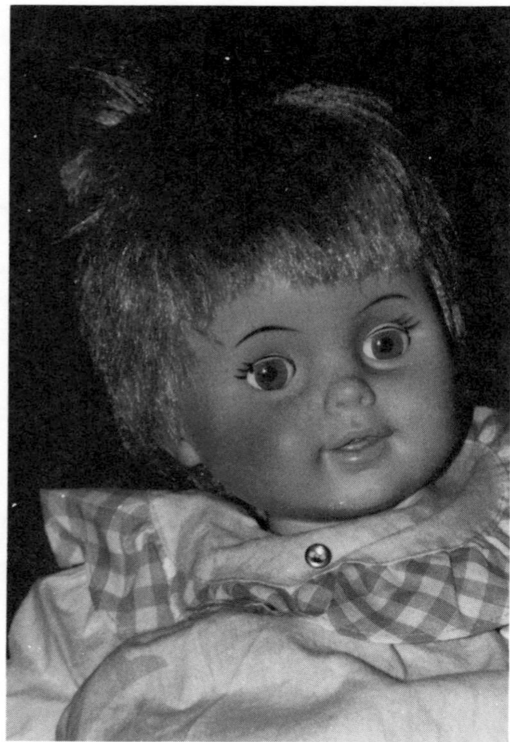

Eegee--16" "Newborn Baby Doll" Cloth with vinyl head and limbs. Sleep eyes. Open closed mouth/molded tongue. Marks: Eegee Co./173. 1963. $6.00. (Courtesy Elaine Kaminsky)

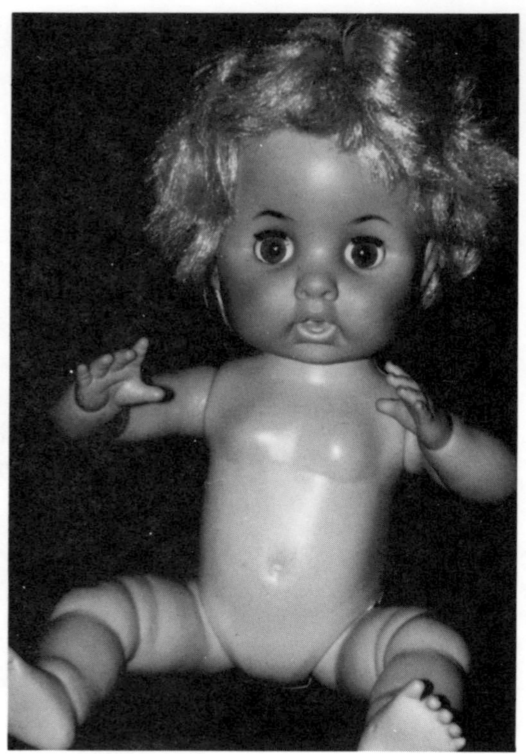

Eegee--12" "Sniffles" Plastic body. Vinyl arms, legs and head. Open mouth/nurser. Blue sleep eyes/lashes. Came with layette. Marks: 13/14 AA/Eegee Co. 1963. $4.00.

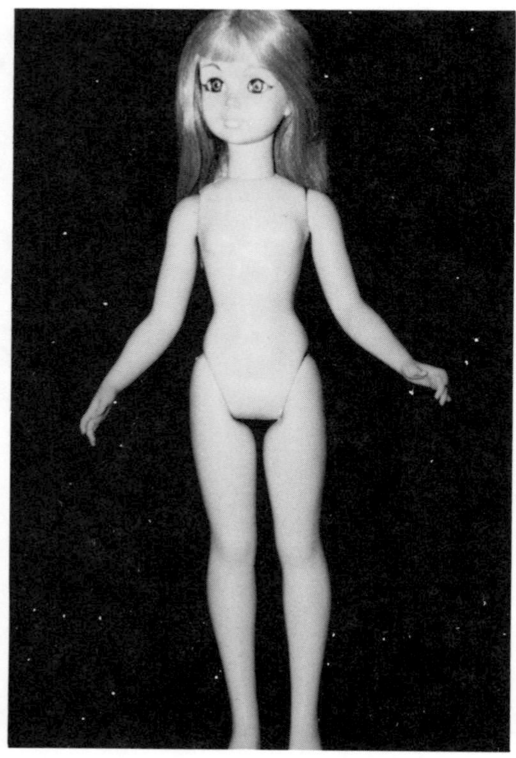

Eegee--15" "Gemette" to show body. Marks: Eegee, on head. 1963/Eegee Co., on back. This doll has been used for several personalities. $4.00.

Eegee--16" "Rose Red Flowerkin" Plastic and vinyl. Blue sleep eyes. All original. Marks: 8/F2/ Eegee, on head. Goldberger Doll/Mfg. Co. Inc./ Pat. Pend. on back. 1963. $12.00.

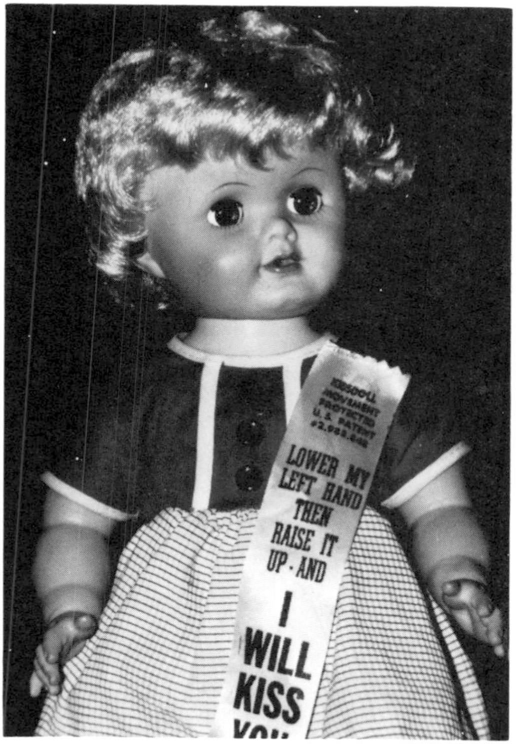


Eegee--17" "Kiss Me" Plastic with vinyl arms and head. Raise left arm and mouth "kisses." Blue sleep eyes. Original. Marks: 14-16/Eegee, on head. 16 inside left arm and New/16 inside right arm. Tag: Kiss Me movement protected U.S. Patent #2,988, 843. 1963. $5.00.

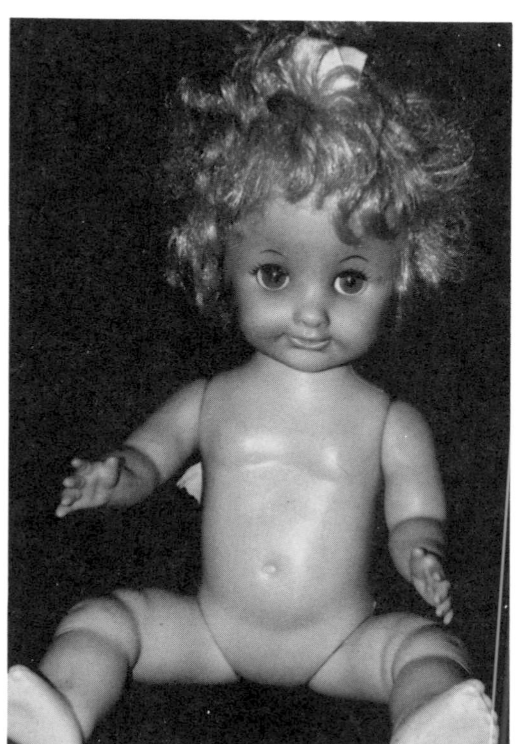

Eegee--10" "Darling Baby" Plastic and vinyl. Blue sleep eyes. Open mouth/nurser. Marks: 25/10T/Eegee Co. 1964. $3.00.

Eegee--31" "Bonnie Ballerina" Plastic and vinyl. Jointed ankles, hips, waist, shoulders and neck. Sleep eyes. Original. Marks: Eegee/5, on head. 1964. $18.00. (Courtesy Alice Capps)

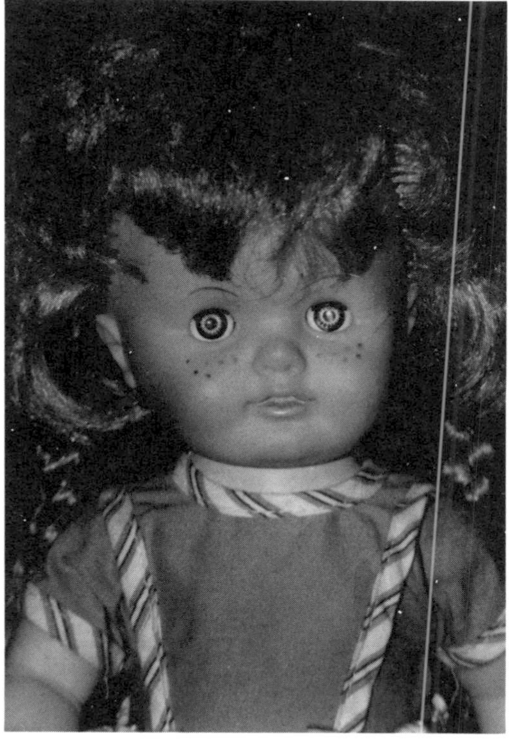

Eegee--12" Plastic and vinyl. Hair rooted in ponytails. Freckles. Sleep eyes. Marks: 12 12K/Eegee. $6.00. (Courtesy Cecelia Eades)

Eegee--21½" "Carol" Plastic and vinyl. Flat feet. Pre-teen body. Sleep eyes. Marks: Eegee Co./ 15 PM/1B or 8. 1968. $9.00. (Courtesy Phyllis Houston)

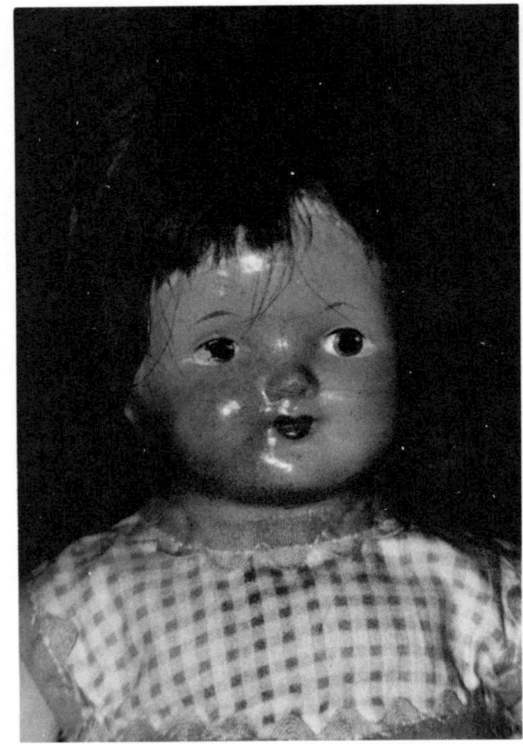

Effanbee--15" "Baby Dainty" Cloth with composition shoulderplate. Painted blue eyes. Mohair over molded hair. Marks: Effanbee/Baby Dainty. $50.00. (Courtesy Marie Ernst)

For complete Effanbee Company information refer to Series I, Page 83.

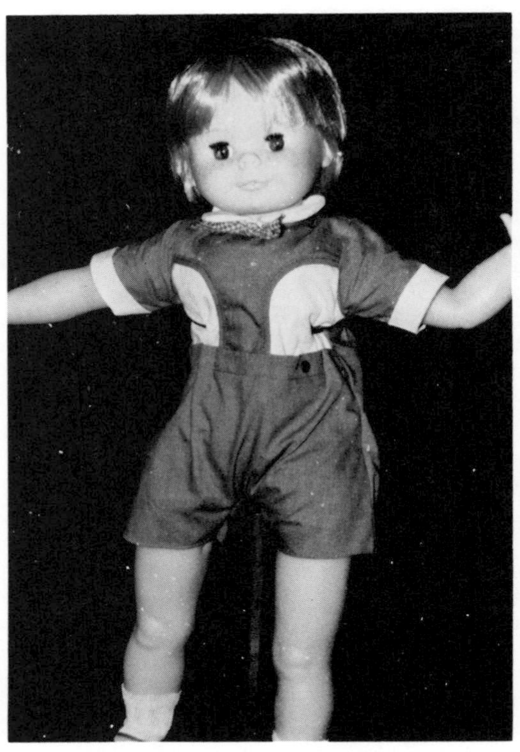

Eegee--23" "Georgie" Twin to "Georgette" Refer to Vol. II, page 86. Green sleep eyes. Freckles. Cloth body. Orange hair. Original. Marks: 17/ RNG/Eegee. 1971. $8.00. (Courtesy Marie Ernst)

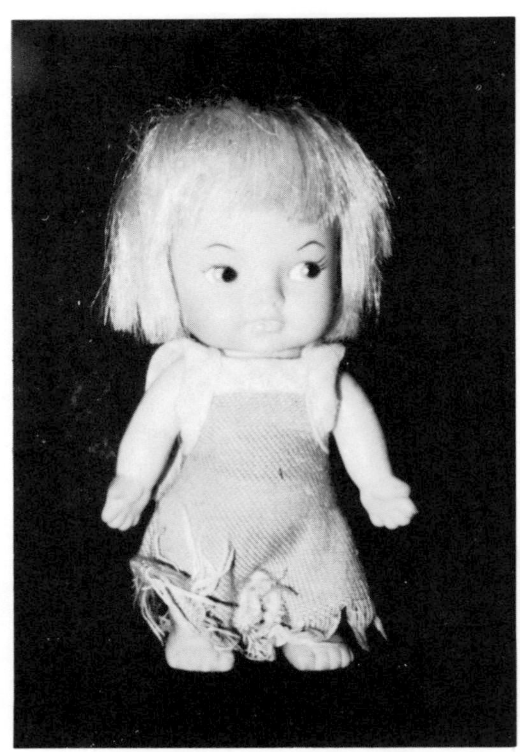

Eegee--3½" All vinyl. Jointed neck only. Rooted white hair. Painted blue eyes. Marks: Eegee Co. 1966. $2.00.

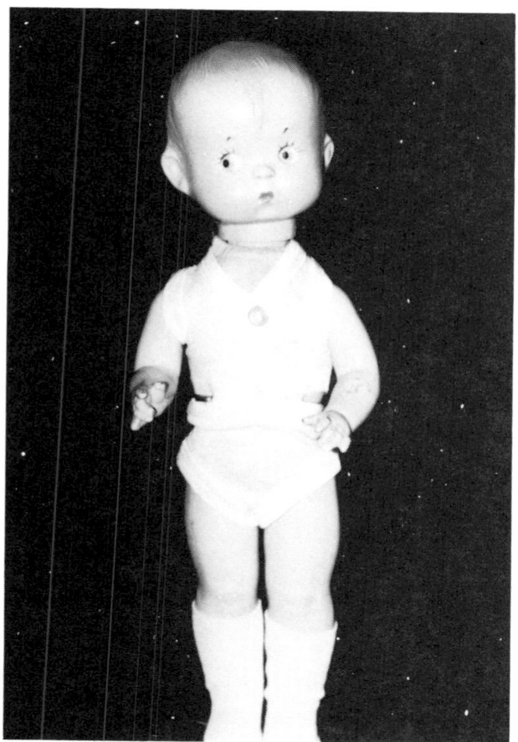

Effanbee--14" "Skippy" Cloth body with composition head and limbs. Wood block neck. Molded hair with one lock down forehead. Marks: Skippy/Effanbee. $55.00.

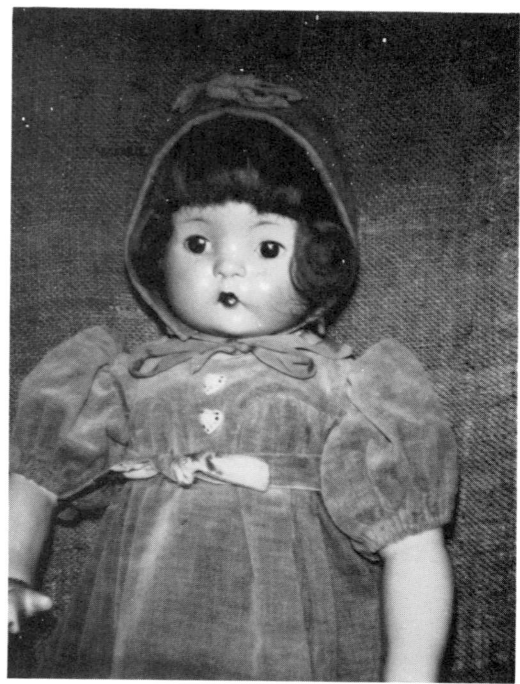

Effanbee--27" "Patsy Ruth" Cloth body with composition limbs and head. Brown sleep eyes. Human hair wig. All original. Marks: Effanbee/Patsy Ruth. 1935. $150.00.

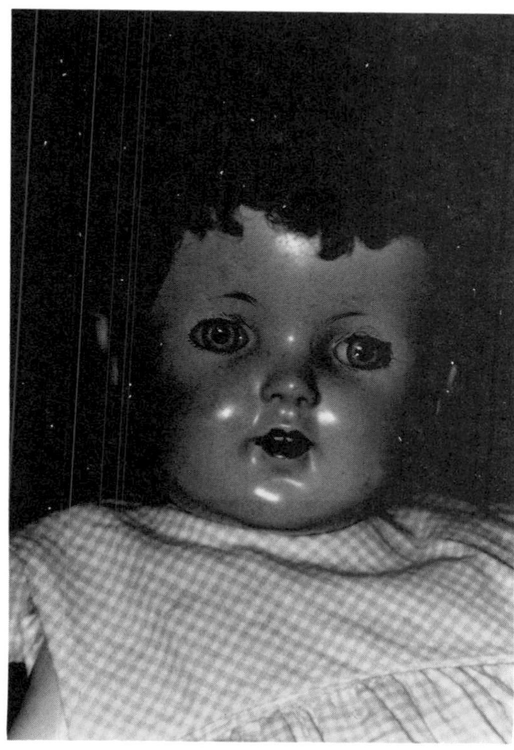

Effanbee--16" "Mary Lee" All composition. Sleep eyes/lashes. Open mouth/4 teeth and felt tongue. Marks: Mary Lee on head. Effanbee/Patsy Joan, on back. $75.00. (Courtesy Alice Capps)

Effanbee--8" "Button Nose" All composition with painted brown eyes and molded hair. Marks: None. Button: Blue Bird/Effanbee Dolls/Finest and Best. Refer to Vol. II, page 89. 1943. $35.00.

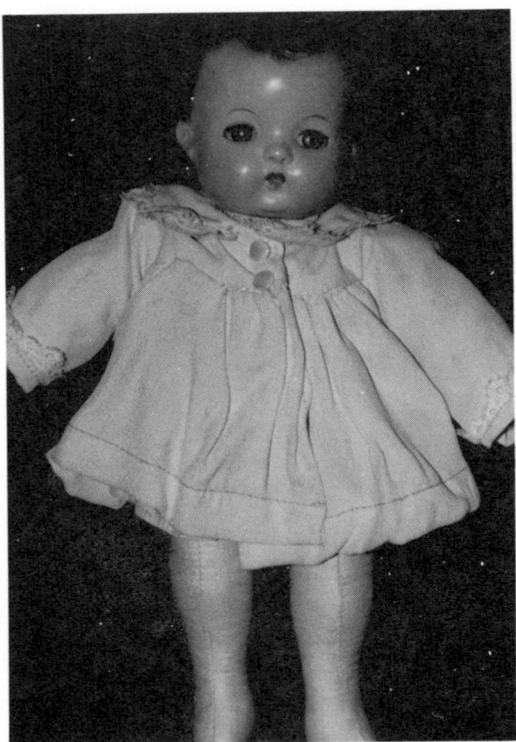

Effanbee--10" "Patsy Baby" Cloth body, legs and arms with gauntlet celluloid hands. Composition head. Sleep eyes. Original clothes minus bonnet. $45.00.

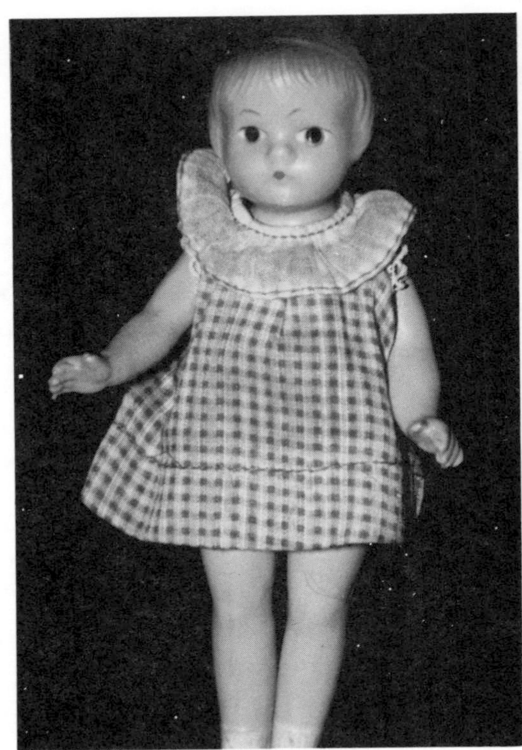

Effanbee--5½" "Wee Patsy" All composition. Molded on hair band, shoes and socks. Original. $85.00. (Courtesy Helen Draves)

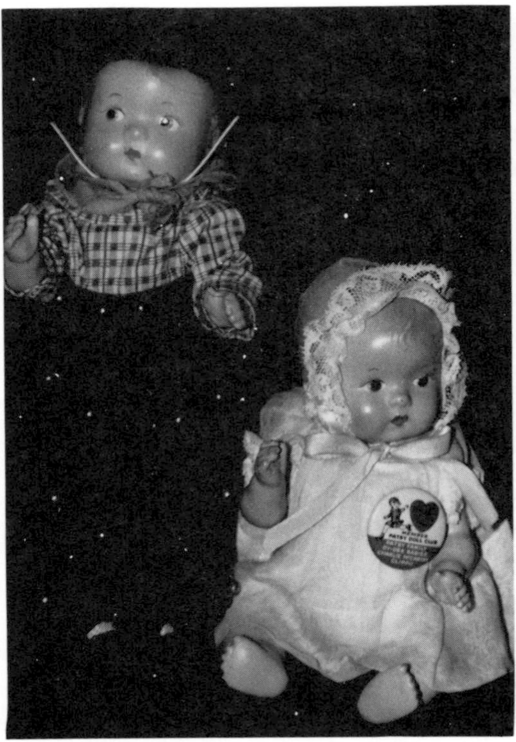

Effanbee--8" "Baby Tinyette" All composition. Came in both straight and bent baby legs. Marks: Effanbee/Baby Tinyette, on back. Effanbee, on head. Original. 1933-36. $50 each. (Courtesy Marge Meisinger)

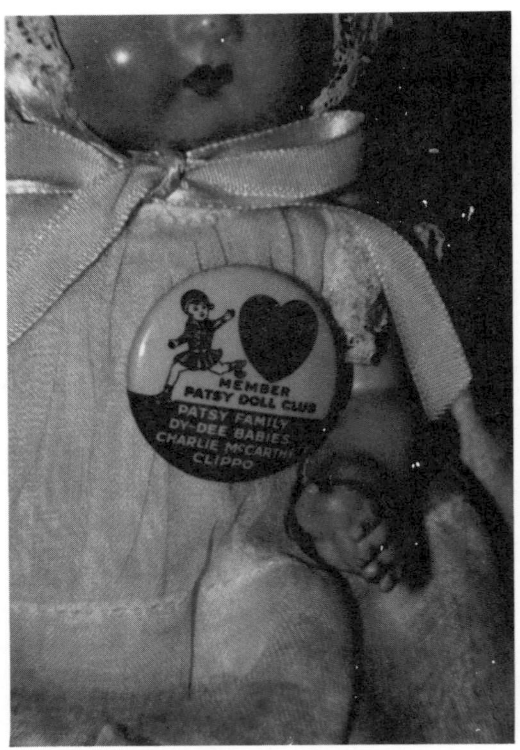


Effanbee--Shows close up of the Patsy Doll Club pin worn by Baby Tinyette. (Courtesy Marge Meisinger)

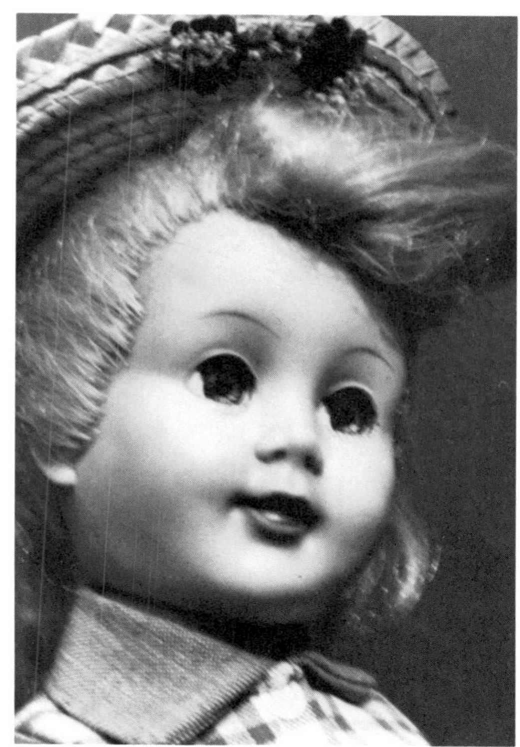

Effanbee--18½" Hard plastic body and limbs. Vinyl head. Blue sleep eyes with molded eyelids. Smile mouth. Original. Marks: Effanbee, on head. $22.00. (Courtesy Phyllis Houston)

Effanbee--Shows interesting hairline of the 18½" girl.

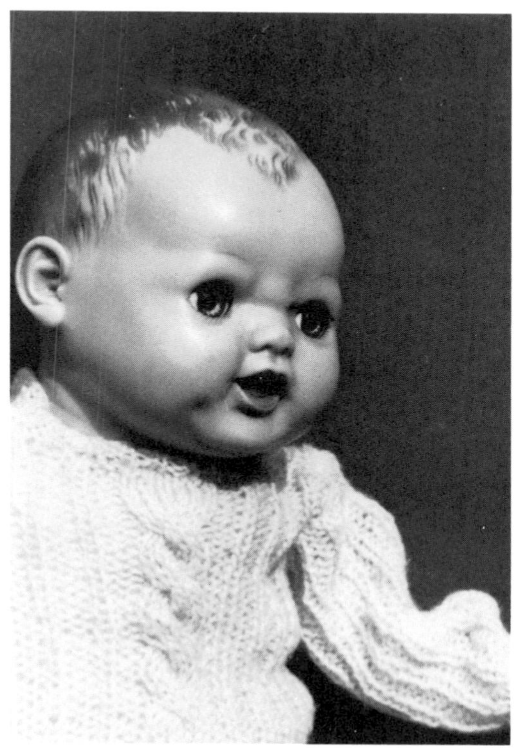

Effanbee--16" "Lil Darlin" Sleep eye version. Cloth body with cry box. Sticky early vinyl head and ¾ arms and legs. Marks: Effanbee, on head. $15.00. (Courtesy Phyllis Houston)

Effanbee--12" "Baby Cup Cake" 1964 through Sears. Plastic and vinyl. Blue sleep eyes. Deep dimples. Open mouth but no wetting hole. Marks: Effanbee/1963, back and head. $5.00. (Courtesy Phyllis Houston)

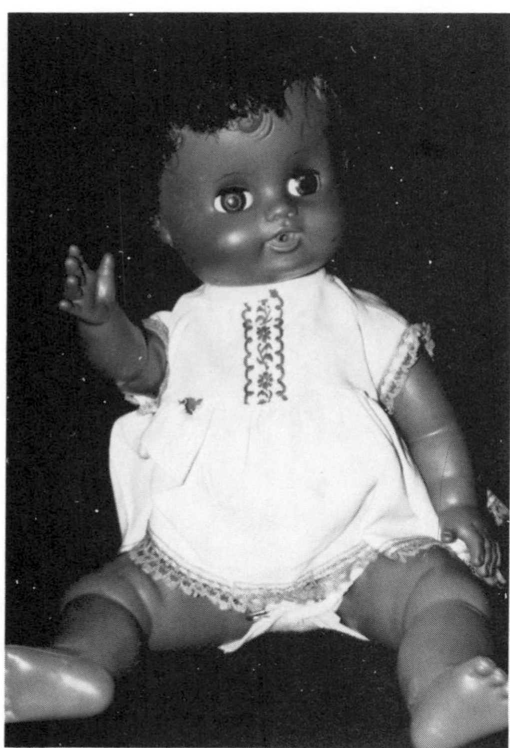

Eugene--12" "Baby Sarah Lee" Plastic body and legs. Vinyl arms and head. Rooted black hair over molded hair. Original. Marks: Eugene, on head. 1965. $4.00.

Eugene--9½" "Baby Missey" Cloth with vinyl arms, legs and head. Blue sleep eyes. Rooted brown hair. Marks: Tag: Eugene Doll Co. 91, inside arms. 91/14, inside legs. 960/Made in Taiwan/8 Eye/5, on head. $2.00.

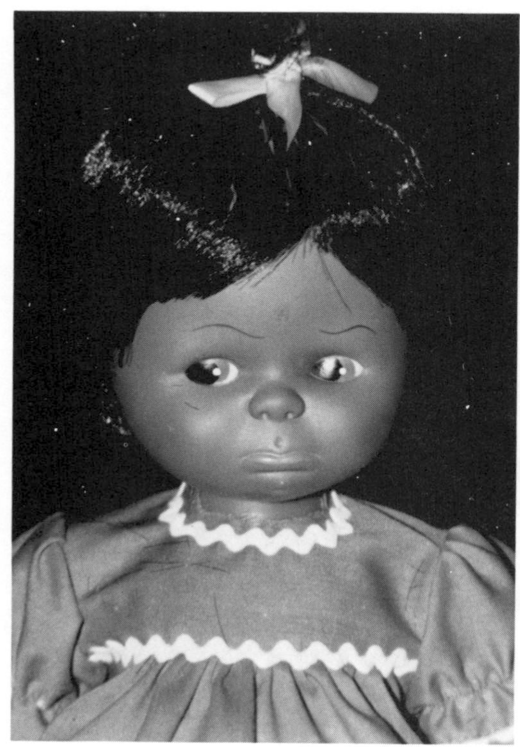

Eugene--Check under Lorrie for more dolls by this company. The company name is Eugene but the dolls are marked Lorrie.
12" "Bitter-Sweet" Pouty. Plastic and vinyl. Painted eyes. Also comes in white version. Marks: P/Lorrie Doll Co/1974. Eugene on box. $18.00.

Eugene--12" "Sweet-ee" Plastic and vinyl. Character face. Painted eyes. Marks: G/Lorrie Doll Co/1974, on head. Eugene on box. $18.00.

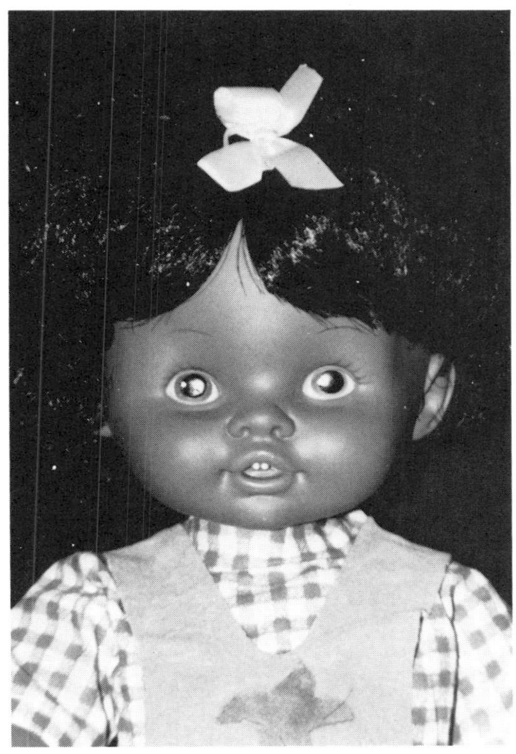

Eugene--12" "Taffy" Plastic and vinyl. Open/closed mouth with two molded and painted upper teeth. Marks: T/Lorrie Doll Co./1974, on head. Eugene on box. $18.00.

Eugene--7" "Pit & Pat" Plastic with vinyl heads. Painted features. Marks: Taiwan, on head. Made in Taiwan, on backs. $4.00.

Eugenia--6½" "Eugenia" dressed in "Goes To A Party." All composition. Jointed arms only. Painted on black shoes. Painted blue eyes. Marks: None. Box: A Touch of Paris/picture of Eiffel Tower/Copyright 1945. $12.00.

Eugenia--6½" "Friday-Eugenia Goes To The U.S.O." All composition. Jointed arms only. Painted blue eyes. Painted on black shoes. Marks: None. Box: A Touch of Paris, picture of Eiffel Tower/Copyright 1945. Friday Eugenia Goes To The U.S.O. $12.00.

Eugenia--6½" "Eugenia's Bridesmaid" All composition. Jointed at arms only. Painted blue eyes. Painted on black shoes. Marks: None. Box: A Touch of Paris/picture of Eiffel Tower/Copyright 1945/Eugenia's Bridesmaid. $12.00.

Excel--9½" "Pochahontas" Rigid plastic with vinyl head. Jointed action figure. Ball jointed waist. Molded black hair. Marks: Excel Toy Corp/Hong Kong, on head. Available in some areas.

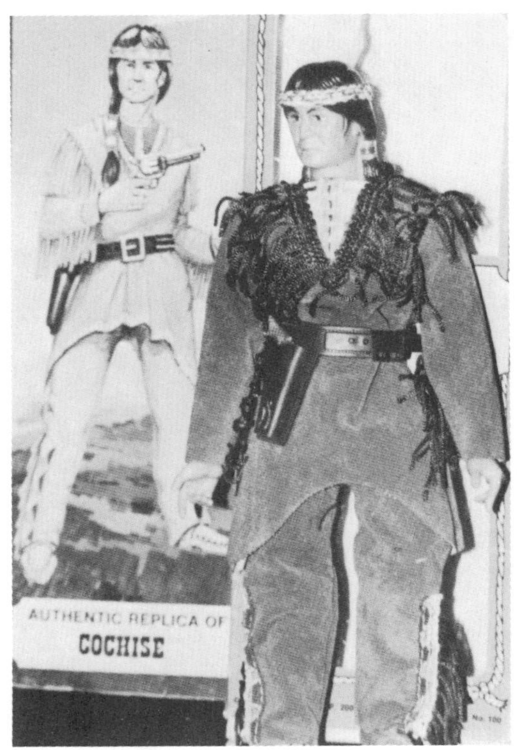


Excel--9½" "Cochise" Action figure. Marks: Excel Toy Corp/Hong Kong, on head. Available in some areas.

Excel--9½" "Annie Oakley" Rigid plastic with vinyl head. Jointed action figure. Ball jointed waist. Molded blonde hair. Marks: Excel Toy Corp/Hong Kong, on head. Available in some areas.

Excel--9½" "Wild Bill Hickok" Action figure. Marks: Excel Toy Corp/Hong Kong, on head. Available in some areas.

Excel--9½" "Calamity Jane" Rigid plastic with vinyl head. Jointed action figure. Ball jointed waist. Molded dark blonde hair. Marks: Excel Toy Corp/Hong Kong, on head. Available in some areas.

Excel--9½" "Buffalo Bill Cody" Action figure. Marks: Excel Toy Corp/Hong Kong, on head. Available in some areas.

Excel--9½" "Deadwood Dick" Action figure. Marks: Excel Toy Corp./Hong Kong, on head. Available in some areas.

Excel--9½" "Belle Starr" Rigid plastic with vinyl head. Jointed action figure. Ball jointed waist. Molded brown hair. Marks: Excel Toy Corp/ Hong Kong, on head. Men in set: Deadwood Dick, Jessie James, Buffalo Bill Cody, Cochise, Wyatt Earp, Wild Bill Cody, Davy Crockett. Available in some areas.

Excel--9½" "Davy Crockett" Action figure. Marks: Excel Toy Corp/Hong Kong, on head. Still available in some areas.

Excel--9½" "Jessie James" Action figure. Marks: Excel Toy Corp/Hong Kong, on head. Available in some areas.

Excel-9½" "Wyatt Earp" Action figure. Marks: Excel Toy Corp/Hong Kong, on head. Available in some areas.

Excel--12" "George Washington" 1732-1799. Marks: Same as Gen. Lee. Available in some areas.

Excel--12" "Ulysses S. Grant" 1822-1885. Same marks as Gen. Lee. Available in some areas.

Excel--12" "Lt. Col. Theodore Roosevelt" 1858-1919. Marks same as Gen. Lee. Available in some areas.

Excel--12" "Gen. John. J. Pershing" 1860-1948. Marks same as Gen. Lee. Available in some areas.

Excel--12" "Lt. Col. Paul Revere" 1735-1818. Marks same as Gen. Lee. Available in some areas.

Excel--12" "Gen. Robert E. Lee" Plastic and vinyl. Fully jointed action figure. Excellent modeling. Marks: Excel Toy Corp/Hong Kong. Box: 1974. Available in some areas.

Excel--12" "Gen. Joseph W. Stillwell" 1883-1946. Marked same as Gen. Lee. Available in some areas.

Excel--12" "Gen. Douglas MacArthur" 1880-1964 Marks same as Gen. Lee. Available in some areas.

Excel--12" "Admiral William F. Halsey" 1882-1959. Marks same as Gen. Lee. Available in some areas.

Excel--12" "Dwight D. Eisenhower" 1890-1969. Marks same as Gen. Lee. Available in some areas.

Excel--12" "Gen. Claire L. Chinnault" 1890-1964. Marked same as Gen. Lee. Available in some areas.

Excel--12" "Gen. George S. Patton" 1884-1945. Marked same as Gen. Lee. Available in some areas.

Flagg--6½" "Cowgirl" All vinyl and posable. Molded blonde hair in bun in back. All original. Vest removable only. Marks: None. $7.00.

Flagg--7" "Egyptian" Glued on hair. Painted features. All vinyl that is made in one piece and is bendable. $7.00. (Courtesy Marge Meisinger)

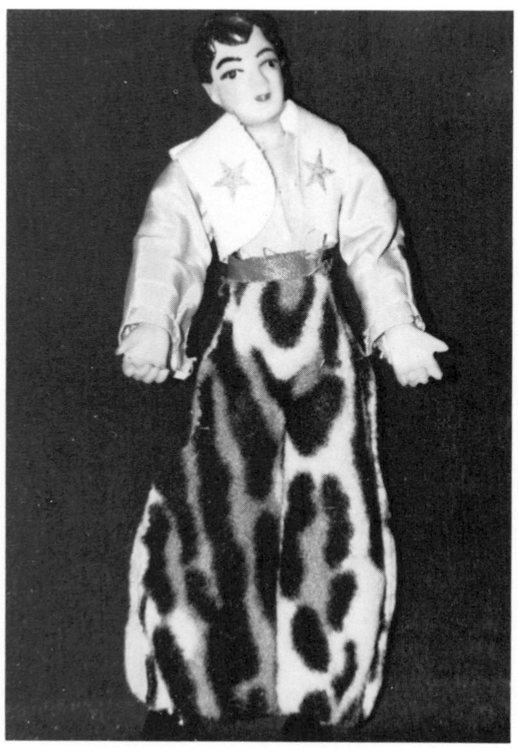

Flagg--7" "Cowboy" All bendable one piece vinyl. Molded hair and painted eyes. Original except hat. $7.00. (Courtesy Marge Meisinger)

Flagg--7" "Calypso Dancer" All posable vinyl. Molded black hair. Stapled on clothes. Marks: None. $7.00.

Flagg--7" "Flagg Dancer" Given to dance students of the Charlotte School of Dance. $7.00. (Courtesy Alice Capps)

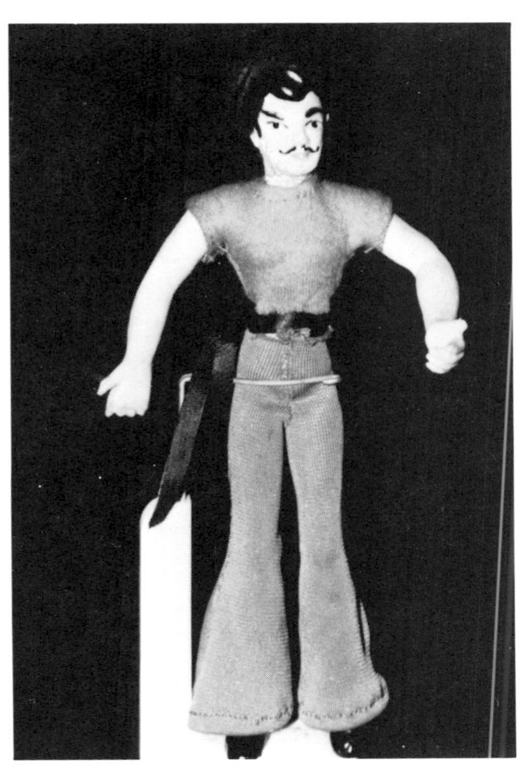

Flagg--7" "Frenchman" ca. 1947. $7.00. (Courtesy Alice Capps)

Flagg--3" "Children" Boy and girl. All one piece vinyl that is posable. Molded hair and painted features. Girl is original. $3.00 each. (Courtesy Marge Meisinger)

Flanders, Harriet--11" All composition. Painted blue eyes. Yellow molded and glued on yarn hair. Marks: Harriet Flanders/1937. $35.00. (Courtesy Jay Minter)

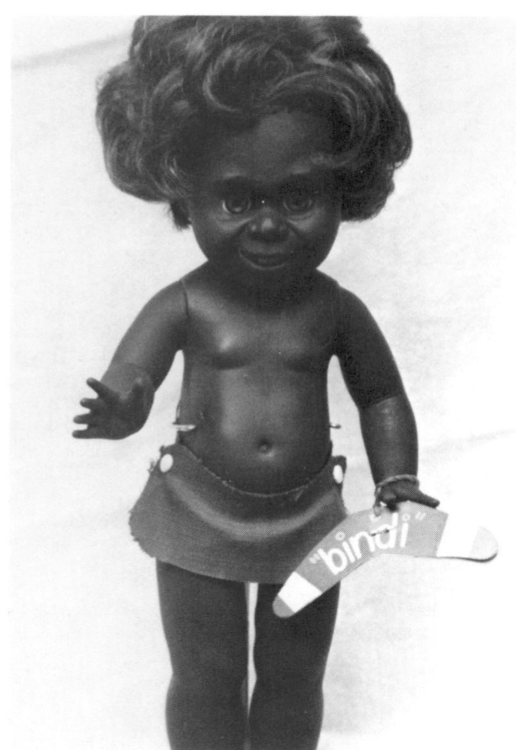


Australia--13" "Bindi" All vinyl with amber/orange sleep eyes. Streaked hair. Painted/molded teeth. Marks: Metti/Autralia. $45.00. (Courtesy Marie Ernst)

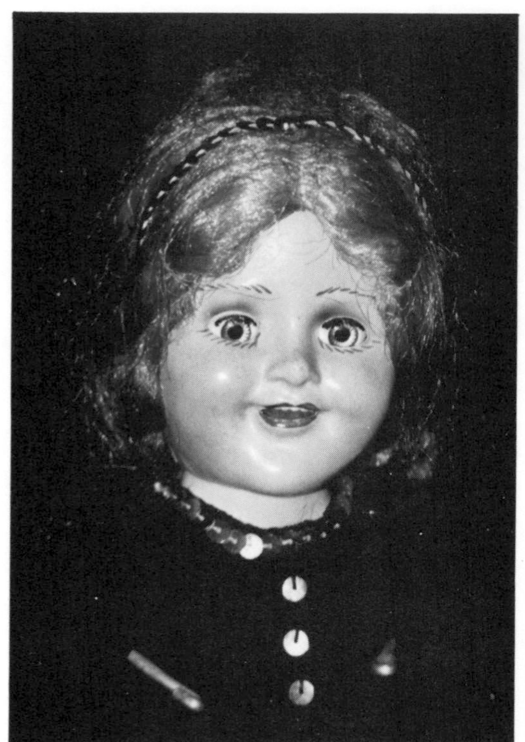

Canada--14" "Barbara Ann Scott" All composition. Blue sleep eyes. Open mouth with six teeth. Marks: Reliable of Canada. $75.00. (Courtesy Helen Garrett)

China--9" Character doll. All composition. Molded, painted hair. Painted dark green eyes. Marks: Box: Made in the People's Republic of China. $30.00. (Courtesy Dodie Shapiro)

China--12" All composition. A beautiful quality doll. Marks: Box: Made in China. $35.00. (Courtesy Dodie Shapiro)

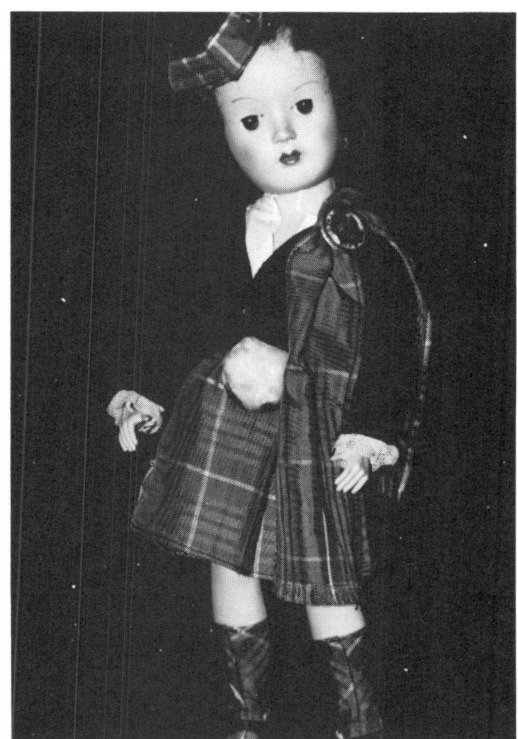

England--14" "Glasgon Scotland" All hard plastic with a matt finish on head. Brown sleep eyes/long lashes. Glued on red mohair. Doll is strung. Original. Marks: Politoy/35/Made in England. $15.00. (Courtesy Mary Partridge)

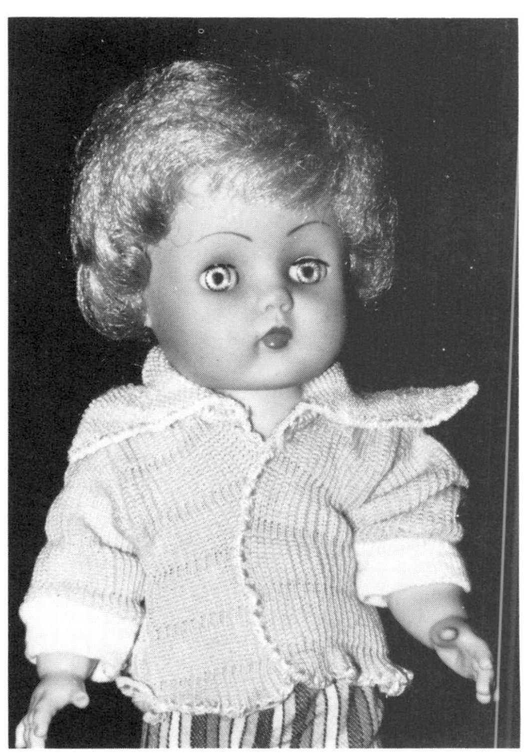

England--11½" "Tricia" All very good quality vinyl. Blue sleep eyes with blue eyeshadow all around eyes. Marks: Chiltern/Made in England, on back. 1961. Sold thorugh Marshall Fields. $6.00. (Courtesy Mary Partridge)

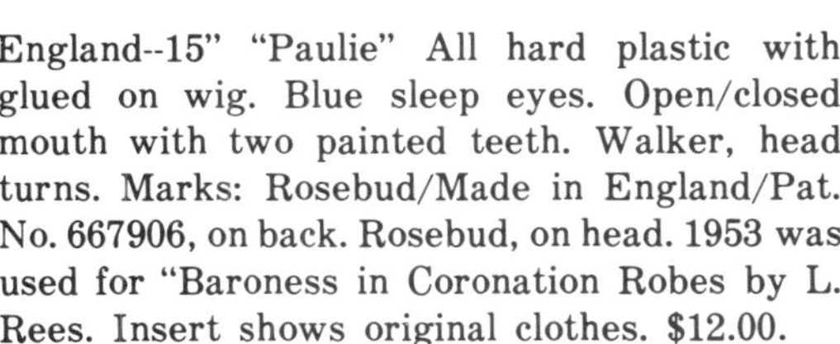

England--15" "Paulie" All hard plastic with glued on wig. Blue sleep eyes. Open/closed mouth with two painted teeth. Walker, head turns. Marks: Rosebud/Made in England/Pat. No. 667906, on back. Rosebud, on head. 1953 was used for "Baroness in Coronation Robes by L. Rees. Insert shows original clothes. $12.00.

England--7" "Twins" All hard plastic with pale blue sleep eyes/no lashes. Wide spread fingers. Painted on shoes and socks. Original velvet "dance" outfits. Marks: Pedigree, in a triangle/ Made in/England. ca. 1960. $3.00 each.

England--21" "Lucky Lisa" Plastic body, legs and right arm. Vinyl left arm and head. Blue sleep eyes. Painted teeth, "Plug in" in right hand. Battery operated. Jointed right wrist. Original. Marks: 030-00, on head. Dress Tag: Pedigree/Made in England. 1971. Holds dice cup. $8.00.

England--7½" "Chad Valley" All rubber. Painted brown eyes. Painted on black shoes. Glued on mohair. Marks: Chad Valley/Pat. 517252/Made in/England. Tag on slip: Hygienic Toys/Made in England by/Chad Valley Co. Ltd. $10.00. (Courtesy Mary Partridge)

## Peggy Nisbet Dolls

The Peggy Nisbet dolls are made in the seaside town of Westonsuper-Mare in the West Country of England. Mrs. Nisbet began making dolls in 1953 (Coronation year). The dolls listed below are currently available: The numbers following them are order numbers.

THE ROYAL FAMILY
Queen Elizabeth in state robes P400
Queen Elizabeth in Garter Robes P401
Queen Elizabeth in Thistle Robes P406
Princes Charles in Garter Robes P402
Queen Elizabeth, The Queen Mother (Garter) P403
Princess Anne in Wedding Dress P405

THE PLANTAGANETS
King Henry VI P642
Margaret of Anjou P643

THE HOUSE OF TUDOR
King Henry VIII H218
Katherine of Aragon H219
Anne Boleyn H217
Jane Seymour H220
Anne of Cleves H222
Catherine Howard H221
Catherine Parr H223
Queen Elizabeth I H214
Lady Jane Grey H216
William Shakespeare P617

THE HOUSE OF STUART
King Charles I P609
Henrietta Maria H239
King Charles II P639
Catherine of Braganza H286
Nell Gwyn, Mistress of H275
King Charles II
Lady Randolph Churchill P592
Sir Winston Churchill P615
King George VI P712
Queen Elizabeth (State robes) P713
King Edward VIII P711
King George V P709
Queen Mary (State robes) P710
Queen Victoria (State robes) P708
King Edward VII P611
Queen Alexandra P612
Queen Victoria (widow) P610
Prince Albert P624

SCOTTISH KINGS & QUEENS &
HISTORICAL CHARACTERS
King James IV P559
Margaret Tudor P238
Mary Queen of Scots H209
Mary Queen of Scots (wedding) P608
Mary Seaton H247
Mary Fleming H248
Charles Edward Stuart P210
Flora MacDonald H224
King James VI P638
Anne of Denmark P249

SCOTTISH COSTUMES
Bonnie Mary BR241
Scots Lassie BR311
Scots Laddie BR312
Scottish Piper BR339
Pipper of the Royal Highlanders BR325

CRIES OF LONDON
Lavender Girl BR304
Orange Seller BR305
Cherry Ripe BR306
Flower Girl BR309
Pretty Ribbons BR378

COSTUMES OF THE WORLD
Argentine N146
Austria N108
France N101
Germany N123
Holland N109
Hungary N102
Italy N104
Japan N116
Jersy N160
Norway N114
Spain N112
Switzerland N107

COSTUMES AND UNIFORMS
OF GREAT BRITAIN
England BR376
Wales BR301
Ireland BR302
Pearly King BR314
Pearly Queen BR315
Grenadier Guardsman BR317
Yeoman Warder (Beefeater) BR330

SOUVENIR RANGE
Donald (Scottish Dancer) S501
Meg (Scottish Dancer) S502
Stewart (Piper) S503
Molly S504
Blodwen S505
Susan S506
Thomas (Guardsman) S507
James (Beefeater) S508

MODELS OF YESTERYEAR
These are no longer in production
but may be reintroduced in years to come.
Elysabeth of York
Cardinal Wolsey
Pope John XXIII
Lord Darnley
James Hepburn, Earl of Bothwell
Robert Burns
Richard III
Queen Anne
William the Conqueror
Queen Matilda
Frances, Countess of Warwick
King Edward II
Queen Isabella
King Henry V
Queen Catherine
Princess Margaret
Catherine, Empress of Russia
Hengrist, Chief of the Angles
Lord Nelson
Lady Hamilton
Georgiana, Dutchess of Devonshire

BICENTENARY
Gen. George Washington P702
Martha Washington P703
Betsy Ross H226
Paul Revere P704
The Famous Minutemen H814
Minuteman's Wife H815
American Trooper H816
Indian Warrior P705
King George III (State robes) P706
British Redcoat 1776 H817
Queen Charlotte P707

THE FRENCH COURT
Marie Antoinette H215
Madame Pompadour H227
Madame DuBerry H271

CENTURY LADIES
15th Century Medieval Lady H211
16th Century Elizabethan Lady H202
18th Century Georgian Lady H204
19th Century Victorian Lady (Crinoline) H225
19th Century Victorian Lady H258
20th Century Edwardian Lady H801
Peeress of the Realm H811

SPECIAL COLLECTOR'S SETS
Each is autographed by Mrs. Peggy Nisbet. Editions are limited to 350. A set comprises 3 to 5 models. Set No. 10 was introduced March 1975 and set No. 11 was available June 1975.
King John and his Barons
War of the Roses (Part I)
War of the Roses (Part II)
The Spanish Armada
The Battle of Waterloo
Three Tragic Queens
Louis XIV-The Sun King
Bloody Mary-Mary Tudor
King William IV
Regency Period
The Court of King Arthur

England--8" "H.M. Queen Elizabeth II" Made by Peggy Nisbet in 1971. (#1395). $25.00. (Courtesy Marie Ernst)

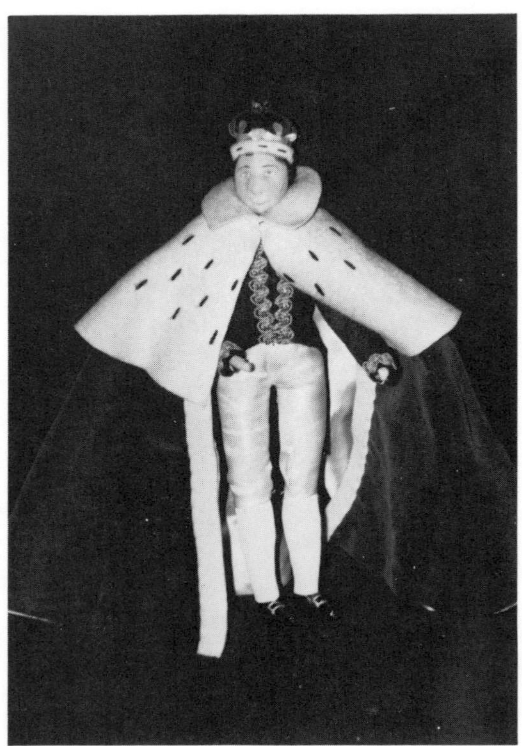

England--8½" "King" All cloth with wired arms. Original. Tag: Liberty/Made in England. $18.00. (Courtesy Barbara Coker)

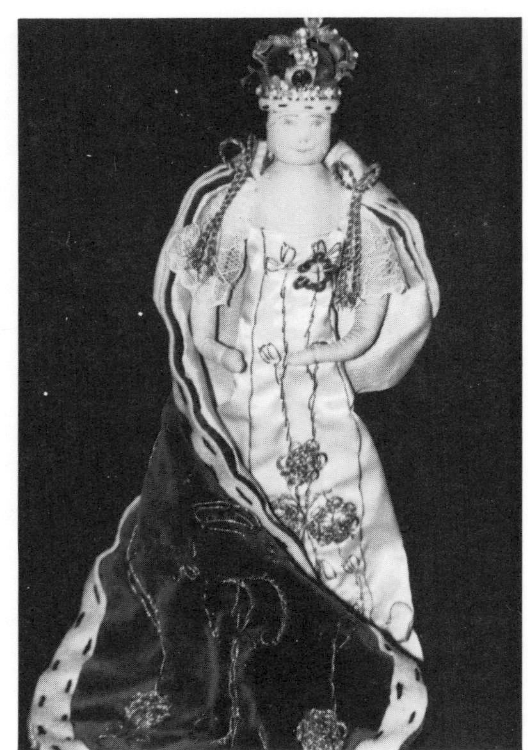

England--8½" "Queen" All cloth with wired arms. Original. Tag: Liberty/Made in England. $18.00. (Courtesy Barbara Coker)

France--30" "Oriental" Plastic and vinyl with molded paper head and paper hair. Body is in two sections which allows it to "move." Original. Used in a window display. Made by G. Giroud & Cie, France. 1960. $30.00. (Courtesy Karen Penner)

France--12" All vinyl. Jointed neck, shoulders and hips. Inset eyes/lashes. Open/closed mouth. Marks: M/P, on head. ca. 1962. Original. $4.00. (Courtesy Mary Partridge)

Germany--7" All vinyl with jointed neck. No ears. Dark sun tan color with rooted white hair. Painted black eyes. 1963. Marks: Heico/H/Made in Western/Germany, seal on bottom. Necklace: Original/Western Germany. $4.00.

Germany--12" "Gucki" Rubber and felt. Tag: Mollenecht Durch/Eulan/Bayer/ Leverrisen. $8.00. (Courtesy Jay Minter)

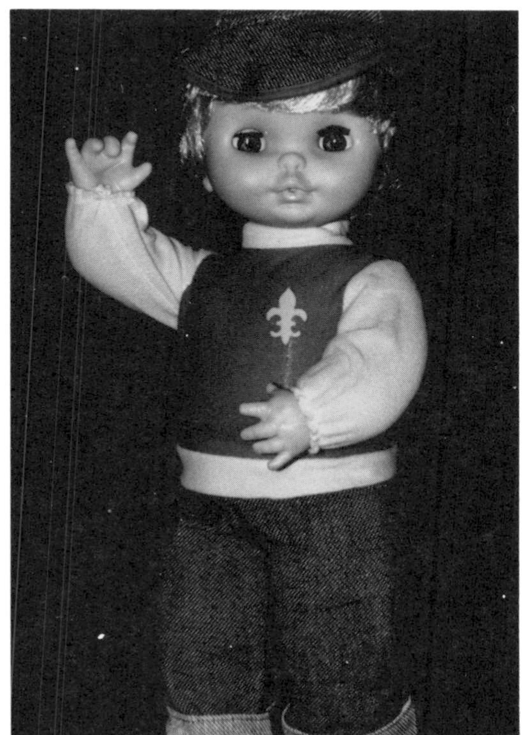

France--16" "Edmond" Plastic body. Vinyl arms. legs and head. Golden brown sleep eyes. Bent baby legs. Individual large toes. Tiny hole in mouth/nurser. Marks: Clodrey/2018-6926, on head. Original clothes. 1972-73 and 74. $22.00.

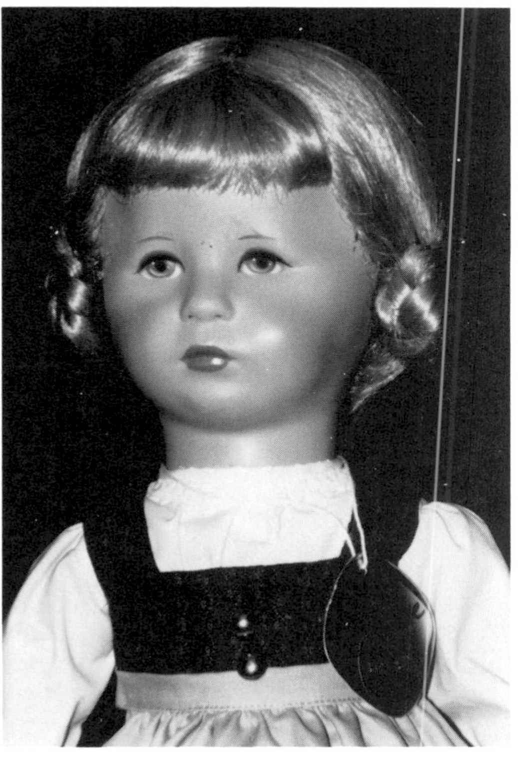

Germany--19" "Riekchen" 1970. Cloth and rigid plastic. Painted blue eyes. Marks: Tag: Kathe Kruse/Exclusive for Neiman-Marcus. $28.00. (Courtesy Jay Minter)

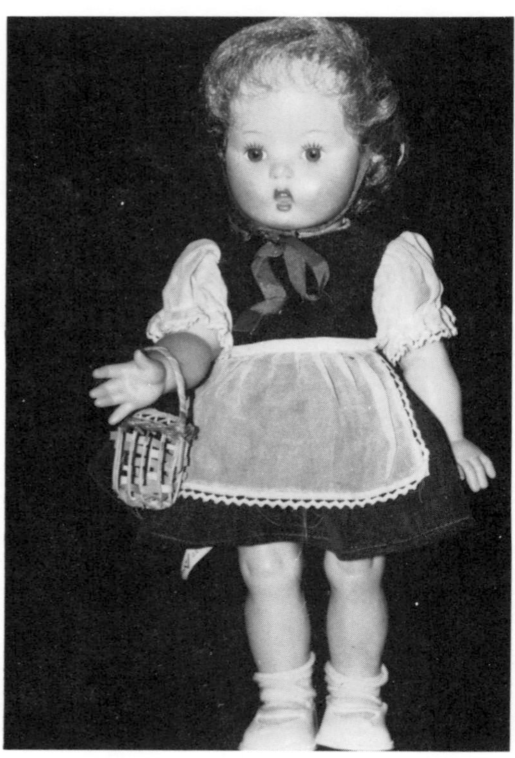

Germany--14" "Hummel" Vinyl with open/closed mouth. Inset eyes. $8.00. (Courtesy Jay Minter)

Germany--18" Cloth over foam. Vinyl gauntlet hands. Vinyl head with inset blue eyes. Marks: None. 1968. $16.00. (Courtesy Julia Rogers)

Germany--5½" "Hummel" Painted green eyes. Plastic and vinyl. Marks: Bee in V 2914/2/ Charlotte Byj/1966 W. Goebel., on head. Bee in V/W. Goebel/1966/Charlotte Byj/2914/1x2/W. Germany, on back. $3.00. (Courtesy Phyllis Houston)

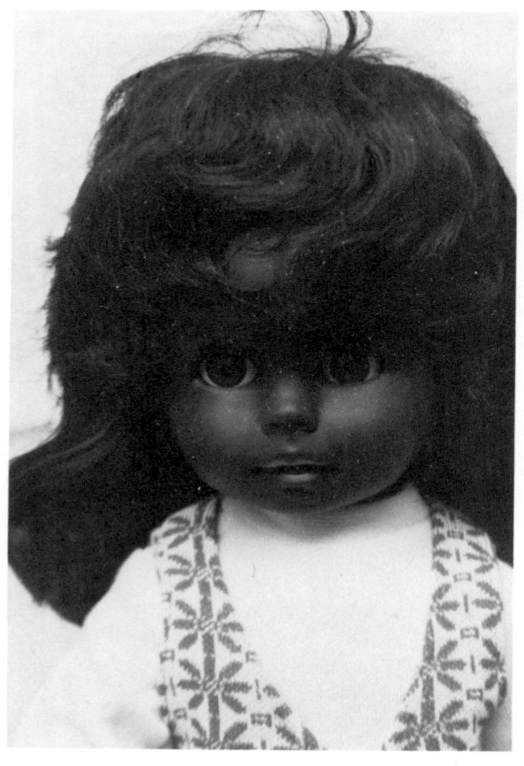

Germany--11" "Shirley Jean" Black painted eye version. Marks: 30/Made in/W. Germany, on back. Turtle mark, on head. (Courtesy Phyllis Houston)

Germany--11" "Shirley Jean" 1958-59. Plastic body, arms and legs. Vinyl head with blue sleep eyes/lashes. Open/closed mouth with two molded painted upper teeth. Deep dimples. Original sailor dress. Marks: 30/Made in/W. Germany, on back. Turtle mark, on head. $6.00. (Courtesy Mary Partridge)

Germany--11" "Shirley Jean" Plastic and vinyl. Painted very pale blue eyes. Original. Marks: Turtlemark/30/Made in/W. Germany. $6.00. (Courtesy Phyllis Houston)

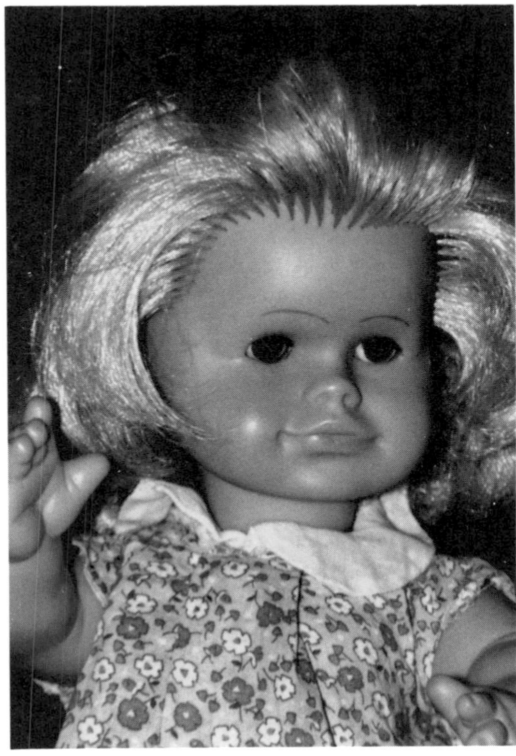

Germany--16" "Gret" All vinyl with brown sleep eyes/lashes. Original. 1968. Marks: Gotz Puppe. $12.00. (Courtesy Marie Ernst)

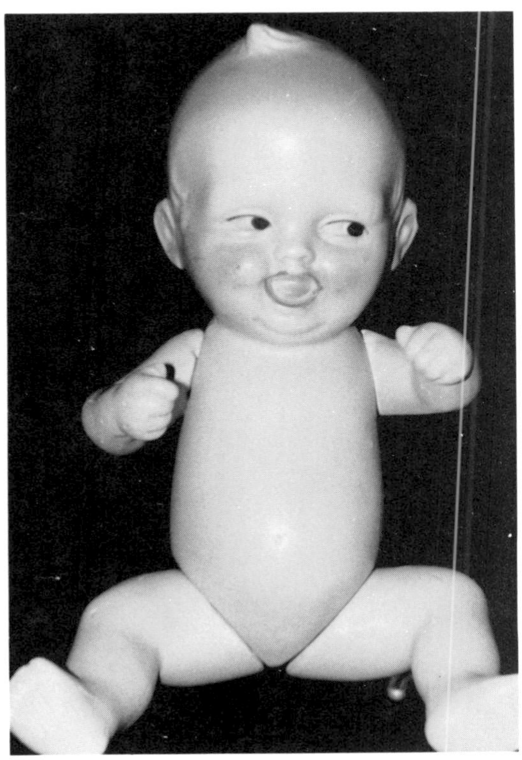

Germany--6" "Baby Sandy" (Sandra Henville) Painted bisque. Blue painted eyes. Open/closed mouth. Dimples. (Marks: Germany, on back. $65.00. (Courtesy Maxine Heitt)

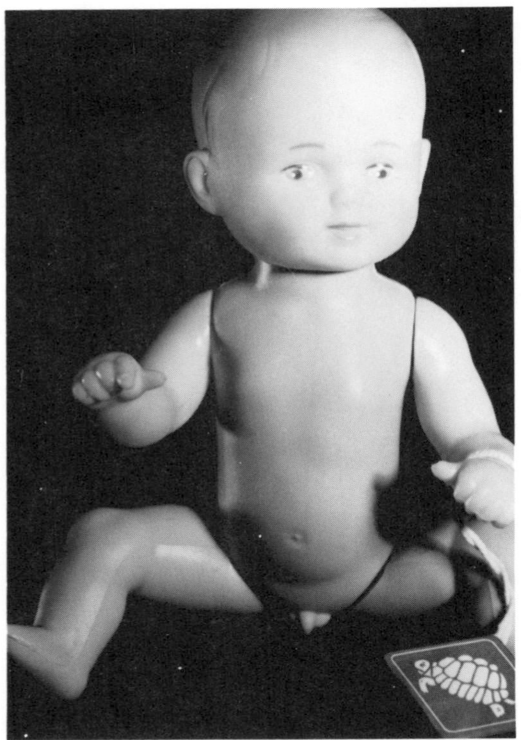

Germany--16" All vinyl with sleep eyes. Closed mouth. Marks: 36/Gotz/B. $8.00. (Courtesy Kathy Walker)

Greece--The Kehagias dolls are like most Furga's and Alexanders. The doll is the same but the outfit has name. For example this 12" doll shown is dressed as Adriadne, Sylvia, Isabella, Betty and Rania. The dolls appear to be made of above average quality materials. All I have seen have been completely unmarked. $9.00.

Greece--7" "Natalie" #7021. All vinyl with inset blue eyes. Open/closed mouth. Posable head. Original. Marks: None. Made by Kehagias, Greece. $8.00. (Courtesy Mary Partridge)

Greece--13" "Lena" Plastic and vinyl. Brown sleep eyes. Open/closed mouth, molded upper teeth unpainted. Excellent quality clothes. Marks: None. Box: Made by Kehagia and distributed by M&S Shillman Inc. Catalog shows this outfit also called: Tina, Venia, Maria and Joanna (boy: John). $9.00. (Courtesy Bessie Carson)

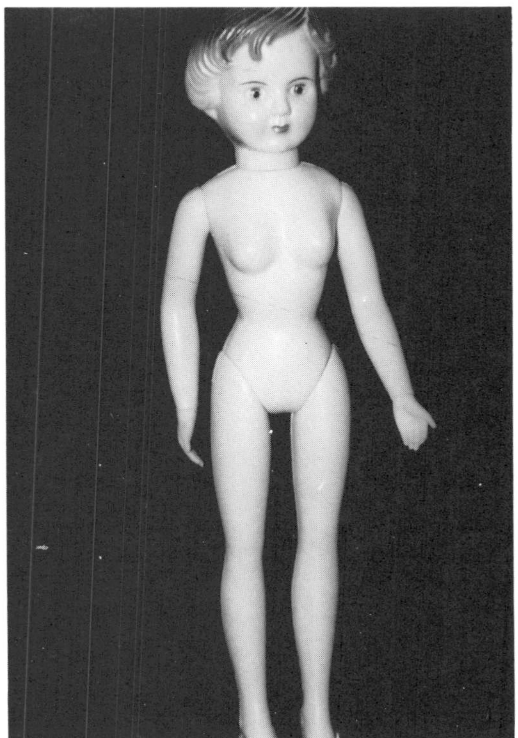

Hong Kong--14½" "Hillery" 1969. All plastic with jointed wrists. Blue sleep eyes/molded lashes. High heel feet. Marks: Evergreen/Made in/Hong Kong/9150. $3.00. (Courtesy Mary Partridge)

Hong Kong--14" Pregnant doll. Plastic and vinyl. Rooted hair. Blue sleep eyes. Original clothes. Marks: Perfekta/Made in Hong Kong, on head. $8.00. (Courtesy Sally Bethscheider)

Hong Kong--17" "Rhonda" Plastic body and legs. Vinyl arms and head. Right leg molded slightly bent at the knee. Jointed waist. Painted blue eyes. Mf'd for SS Kresge Co. Came in 5 different original outfits. Marks: Blue Girl, picture of head of girl, Hong Kong, on head. Hong Kong/ Blue Girl, on back. 1974. $7.00.

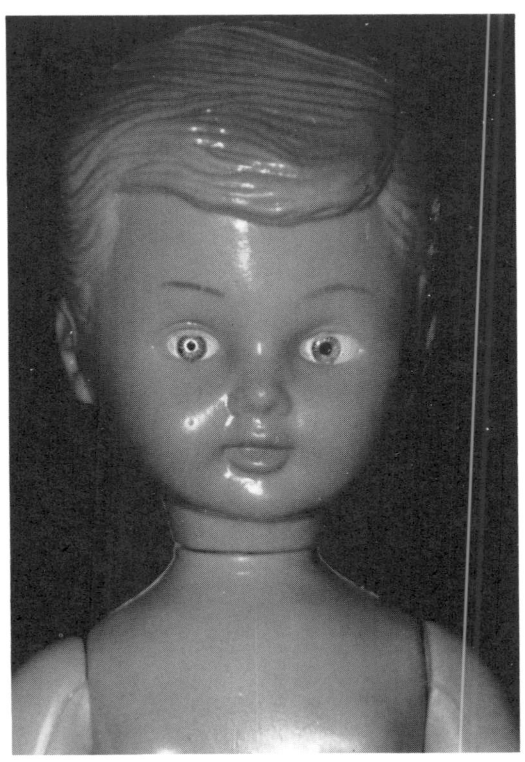

Hong Kong--20" "Robbie" All thin plastic. Inset blue eyes. Molded hair. 1967. Marks: large "M"/ PF, in a circle/Made in Hong Kong. $6.00. (Courtesy Marie Ernst)

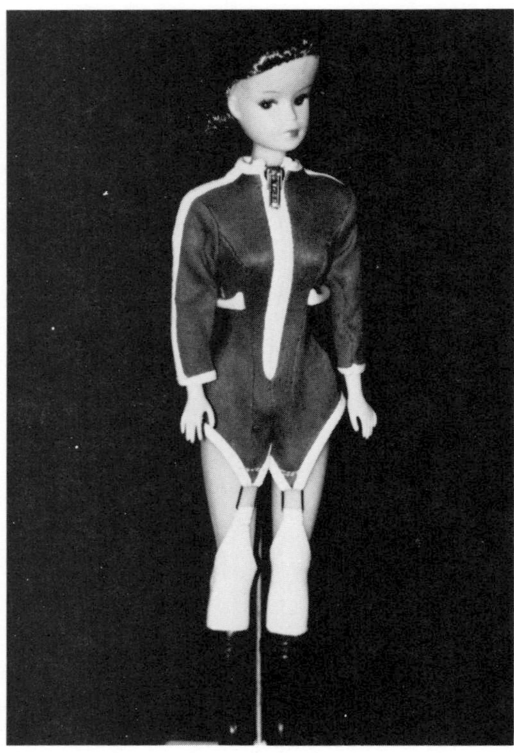

Teen--11½" "Emma Peel" Plastic and vinyl. Painted brown eyes. Brown hair. Original. Marks: Made In/Hong Kong, on back. Emma Peel, on stand. $18.00. (Courtesy B. Mongelluzzi)

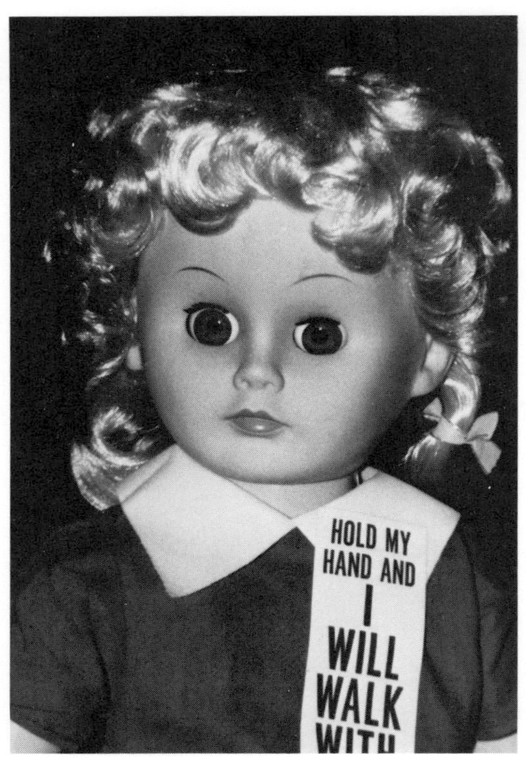


Hong Kong--23" "Babs Walker" Plastic with vinyl head. Blue sleep eyes. Yellow hair. Walker. Original. Paper sticker: Made in Kong Kong. $3.00.

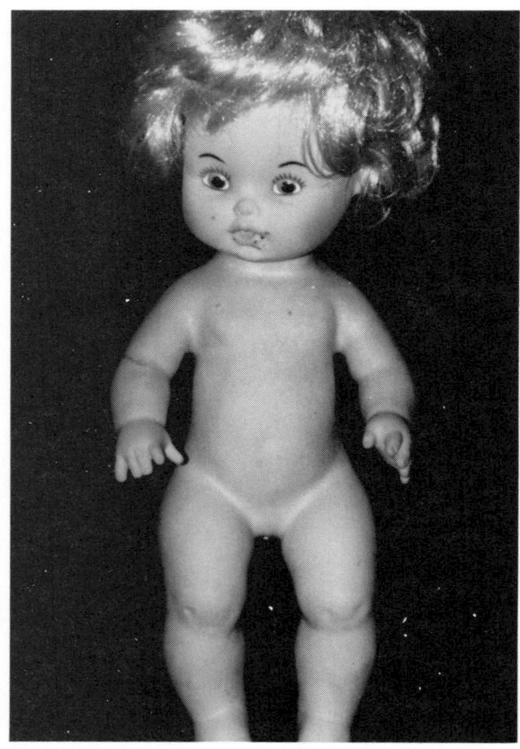

Hong Kong--11" "Lovely Baby" Poly-foam one piece body arms and legs. Vinyl head. Painted blue eyes. Open mouth/nurser. Marks: Hong Kong, picture of world in an oval, on back. Hong Kong, on head. $2.00.

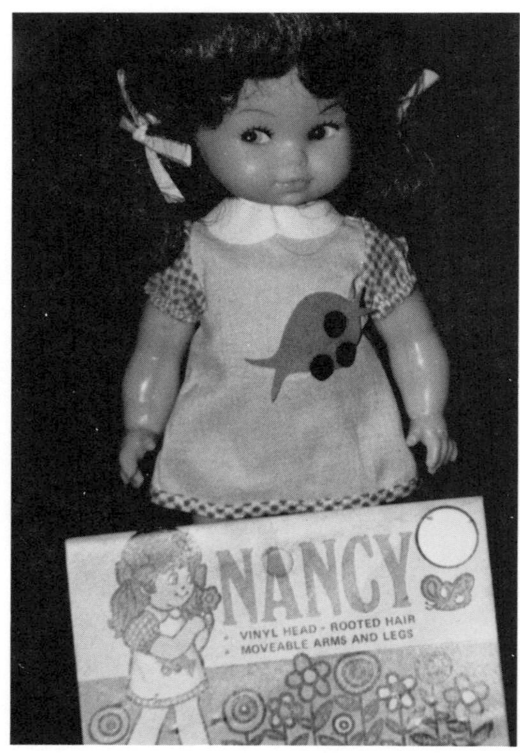


Hong Kong--9" "Nancy" Plastic and vinyl. Blue sleep eyes. Posable head. Original. 1969. Marks: Hong Kong, on back. $3.00. (Courtesy Marie Ernst)

Hong Kong--3" "Vampire Troll" All vinyl. Jointed neck only. Fangs. Marks: Made In/Hong Kong, on head and back. 1966. $3.00. (Courtesy Marie Ernst)

7½" "Patches" Plastic and vinyl with painted blue eyes. Posable heads. Original. 1974. Marks: Made in Hong Kong, on back. Sack: Made for P. Kronow & Co. $2.00 each.

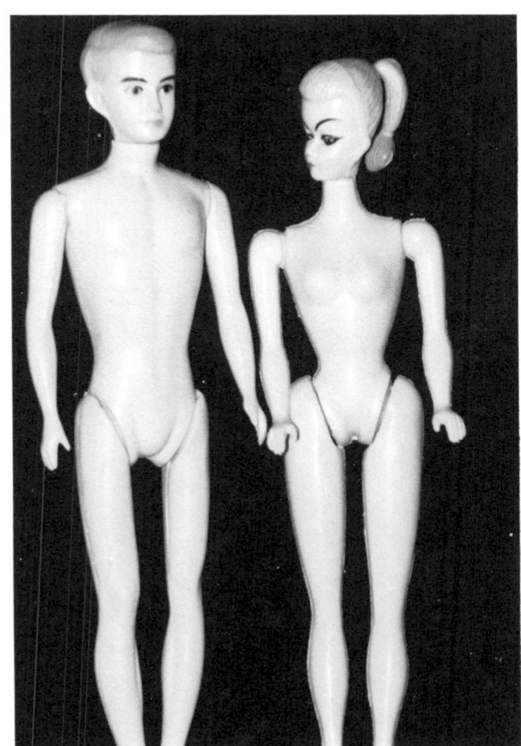

Teen--11½" "Mod Jerry & Mod Judy" All plastic. Judy: Black heavy brows. Plastic pony tail socketed to rotate. Jerry: Molded red hair. Painted blue eyes. Marks: Made In/Hong Kong, lower back. Made for Australia. $4.00. (Courtesy Marie Ernst)

Teen--"Three Generation Family" Man:12" red molded hair. Blue painted eyes. Lady: 11½" brown with mixed grey hair. Blue painted eyes. Young Girl 11½" Open/closed mouth, painted teeth, jointed like action. 4" Baby, jointed neck only. Nurser. All have jointed waists. Marks: Hong Kong. $25.00 set. (Courtesy Marie Ernst)

Teen--12" "Pool Dolls" (girl is 11½"). Plastic with vinyl heads. Man is suntanned. Reddish brown molded hair and painted teeth. Girl: Blue painted eyes to left. Came with swimming pool. Marks; Made in/Hong Kong, on back. $16.00 set. (Courtesy Marie Ernst)

Hong Kong--7½" "John Paul Jones" One of the Heroes of the American Revolution sets sold through Montgomery Wards and Kresge. This and following 6 are plastic with vinyl heads. They have jointed waists. Marks: Made in Hong Kong, on backs. RT-Hong Kong, on boxes.

Hong Kong--7½" "George Washington" Marked same as John Paul Jones.

Hong Kong--7½" "Paul Revere" Marked same as John Paul Jones.

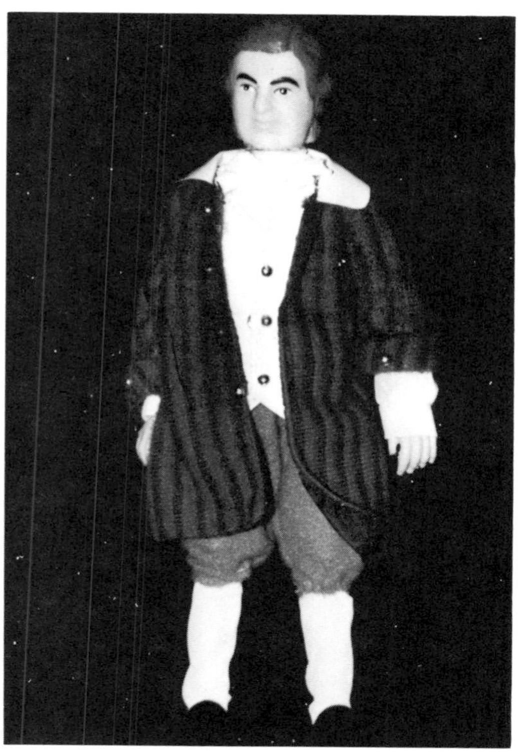

Hong Kong--7½" "Thomas Jefferson" Marked same as John Paul Jones.

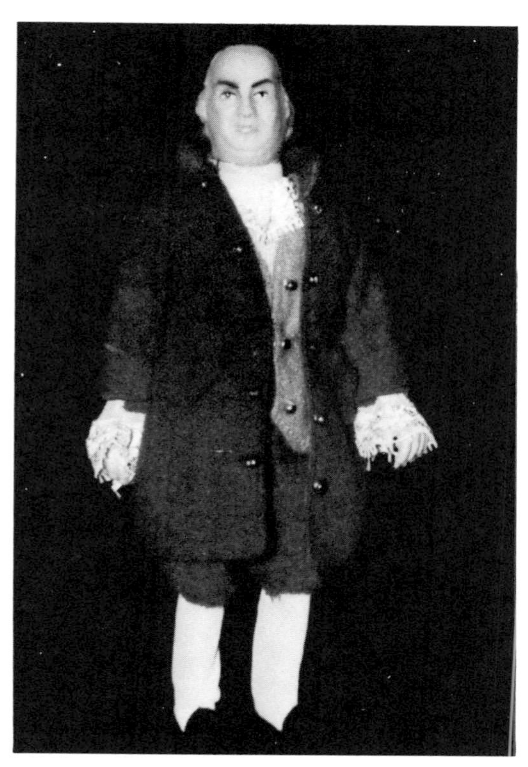

Hong Kong--7½" "Benjamin Franklin" Marked same as John Paul Jones.

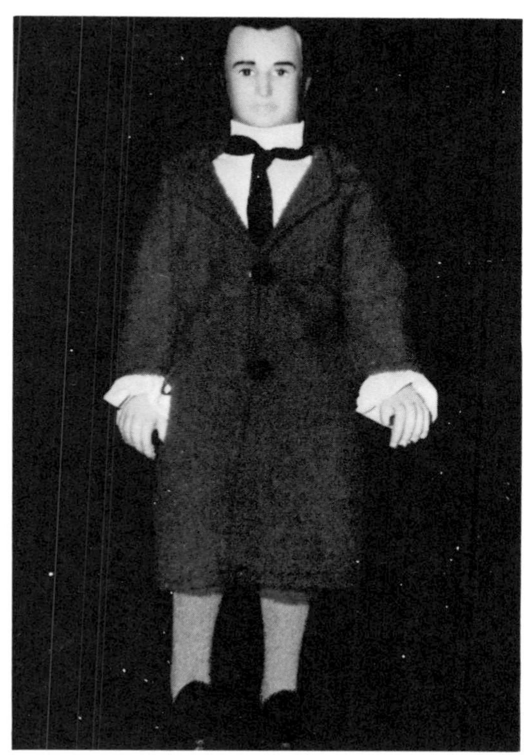

Hong Kong--7½" "Patrick Henry" Marked same as John Paul Jones.

Hong Kong--7½" "Nathan Hale" Marked same as John Paul Jones.

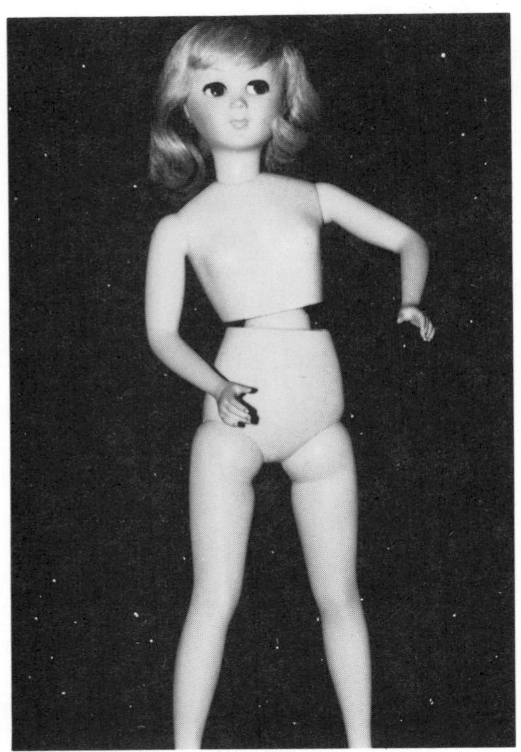

Italy--19" "Lizabetta" All rigid plastic. Ball jointed waist. Human hair wig. Flirty/sleep deep green eyes/lashes. Doll is strung. 1962. Marks: Bonomi/Italy, on head and back. Tag: Poupee/Originale/Bonomi/Fabriquee in /Italie. $30.00. (Courtesy Bessie Carson)

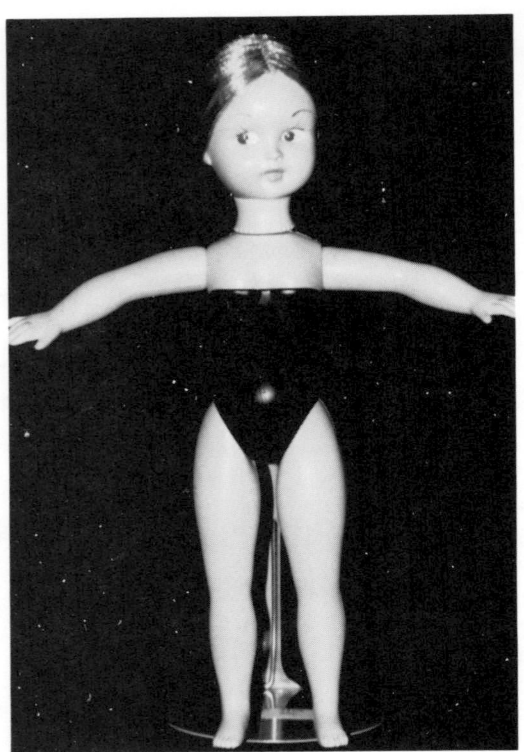

Teen--8" "Collette" Copied from a French idea. "Pop" apart plastic and vinyl. Came with cut out (non-sew) costumes. Sold through Sears 1961. Marks: Hong Kong, on back. $7.00.

Iran--8" "Iran" All vinyl. Blue sleep eyes. Original. Very good quality. Marks: None. $9.00. (Courtesy Marie Ernst)

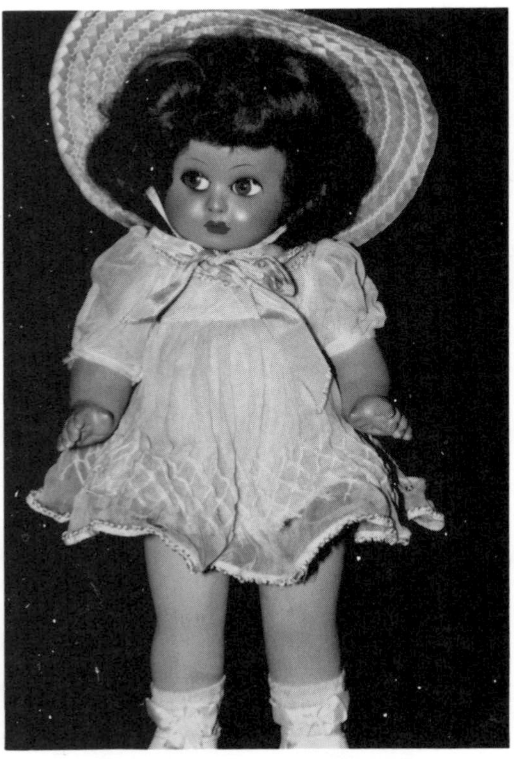

Italy--12" "Little One" (translation). All painted heavy plastic. Flirty eyes/lashes. Polished nails. Original. $45.00. (Courtesy Marge Meisinger)

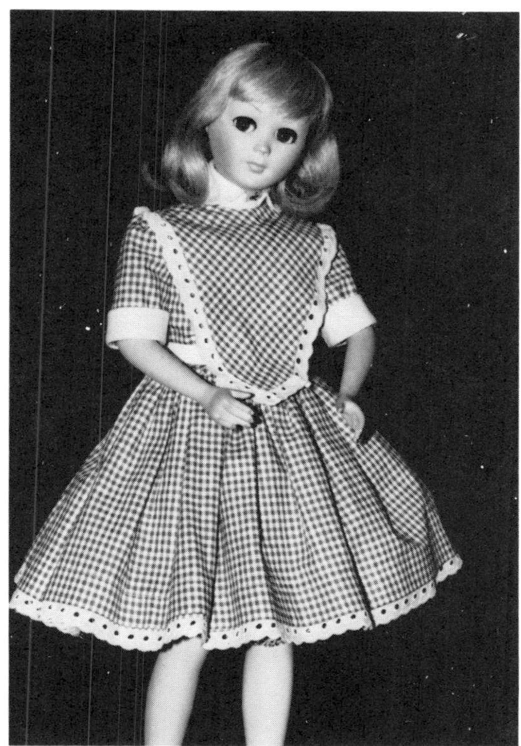

Italy--19" "Lizabetta" Shows one of her original outfits. Red/white check. Individual white collar.

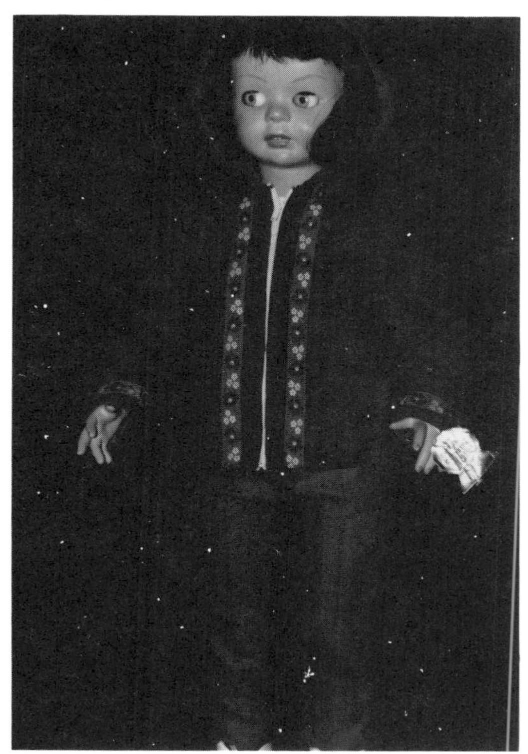

Italy--22" "Handora" Rigid plastic. Flirty/blue sleep eyes. Ball jointed waist. Open crown with cryer box in head. Closed mouth, two painted upper teeth. Human hair black wig. Ca. 1961. Marks: Bonomi/Italy, on back. Bonomi/Italy, on head. Tag: Poupee/Originale/Bonomi/Fabriqee in/Itale. $28.00. (Courtesy Bessie Carson)

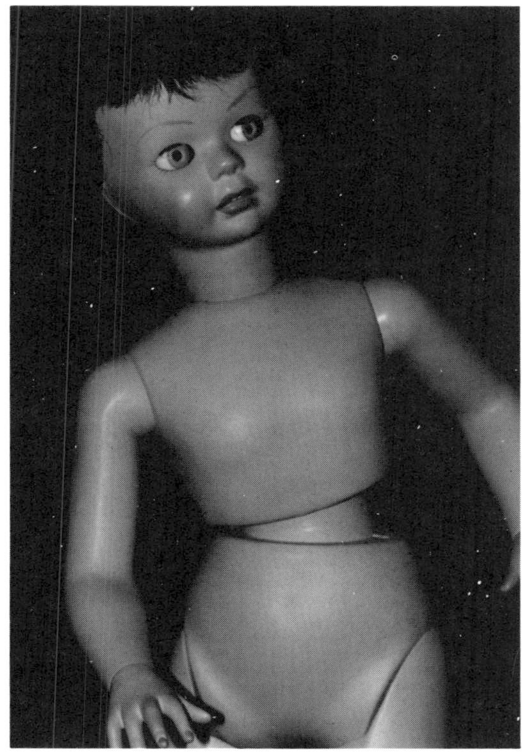

Italy--22" "Handora" Shows body construction. Same as the Vogue "Brikette."

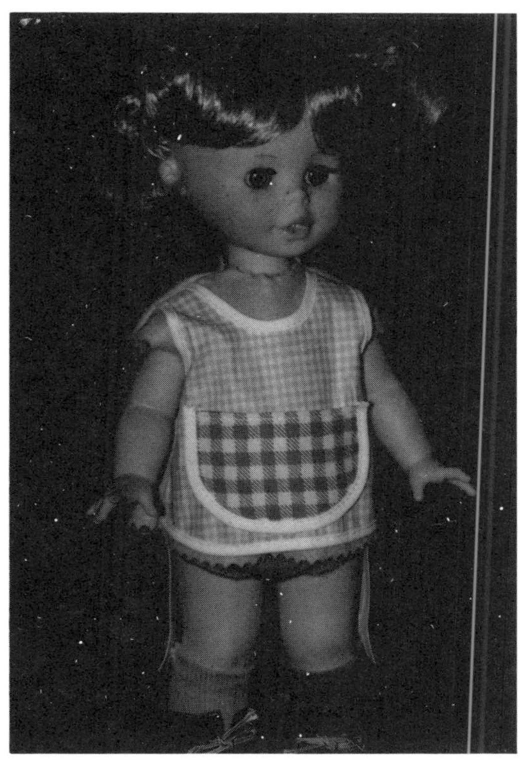

Italy--12" "Pipi Long Stockings" Vinyl with plastic body. Blue sleep eyes. Orange rooted hair. Freckles. All original. Marks: Italy/1-C in square. $12.00. (Courtesy Marie Ernst)

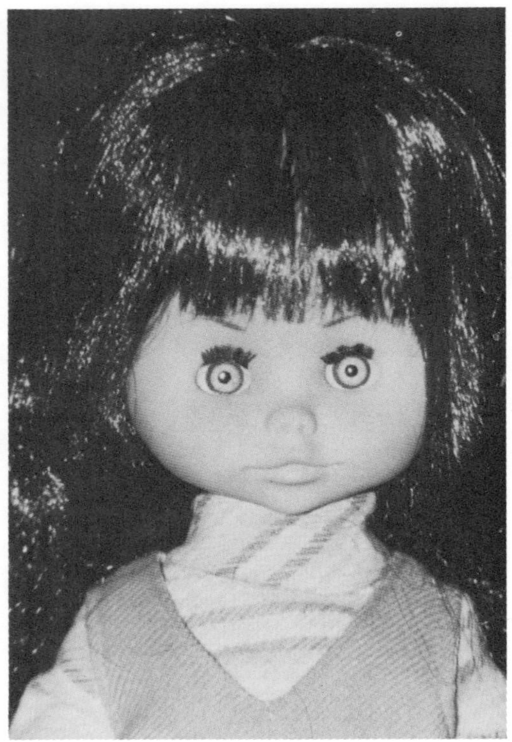

Italy--15" "Denita" All vinyl with blue sleep eyes. Original. Marks: IC, in square/1969. $12.00. (Courtesy Marie Ernst)

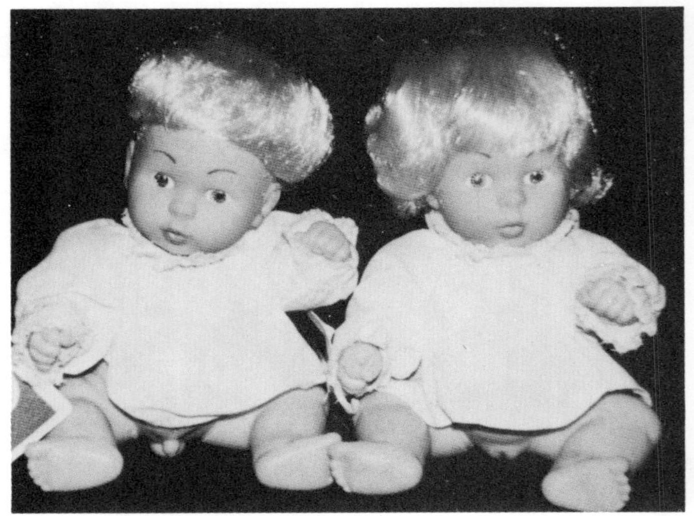

Italy--5" "Nina & Nino" All vinyl. Inset plastic blue eyes. Original. Made by Italocremona. Marks: IC, in a square/1967. $25.00 set. (Courtesy Cindy Karsti)

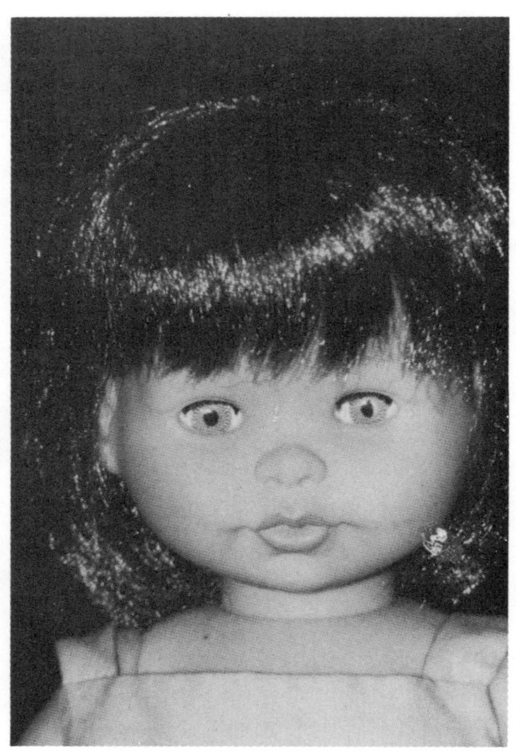

Italy--16" "Rennetta" All vinyl with set blue eyes/lashes. Marks: girl holding an "M", in a circle: Italy/Miglioratti, on head and body. $12.00. (Courtesy Marie Ernst)

Italy--12" "Sabrina" Manufactured just for SS Kresge Co. $12.00. (Courtesy Marie Ernst)

Italy--12" "Mirella" Made just for the SS Kresge Co. Marks: IC, in square. $12.00. (Courtesy Marie Ernst)

Italy--16" "Suzabette" All vinyl with sleep blue eyes. Original. Marks: IC, in square./Made in/ Italy. $12.00. (Courtesy Marie Ernst)

Italy--6½" "Twins: Lella & Lulu" All vinyl with sleep eyes. Original. Marks: 11701/Furga/Italy. $6.00 each. (Courtesy Marie Ernst)

Italy--10" "Muzzi" of the twins Muzzi & Mizzi. Plastic body. Vinyl arms, legs and head. Bright blue sleep eyes/lashes. One arm bent. Original. Marks: Furga Italy, on head. $8.00. (Courtesy Bessie Carson)

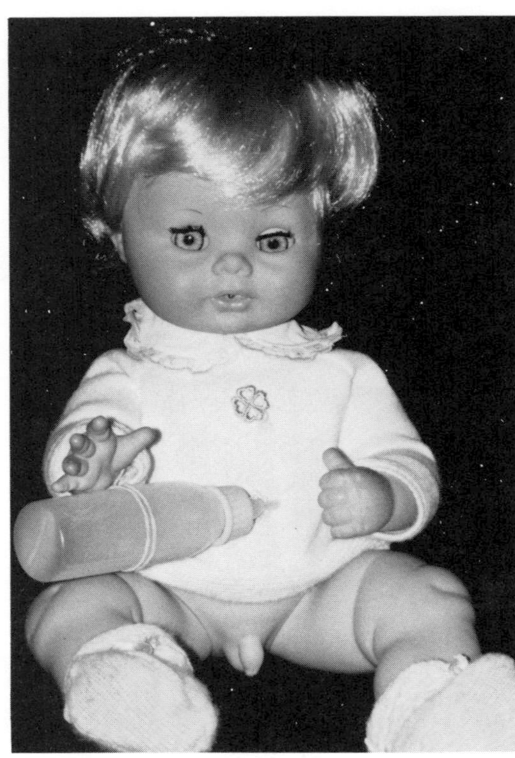

Furga--16" All vinyl with blue sleep eyes. Open/ mouth nurser. Original. Marks: 1240/Furga/ Italy, in a square. $35.00. (Courtesy Julia Rogers)

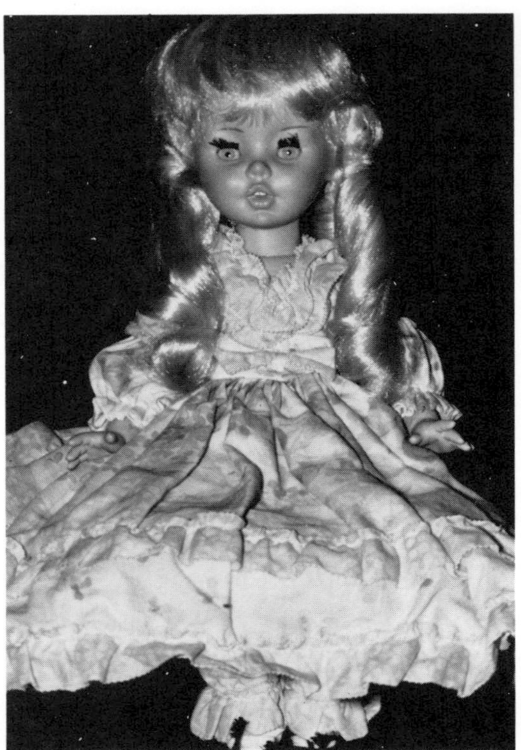

Italy--15" "Guendalina" Plastic and vinyl. Had feathered hat and umbrella. Dress colors are blue/white with a touch of yellow. Marks: Furga Italy, on head. Italy/Furga, on body. $50.00.

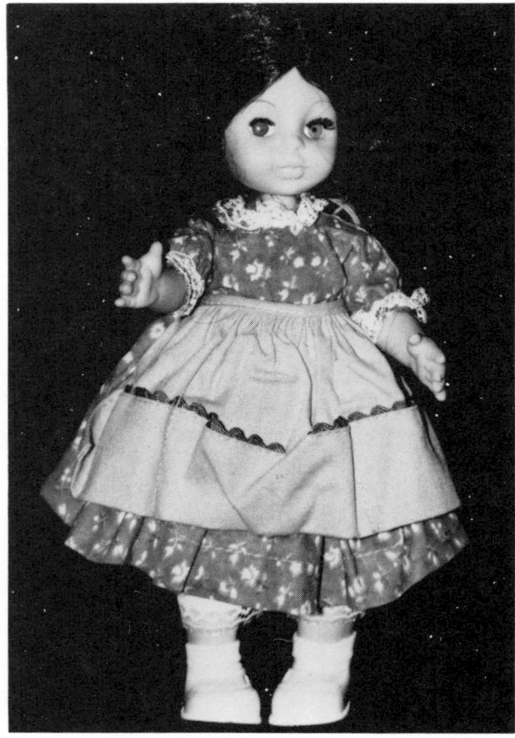

Italy--9" "Mary, Mary" Plastic and vinyl. Brown hair with blue eyes. Marks: Furga/Italy. 1974. Still available.

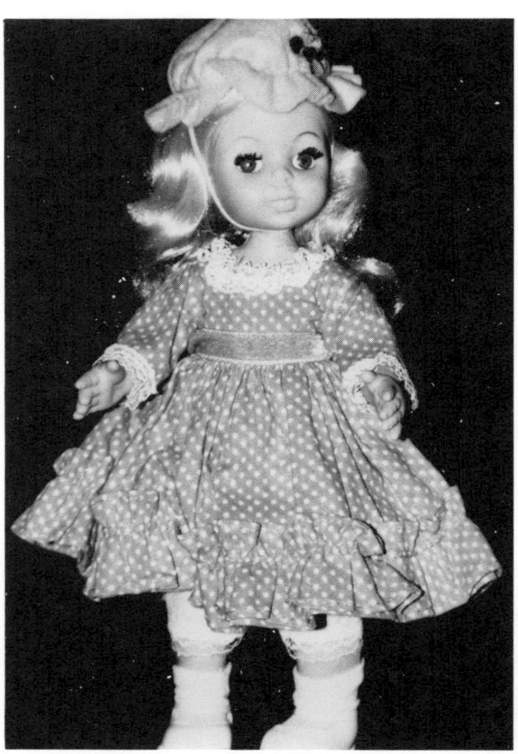

Italy--9" "Cinderella" Plastic and vinyl. White hair with blue eyes. Marks: Furga/Italy. 1974. Still available.

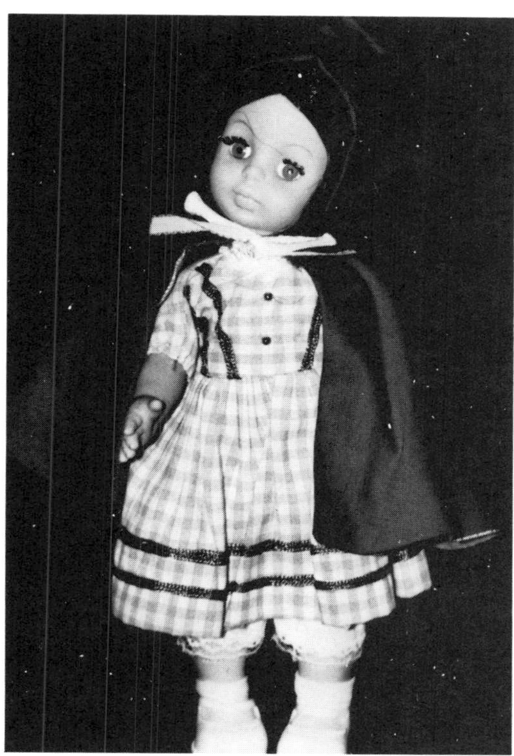

Italy--9" "Red Riding Hood" Plastic and vinyl. Brown hair and blue eyes. Marks: Furga/Italy. 1974. Still available.

Italy--9" "Miss Muffet" Plastic and vinyl. White hair and blue eyes. Marks: Furga/Italy. 1974. Still available.

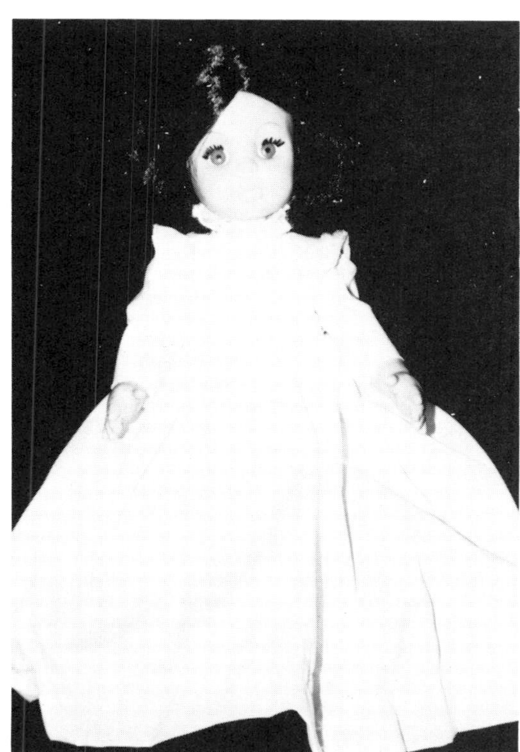

Italy--9" "Snow White" Plastic and vinyl. Brown hair and blue eyes. All white dress. Marks: Furga/Italy. 1974. Still available.

Italy--9" "Gretel" Plastic and vinyl. White hair with blue eyes. Marks: Furga/Italy. 1974. Still available.

Furga--14" "Zefirina" Flannel filled with foam. A "flat" doll. Stitched mohair. Removable clothes. Elastic in top of head for hanging. Marks: None on doll. $4.00.

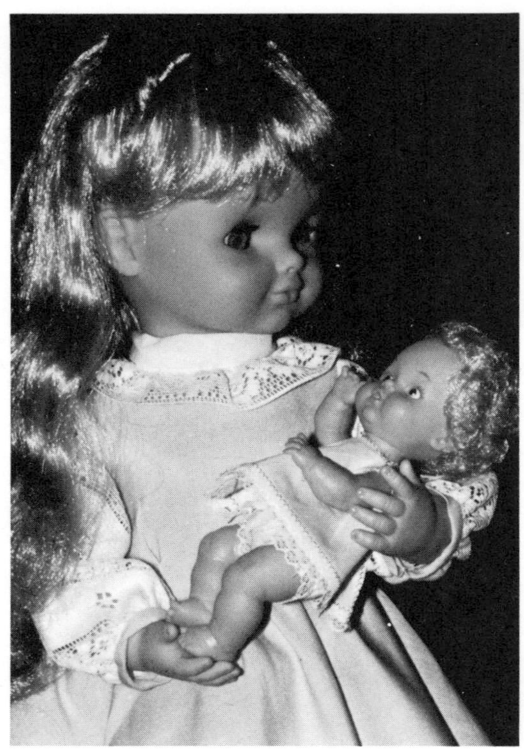

Italy--21" "Titti" and son 7" "Cialdino" Baby is all vinyl with painted blue eyes. Nurser. "Titti" is plastic and vinyl with jointed waist. Key wind. Rocks baby, eyes open and close. Head lowers and raises. Marks: Baby: Made Italy/Sebino. Titti: Sebino/Made Italy, head and body. Original. Sold since 1972. $45.00.

Italy--12" "Mioa, Mioa" All vinyl. Blue sleep eyes. Original clothes representing a kitten. Sebino. 1974. $25.00.

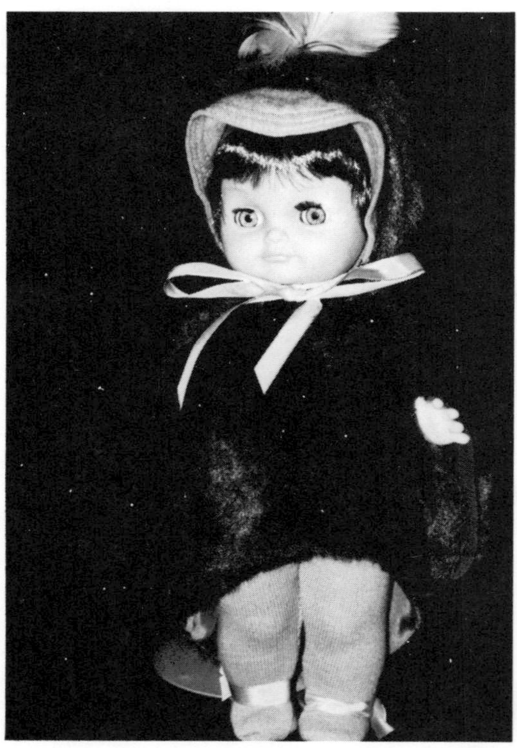

Italy--12" "Qua, Qua" All vinyl with blue sleep eyes. Original clothes representing a duck. Sebino. 1974. $25.00.

Japan--8" "Mrs. Claus" All vinyl, jointed neck and shoulders. Painted features. Marks: Made in Japan. $3.00.

Japan--7½" All vinyl with rooted black hair. Painted features. Sideward smile. Marks: Japan, on foot. 532/B/SH1BA, on head. $2.00.

Japan--7" "Patty Jean" Good quality. Excellent toe detail. Rooted orange hair. Painted blue/black eyes. Original. Marks: Japan, bottom of foot. $2.00.

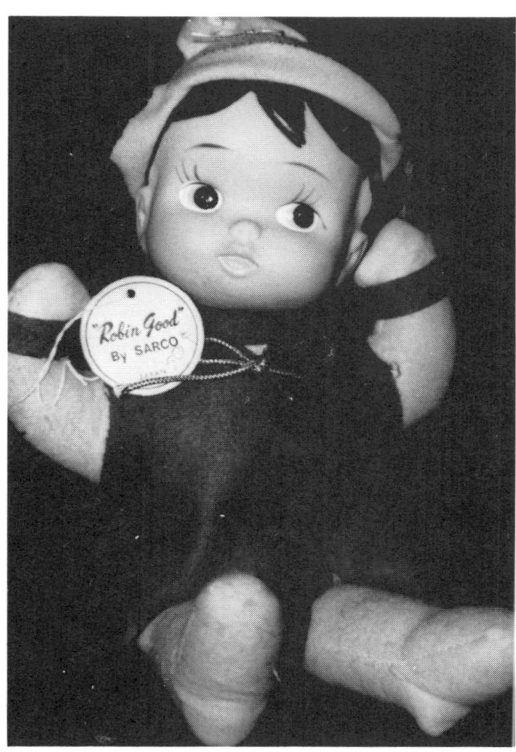


Japan--10½" "Robin Good" All stuffed felt. Vinyl head. Painted features. Open/closed mouth with molded tongue. Marks: None. Tag: "Robin Good" by Sarco/Japan. $2.00. (Courtesy Mary Partridge)

Japan--7" "Moari" doll. New Zealand aborigine with baby. All hard plastic. Sleep eyes. Full joints: baby is one piece. Moari dolls are made in Japan. $8.00. (Courtesy Phyllis Houston)

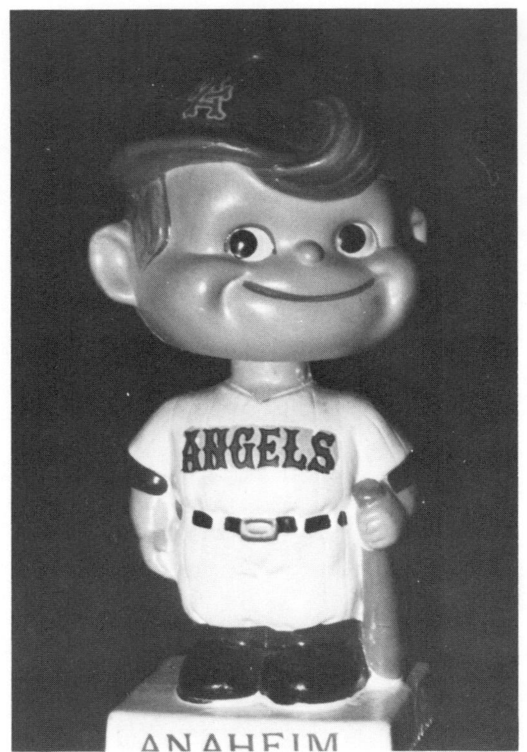


Japan--6" "Angels Nodder" Plaster and paper mache. Painted and molded on clothes, hair and features. Marks: Paper sticker on bottom/Japan La, on cap. Angels, on shirt. Paper sticker: Anaheim, over "Los Angeles". Between 1961 and 1966. $4.00. (Courtesy Edith Goldsworthy)

Japan--Shows the end of the "Junior Margaret" box. Doll was sold in several "original" outfits.

Japan--15" "Junior Margaret" Plastic and vinyl. Posable head. An excellent quality doll. Pull string talker, with a pearl keeping the string from going in too far. She talks in Japanese. Marks: ☆ Made in Japan, on head. Same on back plus: Pat. P.O. 27057. 1972. Original including glasses. $22.00.

Japan--9" "Bizzy Buzz Buzz" All vinyl. Red rooted hair and painted eyes. Original clothes. Marks: King Features Synd/Gund Mfg Co., on head. A "M" in a Diamond/Japan, on back. Tag: Bizzy/Buzz Buzz/King Features Syndicate/J. Swedlin, Inc. $4.00. (Courtesy Phyllis Houston)

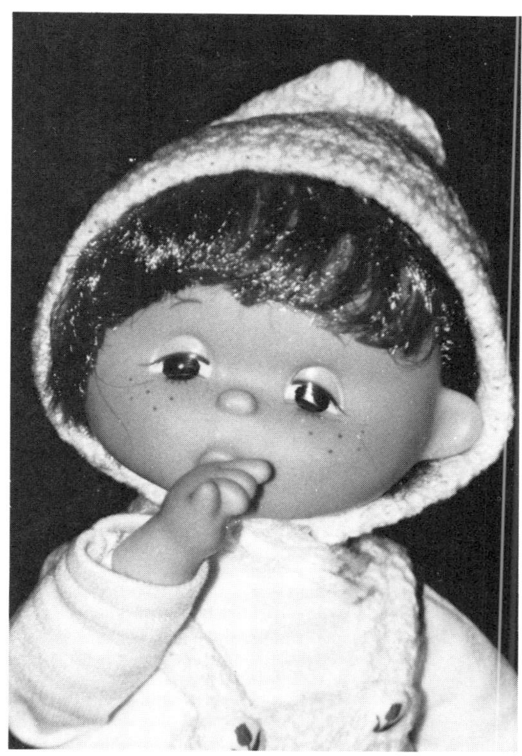

Japan--13" "Sucking Thumb Baby" All cloth with gauntlet vinyl hands. Vinyl head with very protruding ears. Round open/closed mouth. Freckles. Painted half closed eyes. An FAO Swartz exclusive for 1975. Marks: Tag on doll: Seikiguchi and picture of child with crown. Tag on bootie: Sakai & Co. Ltd/Japan. Box: Petite Poupee/Seki-Guchi. Original clothes. $22.00.

Cloth--9½" "Dennis the Menace" All stockinette. Original. Paper tag: Made in Japan, on foot. $6.00. (Courtesy Bev. Gardner)

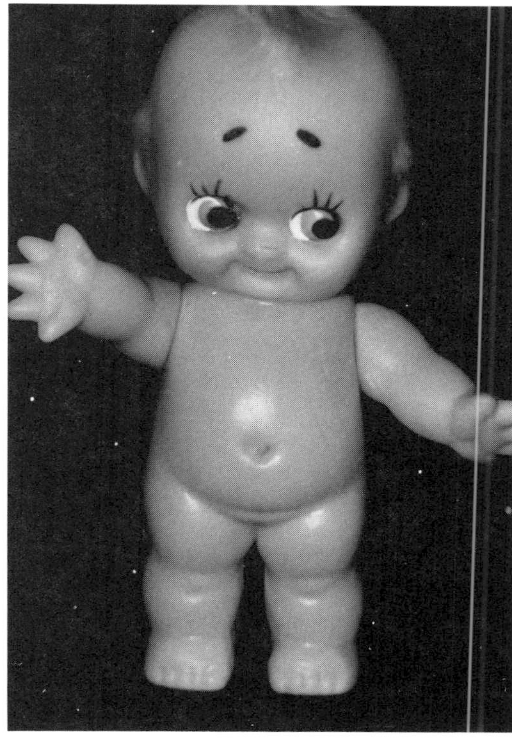

Japan--5" Made in Japan and re-issued 1975. Jointed arms and neck. Red curly top knot. Unpainted wings. Still available.

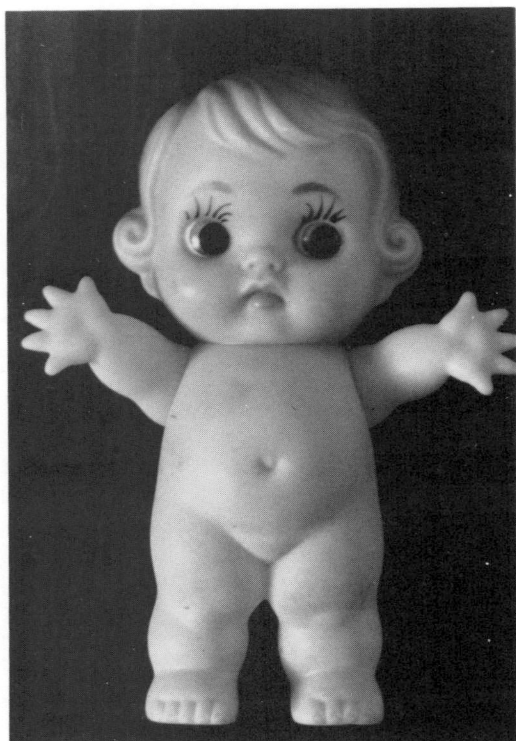

Japan--7½" All vinyl girl. Green wings. Marks: None. $3.00. (Courtesy Phyllis Houston)

Manufacturer Unknown--9½" "Artist" Silk covered wire armature. Composition type head. Original.

Foreign--5" Rooted hair, molded on clothes and brown "skin." A very small "sexed" doll. Was a gift from New Zealand. $6.00. (Courtesy Phyllis Houston)

Japan--12½" Posable silk stockinette doll. Jersey and felt clothes. Woolen hat. Painted features. Yarn hair. On self stand. Tag: Sonsco Toys/Japan. (Courtesy Phyllis Houston)

Korea--17" "Dance Group" Set of five fan dancers. Sold through Military P.X.'s in 1973. $65.00. (Courtesy Ruth Brocha)

Korea--27" Called French Type Doll. Sold through Military P.X.'s in 1973. $20.00. (Courtesy Ruch Brocha)

Korea--17" Called "Sisters" and shows the traditional carrage of children. Sold through Military P.X.'s in 1973. $22.00. (Courtesy Ruth Brocha)

Poland--15" "Little Lulu" Cloth with jointed shoulders/hips. Plastic face mask. Floss type hair. Marks: Poland, stamped on back of leg. $28.00. (Courtesy B. Mongelluzzi)

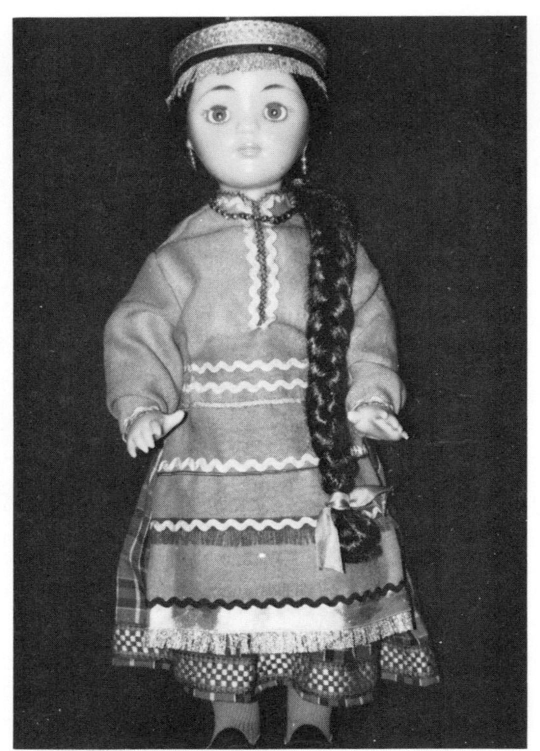

Russia--21" "Takmeobckom" Excellent quality. Green sleep eyes. Glued on wig. All hand painted features (other than eyes). Has the look of wax but is vinyl. Tag: Tameobckom and other Russian characters, plus Made In USSR. $35.00. (Courtesy Dodie Shapiro)

Spain--18" All felt with felt mouth, lashes and clothes. Real fur hat (hair?). Paper eyes. $22.00. (Courtesy Virginia Jones)

Spain--16" All vinyl. Tag: Marin Chiclana/ Made in Spain. 1974. (Courtesy Louise Alonso)

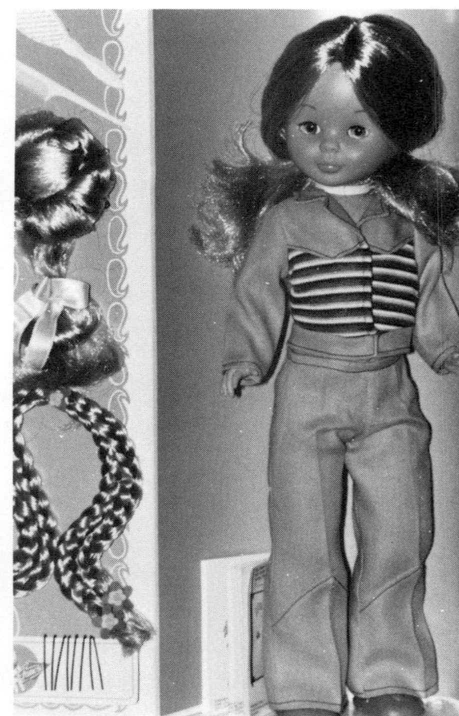

Spain--16" "Nancy" Plastic and vinyl. Legs have fat calfs and very fat ankles. Pale brown sleep eyes. Came with extra hair pieces. Had many outfits available. Marks: Famosa, on head, shoes. Tag: Munecas/ Famosa/Made in Spain. $20.00. (Courtesy Bessie Carson)

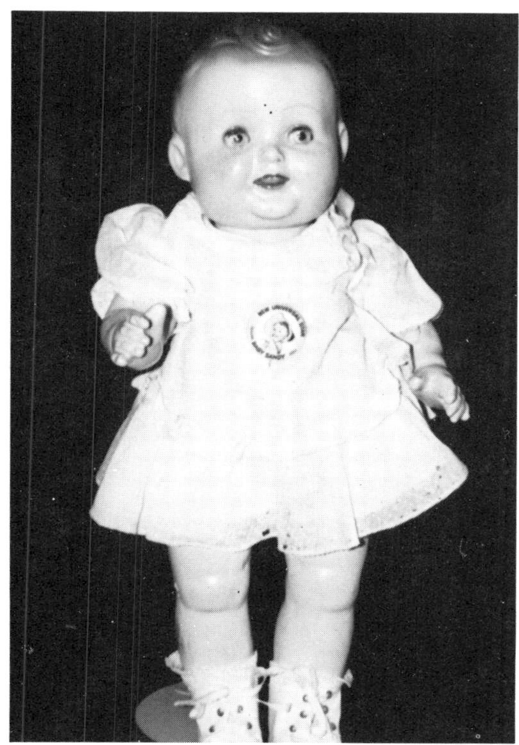

Freundlich, Ralph--16" "Sandy Henville" child movie star. All composition. Sleep eyes/lashes. Open mouth. Molded hair. All original including pin. $85.00. (Courtesy Kimport Dolls)

Fun World--6" "I Saw A Ship A-Sailing" Mother Goose Picture Book and Doll Series. Set includes: "What Are Little Girls Made Of," "Jack & Jill" & "The Queen of Hearts." Plastic and vinyl. Fully jointed. Her hair is orange and his is dark blonde. Marks: Made In/Hong Kong, on head. $4.00.

Fun World--6½" "Cissy Swinger" Bean bag style with vinyl head. Molded hair on front only. Jointed neck. Painted blue eyes. Open/closed mouth. Marks: Hong Kong, on neck. Tag: Fun World/Inc. 1975. $3.00.

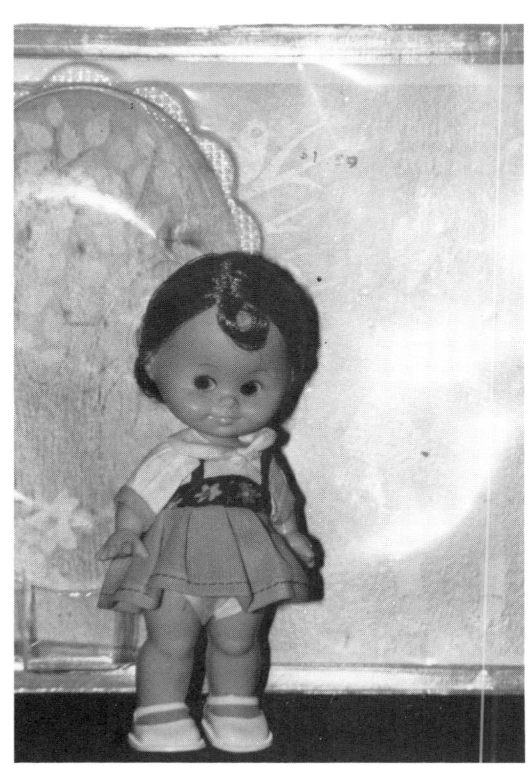

Fun World--7½" "A Little Girl With a Curl" Mother Goose Storybook doll. Plastic with vinyl head. One of a series. Marks: None. $4.00.

Gilbert--3½" "007" played by Sean Connery, shown in Tux and with rifle. "Goldfinger," played by Gert Frobe in movie. Dolls not marked. Box: 1965 Gledrose Productions Ltd. and/Eon Production Ltd./1965 A.C. Gilbert Co. U.S. Patent Pending. Made in Portugal. $2.00 each.

Gilbert--3½" "Odd Job" played by Harold Sakata in Goldfinger. Next is "Domino" played by Claudine Auger in Thunderball. Next is "Emilio Largo" played by Adolfo Celi in Thunderball. Last is "Moneypenny" (loyal gal-Friday to 007-James Bond) played by Lois Maxwell in Goldfinger. $2.00 each.

Gilbert--3½" "007-James Bond" in the scuba gear from Thunderball as played by Sean Connery. Next is "M" Bond's boss played by Bernard Lee in Goldfinger. "Dr. No" played by Joseph Wiseman. $2.00 each.

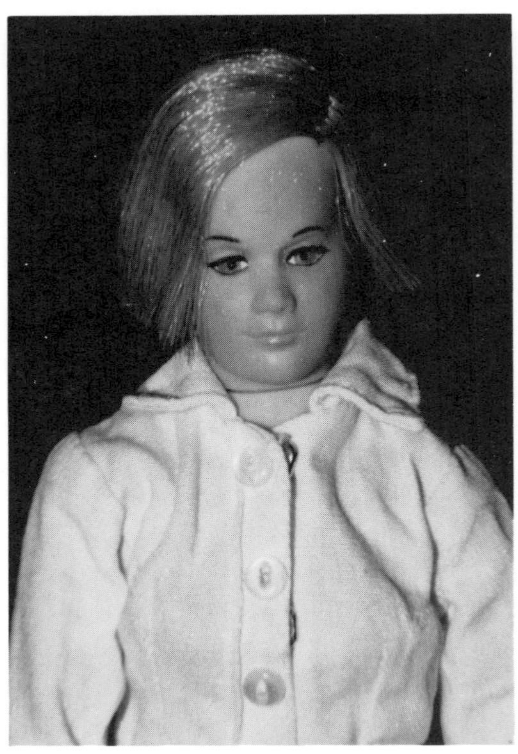

Hasbro--11" "GI Joe Nurse Jane" Green painted eyes/black lashes. Marks: Patent Pend/1967 Hasbro/Made in Hong Kong. Tag: G.I. Nurse/ By Hasbro/Hong Kong. $25.00.

# G. I. Joe Series

The following information comes from Joseph L. Bourgeois who has spent many hours researching the G.I. Joe Action Figures.

"In order to show the sequence of development and changes in the G.I. Joes, I have set up my list into nine series. It isn't likely that the Hasbro company would recognize this many series as their model numbers remain the same for several of my series. A serious collector of Action Figures needs this information to catalogue his mannequins. Fortunately the Hasbro people have produced mannequins with sufficient differences, between models and series, for identification. Even with these differences there are no problems in identifying G.I. Joe Action Sailors from G.I. Joe Action Marine without their original uniforms. The same G.I. Joe is used for both categories.

The first series of G.I. Joes are identified by the letters TM (Trademark) in their mark. They are distinguished one from the other by the color of their hair and eyes, with the exception of G.I. Joe Sailor and G.I. Joe Marne that are the same mannequin.

The second series of G.I. Joes are similar to the first series. The difference is the mark. The TM has been dropped and ® has been added indicating that the name G.I. Joe has been registered. It is this second series that the first Black G.I. Joe is introduced.

In the third series we find that G.I. Joe no longer has a scar on his face. The lack of a scar is the identifying feature. The mark is the same as the second series.

The fourth series is also identified by not having the scar on the face as well as having a change in the mark. The words "Patent Pending" have been removed from the mark and the "Pat. No. 3,2777,602" has been added. It should be noted that the scarless faces of the third and fourth series have a thinner and more "nordic" appearance. It is also in this series that Hasbro introduces their first talking model.

The scar returning to the face identifies the fifth series. The face is also a little rounder. The mark is the same as the fourth series. This is also the last series in which G.I. Joe is packaged with a military designation. (Soldier, sailor, etc.)

In the sixth series G.I. Joe takes on various adventures notably lacking in military flavor. For example he is now a research archeologist searching for "the secret of the mummy's tomb" or he is a deep sea diver in "Eight ropes of danger," etc. With his new adventures, G.I. Joe also takes on a new appearance. He now has flocked hair and a beard. The mark remains the same as series four and five.

The seventh series gives us a taller G.I. Joe. He is now 11¾" tall (all previous models are 11½" tall). He also has new hands called "Kung Fu grips" with which he can easily grasp things. The mark remains the same as in series four, five and six.

There is only one model in the eighth series. It is readily identifiable by its own characteristics. The mark on the right hip is the same as in series four, five, six and seven. For the first time there is a mark on the back of the head of a G.I. Joe.

The ninth series brings out an entirely new G.I. Joe. The body is now more robust and muscleman like when compared to all the previous series. Swimming trunks are molded on as part of the hip section of the body. There is also a new method of articulating the limbs. The new mark is now located in the small of the back.

I feel that the above notes and the following list give a collector sufficient information in identifying his G.I. Joes. This information has been gleened through the examination of hundreds of G.I. Joes and their packagings. I have also had model numbers verified by the Hasbro Company. I hope I've made no errors in transcribing the information. I am still researching G.I. Joe for who designed it, etc.

| | Size: | Name and Particulars | Mold mark located on lower back | |
|---|---|---|---|---|
| | | (1st Series--4 models | | |
| 7500 | 11½" | G.I. Joe Action Soldier (white)<br>Black molded hair, blue eyes | | 1964 |
| 7600 | 11½" | G.I. Joe Action Sailor (white)<br>Brown molded hair, brown eyes | G.I. Joe TM<br>Copyright 1964<br>By Hasbro®<br>Patent Pending<br>Made in U.S.A. | 1964 |
| 7700 | 11½" | G.I. Joe Action Marine (white)<br>Brown molded hair, brown eyes | | 1964 |
| 7800 | 11½" | G.I. Joe Action Pilot (white)<br>Blonde molded hair, brown eyes | | 1964 |

| | Size | Name and Particulars | Mold mark located on lower back | |
|---|---|---|---|---|
| | | (2nd Series--5 models) | | |
| 7500 | 11½" | G.I. Joe Action Soldier (white)<br>Black molded hair, blue eyes | | 1965 |
| 7600 | 11½" | G.I. Joe Action Sailor (white)<br>Brown molded hair, brown eyes | | 1965 |
| 7700 | 11½" | G.I. Joe Action Marine (white)<br>Brown molded hair, brown eyes | G.I. Joe®<br>Copyright 1964<br>By Hasbro®<br>Patent Pending<br>Made in U.S.A. | 1965 |
| 7800 | 11½" | G.I. Joe Action Pilot (white)<br>Blonde molded hair, brown eyes | | 1965 |
| 7900 | 11½" | G.I. Joe Action Soldier (black)<br>Black molded hair, brown eyes | | 1965 |
| | | (3rd Series--5 models--no scar on face) | | |
| 7500 | 11½" | G.I. Joe Action Soldier (white)<br>Black molded hair, blue eyes | | 1966 |
| 7600 | 11½" | G.I, Joe Action Sailor (white)<br>Brown molded hair, brown eyes | | 1966 |
| 7700 | 11½" | G.I. Joe Action Marien (white)<br>Brown molded hair, brown eyes | G.I. Joe®<br>Copyright 1964<br>By Hasbro®<br>Patent Pending<br>Made in U.S.A. | 1966 |
| 7800 | 11½" | G.I. Joe Action Pilot (white)<br>Blonde molded hair, brown eyes | | 1966 |
| 7900 | 11½" | G.I. Joe Action Soldier (black)<br>Black molded hair, brown eyes | | 1966 |
| | | (4th Series--6 models--no scar on face 1st Talking model) | | |
| 7500 | 11½" | G.I. Joe Action Soldier (white)<br>Black molded hair, blue eyes | | 1967 |
| 7600 | 11½" | G.I. Joe Action Sailor (white)<br>Brown molded hair, brown eyes | | 1967 |
| 7700 | 11½" | G.I. Joe Action Marine (white)<br>Brown molded hair, brown eyes | G.I. Joe®<br>Copyright 1964<br>By Hasbro®<br>Pat. No. 3,277,602<br>Made in U.S.A. | 1967 |
| 7800 | 11½" | G.I. Joe Action Pilot (white)<br>Blonde molded hair, brown eyes | | 1967 |
| 7900 | 11½" | G.I. Joe Action Soldier (black)<br>Black molded hair, brown eyes | | 1967 |
| 7900 | 11½" | G.I. Joe Talking Commander (white)<br>Blonde molded hair, brown eyes | | 1967 |

| | Size | Name and Particulars | Mold mark located on lower back | |
|---|---|---|---|---|
| | | (5th Series--6 models--Scar on face) | | |
| 7500 | 11½" | G.I. Joe Action Soldier (white)<br>Black molded hair, blue eyes | | 1968 |
| 7600 | 11½" | G.I. Joe Action Sailor (white)<br>Brown molded hair, brown eyes | | 1968 |
| 7700 | 11½" | G.I. Joe Action Marine (white)<br>Brown molded hair, brown eyes | G.I. Joe®<br>Copyright 1964<br>By Hasbro®<br>Pat. No. 3,277,602<br>Made in U.S.A. | 1968 |
| 7800 | 11½" | G.I. Joe Action Pilot (white)<br>Blonde molded hair, brown eyes | | 1968 |
| 7900 | 11½" | G.I. Joe Action Soldier (black)<br>Black molded hair, brown eyes | | 1968 |
| 7900 | 11½" | G.I. Joe Talking Commander (white)<br>Blonde molded hair, brown eyes | | 1968 |
| | | (6th Series--9 models)<br>Life-like hair and/or beard Adventure team) | | |
| 7400 | 11½" | G.I. Joe Adventure Team Talking Commander (white)<br>Blonde life-like hair and beard | | 1970 |
| 7400 | 11½" | G.I. Joe Adventure Team Talking Commander (black)<br>Black life-like hair and beard | | 1970 |
| 7400 | 11½" | G.I. Joe Adventure Team Talking Commander (white)<br>Blonde life-like hair, no beard | | 1970 |
| 7401 | 11½" | G. I. Joe Land Adventurer (white)<br>Brown life-like hair and beard | | 1970 |
| 7402 | 11½" | G.I. Joe Sea Adventurer (white<br>Red life-like hair and beard | G.I. Joe®<br>Copyright 1964<br>By Hasbro®<br>Pat. No. 3,277,602<br>Made in U.S.A. | 1970 |
| 7403 | 11½" | G.I. Joe Air Adventurer (white)<br>Blonde life-like hair and beard | | 1970 |
| 7404 | 11½" | G.I. Joe Adventurer (black)<br>Black life-like hair, no beard | | 1970 |
| 7405 | 11½" | G.I. Joe Astronaut (white)<br>Blonde life-like hair, no beard | | 1970 |
| 7590 | 11½" | G.I. Joe Talking | | 1970 |
| | | (7th Series--8 models--Kung Fu Grip) | | |
| 7280 | 11¾" | G.I. Joe Land Adventurer (white)<br>Black life-like hair and beard | G.I. Joe®<br>Copyright 1964<br>By Hasbro®<br>Pat. No. 3,277,602<br>Made in U.S.A. | 1974 |
| 7281 | 11¾" | G.I. Joe Sea Adventurer (white)<br>Red life-like hair and beard | | 1974 |

| | Size | Name and Particulars | Mold mark located on lower back | |
|---|---|---|---|---|
| 7282 | 11¾" | G.I. Joe Air Adventurer (white)<br>Blonde life-like hair and beard | | 1974 |
| 7283 | 11¾" | G.I. Joe Adventurer (black)<br>Black life-like hair, no beard | | 1974 |
| 7284 | 11¾" | G.I. Joe Man of Action<br>Black life-like hair, no beard | G.I. Joe®<br>Copyright 1964<br>By Hasbro®<br>Pat. 3,277,602<br>Made in U.S.A. | 1974 |
| 7290 | 11¾" | G.I. Joe Talking Adventure Team Commander (white)<br>Brown life-like hair and beard | | 1974 |
| 7291 | 11¾" | G.I. Joe Talking Adventure Team Commander (black)<br>Black life-like hair and beard | | 1974 |
| 7292 | 11¾" | G.I. Joe Talking Man of Action<br>Brown life-like hair, no beard | | 1975 |
| | | (8th Series--1 model--Atomic Man)<br>See through right arm and left leg | | |
| 8025 | 11½" | Mike Power, Atomic Man<br>G.I. Joe Adventure Team (white)<br>Brown molded hair, no beard, blue eyes | G.I. Joe®<br>Copyright 1964<br>By Hasbro®<br>Pat. No. 3,277,602<br>Made in U.S.A.<br>on back of head:<br>©Hasbro Ind. Inc. 1975<br>Made in Hong Kong | 1975 |
| | | (9th Series--8 models<br>New life like (Muscle man bodies | | |
| 1-7280 | 11¾" | G.I. Joe New Life-like Land Adventurer (white)<br>Brown life-like hair and beard, blue eyes | | 1975 |
| 7281 | 11¾" | G.I. Joe New Life-like Sea Adventurer (white)<br>Red life-like hair and beard, brown eyes | | 1975 |
| 1-7282 | 11¾" | G.I. Joe New Life-like Air Adventurer (white)<br>Blonde life-like hair and beard, brown eyes | | 1975 |
| 7283 | 11¾" | G.I. Joe New Life-like Black Adventurer (black)<br>Black life-like hair, no beard, brown eyes | Mark is now on<br>small of back:<br>©1975 Hasbro®<br>Pat. Pend. Pawt. R.I. | 1975 |
| 7284 | 11¾" | G.I. Joe New Life-like Man of Action (white)<br>Brown life-like hair, no beard, blue eyes | | 1975 |
| 1-7290 | 11¾" | G.I. Joe New Life-like Talking Commander (white)<br>Brown life-like hair and beard, blue eyes | | 1975 |
| 7291 | 11¾" | G.I. Joe New Life-like Talking Black Commander (black)<br>Black life-like hair and beard, brown eyes | | 1975 |
| 1-7292 | 11¾" | G.I. Joe New Life-like Talking Man of Action (white)<br>Brown life-like hair, no beard, blue eyes | | 1975 |

Hasbro--11½" "Russian/G.I. Joe" All plastic and fully jointed. Original Russian outfit. Marks: G.I. Joe/Copyright 1964/By Hasbro/Patent Pending/Made In U.S.A. $18.00

Hasbro--4½" "John" of the Dolly Darling Hat Box Series. Marks: 1965/Hasbro/Japan, on back. Tag: Dolly Darling/By Hasbro/Japan. $2.00. (Courtesy Joan Amundsen)

Hasbro--3½" "Mother Hubbard" All vinyl with rooted white hair. Painted features. Original. Marks: 1967/Hasbro/Hong Kong, on head. $3.00.

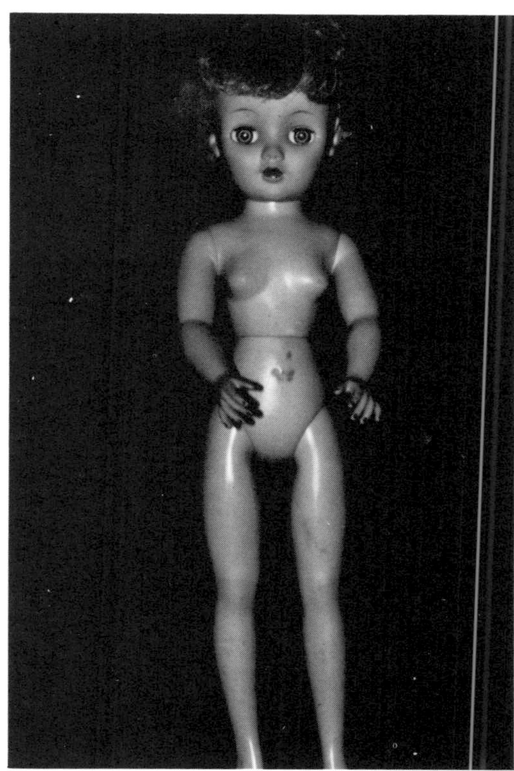

Hill Mfg.--21" "Movie Queen Natalie" All rigid vinyl, softer vinyl head. Sleep eyes, jointed waist. 1959. Marks: Made in U.S.A. mid back. Same doll used for several personalities. Clothes: Natalie: Pink ankle length, lace net overskirt, white "fur" stole. Felice Model: Gold/white X just below knee tight dress. Brown stole lined in dress material. Miss Julie: Long pink satin gown. Coat that is silver with pink lining and hood. Susan Prom Queen: Ankle length yellow ball gown. Flowers on each shoulder and at waist. $12.00.

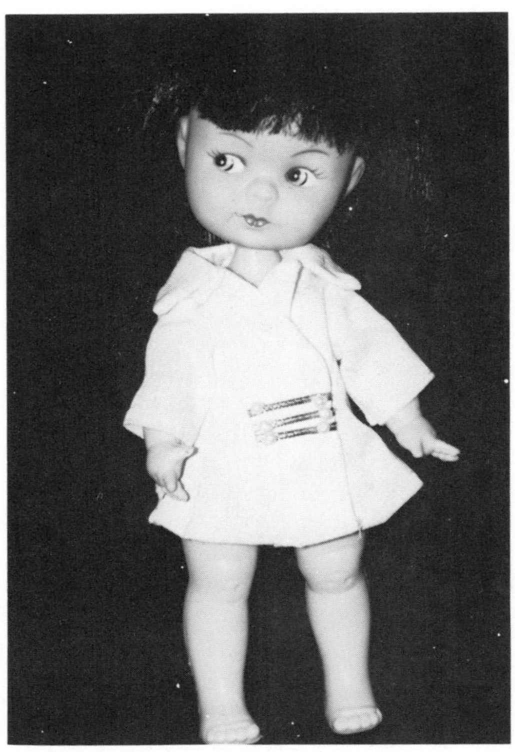

Holiday Fair--9" "Terry" All plastic with vinyl head. Black rooted hair. Painted blue eyes. Marks: Holiday Fair, Inc./Made in Hong Kong, on back. Made in Hong Kong, on head. $2.00.

Holiday Fair--6½" "Luva Girl" Plastic body. Jointed neck only. Vinyl head. Black hair. Blue painted eyes. Earrings. Original. Marks: Made in Hong Kong. $5.00.

For complete information on the Horsman Doll Co. refer to Series I, page 136.

Horsman--20" Composition head and limbs. Cloth body. Blue tin sleep eyes. Original. Open mouth/2 upper teeth. Marks: E.I.H. Co./Horsman. $37.00. (Courtesy Jay Minter)

Horsman--Right: Cloth with composition head, arms and legs. Swivel shoulder plate. Completely original. Blue tin sleep eyes. Marks: Rosebud, on neck. Dress tag: Horsman. Doll on left is also marked: Rosebud. Has brown sleep eyes. $45.00. (Courtesy Flacks)

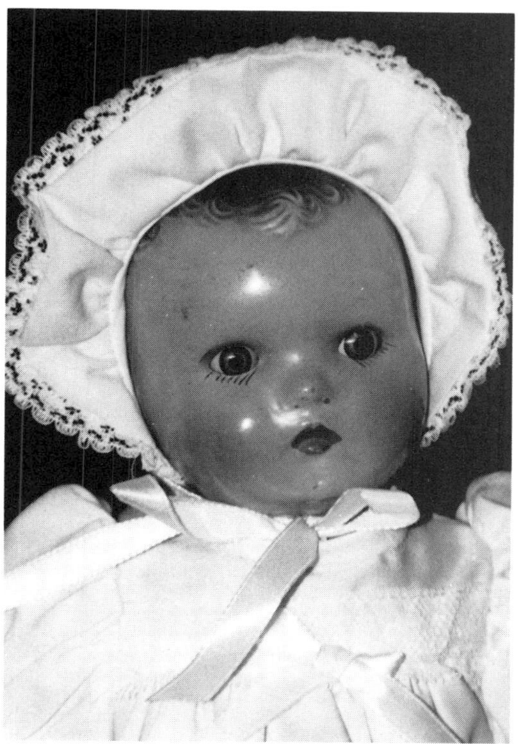

Horsman--14½" Cloth body. Composition arms, legs and head. Brown tin sleep eyes. Curly molded hair. Marks: A/Horsman/Doll. $37.00. (Courtesy Maxine Heitt)

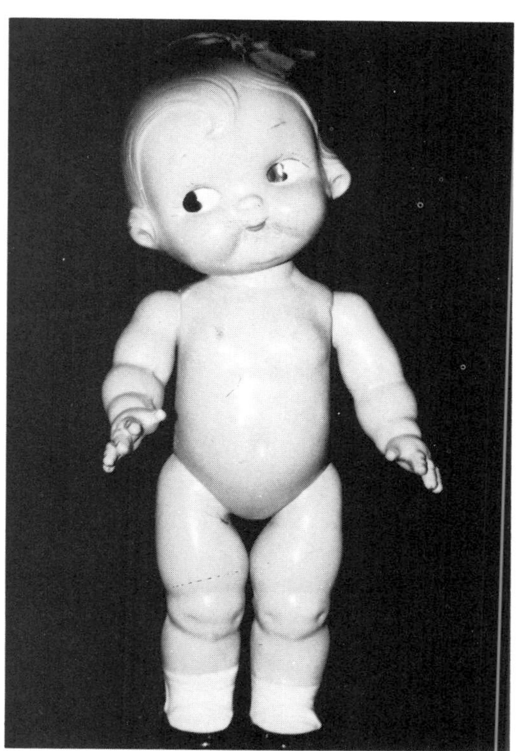

Horsman--12" Campbell Kid" All composition. Painted on shoes and socks. Stapled on ribbon. 1948. $65.00. (Courtesy Kimport Dolls)

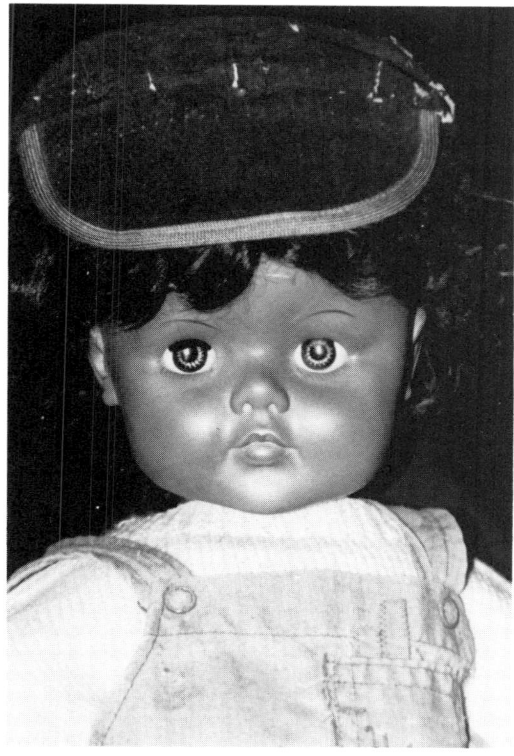

Horsman--22" One piece stuffed vinyl body and limbs. Vinyl head. Brown sleep eyes. Marks: 96/ Horsman. ca. 1955. $15.00.

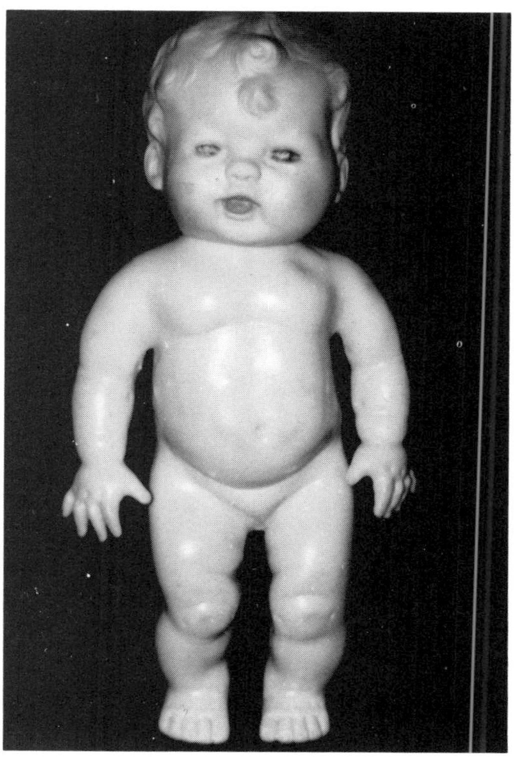

Horsman--7" One piece vinyl with softer vinyl head. Puckered crying face. Painted blue eyes. Marks: HD, on head. $3.00.

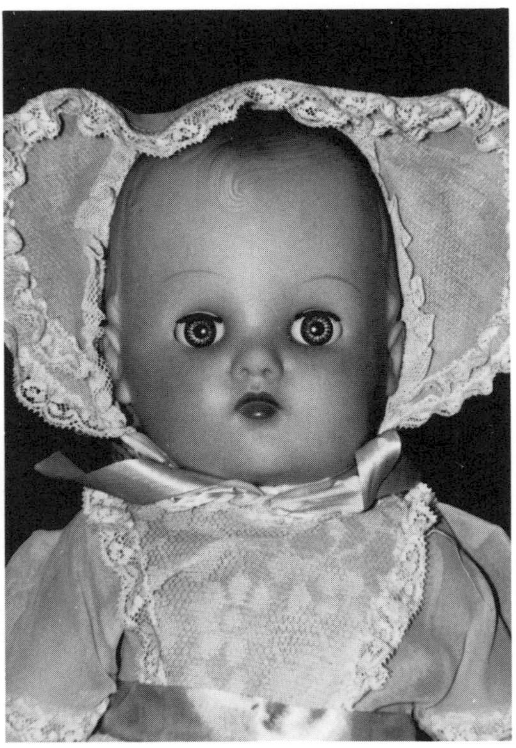

Horsman--18" "Fairy Skin Doll" One piece body and limbs. Molded hair. Sleep eyes. Marks: four dots and Horsman, on head. Tag: Horsman's/ Fairy Skin/Doll/Made Entirely/Of Soft/Vinyl Plastic. $12.00. (Courtesy Alice Capps)

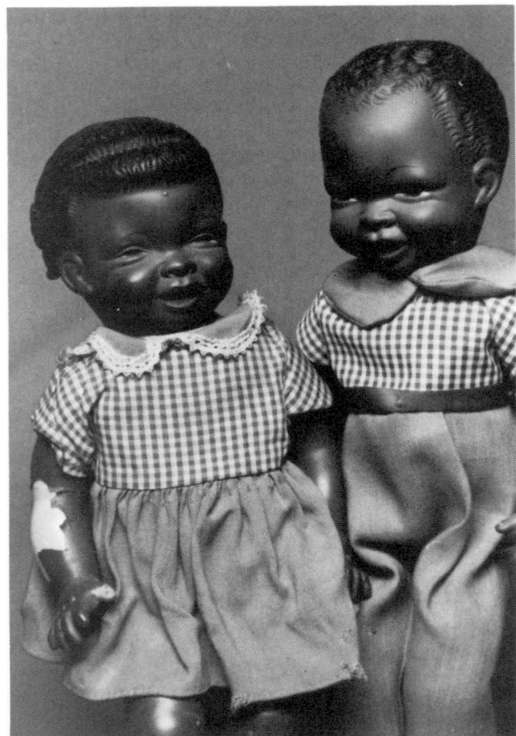

Horsman--13" "Polly and Pete" One piece stuffed vinyl body and limbs. Top layer on body will peel. Vinyl head with molded hair and painted features. Marks: Horsman, on head. 1957. $65.00 each. (Courtesy Alice Capps)

Horsman--26" "Dolly Walks" (Also the Head for Thirstee Walker when mouth is cut open) 8" Baby. Unmarked. Molded hair under rooted hair. Large one is marked: Horsman Dolls Inc./ 1962 CB 25. Both original. $18.00 pair. (Courtesy Tillie Kobe)

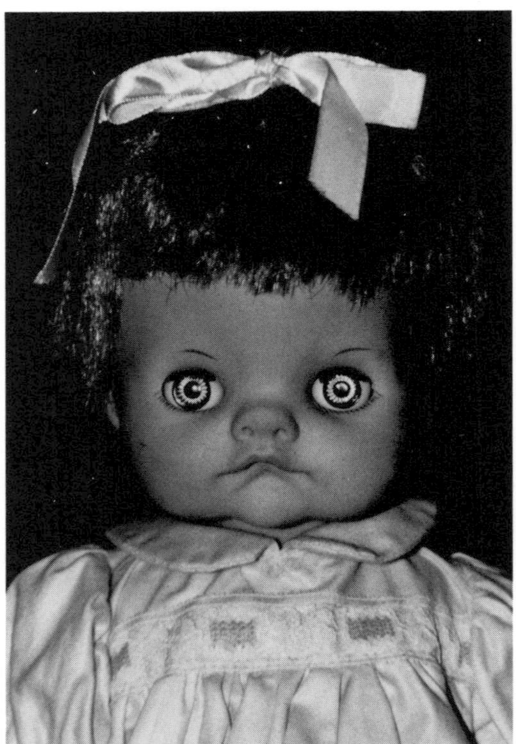

Horsman--15" "Jody" Plastic body and legs. Vinyl arms and head. Blue sleep eyes/lashes. Lower lip sucked under upper one. Marks: Horsman Dolls/1964/T13. By Irene Szors. $8.00. (Courtesy Jayn Allen)

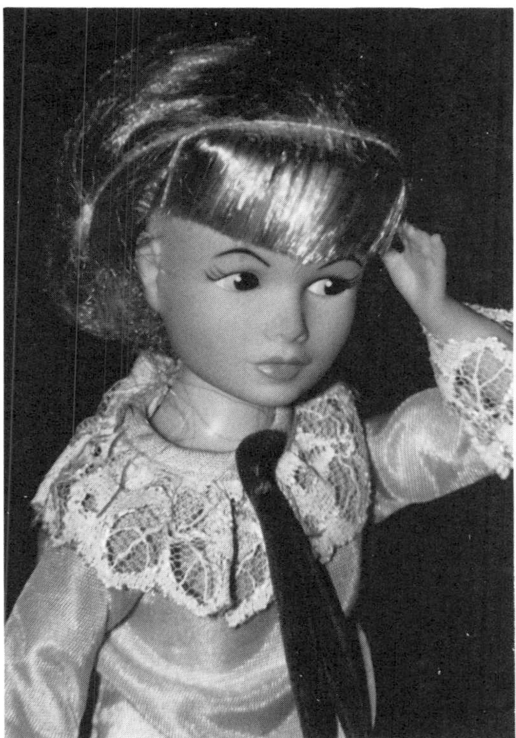

Horsman--12" "Patty Duke" Posable arms and legs. Blue eyes to side (painted). An Irene Szor design. 1965. Marks: Horsman Doll/6211. $16.00. (Courtesy Marie Ernst)

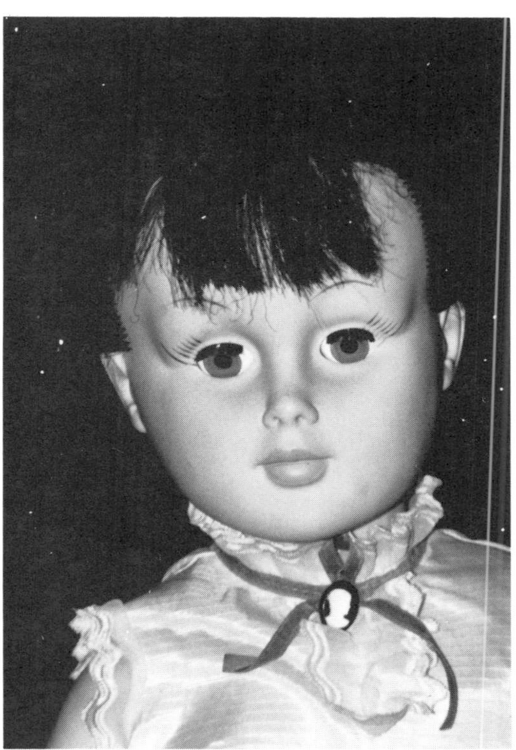

Horsman--26" "Mary Poppins" Walker. Plastic body, arms and legs. Vinyl head. Sleep eyes. Marks: 5/Horsman Dolls Inc./1966/66271. $25.00. (Courtesy Alice Capps)

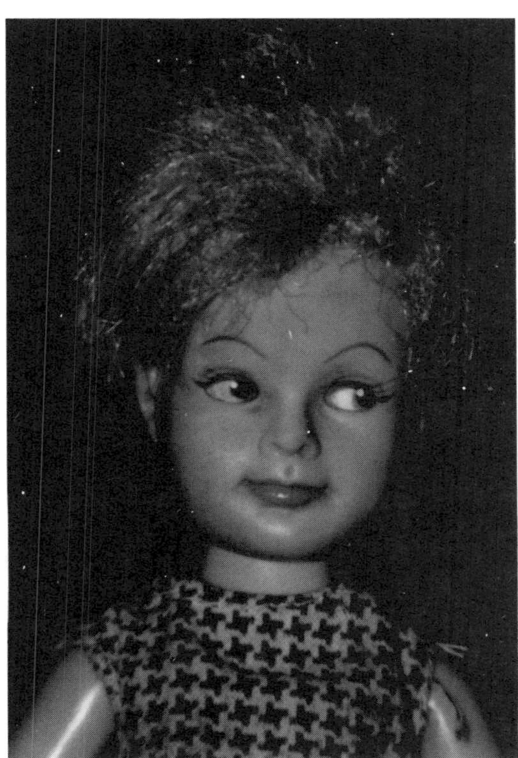

Horsman--8" "Michael" from the Mary Poppins set. Plastic and vinyl. Painted blue eyes. Marks: C.T./Horsman Dolls Inc/6682. $15.00. (Courtesy Cecelia Eades)

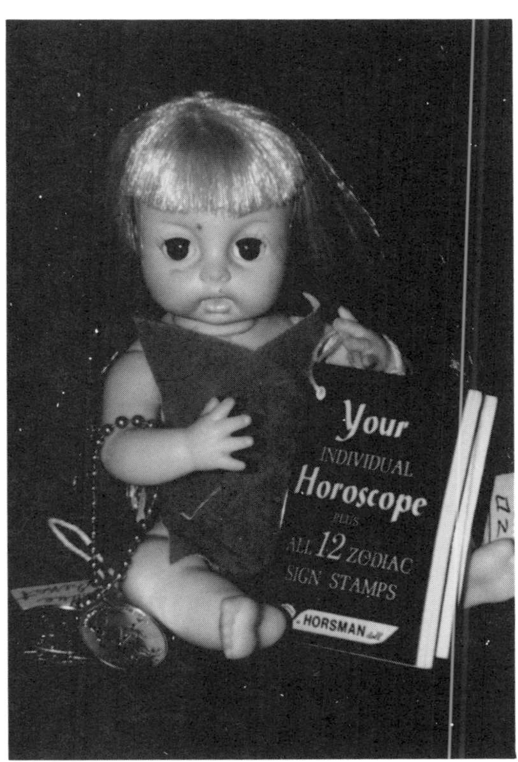


Horsman--6" "Zodiac Baby" All vinyl. Long rooted pink hair. Also came with white hair. Set black eyes. Open/closed mouth. Came with charm bracelet with signs of the Zodiac. Marks: Horsman Dolls Inc/1968, on head. $6.00. (Courtesy Marie Ernst)

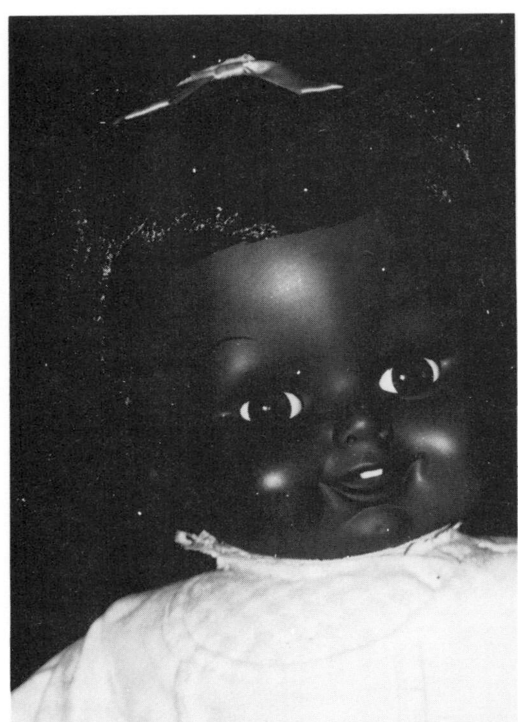

Horsman--21" "Happy Baby" Cloth and vinyl. Zipper down back to get to battery box. Throw her up in the air or bounce on knee and she laughs. Turns itself off. Cheek and chin dimples. Sleep eyes. Open/closed mouth with two upper molded painted teeth. Original. Marks: Horsman Doll Inc./1974. Still available.

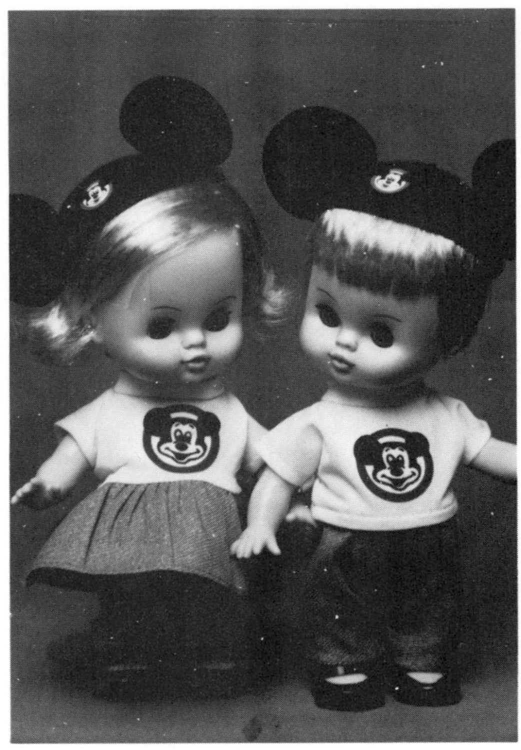

Horsman--8" "Mousketeer" boy and girl. All vinyl with one piece body and legs. Blue sleep eyes. Mousketeer hats "pinned" to heads. Girl is blonde, boy is orange haired. Marks: 1273/10 Eye/33/Horsman Dolls Inc/1971, on head. 10, on back. Box: An Irene Szor design. Still available.

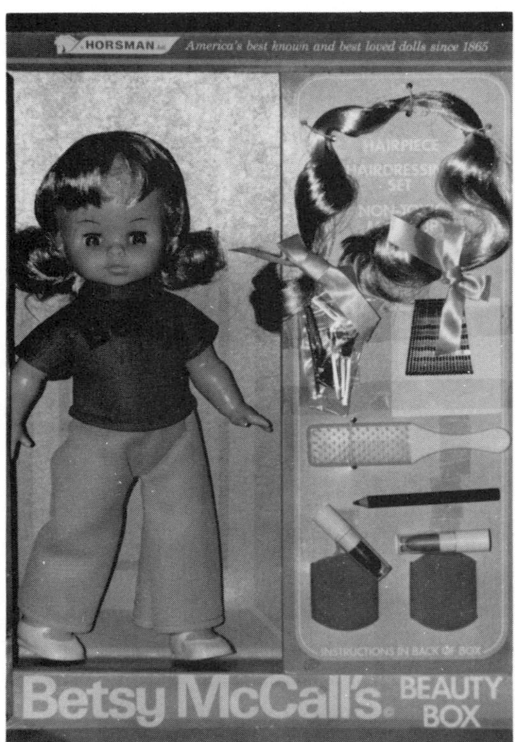


Horsman--13" "Betsy McCall" New for 1975. One piece green/pink jumpsuit. Doll is an earlier issue doll. Marks: Horsman Dolls Inc/Pat. Pending, on back. 1/Horsman Dolls Inc./1967, on head. Box: An Irene Szor Design.

Hoyer--15" "Margie" Plastic body and legs. Vinyl arms and head. Blue sleep eyes. Marks: AE18. Gift from Carolyn Powers.

For complete information on the Ideal Toy Corp. refer to Series I, page 153. Complete information on the Shirley Temple doll is located in Series I, page 179.

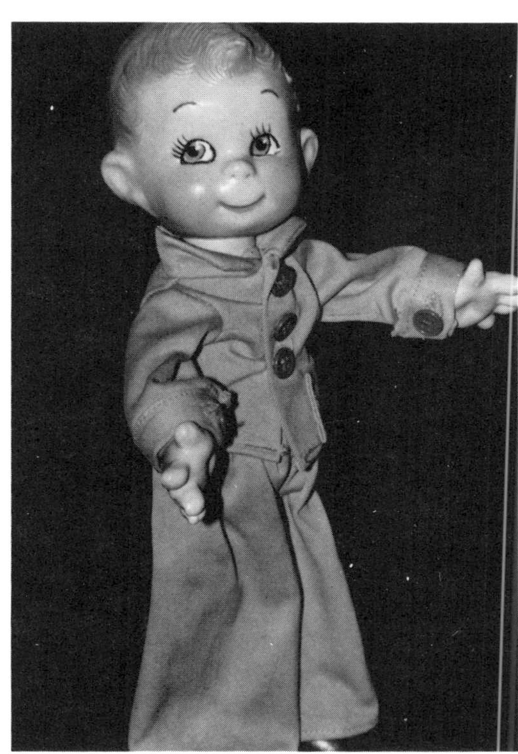

Ideal--13" "Flexy Soldier" All composition and wire. Wood feet. W.W.II doll. Marks: Ideal Doll, on head. $38.00. (Courtesy Barbara Coker)

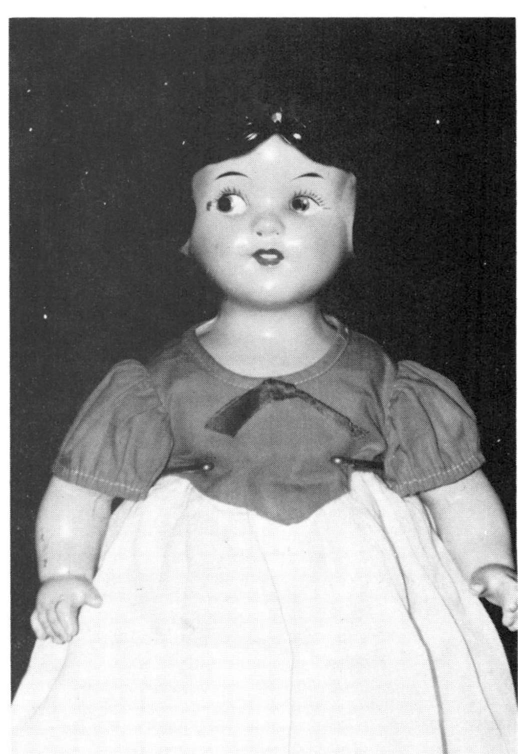

Ideal--18" "Snow White" Cloth body. Composition shoulder plate and limbs. Molded bow painted red. Marks: Ideal, on head. Original. $50.00. (Courtesy Kimport Dolls)

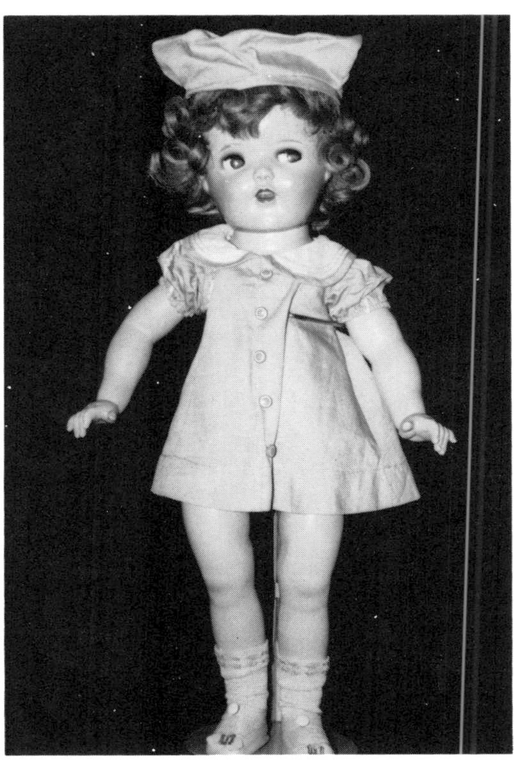

Ideal--18" "Mary Jane" All composition. Flirty brown sleep eyes. Blonde mohair wig. Original. Marks: Ideal 18, on head. (Courtesy Cecelia Eades)

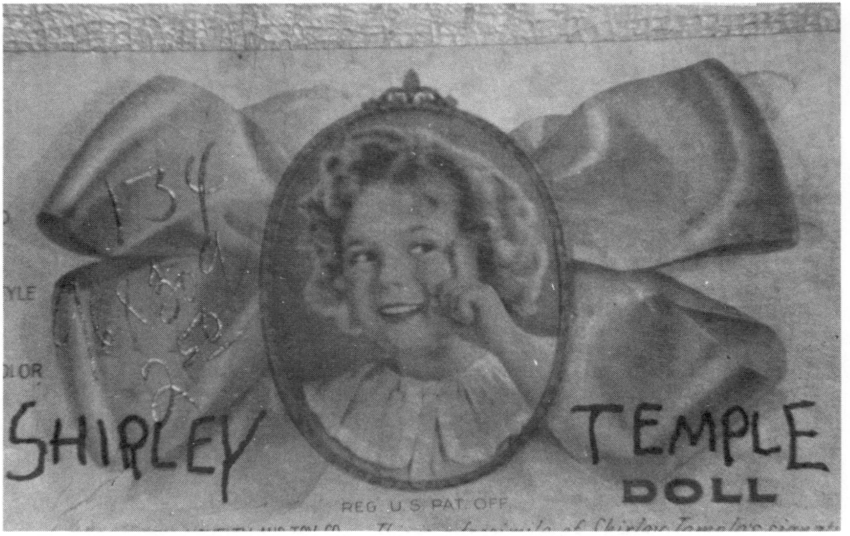


Ideal--Shows end of original Ideal Shirley Temple box.

Ideal--This is the real Deanna Durbin holding one of the first issues of the doll made after her.

## Shirley Temple Prices

Composition: 25" Toddler. Marks: 73/Shirley Temple. $300.00.
23" Toddler with cloth body. Marks: #1 and/or Shirley Temple. $100.00.
16" Baby. Shirley Temple, on head. $125.00.
17" Baby. Shirley Temple, on head. $125.00.
18" Baby. Shirley Temple, on head. $140.00.
22" Baby. Shirley Temple, on head. $160.00.
25" Baby. Shirley Temple, on head. $185.00.
27" Baby. Shirley Temple, on head. $195.00.
All composition dolls:
27" Marked. $200.00.
25" Marked. $110.00.
23" Marked. $95.00.
22" Marked. $85.00.
18" Marked. $85.00.
17" Marked. $85.00.
16" Marked. $85.00.
15" Marked. $85.00.
13" Marked. $75.00.
11" Marked. $140.00.
Any size Hiwaiian. $110.00.
Soap Shirley $30.00.
Plaster Shirley. $15.00.
Reliable of Canada Shirley $45.00.
Mechanical Display Shirley's $1,000.00 up.
9" all compo. molded hair. Closed mouth. Ideal Doll, on back. $60.00.
35" Vinyl and plastic. $365.00.
19" Vinyl. Flirty eyes. $65.00.
17" Vinyl $45.00.
12" Vinyl $25.00.

Ideal--This photo is from the October 1939 issue of Screen Guide and says the photo was made in December 1938. $95.00 up.

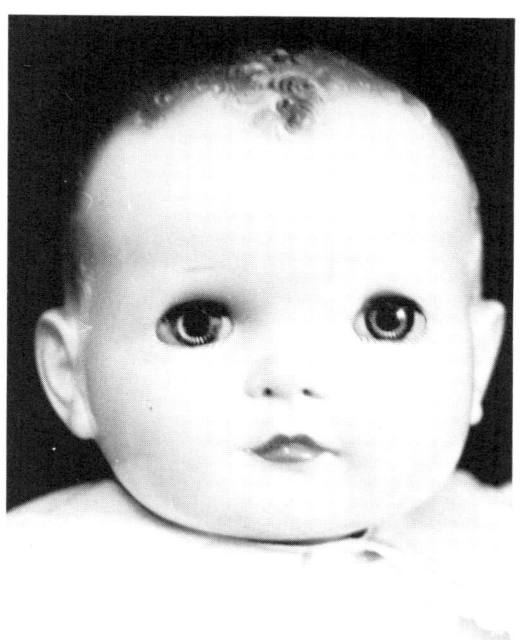

Ideal--30" "Magic Squeezums" Latex body with pin jointed arms and legs. Hard plastic head. Sleep eyes. Molded hair. Marks: Ideal Doll/ Made in USA. 1950. $22.00. (Courtesy Alice Capps)

Ideal--Shows interior of the Ideal Butterick pattern set with 12" manniken. $22.00. (Courtesy Marge Meisinger)

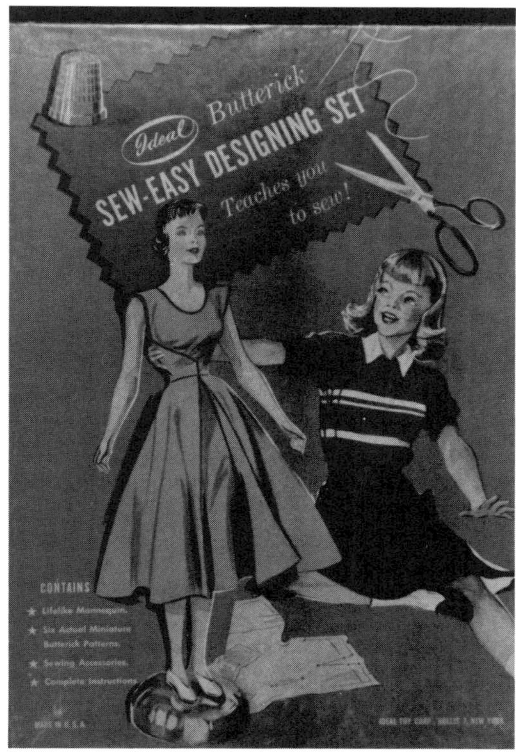


Ideal--Shows box top to Ideal Butterick pattern set. (Courtesy Marge Meisinger)

Ideal--18" "Judy Splinters" Latex arms and legs. Cloth body. Early vinyl head. Black yarn hair. Brown painted eyes. Open/closed mouth with molded tongue. Original. Marks: Ideal Doll, on head. 1951. $30.00.

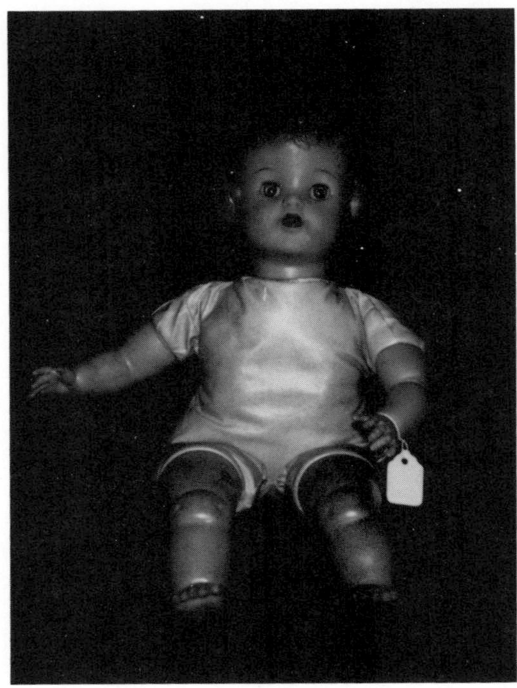

Ideal--15" "Huggee Girl" Vinyl with oil cloth body. Blue sleep eyes. Open/closed mouth. Molded curly hair. Marks: Ideal Doll/BC 16, on head. 1952. $12.00. (Courtesy Carolyn Powers)

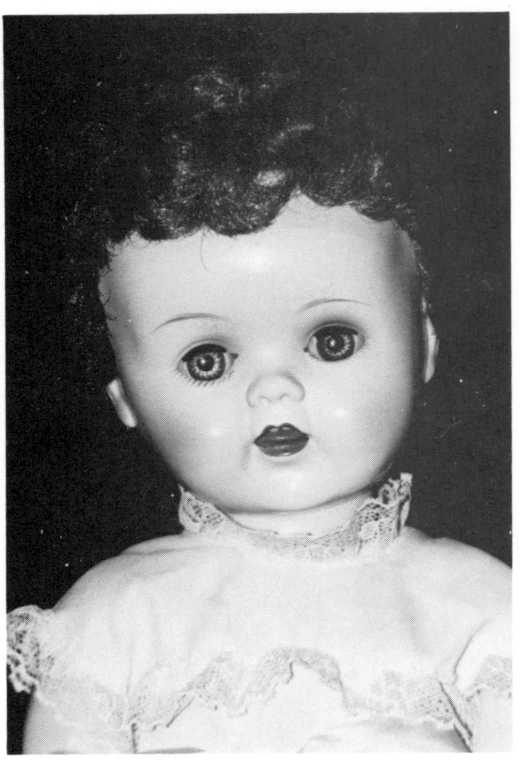

Ideal--17" "Bonnie Walker" All hard plastic with cryer in stomach. Pin hip walker. Blue sleep eyes. Open mouth/2 upper teeth and molded tongue. Marks: Ideal Doll/W16, on head and back. $16.00. (Courtesy Joan Amundsen)

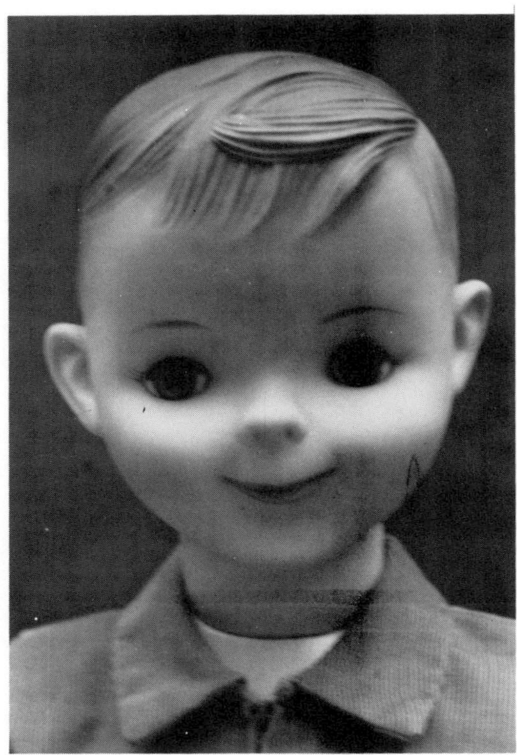

Ideal--36" "Sandy McCall" Molded hair. Sleep eyes. Marked On Head: McCall/Corp 1959. $75.00. (Courtesy Phyllis Houston)

The following is the account of Phyllis Houston and her discovery of Sandy McCall.

The standing picture of Sandy McCall is enclosed for just one reason and that is his stand. Sandy and I came together under the most unusual circumstances. I was going downtown one day for a ladylike luncheon and some shopping when I had to pause between the car park and department store for a "Don't Walk" light. Glancing idly about I met a familiar pair of eyes peering out of a 5&10 display window. It must have been the classic doubletake when I whirled and went in...Sandy McCall, no less, and I had To Have Him. After talking to several people who all giggled, said no he wasn't for sale, implying silly woman, I finally reached the store manager who also giggled and wiggled and then I told them what I would pay for Sandy. Smiles disappeared and he was mine, all 36 naked inches of him. You can imagine the looks we drew, me in white gloves and Sandy in a paper bag around his middle.

Anyway-to be used as a mannequin, they had drilled holes in his shoes, giving them first extra strength by slipping in thin pieces of plywood. The heavy block of wood which is his stand also has holes in it and screws with wing nuts at the bottom allow him to be taken loose for redressing. What a marvelous idea for all my large dolls, who will shortly all wear holey shoes.

Ideal--This shows the "Sandy McCall" on display stand just as Phyllis Houston found him.

Ideal--15" "Carol Brent" Made for Montgomery Wards in 1961. Marks: Ideal Toy Corp/M-15-L, on head. Ideal Toy Corp./M-15, on body. $20.00. (Courtesy Marie Ernst)

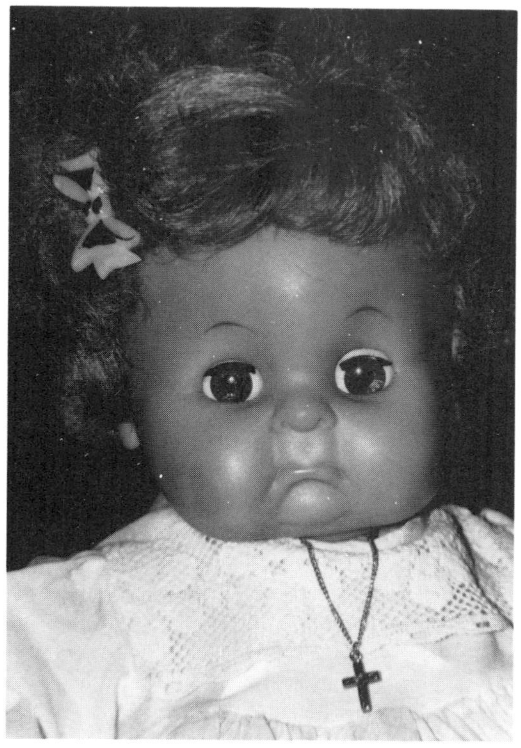

Ideal--15" "Twins" Other is boy. Cloth with vinyl arms, legs and head. Pouty mouth. Blue sleep eyes/lashes. Marks: Ideal Toy Corp./TW-14-2-U, on head. $20.00. (Courtesy Diana Sorenson)

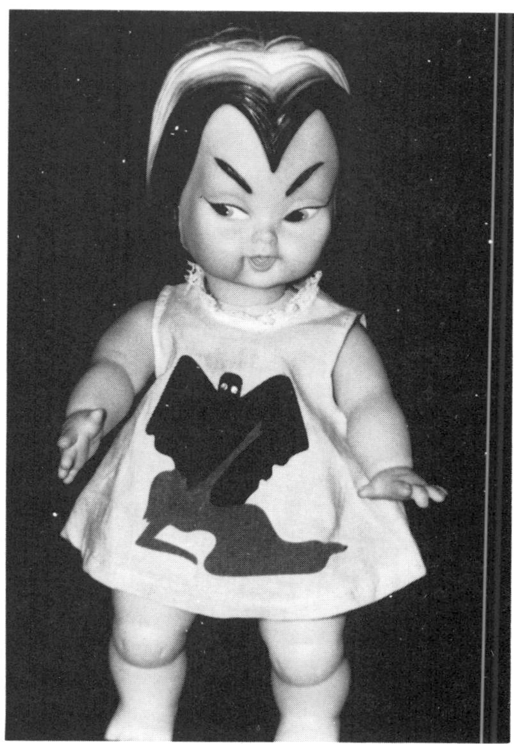

Ideal--9" "Mini Monster" Plastic with vinyl arms and head. Molded eyelids, open/closed mouth and designed on same body as used on one model of Pebbles doll. Original dress. One in set of several. Marks: 1966/Ideal Toy Corp, on head. Made in Japan, on back. Dress Tag: Mini Monster/Ideal, in oval Japan. $6.00. (Courtesy Joan Amundsen)

Ideal--17" "Katie Kachoo" All vinyl. Raise her arm and she sneezes into hankie. Open mouth. Marks: 1968/Ideal Toy Corp/SN-17-EH-37. $20.00. (Courtesy Susan Goetz)

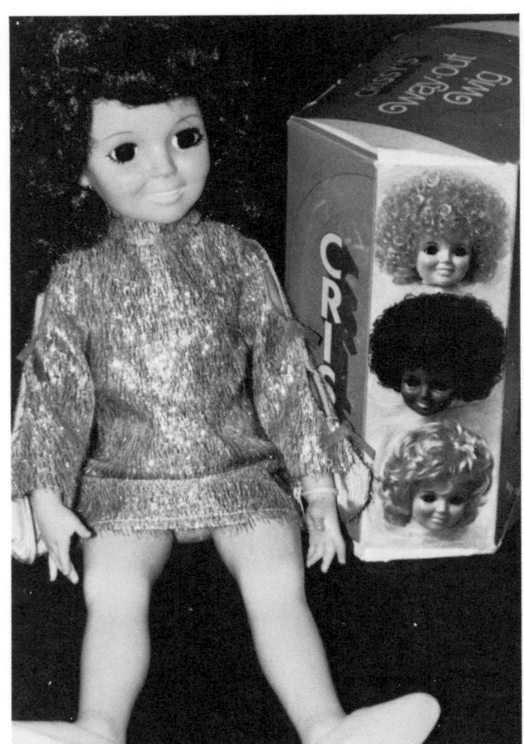

Ideal--Shows a Crissy with her new wig from the Crissy replacement wig set. 1970. (Courtesy Marie Ernst)

Ideal--11" "Dr. Evil" Action figure. Came with various face masks. 1965. $6.00.

Ideal--18" "Tiffany Taylor" Teen fashion model. Plastic and vinyl. Painted blue eyes/long lashes. Top of head swivels to change hair color from blonde to brunette. Original. Marks: 1974/Ideal, in an oval, Hollis, NY 11423/2M 5854-01/2, on lower back. 1973/CG-19-H-230 Hong Kong. Dress Tag: Ideal, in oval. Tiffany Taylor.

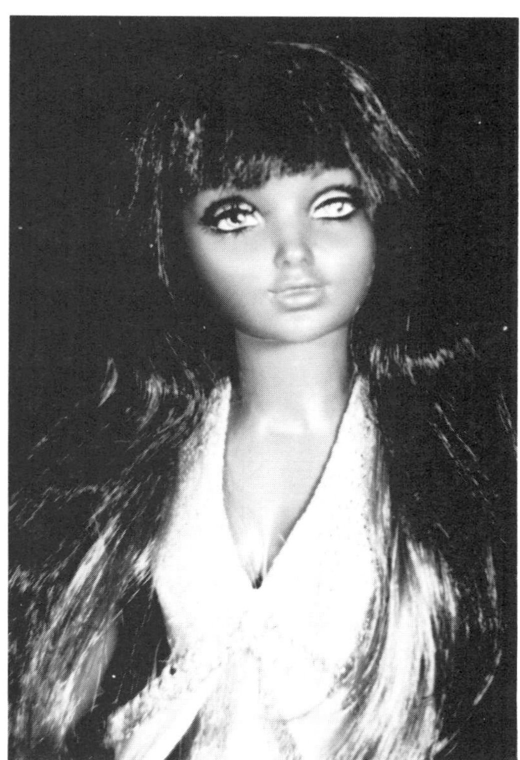

Ideal--18" Black version of "Tiffany Taylor" Hair turns from black to deep red. Still available.

Ideal--18" "Tiffany Taylor" Full length view with hair turned to brunette.

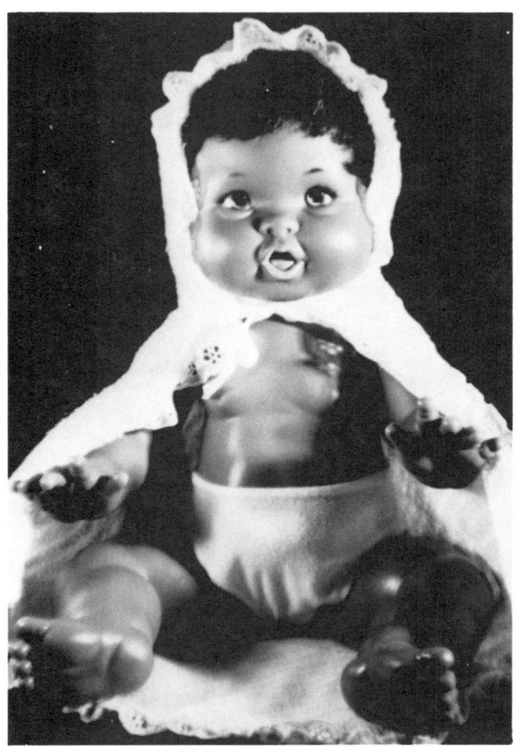

Ideal--17" "Rub A Dub Baby" Plastic body. Vinyl arms, legs and head. Open/closed mouth. Original. Marks: 1973/Ideal Toy Corp/Rad-16-H233, head. 1973/Ideal Toy Corp/HOLLIS NY 11423/RAD 17/2M-5852-01/2., on body. Still available.

Teens--"Family Rider" 10" man: woman: Plastic and vinyl. Jointed knees. Man has molded on black boots, she has molded on white shoes. Both marked: Hong Kong, that runs vertically up backs. 2½" all vinyl baby is molded in one piece in a sitting position. Battery operated. Box: An Illco Toy. Still available.

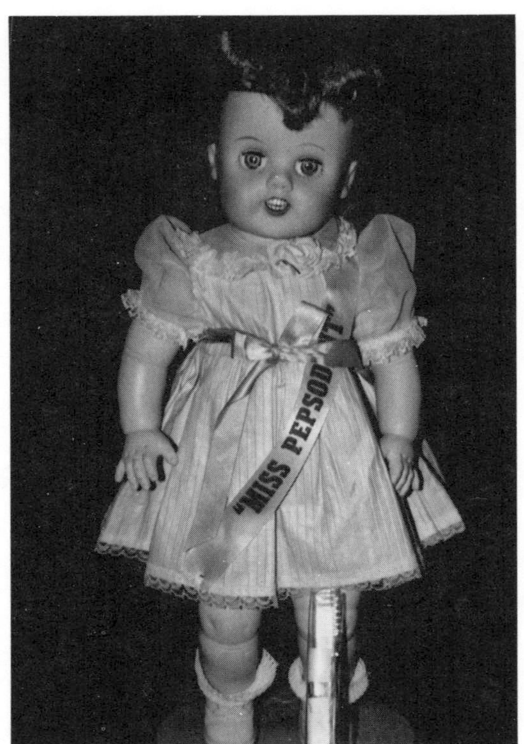


Imperial Crown--23" "Miss Pepsodent" All vinyl. Blue sleep eyes. Open mouth with rolling teeth. When laying down teeth are yellow, when sitting up, they rotate to white. All original.

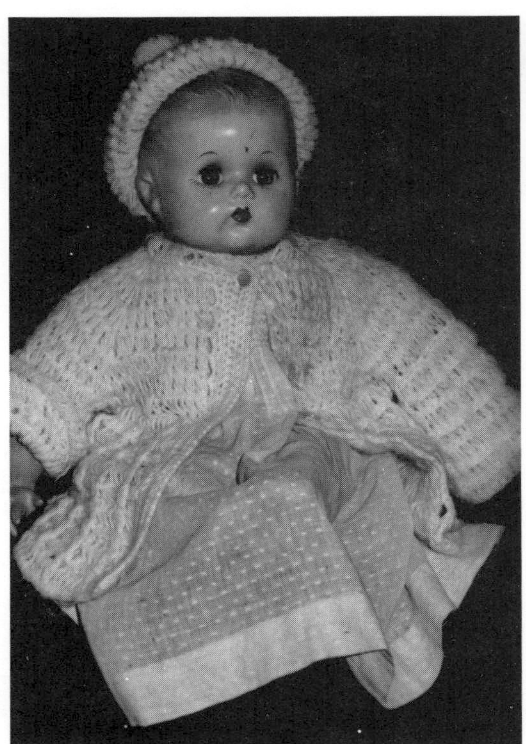

Impco--21" "Baby Bubbles" Composition head. Cloth body. Latex arms and legs. Molded light brown hair. Blue sleep eyes. Cryer. Marks: None. Original dress. 1950. Made by Imperial Crown. $10.00.

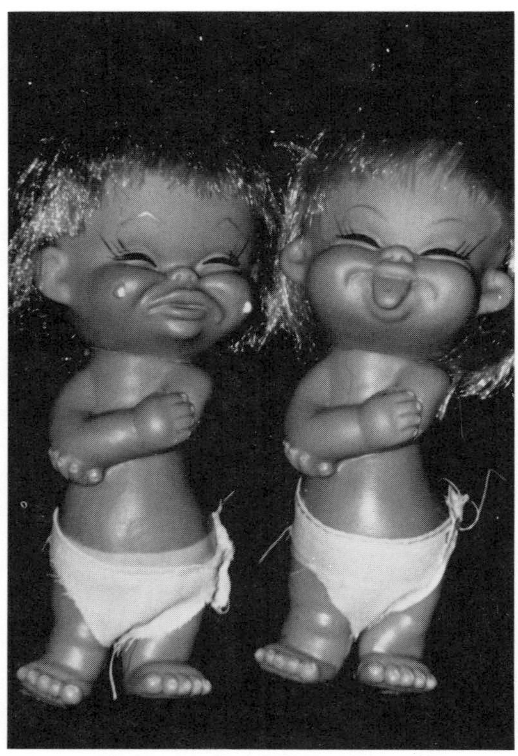

Imperial Toy--5" "Sunny Surfers" All brown vinyl. Jointed neck only. Yellow painted under shorts. Marks: Some have Hong Kong, on foot. 1975. $2.00 each.

Imperial Toy--5" "Sunny Surfers" All brown vinyl. Jointed neck only. Yellow painted under shorts. Marks: Some have Hong Kong, on foot. 1975. $2.00 each.

Imperial Toy--5" "Sunny Surfers" All brown vinyl. Jointed neck only. Yellow painted under shorts. Marks: Some have Hong Kong, on foot. 1975. $2.00 each.

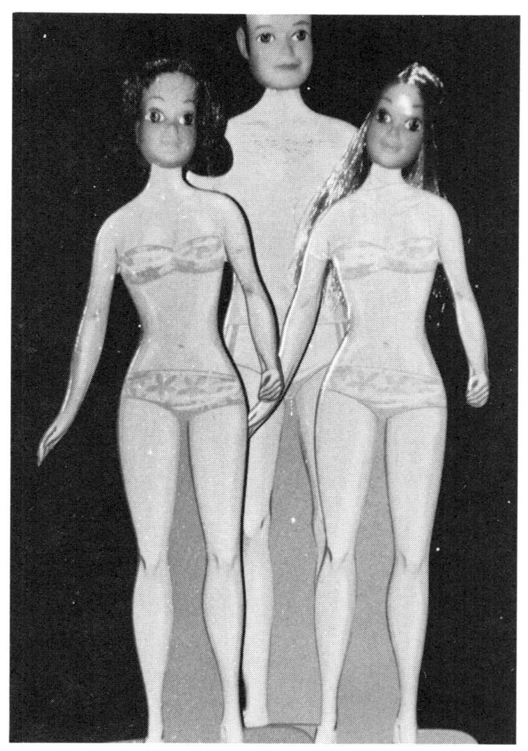

Janex Corp.--"Pretty Quix" dolls. 9" Ivy: Brown hair. 10" Glenn: brown molded hair and 8½" Holly: blonde hair. Vinyl heads with cardboard bodies. Press on fashions of fabric. Made by Janex Corp. $7.00. (Courtesy Marie Ernst)

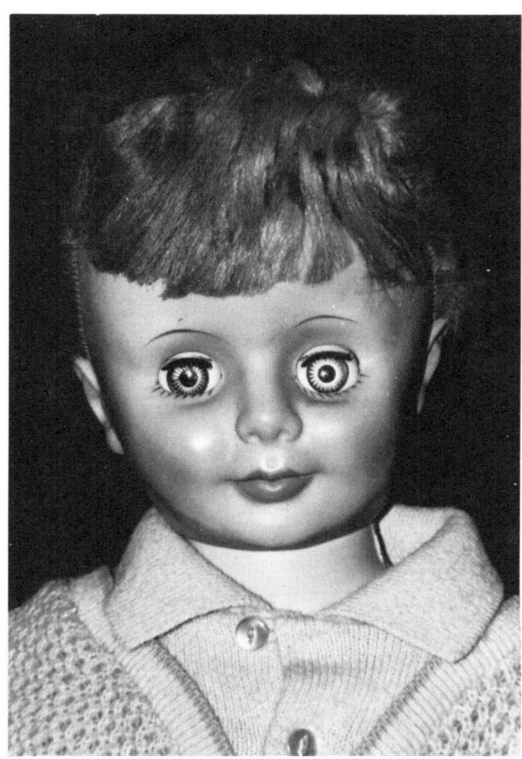

J. Cey--27" Plastic with vinyl arms and head. Smile mouth. Blue sleep eyes. Left eye hole molded larger than right. Marks: J-Cey, on head. $20.00.

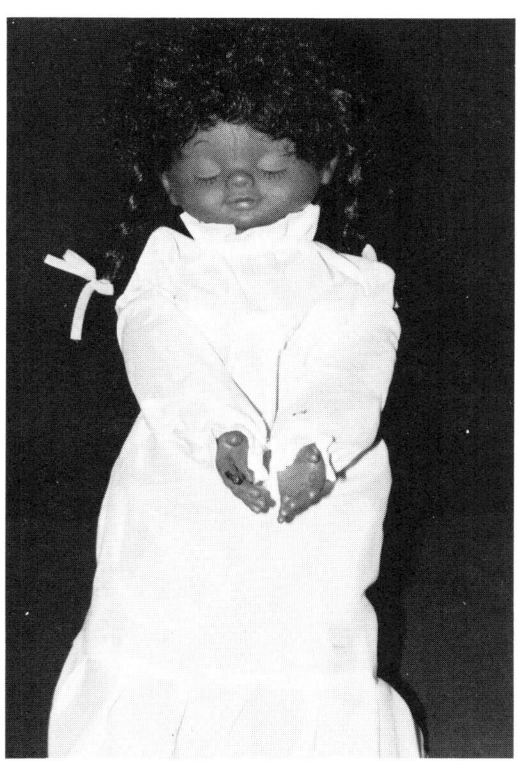

Jilmar--18" "Praying Patti" and also called "Sleepy Angel." Vinyl head with painted closed eyes. Gauntlet rigid vinyl hands. Cloth body with sewn on flannette slippers. Zipper in back for battery pack. Operation button in front. Says prayers. Sold by Niresk Industries. Marks: Tag: Sleepy Angel TM by Jilmar Co. $15.00.

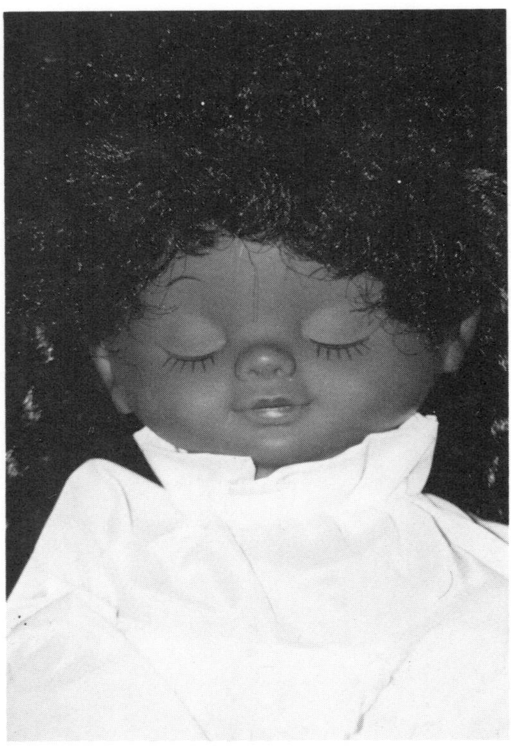

Jilmar--All original Sleep Angel. Snaps on gown hold the arms together.

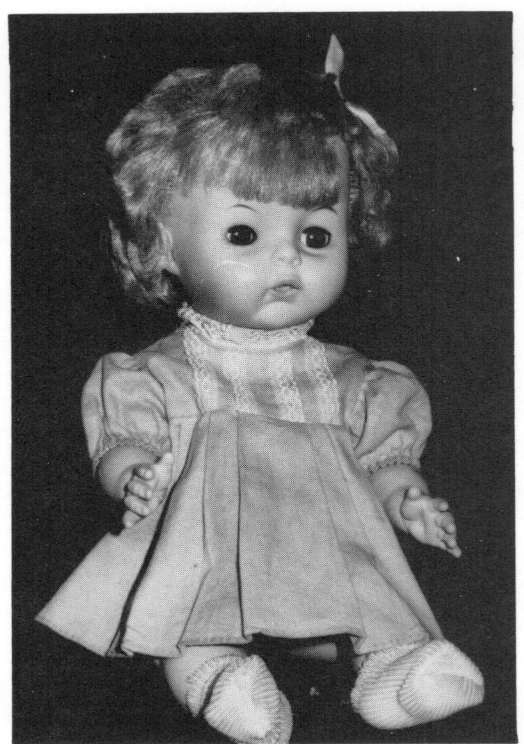

Jolly Toys--16" "Baby Angel" Plastic and vinyl. Blue sleep eyes/lashes. Open mouth/nurser. Marks: Jolly Toys Inc., on head. A reversed AE on body. 1961. $2.00.

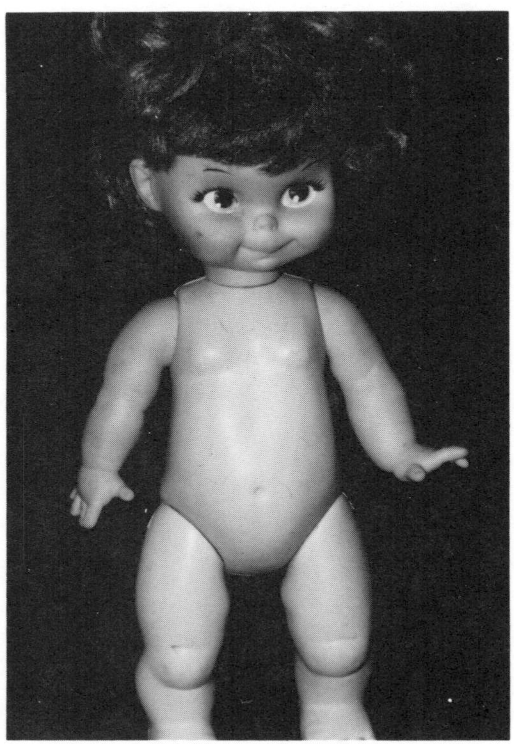

Jolly--11" Painted eyes version of "Jolly." Plastic and vinyl. Painted blue eyes. Upper lip over lower. Marks: L3. ca. mid 1960's. $3.00.

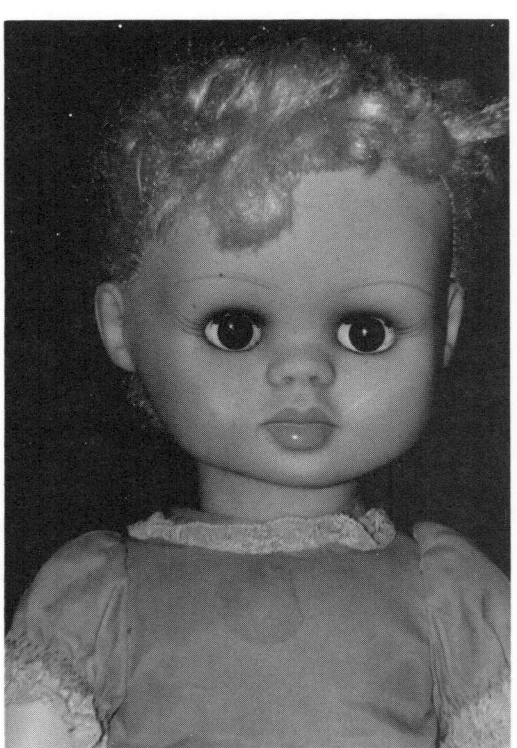

Jolly--19" "Dixie Pixie" Closed mouth version. All vinyl. Black sleep eyes/lashes. Large mouth. White rooted hair. Marks: None, except FR-18, on left arm. 1963. (Courtesy Barbara Coker)

Jolly Toy--17" "Suzanna Ballerina" Plastic and vinyl with rooted blonde hair. Blue sleep eyes. Blue eyeshadow. Marks: Jolly Toy/1965, on head.

Jolly Toys--11" "Judy Playmate" Plastic and vinyl. Blue sleep eyes/molded lashes. Open/closed mouth with molded tongue. Original dress. Hair has been cut. Marks: Jolly Toy/1968, on head. Made in Hong Kong, on back.

Jolly--7½" "Little Lil Lil" All vinyl. Painted eyes. Painted on shoes and socks. Original. Marks: None. Take off of Little Lulu. (Courtesy Cecelia Eades)

Joy Doll--14½" "Marlene Dietrich" All composition. No molded hair under wig. Blue sleep eyes. Stapled on clothes. Golden blonde mohair wig. Gold dress/white net shawl. Deep purple flower on top and in hair. 1945. $45.00. (Courtesy Mary Partridge)

Joy Doll--14½" "Colonial Lady" All composition with yellow mohair wig. Blue sleep eyes. Original. Marks: None. $18.00.

Joy Doll--14½" "Prom Queen" All composition. Blue sleep eyes. Light red mohair. Original. 1939. $18.00.

Junel--11" "Mary Lincoln" All composition. Fully jointed. Painted blue eyes to side. Both arms fairly straight. Original deep blue velvet dress/gold trim. Tag: Copy of Dress worn by Mary Lincoln 1861/Junel Novelties Inc. NY. $18.00.

# Kamar, Inc.

Of the 102 letters to various companies for resumes, I received a packet and a nice letter from the Kamar company. They make only a few dolls but the quality of the dolls is good and they are character ones rather than the "dolly" kind. To future generations the Kamar dolls will be like the "novelty" dolls of the early years of this century. This company produces the FINEST of stuffed toys and it is very difficult to locate any of their animals as the quality is so good that they are kept as prize possessions and rarely are on the "used" market.

This company is so progressive for example: They developed a teddy bear, "Dear Heart" that has a heart beat, before the scientific study involving two separate groups of newborn infants in a New York hospital. Group A was presented with the sound of the human heartbeat, through a recording. Group B was monitored at the same time in the same hospital without the heartbeat. Results: The food intake was the same but Group A gained weight, while Group B showed an overall weight loss. Group A cried less than 40 percent of the time and Group B cried about 60 percent of the time. The results of such studies show that infants need to continue the sound of heartbeats, the only sound they are familiar with (before birth). Kamar's "Dear Heart" fills this need. I will include a photo of this teddy bear in this section, along with ones of a few of the delightful, unique and original stuffed toys by Kamar.

All Kamar toys are handmade and of uncompromising quality. They produce more than 250 items that are distributed in 50 states and 32 foreign countries. These toys are produced in Japan, Portugal, Taiwan, Mexico and Korea, with the firm's home office in Gardena, California...Kamar is a privately held corporation and sells directly to the retailer. The toys range in price from $1 to $150.

The following is part of the "fact sheet" from Kamar and should be of interest to all doll/toy collectors:

# Astrid Elaine Wennemark Kamar: Wife, Mother and Super-Executive

Astrid (pronounced Ah-strid) Kamar, the attractive executive vice president of Kamar, Inc., has realized a multitude of dreams and has achieved something thousands of individuals have tried to attain--overwhelming success in a multi-million dollar business she helped develop from scratch less than 15 years ago.

At the same time she is a busy mother of three children and the wife of one of the world's most talented toy designers.

As a youngster growing up in her native California, Astrid "knew" she could never be content with a hum-drum life. "Life has always been exciting," she said. "I've always reached towards a goal--sometimes I guess my goals were more romantic than realistic, but there was always that exciting challenge to try to achieve them."

Her goal as a young woman out of business school was to use her business skills in as exciting a way as she could; so she joined the U.S. Foreign Service and worked in Washington, D.C., and Jamaica as a cryptographic clerk for 18 months.

Unfortunately, the Foreign Service did not prove to be the exciting venture she had envisioned. Several years and two jobs later, Astrid met an unusual young man, Pascal Kamar (P.K.). His life had been anything but hum-drum, having recently arrived in the United States from war-torn Jerusalem. P.K. had achieved enormous success in Jerusalem as a well-known musician; however, he was not able to become established in the music world in America. To survive and make a living, he had become a salesman in the garment industry at the time Astrid met him.

P.K. had a dream of creating something exciting and original, and Astrid shared this dream. They soon embarked on a small gift-importing business while P.K. continued his work in garment sales. The importing enterprise became a partnership when Astrid and P.K were married. They enlarged the business by importing unusual gifts from Africa and the Middle East and later became the first to import hand carved teak animals from African artisans.

The explosion into success, however, came with the "birth" of Hexter, the first doll designed by P.K. It was a wild-eyed, long-haired gangling predecessor to the troll doll; and, it was an overnight success.

Assuming at first that they had somehow run onto a wonderful, simple situation...that all dolls would sell in the same run-away manner Hexter had...the Kamars put together every scrap of cash and credit they could manage and ordered all the dolls and animals they could afford from the factories in Japan. Then, they watched them languish under dust on shelves in a rented warehouse. The truth didn't escape them for very long, however. It was soon determined that the secret of success in the business was in design...original design by P.K. He began designing more and more dolls and dropping more and more gift imports. By 1963, Kamar was solely in the stuffed doll and animal business running hard to keep up with the demand for Kamar originals.

To keep up with toy production, Astrid began a search for good plants that would produce the toys in quantity but retain the fully hand-made aspect of the toys that is so important to the Kamar quality. Her hunt for production plants took her around the world. Today Kamar has plants in Korea, Taiwan, and Japan; and Astrid established plants in Mexico and Portugal.

"One of the most interesting and rewarding experiences in my life involves establishing our plant in Portugal," recalls Astrid. In southern Portugal, there is a small remote village, Messejana, near the top of Mt. Baixo Alenjo. It is only in the last three years that Messejana has appeared on any maps of Portugal. It was a poor village which offered the villagers little hope. Food was virtually scratched from the ground and each year the supply became more meager.

The local priest, desperate to keep the villagers from near starvation the next winter, began looking into "modern" ways in which the people could earn a living. As an attempt to aid the villagers in supporting themselves, he made a small personal investment in large amounts of yarn and encouraged the local women to knit baby and children wear. Three years ago a crude "factory" was established an today the women of Messejana produce some of the finest hand-made children knit wear in the world.

At approximately the same time as the building of the "factory," Astrid met the priest and discussed her need for toy production. She was specifically looking for a plant in Portugal, for Portugal produces the finest leather in the world, a necessary item for many of the Kamar toys. Today the crude knitting factory of Messejana has expanded to include the production of Kamar leather toys, which in turn has helped assure the residents of Messejana a greater measure of security.

Not long ago, the Kamars brought the priest to the United States for a visit--the first time he had been out of his small region in Portugal--so that he might see additional toy factories and discover a broader outlook on the world. In Messejana he not only is the priest, but is the village's only teacher, doctor, and engineer.

As executive vice president of Kamar, Inc., Astrid directs marketing, shipping and internal purchasing and procedures. She has never contributed to the design of the toys. "I leave all of that to P.K.," she explained. "The design of each and every toy is his life. Besides, I'd probably end up with a five-legged cat or a bunny with no tail."

Five years ago Astrid became one of the first flying, traveling salesladies on the American business scene. At her instigation the company purchased a twin-engine Beechcraft and converted it to a flying showroom. In this manner Astrid flies into city after city meeting customers and buyers and conducting sales presentations while serving lunches and refreshments--all from 4,000 feet.

Astrid, P.K., and their children, Laurie Lynn, 4; Jenny Lynn, 10; and Christopher, 13, live in Palos Verdes (Calif.) on a cliff overlooking the Pacific.

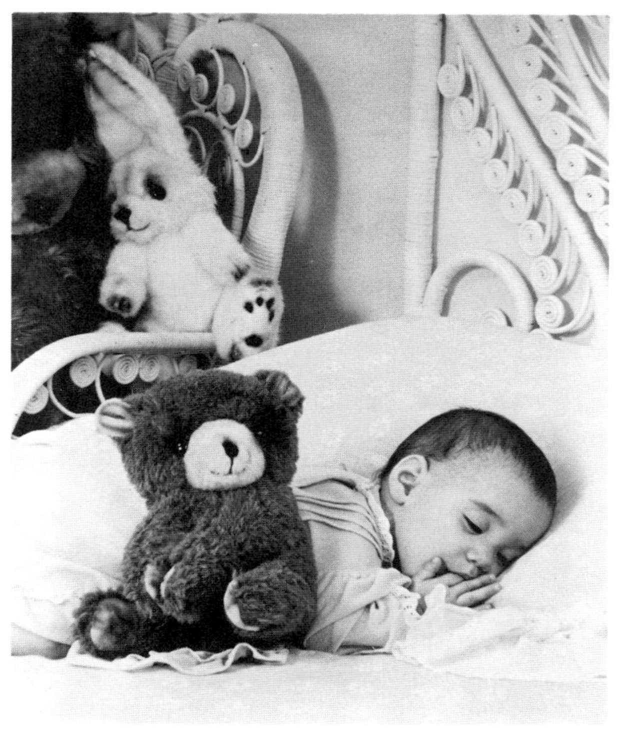

DEAR HEART...THE WORLD'S FIRST TEDDY BEAR WITH A HEARTBEAT. Recent scientific studies have indicated that the sound of a heartbeat is soothing and relaxing to infants. Dear Heart, available in almost every store and shop that sells toys, is produced by Kamar, Inc.

"KAMAR'S WILD THINGS" numbering nearly 100 items are designed by Pascal Kamar president of the firm. The line which is changed by nearly 40 per cent twice a year is now sold in all 50 states and 36 foreign countries.

SUPER-EXECUTIVE AND REAL-LIVE DOLL...is Mrs. Astrid Kamar, executive vice president of Kamar, Inc., California producers of quality, handmade stuffed toys. She and her husband, Pascal, developed their hobby into a multimillion dollar company in less than 15 years.

Kamar--13" "John F. Kennedy" Vinyl head, hands and shoes. "Wired" so that arms and legs can be posed. Sits in rocking chair. Reads newspaper with articles about wife, Jackie and children. A music box (key wound) plays and chair rocks. $22.00. (Courtesy Virginia Jones)

Kamar--13" "Jock" Non removabale clothes. Glued tuffs of mohair. Marks: 1966 Kamar/Made in Japan, on tag. Japan, on head. $3.00.

Kamar--4½" "Ana" All vinyl. One piece body, legs and arms. Jointed neck. Beautiful hand detail. Two cutouts in back for original wings. Marks: Japan, on head. Tag: 1967 Kamar/Made in Japan. $2.00.

Kamar--10" "Clown" All stuffed with vinyl head. Glued on mohair. Tag: 1967 Kamar/Made in Japan. $2.00. (Courtesy Ellie Haynes)

Kamar--8" "Tia Marie" Came in brunette, blonde and red. All vinyl. Sculptured, painted brown eyes. Fully jointed. Painted on green shoes. Original. Marks: 1968 Kamar Inc./Japan. $3.00.

Kamar--9" "Mona" All vinyl with glued on vinyl hat. Also shows top of head on the second doll, without her hat. Marks: Japan. $3.00. (Courtesy Ellie Haynes)

Kamar--5" "K-Tot" All white and vinyl with "fur." Jointed neck. Tag: 1969/Kamar Ink/Japan. $2.00. (Courtesy Ellie Haynes)

Kamar--5" "April" Came in redhead, silver, blonde and brunette. All vinyl. Dimples. Sculptured, painted dark blue eyes. Molded flowers. Jointed neck only. Marks: 1968 Kamar Inc./Japan. $2.00.

Kamar--5" "Nobo" Jointed neck and shoulders. Glued on "fur." Excellent molding of feet and hands. Brown/black sculptured painted eyes. Marks: 1969/Kamar Inc/Japan, on bottom of foot. $3.00. (Courtesy Virginia Jones)

Kamar--6½" Wire/felt. "Red fur" dress. Vinyl head. Marks: 1968/Kamar/Japan, on head. Tag: 1968 Kamar/Made in Japan. $2.00.

## Kaysam

Kaysam--There seem to be rumors that all Kaysam dolls were personalities and this seems to be in error. Kaysam, was a method of injecting molding and was the material used. Kaysam, was a part of the Jolly Toy Company.

Kaysam--15" "Red Cross Nurse" Plastic body and legs. Vinyl arms and head with rooted brown hair. Blue sleep eyes/molded lashes. Blue eyeshadow. Adult figure. High heel feet. Marks: Kaysam/1961, on head. Original clothes. $18.00.

Kaysam--24" This is a Kaysam doll 1961, that is all original and bears the tag: Another Jolly Doll. Doll is marked 1961/Kaysam. This same doll sold in Alden's (1962) and 15" as June Bride, 25" as Jackie and in 16" version as Cynthia and Gerri. $22.00. (Courtesy Marie Ernst)

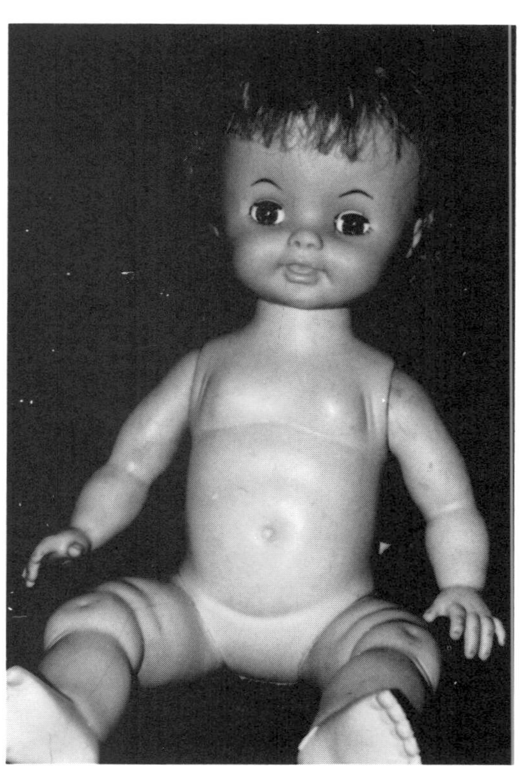

Kaysam--15" "Baby Judy" Plastic and vinyl. Open mouth/nurser. Blue sleep eyes/lashes. Marks: 6514/Kaysam, lower back. HD/20, on head. 1963. $4.00.

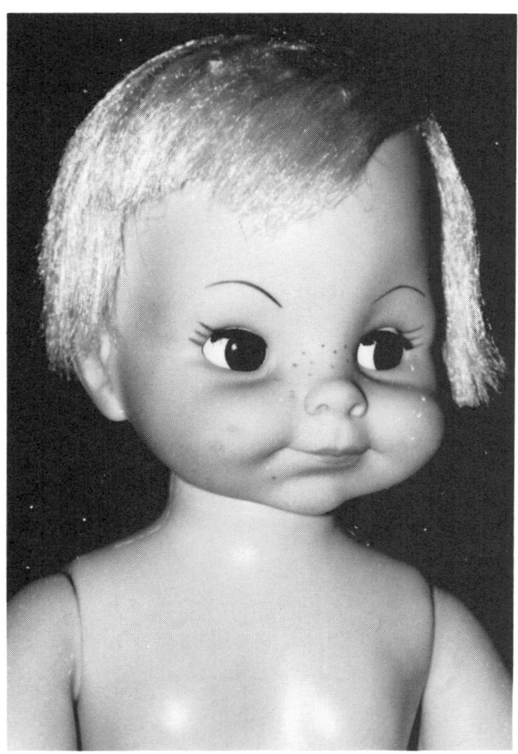

Kaysam--19" Plastic with vinyl arms and head. Black sleep eyes to side. Freckles across nose. Rooted white hair. Marks: Kaysam 4379/1966 20, on head. 6419, lower back. K24 under left arm. K33 under right arm. $10.00.

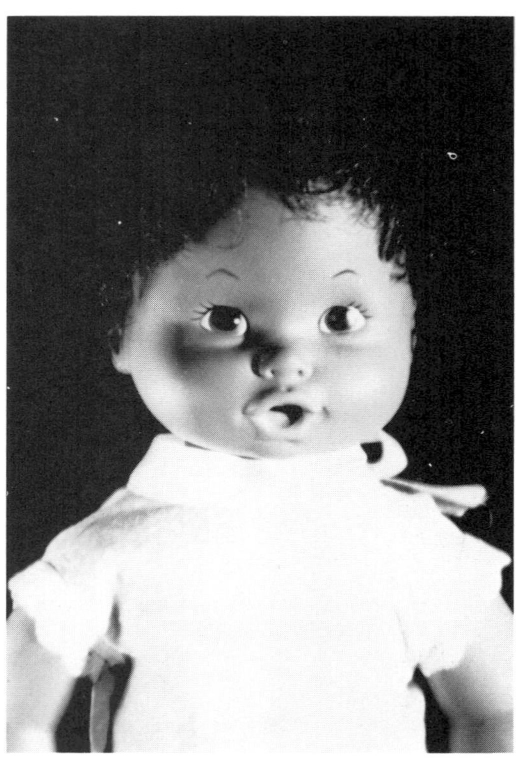

Kenner--16" "Baby Alive" One piece dublon with jointed neck only. Rooted hair in vinyl skull cap sealed over dublon head. Painted eyes. Came in white and black. Open mouth nurser and eater. Battery operated. Had special formula to feed doll. Marks: 3564/P13/Kenner Prod./1973. Still available.

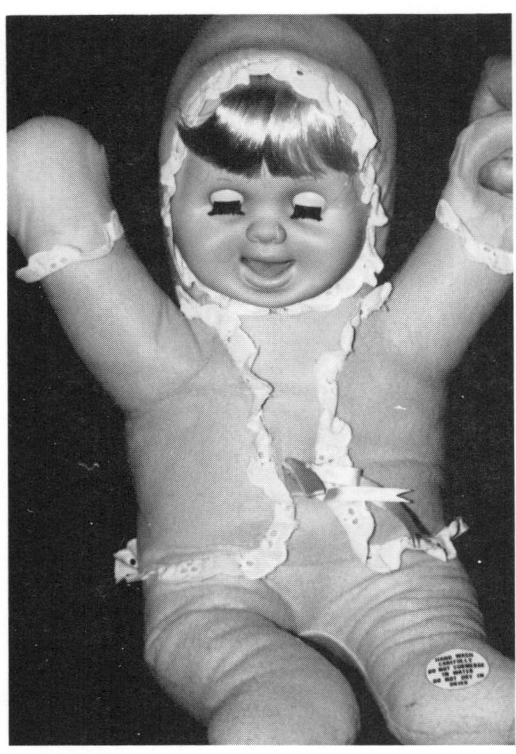

Kenner--15" "Baby Yawnie" Bellows type bulb in left hand. Squeeze and eyes close and mouth yawns. Still available.

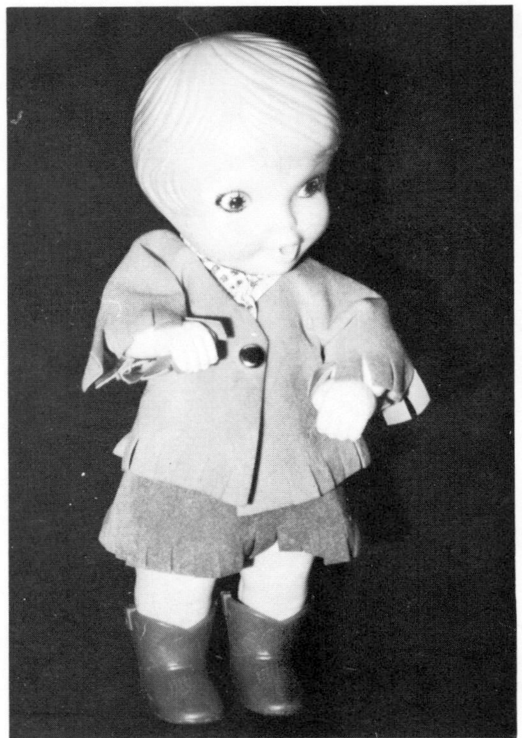

Kenner--6" "Sippin' Sue" Plastic and vinyl with molded yellow hair. Painted blue eyes. Open mouth/not nurser. Original. Marks: 1972/General Mills/Fun Group Inc. These dolls were sold with straws/glass and could stand next to child as they sipped through their own straw. $2.00.

Keebler Co.--6½" "Keebler Elf" All vinyl jointed only at neck. Molded clothes. Painted features. Marks: 1974/Keebler Co. Premium doll. $3.00.

King--9" "Henry" All early rubber vinyl with painted features, and clothes. Marks: KF, on bottom of foot. 1950. $8.00. (Courtesy Edith Goldsworthy)

Knickerbacher--15" "Princess Glory of Lilliput" (Gulliver's Travels) All composition. Eye-shadow/sleep eyes. Bent right arm. Very long hair. Same doll with boy hair style is Prince David of Flefuscu (Gulliver's Travels). $48.00. (Courtesy Mary Partridge)

Knickerbacher--15" "Oh! Susanna" All composition with brown sleep eyes. Open mouth/three teeth. Bent right arm. Marks: Knickerbacher, on backs of some. 1937. $48.00. (Courtesy Jay Minter)

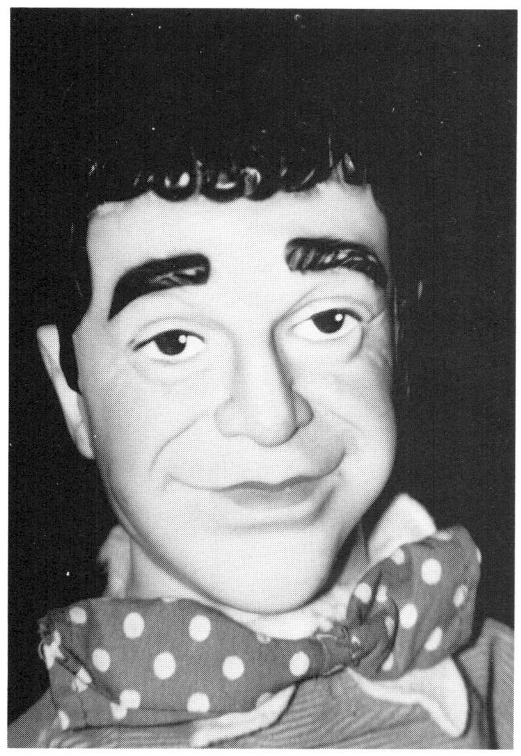

Knickerbacher--13" "Soupy Sales" Vinyl head with cloth body and non-removable clothes. Marks: 1965 Knickerbacher, on head. Tag: Soupy Sales/1966 Soupy Sales, W.M.C. $35.00. (Courtesy Barbara Coker)

Knickerbacher--14" "Theodore & Alvin (Hat)" Chipmonks. Cloth with vinyl heads. Marks: Ross Bagasarin. $10.00 each. (Courtesy B. Mongelluzzi)

Knickerbacher--"Holly Hobbie" Comes in 9½", 16", 27" and 33" also the 7" that is put out in the purse. Still available. (Courtesy 1975 Knickerbacher Catalog)

Knickerbacher--"Heater" Comes in 9½", 16", 27" and 33." Heater is Holly Hobbie's friend. Still available. (Courtesy 1975 Knickerbacher Catalog)

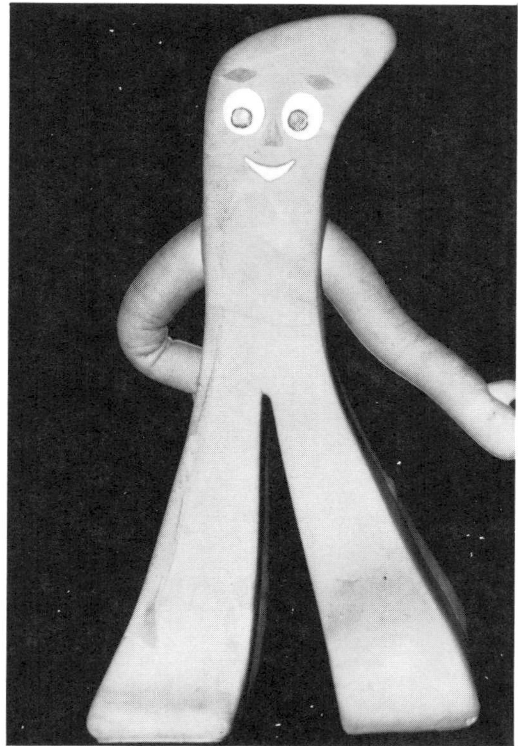

Lakeside--13" "Gumby" All green foam over wire armature. White/red foam eyes. Yellow foam mouth. Came with horse called "Pokey" and with accessories such as guns, guitar, hats, etc. Marks: Gumby/Mfg. By/Lakeside Ind. Inc/LIC. by/Newfeld Ltd./Of England. 1965, 66 and 67. $4.00.

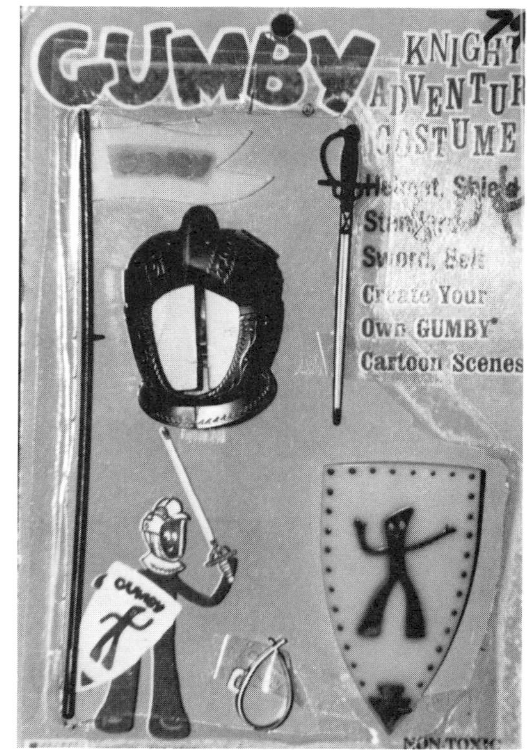


Lakeside--"Gumby" Knight Adventure Set. Yellow/green shield. Silver helmet. Brown standard with yellow flag. Sword is silver and black. 1965, 66 and 67. $2.00.

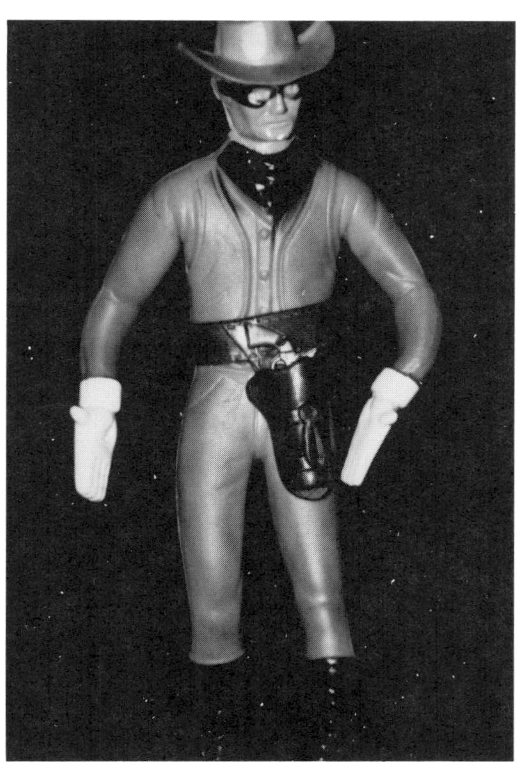

Lakeside--6" "Lone Ranger" All vinyl and completely posable. Molded on clothes, except gun/belt. Marks: 24/1966/Lakeside/Ind. Inc, on back. Box: Wrather Corp/Lakeside Toys Division of Lakeside/Industries Inc. $2.00.

Lesney--5" "Sailor Sue" All vinyl. Rooted red hair and painted brown eyes. Marks: Lesney/1973, on head. Lesney/Products/Hong Kong, on back. $4.00. (Courtesy Marge Meisinger)

Lesney--5" "Alice in Wonderland" All vinyl with rooted blonde hair. Painted blue eyes. Marks: Lesney/1973, on head. Lesney Products/Hong Kong, on body. $4.00. (Courtesy Marge Meisinger)

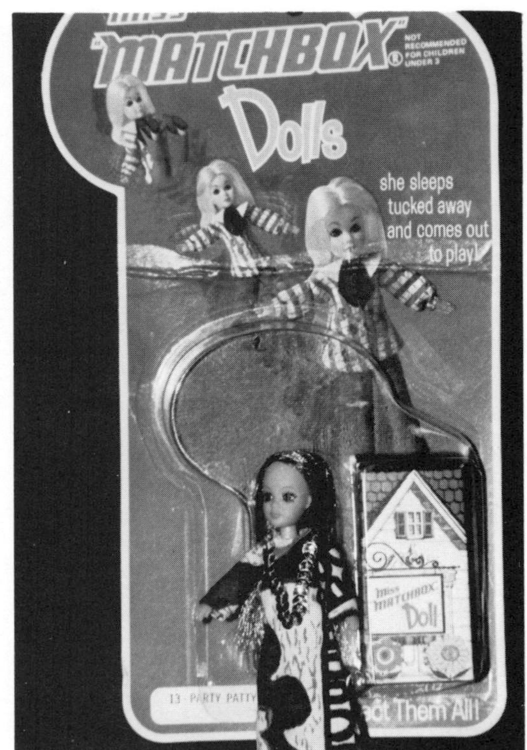


Lesney--5" "Party Patty" All vinyl with red rooted hair and brown eyes. Marks: Lesney/1973, on head. Lesney/Products/Hong Kong, on back. $4.00. (Courtesy Marge Meisinger)

Lincoln International--9½" "Carl," 9" "Carol" & 3" "Baby Cutes" all of the Our Cheerful Family. Plastic with vinyl arms and heads. Inset eyes. Baby: one piece body, arms and legs. Painted eyes. Marks: Made in Hong Kong, on backs. Made by Lincoln International. Still available.

Lorrie--9" "Lucy" Brown sleep eyes/Molded lashes. All soft vinyl. Marks: 9, on head. 9/Lorrie Doll/1971/Made in Taiwan, on back. $4.00. (Courtesy Marie Ernst)

Lorrie--12" Plastic body and legs. Vinyl head and arms. Open/closed mouth with molded tongue. Same body that was used for "Stoneage Baby." Marks: Lorrie Doll, on head and Reliable in oval on back. $3.00. (Courtesy Phyllis Houston)

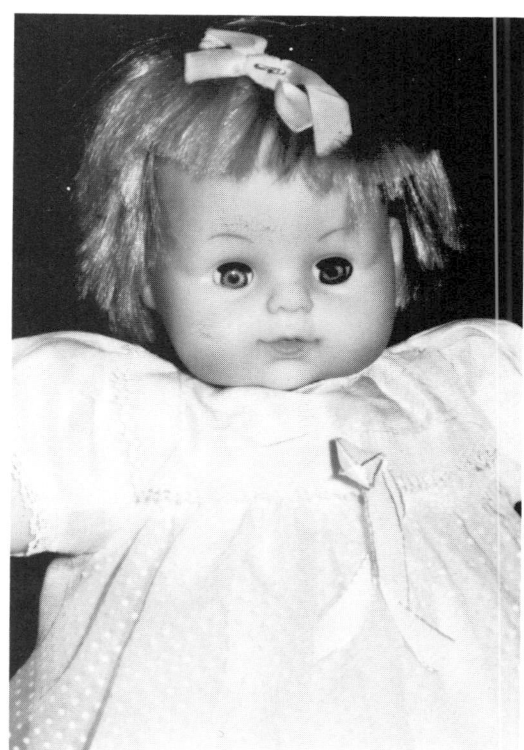

Lorrie--14" "Etty Bitty" Cloth body with vinyl arms, legs and head. Rooted blonde hair. Blue sleep eyes/lashes. Marks: Lorrie Doll/1968/3, on head. Tag: Made in Taiwan/Mfg for Eugene Doll Co. Original clothes. See Eugene Section for other Lorrie Dolls. $3.00.

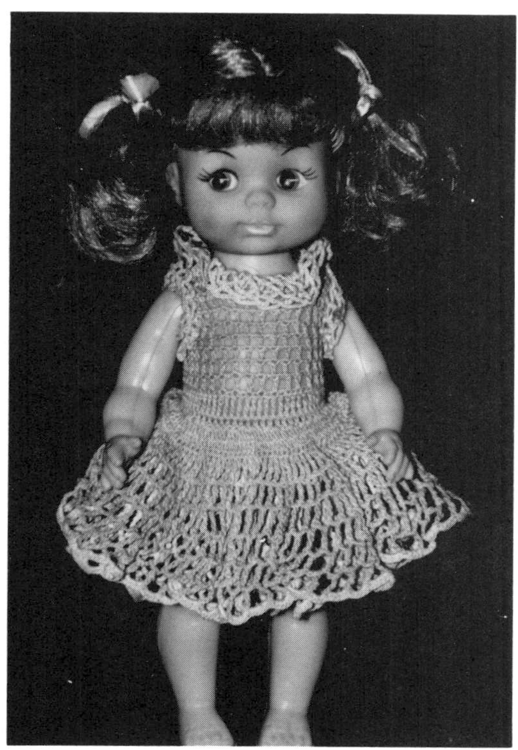

Lorrie--9" "Sandy" Plastic with vinyl head. Painted blue eyes. Marks: Made in/Hong Kong, on back. 26/Lorrie Doll/1969, on head. $3.00.

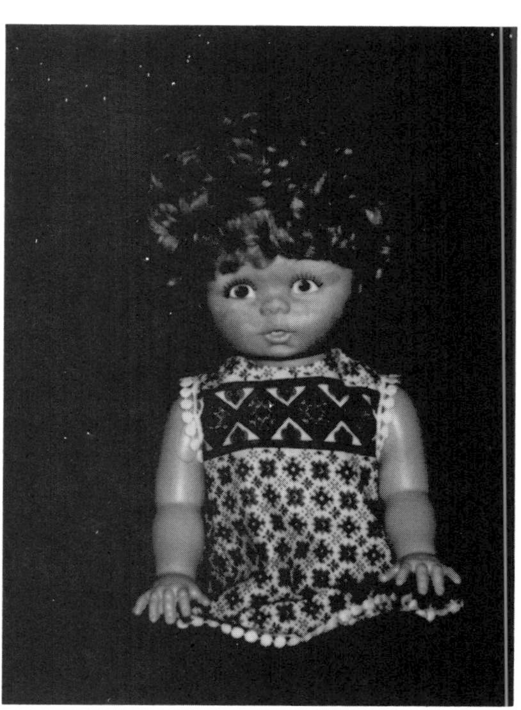

Lovee--23" Plastic with vinyl head. Open mouth/nurser. Blue painted eyes. Marks: 1974/Lovee Doll, on head. $3.00. (Courtesy Carolyn Powers)

Lovee--14" Plastic with vinyl arms and head. White rooted hair. Blue sleep eyes. Open mouth with molded tongue. Marks: Lovee, Made In/ Hong Kong, on back. $2.00. (Courtesy Carolyn Powers)

Lovee--11½" "Daisy-Luv" Plastic body and limbs. Vinyl head. Blue decal eyes. Open/closed mouth with two upper and lower molded teeth. Marks: Made in Hong Kong/No. 2618, on back. 1967 Mattel Inc./Japan, on head. This mold is one of Mattel's old ones and is currently being used. Many older Mattel parts are on the market. (Courtesy Phyllis Houston)

Lyon--8" "Sweet Valentine" Cloth with wire through legs to make them bendable. Vinyl head with glued on white mohair. Painted features. Marks: Rene D. Lyon/Richmond Hill NY, on bottom of foot. Came with box of Whitman's Sampler candy. 1970. $2.00.

Mfg. Unknown--14" All composition. Blue sleep tin eyes. Pouty type mouth. Jointed neck, shoulders and hips. Human hair wig. Marks: None. ca. 1934. $30.00.

Mfg. Unknown--23" "Display Mannikin" All rubber. Molded hair and painted features. Painted and molded on high heel shoes with holes to be placed on a stand. Marks: None. ca. late 1930's. $28.00.

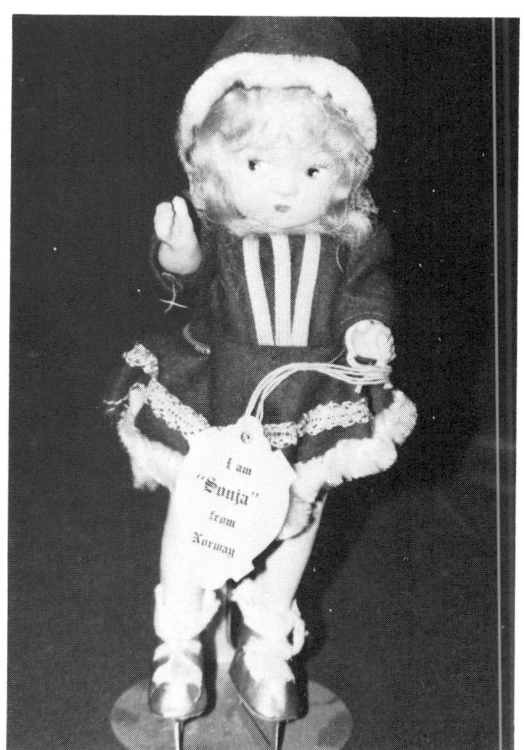


Mfg. Unknown--8" All composition. Painted brown eyes. Fully jointed. Tag: I am Sonja from Norway. $10.00. (Courtesy Maxine Heitt)

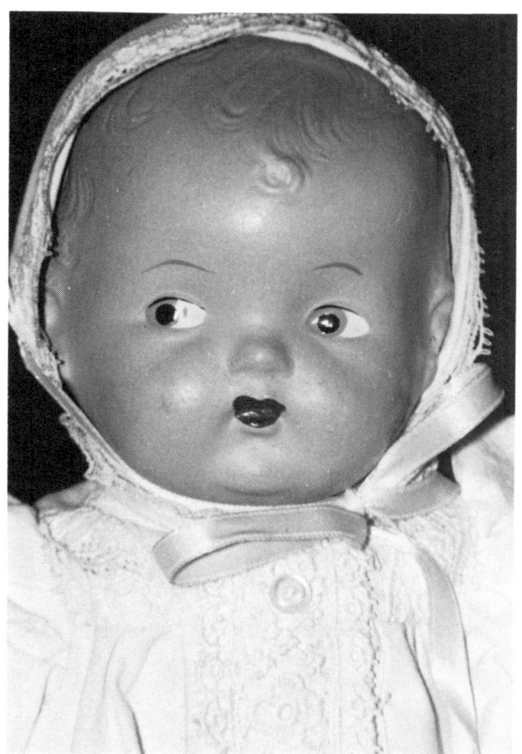

Mfg. Unknown--14" "Peter B. Good" All composition. Painted blue eyes. Orange molded hair. One piece body and head. 1941. Peter B. Good was the baby in Brother Rat & The Baby. Eddie Albert and Jane Bryan were also in the movie by Warner Bros. $12.00. (Courtesy Marie Ernst)

Mfg. Unknown--17" "Pinafore Sally" All composition. Blue sleep eyes. Open mouth/four teeth. Original. Marks: A, in a circle on head. Body: Shirley Temple/17. 1946. $30.00. (Courtesy Marie Ernst)

Mfg. Unknown--16" "Rosaland" All composition with brown sleep eyes. Human hair wig. All original. Sold through Wanamaker's 1947. Marks: X, in circle. $25.00.

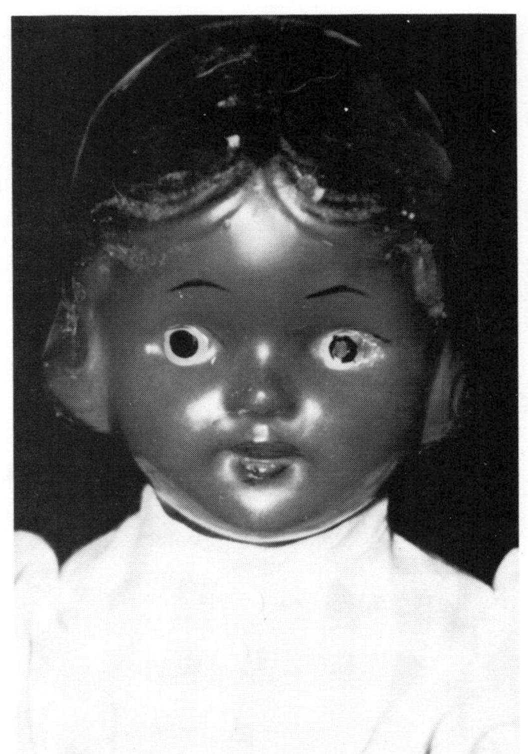

Mfg. Unknown--13½" All composition. Came with molded as well as wigged hair. No molded ribbon. Marks: W.O.L., on head. 1939. $22.00. (Courtesy Maxine Heitt)

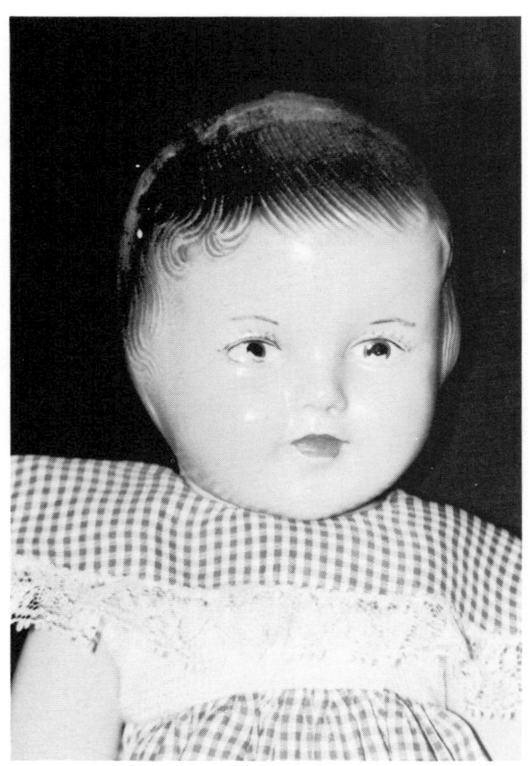

Mfg. Unkown--14" "Marcia Mae" All composition with straight legs. Brown decal eyes. Open/ closed mouth. Sculptured black hair and had a wig over back of hair with molded bangs showing. 1941. $30.00. (Courtesy Diana Soreson)

Mfg. Unknown--13" "Maggie Ann" All composition with glued on blonde mohair. Blue sleep eyes. Open mouth/4 teeth. Marks: R, on head. Shirley Temple (very light and curved)/13, on back. Sold in catalog outlets in 1945. Original. $22.00.

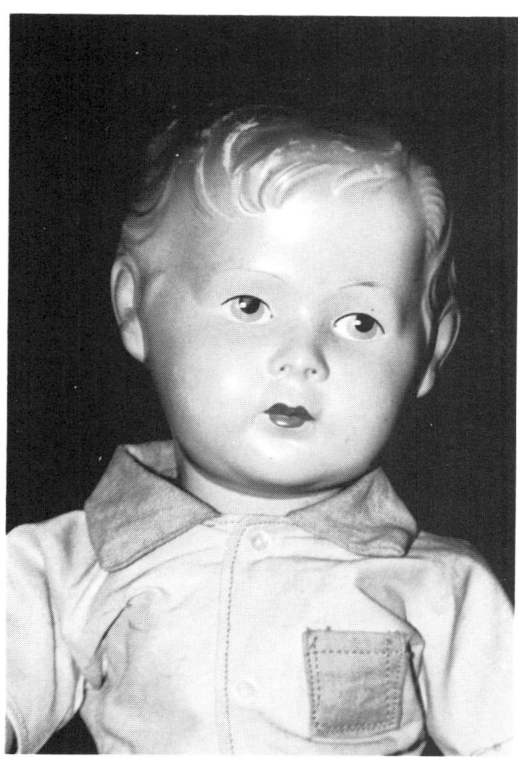

Mfg. Unknown--17" Boy of all hard plastic that is painted. Strung limbs and head. Molded hair. Painted blue eyes. Closed mouth. Original. Marks: None. ca. 1949-52. $65.00. (Courtesy Joan Amundsen)

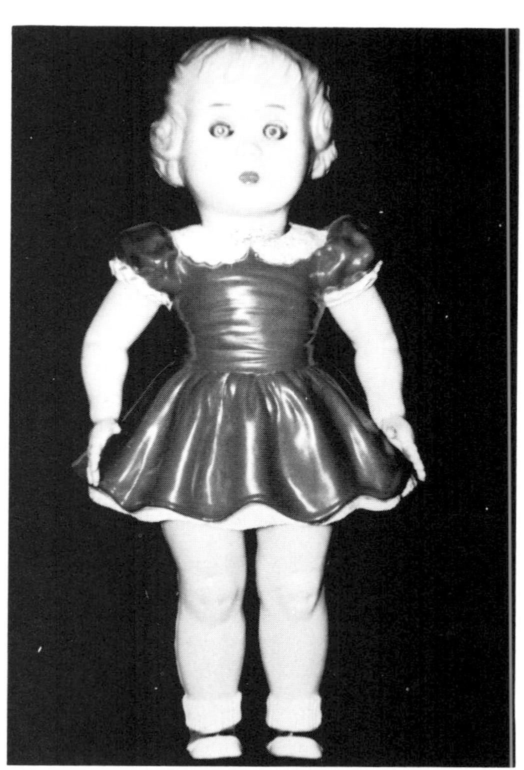

Mfg. Unknown--9½" All plastic. Blue sleep eyes. Pin jointed walker. Head turns and arms move. Molded on clothes. Excellent quality. Marks: None. $4.00. (Courtesy B. Mongelluzzi)

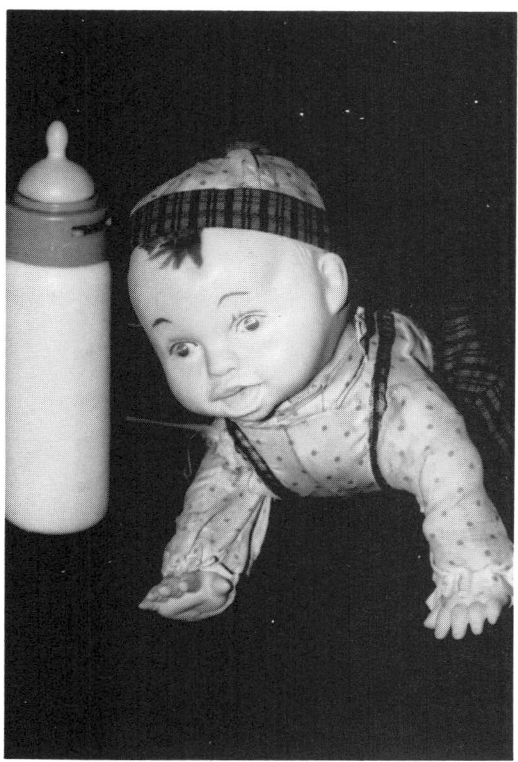

Mfg. Unknown--12" Vinyl hands, head and feet. Metal body. Bottle takes batteries, for baby to crawl. Clothing sewed on. $8.00. (Courtesy Alice Capps)

Mfg. Unknown--15" Vinyl head with large painted blue eyes. Cloth body is wired so it is posable. Gauntlet vinyl hands. Right hand cupped to hold something. Non removable clothes. Marks: None except PRR, on hat. $6.00. (Courtesy Mary Partridge)

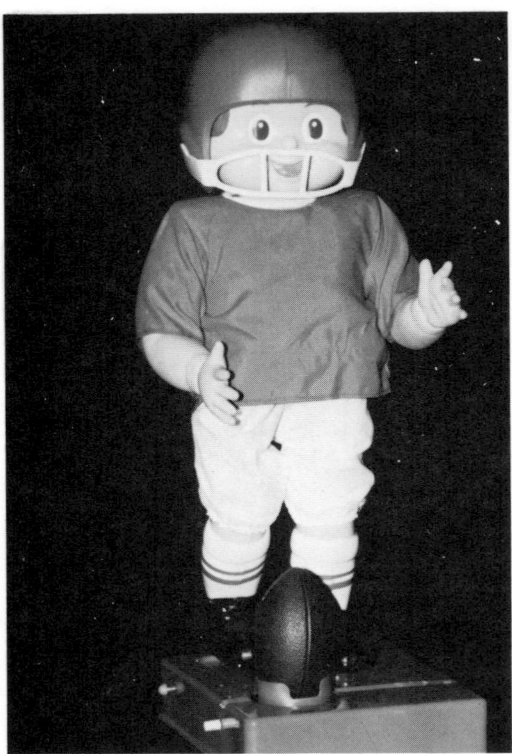

Mfg. Unknown--20" Mechanical football player. Uses batteries. Vinyl head and arms. Plastic and metal body. Plastic legs. Sold from Sears in 1973. $20.00. (Courtesy Alice Capps)

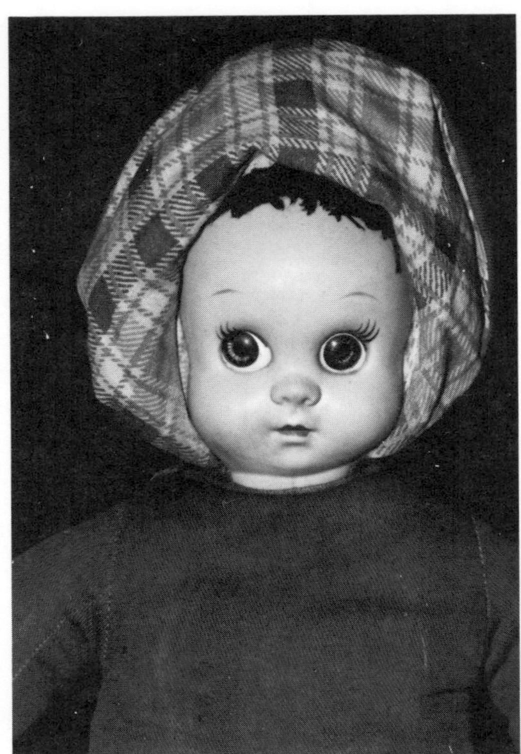

Mfg. Unknown--23" "Googly" Cloth with vinyl face mask. Inset brown eyes. Black yarn hair. Crank talker. Has record player in back. Marks: Tag Gone. ca. later 1950's. $6.00.

Mfg. Unknown--22" Bed doll. Cloth with vinyl full legs and arms. Vinyl head with molded eyelids. Painted blue eyes. Blue pastel hair. Marks: RJ/1961. $8.00. (Courtesy Barbara Coker)

Mfg. Unknown--12" "Clown" Cloth with plastic head. Chain mouth and eyes move by pulling mouth chain. Vinyl hands. Marks: A tag, I can not read. $6.00. (Courtesy Marie Ernst)

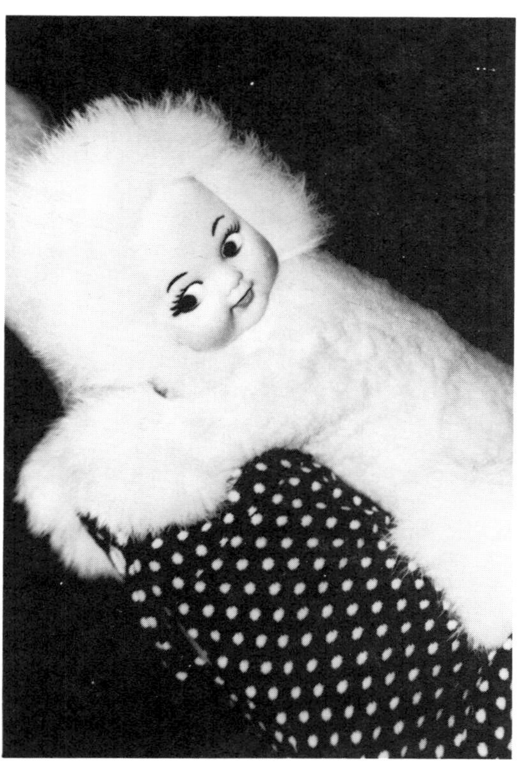

Mfg. Unknown--10" "Cuddle Bun" All stuffed plush. Vinyl face mask. Painted blue eyes. 1" wide metal bands forms arms to "hold" rabbit fur trim. Marks: None. $5.00.

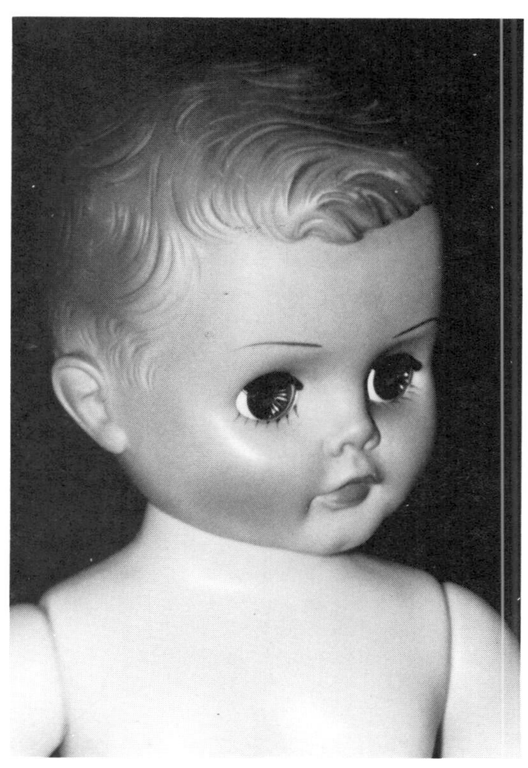

Mfg. Unknown--20" Plastic and vinyl. Blue sleep eyes. Molded light brown hair. Marks: F, in a circle on head. Tag, on underwear: The Forsyth/ Pat. 1927/For Belt. $18.00. (Courtesy Marion Thuma)

# Mattel, Inc.

Complete information on the Mattel Corp. is located in Series I, page 195 and Series II, page 187.

One of the funniest ladies in our nation is Erma Bombeck, who writes articles for the newspapers and I would like to quote one that she wrote in 1974:

'A small item in the newspaper the other day caught my eye. Barbie (as a doll) just celebrated her 16th birthday.

Usually I don't get too choked up about toy people's birthdays, but as I read on I realized how significant this could be to our nation.

In honor of the occasion, her manufacturer threw a "Sweet Sixteen" party for 400 grade school children and at the end of the bash gave each child a stripped-down Barbie.

Now, here's the significant part. If each of those 400 children bought Barbie just one girdle...one skating outfit... or one After 5 dress, the economy of this country could get moving again.

Sixteen years ago, naive people thought General Motors and U.S. Steel were keeping this country solvent. Actually it was the introduction of Barbie.

I first met Barbie when my daughter stood in front of a counter in a department store and pleaded, "Look, Mommy, here's a doll built just like you."

I looked at her two-inch bust, her three-inch hips and two legs that looked like two Benson & Hedges without tobacco and said, "She looks like a woman who whipped through puberty in 15 minutes."

"I want her," she sobbed clutching the doll to her bosom.

Barbie was in the house two days when it became apparent she wasn't just another doll. Barbie has needs. With the baby dolls, you could fill 'em up with water, burp them, tell them they were sleepy and sling them under a bed for a week or so.

Not Barbie. She moved, and she needed a wardrobe to do it. Barbie went skiing ($7.95 not including ski poles). Barbie was in a wedding ($10.95). Barbie needed lounging pajamas ($8.50).

We eventually bought Barbie her own car ($12.95), a house ($22.95) and two friends ($5.00 each) in the buff.

One day when my husband became entangled in Barbie's peignoir drying in the bathroom (she was spending a weekend with Ken at Ohio State) he said, "What's with this doll? When does it all stop?"

"Look at it this way," I said. "We aren't supporting just another doll, we are stabilizing the economy."

It doesn't take an economics major to figure out that if 400 Barbie dolls were outfitted for college, the stock market would soar, employment would rise, the value of the dollar would be restored, and 800 parents would start living above their means again. And that's what economy is all about.

The following is reprinted from the Los Angeles Times (c) 1973 and was written by Art Buchwald.

The Saga of Barbie and Ken

We have nothing against toy companies. They have a right to live just like everybody else. In their own way they bring happiness to the hearts of our young ones, and they give employment to thousands of people all over the country. It is only when they try to bankrupt us that we feel we should speak out. If our situation is duplicated around the country, every father who has a daughter between the ages of 4 and 12 is going to have to apply for relief.

This is what happened.

Our 7 year old daughter requested, four months ago, a Barbie doll. Now, as far as we're concerned, one doll is just like another, and since the Barbie doll cost only $3.00 we were happy to oblige.

We brought the doll home and thought nothing more of it until a week later our daughter came in and said, "Barbie needs a negligee."

"So does your mother," we replied.

"But there is one in the catalogue for only $3," she cried.

"What catalogue?"

"The one that came with the doll."

We grabbed the catalogue and much to our horror discovered what the sellers of Barbie were up to. They let you have the doll for $3 but you have to buy the clothes for her at an average of $3 a crack. They have about 200 outfits, from ice-skating skirts to mink jackets, and a girl's status in the community is based on how many Barbie clothes she has for her doll.

The first time we took our daughter to the store we spent $3 on a dress for her and $25 to outfit her Barbie doll.

A week later our daughter came in and said, "Barbie wants to be an airline stewardess."

"So let her be an airline stewardess," we said.

"She needs a uniform. It's only $3.50."

We gave her the $3.50.

Barbie didn't stay a stewardess long. She decided she wanted to be a nurse ($3), then a singer in a nightclub ($3), then a professional dancer ($3).

One day our daughter walked in and said, "Barbie's lonely."

"Let her join a sorority," we said.

"She wants Ken."

"Who is Ken?"

She showed us the catalogue. Sure enough there was a doll named Ken, the same size as Barbie, with a crew-cut hair, a vinyl plastic chest and movable arms and legs.

"If you don't get Ken," our daughter cried, "Barbie will grow up to be an old maid."

So we went out and bought Ken ($3.50). Ken needed a tuxedo ($5), a raincoat ($2.50), a terry-cloth robe and an electric razor ($1), tennis togs ($3), pajamas ($1.50), and several single-breasted suits ($27).

Pretty soon we had to put up $400 to protect our original $3 investment.

Then one evening our daughter came in with a shocker. "Barbie and Ken are getting married."

"Who's paying for the wedding?"

"They'll need a house to live in. Here's Barbie's Dream House."

"Seven ninety-five?" we shouted. "Why can't they live on a shelf like the rest of your dolls?"

The tears started to flow. "They want to live together as man and wife."

Well, Barbie and Ken are now happily married and living in their Dream House with $3,000 worth of clothes hanging in the closet. We wish we could say that all was well, but yesterday our daughter announced that Midge ($3), put out by the same toy firm, was coming to visit them. And she doesn't have a thing to wear.

The Los Angeles Times has reported the results of a special report by the Securities and Exchange Commission on the Mattel Company. The report lays the blame for Mattel's financial manipulations, falsification of sales, etc. at the feet of the founders, Ruth and Elliot Handler and their Executive Vice President Seymour Rosenberg. On Oct. 17, the Handlers resigned from the board of Mattel and since 1973 they have been figure heads with no real power. Seymour Rosenberg resigned from Mattel in the summer of 1972. The SEC began investigating Mattel in 1973.

Mattel--11½" "Lilli" Made in West Germany and known to be on the market in 1957-58. Called the "proto-type" for the Barbie doll. An excellent quality rigid plastic. Jointed at the shoulders and neck. Molded on shoes with holes to fit circular stand. Doll is not marked. $100 and up.

Mattel--First Barbie: Ponytail with curly bangs. White irises and pointed eyebrows. Holes in feet to fit prones of stand. Heavy, solid torso, marked: Barbie/Pats. Pend./MCMLVIII/By/ Mattel/Inc. Bright red lips and nails. Black and white stripe bathing suit. Gold hoop earrings. $100 and up. (Courtesy Sibyl DeWein)

Mattel--The 1960 second Barbie is basically the same doll except the holes in the feet are no longer there. This same year saw the #3 Barbie, who now has blue irises, curved eyebrows and no holes in the feet. $50.00. (Courtesy Sibyl DeWein)

Mattel--The #4 Barbie has longer eyebrows, smaller pupils and lighter lip color. $35.00. (Courtesy Marie Ernst)

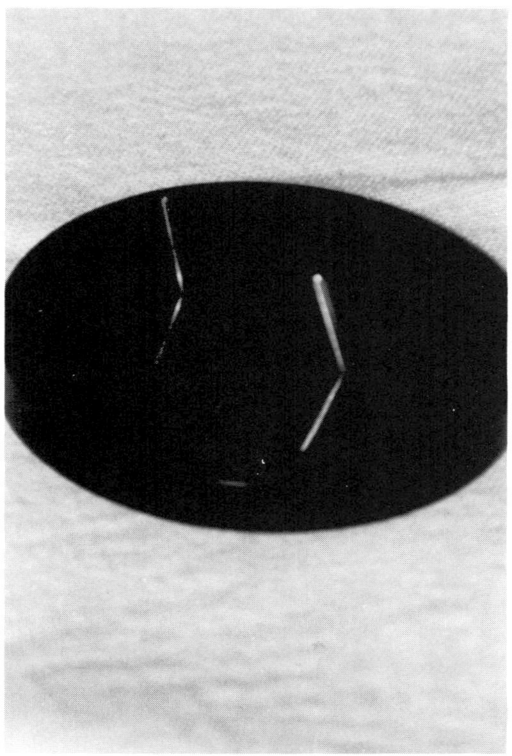

Mattel--Shows the original Barbie stand. These cylinders fit the holes in the feet of the first Barbies. $20.00. (Courtesy Marie Ernst)

Mattel--Barbie clock sold in 1964. Marked: Made in W. Germany. $12.00. (Courtesy Marie Ernst)

Mattel--Barbie Car. Marks: Mattel Inc. $15.00.

Mattel--1962 "Ken" shown in original outfit and box, and called "Dr. Ken." $18.00.

Mattel--11½" "Barbie" Shown in her Airline Stewardess outfit. 1962. $18.00. (Courtesy Marie Ernst)

Mattel--Barbie's first plane called Ken's Sports Plane. Made by Irwin Corp./Custom Designed For/Barbie & Ken & Midge/Mattel 1964. $15.00. (Courtesy Joan Ashabraner)

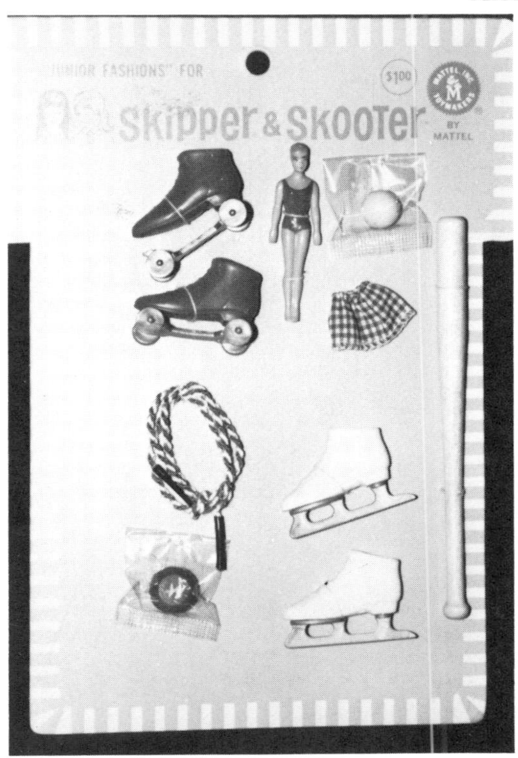


Mattel--Skipper & Skooter 1964 pac with the Tiny Barbie doll. $10.00.

Mattel--Trade in Barbie Box, 1966. (Courtesy Bessie Carson)

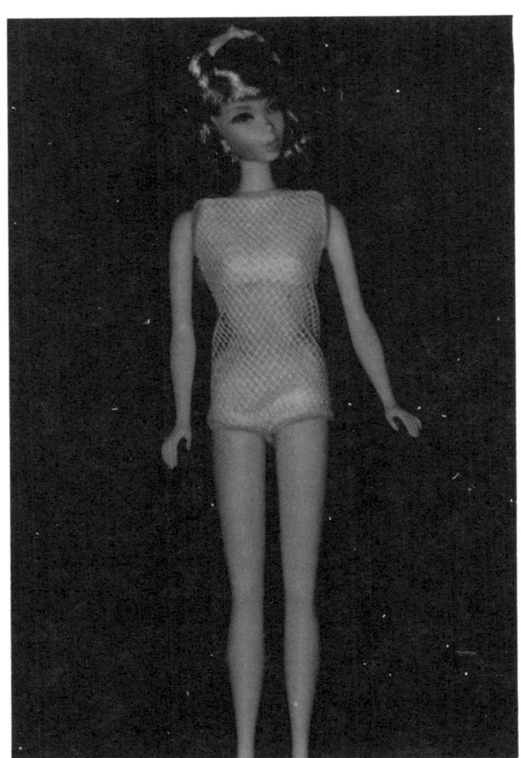

Mattel--11½" "Trade In Barbie" Jointed waist. Bend knees. Pierced ears. Long lashes. Orange 2 piece suit with white/orange trim "Oversuit." Orange earrings. Marks: 1966/Mattel Inc./U.S. Patented/U.S. Pat. Pend./Made In/Japan, on hip. $15.00. (Courtesy Bessie Carson)

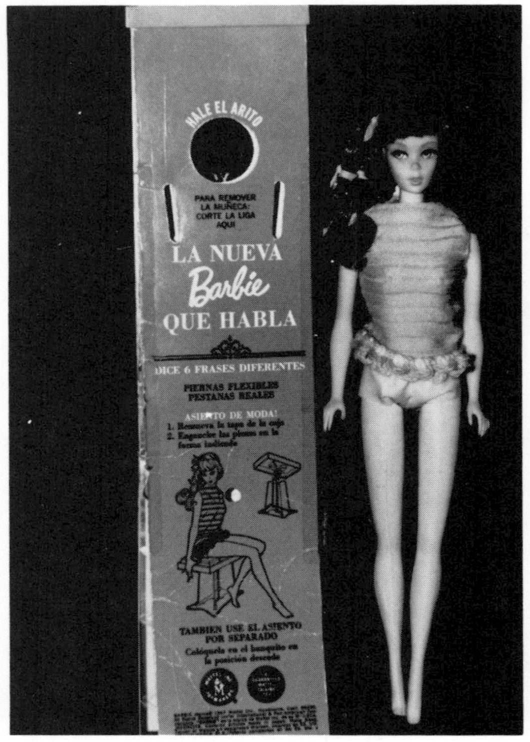


Mattel--11½" "Spanish Talking Barbie" Pink/rose and yellow. Marks: 1967/Mattel Inc/U.S. & Foreign/Pats. Pend./Mexico. $18.00.

Mattel--½" "Mini Kiddles" that go in Popups: Left to right: Soda Parlor, Fairytale, Castle and Gingerbread House.

Mattel--1967 Mini-Kiddles Popup Gingerbread House. $3.00.

Mattel--Liddle Kiddles Talking Townhouse. Plastic with built in furniture. Front comes down. Chatty ring at lower rear at side. The elevator works on elastic band. $4.00. (Courtesy Phyllis Houston)

Mattel--Liddle Kiddles Klub. Cardboard front comes down and case has molded plastic furniture. $4.00. (Courtesy Phyllis Houston)

Mattel--"Francie & Becky" #3448. "With It Whites" 3 pieces white. Red blouse/shoes/belt. Gold rings. Red top-stitched on white pieces. The Becky doll was never produced and the prototype was sold to the Shindana Toy Co. (Operation Bootstraps)

Mattel--Barbie Fan Club Membership pac of 1969. Included "Salute to Silver Dress," Family portrait, Card and certificate, "Barbie Talk" club magazine. (Courtesy Bessie Carson)

Mattel--Family portrait from the 1969 Barbie Fan Club pac. (Courtesy Bessie Carson)

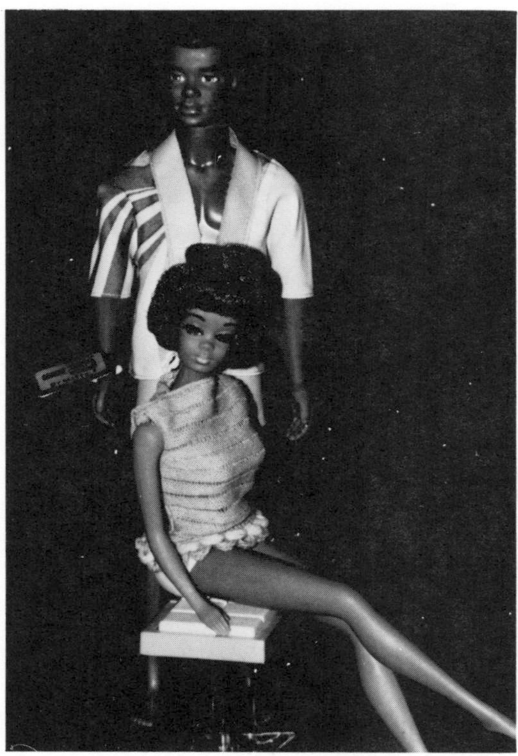

Mattel--12" "Talking Brad" Marks: 1968/Mattel Inc/US & For. Pat'd/Other Pats. Pend/Mexico, on hip. 1969 Mattel Inc., on head. 11½" "Talking Christie" Marks: 1967/Mattel Inc/U.S. & Foreign/Pats. Pend./Mexico. $9.00 each.

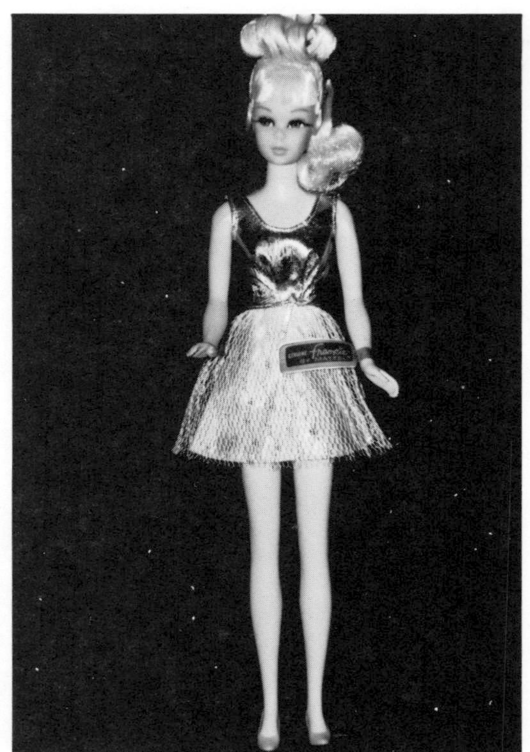

Mattel--1970 "Francie" with growin' Pretty hair. Bendable knees. Gold top with rose skirt (1 pc.). $7.00.

Mattel--11½" "Francie" A rarer one with no bangs and orange head band. Brown eyes/lashes 1971. $9.00. (Courtesy Marie Ernst)

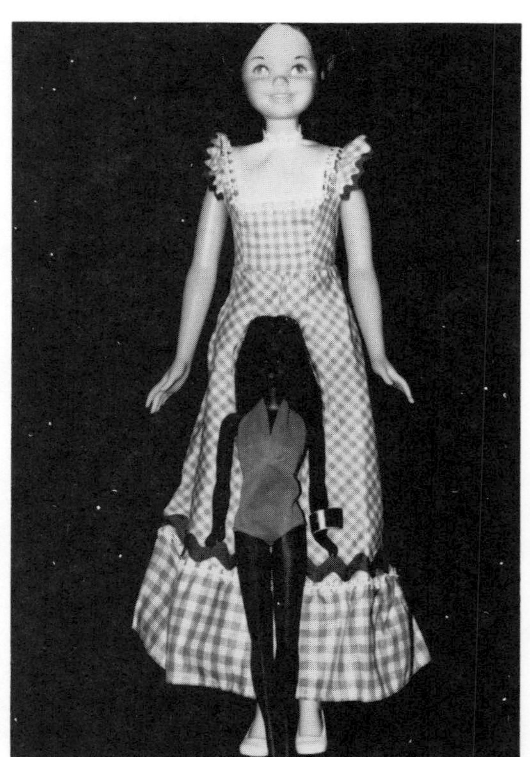

Mattel--19" "Quick Curl Casey" #8663. 1973. Marks: 1971 Mattel Inc./Hong Kong, on head. 1971 Mattel Inc/U.S.A./U.S. Patent Pending, on back. 11½" "Malibu Christie" Skin tones are darker than the regular "Christie." Twist and Turn with bendable knees. $9.00.

Mattel--4" "Teener-Doreen" #4002. Golden blonde in pink suit. Marks: 1971/Mattel/Inc./Hong/Kong, on hip. $6.00.

Mattel--4" "Teener-Coreen" #4001. White hair in yellow suit. Marks: 1971/Mattel/Inc./Hong/Kong, on hip. $6.00.

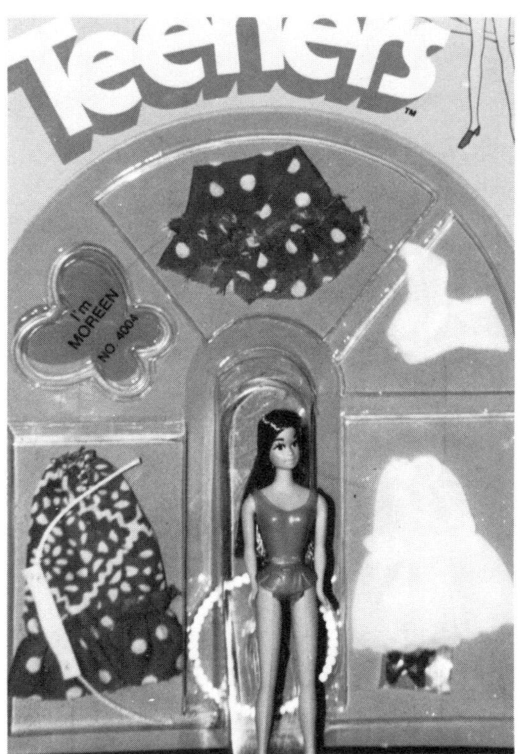


Mattel--4" "Teener-Moreen" #4004, in green suit with red hair. The Mattel 1972 catalog shows "Moreen" changed to "Maxeen" with darker skin tones than the other three. Marks: 1971/Mattel/Inc./Hong/Kong, on hip. $6.00.

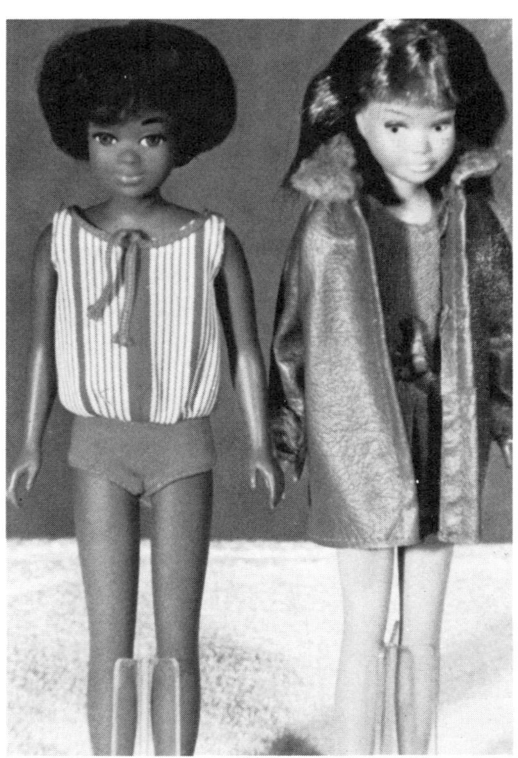

Mattel--This is photograph of a photograph of the Black Skipper that was to be made and never put on the market so this one could be called a "prototype." It now belongs to Joan Ashabraner and the photo belongs to Sibyl DeWein.

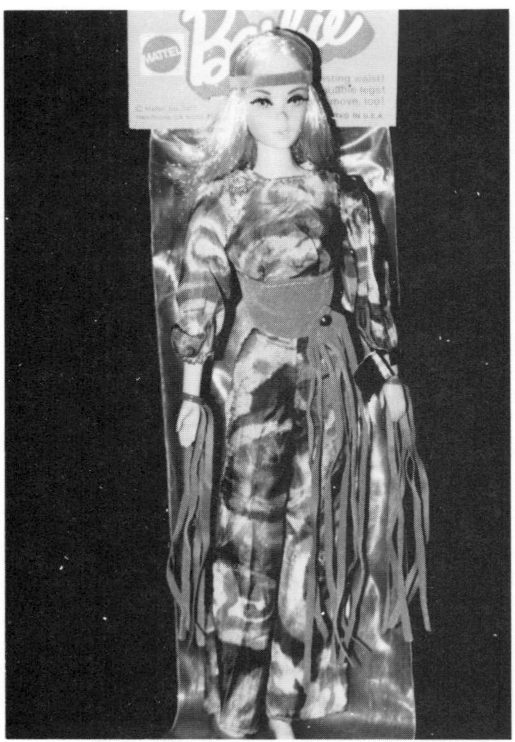


Mattel--"Action Barbie" Sold in 1973 in this plastic sack. $8.00.

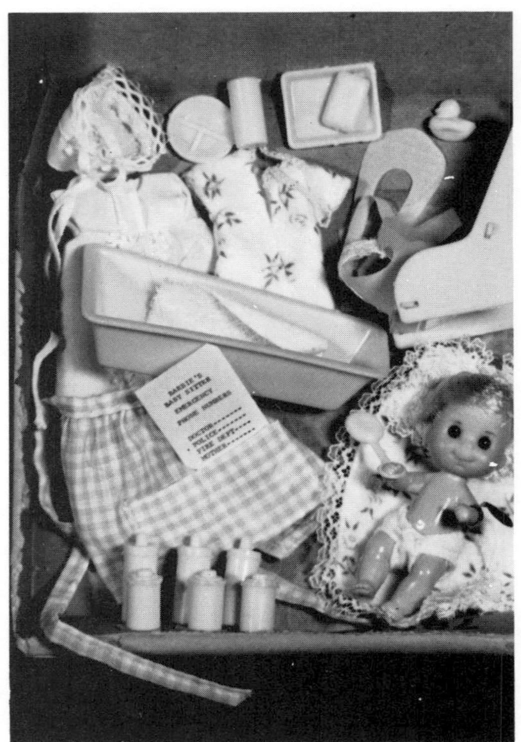

Mattel--"Barbie Baby Sits" 3" "Little Sweets" from the Sunshine Family. Body is unjointed rigid vinyl. Softer vinyl head. Inset blue eyes. Rooted blonde hair. Marks: 1973 Mattel Inc., on head. 1973 Mattel Inc./Taiwan, on back. $7.00.

Mattel--12" "Bucky Love Notes" Cloth with vinyl head. Blue decal eyes. Freckles. Press arms, legs and stomach and he plays 8 different tunes. Comes with song book. Each part of him is color coded to match song book. Marks: 1974 Mattel Inc, on head. Tag: Mattel Inc. 1974, etc. Still available.

Mattel--"Little Sweets" of the Sunshine Family #7258. This one has red hair. Still available. (Courtesy Sibyl DeWein)

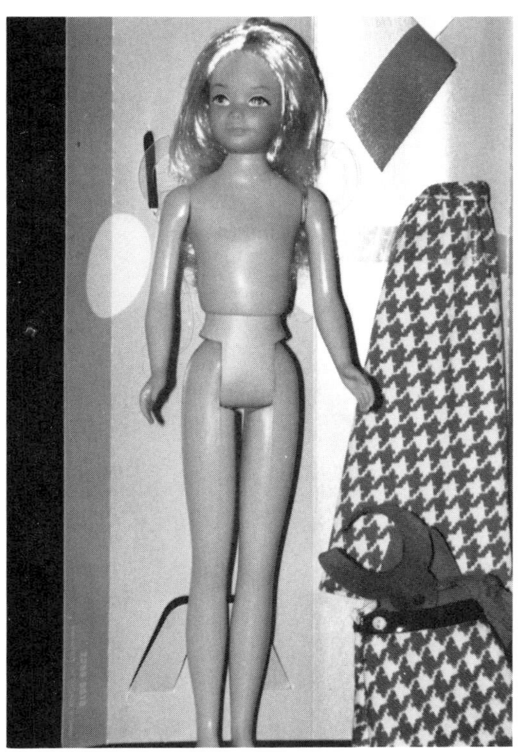

Mattel--Growing Up Skipper. Marks: 1967/Mattel Inc/Hong Kong/US & For. Pat., on hip. Issued Spring 1975. Shows original red/white outfits. Still available.

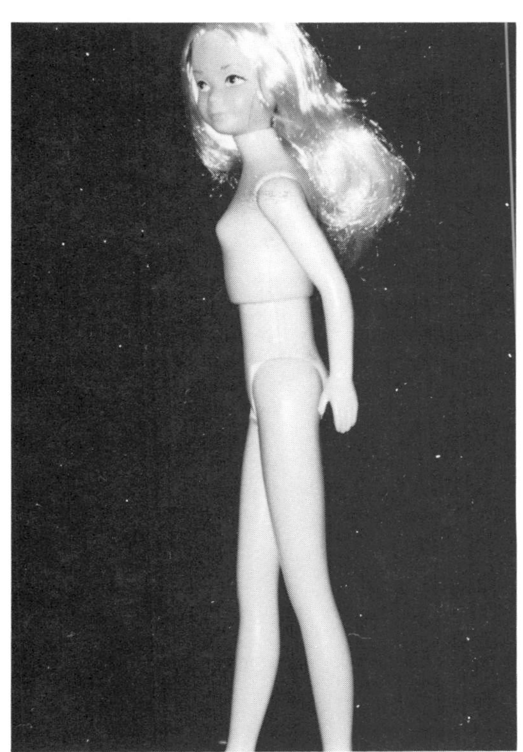

Mattel--Shows "Growing Up Skipper" as an older girl. Waist gets longer and small breasts appear, by rotating arm.

Mattel--3" "Hero's In Action" Grenade thrower. Lever moves to make and hear noise, also moves upper half of figure. Marks: Stand: Mattel Inc./ Hong Kong/Patent Pending. Set of 14: Point Man, Rifleman, Company Commander, Cleanup man, Ranger, Flame Thrower, Sniper, Infantryman, Marksman, Sharpshooter, Recon Officer, Heavy Weapons and Bazookaman.

Mattel--9" and 8½" "Jazz Performers:" Mellie and Louis Harris. Other couples: Liberty Patriots: Regina and Richard Stanton and Thanksgiving Pilgrams: James and Louisa Winthrope. Still available. (Courtesy Sibyl DeWein)

Mattel--8½" "Colonial Girl" (Miss Alison Thompson) Hard plastic with jointed knees. Inset blue eyes. Vinyl head. Marks: 1973 Mattel Inc., on head. Still available.

Mattel--8½" "Indian Maiden" (Smiling Eyes) Hard plastic with jointed knees. Inset brown eyes. Vinyl head. Marks: 1973 Mattel Inc, on head. Still available.

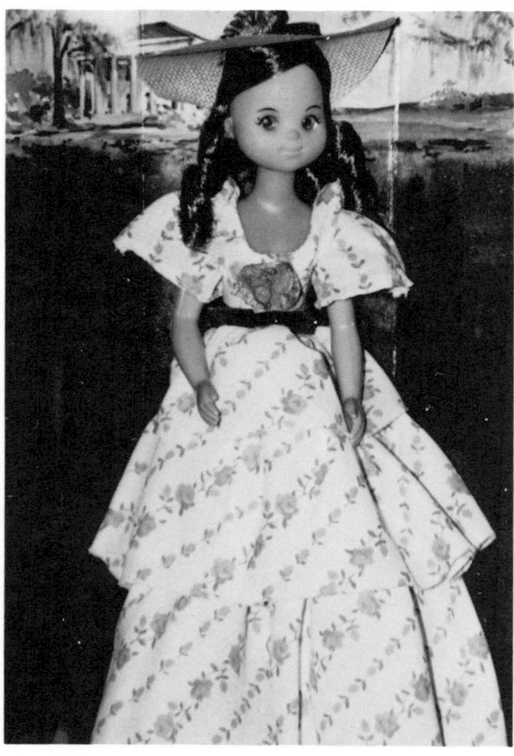

Mattel--8½" "Southern Belle" (Rosa Lee Linden) Hard plastic with jointed knees. Inset blue eyes. Vinyl head. Marks: 1973 Mattel Inc., on head. Still available.

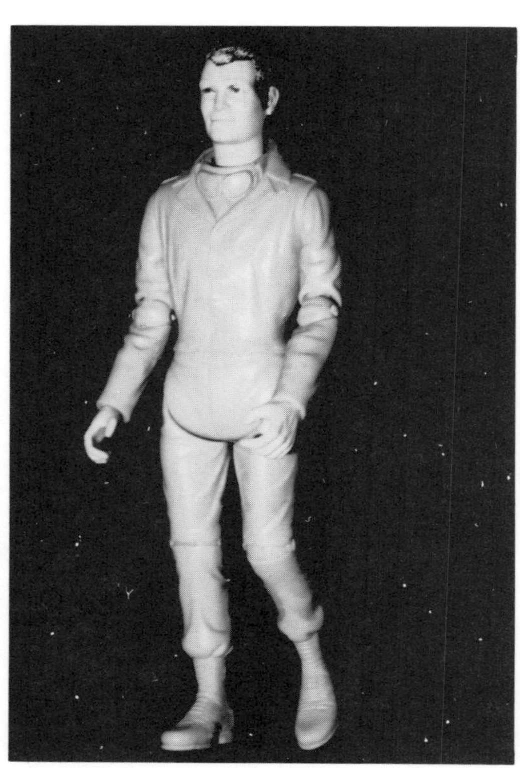

Marx--11" "Tank Driver" All heavy solid vinyl. Molded on clothes. Jointed neck, shoulders and elbows and wrists. Arms and head are strung. Soft vinyl hands. Marks: Marx/Toys, in a circle, on back. $3.00.

Marx--12" "Viking" All rigid vinyl. Marks: Louis Marx & Co/MCMLXIX/Made in U.S.A. $3.00.

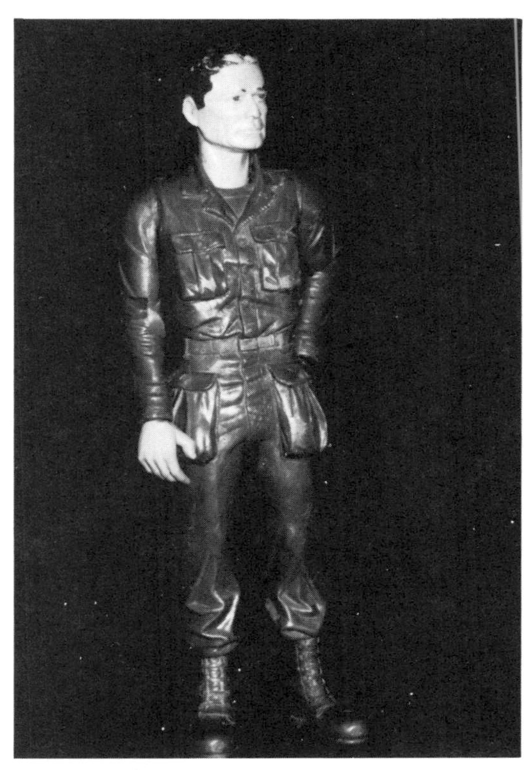

Marx--11" "Stony "Stonewall" Smith" All heavy solid vinyl with molded on clothes. Arms and head are strung. Fully jointed. Marks: Marx/ Toys, in a circle. 1964. $3.00.

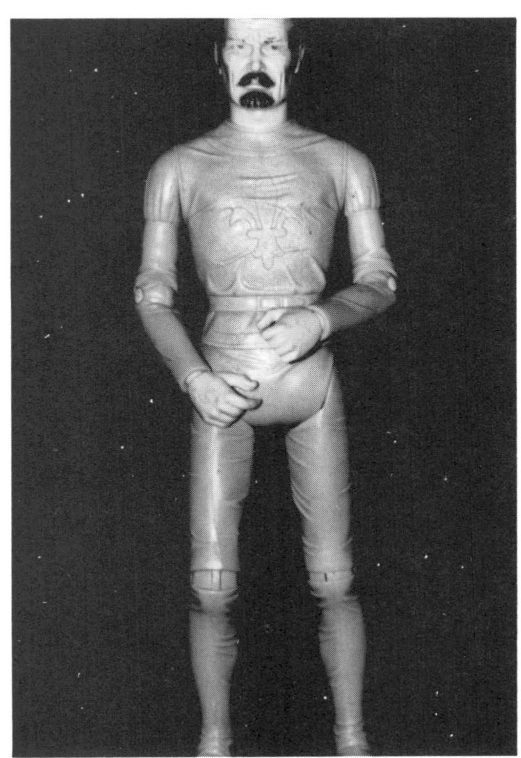

Marx--12" "Knight" All rigid vinyl Marks: Louis Marx & Co/MCMLXVII/Made in U.S.A. $3.00.

Mego--8" "Supergirl & Batgirl" Marked the same as Wonderwomen and Catwomen. Available in some areas.

Mego--8" "Wonderwomen & Catwomen" Marks: NPP Inc/1973, on head. Mego Corp/MCMLXX-II/Pat. Pending/Made in/Hong Kong, on back. Available in some areas.

Mego--8" "Sitting Bull" Original. Marks: Mego Corp 1973, on head. Mego Corp/Reg. US Pat. Off./Pat. Pending/Hong Kong/MCMLXXI. Available in some areas.

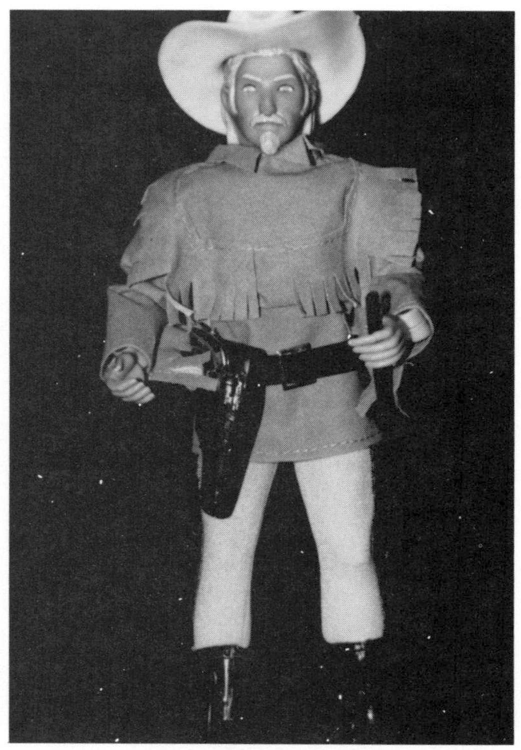

Mego--8" "Buffalo Bill Cody" Original. Marks: Mego Corp 1973, on head. Mego Corp./Reg. U.S. Pat. Off./Pat. Pending/Hong Kong/MCMLXXI. Available in some areas.

Mego--8" "Wyatt Earp" Original. Marks: Mego Corp 1973, on head. Mego Corp/Reg. U.S. Pat Off./Pat. Pending/Hong Kong/MCMLXXI. Available in some areas.

Mego--8" "Davey Crockett" Original. Marks: Mego Corp 1973, on head. Mego Corp./Reg. U.S. Pat. Off./Pat. Pending/Hong Kong/MCMLXXI. Available in some areas.

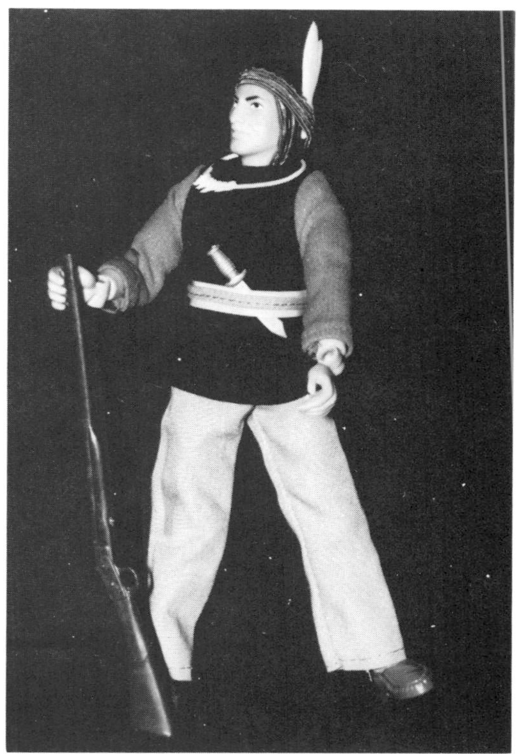

Mego--8" "Cochise" Original. Marks: Mego Corp 1973, on head. Mego Corp/Reg. US Pat. Off./ Pat. Pending/Hong Kong/MCMLXXI. Available in some areas.

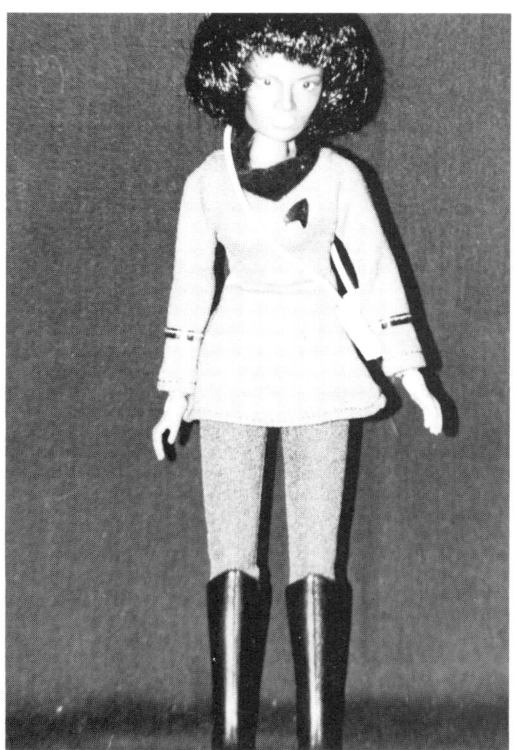

Mego--8" "Lt. Uhura" Full jointed action figure. Marks: 1974/Paramount/Pic. Corp. on head. Mego Corp/MCMLXXII/Pat. Pending/Made In/Kong Kong, on back. See color section for the other members of Star Trek. Still available in some areas.

Mego--8" "Ivanhoe" Action figure. Marks: Mego Corp/1974. Available in some areas.

Mego-8" "King Arthur" Action figure. Head marked: Mego Corp/1974. Available in some areas.

Mego-8" "Sir Lancelot" Action figure. Marks: Mego Corp/1974. Available in some areas.

Mego-8" "Long John Silver" and "Jean Lafitte" Action figures. Marks: Mego Corp/Reg. US Pat. Off./Patent Pending/Hong Kong/MCMMLXXI. 1975. Available in some areas.

Mego-8" "Captain Patch" and "Black Beard" Action figures. Marks: Mego Corp./Reg. U.S. Pat. Off./Patent Pending/Hong Kong/MCMLX-XI. 1975. Available in some areas.

Mego--8" "Friar Tuck," "Will Scarlet" and "Little John" All Action figures. All original. Marks: Mego Corp./Reg. U.S. Pat. Off./Patent Pending/Hong Kong/MCMLXXI. 1975. Available in some areas.

Mego--8" "Dorothy & Toto" and 8" "Scarecrow" Plastic and vinyl. Marks: Mego Corp/MCMLXXII/Pat. Pending/Made in Hong Kong, on back. 1974. M.G.M./Inc., on head. Toto: M.G.M. Inc. Available in some areas.

Mego--7" "Wicked Witch" All green. Plastic and vinyl. Marks: Mego Corp/MCMLXXII/Pat. Pending/Made in Hong Kong, on back. 1974. M.G.M./Inc., on head. Played by Margaret Hamilton. Available in some areas.

Mego--8" "Glenda, The Good Witch" Plastic and vinyl action figure. Hole in head for crown. Marks: 1974 Mego/Inc., on head. Played by Billie Burke. Available in some areas.

Mego--8" "Wizard of Oz" Same markings as the others. You can only purchase this doll when you buy the "Oz City" and the purchase price is fairly high. This head also used for Mr. Mxytpet. Available in some areas.

Mego--8" "Tin Woodsman" and "Cowardly Lion" Plastic and vinyl. Marks: Mego Corp/MCML-XXII/Pat. Pending/Made in Hong Kong, on back. 1974 M.G.M./Inc, on head. Available in some areas.

Mego--Shows the original cast of the much loved movie "Wizard of Oz" by Metro Goldwyn-Mayer.

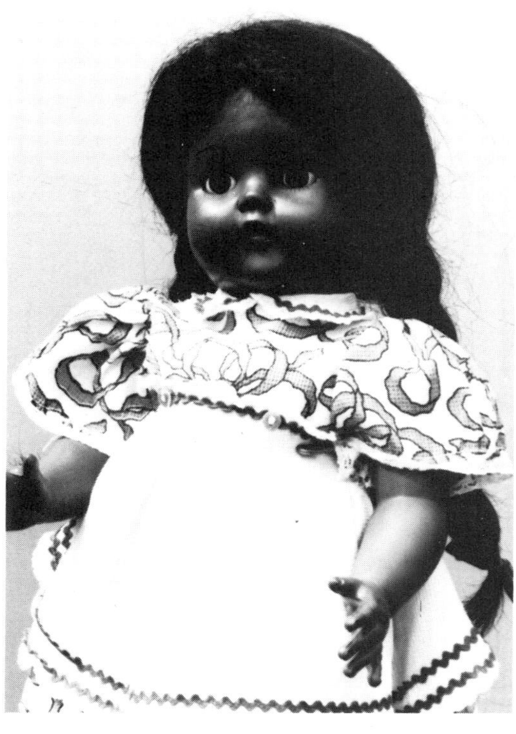

Miller Rubber--22" "Honeybunch" Dark hard plastic walker (exactly like Ideal's Saucy Walker). Vinyl rubber head with dark layer of "skin." Brown sleep eyes. Open mouth. 1956. (Courtesy Phyllis Houston)

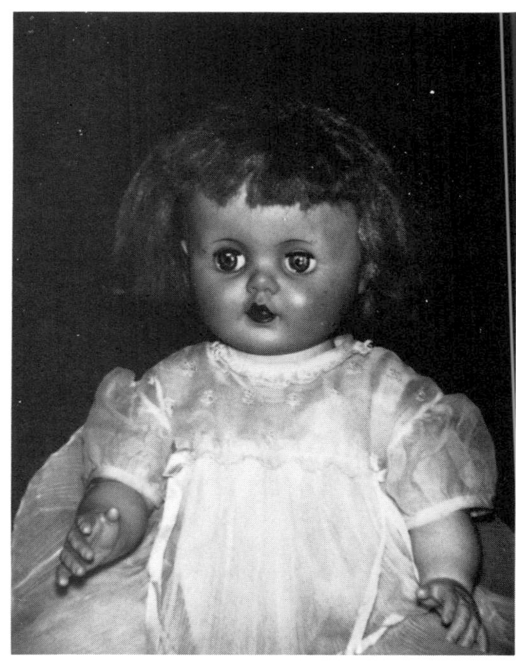

Midwestern--24" "Darleen" (Speigels 1961) Plastic and vinyl. Blue sleep eyes. Open/closed mouth with molded tongue. Molded hair under rooted hair. Marks: Form of a flying bird, on head. 25-6/AE, lower back. $3.00. (Courtesy Carolyn Powers)

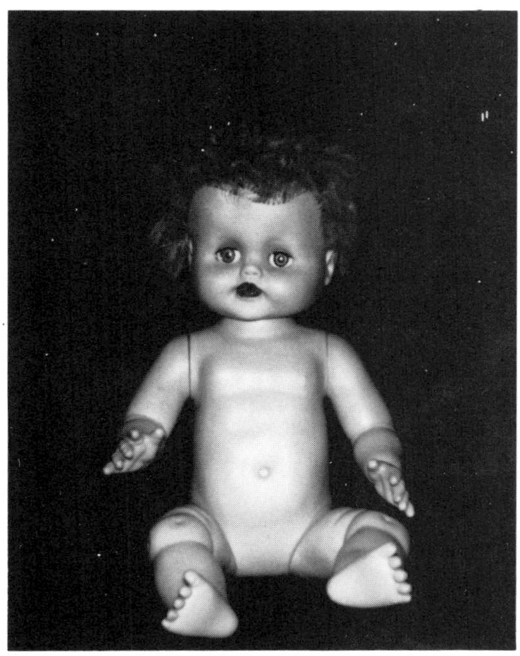

Midwestern--15" "Tiny Little" All vinyl with molded hair under rooted hair. Open mouth/nurser. Sleep eyes/lashes. Marks: PTN/18, on head. 1964. $2.00. (Courtesy Carolyn Powers)

Nancy Ann--8" "Muffie" dressed in her original Daniel Boone clothes. 1954. $15.00. (Courtesy Marge Meisinger)

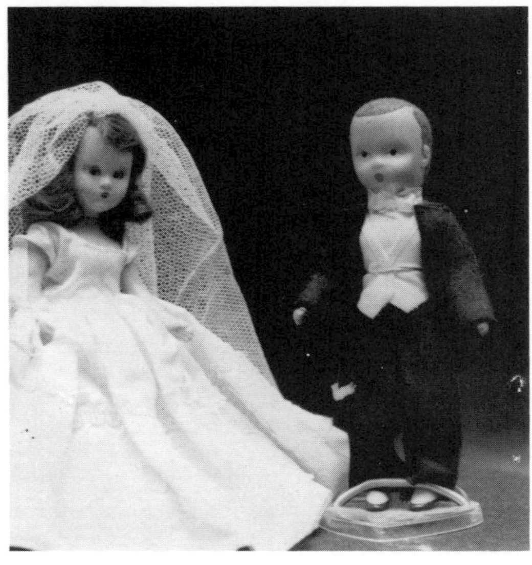

Nancy Ann--6" Hard plastic. All original. Bride has sleep eyes. Groom has painted eyes. Marks: Nancy Ann Storybook Dolls. $12.00 each. (Courtesy Phyllis Houston)

Nancy Ann--5½" "Valentine" Painted bisque. All original. $12.00. (Courtesy Phyllis Houston)

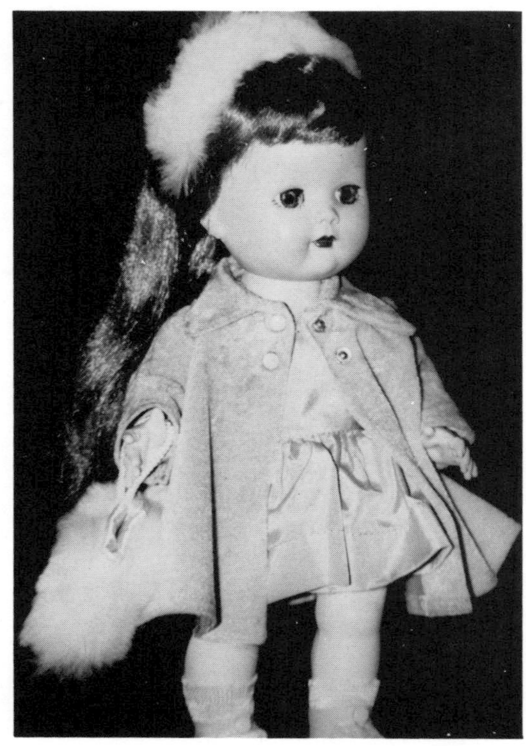

Nancy Ann--10½" "Debbie" All hard plastic. Walker, head turns. Marks: Nancy Ann, on head. Pale blue valour coat. White rabbit head band and muff. Pale blue dress, snap shoes and socks. $10.00. (Courtesy Bessie Carson)

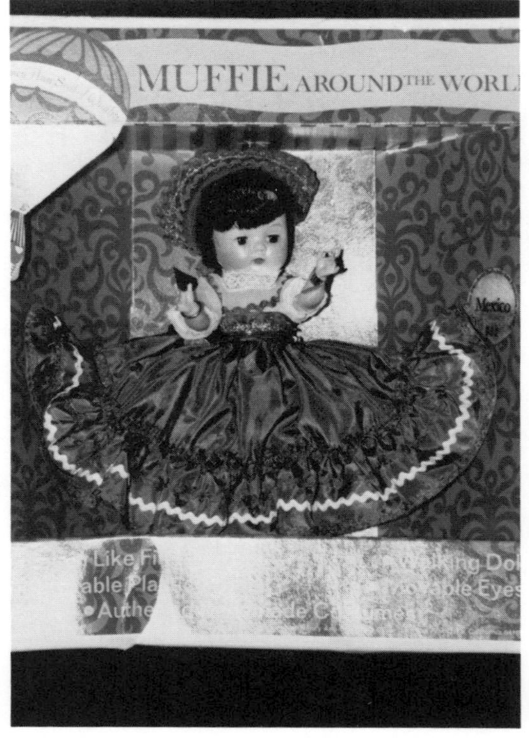


Nancy Ann--8" "Muffie" as Mexico. Re-issue of 1968-69. All hard plastic. $8.00. (Courtesy Marge Meisinger)

Nancy Ann--8" "Muffie" as Peru. Re-issue of 1968-69. All hard plastic. $8.00. (Courtesy Marge Meisinger)

Nancy Ann--8" "Muffie" as Poland. This is the re-issue of 1968-69. Doll is hard plastic. $8.00. (Courtesy Marge Meisinger)

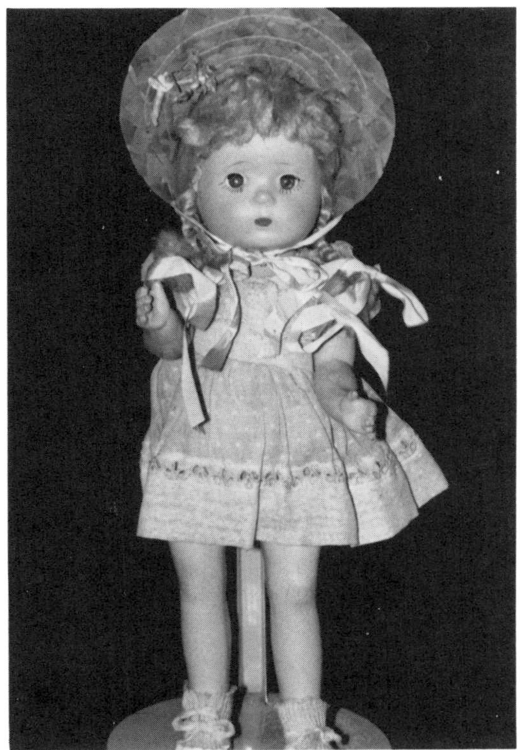

Nasco--14" "Debbie Lou" All composition. Fully jointed. Blue sleep eyes/lashes. Original. 1944. $22.00. (Courtesy Maxine Heitt)

Nasco--24" "Raggedy Ann & Andy" Rooted yarn hair in vinyl heads. Plastic bodies. Original. Marks: Nasco Doll Inc./The Hobbs-Merrill Inc./ 1973. $7.00 each. (Courtesy Marie Ernst)

Nasco--15" "Grow Hair Angie" Plastic and vinyl. Blue sleep eyes. Head is strung with the long hair attached to legs. Marks: Nasco, high on head. Nasco/Made in Hong Kong, on back. 1967. $4.00.

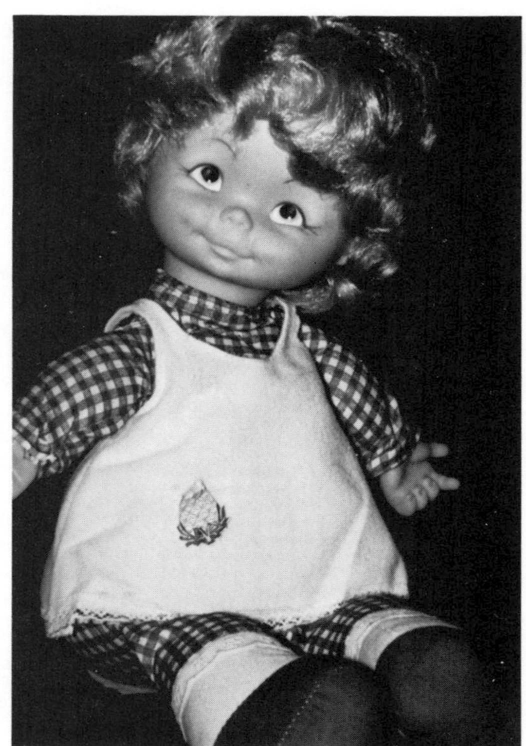

Nasco--13" "Stumbles" All cloth with vinyl head. Gauntlet vinyl hands. Painted blue eyes. Dimples. Sold as a floppy "walking" doll. Hold at back of neck and cloth legs will "walk." Marks: Nasco Doll Co Inc/Taiwan. $6.00.

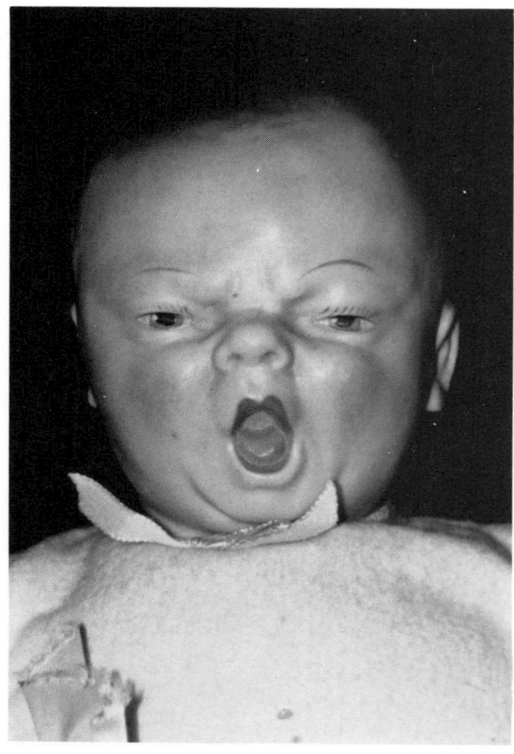

Natural Doll Co.--23" "Baby Jasmine" Cloth body with cryer in stomach. Vinyl head and limbs. Open/Closed mouth. Painted blue eyes. 1952. Made by Natural Doll Co. Marks: N'52. $20.00. (Courtesy Joan Amundsen)

Natural Doll Co.--17" "Miss Ritzi" All vinyl. Blue sleep eyes. Marks: A/14RA, on head. B-18, on back. Pat. Pend., on lower waist. 1959. $8.00.

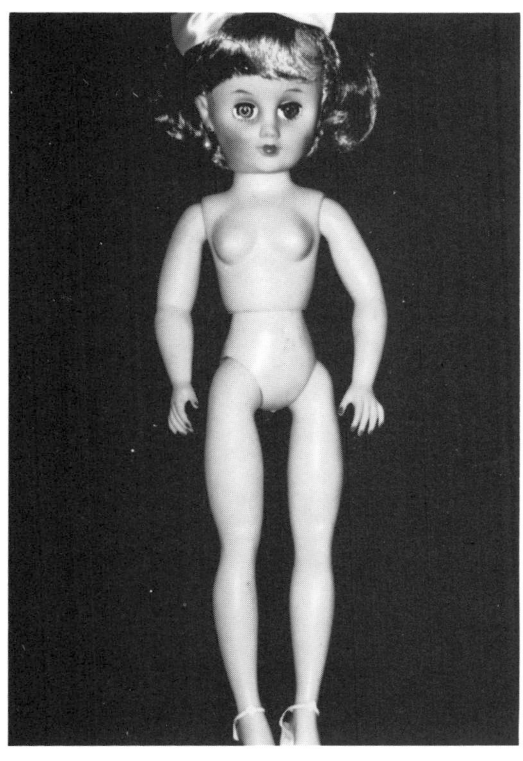

Natural Doll--17" "Miss Ritzi" (also came in 14"). To show body view of the doll.

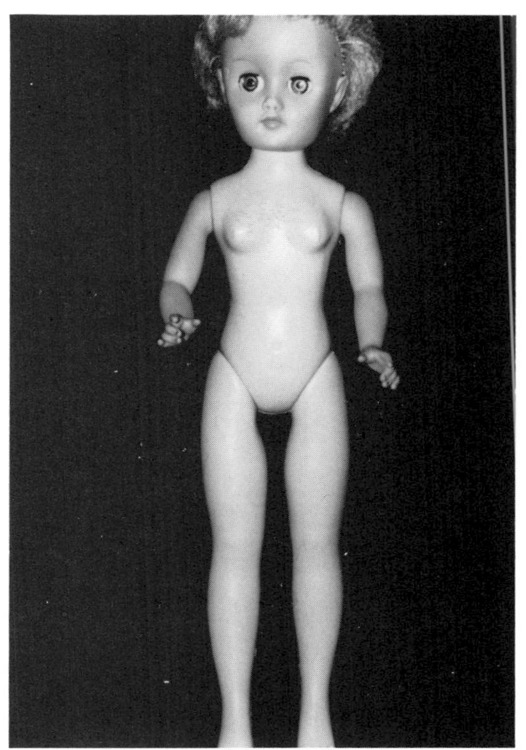

Natural Doll--14" All vinyl. Marks: None, except 15, on back of arms.

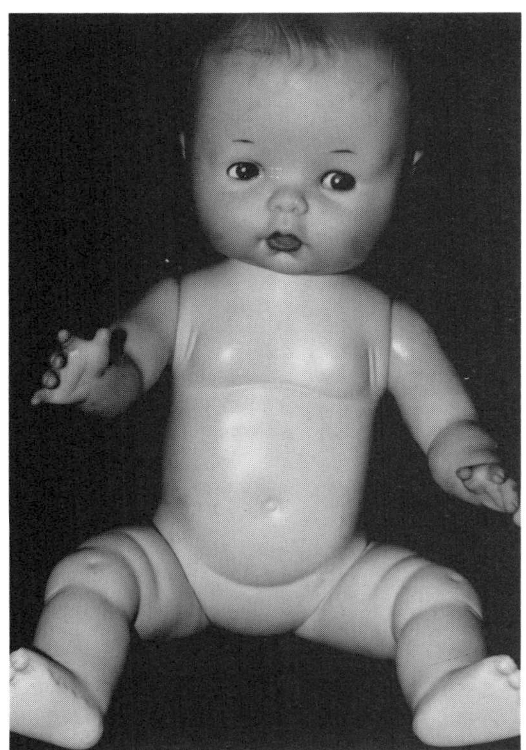

Natural--13" "Baby" Plastic and vinyl. Painted black eyes. Open/closed mouth. Marks: None. 1967.

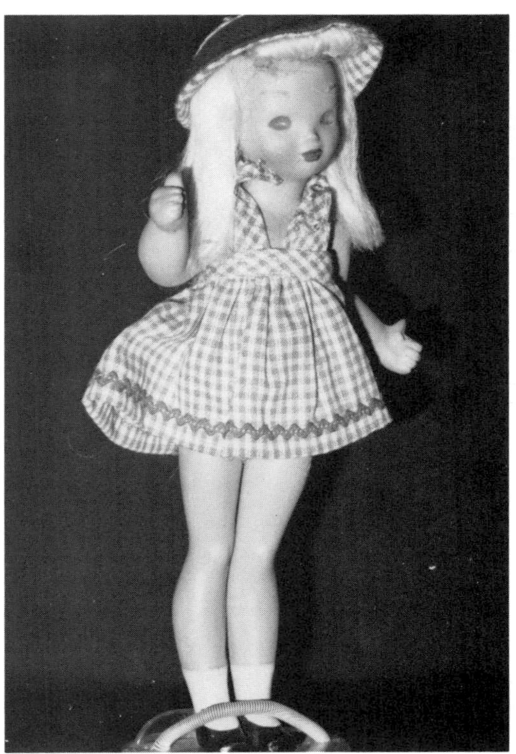

Nilsen, Margit--7½" "Thumbs Up Victory Doll" Complete one piece construction made of Lasticoid, non flexible. Open crown under wig. Painted features. Dolls sold for the purchase of ambulances for Britain. 1940. An original outfit. Marks: None. (Courtesy Pearl Clasby)

Ocean Toys--9½" "The Happy Family" Dad: Brown inset eyes. All plastic with vinyl head. 9" Mom: Blue painted eyes. All plastic with vinyl head. 3" Baby: Painted blue eyes. All plastic one piece body. Vinyl head. Extra nice quality clothes. Marks: All: Hong Kong, on back. Box: Ocean Toys.

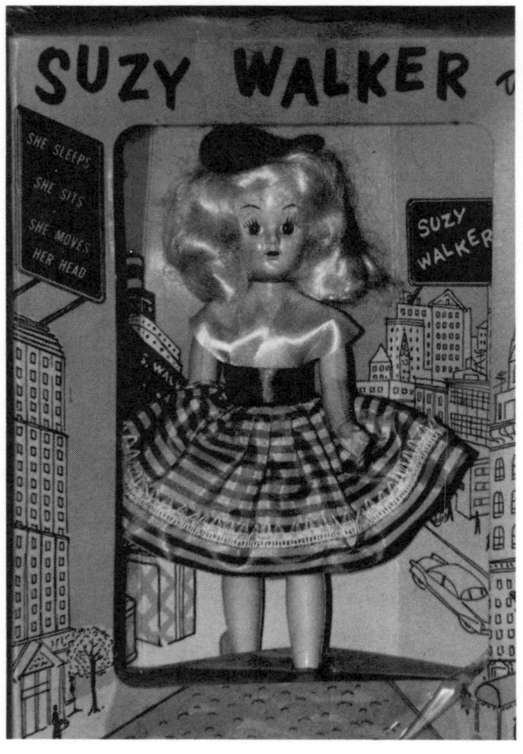


Plastic Molded Arts--8" "Suzy Walker" All hard plastic with blue sleep eyes. Walker head turns. Marks: None. $3.00. (Courtesy Barbara Coker)

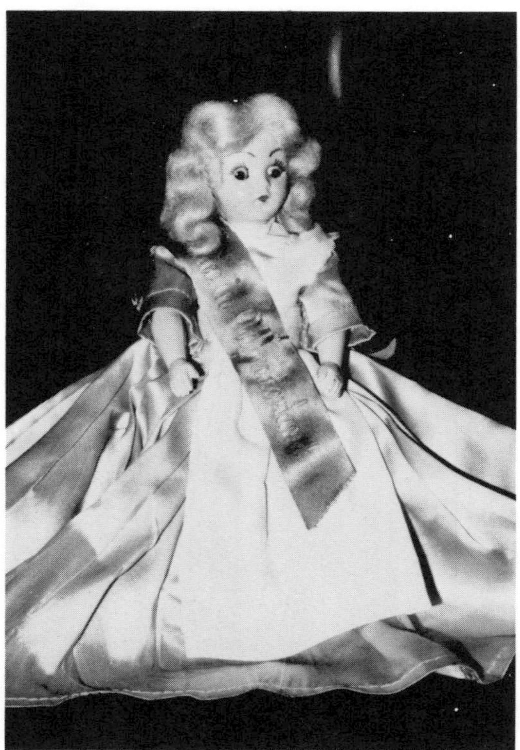

Plastic Molded Arts--7½" "Alice in Wonderland" All hard plastic with glued on blonde hair. Blue sleep eyes. Original. $2.00.

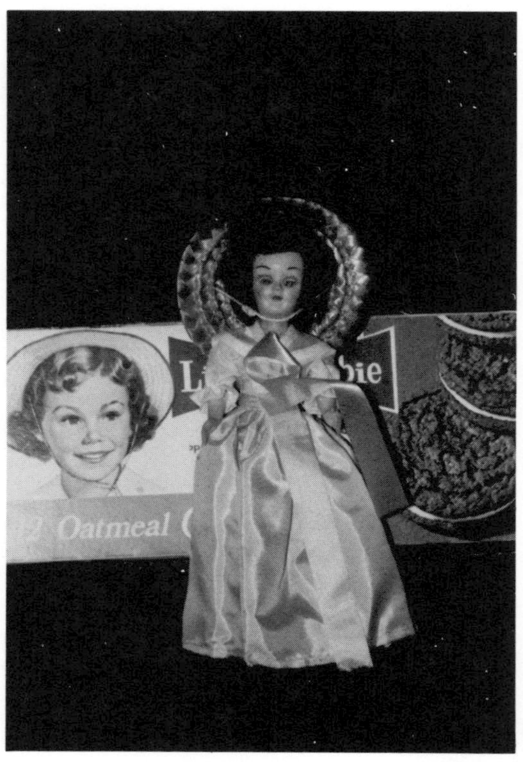


Plastic Molded Arts--8" "Debbie Cakes" Advertising doll. All plastic with stapled on clothes. Jointed neck and shoulders. $3.00. (Courtesy Marie Ernst)

Playthings--20" "Nancy" One piece vinyl with stuffed vinyl head. Rooted blonde hair. Blue sleep eyes. Blue eyeshadow. Pierced ears and high heel feet. Marks: 25/Plaything, on head. 1954. $3.00.

Playmates--8½" "Toddler Twins" Premium for tops from two Raisin Bran and $3.50. 1974. Boy, painted brown eyes. Girl, painted blue eyes. Boy has freckles. Original. Marks: Hong Kong, on head. By Playmates, in a circle/Hong Kong/ 5092, on backs. $2.00 each.

Playmates--14" "Shelly" Plastic and vinyl. Brunette is dressed in pink and Yellow blonde is dressed in yellow. $3.00 each. (Courtesy Marie Ernst)

P&M Sales--12½" "Lotus Blossom" All vinyl with brown sleep eyes. Beauty spot on left cheek. Orange satin trousers and print cotton top original. 1966. $4.00. (Courtesy Phyllis Houston)

P&M Sales--14" Plastic body and legs. Vinyl arms and head. Rooted black hair. Black sleep eyes to side/lashes. Molded eyelids and brows. Large nose and ears. Original. Has two pearl necklaces and two pearl "pierced" earrings. Molded breast and high heel feet. Marks: 2040/ 10 Eye/New/1967. Backward AE, lower back. 15, inside arms. $22.00.

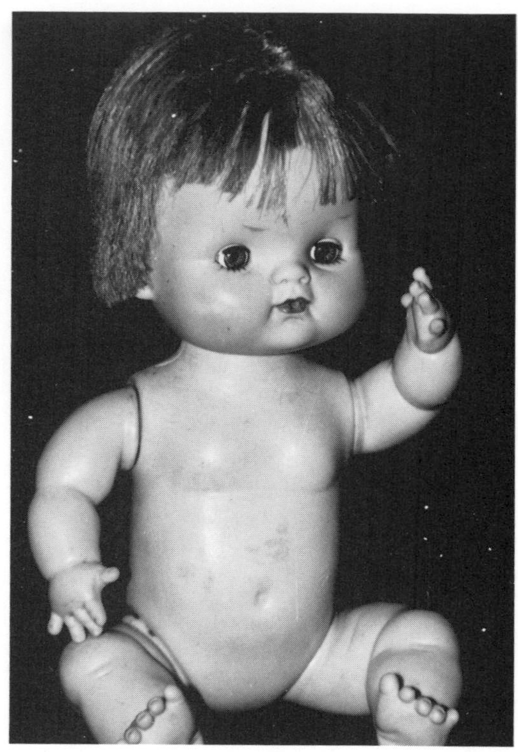

P&M Sales--11" "Baby Buttons" Plastic body, rest vinyl. Blue sleep eyes/molded lashes. Open mouth/nurser. Came also with painted eyes. Marks: None. 1966. $3.00.

Product People Inc--7" "Charlie The Tuna" All vinyl with molded on hat. Painted features. Marks: 1973/Star-Kist Foods Inc. on bottom of feet. $2.00.

Puppet--10" "Gene Autry" puppet. Cloth and rubber with molded on hat. Painted eyes. Marks: None on puppet. Box: National Mask &/ Puppet Corp. $18.00. (Courtesy Marge Meisinger)

Puppet--12" Cloth and composition. Marks: P. Puppet, on head. Box: Peter Puppet Playthings Inc./Designed By/Raye Copalan. $18.00. (Courtesy Joan Amundsen)

Puppet--11" "Oliver Hardy" Cloth body puppet. Vinyl head with molded on hat. Marks: Knicherbacher/1965/Japan, on head. Licensed by Harmon Pic. Corp. $5.00.

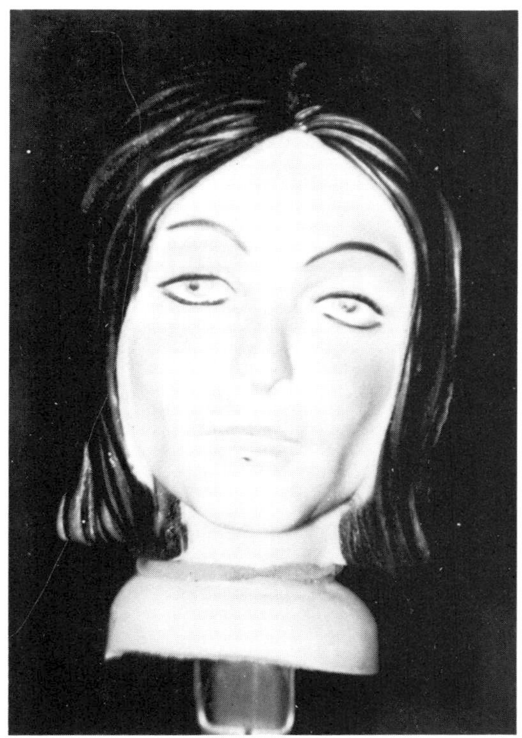

Puppet--9" "Lilly Munster" Black molded hair. Blue painted eyes with lavender eyeshadow. Marks: Filmways TV Productions Inc./1964. $4.00. (Courtesy Marie Ernst)

# Remco Industries, Inc.

The Remco Company was founded by Sol Robbins, and was a successful company for many years and never seemed to lack in design and modeling. For example in 1968, Annuel McBurroughs, a Negro artist helped to design an "ethically correct" line of dolls for Remco. The series included: Tippy Tumbles, Polly Puff, Tiny Tumbles, Baby Laugh-a-lot, L'il Winking Winny, Growing Sally, Baby Know It All, Tina, Baby Whistle, Jumpsy, Billy, Baby Grow-A-Tooth, Bunny Baby and Tumbling Tomboy. The dolls were made all in the White versions but none became too popular and were shortly discontinued.

Many of the items for Remco were made in Canada by the Playcraft Toys Inc. With the closing of the Remco Co. doors (1974) the Miner Industries bought the "Sweet April" doll and accessories. Azrak-Hamway Int'l. purchased the name Remco, Remco Industries, Inc. and Remcraft and are sole owners of the U.S. Trademarks: 848,973; 711,485; 862,678 and corresponding Trademarks throughout the world, and is now called Remco Industries, Inc. A Division of Azark-Hamway International, Inc. The above information appeared in the January 1975 Playthings magazine, so it may be possible they will produce dolls under the Remco name at some future date.

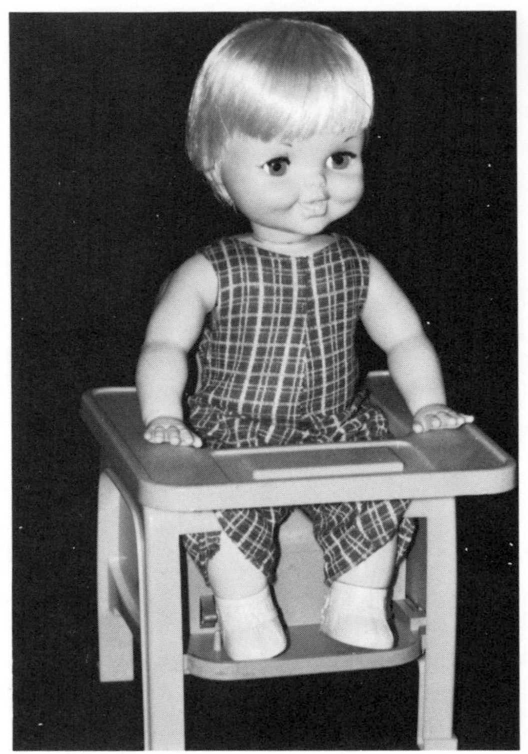

Remco--17" "Baby Know It All" Plastic and vinyl. Set blue eyes. Molded on shoes. Open/closed mouth with two lower teeth. Marks: Remco Ind. Inc./1969. $5.00. (Courtesy Ruth Clarke)

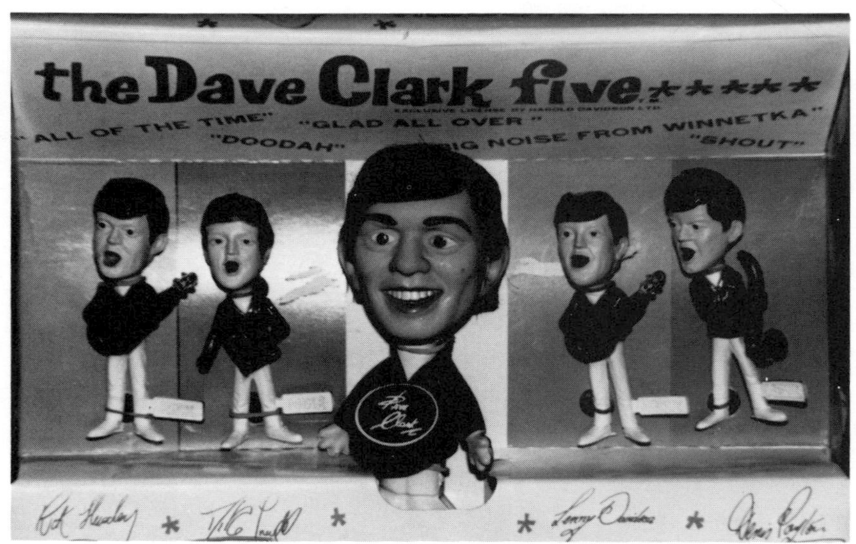


Remco--4½" "Dave Clark" and 3" "Rick, Mike, Lenny & Dennis" The small ones are all plastic. Molded hair. All have open/closed mouths. No marks: Dave Clark: has vinyl head with rooted and lacquered hair. Painted teeth. Marks: Dave Clark/5/1964 Remco Inc., on back. 22/Dave Clark/1964/Remco Ind. Inc., on head. $22.00. (Courtesy Bessie Carson)

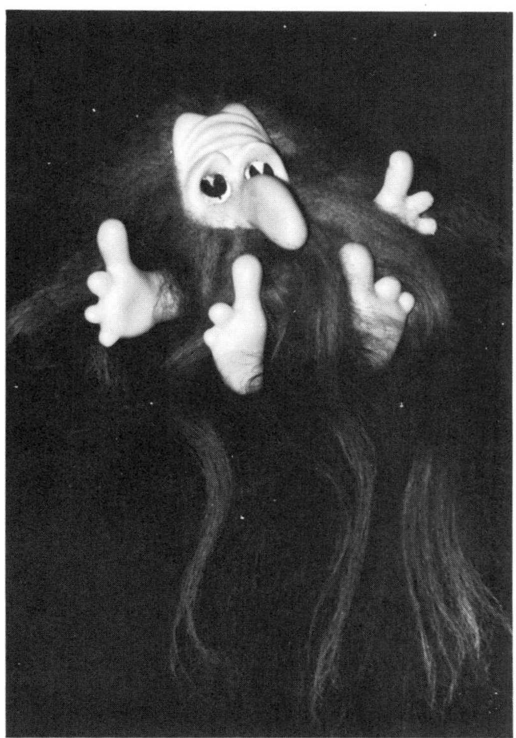

RDF--3½" "Tiny Tim" All vinyl in sitting position. Unjointed. Very long nose. Glued on long mohair. Felt eyes. Marks: RDF '67, on foot. 1967. $8.00.

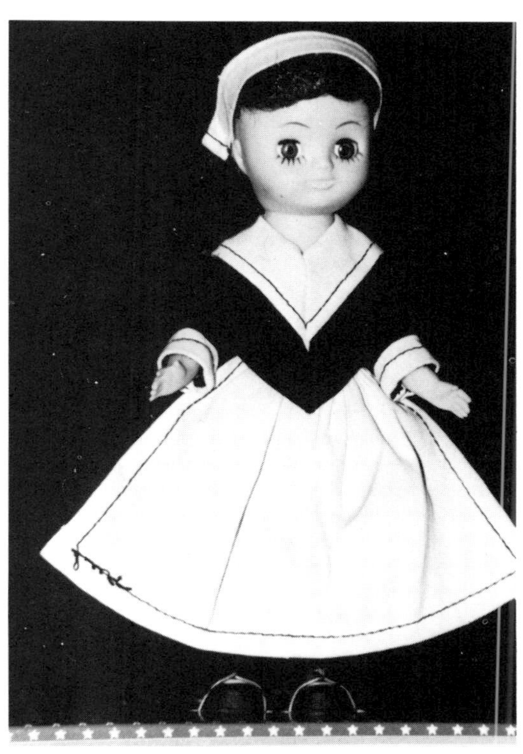

Richard Toy Co.--8" "Pilgrim-1620" Marks: Hong Kong, on head. Dress tag: Bicentennial/Fashion Friends. Other side: Made in Hong Kong/Richard Toy Co. Ltd. 1975. Available in some areas.

Richard Toy Co.--8" "Colonist-1740" Marks: Hong Kong, on back. Dress tag: Bicentennial/ Fashion Friends. Other side: Made in Hong Kong/Richard Toy Co. Ltd. 1975. Available in some areas.

Richard Toy Co.--8" "Independence-1776" Marks: Hong Kong, on back. Dress tag: Bicentennia/Fashion Friends. Other side: Made in Hong Kong/Richard Toy Co. Ltd. 1975. Available in some areas.

Richard Toy Co.--8" "First Lady-1789" Plastic and vinyl. Blue sleep eyes. White floss hair. Marks: Hong Kong, on back. Tag: Made in Hong Kong/Richard Toy Co. Ltd. Other side: Bicentennial/Fashion Friends. TM. Available in some areas. (Courtesy Virginia Jones)

Richard Toy Co.--8" "Frontier-1848" Marks: Hong Kong, on head. Dress tag: Bicentennial/ Fashion Friends. Other side: Made in Hong Kong/Richard Toy Co. Ltd. 1975. Available in some areas.

Richard Toy Co.--8" "Southern Belle-1861" of the Bicentennial Fashion Friends. Marks: Hong Kong, on back. Dress tag: Bicentennial/Fashion Friends. Other side: Made in Hong Kong/Richard Toy Co. Ltd. 1975. Available in some areas.

Richard Toy Co.--8" "Gibson Girl-1900" Marks: Hong Kong, on back. Dress tag: Bicentennial/ Fashion Friends. Other side: Made in Hong Kong/Richard Toy Co. Ltd. 1975. Available in some areas.

Richard Toy Co.--8" "Flapper-1925" Marks: Hong Kong, on back. Dress Tag: Bicentennial/ Fashion Friends. Other side: Made in Hong Kong/Richard Toy Co. Ltd. 1975. Available in some areas.

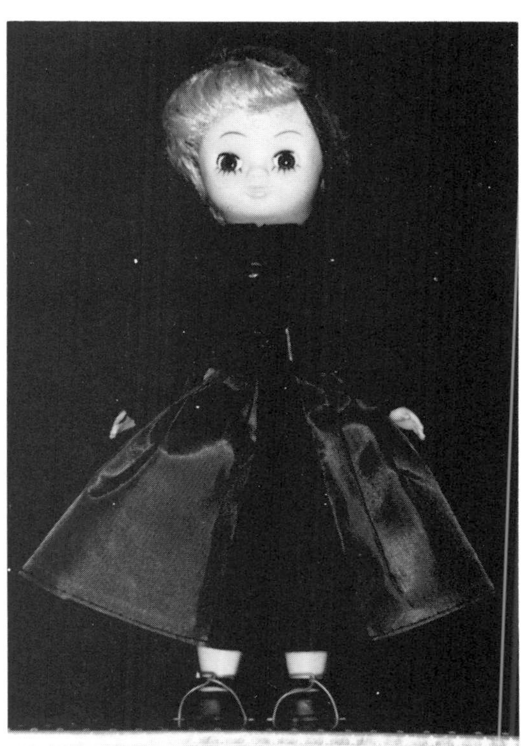

Richard Toy Co.--8" "New Look-1947" Marks: Hong Kong, on back. Dress Tag: Bicentennial/ Fashion Friends. Other side: Made in Hong Kong/Richard Toy Co. Ltd. 1975. Available in some areas.

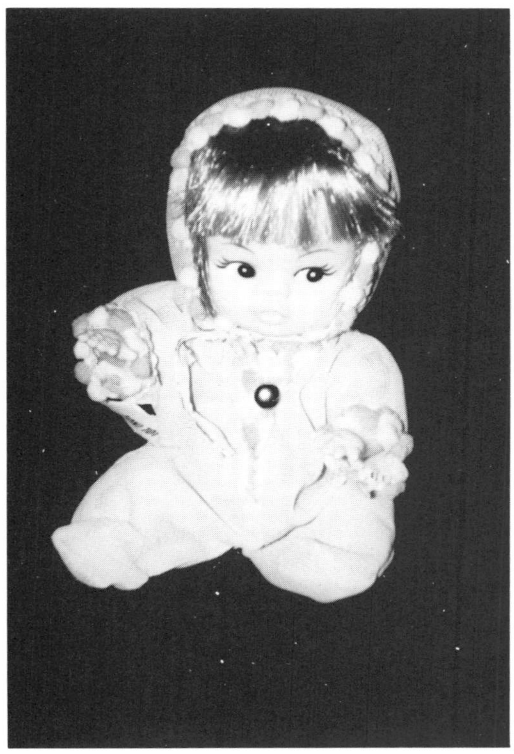

Richard Toy Co.--6" "Toni Tot" Plastic with vinyl head. Painted blue eyes. Original. Marks: Hong Kong, on head and back. Clothes Tag: Toni Tot/other side: Made in Hong Kong/Richard Toy Co. Ltd. $2.00.

Richwood Toys--Sandra Sue was created by the famous sculptor Agop Agopoff. Mr. Agopoff is known for his famous bust of Will Rogers and Anton Dvorak, the Czech composer. Sandra Sue outfits included Louisa May Alcott Little Women outfits. She also had a four poster colonial wooden bed and wardrobe.

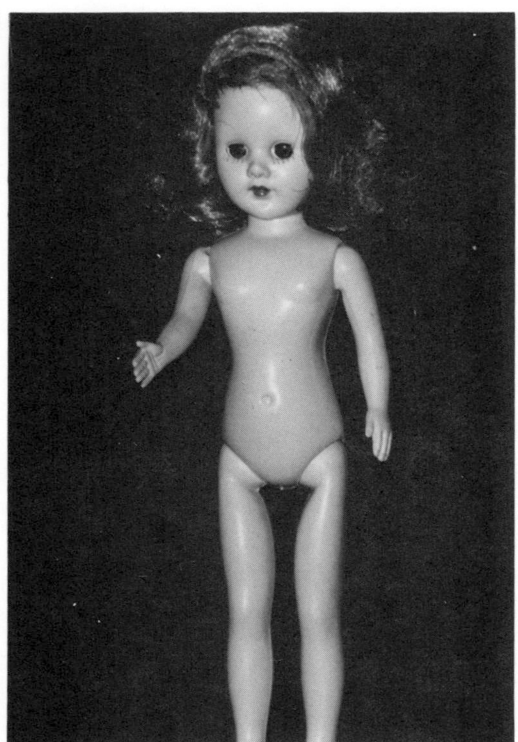

Richwood Toys--8" "Sandra Sue" All hard plastic. Walker mechanisms. (Head doesn't turn.) Blue sleep eyes, painted red lashes, red "fly away" brows. Full red mouth. Fingers straight. Looks like formed soles on plain molded feet. Clothes are excellent quality. Marks: #1, left arm. 2, right arm. (Courtesy Jeanne Niswonger)

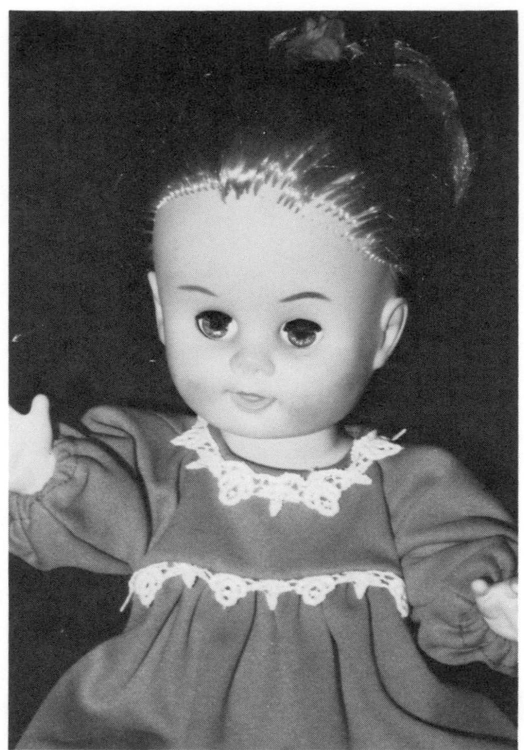

Roberta--13" "Baby Beth" All vinyl with rooted blonde hair. Blue sleep eyes. 1961. Marks: Roberta/13, on head. $3.00.

Roberta--14" "Model" All hard plastic with glued on red mohair. Blue sleep eyes/molded lashes. Early walker with pin joints. Head turns. Marks: 14, on head. Made in USA, in circle on back. 1952. Sold with 22 piece wardrobe. $6.00.

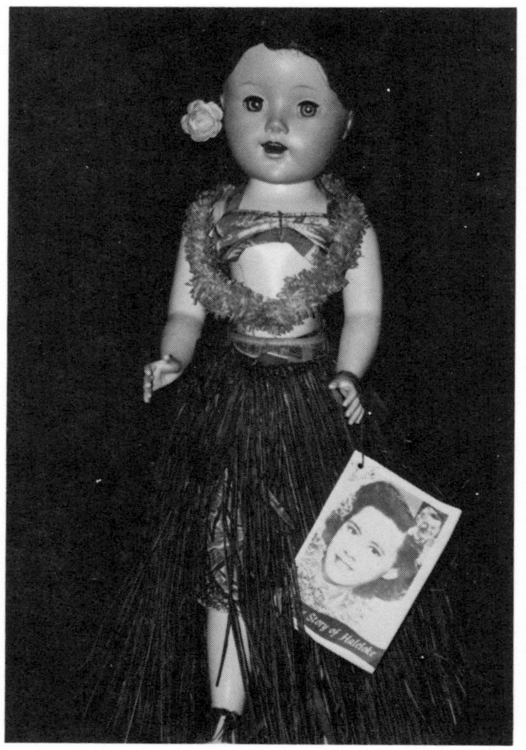

Roberta--17" "Haleoke" From Arthur Godfrey Show. All hard plastic walker, head doesn't turn. Blue sleep eyes/lashes. Skin tones on head only are suntan. Glued on black saran hair. Marks: Made in U.S.A., on back. Clothes made in Hawaiian Islands, with Uke/shoes and hose extra. Dist. by Cast Distributing Corp. NY. $45.00. (Courtesy DeAngelo Collection)

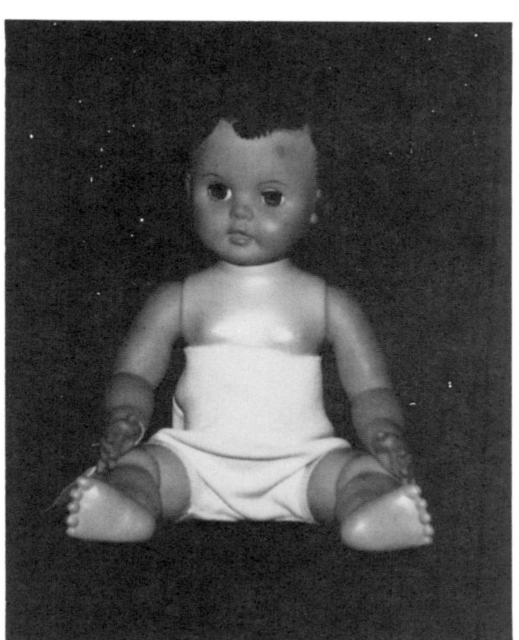

Roberta--16" "Tear Drop" Plastic and vinyl. Blue sleep eyes/lashes. Open mouth/nurser. 1966. Marks: 14-5W, on head. Backward "D", lower back. (Courtesy Carolyn Powers)

Ronald Trading Co.--6½" Plastic head. "Bean bag" (foam pellets) body. Marks: Made in/Hong Kong, on head. Bag: Ronald Trading Co. Ltd. $2.00.

Cloth--8" "Gramps" and 7½" "Granny" Vinyl heads with molded on glasses. Printed cloth bodies. Marks: Made in Hong Kong, on head. Tag: Li'l Stuffs/Made in Hong Kong for/Ronald Trading, Ltd. Still available.

Cloth--7" "Grandaughter" Vinyl head. Printed cloth body. Marks: Hong Kong, on head. Tag: Li'l Stuffs/Made in Hong Kong For/Ronald Trading Co. Ltd. Still available.

Rushton--13" "Connie" Cloth, foam stuffed. Vinyl gauntlet feet and hands. Vinyl face mask with molded blonde hair. Painted features. Yellow yarn hair glued to cloth back of head. Pants removable only. Tag: Connie. Cloth tag: A Rushton Star Creation. Top of Head: White Provision Co. $22.00. (Courtesy Mary Partridge)

Rushton--15½" "Musical Mistress Mary" Cloth body arms and legs. Felt feet. Gauntlet vinyl hands. Vinyl head with rooted orange yarn/molded hair. Side glancing blue eyes. Key wind music box in center of back. Marks: None. 1964. Set of five: Jack, Jill, Little Boy Blue, Little Bo Peep. $13.00.

Rushton--15½" "Little Bo Peep" 1964. $13.00. (Courtesy Alice Capps)

Rushton--19" "Nap Time Pal" 1961. Plush with vinyl gauntlet hands and vinyl face mask. Painted features. Marks: Rushton Co. $3.00.

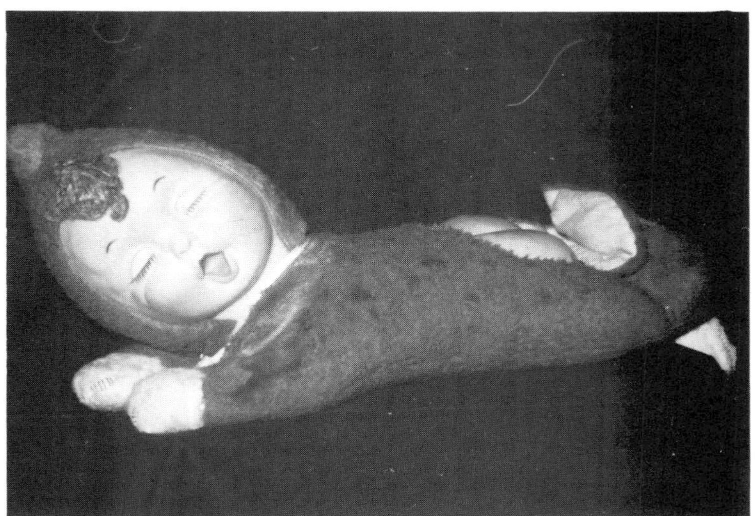

Rushton--22" "Sleepy" Plush with vinyl head on bottom. Rooted hair. Painted closed eyes. Squeeker in bottom flap. Zipper in stomach. Marks: ©, on neck. $4.00.

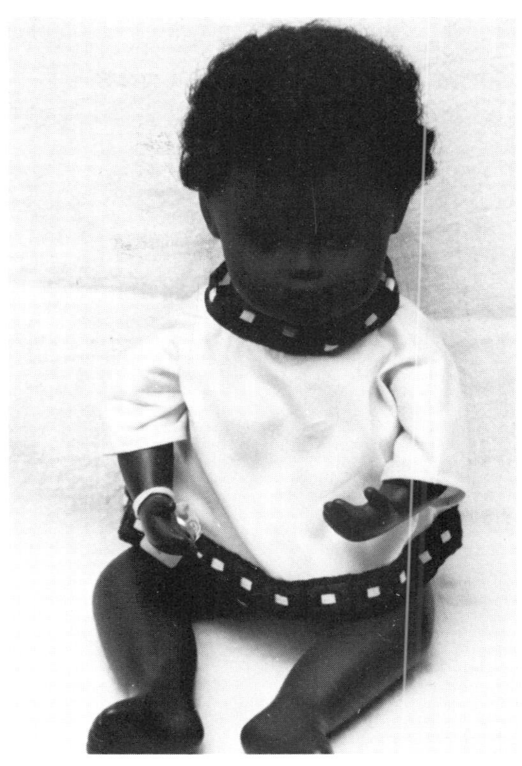

Sasha--"Sasha" Baby" These babies are just slightly sexed. Still available. (Courtesy Marie Ernst)

RUSHTON

SASHA

SAYCO

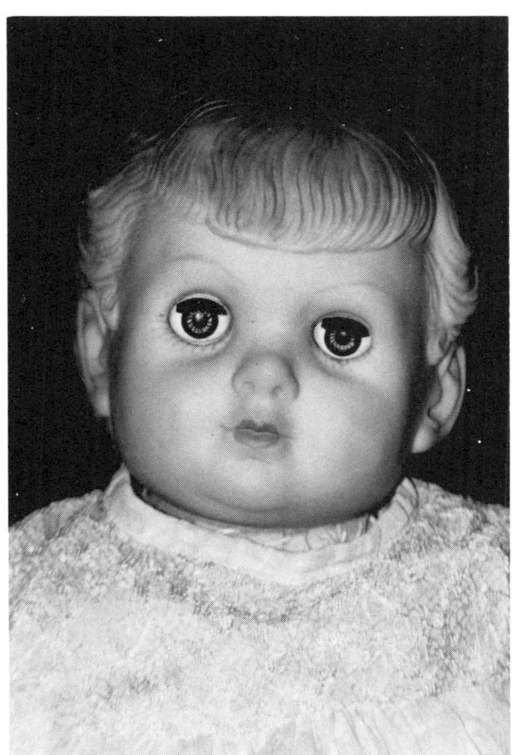

Sayco--20" "Melissa" Brown sleep eyes/lashes. Cloth body with vinyl arms, legs and head. Sculptured hair. Marks: Sayco/18-D. $40.00. (Courtesy Barbara Coker)

Sayco--20" "Melissa" Shows back of sculptured hair. (Courtesy Barbara Coker)

Sayco--17" "Laura" Hard plastic with a vinyl head. Dark brown rooted hair. Blue sleep eyes. Marks: Sayco, on head.

Sayco--14" "Bride" Rigid vinyl with softer vinyl head. High heel feet. Jointed waist. All original except bouquet. 1957. $15.00. (Courtesy Phyllis Houston)

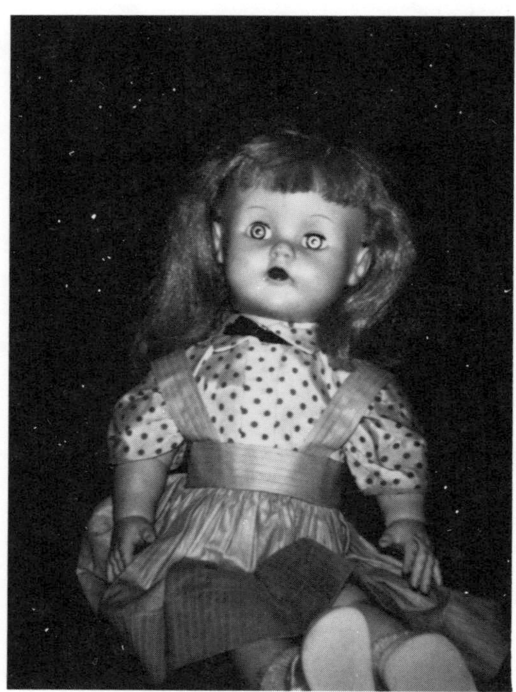

Sayco--20" "Sherry Ann" One piece stuffed vinly body and limbs. Blue sleep eyes. Very tight outside row of hair. Was in up/back sweep. Open/closed mouth. Original. 1956. Marks: 74, on head. (Courtesy Carolyn Powers)

# Shindana Toys

Shindana is a black community owned toy company, in the Watts section of Los Angeles. The President of the company is Lou Smith, who says, "It's totally unrealistic to expect black kids to play with blonde, blue eyed dolls when they, nor their children, will not grow up to look that way. Instead of making "suntanned" dolls, we use the ethnic characteristics of black people."

To give the dolls a kinky Afro hairdo, the company had to order a curling machine from Italy, as no such machine could be found that was made in the U.S. and the company's first doll, "Baby Nancy" came off the assembly line with straight black hair.

According to Herman Thompson, director of sales and marketing for Shindana, the making of a "truly black doll" came about only after a study by a black psychiatrist which showed that black children, when given a choice, preferred white dolls over black ones and stated, "We saw this as an expression of a lack of love and understanding these children held for themselves. We tackled this problem by producing and marketing 21 black dolls that black and white children can learn to relate to a very early age."

Shindana was founded without government subsidy. When Lou Smith and his partner Robert Hall, an official of the Congress of Racial Equality, started the toy company in Watts after the 1968 riots, Smith went to Mattel, Inc. for financial backing and advice. Mattel was responsive to Smith's idea and gave him $300,000 initial capital and technical advice to begin the enterprise. "There were no strings attached." Smith said. Mr. Hall, his partner died in 1973, a man in his 30's who had literally worked himself to death.

Shindana Toys is the economic arm of Operation Bootstraps, a non-profit self help business organization whose goals are to establish businesses in the riot torn Watts area.

Shindana means "complete" in Swahili and began eight years ago with one doll "Baby Nancy" and today it is a $1,300,000 a year company that makes 21 different dolls and eight educational games.

Smith did not believe the poverty programs of the '60's would work but believed that the ghettos must be changed from within. He says, "You have to establish an economic base, an educational base, a self-esteem and self-love and all this must come from within the community. Instead of going to Washington for handouts, we have to build industry to employ and train people right in the ghetto and we must manufacture products that society wants and needs."

"For example, one Shindana doll, "Wanda the Career Girl" is an off-shoot of the Mattel's white Barbie doll. But instead of just giving her a beautiful wardrobe, we use the black doll as a career woman to introduce career ideas and opportunities to black children. In the ghetto, black people aren't aware of the careers open to them."

There are three Wanda dolls on the market, the Nurse, the Ballerina and the Airline Stewardess. These careers were chosen first, as they have distinct costumes to coincide with the career but Shindana plans to introduce other professions.

Each doll (Wanda) comes with a booklet with a picture from, a successful black woman in each of the three fields. For example, Wanda the Airline Stewartess booklet has a message from Bernadette, Wanda's friend. Bernadette Gossey is a real person and actually works for TWA and she tells the youngsters about her career and why she enjoys it.

Wanda also has a Career Club. Each month, more than 5,000 career club members receive a free newsletter about careers from interior decorating to journalism.

Dolls by Shindana, a member of Operation Bootstraps, has always been of interest to the doll collector because of the beauty of the dolls themselves and for the high quality of the vinyl and of the clothes. These dolls can only enhance a collection.

Shindana--23""J.J." Talking character doll, based on J.J. Evans of the T.V. show "Good Times." Played by actor Jimmy Walker. Says ten things and is pull string operated. (Courtesy Harshe-Rotman & Druck, Inc. Public Relations firm for Shindana)

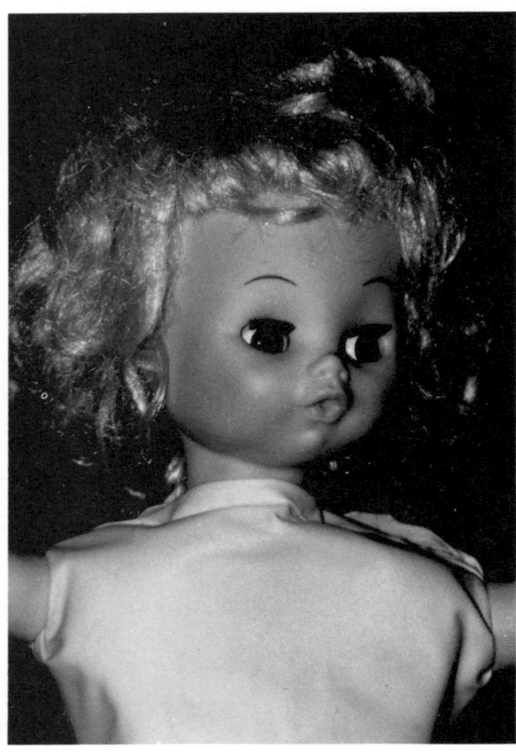

Singer--14" Pink plastic covered foam body. Vinyl head, arms and legs. Open mouth/nurser. Blue sleep eyes/long lashes. Marks: Singer Crafts/Patterson N.J./Mass T 984/Polyfoam/ Made in Hong Kong. $6.00.

Skippy--17½" "Julia" Plastic and vinyl. Blue sleep eyes. Closed mouth. Marks: A Skippy Doll/1967, on head. AE, on back and a backward AE, lower on back. $6.00. (Courtesy Carolyn Powers)

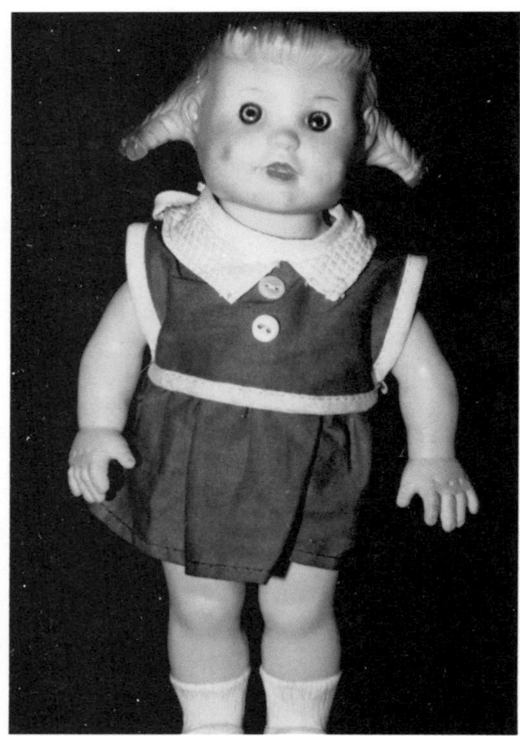

Squeeze Toy--9" "Annie" All vinyl with molded on underwear, shoes and socks. Molded brown hair. Inset blue eyes. Open/closed mouth. Jointed neck only. Marks: The Sun Rubber Co./ 1965, on back. $2.00.

Squeeze Toy--10" "Sweetie Pie" All vinyl, unjointed. Molded on clothes. Doll is dressed and looks just like her. Marks( Sweetie Pie/A Stern Toy/N.E.A. 1959. $3.00.

Squeeze Toy--6" "Googly" Press stomach and eyes twirl. All vinyl. Jointed neck only. Rooted hair. Marks: U.S. Pat. No. 3451160, on head. #1012/Copyrighted 1969/Parksmith Corporation/ Japan. $2.00.

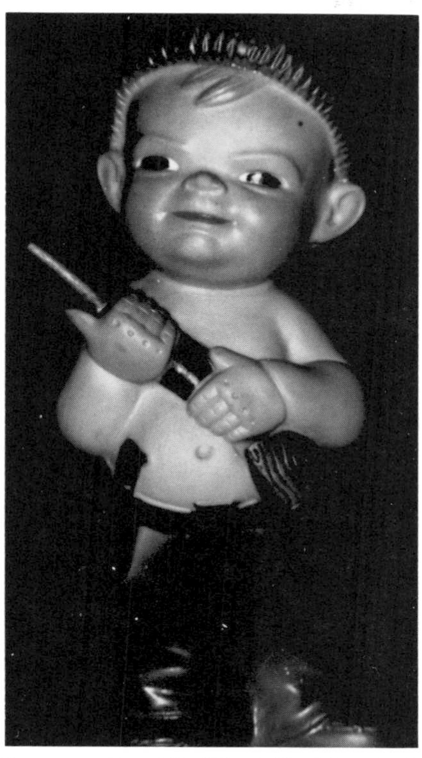

Squeeze Toy--8" "Daniel" All vinyl. Marks: None. $2.00.

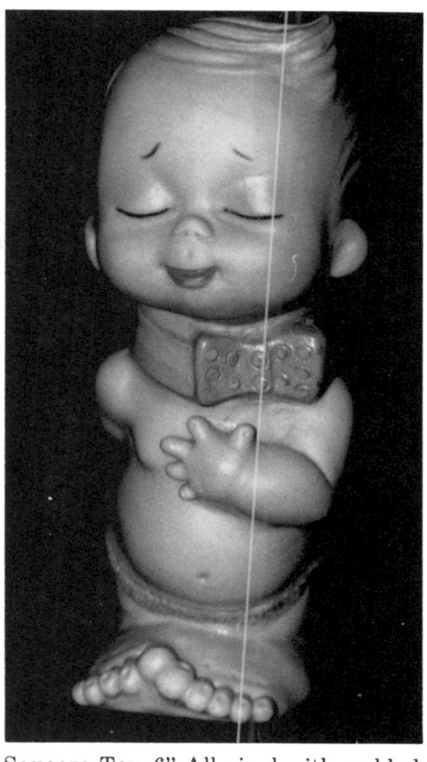

Squeeze Toy--6" All vinyl with molded orange hair. Has two "daisys" behind back. Marks: 1966/Ideal Toy Corp/I-D-5, on lower back legs. 1966/Ideal Toy Corp/Portugal, on bottom. $2.00. (Courtesy Virginia Jones)



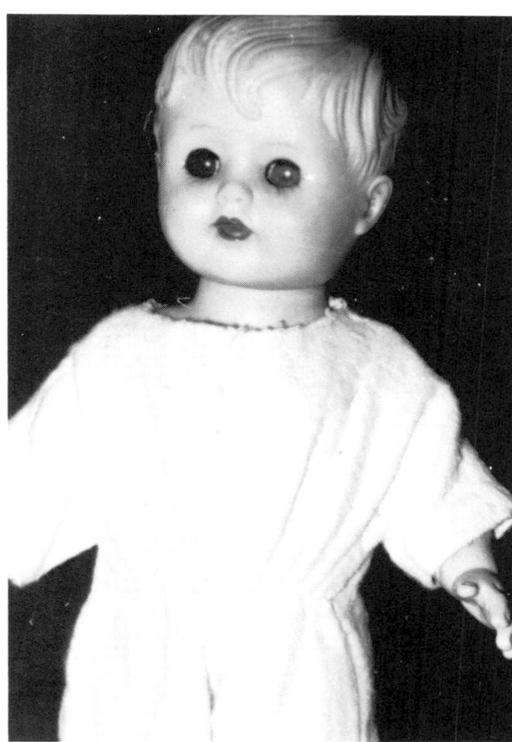

Super Doll--12" "Little Debbie Eve's Brother" Rigid vinyl body, arms and legs. Blue sleep eyes. 1960. Marks: 12-D, on lower back. $2.00.

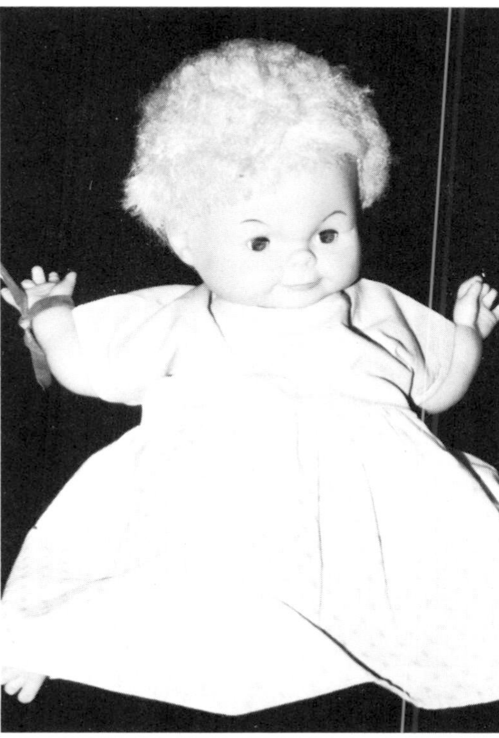

Super Doll--14" "New Born" (with rocking plastic cradle). Cloth and vinyl with rooted white hair. Blue sleep eyes. Cryer. Marks: SD/ 18, on head. 1964. $1.00.

# The Story of Terri Lee

The following article was prepared by Lula May Close. Mrs. Close is a member of the Capitol City Doll Club of Ohio. The article was written in 1968 and the author cbtained her information from Mrs. Violet Gradwohl herself.

It was a cloudy bleak December afternoon in Lincoln, Nebraska, in 1944 when a group of housewives were gathered around a huge table mending dolls for the needy. Violet Gradwohl was rather tired, having spent a busy morning at the U.S.O. and today was typical of almost every other day she had spent since the beginning of the war.

As she cemented together the jagged pieces of a broken leg, taking care not to interfer with the walking mechanism, she sighed, "Why don't they make a doll in a little girl's image, uncomplicated, with which a child can use her imagination? Dolls with eyes that can't be gouged out, without walking devices that soon stop running, with chubby legs and slightly protruding tummies, such as every little girl has?" The more she thought about it the more she felt that someone should create a doll that looked like a human being, and that did not have all the faults she felt every doll that has been manufactured so far had. For this reason Violet Gradwohl decided to enter the doll manufacturing business herself.

She began to form her own ideas of what a doll should be in order to become a durable darling of a child's heart. It was an ideal, to be sure, but Mrs. Gradwohl set out to make it a reality.

Soon after the war Mrs. Gradwohl found time hanging heavily on her hands and set about creating a model for a doll that would combine her observations, experiences and ideals; a doll with a new sytle body that would not break, durable, with an attractive appearance and plenty of pretty clothes. It was sculptured in plaster by her niece, Maxine Stevens, a California sculptress who used her own two year old daughter Adrienne as a model. For a name Mrs. Gradwohl took that of her daughter, Terri Lee.

(You will note that this contradicts with the following, which was also from Mrs. Gradwohl).

By 1946 she had accomplished several things toward making her dream a reality. From photographs of her daughter taken in childhood, she had a model and then a mold made. Because she wanted the doll to last with the child, she wanted to protect it from unsightly broken fingers and sightless eyes. She combed the market for a plastic that had a life-like appearance and selected rigid plastic for the doll parts. The head was molded so that the eyes were part of the head itself, and she selected artists to paint the eyes and all the features so that it retained humanness. There had never been a doll like Terri Lee. She was the first made of plastic which was guaranteed for life as unbreakable. Mrs. Gradwohl had seen her child in tears over a broken doll, and felt it was important for the child to have something to love, that would not break. She believed in making things beautiful, sturdy and practical for children.

Her next job was to find a wig that could be shampooed, combed and curled. Terri Lee was not only the first doll with a lifetime guarantee, but also the first doll to have a wig of this type. The finished product was so charming and beautiful, it cried out for charming and beautiful clothing. Vi Gradwohl's daughter, Terri Lee, who was also very talented, and her mother put their heads together and designed a wardrobe such as any child would like to have, and made of materials like children wear, with buttons and snaps and lovely ribbons and laces. Later, formals and Bride's dresses were added because all little girls like to play that they are grown up. Terri Lee was the first doll with a complete wardrobe and has always been America's best dressed doll.

The doll called Terri Lee suggested a brother, Jerri, which was made on the same mold, with a different wig. Next, Mrs. Gradwohl felt Negro children would like dolls made in their own likeness with the same chubby legs and pretty clothes. Vi chose a warm exotic beige brown paint and went to work with a spray gun. The result was Bonnie Lu and Benjie; then came Patty Jo, a cartoon character developed by Jackie Ormes. Next was Nanook, a slightly lighter color..an Eskimo child. The Baby Linda was brought into being, designed to be a baby's first doll, made in soft vinyl plastic 11" long. The production of Linda is a story in itself, the very first soft plastic doll completely articulated. Later on there was Tiny Terri and Tiny Jerry.

Mrs. Gradwohl, with no knowledge of the doll business, took the beautifully dressed plaster model Terri Lee to a New York doll show in March 1946, only to discover that just manufacturers could exhibit. However, Inez Holland, a manufacturer and manufacturer's representative, showed Terri Lee.

Mrs. Gradwohl spent six weeks in New York, learning about the doll business and finding out what she needed to get into business.

She encountered innumerable difficulties at the outset. With no backing other than her own determination, she walked into a large textile house and announced that she was going to manufacture a new doll and desired to purchase materials in quanity. This was in 1946, with most production was still on the war-era basis, and she was informed that no one could buy a yard of material except on quota. Manufacturers of garments, whether for humans or dolls, were being allocated materials only on the basis of past production and even that was limited. They informed her they could not supply her with raw materials since she did not have an established company, but before she left, she had somehow charmed the textile company into promising her a quota of materials if she could provide a satisfactory rating from Dun and Bradstreet. She didn't know what they were talking about, but promised anyway.

Several doll parts manufacturers refused her business, and she was told that the doll she wanted to manufacture had a funny face that nobody would buy. Finally, one consented to make parts for her, though informing her ominously that she would lose money.

Mrs. Violet Gradwohl went into the doll business in Lincoln, Nebraska in August 1946, with ten employees, working in one room. The Terri Lee doll was a success from the first.

Although Mrs. Gradwohl had planned to make the dolls of plastic (there were no plastic dolls on the market then), the first dolls were composition. Within the next year or so an Omaha firm pressed the dolls from "Unbreakable" plastic. (Lulu Cose comments that she has several Terri Lees which are made out of a whitish soft rubber, or soft plastic, probably an experimental medium in the transition from composition to hard plastic.)

Within the next several years the business had expanded so that the plant in Lincoln, with 23 employees in full production, could turn out 1,000 dolls a week, and in the peak season approximately 75 seamstresses were employed in making doll clothes. An extensive wardrobe for every season was available. Girl dolls had 20 different outfits to choose from, and boy dolls had 12. A Lincoln firm called Ben, Your Hairdresser, sub-contracted to make the wigs, and employed 7 or 8 persons making wigs during the peak season. The hair for the wigs was from Mrs. Gradwohl's own patented process from celanese yarn woven into artificial hair. This was a secret process and was never commercialized despite offers from other doll manufacturers.

By the year 1948, the Terri Lee firm had an assortment of dolls: Jerri, Bonnie, Benjie, Chiquita. They all had the same body (marked Terri Lee) but there were appropriate changes in wigs and coloring.

During an interview around the close of the second year of the venture, Mrs. Gradwohl said that Terri Lee was the first doll in the business to have real buttons, snaps and button holes in her clothes. It was attention to detail, she thought, that was partly responsible for the success of the dolls.

Besides the hairdresser-wig maker, Ben, another Lincoln firm which contributed to the Terri Lee line was Dewey and Wilson, who made the motor driven merry-go-rounds which stores used to make permanent doll displays.

Terri Lee dolls were featured in newsreels, movie shorts and television programs by 1948. She was written up in Negro Digest, Ebony and other National Publications. "Jr. Magazine" for children featured Terri Lee monthly. The American Association of University Women recommended Terri Lee dolls. In the fall of 1948 Terri Lee appeared in the uniform of the Girl Scouts of America, by whom she had been adopted.

During this time the company maintained representatives in Chicago, St. Paul, Dallas, Denver, Salt Lake City, Portland (Oregon), and High Point (N.C.). During 1948 a large shipment of dolls was sent to Durbin, South Africa. Terri Lee dolls had been sold in every state in the Union and in Liberia, Norway, Switzerland, Hawaii, Nicaragua and Canada.

Within 5 years of its beginning, in 1951, Terri Lee, Inc. was one of the leading doll companies in the country, and the doll that "nobody would buy" sold at the rate of 3,000 per week, and was made in a two floor factory in Lincoln with almost 190 employees, a day and night shift, and more orders that could be filled.

At that time everything was manufactured and finished in Lincoln, except the moulding of the plastic and the production of the doll shoes, stockings, and straw hats.

Although the demand for Terri Lee dolls almost doubled every year the going for her creator was not always easy. Soon after Mrs. Gradwohl managed to acquire adequate space for efficient production, the factory was burned to the ground. The catastrophe happened just before Christmas 1951, near the end of the rush season.

Mrs. Gradwohl suffered exposure when records of the doll factory were removed from the flaming building by firemen and her husband, Dr. Harry Gradwohl. Mrs. Gradwohl went to the hospital in a state of nervous collapse.

The plant was a total loss, $75,000, and was not completely covered by insurance. Mrs. Gradwohl said that among items lost in the fire was a special luxury order doll dressed in a $250.00 mink coat.

The plant had "thousands" of small cash orders to be filled over one week-end, the plant manager said, and the plant would have shipped more than a carload of merchandise at the first of the week had they not had the fire.

However, the company received numerous letters and telegrams in regard to dolls that had been sent to the Terri Lee "hospital" for repairs, and the plant manager said these dolls were the greatest loss because of the value attached to them by their youthful owners. He said approximately 150 dolls were in the plant for repairs at the time.

Terri Lee, Inc. had scouted other business locations to house the growing doll business, and the firm was ready to build its own factory except for the current difficulties in securing construction materials.

Mrs. Gradwohl returned home from the hospital on Christmas Eve, determined to get out of business. In a corner of her living room stood two bushel baskets overflowing with letters from children, mothers and fathers, and merchants all over the country who had ordered dolls and hadn't received them because of the fire. All assured her that they would wait until she could deliver, no matter how long. She was soon in business again, filling these orders.

On May 9, 1952, Mrs. Gradwohl opened a plastic doll factory in Apple Valley in the Mojave Desert of Southern California, once the crossroads of four historic pioneer trails, with 32 persons in the assembly of her Terri Lee dolls. The business progressed and in 1953, seven years from the start of the venture in Lincoln, the company had grown to become one of something like 300 major doll manufacturing companies in the country and to hold the rank of fifth in production..more than 100,000 dolls a year.

The dolls were manufactured in Apple Valley, and the Lincoln plant which had been destroyed by fire was replaced by a plant to manufacture garments for the dolls. The Apple Valley plant also did a big business in wardrobes for the dolls and in the year 1953 sold three mink coats for them at $295 each.

From Independent Woman, November 21, 1954, was taken the following: "Alice in Wonderland never stepped into a more fantastic setting than that of the Doll House of Apple Valley. The building, which looks like a huge pink frosted birthday cake, stands in the midst of the vast golden California desert surrounded by Joshua trees. These trees, which are native to the area but which are nowhere else to be found except Palestine, add to the unreality of the scene by the incredible and amusing shapes of make-believe animals they make.

The loftiest peaks of the mountains that guard this valley of enchantment wears snow caps all year, but the valley itself is always warm with sunshine tempered by soft breezes, and the people who live there are happy. The people who work in the Doll House are probably happiest of all. The long modern building may be seen for miles around, and everyone who knows the community points it out with pride that is partly fond amusement and partly incredulity. It is difficult for them to believe that this magnificent and fantastic factory has come to stay in their midst. It is a little bit like something wonderful which has appeared by magic and might disappear just as suddenly.

But the Doll House is real and very permanent in Apple Valley. Viola Gradwohl, who called it into being, not by a wave of a fairy wand, but by good hard work, thinks there is no other place so delightful for living, and for earning a living making dolls for little girls.

Because the factory is located over a hundred miles from any large city and is the only industry in the area, the first great difficulty to be overcome was communications. "But I had fallen in love with this place on my first visit and was determined to locate here," said the Doll Lady, as she is affectionately called by everyone. She dismissed that problem with the quip, "The only thing lacking, really, was carrier pigeons."

"I have found you can't make a success of anything unless you live, eat and sleep it. In establishing a new business, there are times when all you have left is courage, and it takes a lot of courage. The manufacturing business is a man's world. A woman must learn to look at all problems as a man would, without emotion or hurt feelings. If this business were not so full of fun and challenge but it is fun to meet their faith with everything they expect of you."

Furthermore, I believe it is not necessary for a doll to have all the human attributes. In imagination children endow their playthings with every quality and function they wish. Also, I have discovered that children do not want a doll to resemble an adult. Several years ago we featured a Gene Autry doll but it was not a real success. The Gene Autry costumes which may be changed for others are much more popular.

Terri Lee wears beautiful and fashionable costumes, well made and well designed in the best available materials. Nylon, laces and nets, satin, cotton, linen of the best quality and even several kinds of fur are used to fashion her 150 varied and complete ensembles. If a capricious owner should douse Terri Lee's splendid formal gown in a basin of water, it would soon dry and be as good as new again.

Everyone who works at the Doll House radiates happiness. This work seems to have therapeutic quality. One of the girls who paints the doll's faces is a deaf mute whose personality has changed completely since she came to work at the Doll House. She is now even able to talk a little. Of the children who receive the dolls, Mrs. Gradwohl says, "The best way to teach children love and respect for possessions is to provide them with beautiful and durable things and then encourage them to care for their treasures."

This program is initiated by literature which accompanies the dolls and is maintanied by a monthly magazine sent to every owner of a Terri Lee doll as a life member of her Friendship Club. Colorful and timely, this miniature publication contains all the usual features of adult magazines slanted to juvenile readers. Terri Lee is the official Girl Scout and Campfire Girl's doll, and has her own authentic uniforms. Her philantrophies are many and varied.

Psychology is at work on a large scale in Viola Gradwohl's enterprise in exerting influence for good upon some 400 employees and the thousands of recipients of Terri Lee dolls.

During 1955, a series of fashion shows were put on by the three "City of Paris" stores in San Francisco, Vallejo and San Mateo, and proved to be a wonderful event. Thirteen nine-year-old girls were dressed exactly like the Terri Lee dolls they carried in their arms."

On November 10, 1955, forty thousand square feet of additional factory space was opened in Apple Valley by an entertainment and a conducted tour of the new plant and its facilities. The Terri Lee Sales Corporation now occupied 50,000 square feet of space. One sewing department, a molding, painting, wigging, assembling and packing units were now housed in the addition.

Five hundred to six hundred employees were required during the busy season at Apple Valley and 300 more at the sewing plant in Lincoln, Nebraska. Terri Lee Schrepel still designed the beautifully made fashions.

In 1956, there were four basic dolls in the series: Terri Lee, a 17" all plastic doll (with Jerri Lee, a brother, like Terri in size and construction); Connie Lynn, a 20" all plastic sleeping doll with long natural eye lashes and curly soft hair; Baby Linda, 11," fully articulated vinyl baby doll; and Tiny Terri Lee (with Tiny Jerri, brother to Tiny Terri). The Tiny Terri had thirty costumes, all exactly like those of big sister Terri, and this small doll sat, walked and had movable eyes with long, sweeping eyelashes.

Somewhere along the line someone must have changed their minds about movable eyes, since both Connie Lynn and Tiny Terri and Jerri had sleeping eyes. The eyes of Connie Lynn were not guaranteed, however, and the lifetime guarantee did not cover Baby Linda nor the Tiny Terri and Jerri.

Every buyer was reportedly given a birth certificate with finger and footprints, and hospitals were maintained for sick Terri Lees. For only the bare cost of labor a practically new doll was returned to the little mother whose doll had been sent a Terri Lee Hospital.

To assure that lifetime guarantee, Mrs. Gradwohl maintained two doll hospitals during this period where for a small fee Terri Lee dolls that showed signs of aging could be rejuvenated. Repairs included new hair, repainting features or anything else necessary to restore the doll to her original perfection. One fact that pleased Terri Lee's creator is that not one Terri Lee came in with broken fingers. The hospital for dolls living east of the Rocky Mountains was located in Lincoln, Neb. and for west coast dolls in Apple Valley.

Indeed the Terri Lee, with its lifetime guarantee and hospital for sick Terri Lees would appeal to children, and the monthly magazine sent to owners, which carried patterns, stories, games and contests, together with the birthday clubs and special Terri Lee birthday cards, would keep up their interest. Note the instructions to the mother of a sick Terri Lee..."Send your dolly undressed so the doctor can put her right to bed." From the literature available you can see that there was no "talking down" to the children, but everything was in language they could understand. It has been reported that in one year alone the "mamas" of Terri Lee dolls wrote more than 300,000 letters to the "Lovely Lady." Little girls wrote, told her riddles and jokes and every letter was answered.

But misfortune struck again. Not much information can be obtained as to the demise of the Terri Lee venture in Apple Valley. It has been rumored that they had another fire there, which destroyed the Apple Valley plant; also that Terri Lee was forced into bankruptcy by the government in 1958 and all equipment and buildings in Apple Valley were sold at auction. Whatever happened to the Lincoln plant is unknown, and evidently it was closed also.

But Mrs. Gradwohl was not beaten yet. In the year 1962, Terri Lee dolls were made by I. and S. Industries in Glendale, California, and sold by Mar-fan Company of Glendale, Calif. The lifetime guarantee was still in effect and sick Terri Lees were to be sent to Mar-fan.

And something new was added. Some of the Terri Lees made by I&S had a voice. A phonograph jack was inserted in the back of the head under the hair line and a cord from the jack to the phonograph, with a Terri Lee record playing, seemed to give life to the doll. Several records by Terri Lee were available. These later dolls had softer hair, somewhat like dynel.

Although Terri Lee dolls were always in a fairly high price bracket, $12.95 and up, depending on costumes, (the dolls with voice were $8.00 more) the hospital charges were quite reasonable.

I have not been able to ascertain how long I&S Industries and Mar-fan sold Terri Lees. As said above, the hospital plan was still in effect in 1962, as well as the monthly magazine but evidently this was about the end of the Terri Lee manufacture as research reveals no further information.

It has been rumored that Terri Lees may be manufactured again, and evidently it may possibly be true as Mrs. Gradwohl wrote me the first of this year (1968)..."Am trying to get back into the manufacture of Terri Lee. If I can get the required financing, this I will do. I believe from the shabby doll clothes I see on the market that Terri Lee can again be popular, even without all the mechanical gadgets so many of the new dolls have."

The Terri Lee dolls are different and are sought after by many doll collectors, also the accessories made for the doll such as strollers that were sold for the Terri Lee dolls; Connie and Linda purses for little girls; Terri Lee lamps with a picture of Terri Lee on the shades; and Tiny Terri and Jerri kits with doll parts and dresses for children to put together and dress.

This ends Lulu Close's article and we continue with the story of Terri Lee as told in the fashion booklets that came with the dolls:

# The Story of Terri Lee

"Once upon a time, not long ago, there was a Lovely Lady who had a beautiful little girl with shining curls and bright eyes like stars and oh! so many pretty clothes! This little girl's name was Terri Lee. The Lovely Lady thought, "How nice it would be if there was a doll just like my Terri Lee!" And she made a doll that looked like the real little girl. Then she thought, "How nice it would be if this pretty doll had lots of costumes!" And she made lots of costumes for the pretty doll. Then she thought, "How nice it would be if every little girl in the whole country could have a doll exactly like this one, with pretty clothes!" And that's how Terri Lee Dolls and their many beautiful costumes came to be.

The Lovely Lady thought of important things like how dolls get broken when they're loved too hard, how their clothes get mussed and soiled from being played with, and how their hair becomes all shabby after a little while. She wondered what she could do to be sure the Terri Lee Dolls would be lastingly beautiful. So she had the dolls made of fine, durable plastic that would be unbreakable. The material she selected for the hair was silky and lifelike and could be shampooed and set. And the costumes? She made them of the finest materials, with fur and lace and handwork on some, and she sewed them beautifully so they could be cleaned over and over, like a child's own garments.

Then she thought of having a real Doll Hospital and Lifetime Guarantee for the Terri Lee Dolls, where Little Mothers could send them in case anything happened to them, or where they could have new wigs put on them. That's how the Terri Lee Doll Hospital at Apple Valley, California, came to be.

And then the Lovely Lady thought, "Terri ought to have a brother!" So she made Jerri Lee, and designed all sorts of wonderful outfits for him, after that came the rest of the beautiful dolls in the Terri Lee circle, including Linda Baby. Linda Baby is the beautiful baby sister of Terri and Jerri, who is made of Rose-petal Vinyl and looks like Terri, too. There were costumes made for Linda, just like real babies wear.

And then she planned and created the monthly Terri Lee Magazines to send to all Little Mothers; the Birthday Club, the Terri Lee Thrift Club and the wonderful accessories: the Wardrobe Trunks, the Fashion Racks, the Terri Lee Records, the Bassinettes and Play Pen and Nursery Chair for Linda Baby; the Terri Lee Walker and all the rest. There were so many wonderful things to make and it seemed that every little girl wanted them, so there had to be a special place to make all these things. That's how the Terri Lee Doll House in Apple Valley came to be! If you could see the hundreds of wonderful dolls, the thousands of beautiful costumes and accessories in the Doll House, you'd think you were truly in Santa's Palace! There's a Beauty Salon, where Terri's new hair styles are designed and made; the place where each and every Terri, Jerri and Linda's face is specially, separately hand painted on; the rows and rows of Terri Lee dressed in their finest on a shelf for all to see...and everywhere you would feel the Fairyland magic that surrounds all things Terri Lee! Then, finally, she thought how nice it would be to create playmates for this little family of dolls. If you do not know the new members of the Terri Lee family, write us for information. There is Tiny Terri, available in all the costumes that Terri wears; Tiny Jerri, with a special wardrobe too; Connie Lynn...Sleepy Baby, with a very complete wardrobe all her own.

The Lovely Lady waved her magic wand and created all this from her loving thoughts...and she thought of everything, didn't she?"

The above "The Story of Terri Lee" was written for children and is conntained in some of the Terri Lee Fashion booklets with the address of Apple Valley, California. The following is a copy of the cover on one of the Fashion booklets and shows the real Terri, Connie Lynn and Linda.

TERRI LEE FASHION PARADE
Meet the Terri Lee family
The original Connie Lynn, Terri Lee and Linda
Terri Lee SALES CORP.
APPLE VALLEY, CALIFORNIA
Copyright TERRI LEE SALES CORP. 1956


A 1956 booklet has this: "This is the Story of Tiny Terri Lee"

"Terri Lee, as you know, is a real little girl, just like you. However, like all little girls, Terri Lee wished to be something else. So, Terri Lee wished to become a very tiny little girl. Princess Tinkle had given her a magic wishing stone, so Terri Lee rubs the wishing stone and Princess Tinkle appears and makes her into a tiny little doll.

Tiny Terri Lee can walk, she has closing eyes, she has hair that you may shampoo and it still will have a permanent like yours when you have a permanent. Tiny Terri Lee has many beautiful costumes, exactly the same number and kind of costumes as Terri Lee."

There is a dimensional "paper doll" that looks exactly like the 16" Terri Lee except it is about 12" tall. It was made during the early years of the doll and by a company unknown in this line. I have only seen one, and never heard of any more. No doubt there are more and will be seen in other paper doll collections in the future."

Now let us return to the begining and see what we have. Founder and designer (doll) is Mrs. Violet Lee Gradwohl of Lincoln, Nebraska, the "Lovely Lady" of the children's story of the Terri Lee doll. Terri Lee was named after Mrs. Gradwohl's first daughter by the same name. Her second daughter was Linda Lee and a trademark for this name was issued in 1951 (see below) and her third daughter was Connie Lynn.

1946: Lincoln, Nebraska...Terri Lee Doll (Composition) and not trademarked until 1948.

1948: Trademark for Jerri Lee: #528,824 on November 30. Both Terri and Jerri in composition.

1949: Dolls in hard plastic: Colored Bonnie Lu and Benjie and Eskimo Nanook.

1950: Look-a-like paper doll added to line. Patty Jo, character by Jackie Ormes.

1951: Obtained patent (trademark) #618,471 on September 19, for the use of tradename: Linda Lee It is not known if a doll was made but there is labeled clothing for "Linda Lee."

1951: November 10...fire destroys Lincoln operation.

1953: Reopen in Apple Valley, California Terri Lee and Jerri Lee made in early vinyl...the type that becomes "sticky" with age.

1955: Trademark #694,933 was taken out for Connie Lynn (Sept. 19)

1956: Tiny Terri and Jerri Lee were presented to the market.

1957: Trademark #28,667 for So Sleepy on April 22 but not introduced unti 1960.

1960: The factory moved to Glendale, California under the name "Mar-Fan." Introduces So Sleepy and Talking Terri Lee. Re-starts "Friendship Club." Linda Baby added.

1962: Still operating as Mar-Fan, using advertising stating "American made for American Maids." Address was 1708 Standard Street, Glendale, Calif. and Violet Lee Gradwohl is signing company letters as "Vice-President." Exchange heads to make Terri Lee "talk" are offered for $8.00. The doll could be taken to any of the Terri Lee stores and "made to talk."

The exact date that Mar-Fan closed their doors is unknown. It is known that a large California dealer bought the remaining stock.

The Terri Lee Doll Company was plagued with misfortune...some printable and others unprintable. Many rumors still abound. It is known that Mrs. Gradwohl died in 1972 in the State of Virginia.

The Terri Lee doll had a pet. It was a monkey and came as a boy or girl...dressed in boy or girl's clothing. The girl monkey's name is Penelope and the boy monkey's name is Tony. About 4" tall, fur covered except the face is all I can tell you about these pets. Terri Lee's "pet" dress is covered with umbrellas as is Jerri's one piece short suit.

Accessories for Terri Lee include: Trunks, both metal and cardboard. Hair dress kit, Wooden fashion rack/hangers with "Terri Lee" on side. Wardrobe chest, bassinete, walker...metal with rubber tires, with dolls feet placed in base and doll is strapped to stand and as walker is moved, the dolls legs move back and forth, baglets, made of imported kidskin, lamp with picture of Terri Lee, a play pen for Linda Baby, Nursery chair and baby bed...all pieces in wood.

The very early clothes tags were printed on and had a tendency to fray at the end. Late ones are embroidery. Special outfits made included: a full length mink coat, Alice in Wonderland, Scout and Brownie uniforms, Camp Fire and Blue Bird uniforms, masquerade costumes, Hula costume, Dutch girl, Dutch boy and calypso costume, Scotch costume, Nurse and Doctor uniforms, Southern Belle outfit, Engineer suit, along with cowgirl and cowboy outfits and those of



*Refer to Luella Hart's U.S. Tradmarks

cheerleaders and majorettes.

It is known that the Terri Lee Co. bought 15,000 dolls (8") from the Cosmopolitan Doll Co. (Ginger). They were dressed in the uniforms of Girl Scouts, Brownies and Blue Birds. The clothes bear the Terri Lee tag and the box information is included into this section (refer to photo) and contains the Apple Valley address.

The so called 16" "Terri Lee Walker" was actually named "Mary Jane" and has been reported to have been made by three different companies: Richwood Dolls, Cosmopolitan and Reliable of Canada. Someday one will show up that is in the original box and we will know for sure who made her. I have had 5 of them and all had black hair and very black eyebrows. A picture is included in the color section.

To sum up, the Terri Lee Company could be said to have gone out of business because of their guarantee! The doll is so indestructible as to last a life time...but some did break, many had to be restrung and repainted plus thousands of wigs had to be replaced. The only things that seemed to be left out of the guarantee was parts lost, chewed by a dog or covered with nail polish and crayons. Each doll came with an "Admission Card" to the Terri Lee Hospital. Repairs had to be taken care of because the reputation of the doll stood on the guarantee of the company.

There are reports of someone having made a mold from an original Terri Lee during the years of 1952 and 1955. This may be true as we have found Terri Lee dolls that are slightly smaller than the official ones and this would indicate a mold being taken from a doll itself. I will show the one belonging to Marge Meisinger for comparison.

Terri Lee--Mrs. Reatha Jackson reports that when her daughter was seven in 1954, she bought her a "Mary Jane" and in 1955 a friend wanted one for her daughter so Mrs. Jackson returned to the store to buy one and was told by the store manager that they were no longer being made. He said a woman who had worked at the Terri Lee factory had designed the "Mary Jane" but was made to stop production. To date we have no other information.

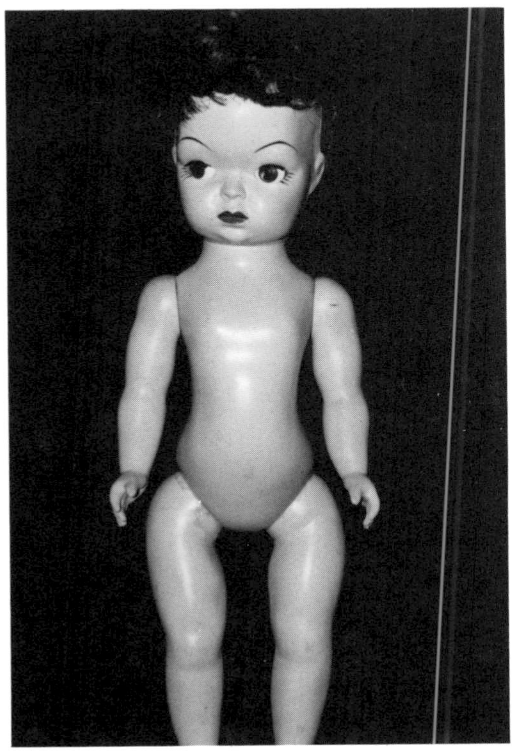

Terri Lee--16" "Mary Jane" All hard plastic. Flirty, blue sleep eyes. Walker, head turns. Has long plastic lashes. Marks: None. (Courtesy Marie Ernst)

# Terri Lee Family

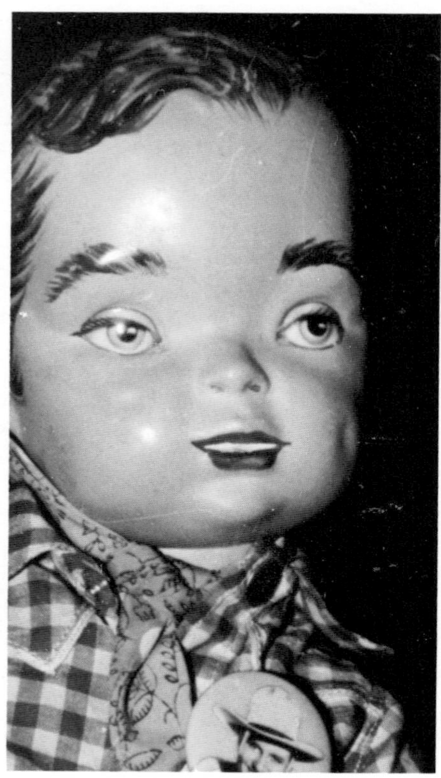

Terri Lee--16" "Gene Autry" All rigid plastic. Hand painted. Marks: Terri Lee/Pats. Pending, on back. $165.00.

Terri Lee--"Talking Terri Lee." See Series I, Terri Lee section for full description. "Jack" at base of neck in back. $50.00.

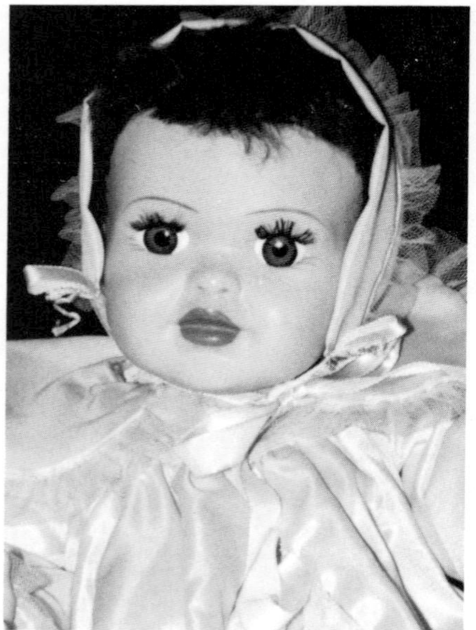

Terri Lee--"Connie Lynn" All rigid plastic. Inset eyes with long lashes. Caracul wig. $45.00. (Courtesy Jay Minter)

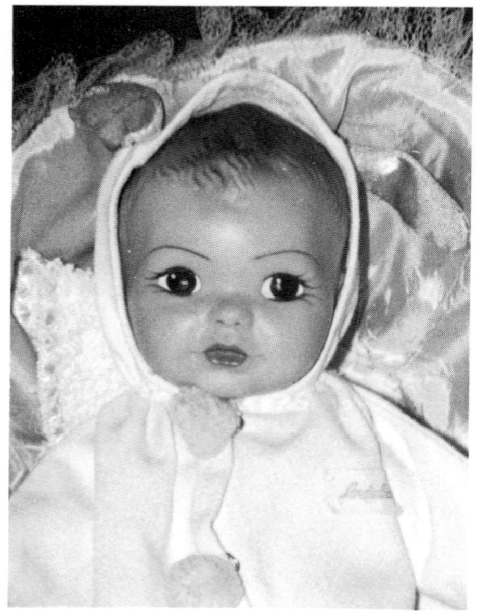

Terri Lee--All original "Linda Baby" All vinyl. $35.00. (Courtesy Jay Minter)

Terri Lee--7½" "Girl Scout" All hard plastic. Walker, head turns. Blue sleep eyes/long molded lashes. Tagged Terri Lee uniform. This is "Ginger" by Cosmopolitan. (Courtesy Bessie Carson)

Terri Lee--7½" "Brownie" Close up of "Ginger" face.

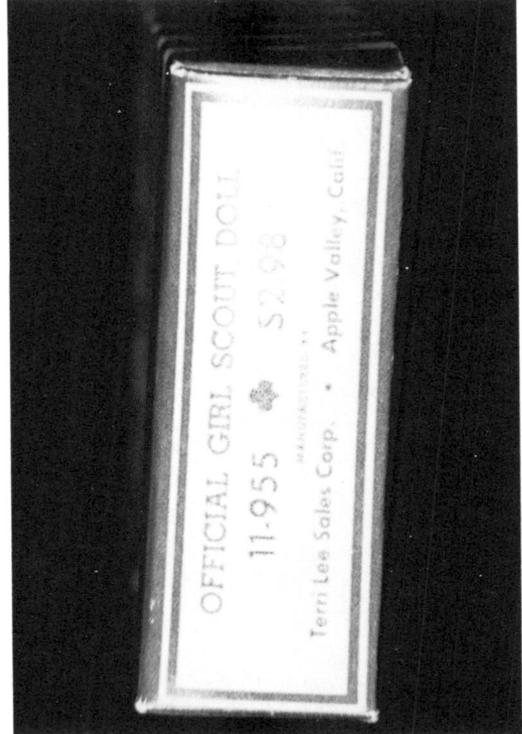


Terri Lee--Shows box end of the Terri Lee Scout doll, made by Cosmopolitan (Ginger). (Courtesy Bessie Carson)

## Terri Lee Prices

16" Terri Lee $35.00; Compo, $45.00; Colored, $45.00; Brown, $45.00; Oriental, $50.00
16" Jerri Lee, $50.00; Colored, $60.00; Brown, $60.00; Oriental, $65.00
16" Early Terri Lee in vinyl. Weights in feet. $35.00.
10" Tiny Terri Lee $25.00.
10" Tiny Jerri Lee $35.00.
12" Linda Lee. All early vinyl, $55.00.
9½" So Sleepy, $30.00.

Terri Lee--1 inch "Terri Lee Friendship Club pin." (Courtesy Bessie Carson)

Terri Lee--Terri and Jerri Lee's Pet. The monkey dressed as a girl is "Penelope" and the one dressed as a boy is "Tony."

Terri Lee--Terri Lee shown with her pet monkey which could be either Penelope or Tony. Clothes are gone except shoes.

Terri Lee--16" "Terri Lee" shown in an original trunk. Trunk is metal and red with white boarder trim. (Courtesy Irene Gann)

Terri Lee--Box top showing Terri Lee Fashions. (Courtesy Bessie Carson)

Terri Lee--Terri Lee Fashion Pac containing sleepwear tagged "Linda Baby and Connie Lynn"

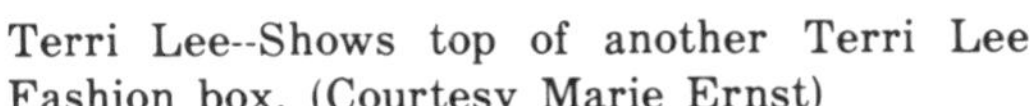
Terri Lee--Shows top of another Terri Lee Fashion box. (Courtesy Marie Ernst)

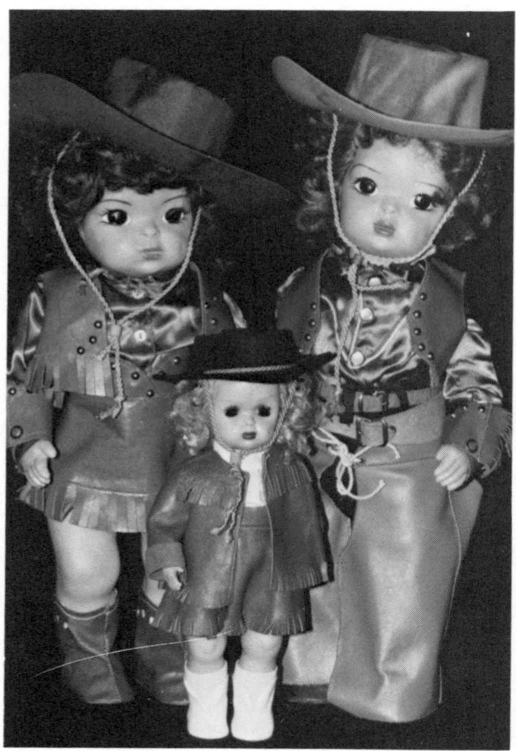

Terri Lee--Shows the Fake Terri Lee, the real 16" one and the Tiny Terri Lee, all in original Terri Lee western outfits. (Courtesy Marge Meisinger)

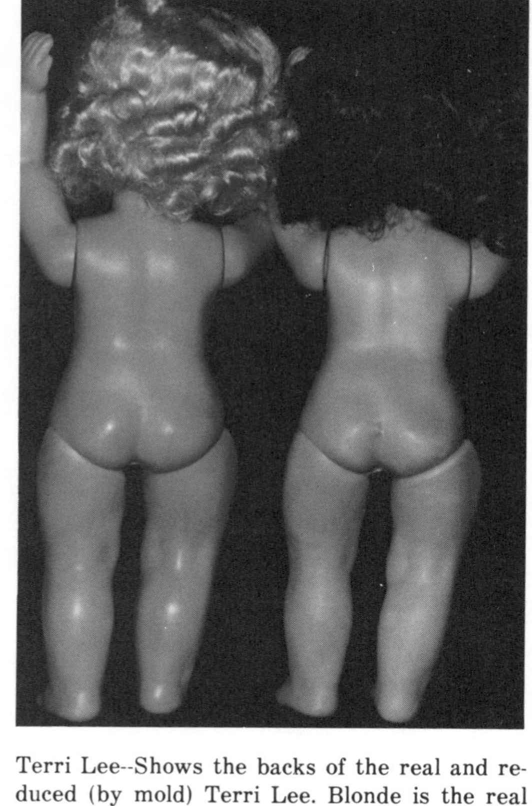

Terri Lee--Shows the backs of the real and reduced (by mold) Terri Lee. Blonde is the real one. Real: 9¾" at waist, 5½" at calf and is 16" tall. Fake: 9¼" at waist, 5¼" at calfs and is 15½" tall and has holes in feet. (Courtesy Marge Meisinger)

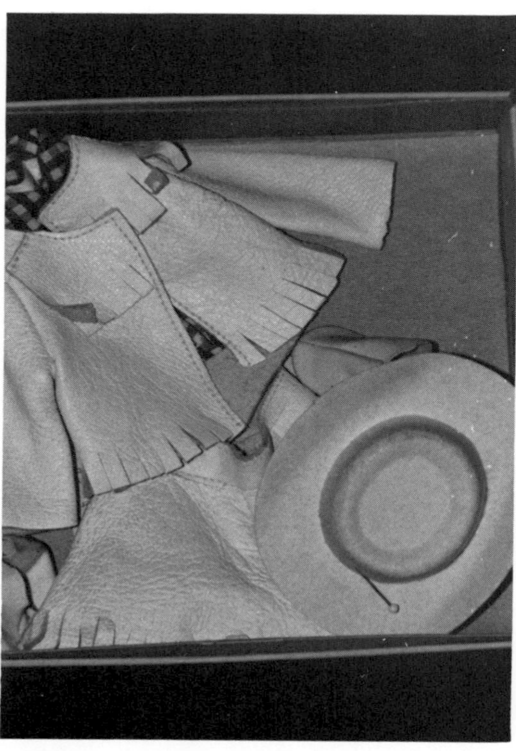

Terri Lee--Tiny Terri Lee's original boxed white cowgirl outfit. (Courtesy Marge Meisinger)

Terri Lee--Terri Lee as Cowgirl. Dark green satin shirt. White leather skirt and vest. (Courtesy Irene Gann)

Terri Lee--10" "Tiny Terri Lee" Shown in her original case. Red checkered and made of pressed carboard. (Courtesy Laura Gann)

Terri Lee--16" "Terri Lee" Shown in her real mink coat. I have heard a price tag of $300.00 for this coat but seems more reasonable that it was a lot less.

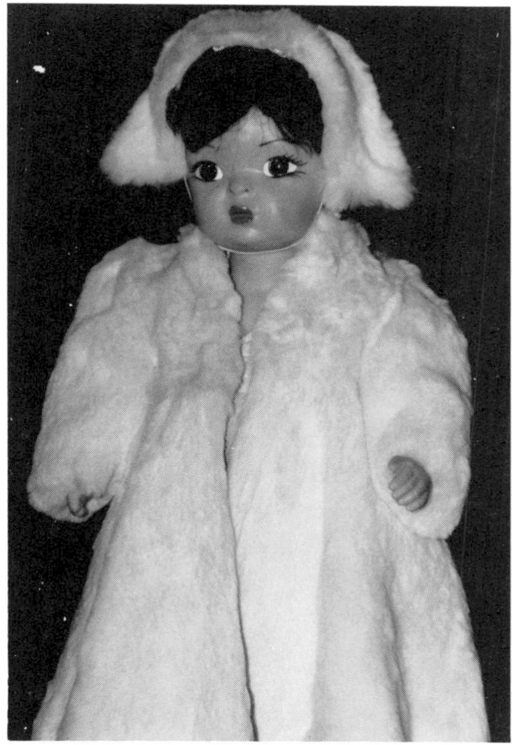

Terri Lee--Shows Terri Lee in an original full length coat of white fur and cap. (Courtesy Marge Meisinger)

Terri Lee--Shows Terri lee in her original full length blue coat. (Courtesy Marge Meisinger)

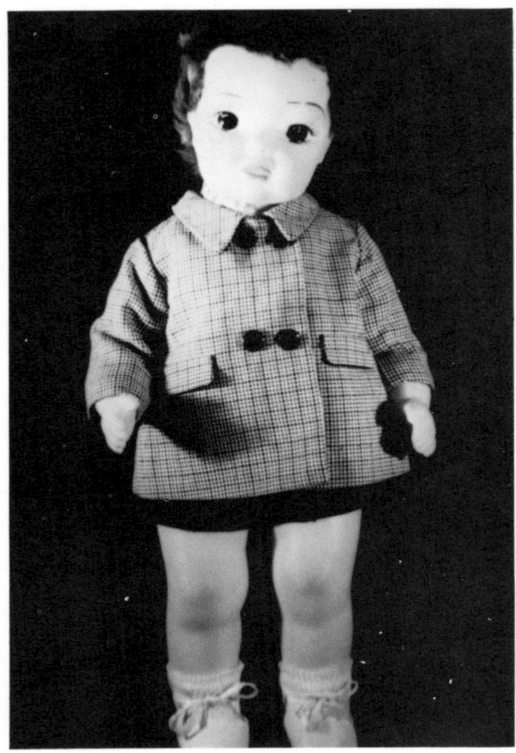

Terri Lee--Jerri Lee in Spring Coat #3590. Black/blue check on white. Black buttons. Navy lining.

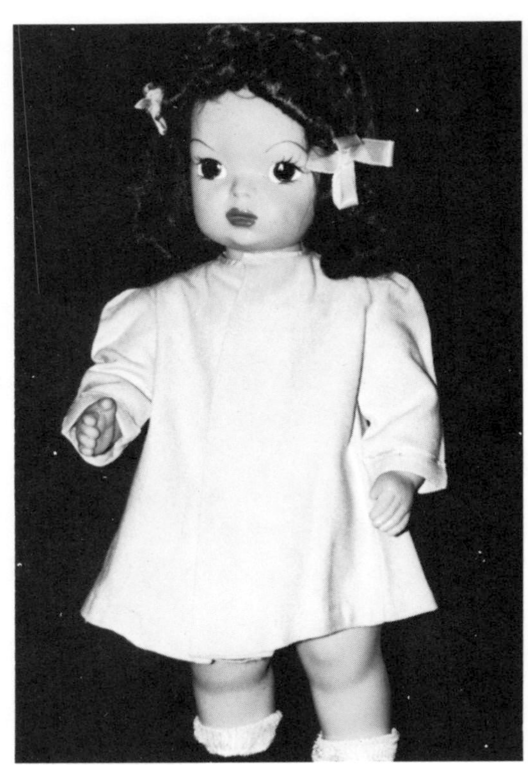

Terri Lee--Early pink coat with pale blue piping.

Terri Lee--White coat and bonnet with red lamb and trim. May belong to Connie Lynn although tag is for Terri Lee.

Terri Lee--Terri Lee in red with white polka dots rain coat/hood. #1839. (Courtesy Irene Gann)

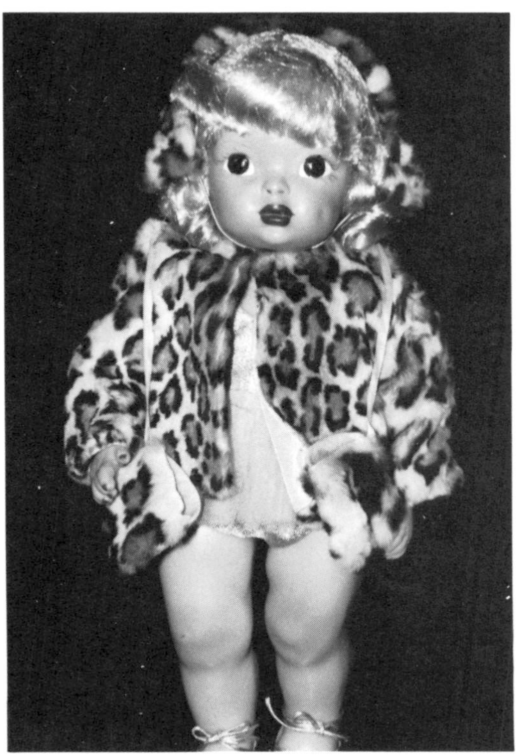

Terri Lee--This is Terri Lee's original fur jacket, cap and muff. (Courtesy Marge Meisinger)

Terri Lee--#3504. Pale aqua with white cuffs. White blouse.

Terri Lee--Pale rose formal with pink overnet skirt.

Terri Lee--Pink and lavender flowers on a pink formal.

Terri Lee--#1380 Bridesmaid dress of pale pink. Pink flowers in head band. (Dress courtesy Mary Partridge)

Terri Lee--Yellow with yellow flowers and black sequin trim and ribbon tie.

Terri Lee--#3560P. White blouse with lace trim. Navy pleated skirt.

Terri Lee--Navy blue dress with white color and cuffs. White flowers on end of belt.

Terri Lee--#3520F Pique sport dress with matching panties. Navy blue/white. White plastic belt is missing.

Terri Lee--#3519D Play Dress. Blue with rose sleeves and collar. Birds on dress are rose and pale blue/white.

Terri lee--Terri Lee in #3332 and 1357 Organdy Party Dress. Hat missing. Pale blue with white collar and small flowers.

Terri Lee--Terri Lee in pinafore #3520H and 1316. Pale pink with white shoulder straps. Pink ribbon at waist.

Terri Lee--Red polka dots on top. Rest red. White/red polka dot matching panties.

Terri Lee--Terri Lee in school dress. All red with white collar. (Courtesy Irene Gann)

Terri Lee--Terri Lee in her rose-pink dress with white lace trim. "School Dress" #T-1330. (Courtesy Irene Gann)

Terri Lee--#4520F. Sport Set. White top with red dots. Navy pants.

Terri Lee--#4311. Red/white checkered shirt. Navy blue jeans. Brown belt.

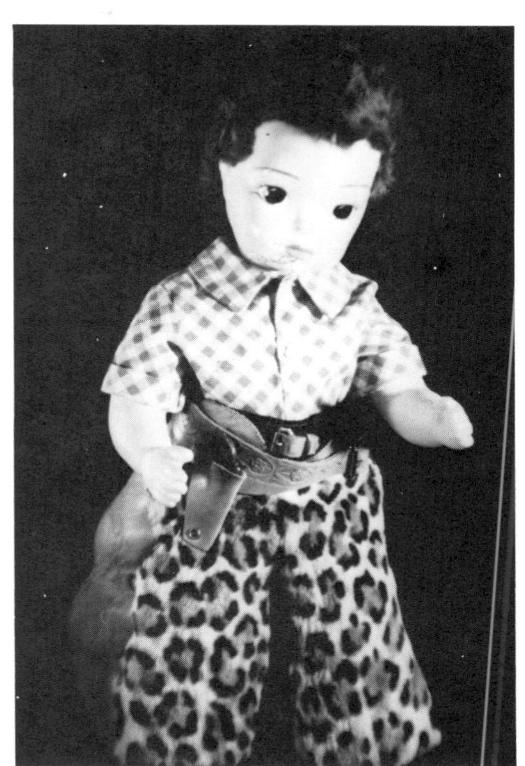

Terri Lee--#4311 plus chaps and gun belt.

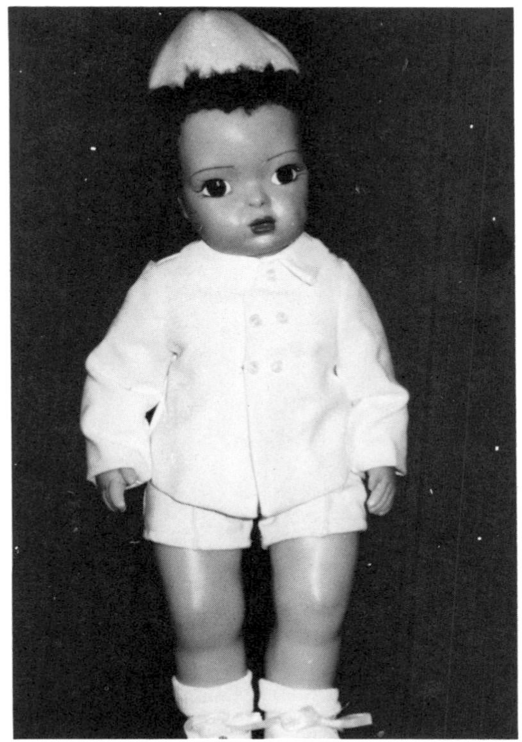

Terri Lee--Jerri Lee in white Summer Suit. #2321.

Terri Lee--Terri Lee in #35401 Brownie uniform. Belt and tam missing. Also #3351 and 1351.

Terri Lee--#3520C Pedal Pushers. Blue denim with red/white checks.

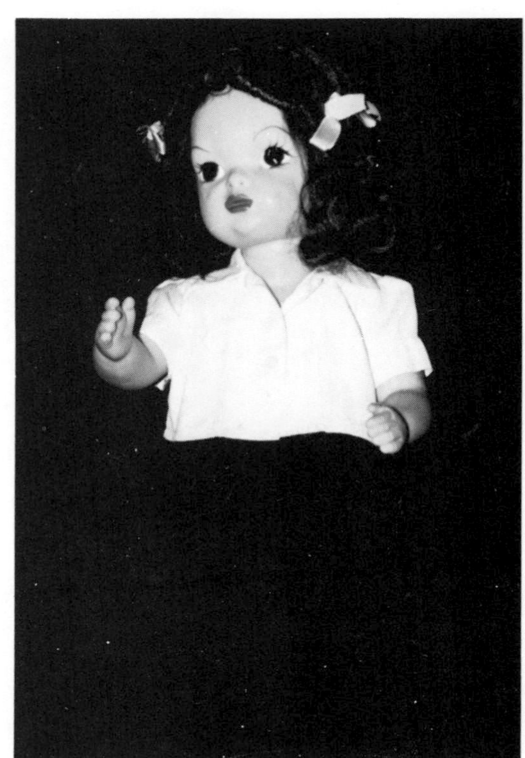

Terri Lee--White short waisted blouse (cotton) and blue jeans.

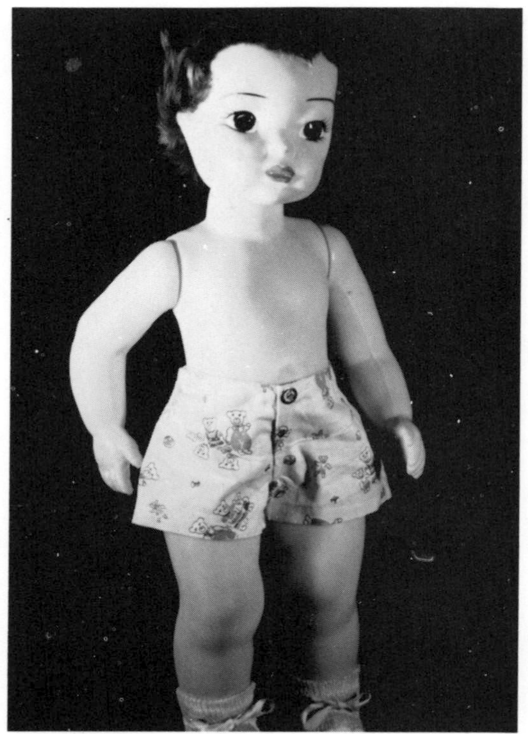

Terri Lee--Jerri Lee in shorts #4300 and 2300.

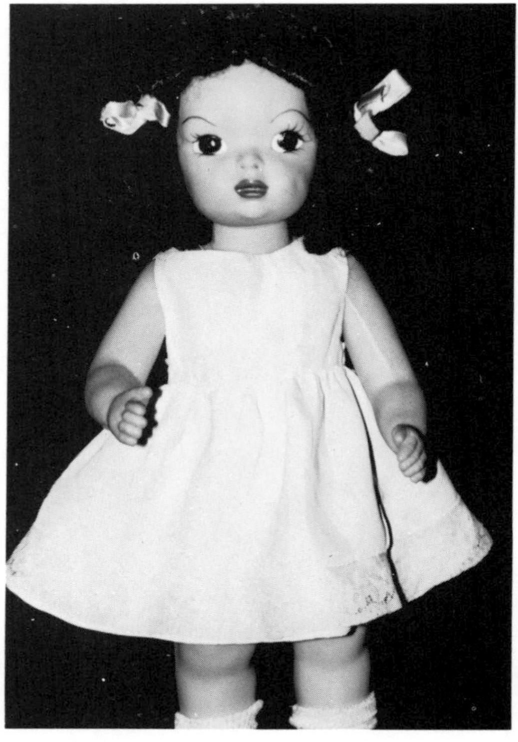

Terri Lee--Terri Lee in slip #510G. Pink.

Terri Lee--Can Can #500C. Pink.

Terri Lee--Terri Lee in red/white checkered sundress. (Courtesy Irene Gann)

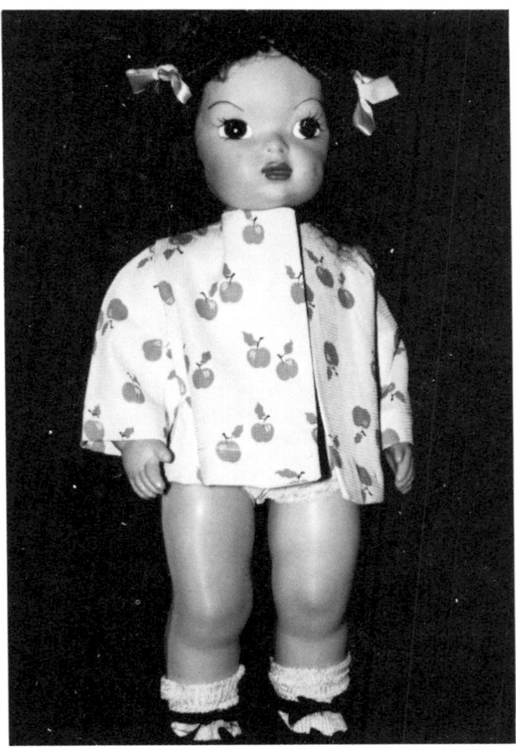

Terri Lee--#3311. Beach jacket. White with orange/blue apples.

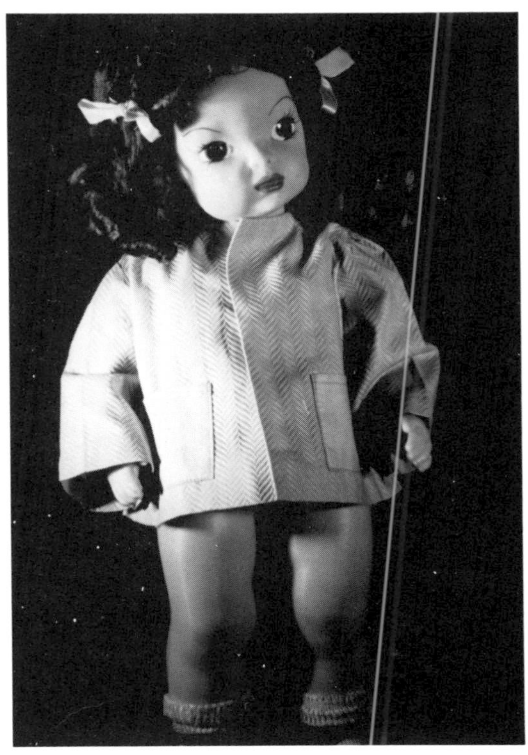

Terri Lee--#3310. Beach jacket of light blue.

Terri Lee--16" "Terri Lee" in dark green bathing suit with white trim. Green dark glasses. (Courtesy Irene Gann)

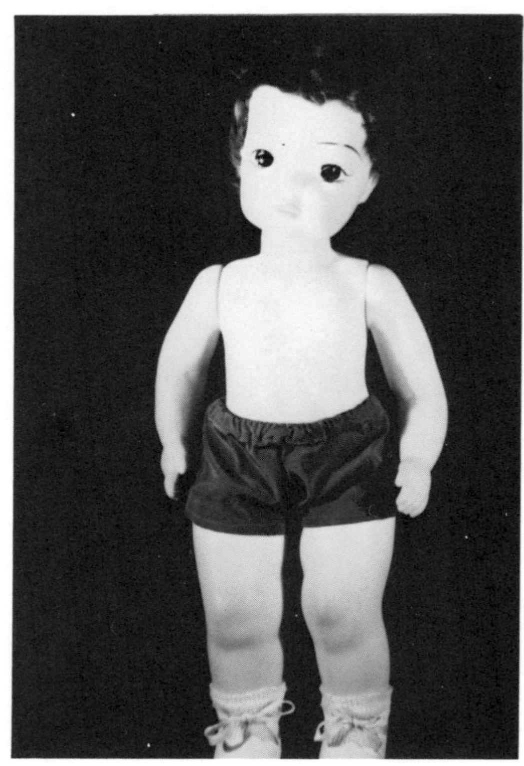

Terri Lee--#4301. Swim trunks that are royal blue.

Terri Lee--Terri Lee in pajamas with lavender roses. (Courtesy Irene Gann)

Terri Lee--Terri Lee in her pink Terry Cloth bathrobe. (Courtesy Irene Gann)

Terri Lee--Terri Lee in pedal pushers. Lavender/white checkered top and cuffs. Lavender pants. (Courtesy Irene Gann)

Terri Lee--Terri Lee in her original Hawaiian outfit. (Courtesy Marge Meisinger)

Terri Lee--16" "Jerri Lee in original Davy Crockett outfit. (Courtesy Marge Meisinger)

Terri Lee--Terri Lee has on Tea Party Dress, minus purse. #1367. Pale yellow with white insert down front. Jerri Lee has on pink pants/tam. Blue/pink/black stripe on cap bill and jacket.

Terri Lee--Terri in one piece pink chamise. Jerri in two piece shorts and T shirt of white with pink trim.

Terri Lee--Terri Lee is in pink dress with white polka dots and white insert. Jerri Lee has on an aqua #2306 suit with black stripes.

Terri Lee--Terri Lee in Birthday Dress. White with blue/white checkered top and half sleeves. Attached slip. Jerri Lee has on orange pants. Yellow shirt with orange collar. Carrots and rabbits on top are orange and grey.

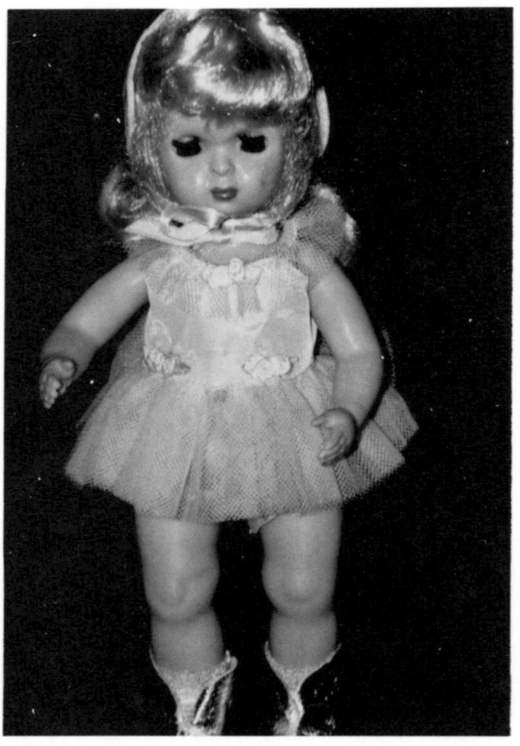

Terri Lee--Tiny Terri Lee in her ballerina outfit and shows her roller skates. (Courtesy Marge Meisinger)

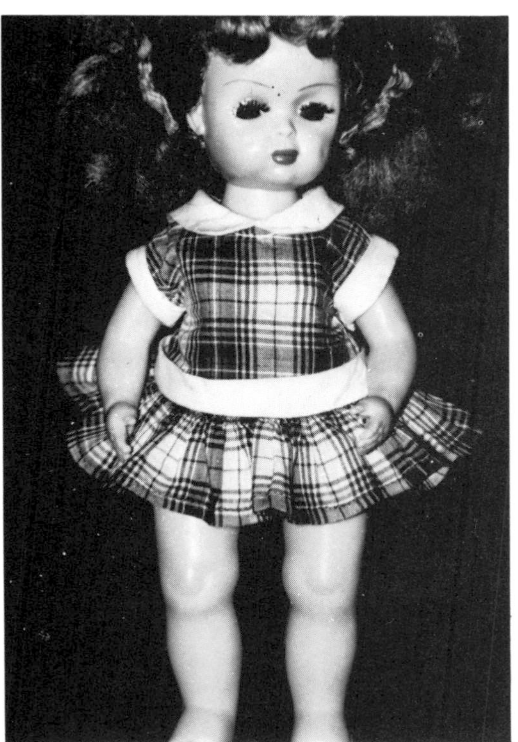

Terri Lee--Tiny Terri Lee in #3335 "School Dress" Red/green/blue/checkered with white trim. (Courtesy Laura Gann)

Terri Lee--Tiny Terri Lee shown in her original Majorette outfit. (Courtesy Marge Meisinger)

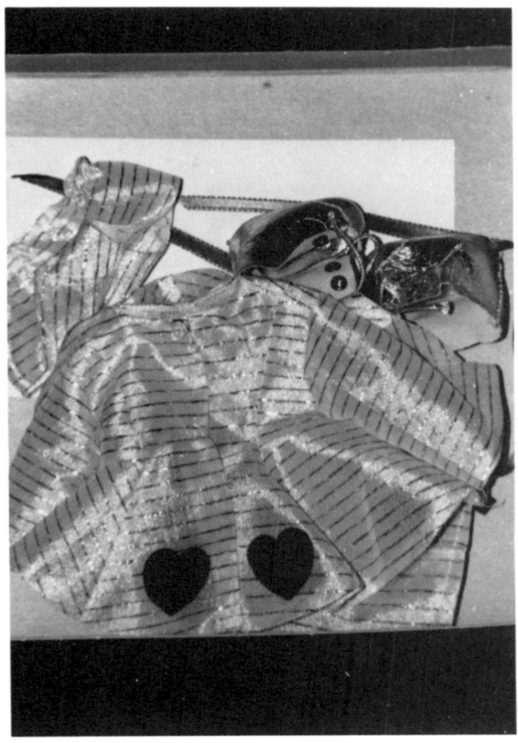

Terri Lee--Tiny Terri Lee's Ice Skating outfit shown in original box. (Courtesy Marge Meisinger)

Terri Lee--Tiny Terri Lee in one of her original Bride outfits. (Courtesy Marge Meisinger)

Terri Lee--Tiny Terri Lee in #TT3321 "Squaw Dress." Navy blue. 2 piece. (Courtesy Laura Gann)

Terri Lee--Tiny Terri Lee in Pinafore Party #3316. Pink with white top. Pink panties. (Courtesy Laura Gann)

Terri Lee--Tiny Terri Lee in her #3805 Clown pajamas. (Courtesy Laura Gann)

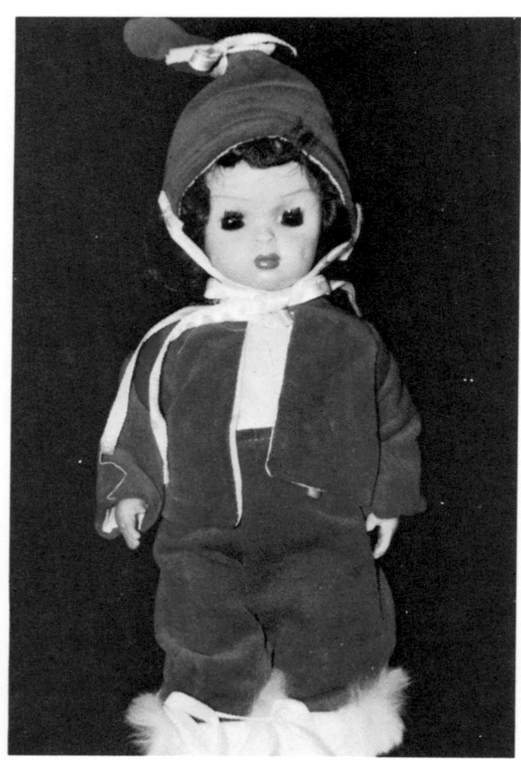

Terri Lee--Tiny Terri Lee in an original snow suit. (Courtesy Marge Meisinger)

Terri Lee--Tiny Terri Lee in her Cowgirl Outfit. Hat and shoes missing. Blue/white with brown plastic trim. (Courtesy Laura Gann)

Togs and Dolls--12" "Penny Walker" All hard plastic with glued on brown hair. Chubby build. Blue sleep eyes. Walker, head turns. Marks: Pat. Pend., on head. Tag: Penny Walker. Box: Togs & Dolls Corp/New York 1, NY/Factory at Greensboro N.C. 1951. $8.00. (Courtesy Virginia Jones)

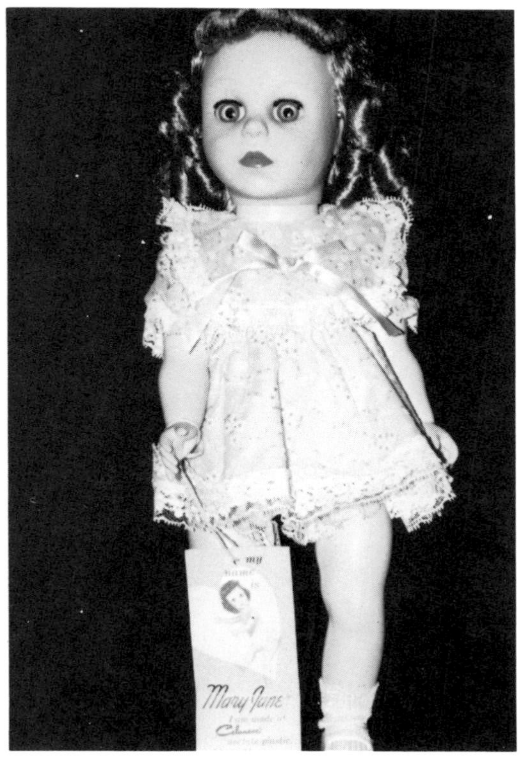


Togs and Dolls--17" "Mary Jane" Hard plastic walker, head turns. Arms only raise to shoulder high. Vinyl head. Blue sleep eyes/lashes. Marks: None. Tag: My Name is/Mary Jane. I am made of Celanese/Acetate Plastic. I have 36 pretty outfits. $45.00.

Togs and Dolls--Close up of 17" "Mary Jane" head.

Tomy--12½" "Ricky" Tin body and legs. Plastic non-removable shoes. Pants glued on. Vinyl arms, holding bell. Vinyl head. Molded hair. Painted blue eyes. Walker (battery), bell rings. Marks: Box: Ricky the Walking Toddler/By Amico. Paper label on back has drawing of boy and girl/Tomy/Made in Japan. $8.00. (Courtesy Edith DeAngelo)

UFS--16" "Charlie Brown" Blow up balloon type doll. Marks: 1969 United Feature Syndicate Inc. $2.00.

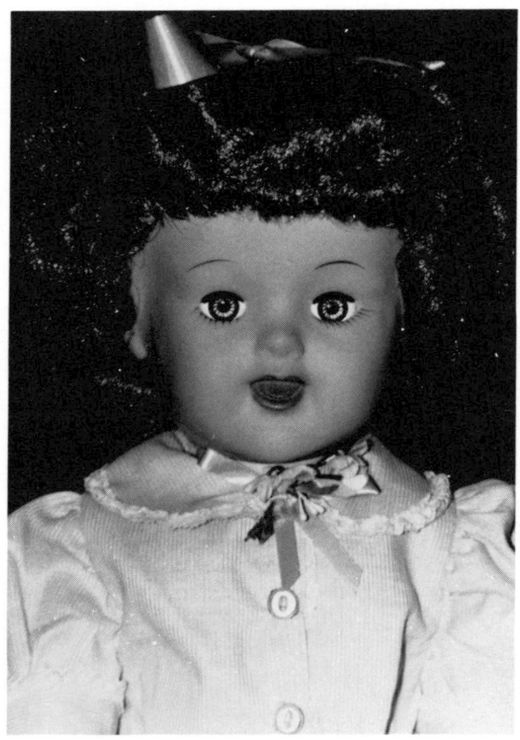

Uneeda--21" "Toddles" Hard plastic walker. Original clothes. Vinyl head. Blue sleep eyes. Wide open/closed mouth. Marks: Uneeda, on head. $9.00. (Courtesy Alice Capps)

Information on the Uneeda Doll Co. will be found in Series I, page 279.

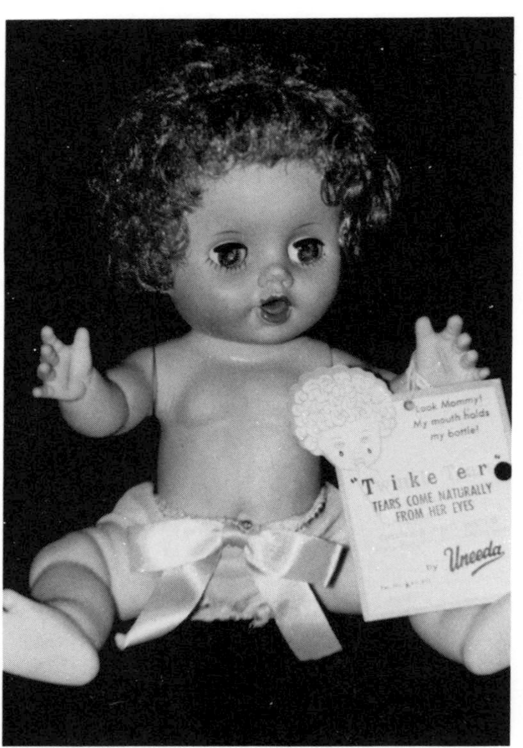


Uneeda--12" "Twinkle Tears" All vinyl. Mouth designed to hold bottle without hands. After "feeding," sit doll up and slightly forward and squeeze body and tears will start. Original. Same doll as "Yummy" but without "sucking" mechanism. 1961. Marks: None. $3.00. (Courtesy Edith DeAngelo)

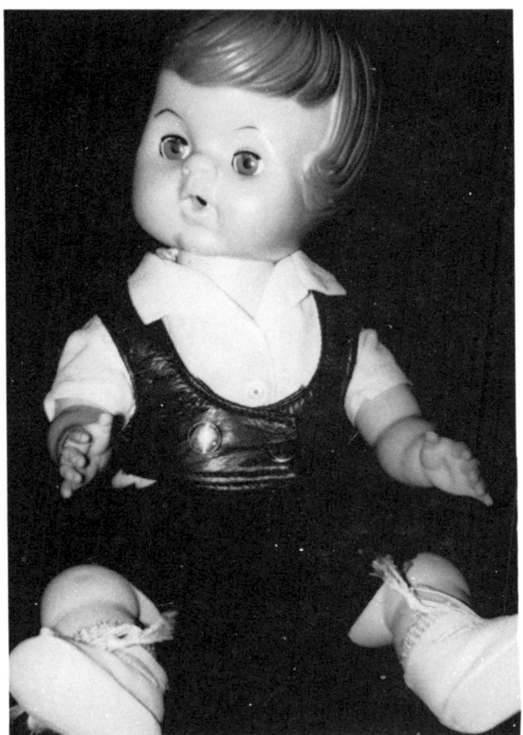

Uneeda--11" "Twins" Came as boy or girl. Plastic and vinyl. Molded hair. Bright blue sleep eyes/molded lashes. Open mouth/nurser. Bent baby legs. Marks:11/Uneeda/1965. $4.00. (Courtesy Bessie Carson)

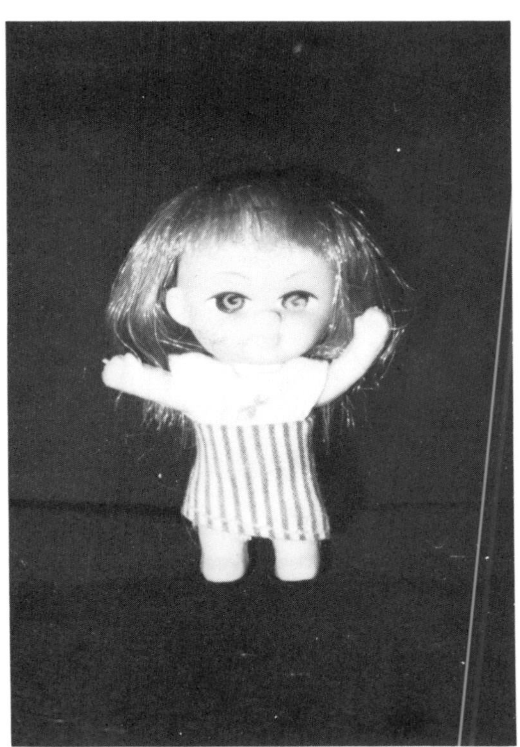

Uneeda--2½" "Nurse Keywee" Sold in pocket purse with key chain. 1968. Marks: None. $2.00.

Uneeda--3" "Troll" All vinyl with red mohair. Inset yellow eyes. Dressed in Pee Wee outfit called Gardentime. 1966. $2.00.

Uneeda--6" "Troll Wishnik" Lavender hair. Jointed neck only. All vinyl. Marks: Uneeda/Wish-Nik TM/Pat. #. $2.00.

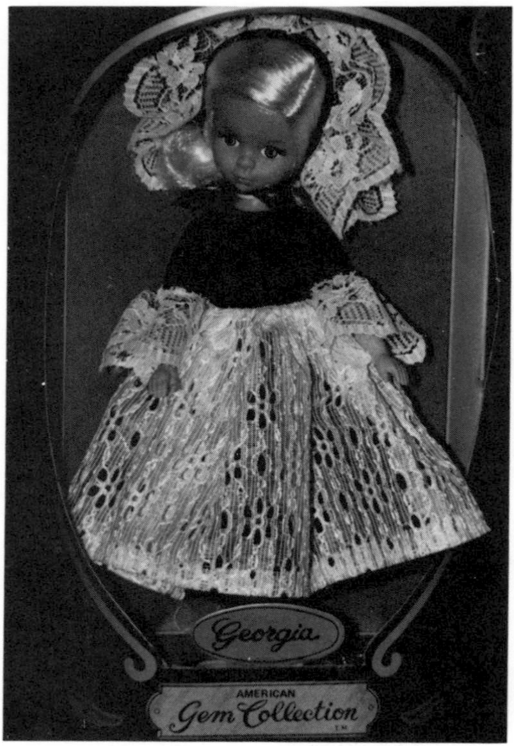


Uneeda--8½" "Georgia" Blue eyes. White hair. Marks: U.D.Co. Inc./MCMLXXI/Made in Hong Kong, head and body. Box: MCMLXIV/Dist. 1975. American Gem Collection. Available in some areas.

Uneeda--8½" "Carolina" Blue eyes. White hair. American Gem Collection. Available in some areas.

Uneeda--8½" "Patience" Blue eyes. Brown hair. American Gem Collection. Available in some areas.

Uneeda--8½" "Prudence" Blue eyes. Red hair. American Gem Collection. Available in some areas.

Uneeda--8½" "Priscilla" Blue eyes. Brown hair. American Gem Collection. Available in some areas.

Uneeda--8½" "Virginia" Blue eyes. Blonde hair. American Gem Collection. Available in some areas.

Uneeda--6" "Tiny Penelope" Vinyl head with freckles and orange rooted hair. Soft filled body. Removable dress. Marks: UD Co. Inc./MCML-XXIV/Hong Kong, on head. Tag: Undeeda. $2.00.

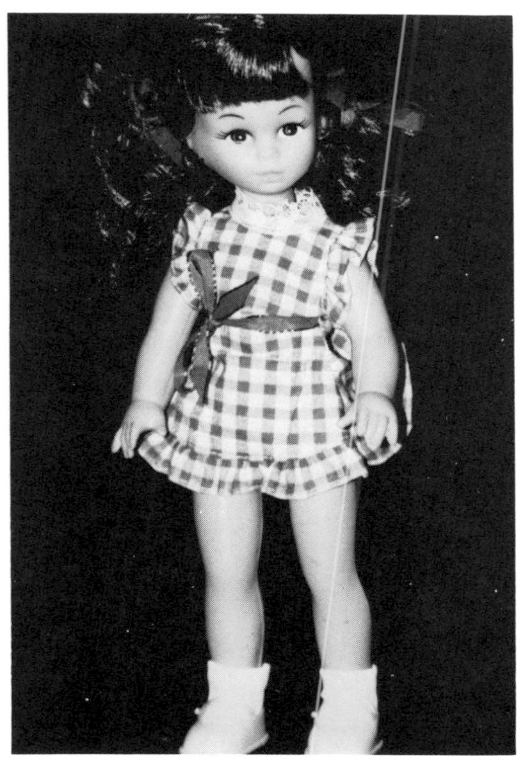

Uneeda--10" "Clover" Plastic with vinyl head. Head sockets into body. Original. Marks: Hong Kong, on back. Available in some areas. (Courtesy Marie Ernst)

Uneeda--6" "Grannykins" Plastic with vinyl arms and head. Black/grey hair. Painted blue eyes with painted on glasses. Original. Marks: U.D. Co. Inc./MCMLXXIV/Hong Kong, on head. Available in some areas. (Courtesy Marie Ernst)

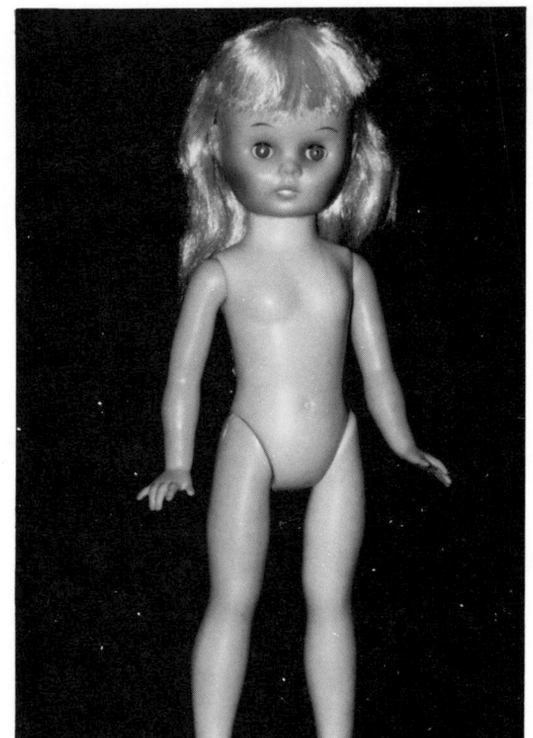

Unique--15" "Margie" Plastic and vinyl with rooted blonde hair. Blue sleep eyes/molded lashes. Marks: Unique/19. This is the same doll as the late and last Mary Hoyer dolls. $2.00.

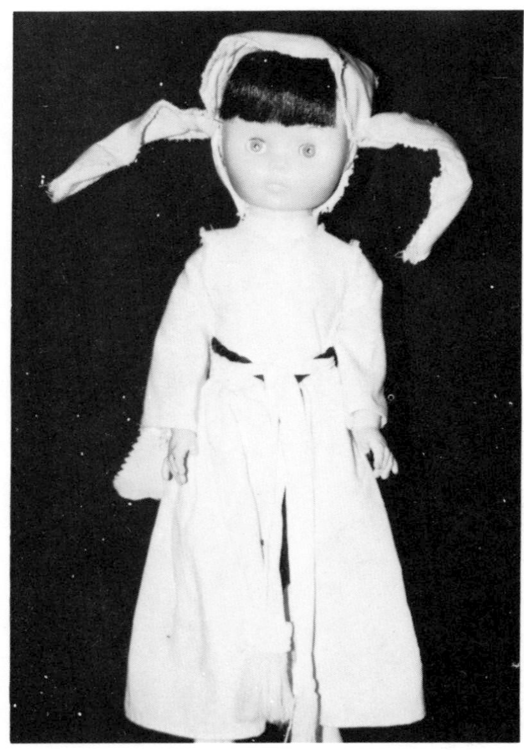

Unique--16" "Flying Nun" Plastic and vinyl. One row of rooted hair in front. Blue sleep eyes/ molded lashes. Original. Marks: Unique/11, on head. $6.00. (Courtesy Virginia Jones)

Universal--"Springtime Family" 9" man, $8^{1/2}$" woman and 3" baby. Man: brown eyes, with or without mustache (painted) plastic and vinyl. Marks: Hong Kong, head and Universal Associated Co. Ltd. vertically down back. Baby has jointed neck only, blue eyes and is smiling. Baby is marked: H.K. in square/Hong Kong, on back. Made for S.S. Kresge. 1975. Still available.

Valentine--14" "Margie Ann" Hard plastic head with glued on blonde wig. Blue sleep eyes. Open/closed mouth. 1949. Marks: 128, on back. $7.00.

Valentine--11½" All hard plastic. Blue sleep eyes/long molded lashes. This doll was used in the "Mona Lisa" series and they were dressed in long gowns. Marks: 12, on head. 12/Made in USA, on back. $6.00. (Courtesy Marie Ernst)

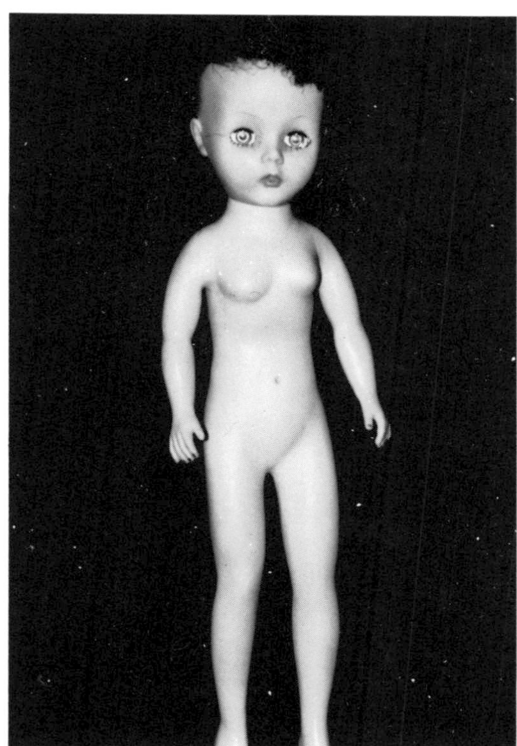

Valentine--13" One piece stuffed vinyl. Marks: AE1406/46, on head. V, on lower back. V-15, back of arms. $5.00.

Valentine--19" "Debbie Reynolds" As grown up "Tammy." All hard plastic. Open mouth/5 teeth. Blue sleep eyes. Red lips/nails. Walker, head turns. Mid high heel feet. Jointed knees/ankles. Pale golden blonde hair glued on. Marks: Made in U.S.A., back. Medium blue on pale blue/white lace trim. (Courtesy Mary Partridge)

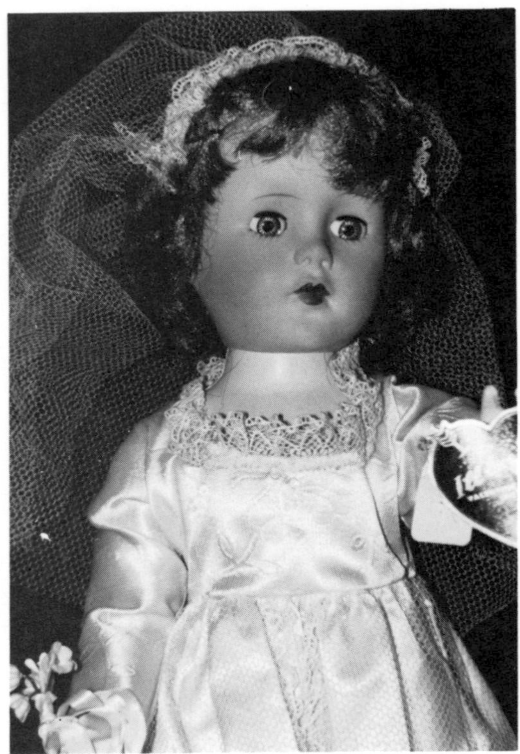

Valentine--18" "Bride" A Mona Lisa Doll. Hard plastic with vinyl head. Blue sleep eyes. Pin jointed hips with rivets. Walker, head turns. Left arm socketed to raise shoulder height only. Original. Marks: Made in USA, on back. 17 VW, on head. Tag: I'll Love You/Valentine Dolls, Inc. $8.00. (Courtesy Edith DeAngelo)

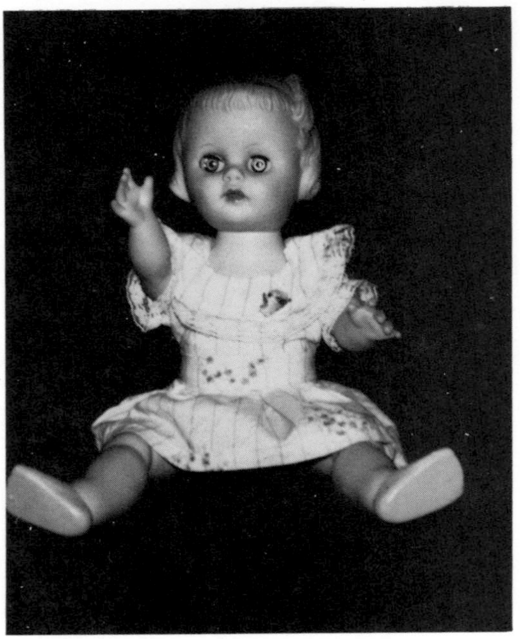

Valentine--15½" "Connie" Plastic with vinyl arms and head. Molded curls with molded hair bow. Manufactured by Eegee for Natural Doll Co. 1963. (Courtesy Carolyn Powers)

Valentine--14" "Ballerina" Hard plastic with vinyl head. Rooted ash blonde hair. Blue sleep eyes. Jointed ankles. Original. Marks: AE, on head. Made in USA/Pat. Pending, on back. 1955.

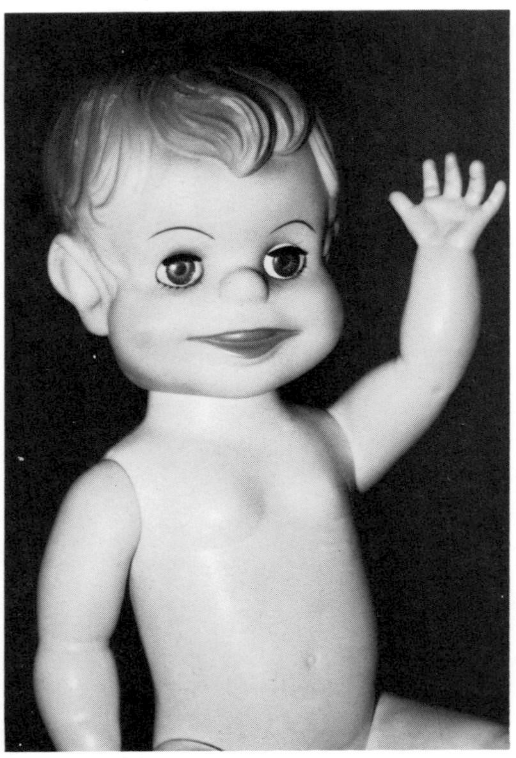

Valentine--15" "Patient" All vinyl. Blue sleep eyes. Open/closed mouth. Same head used for "Dondi" with hair painted black and teeth painted in. This issue was put out with "hospital" items and sold as "Perfect Patient." 1957.

Valentine--15" "Bonnnie" Plastic and vinyl. White rooted hair. Blue sleep eyes. 1964. "Bonnie" was issued as a baby, toddler and teen. $6.00.

Valentine--30" "Susy Walker" Sold through Speigel's in 1960. Plastic and vinyl. Blue sleep eyes. Widespread legs. Marks: AE/3006/16, on head. $18.00. (Courtesy Phyllis Houston)

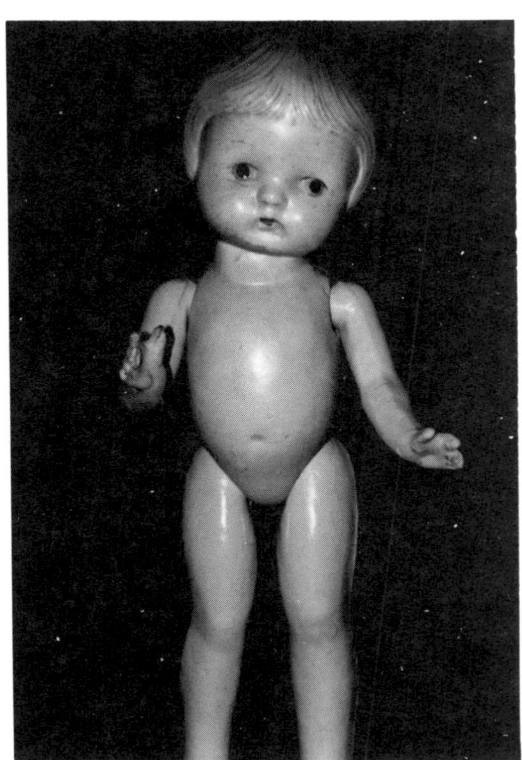

Vanity Doll--11" "Paula" All composition. Bent right arm. Second and third fingers molded together. Blonde molded hair. Painted blue eyes. Marks: None. (Courtesy Mary Partridge)

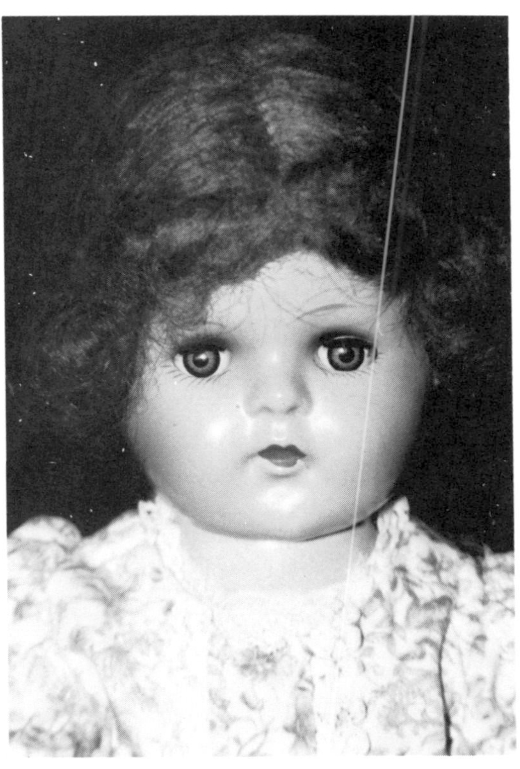

Vanity Doll--13½" "Peggy Ann" (also came in 15" size). All composition. Bent right arm. Brown sleep tin eyes. 1941. Marks: None. (Courtesy Maxine Heitt)

Wood--6" "Girl Scout" and "Brownie" All wood. Nodder type heads. Marks: Japanese, in script on bottom. $3.00. (Courtesy Ellie Haynes)

Wood--2" "Seattle Pioneer Woman/Man, Early 1850's." Carve/painted wood. These miniatures were designed/produced by Mrs. John R. Bringloe, member of the Research Committee of the Seattle Historical Society. Funds from sales further work of the Committee. $15.00 pair. (Courtesy Frances and Mary Jane Anicello)

Wood--3" "Dutch Boy & Girl" All wood. Springs for necks and part of arms. Metal buckets. Braids are stiffened string. Marks: Made/Goula/ In Spain, on feet. $6.00. (Courtesy Frances and Mary Jane Anicello)

Wood--2¾" All wood. Carved from one piece. Unjointed. All painted. Marks: None. $12.00. (Courtesy Frances and Mary Jane Anicello)

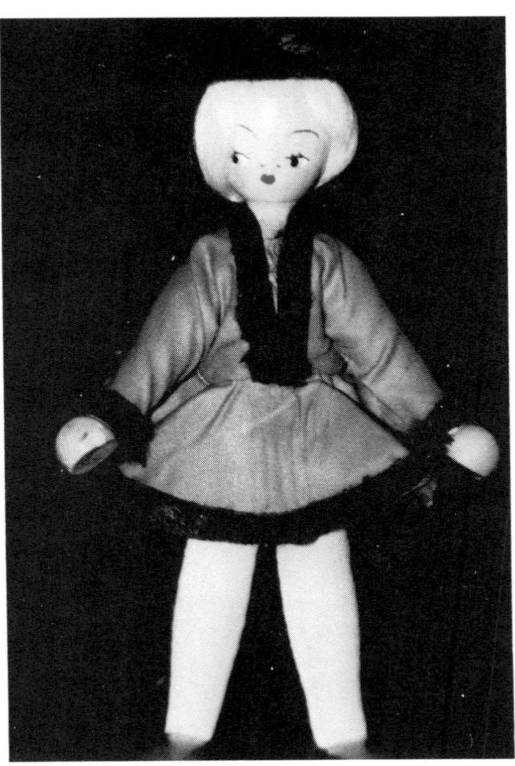

Wood--7¼" "Miski Dancer" All wood. One piece body and head. Painted features. Glued on hair. Non-removable clothes. Marks: Paper tag: Made/In/Poland. (Courtesy Mary Partridge)

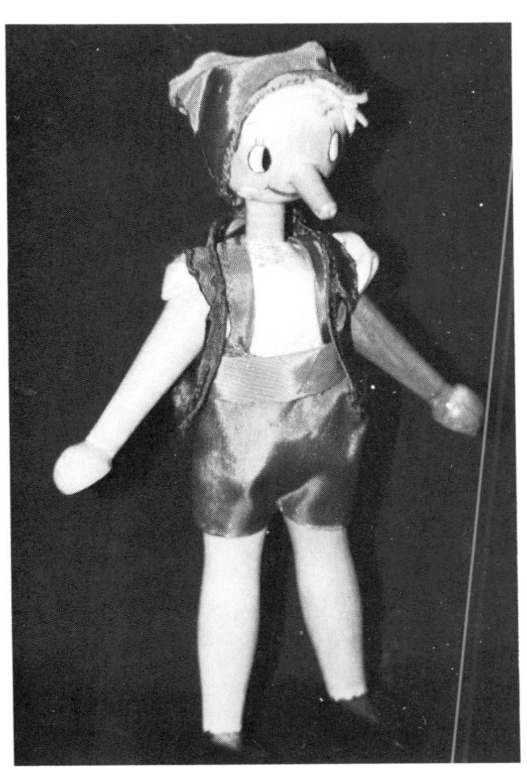

Wood--7½" "Pinochio" All wood. Removable clothes. Yellow yarn hair. Jointed shoulder and hips only. Original. Marks: Pinochio, one foot and Poland, other foot. (Courtesy Mary Partridge)

Wood--9" "Skater" All wood. Jointed shoulders and hips. Non-removable clothes. Marks: None. Sticker: Made in Poland. (Courtesy Ellie Haynes)

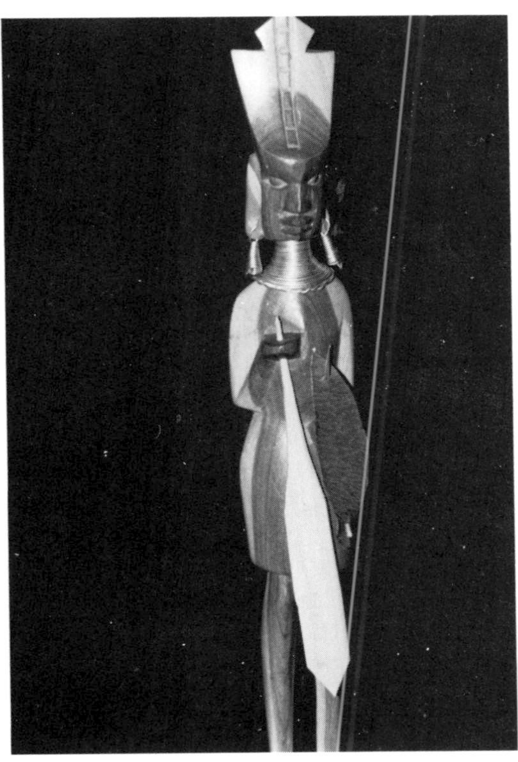

Wood--12" Carved from one piece of wood. Earrings and neck piece are wire. Hide shield and wood spear. From Kenya. (Courtesy Ellie Haynes)

Wood--11" "Koheshi Doll" All wood. Painted features and scene. Dip painted on swirl area. Marks: Made in Japan, on back. (Courtesy Ellie Haynes)

Wood--8" "Ragman" All wood. Jointed shoulders and hips. ca. 1950, although these basic dolls are still available. Marks: sticker: Made in Poland. (Courtesy Mary Partridge)

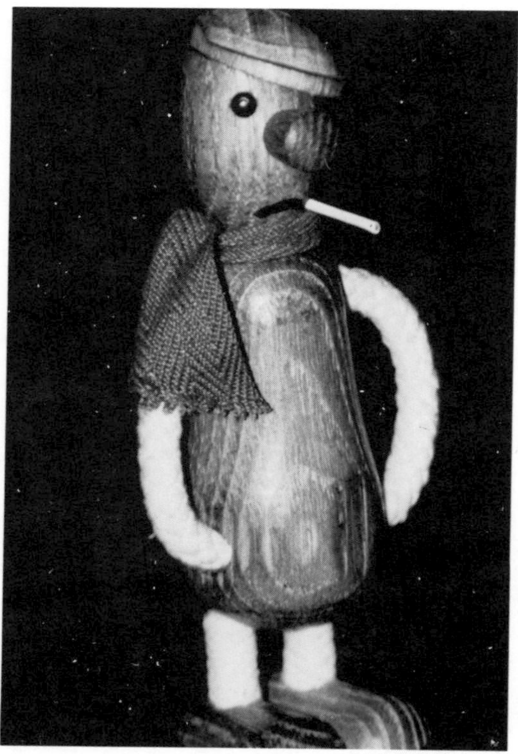

Wood--5" "Alfie Smoker" One piece wood with separate wood hat and shoes. Legs and arms are tightly woven rope. Smokes tiny cigarettes. Made in Denmark. 1963. Marks: None. $4.00. (Courtesy Ellie Haynes)

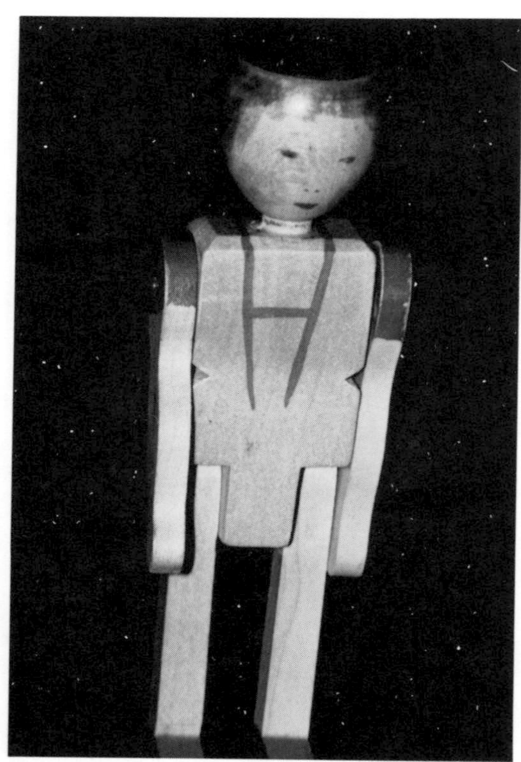

Wood--5½" All wood. Nail pegged shoulders and hips. One piece body, head. Painted features. Marks: None. $3.00. (Courtesy Mary Partridge)

Wood--8" "Pioneer Lady" All wood with one piece body and head. Jointed shoulders and hips. Original. Marks: Tag: Copyright Shackman/ 119591 Japanese Patent No. 208916. Still available. (Courtesy Frances and Mary Jane Anicello)

Wood--12" "Spanish Lady" All wood with floss hair. Marks: None. $12.00. (Courtesy Elaine Kaminsky)

Wood--3½" All one piece. Made in 1963 and carved by Kay Archer, an 80 year old Indian lady of the Hesqwit tribe, Canada. Hand painted. $2.00. (Courtesy Ellie Haynes)

# Picture Index

# Numbers, Letters and Symbol Index

# MODERN COLLECTOR'S DOLLS
# REVISED PRICES FOR SERIES 1 & 2

The following are the revised prices for Series I and Series II. It was designed to be easily used with these books.

It is important to repeat that these prices are based on COMPLETELY ORIGINAL AND IN MINT CONDITION dolls. If your doll is any less than perfect DEDUCT accordingly.

With the tapering off of the doll market by collectors becoming more selective and upgrading their collections and by many collectors "specializing" doll prices have dropped in many areas and have only increased in two areas, those dolls by Alexander and personality dolls. A word about the Madame Alexander area...ALL the 8" dolls shown in these books have BEND KNEES and prices are based on that fact.

A "S.A." behind a price means that the doll is STILL AVAILABLE in some areas.

14..7" Dionne Quints...200.00 set
15..14" Dionne Quints..85.00 each
15..McGuffy Ana..........55.00
15..Princess Alexandria....55.00
15..Butch..................35.00
16..Snow White...........75.00
16..13" Snow White........65.00
16..Princess Elizabeth......70.00
16..McGuffy Ana..........55.00
17..Flora McFlimsey.......95.00
17..Kate Greenway........85.00
17..Sonja Henie...........75.00
17..McGuffy Ana..........35.00
18..Sonja Henie...........75.00
18..W.A.A.C..............55.00
19..Scarlett O'Hara.......100.00
19..Margaret O'Brien.....185.00
19..Baby Genius...........25.00
20..Kathy................55.00
20..Alice................55.00
20..Maggie Mixup.........55.00
20..Annabelle.............50.00
21..McGuffy Ana..........65.00
21..Cissette..............35.00
21..Dumplin Baby.........35.00
22..Rosebud..............40.00
22..Cry Dolly.............40.00
22..Bonnie................40.00
22..Cissy.................35.00
23..Marme................45.00
23..Kathy Cry Dolly.......25.00
23..Princess Ann..........45.00
23..Bonnie Prince Charles..45.00
24..Elise.................45.00
24..Shari Lewis...........85.00
24..Kathy................25.00
24..Little Genius..........35.00
25..Little Shaver..........35.00
25..Marybel..............40.00
25..Edith.................40.00
25..Kathy Tears...........25.00
26..Genius Baby..........30.00
26..Little Cherub..........30.00
26..Queen................60.00
26..Melanie..............125.00
27..Godey...............125.00
27..Chatterbox...........45.00
27..Melinda..............45.00
27..Laurie..........17.00 (S.A.)
28..Little Huggums...9.00 (S.A.)
28..Big Huggums....22.00 (S.A.)
28..Sugar Darlin'..........35.00
29..Sweet Tears.....13.00 (S.A.)
29..Bo Peep.........18.00 (S.A.)
29..Pussy Cat.......16.00 (S.A.)
29..Sugar Darlin'..........35.00
30..Alice In Wonderland...16.00 (S.A.)
30..Leslie.................65.00
30..Scarlet O'Hara.........24.00
30..Storybook Doll.........35.00
31..Hansel & Gretel........40.00
31..Hungarian.......18.00 (S.A.)
31..India...........18.00 (S.A.)
31..Spanish Friend...18.00 (S.A.)
32..Elise...........22.00 (S.A.)
32..Rebecca.........18.00 (S.A.)
32..Betsy Ross.......18.00 (S.A.)
32..Degas...........18.00 (S.A.)
33..Happy.................45.00
33..Grandma Jane.........40.00
33..Blue Boy........15.00 (S.A.)
33..Red Boy.........10.00 (S.A.)
33..Cinderella.......13.00 (S.A.)
35..Dandy.................10.00
35..Little Love............25.00
35..Miss Chicadee.........15.00
35..Tiny Tears............12.00
36..Baby Lou...............4.00
36..Sweet Susanne........35.00
36..Sweet Sue.............35.00
36..Tiny Tears............12.00
37..Bride.................35.00
37..American Beauty......40.00
37..Sweet Sue.............45.00
37..Sweet Susanne.........25.00
38..Peek a Boo Toodles.....20.00
38..Toodles...............22.00
38..Sweet Sue.............20.00
38..Betsy McCall..........25.00
39..New Born Baby........18.00
39..Tiny Tears............12.00
39..Astronaut.............35.00
39..Graduate..............35.00
40..Whimmsie.............35.00
40..Hedda Get Bedda.......35.00
41..Betsy McCall..........15.00
41..Toodle-Loo............30.00
41..Butterball.............30.00
41..Talking Marie..........25.00
42..Tressy................12.00
42..New Tiny Tears.........4.00
43..Nancy.................32.00
43..Debu-teen.............35.00
44..Little Angel...........20.00
44..Sonja Henie...........45.00
44..Snuggle Doll...........20.00
45..Snuggle Bun............6.00
45..Peachy.................4.00
45..Judy..................35.00
46..Angeline..............35.00
46..Nanette...............35.00
46..17" Nanette...........35.00
46..Dream Bride...........35.00
47..Taffy.................40.00
47..New Happytot..........8.00
47..Nanette...............35.00
48..Francine..............35.00
48..Littlest Angel...........6.00
48..Prom Queen...........35.00
48..Littlest Angel...........6.00
49..My Angel.............22.00
49..Littlest Angel...........8.00
50..21" Skookum..........42.00
50..14" Skookum..........32.00
50..Playful.................5.00
50..Bye-Bye Baby..........10.00
51..Baby Doo...............2.00
51..Candy..................2.00
51..Pretty Lady...........12.00
51..Pouty.................10.00
52..Cindy..................4.00
52..Master.................2.00
52..My Friend..............2.00
52..Little Miss Gadabout...25.00
53..Raving Beauty.........25.00
53..Lov You...............12.00
53..Miss B.................1.00
53..Ballerina Belle..........4.00
54..Belle-Lee...............2.00
54..Jimmy.................2.00
54..Timmy.................2.00
54..Babies First Doll........3.00
55..Rock A Bye Baby........2.00
55..Perky Bright............7.00
55..Poor Pitiful Pearl.......18.00
55..Rusty.................16.00

56 . . Liza . . . 3.00
56 . . Tim . . . 3.00
57 . . Plum . . . 40.00
57 . . Miss Peep . . . 16.00
58 . . New Born Miss Peep . . . 16.00
58 . . Scootles . . . 65.00
58 . . Ragsy . . . 6.00
58 . . Kewpie . . . 4.00
59 . . Kewpie Gal . . . 6.00
59 . . Kewpie . . . 18.00
59 . . Sad Eyes . . . 3.00
59 . . Cleaning Day . . . 2.00
60 . . Bride . . . 2.00
60 . . Gloria . . . 15.00
60 . . Emily . . . 20.00
60 . . Pam . . . 20.00
61 . . Paula Marie . . . 16.00
61 . . Baby Brite . . . 8.00
62 . . Penny Brite . . . 4.00
62 . . Bonnie Bride . . . 4.00
62 . . Susie Cute . . . 4.00
62 . . Baby Boo . . . 6.00
63 . . Baby Magic . . . 7.00
63 . . Cool Cat . . . 5.00
63 . . Baby Tickle Tears . . . 7.00
64 . . Susie Homemaker . . . 6.00
64 . . Party Time . . . 5.00
64 . . Lil Miss Fussy . . . 5.00
65 . . Tickles . . . 5.00
65 . . Bikey . . . 7.00
65 . . Baby Catch A Ball . . . 18.00
65 . . Baby Peek 'n Play . . . 8.00
66 . . Baby Bunny . . . 5.00
66 . . Dawn . . . 4.00
66 . . Smarty Pants . . . 5.00
67 . . Sunny . . . 125.00
67 . . Prince Ranier . . . 150.00
67 . . Liz Taylor . . . 165.00
68 . . Gypsy Mother&Child . . 365.00
68 . . Uncle Sam . . . 115.00
68 . . Little Women . . . 95.00 set
69 . . Little Women . . . 95.00 set
69 . . Boy . . . 35.00
70 . . John Kennedy . . . 35.00
70 . . Good Luck Troll . . . 2.00
70 . . May . . . 1.00
70 . . Cinderella . . . 2.00
71 . . Scotch Miss . . . 1.00
71 . . Martha Washington . . . 1.00
71 . . Scarlet . . . 2.00
71 . . Carmen . . . 1.00
72 . . Tinker Bell . . . 3.00
72 . . Peter Pan . . . 3.00
72 . . Miss Hollywood . . . 1.00
72 . . Danny Groom . . . 2.00
73 . . Miss Tastee Freeze . . . 2.00
73 . . Miss North America . . . 2.00
74 . . Miss Charming . . . 45.00
74 . . Gigi Perreaux . . . 45.00
75 . . Bobby . . . 25.00
75 . . Robert . . . 32.00
75 . . Lil Susan . . . 5.00
75 . . Grace . . . 12.00
76 . . Luvable Susan . . . 5.00
76 . . Little Debutante . . . 25.00
76 . . Baby Susan . . . 3.00
76 . . Tina . . . 5.00
77 . . Lil Susan . . . 2.00
77 . . Tandy Talks . . . 18.00
77 . . Andy . . . 5.00
77 . . Little Miss . . . 5.00
78 . . Gemette . . . 4.00
78 . . Daisy Darlin . . . 12.00
78 . . Flowerkin . . . 12.00
78 . . Sandi . . . 5.00
79 . . Bundle of Joy . . . 4.00
79 . . Pix-i-Posie . . . 4.00
79 . . Annette . . . 6.00
79 . . Musical Baby . . . 4.00
80 . . Susan . . . 4.00
80 . . Bundle of Joy . . . 2.00
80 . . Adorable . . . 3.00
80 . . Baby Sniffles . . . 3.00
81 . . Sleepy . . . 10.00
81 . . Posi-Playmate . . . 5.00
81 . . Softina . . . 3.00
81 . . Baby Softina . . . 3.00
82 . . Cuddlekins . . . 2.00
85 . . Patricia . . . 65.00
85 . . Anne of Green Gables . . . 55.00
85 . . Ann Shirley . . . 60.00
86 . . Suzanne . . . 40.00
86 . . Little Lady . . . 45.00
86 . . Candy Kid . . . 45.00
86 . . Patsy Joan . . . 50.00
87 . . DyDee Baby . . . 12.00
87 . . Lil Darlin' . . . 15.00
87 . . Honey Girl . . . 18.00
87 . . Tintair . . . 35.00
88 . . Mommy's Baby . . . 12.00
88 . . Baby Cuddle Up . . . 20.00
88 . . Fluffy . . . 6.00
88 . . Polka Dottie . . . 32.00
89 . . Candy Twins . . . 35.00 set
89 . . Mickey . . . 5.00
89 . . Fluffy . . . 6.00
89 . . Katie . . . 16.00
90 . . My Fair Baby . . . 9.00
90 . . Twinkie . . . 5.00
90 . . Patsy Ann . . . 18.00
91 . . My Precious Baby . . . 5.00
91 . . Suzie Sunshine . . . 20.00
91 . . Gumdrop . . . 20.00
91 . . Precious New Born . . . 9.00
92 . . Baby Butterball . . . 3.00
92 . . Baby Sweetie . . . 3.00
92 . . Babykin . . . 2.00
92 . . My Fair Baby . . . 3.00
93 . . Miss Chips . . . 15.00
93 . . Peaches . . . 16.00
93 . . Thumpkin' . . . 4.00
93 . . Chipper . . . 15.00
94 . . Pum'kin . . . 4.00
94 . . Half Pint . . . 5.00
94 . . New Dy Dee Baby . . . 5.00
94 . . Honey Bun . . . 9.00
95 . . Lil Sweetie . . . 12.00
95 . . Tiny Tubber . . . 7.00
95 . . Baby Face . . . 4.00
95 . . Button Nose . . . 16.00
96 . . Butterball . . . 6.00
96 . . Little Luv . . . 7.00
97 . . Color Me . . . 3.00
97 . . Personality Playmate . . . 35.00
97 . . Sandra . . . 30.00
97 . . Precious . . . 12.00
98 . . Curly . . . 4.00
98 . . Winkin' . . . 2.00
98 . . Sissy . . . 3.00
99 . . Fredel . . . 10.00
99 . . Trudila . . . 10.00
99 . . Bettina . . . 10.00
99 . . Jamie . . . 30.00
100 . . Dee Dee . . . 8.00
100 . . Nantoc . . . 16.00
100 . . Eskimo . . . 12.00
100 . . Col. Sanders . . . 7.00
101 . . Swimmer . . . 40.00
101 . . Janie . . . 10.00
101 . . Rosette . . . 20.00
102 . . Mariann . . . 9.00
102 . . Flirty . . . 9.00
102 . . Cindy . . . 16.00
102 . . Rose . . . 12.00
103 . . Beatles . . . 35.00
103 . . Sonja . . . 15.00
104 . . Andra . . . 10.00
104 . . Jumeau . . . 225.00
105 . . Lorraine . . . 80.00
105 . . Bella Bee . . . 25.00
105 . . Lynette . . . 10.00
105 . . GeGe . . . 20.00
106 . . Polly . . . 10.00
106 . . Soupee . . . 18.00
106 . . El Poupee . . . 12.00
106 . . Soupee Bella . . . 20.00
107 . . Rosemund . . . 30.00
107 . . Michella . . . 20.00
107 . . Claudette . . . 32.00
107 . . Pretty . . . 12.00
108 . . Pauline . . . 85.00
109 . . Crawler . . . 8.00
109 . . Katinka . . . 18.00
109 . . Peasant Family . . . 5.00
109 . . Gura . . . 10.00
110 . . Gretchen . . . 9.00
110 . . Barbel . . . 7.00
110 . . Pride . . . 80.00
111 . . Lonee . . . 4.00
111 . . Freckles . . . 3.00
111 . . BeeBee . . . 2.00
111 . . Lovely . . . 3.00
112 . . Eggie . . . 2.00
112 . . Jane . . . 1.00
112 . . Lily . . . 4.00
112 . . Clown . . . 2.00

113 . . Junie . . . . . . . . . . . . . . . . . . 4.00
113 . . My Little Girl . . . . . . . . . . . 2.00
113 . . Mod . . . . . . . . . . . . . . . . . . . 4.00
113 . . Lil Bit . . . . . . . . . . . . . . . . . 2.00
114 . . Little Guy . . . . . . . . . . . . . . 2.00
114 . . Baby Jane . . . . . . . . . . . . . . 2.00
114 . . Liza . . . . . . . . . . . . . . . . . . . 2.00
114 . . Picture This . . . . . . . . . . . . 3.00
115 . . Miss India . . . . . . . . . . . . . 18.00
115 . . Red Riding Hood . . . . . . . . 4.00
115 . . Carolina . . . . . . . . . . . . . . 18.00
115 . . Angelica . . . . . . . . . . . . . . 16.00
116 . . Betta . . . . . . . . . . . . . . . . . 6.00
116 . . Sweet Adraina . . . . . . . . . 35.00
116 . . Bride . . . . . . . . . . . . . . . . 35.00
116 . . Valentina . . . . . . . . . . . . . 15.00
117 . . Anita . . . . . . . . . . . . . . . . . 35.00
117 . . Guilietta . . . . . . . . . . . . . . 20.00
117 . . Alicia . . . . . . . . . . . . . . . . 65.00
117 . . Gabriella . . . . . . . . . . . . . . 50.00
118 . . Florenza . . . . . . . . . . . . . . 50.00
118 . . Bonomi . . . . . . . . . . . . . . . 10.00
118 . . Vanessa . . . . . . . . . . . . . . . 9.00
119 . . Nina . . . . . . . . . . . . . . . . . 12.00
119 . . Lizza . . . . . . . . . . . . . . . . . 9.00
119 . . Mariella . . . . . . . . . . . . . . 10.00
119 . . Christina . . . . . . . . . . . . . 20.00
120 . . Dama . . . . . . . . . . . . . . . . . 30.00
120 . . Mia . . . . . . . . . . . . . . . . . . . 5.00
120 . . Kitten . . . . . . . . . . . . . . . . . 7.00
120 . . Christina . . . . . . . . . . . . . 28.00
121 . . Bed Doll . . . . . . . . . . . . . . 30.00
121 . . Kewpie . . . . . . . . . . . . . . . 12.00
121 . . Playmate . . . . . . . . . . . . . . . 7.00
121 . . Sailor . . . . . . . . . . . . . . . . 12.00
122 . . Monkey . . . . . . . . . . . . . . . 12.00
122 . . Baby . . . . . . . . . . . . . . . . . 15.00
122 . . Kewpie Type . . . . . . . . . . 18.00
122 . . Indy . . . . . . . . . . . . . . . . . . 1.00
123 . . Santa Claus . . . . . . . . . . . . 12.00
123 . . Eskimo & Patty . . . . . . . . . 1.00
123 . . Kutie . . . . . . . . . . . . . . . . . 11.00
123 . . Edy . . . . . . . . . . . . . . . . . . 1.00
124 . . Swimmer . . . . . . . . . . . . . . 4.00
124 . . Doris . . . . . . . . . . . . . . . . . 1.00
124 . . Mary Mary . . . . . . . . . . . . . 1.00
124 . . Crawler . . . . . . . . . . . . . . . 15.00
125 . . Tiny . . . . . . . . . . . . . . . . . . 1.00
125 . . Brat . . . . . . . . . . . . . . . . . . 2.00
125 . . Charleen . . . . . . . . . . . . . . 25.00
125 . . Wind Song . . . . . . . . . . . . . 28.00
126 . . Cisco Kid . . . . . . . . . . . . . 12.00
126 . . Romona . . . . . . . . . . . . . . . 6.00
126 . . Americana . . . . . . . . . . . . . 4.00
126 . . Juanita . . . . . . . . . . . . . . . 4.00
127 . . Pam . . . . . . . . . . . . . . . . . . 5.00
127 . . Cowgirl Pam . . . . . . . . . . . 7.00
127 . . Sleepy Head . . . . . . . . . . . . 2.00
127 . . Soul Sister . . . . . . . . . . . . 2.00
128 . . Huggles . . . . . . . . . . . . . . . 1.00
128 . . Chubby Kid . . . . . . . . . . . 32.00
128 . . Emerald . . . . . . . . . . . . . . 20.00
128 . . Dress Me Doll . . . . . . . . . . 2.00
129 . . Buddy Lee, hard plastic . 55.00
129 . . Buddy Lee, composition . 75.00
130 . . Doll House Mother . . . . . . 1.00
130 . . Poodle-oodle . . . . . . . . . . . 2.00
130 . . G.I. Joe . . . . . . . . . . 5.00 (S.A.)
131 . . Sunday . . . . . . . . . . . . . . . . 2.00
131 . . Little Miss No Name . . . . 26.00
131 . . Flying Nun . . . . . . . . . . . . 12.00
132 . . Sleeping Beauty . . . . . . . . 6.00
132 . . Rumpelstilskin . . . . . . . . . 6.00
132 . . Goldilocks . . . . . . . . . . . . . 6.00
132 . . Snow White/Dwarfs . . . . . 9.00
133 . . Prince Charming . . . . . . . . 6.00
133 . . Michelle . . . . . . . . . . . . . . . 8.00
133 . . World of Love . . . . . . . . . . 5.00
133 . . Baby Ruth . . . . . . . . . . . . . 4.00
134 . . Little Miss Muffet . . . . . . . 8.00
135 . . Masquerade . . . . . . . . . . . . 8.00
135 . . Bonnie Blue Bell . . . . . . . . 8.00
135 . . Red Riding Hood . . . . . . . . 8.00
135 . . Sweet Janice . . . . . . . . . . . 6.00
137 . . JoJo . . . . . . . . . . . . . . . . . 40.00
137 . . Baby Chubby . . . . . . . . . . 22.00
137 . . Shadow Wave Baby . . . . 25.00
137 . . Cindy Kay . . . . . . . . . . . . . 20.00
138 . . Betty Ann . . . . . . . . . . . . . 16.00
138 . . Little Sister . . . . . . . . . . . . 9.00
138 . . Dolly . . . . . . . . . . . . . . . . . 20.00
138 . . Gold Medal Doll . . . . . . . . 85.00
139 . . Pretty Betty . . . . . . . . . . . 10.00
139 . . Chubby Baby . . . . . . . . . . . 8.00
139 . . Betty . . . . . . . . . . . . . . . . . 6.00
140 . . Cindy Kay . . . . . . . . . . . . . 25.00
140 . . Little Miss Betty . . . . . . . . 4.00
140 . . Baby Precious . . . . . . . . . . 8.00
140 . . Peggy . . . . . . . . . . . . . . . . 35.00
141 . . Ruthie . . . . . . . . . . . . . . . . 6.00
141 . . Cindy . . . . . . . . . . . . . . . . . 9.00
141 . . Fair Skin Doll . . . . . . . . . . 6.00
141 . . Ruth's Sister . . . . . . . . . . 22.00
142 . . Flopsie . . . . . . . . . . . . . . . 10.00
142 . . Little Happy Fella . . . . . . 22.00
142 . . Kathy . . . . . . . . . . . . . . . . . 6.00
142 . . Betty Jo . . . . . . . . . . . . . . 10.00
143 . . Grown Up Miss . . . . . . . . . 6.00
143 . . Gloria Jean . . . . . . . . . . . . 3.00
143 . . Princess . . . . . . . . . . . . . . 30.00
143 . . Poor Pitiful Pearl . . . . . . . 16.00
144 . . Buttercup . . . . . . . . . . . . . . 3.00
144 . . Thirstee Baby . . . . . . . . . . 3.00
144 . . Tynie Toddler . . . . . . . . . . 2.00
144 . . Lullabye Baby . . . . . . . . . . 2.00
145 . . Baby Buttercup . . . . . . . . . 1.00
145 . . Betty . . . . . . . . . . . . . . . . . 2.00
145 . . Mary Poppins . . . . . . . . . . 18.00
145 . . My Ruthie . . . . . . . . . . . . . 4.00
146 . . Softie Baby . . . . . . . . . . . . 2.00
146 . . Toddler Baby . . . . . . . . . . . 2.00
146 . . Sleepy Baby . . . . . . . . . . . 18.00
146 . . Answer Doll . . . . . . . . . . . . 3.00
147 . . Baby Darling . . . . . . . . . . . 2.00
147 . . Teensie Baby . . . . . . . . . . . 2.00
147 . . Ruthie . . . . . . . . . . . . . . . 10.00
147 . . Tuffie . . . . . . . . . . . . . . . . 12.00
148 . . Mommy's Darling . . . . . . . 8.00
148 . . Ruthie . . . . . . . . . . . . . . . . 4.00
148 . . Ruthie Baby . . . . . . . . . . . . 6.00
148 . . Walker Ruth . . . . . . . . . . . . 2.00
149 . . Baby Tweaks . . . . . . . . . . 10.00
149 . . Lullabye Baby . . . . . . . . . . 4.00
149 . . Songster . . . . . . . . . . . . . . 10.00
149 . . Twistie . . . . . . . . . . . . . . . . 2.00
150 . . Athlete . . . . . . . . . . . . . . . 2.00
150 . . My Baby . . . . . . . . . . . . . . . 2.00
150 . . Lil Softee . . . . . . . . . . . . . . 2.00
150 . . Softee Baby . . . . . . . . . . . . 3.00
151 . . Love Me Baby . . . . . . . . . . 2.00
151 . . Pooty Tat . . . . . . . . . . . . . . 1.00
151 . . Bootsie . . . . . . . . . . . . . . . 6.00
151 . . Cindy . . . . . . . . . . . . . . . . . 2.00
152 . . Buttercup . . . . . . . . . . . . . . 1.00
152 . . Bi Lo . . . . . . . . . . . . . 9.00 (S.A.)
154 . . Deanna Durbin . . . . . . 95.00 up
154 . . 21" Deanna Durbin . . 95.00 up
155 . . Judy Garland . . . . . . . . . . 85.00
155 . . Magic Skin Baby . . . . . . . . 5.00
155 . . Georgous . . . . . . . . . . . . . . 16.00
156 . . Magic Skin Doll . . . . . . . . . 8.00
156 . . Miss Deb . . . . . . . . . . . . . . 22.00
156 . . Flexy Soldier . . . . . . . . . . 38.00
156 . . Sparkle Plenty . . . . . . . . . 22.00
157 . . Baby Coos . . . . . . . . . . . . . 25.00
157 . . Tickletoes . . . . . . . . . . . . . . 9.00
157 . . Tickletoes . . . . . . . . . . . . . 12.00
157 . . Plassie . . . . . . . . . . . . . . . 16.00
158 . . Magic Skin Baby . . . . . . . . 5.00
158 . . Toni . . . . . . . . . . . . . . . . . 22.00
158 . . 15" Toni . . . . . . . . . . . . . . 22.00
159 . . Toni Walker . . . . . . . . . . . 26.00
159 . . Tiny Girl . . . . . . . . . . . . . . . 2.00
159 . . Pete . . . . . . . . . . . . . . . . . . 2.00
159 . . Saucy Walker . . . . . . . . . . 18.00
160 . . Kiss Me . . . . . . . . . . . . . . . 22.00
160 . . Bonnie Braids . . . . . . . . . . 18.00
160 . . Miss Curity . . . . . . . . . . . . 25.00
160 . . Betsy McCall . . . . . . . . . . 24.00
161 . . Saucy Walker . . . . . . . . . . 18.00
161 . . Harriet Hubbard Ayers . 35.00
161 . . 18" H.H. Ayers . . . . . . . . . 40.00
161 . . Baby Big Eyes . . . . . . . . . 25.00
162 . . Princess Mary . . . . . . . . . 12.00
162 . . Saucy Walker . . . . . . . . . . 18.00
162 . . Betsy Wetsy . . . . . . . . . . . 12.00
162 . . Magic Lips . . . . . . . . . . . . 40.00
163 . . Miss Revlon . . . . . . . . . . . 22.00
163 . . Baby June . . . . . . . . . . . . . 25.00
163 . . Betsy Wetsy . . . . . . . . . . . . 5.00
164 . . Little Miss Revlon . . . . . . 14.00
164 . . Miss Revlon . . . . . . . . . . . 18.00
164 . . 19" Miss Revlon . . . . . . . . 18.00
164 . . Mrs. Revlon . . . . . . . . . . . 22.00
165 . . Betsy Wetsy . . . . . . . . . . . . 4.00
165 . . Penny Playpal . . . . . . . . . 50.00

165..Betsy Wetsy..........16.00
165..Miss Ideal..........32.00
166..Pattie Playpal..........26.00
166..Cream Puff..........18.00
166..Betsy Wetsy..........8.00
166..Dew Drop..........4.00
167..Tiny Kissey..........22.00
167..Thumblina..........16.00
167..Tammy..........5.00
167..Betsy Wetsy..........5.00
168..Ted..........8.00
168..Pepper..........5.00
168..Pebbles..........8.00
168..BamBam..........9.00
169..Pebbles..........9.00
169..Cuddly Kissey..........22.00
169..Baby Betsy Wetsy..........4.00
169..James Bond..........25.00
170..Illya Kuryakin..........25.00
170..Miss Clairol..........8.00
170..Honeymoon..........22.00
170..Goody Two Shoes..........25.00
171..Betsy Wetsy..........20.00
171..Baby Snoozie..........16.00
171..Pebbles..........5.00
171..Tabatha..........40.00
172..Honeyball..........2.00
172..Tearful Thumblina..........18.00
172..Baby Giggles..........26.00
172..Tiny Baby Kissy..........8.00
173..Tubsy..........12.00
173..Giggles, White..........25.00
173..Giggles, Colored..........30.00
173..Daisy..........4.00
174..Pixie..........5.00
174..Newborn Thumblina, Colored....7.00
174..Newborn Thumblina, White....5.00
174..Tearie Betsy..........4.00
175..Toddler Thumblina..........6.00
175..April Showers..........12.00
175..Little Lost Baby..........25.00
176..Crissy, White..........6.00
176..Crissy, Colored..........9.00
176..Velvet..........6.00
176..Dale..........3.00
177..Lissing Thumblina..........4.00
177..Tiny Thumblina..........4.00
177..In a Minute Thumblina..........5.00
177..Patti Playful..........20.00
178..Baby Belly Button..........2.00
178..Play N Jane..........9.00
178..Dina..........30.00
178..Lazy Dazy..........3.00
181..13" Shirley Temple..........75.00
181..17" Shirley Temple..........75.00
182..16" Shirley Temple..........85.00
182..22" Shirley Temple..........85.00
182..27" Shirley Temple..........200.00
183..17" Shirley Temple Baby...125.00
183..Hawaiian Shirley Temple...110.00
183..12" Shirley Temple..........25.00
183..15" Shirley Temple..........35.00
184..17" Shirley Temple..........45.00
184..1972 17" Shirley Temple...25.00
186..Love Me..........6.00
186..Dolly..........2.00
186..Tiny Bubbles..........9.00
186..Bashful Boy..........2.00
187..Sherri..........4.00
187..Trudy..........4.00
187..Pretty Girl..........3.00
187..Twistee..........2.00
188..Nikki..........5.00
188..Jolly..........6.00
188..Cuties..........8.00
188..Judy..........3.00
189..Playpen Doll..........2.00
189..Cutie Pie..........2.00
189..Timmy..........6.00
189..Linda..........9.00
190..Lil Lil..........2.00
190..Catherine..........22.00
190..Miss Sweet..........2.00
190..Pumpkin..........2.00
191..Snow White..........48.00
191..Raggedy Ann & Andy..........4.00
191..My Baby..........4.00
191..Cuddly Infant..........2.00
192..Baby..........2.00
192..Louise..........4.00
192..Pastel Miss..........2.00
192..Delightful..........4.00
193..Lorrie..........2.00
193..Marsha..........2.00
193..Little Linda..........3.00
193..Miss Toddler..........20.00
194..Twinkie..........6.00
194..Jamie West..........3.00 (S.A.)
194..Mary Hoyer..........25.00
196..Barbie..........5.00
196..Mattie..........22.00
197..Sister Belle..........22.00
197..Charming Chatty..........25.00
197..Chatty Cathy..........18.00
197..Midge..........7.00
198..Shrinking Violet..........45.00
198..Rickey..........7.00
198..Skooter..........9.00
198..Skipper..........5.00
199..Baby Pattaburp..........12.00
199..Singing Chatty..........12.00
199..Baby First Step..........15.00
199..Talking Baby First Step..........15.00
200..Scooba Doo..........25.00
200..Baby Cheryl..........8.00
200..Casper The Ghost..........22.00
200..Baby Teenie Talk..........6.00
201..Cheerful-Tearful..........6.00
201..Baby Secret..........12.00
201..Bunson Bernie..........8.00
202..Lola Liddle..........8.00
202..Cinderella..........8.00
202..Liddle Diddle..........8.00
202..Florence Niddle..........8.00
203..Casey..........5.00
203..Francie..........5.00
203..New Barbie..........5.00
203..Julia..........10.00
204..Tiny Cheerful-Tearful..........6.00
204..Drowsy..........6.00 (S.A.)
204..Baby See N Say..........9.00
205..Baby's Hungry..........9.00
205..Buffie..........10.00
205..Randy Reader..........12.00
205..Sleeping Beauty..........8.00
206..Sister Small Talk..........5.00
206..Small Talk..........5.00
206..Doctor Doolittle..........12.00
206..22½" Dr. Doolittle..........25.00
207..Shelia Skediddle..........3.00
207..Tippy Toes..........8.00
207..Busy Ken..........8.00
207..Dancerina..........12.00
208..Bouncy Baby..........3.00
208..Baby Tenderlove..........3.00
208..Chatty Tell..........16.00
208..Baby Sing A Song..........16.00
209..Beany..........22.00
209..Charlie Brown Skediddle..........3.00
209..Breezy Bridgit..........1.00
209..Dressy..........3.00
210..Big Jack..........4.00 (S.A.)
210..Kretor & Zark..........12.00
211..Haddie Mod..........4.00
211..Joe Namath..........8.00
211..Nun Nurse..........3.00
211..Molly..........12.00
212..Monica..........60.00
212..Christening Baby..........5.00
212..Claudette..........4.00
212..Topsy-Turvy..........22.00
213..Happy Toddler..........20.00
213..Walker..........65.00
213..Lone Ranger..........145.00
214..Eva..........20.00
214..American Child..........65.00
214..Lois Jane..........42.00
215..Dutch Girls..........6.00
215..Betty Grable..........65.00
216..False Snow White..........10.00
216..Happy Baby..........6.00
216..Air Force..........35.00
216..Henry..........25.00
217..Henrette..........25.00
217..Topsy..........15.00
217..Big Boy..........8.00
217..Gingham Gal..........16.00
218..Lollypop Kid..........3.00
218..Abbi-Gail..........35.00
218..Dream Doll..........12.00
219..Pauline..........10.00

219..Crying Baby...15.00
219..Pretty Baby...6.00
219..Baby Benny...5.00
220..Bendee...12.00
220..Johnny...3.00
220..Dimply Baby...4.00
220..Polly...15.00
221..Little Traveler...6.00
221..Janie...2.00
221..Teena...4.00
221..Miss Curity...10.00
222..Little Sister...6.00
222..Nun...2.00
222..World Traveler...16.00
222..Mary Lou...10.00
223..Ninette...5.00
223..Rosy Walker...22.00
223..Amy Louise...40.00
223..Pansy...8.00
224..Sweet Lou...12.00
224..Cuddly Kathy...6.00
224..My Baby...6.00
224..Pert & Sassy...4.00
225..Miss Glamour Ann...6.00
225..Kleenex Baby...2.00
225..Baby Bunting...16.00
225..Dream Doll...4.00
226..Yuletide...6.00
226..Angel...9.00
226..Pert Teenager...7.00
226..Bed Doll...20.00
227..Stunning...30.00
227..Baby Beth...2.00
227..Sugar & Spice...2.00
227..Trousseau Bride...6.00
228..Peggy Ann...2.00
228..BeeBee...1.00
228..Campbell Kid...4.00
228..Bonny...2.00
229..Mattie Mame...2.00
229..Pretty Girl...3.00
229..Pixie...3.00
229..Pixie Haircut Baby...3.00
230..Imp...2.00
230..Suzy Smart...7.00
230..Valerie...7.00
230..Amish Boy & Girl...4.00
231..Jockey & Fox Hunter...10.00
231..African Native...3.00
231..Sexed Caveman...5.00
232..Little Joan...12.00
232..Flowergirl...12.00
233..Queen of Hearts...12.00
233..Elsie Marley...12.00
233..Winter...12.00
233..Daffidown Dilly...12.00
234..Miss Muffett...8.00
234..Bride...8.00
234..Doll of Day...8.00
234..Bride...8.00
235..Commencement...8.00
235..Little Sister...12.00
235..Dillar A Dollar...8.00
235..Muffie...10.00
236..Christening Baby...12.00
236..Valentine...8.00
236..Nancy Ann...6.00
236..Linda Williams...12.00
237..Dolly Ann...10.00
237..JoAnn...6.00
237..Belinda...7.00
237..Baby Princess...6.00
238..Royal Princess...3.00
238..Poppin Fresh...1.00
238..Flowergirl...1.00
238..Bride...1.00
239..Captain Hook...3.00
239..Nun...3.00
239..Graduate...2.00
239..Bride...2.00
240..Miss America...1.00
240..Lady Ravencroft...1.00
240..Miss Valentine...1.00
240..Crusader...2.00
241..Polish Girl...1.00
241..Lady Hampshire...2.00
241..Miss 1953...2.00
241..Priscilla Alden...2.00
242..Bride...1.00
242..Greenbrier Maid...3.00
242..Dress Me...1.00
242..Scotch Groom...2.00
243..Nelly...2.00
243..New Baby...3.00
243..Glorious Gold Princess...3.00
243..Flowergirl...3.00
244..Bride...3.00
244..Polish Girl...3.00
244..Pert Pierrette...1.00
244..Red Riding Hood...2.00
246..Emily Ann...55.00
246..Marie...2.00
246..Tomas...2.00
246..Howdy Doody...16.00 (S.A.)
246..Poodle...10.00
246..Dick & Sally...6.00
246..Woody Woodpecker...2.00
247..Teto...1.00
247..Puppetrina...35.00
247..Jiminy Cricket...1.00
247..Donald Duck...2.00
248..Yogi Bear...1.00
248..Pluto...1.00
248..Donald Duck...1.00
248..Sylvester...1.00
249..Tom...2.00
249..Baby...1.00
249..Charlie McCarthy.50.00 (S.A.)
249..Betty Ballerina...1.00
250..Popeye...3.00
250..Dr. Doolittle...4.00
250..Happy Me...2.00
250..ByeLo...95.00
251..Charlie Chaplin...75.00
251..Ling Toy...6.00
251..Chi-Lu...4.00
251..Snow White...60.00
252..Polish Girl...4.00
252..Mammy's Baby...4.00
252..Dutch Girl...3.00
252..Mammy...7.00
253..Marie...6.00
253..Abby...2.00
253..Norah Sue...32.00
253..Miss Smith...18.00
254..Tak-Uki...48.00
254..Soo Ming...3.00
254..Dutch Boy & Girl...2.00
254..Girl & Doll...9.00
255..Dancing Partner...9.00
255..Santa Claus...35.00
255..Little Lulu...35.00
255..Sweet Pea...12.00
256..Popeye...18.00
256..Baby's Doll...2.00
256..Daisy...7.00
256..Flip...4.00
257..Candy Striper...2.00
257..Cindy...1.00
257..Mickey Mouse...6.00
257..Mr. Magoo...5.00
258..Eskimo Pie...2.00
258..Multi-Face...5.00
258..Sleepyhead...2.00
258..Pinocchio...5.00
259..Little Bo Peep...13.00
259..Clown...4.00
259..Mickey Mouse...7.00
259..Scarecrow...8.00
260..Ronald McDonald...1.00
260..Oh My...2.00
260..Little Orphan Annie...15.00
260..Hansel...1.00
261..Lil Soul...2.00
261..Talk A Little...4.00
261..Holly...2.00
262..Gramma...12.00
262..Doughboy...2.00
262..Jolly Green Giant...3.00
262..Mr. Peanut...3.00
263..Eskimo...1.00
263..Louise...2.00
263..Jan...4.00
263..Heidi...3.00
264..Baby Stroll Along...3.00
264..Baby Sad N Glad...6.00
264..Snugglebun...5.00
265..Tippy Tumbles...4.00
265..Heidi...4.00
265..Bottle Baby...2.00
265..Baby Crawalong...7.00
266..Linda Lee...5.00
266..Baby Grow A Tooth...6.00
266..Tumbling Tomboy...5.00
266..Baby Laugh A Lot...6.00
267..Jumpsy...4.00

267..Whistler ...............2.00
267..Sweet April ...........1.00
267..Funny .................1.00
268..Rosa ..................1.00
268..Elmer Fudd ...........4.00
268..First Date .............1.00
268..Lonely Liza...........18.00
269..Joy ..................15.00
269..Valentine Bonnet Toddler...4.00
269..St. Pat's Day Toddler ....4.00
269..Easter Bonnet Toddler...4.00
270..Billy Joe .............25.00
270..New Happytime Baby....6.00
270..Walking Bride ..........5.00
270..Mommy's Baby .........3.00
271..Adorable ...............2.00
271..Bubble Bath Baby .......2.00
271..Indian Troll.............2.00
271..Nurse Troll .............2.00
272..Baby Janie ...........10.00
272..Tamu ............6.00 (S.A.)
272..Flip Wilson .......9.00 (S.A.)
273..Muff Doll ...............2.00
273..Amosandra ...........35.00
273..Betty Bows ...........12.00
273..Tod-L-Dee & Tod-L-Tim..6.00
274..Banister Baby .........20.00
274..Babee Bee ..............6.00
274..Chunky ................2.00
274..Baby ..................1.00
275..Gerber Baby ..........12.00
275..Tod-L-Tee ..............2.00
275..So Wee ................2.00
275..Gerber Baby ..........10.00
276..Little Debbie Eve .......4.00
276..Melody Baby Debbi......3.00
276..Baby Debbie............6.00
276..Talking Terri Lee ......50.00
277..Terri Lee .............35.00
277..Jerri Lee ..............50.00
277..Tiny Jerri Lee .........25.00
277..Tiny Terri Lee .........35.00
278..Baby Linda ...........35.00
278..Mannequin ............12.00
278..Dawk ..................4.00
279..Carmen ...............75.00
280..Sweetum...............6.00
280..Surprise Doll ..........18.00
281..Princess Bride ..........6.00
281..Country Girl...........12.00
281..Dollikins ...............8.00
281..Pri-thilla ...............9.00
282..Baby Dollikins .........16.00
282..Wiggles ..............45.00
282..Betsy McCall ..........26.00
283..Blue Fairy..............4.00
283..Freckles ..............16.00
283..Pollyanna .............45.00
283..Tinyteen ...............5.00
284..Yummy ...............12.00
284..Purty ................12.00
284..Cuddly Baby ............1.00
285..Blabby ...............15.00
285..Miss Debteen ...........6.00
285..Debteen Toddler .......12.00
286..Baby Sweetums .........5.00
286..Bob...................6.00
286..Coquette ...............6.00
286..Bare Bottom Baby .......8.00
287..Posin Elfy ..............2.00
287..Debteen ...............6.00
287..Little Coquette .........4.00
287..Posable Baby Trix .......2.00
288..Needa Toodles ..........2.00
288..Tiny Toodles............1.00
288..Pretty Portrait .........4.00
288..Baby Pee Wee ..........2.00
289..Secret Sue .............6.00
289..50th Anniversary Doll ..20.00
289..Penelope ...............3.00
289..Baby Sweetums .........2.00
290..First Born Baby .........1.00
290..Daffi Dill ...............3.00
290..Dolly Walker ...........2.00
290..Dollikins .........3.00 (S.A.)
291..Bathtub Baby ...........1.00
291..Adorable Cindy .........1.00
291..Debteen ...............2.00
291..New Born Yummy .......1.00
292..Tiny Trix..............1.00
292..Kim ..................2.00
292..Baby Sleep Amber ......4.00
292..Jennifer...............4.00
293..New Gerber Baby .......5.00
293..Happy Pee Wee .........2.00
293..Toe Dancing Ballerina ..18.00
293..Ballerina ..............9.00
294..Big Girl ..............22.00
295..Ginny ................16.00
295..Ginny ................16.00
296..Ginny ................14.00
296..Ginny ................14.00
296..Ginny ................10.00
296..Ginny Baby ...........18.00
297..Jeff..................15.00
297..Jan ..................15.00
297..Jill ..................15.00
297..Brickette..............35.00
298..Baby Dear.............25.00
298..Little Baby Dear ........8.00
298..Ginny ................10.00
298..Ginny Baby ...........16.00
299..Baby Dear.............16.00
299..Baby Dear..............8.00
299..Littlest Angel...........8.00
299..Posie Pixie ............10.00
300..Littlest Angel...........8.00
300..Angel Baby .............8.00
300..Picture Girl.............9.00
300..Star Brite .............25.00
301..Little Miss Ginny ........6.00
301..Dearest One ...........22.00
301..Ginny Baby .............8.00
301..Pinocchio .............45.00
302..Bashful ..............35.00
302..Snow White ...........40.00
302..Tinker Bell ............12.00
302..Mousketeer ...........16.00
303..Christopher Robin......12.00
303..Winnie Pooh............8.00
303..Jiminy Cricket ..........2.00

# REVISED PRICES FOR SERIES 2

1..Mimi .................75.00
4..Lady Hamilton ..........3.00
4..Dainty Dolly............7.00
5..Musical Sweetheart .....4.00
5..Lady Lettie.............3.00
5..Empress Eugenie ......18.00
7..Bobby Q & Susie Q .....85.00
8..China .................35.00
8..Jane Withers .........185.00
8..Little Shaver ..........60.00
9..Scarlett O'Hara .......100.00
9..Ginger Rogers .........85.00
9..W.A.V.E. .............55.00
9..Margaret O'Brien .....185.00
10..Scotch ...............35.00
10..Norwegian ............35.00
10..Swiss................35.00
10..Jeannie Walker ........85.00
11..Bride .................50.00
11..Babs..................65.00
11..Alice in Wonderland ....55.00
11..Nina Ballerina .........50.00
12..Fairy Queen ...........55.00
12..9" Latex ..............18.00
12..Prince Charming .......75.00
12..Cinderella .............75.00
12..Violet................45.00
13..Alice in Wonderland ....55.00
13..Sonja Henie ...........65.00
13..Kathy ................55.00

13..Madeline..............45.00
14..McGuffey Ana.........65.00
15..Cynthia...............85.00
15..Rosebud..............40.00
15..Active Miss............45.00
15..Christening Baby.......30.00
16..Binnie Walker.........40.00
16..Jo....................45.00
16..Queen................45.00
16..Lissy.................45.00
17..Groom................40.00
17..Cissy Queen..........125.00
17..Lissy.................45.00
17..Billy..................45.00
17..Wendy Ann...........35.00
18..Elise Bride............45.00
18..Cisette................35.00
18..Cisette................35.00
18..Sleeping Beauty........55.00
19..Aunt Agatha..........40.00
19..Renoir................75.00
19..Kelly.................45.00
19..Cissette..............35.00
20..Quintuplets.......150.00 set
20..Janie.................35.00
20..Brenda Starr..........45.00
21..Kitten................25.00
21..Jaqueline.............75.00
21..Cissette Ballerina......35.00
21..Lively Huggums.......25.00
22..Cissette Ballerina......35.00
22..Caroline..............75.00
22..Maggie Mixup.........55.00
22..French..........18.00 (S.A.)
23..Sleeping Beauty.......115.00
23..Pollyanna.............45.00
23..Funny...........12.00 (S.A.)
24..Wendy................35.00
24..Wendy................35.00
24..Janie.................35.00
24..Peruvian Boy..........40.00
26..Red Riding Hood .18.00 (S.A.)
26..Polly.................45.00
26..Baby Ellen............30.00
26..Gretel................45.00
27..Maggie...............45.00
27..African...............40.00
27..Hawaiian..............40.00
27..Bride.................40.00
30..Thailand.........18.00 (S.A.)
30..Scarlet................40.00
30..Gidgit................35.00
30..Coco.................150.00
31..Scarlett..............125.00
31..Disneyland
Snow White...20.00 (S.A.)
31..Agatha..............125.00
31..Pumpkin........20.00 (S.A.)
33..Granny...............40.00
33..McGuffy Ana..........40.00
33..Sheri Lewis...........85.00
33..Snow White...........55.00
33..Mary Martin...........65.00
33..Madaline..............45.00
33..Alice in Wonderland....65.00
33..Elise Ballerina.........45.00
34..Agatha...............50.00
34..Scarlet..............150.00
34..Renoir...............125.00
34..Amish Boy & Girl......40.00
34..Spanish Boy...........35.00
34..Spanish Girl.....18.00 (S.A.)
34..Suzy..................50.00
34..Janie.................35.00
34..Rosy..................50.00
35..Cinderella.......22.00 (S.A.)
35..Easter Girl............75.00
35..Scarlett...............40.00
35..Alice in Wonderland....35.00
35..Peter Pan Set......165.00 set
35..Renoir Child...........55.00
36..11" Portretts......65.00 each
37..Cowgirl & Cowboy.....40.00
37..Southern Belle.........40.00
37..Lady Hamilton........125.00
37..Japan.................35.00
38..Rumania........18.00 (S.A.)
38..Finland..........18.00 (S.A.)
38..Godey................65.00
38..Jenny Lind............50.00
39..Wendy................50.00
39..Peter Pan.............50.00
39..Jenny Lind............50.00
39..Heidi...........20.00 (S.A.)
40..Renoir...............125.00
40..Lucinda...............50.00
40..Southern Belle.........40.00
40..Smiley................50.00
41..Renoir Child.....22.00 (S.A.)
41..Janie.................25.00
41..Lucinda.........15.00 (S.A.)
41..Gainsboro............125.00
42..Sally.................45.00
42..Debutante Walker......50.00
42..Jimmy John...........50.00
43..Ricky Jr..............18.00
43..Ricky Jr..............35.00
43..Sweet Sue............35.00
43..Tiny Toodles..........15.00
44..Groom................45.00
44..Betsy McCall..........25.00
44..Whimette..............6.00
44..New Tiny Tears........10.00
45..TeenWeeny Tiny Tears..5.00
45..Sally Says............30.00
45..Cricket...............10.00
45..Margaret Rose.........13.00
46..Freckles...............7.00
46..Hoss Cartright.........40.00
46..Ben Cartright..........35.00
47..Sweet Sue............35.00
47..Toni..................25.00
48..So Big................28.00
48..Baby Donna...........20.00
48..Gloria Jean............65.00
48..Susan.................30.00
50..Nanette...............35.00
50..Nanette...............35.00
50..Nanette...............35.00
50..Miss Coty..............6.00
51..Count Dracula..........3.00
51..Frankenstein...........3.00
51..Wolfman...............3.00
51..The Mummy............3.00
51..Lil Abner..............65.00
54..Betsy McCall, 11½"....22.00
54..Betsy McCall, 22"......26.00
54..Betsy McCall, 29"......35.00
54..Betsy McCall, 36"......75.00
55..Kewpie Doll...........30.00
55..Miss Peep.............20.00
55..Scootles..............75.00
55..Kewpie Beanbag........8.00
57..Carol..................6.00
57..Polly Pond Doll........25.00
58..Ginger.................5.00
58..Miss Ginger............8.00
58..Ginger.................5.00
59..Cowgirl Ginger.........5.00
59..Trike Tike..............2.00
60..Sasha.........Still Available
60..Gregor........Still Available
61..Sweet Rosemary.......12.00
61..Penny Brite............6.00
61..Swinger................5.00
61..Hot Canary.............5.00
62..Yeah, Yeah & Slick Chick.5.00
62..Fancy Feet.............9.00
62..Kevin..................9.00
62..Susie Homemaker.......6.00
62..Dawn..................4.00
63..Dale...................6.00
63..Van...................6.00
63..Angie..................5.00
63..Glori..................5.00
64..Gary..................5.00
64..Longlocks..............6.00
64..Ron...................5.00
64..Dancing Dawn..........4.00
65..Dancing Gary..........5.00
65..Dancing Dale...........6.00
65..Dancing Van............6.00
65..Dancing Longlocks......6.00
66..Dancing Angie.........5.00
66..Dancing Glori..........5.00
66..Dancing Ron...........5.00
66..Kevin..................5.00
67..Denise.................8.00
67..Melanie................8.00
67..Dinah..................8.00
67..Daphne................8.00
68..Connie.................8.00
68..Longlocks..............5.00
68..Dawn..................5.00
68..Maureen...............8.00
69..Dancing Jessica.........5.00

69..Jessica..................5.00
69..Kip......................8.00
69..Dawn Majorette...........8.00
70..Bonnet Head.............55.00
70..Parian..................55.00
70..Parian..................55.00
70..Grandaughter...........110.00
71..Oriental...............165.00
71..Parthenia..............185.00
71..Young Victoria.........265.00
73..Ken Tuck................25.00
73..9½" All Bisque..........60.00
73..7½" All Bisque..........60.00
74..Nicodemius.............125.00
74..Girl...................125.00
74..Pouty...................85.00
74..Bru Jne.................65.00
75..Boutique................40.00
75..Country Mice............40.00
75..Bonnie Bru..............85.00
76..Freckles.................7.00
77..Snow Baby...............45.00
77..By Lo...................35.00
77..American Schoolboy......45.00
77..Tete Jumeau.............55.00
78..Circle Dot Bru..........45.00
78..Negro Bru...............65.00
78..S.F.B.J. 236............55.00
78..S.F.B.J. 252............55.00
79..Bru Jne.................55.00
79..Willie & Millie.........45.00
79..Two Face................50.00
80..165.....................55.00
80..Cut Down 165............45.00
80..Gancho.................225.00
80..Empress Carlotta.......185.00
81..Peggy McCall............22.00
82..Marge....................1.00
82..Kung Fu..................3.00
82..Patty Pigtails...........4.00
82..Junior Miss.............22.00
83..Lisabeth................35.00
83..Miss Charming...........45.00
83..Janie....................5.00
83..Play Pen Pal.............3.00
84..Miss Flexie..............5.00
84..Chubby Schoolgirl........5.00
84..Miss Debby...............6.00
84..Miss Sunbeam............15.00
85..Kid Sister...............3.00
85..Shelly...................4.00
85..Terri Talks..............6.00
85..Playpen Baby.............3.00
86..Babette..................6.00
86..Georgette................6.00
86..Bean Bag.................3.00
86..Mary Kay.................3.00
87..Grumpy..................45.00
87..Baby Evelyn.............45.00
87..Ice Queen...............85.00
87..18".....................60.00
88..Portrait Doll...........35.00
88..Little Lady.............45.00
88..Little Lady Majorette...45.00
88..Honey...................45.00
89..8" Button Nose..........35.00
89..Formal Honey............85.00
89..Honey Walker............30.00
89..Honey Walker,
Ball Gown...30.00
90..Honey Ballerina.........35.00
90..Honey Walker............18.00
90..Happy Boy...............12.00
90..My Fair Baby............25.00
91..Susie Sunshine..........20.00
91..Susie Sunshine, lower...20.00
92..Sugar Plum...............8.00
92..Twinkie..................6.00
92..My Fair Baby.............4.00
92..Sugar Plum...............6.00
93..Yawning John............18.00
93..Baby Ann..........9.00 (S.A.)
93..Audrey............9.00 (S.A.)
93..Natalie...........9.00 (S.A.)
94..Jenny.............9.00 (S.A.)
94..Mary..............9.00 (S.A.)
94..Elizabeth.........9.00 (S.A.)
95..Flagg Dancing Dolls......7.00
95..17".....................18.00
95..Bi-Bye..................16.00
96..Louise...................5.00
96..Love Me Indian...........4.00
96..Nova Scotia..............2.00
96..Mary Baby................3.00
97..New Zealand..............8.00
97..Royal Scot...............4.00
97..Scot Lad................25.00
97..Highland Lass............6.00
98..Husar Guard..............4.00
98..Palace Guard.............4.00
98..Jeannie..................5.00
98..Mice Dolls..............10.00
99..Victorian Girl..........25.00
99..Victorian Girl..........25.00
99..Scots Lass..............25.00
99..Grandma.................25.00
100..Pearly King............25.00
100..Pearly Girl............25.00
100..London Bobby...........25.00
100..India..................12.00
100..Marina..................7.00
101..Poupee Lee..............6.00
101..Claudine................6.00
101..17" Claudine...........22.00
102..Leeka...................5.00
102..My Playmate............25.00
102..Greta..................17.00
102..Lousita................15.00
103..All rubber.............12.00
103..Bettina Lee.............8.00
103..Lisa-Bella.............25.00
103..Oleagh..................4.00
104..Isabell................12.00
104..Terria..................9.00
104..Grandmother.............3.00
104..Pette...................3.00
105..Gretta..................4.00
105..Leialoha................5.00
106..7" All Plastic..........3.00
106..Mariclaire...............4.00
106..Waikki Girl..............5.00
106..5½"......................3.00
107..Pixie....................3.00
107..Tiny Traveler............2.00
107..Betty....................1.00
107..Baby Bright Eyes.........1.00
108..Captain Amos.............8.00
108..Simple Simon.............4.00
108..Hans Brinker.............4.00
108..Heidi & Tomoko...........2.00
109..Taffy....................2.00
109..Texaco...................6.00
109..Picture Jan..............2.00
109..Balloon Blower...........2.00
110..8".......................7.00
110..8".......................7.00
110..8".......................7.00
110..Crolly Doll.............10.00
111..Shawn....................8.00
111..Erin.....................7.00
111..Timothy..................8.00
111..Leprechaun...............9.00
112..Bed Doll.................6.00
112..Daniela.................25.00
112..Bibi.....................7.00
112..Smiling Baby............10.00
113..Mara Beth...............25.00
113..Arabella................25.00
113..Nina....................25.00
113..Rosella.................18.00
114..Sylvie...................8.00
114..Mariana&Modesto .15.00 each
114..Mary Ella...............10.00
114..Claudina................12.00
115..Clementina..............35.00
115..Tenderella..............15.00
115..Tilly....................6.00
115..Fiammetta...............35.00
116..Adrian Bambino...........5.00
116..Mia Nina.................5.00
116..Petro....................3.00
116..Bettina.................15.00
117..Juli.....................9.00
117..Melita...................4.00
117..Happy Andrina...........12.00
117..Dutch Boy & Girl.........6.00
118..Shirley Temple..........45.00
118..Carnival Lady............5.00
118..Suzie May................6.00
118..Character Toddler.......10.00
119..3½".....................10.00
119..5½".....................15.00
119..6"......................15.00
119..3".......................5.00
120..4".......................7.50
120..McDare...................5.00

120. . My Candy . . . . . . . . . . . . . . 2.00
120. . Musical Mimi . . . . . . . . . . . 6.00
121. . Mini Martian . . . . . . . . . . . 5.00
121. . Diana . . . . . . . . . . . . . . . . . 8.00
121. . Bimby . . . . . . . . . . . . . . . . 2.00
121. . Baby Princess . . . . . . . . . 10.00
122. . Twin Dandy . . . . . . . . . . . . 4.00
122. . Twin Tandy . . . . . . . . . . . . 4.00
122. . Popo . . . . . . . . . . . . . . . . . 2.00
122. . Skeetle . . . . . . . . . . . 7.00 (S.A.)
123. . Crying Baby . . . . . . 5.00 (S.A.)
123. . Baby Paula . . . . . . . 2.00 (S.A.)
124. . Fascination . . . . . . . . . . . 15.00
124. . Mannikin . . . . . . . . . 5.00 (S.A.)
124. . Luisa . . . . . . . . . . . . . . . . . 5.00
125. . 9" . . . . . . . . . . . . . . . . . . 22.00
125. . Peruvians . . . . . . . . . . . . 22.00
125. . 6" . . . . . . . . . . . . . . . . . . . 8.00
125. . Welsh . . . . . . . . . . . . . . . 50.00
126. . Pam . . . . . . . . . . . . . . . . . . 8.00
126. . Sparky . . . . . . . . . . . . . . . . 2.00
127. . Flop Tot . . . . . . . . . . . . . . 1.00
127. . Kitty Coed . . . . . . . . 4.00 (S.A.)
127. . Sparky . . . . . . . . . . . . . . . . 2.00
128. . Poland . . . . . . . . . . . 3.00 (S.A.)
128. . Mexico . . . . . . . . . . . 3.00 (S.A.)
128. . My Baby . . . . . . . . . . . . . . 30.00
128. . Honeywest . . . . . . . . . . . . 15.00
129. . G.I. Joe . . . . . . . . . . 5.00 (S.A.)
130. . G.I. Joe . . . . . . . . . . 5.00 (S.A.)
130. . Monkee . . . . . . . . . . . . . . 10.00
130. . Dolly Darling . . . . . . . . . . . 2.00
131. . Jamie . . . . . . . . . . . . . . . . . 3.00
131. . Dolly Darling . . . . . . . . . . . 2.00
132. . That Kid . . . . . . . . . . . . . 25.00
132. . Daisy Darling . . . . . . . . . . . 2.00
132. . Dolly Darling . . . . . . . . . . . 2.00
133. . Lily Darling . . . . . . . . . . . 2.00
133. . Music . . . . . . . . . . . . . . . . . 9.00
133. . Peace . . . . . . . . . . . . . . . . . 5.00
133. . Adam . . . . . . . . . . . . . . . . . 6.00
134. . Flower . . . . . . . . . . . . . . . . 5.00
134. . Peace . . . . . . . . . . . . . . . . . 5.00
134. . Soul . . . . . . . . . . . . . . . . . 6.00
134. . Love . . . . . . . . . . . . . . . . . 5.00
135. . Leggy Sue . . . . . . . . . . . . . 6.00
135. . Leggy Nan . . . . . . . . . . . . . 5.00
135. . Leggy Jill . . . . . . . . . . . . . 5.00
136. . Leggy Kate . . . . . . . . . . . . 5.00
136. . Sweet Cookie . . . . . . . . . . . 5.00
136. . Bonnie Breck . . . . . . . . . . 10.00
136. . Aimee . . . . . . . . . . . . . . . 18.00
137. . 7" . . . . . . . . . . . . . . . . . . 12.00
137. . 8" . . . . . . . . . . . . . . . . . . . 7.00
137. . 9" . . . . . . . . . . . . . . . . . . . 8.00
138. . Joyce . . . . . . . . . . . . . . . . 35.00
138. . Roberta . . . . . . . . . . . . . . 40.00
138. . JoJo . . . . . . . . . . . . . . . . . 40.00
138. . Bright Star . . . . . . . . . . . 25.00
139. . Cindy . . . . . . . . . . . . . . . . 20.00
139. . Life Size Baby . . . . . . . . . 18.00
139. . Cindy . . . . . . . . . . . . . . . . 20.00
139. . Renee . . . . . . . . . . . . . . . 12.00
140. . Perfume Pixie . . . . . . . . . . 2.00
140. . Yvonne . . . . . . . . . . . . . . . 4.00
140. . Cinderella . . . . . . . . . . . . . 5.00
140. . 15" . . . . . . . . . . . . . . . . . . 6.00
141. . Molly . . . . . . . . . . . . . . . . . 8.00
141. . Twin Tot . . . . . . . . . . . . . . 2.00
141. . Wee Bonnie Baby . . . . . . . 2.00
141. . Teensie Baby . . . . . . . . . . . 2.00
142. . Floppy . . . . . . . . . . . . . . . . 5.00
142. . Anthony Pipsqueek . . . . . . 7.00
142. . Marc Pipsqueek . . . . . . . . . 7.00
142. . Cleo Pipsqueek . . . . . . . . . 7.00
143. . Baby Precious . . . . . . . . . . 4.00
143. . New Baby Tweaks . . . . . . . 4.00
143. . Tiny Baby . . . . . . . . . . . . . 2.00
143. . Loonie Lite . . . . . . . . . . . . 3.00
144. . Penny Penpal . . . . . . . . . . . 5.00
144. . Softy Skin . . . . . . . . . . . . . 3.00
144. . Bednobs . . . . . . . . . . . . . 10.00
144. . Pippi Longstockings . . . . 12.00
145. . Lone Ranger . . . . . . 5.00 (S.A.)
145. . Tonto . . . . . . . . . . . . 5.00 (S.A.)
145. . Baby Wet . . . . . . . . . . . . . 4.00
146. . Shirley Temple Baby . . 125.00
146. . Little Princess . . . . . . . . . 65.00
146. . Snow White . . . . . . . . . . . 75.00
146. . Judy Garland . . . . . . 185.00 up
147. . 22" . . . . . . . . . . . . . . . . . 35.00
147. . Shirley . . . . . . . . . . . . . . . 75.00
147. . 18" Shirley . . . . . . . . . . . 85.00
147. . 16" . . . . . . . . . . . . . . . . . 35.00
148. . 18" . . . . . . . . . . . . . . . . . 25.00
148. . Magic Skin Baby . . . . . . . . 6.00
148. . Talking Tot . . . . . . . . . . . 20.00
148. . Baby Snookie . . . . . . . . . . . 4.00
149. . Baby Gurglee . . . . . . . . . . . 9.00
149. . Peggy . . . . . . . . . . . . . . . 35.00
149. . Joan Palooka . . . . . . . . . . 22.00
149. . Sara Ann . . . . . . . . . . . . . 22.00
150. . Mary Hartline . . . . . . . . . 35.00
150. . Saucy Walker . . . . . . . . . . 20.00
150. . Miss Curity . . . . . . . . . . . 25.00
150. . Patty Petite . . . . . . . . . . . 22.00
151. . Posie . . . . . . . . . . . . . . . . 20.00
151. . Miss Revlon . . . . . . . . . . . 22.00
151. . 19" Shirley . . . . . . . . . . . 65.00
151. . 17" Shirley . . . . . . . . . . . 45.00
152. . 35" Shirley . . . . . . . . . . 365.00
152. . Little Miss Revlon . . . . . . 14.00
152. . Mitzi . . . . . . . . . . . . . . . . . 8.00
152. . Patti . . . . . . . . . . . . . . . . . 5.00
153. . 19" . . . . . . . . . . . . . . . . . . 6.00
153. . Patti Playpal . . . . . . . . . . 65.00
153. . Lovely Liz . . . . . . . . . . . . . 8.00
153. . Tammy . . . . . . . . . . . . . . . 5.00
154. . Tammy . . . . . . . . . . . . . . . 5.00
154. . Rock Baby Coos . . . . . . . . . 6.00
154. . Tammy's Mom . . . . . . . . . 12.00
154. . Ted . . . . . . . . . . . . . . . . . . 8.00
155. . PosN Pete . . . . . . . . . . . . . 7.00
155. . Grown Up Tammy . . . . . . . 8.00
155. . Pepper . . . . . . . . . . . . . . . . 5.00
155. . Dodi . . . . . . . . . . . . . . . . . . 7.00
156. . Samantha . . . . . . . . . . . . 12.00
156. . Baby Herman . . . . . . . . . . . 6.00
156. . Real Live Lucy . . . . . . . . . . 6.00
156. . Talking Goody
Two Shoes . . 28.00
157. . Captain Action . . . . . . . . . . 4.00
157. . Trixy Flatsy . . . . . . . . . . . . 7.00
158. . Casey Flatsy . . . . . . . . . . . . 7.00
158. . Tressy . . . . . . . . . . . . . . . . 6.00
158. . Kerry . . . . . . . . . . . . . . . . 15.00
158. . Filly Flatsy . . . . . . . . . . . . . 7.00
159. . Baby Flatsy . . . . . . . . . . . . 2.00
159. . Spinderella Flatsy . . . . . . . 4.00
159. . Lemonade Flatsies . . . . . . 3.00
159. . Play Time Flatsy . . . . . . . . 7.00
160. . Slumbertime Flatsy . . . . . 7.00
160. . Nancy Flatsy . . . . . . . . . . . 7.00
160. . Rally Flatsy . . . . . . . . . . . . 7.00
160. . Bonnie Flatsy . . . . . . . . . . . 7.00
161. . Candy Flatsy . . . . . . . . . . . 7.00
161. . Brandi . . . . . . . . . . . . . . . 15.00
161. . Cookie Flatsy . . . . . . . . . . . 7.00
161. . Mia . . . . . . . . . . . . . . . . . . 15.00
162. . Cricket . . . . . . . . . . . . . . 10.00
162. . Velvet . . . . . . . . . . . . . . . . 6.00
162. . New Tiny Tears . . . . . . . . . 4.00
162. . Baby Belly Button . . . . . . . 4.00
163. . Cinnamon . . . . . . . . . . . . 10.00
163. . Busy Lizy . . . . . . . . . . . . . 22.00
163. . Upsy-Dazy . . . . . . . . . . . . 10.00
163. . Harmony . . . . . . . . . . . . . 20.00
164. . Evel Knievel . . . . . . 4.00 (S.A.)
164. . Look Around Velvet . . . . . 6.00
164. . Look Around Crissy . . . . . 6.00
164. . 17" Shirleys . . 25.00-9.00 (S.A.)
165. . Pan Am . . . . . . . . . . . . . . . 2.00
165. . Jal . . . . . . . . . . . . . . . . . . . 2.00
165. . BOAC . . . . . . . . . . . . . . . . . 2.00
166. . Little Love . . . . . . . . . . . . . 3.00
166. . Lovely Liz . . . . . . . . . . . . . 3.00
166. . Miss Grow Up . . . . . . . . . . 4.00
166. . Kimberly . . . . . . . . . . . . . . 5.00
167. . 8" . . . . . . . . . . . . . . . . . . . 18.00
167. . 8" . . . . . . . . . . . . . . . . . . . 18.00
167. . Miss America . . . . . . . . . . 25.00
167. . Steve Scout . . . . . . . 7.00 (S.A.)
168. . Crumpet . . . . . . . . . . . . . . 5.00
168. . Blythe . . . . . . . . . . . . . . . . 5.00
168. . Gabbigale . . . . . . . . . . . . . . 6.00
168. . Meadow . . . . . . . . . . . . . . . 4.00
169. . Hy Finance . . . . . . . . . . . . . 4.00
169. . Sleeping Beauty . . . . . . . . 48.00
169. . Jeannie . . . . . . . . . . . . . . 20.00
169. . Pamela . . . . . . . . . . . . . . . 6.00
170. . Mister Action . . . . . . . . . . . 4.00
170. . Rookies . . . . . . . . . . 3.00 (S.A.)
170. . Pamela . . . . . . . . . . . . . . . 6.00
171. . Bonnie Jean . . . . . . . . . . . . 4.00
171. . Sweet Candy . . . . . . . . . . . 4.00
171. . Debbie . . . . . . . . . . . . . . . . 6.00

171 . . Mary Jane . . . . . . . . . . . . . 2.00
172 . . Pretty . . . . . . . . . . . . . . . . 4.00
172 . . Powder Puff . . . . . . . . . . . 3.00
173 . . 21" . . . . . . . . . . . . . . . . . . 45.00
173 . . Marie Antoinette . . . . . . . 15.00
173 . . 19" . . . . . . . . . . . . . . . . . . 45.00
173 . . 8" . . . . . . . . . . . . . . . . . . . 15.00
174 . . Chubby Kid . . . . . . . . . . 20.00
174 . . 17" . . . . . . . . . . . . . . . . . . 30.00
174 . . Twins . . . . . . . . . . . . . . . . 18.00
174 . . Rosalie . . . . . . . . . . . . . . . 20.00
175 . . 10" . . . . . . . . . . . . . . . . . . 20.00
175 . . Alice In Thimble . . . . . . . . 5.00
175 . . 27" . . . . . . . . . . . . . . . . . . 40.00
175 . . 9½" Baby . . . . . . . . . . . . 20.00
176 . . Baby Rose . . . . . . . . . . . . . 7.00
176 . . 15" . . . . . . . . . . . . . . . . . . 15.00
176 . . Dude Ranch Cowgirl . . . . . 4.00
176 . . Display Mannikin . . . . . . . 7.00
177 . . Angel Face . . . . . . . . . . . 10.00
177 . . Bundle of Charm . . . . . . . 14.00
177 . . Pretty Miss . . . . . . . . . . . 18.00
177 . . Baby Good . . . . . . . . . . . 14.00
178 . . Christening Baby . . . . . . . . 5.00
178 . . Walking Pretty . . . . . . . . . 4.00
178 . . Miss Echo . . . . . . . . . . . . 25.00
178 . . Snow Baby . . . . . . . . . . . . . 3.00
179 . . Carry Walker . . . . . . . . . . . 3.00
179 . . Mascots . . . . . . . . . . . . . 3.00 set
179 . . Shelly . . . . . . . . . . . . . . . . . 2.00
180 . . Mascots . . . . . . . . . . . . . 3.00 set
180 . . Big Boy . . . . . . . . . . 1.00 (S.A.)
180 . . Lili . . . . . . . . . . . . . . . . . . . 5.00
180 . . Carole Channing . . . . . . . 15.00
181 . . Dollie Grams . . . . . . . . . . . 1.00
181 . . Johnny Hero . . . . . . 3.00 (S.A.)
181 . . Baby Susan . . . . . . . . . . . . . 3.00
181 . . Bonnie Blue Ribbon . . . . . . 6.00
182 . . Mary Hoyer,
Composition . . . 35.00
183 . . Mary Hoyer,
Hard Plastic . . . 25.00
184 . . Mary Hoyer,
Painted Eyes . . . 40.00
185 . . Johnny West . . . . . . 3.00 (S.A.)
185 . . Jane West . . . . . . . . 3.00 (S.A.)
185 . . Miss Seventeen . . . . . . . . 10.00
185 . . Ginny Bones . . . . . . . . . . . 12.00
186 . . Bonnie Walker . . . . . . . . . . 6.00
186 . . Geronimo . . . . . . . . . 3.00 (S.A.)
186 . . General Custer . . . . 3.00 (S.A.)
186 . . Shopping . . . . . . . . . . . . . . . 2.00
203 . . Barbie . . . . . . . . . . . . . . . . 10.00
Outfit . . 1.00
203 . . Barbie . . . . . . . . . . . . . . . . 10.00
Cotton Casual . . . 3.00
203 . . Barbie . . . . . . . . . . . . . . . . . 7.00
Winter Holiday . . . 3.00
203 . . Barbie . . . . . . . . . . . . . . . . 10.00
Knitting Party . . . 5.00
203 . . Barbie . . . . . . . . . . . . . . . . . 7.00
Sheath . . . 2.50
203 . . Ken . . . . . . . . . . . . . . . . . . . 9.00
Campus Hero . . . 3.00
204 . . Ken . . . . . . . . . . . . . . . . . . . 7.00
Saturday Date . . . 3.00
204 . . Ken . . . . . . . . . . . . . . . . . . . 7.00
Dreamboat . . . 3.00
204 . . Ken . . . . . . . . . . . . . . . . . . . 5.00
Sportsman . . . 2.00
204 . . Ken . . . . . . . . . . . . . . . . . . . 9.00
Campus Hero . . . 3.00
204 . . Ken . . . . . . . . . . . . . . . . . . . 7.00
Tuxedo . . . 5.00
204 . . Ken . . . . . . . . . . . . . . . . . . . 7.00
Sleep Set . . . 2.00
204 . . Barbie . . . . . . . . . . . . . . . . . 7.00
Friday Nite Date . . . 3.00
205 . . Baby Sitter . . . . . . . . . . . . 20.00
205 . . Barbie Case 1961 . . . . . . . . 3.00
205 . . Ken Case 1961 . . . . . . . . . . 4.00
206 . . Fashion Queen Barbie . . . 10.00
206 . . 1962 Barbie . . . . . . . . . . . 10.00
206 . . Barbie . . . . . . . . . . . . . . . . . 7.00
Red Flare . . . 5.00
206 . . Barbie . . . . . . . . . . . . . . . . . 7.00
Tennis . . . 5.00
206 . . Ken 1962 . . . . . . . . . . . . . . 7.00
206 . . Ken . . . . . . . . . . . . . . . . . . . 7.00
Yachtsman . . . 3.00
207 . . Barbie Wardrobe . . . . . . . . 6.00
207 . . Dressing Table . . . . . . . . . . 6.00
207 . . Barbie Case 1962 . . . . . . . . 2.00
207 . . Tiny Chatty Baby . . . . . . 15.00
208 . . Barbie . . . . . . . . . . . . . . . . . 7.00
Swinging Easy . . . 3.00
208 . . Barbie . . . . . . . . . . . . . . . . . 7.00
Career Girl . . . 5.00
208 . . Barbie . . . . . . . . . . . . . . . . . 7.00
Movie Date . . . 3.00
208 . . Barbie . . . . . . . . . . . . . . . . . 7.00
Ski Queen . . . 4.00
208 . . Barbie . . . . . . . . . . . . . . . . . 7.00
Knit Sheath . . . 1.00
208 . . 1963 Midge . . . . . . . . . . . . . 7.00
208 . . Ken . . . . . . . . . . . . . . . . . . . 7.00
Going Hunting . . . 2.00
209 . . Skooter . . . . . . . . . . . . . . . . 8.00
Flower Girl . . . 2.00
209 . . Midge . . . . . . . . . . . . . . . . . 7.00
Fancy Free . . . 2.00
209 . . Skooter . . . . . . . . . . . . . . . . 8.00
Dreamland . . . 1.00
209 . . Ken . . . . . . . . . . . . . . . . . . . 7.00
Ski Champion . . . 3.00
209 . . Ken . . . . . . . . . . . . . . . . . . . 7.00
Masquerade . . . 6.00
209 . . Midge . . . . . . . . . . . . . . . . . 7.00
Raincoat . . . 3.00
210 . . Skooter . . . . . . . . . . . . . . . . 8.00
Ballet Lessons . . . 4.00
210 . . Barbie . . . . . . . . . . . . . . . . . 7.00
Midnight Blue . . . 5.00
210 . . Barbie . . . . . . . . . . . . . . . . . 7.00
Drum Majorette . . . 5.00
210 . . Sleep Eye Barbie . . . . . . . 25.00
211 . . Barbie . . . . . . . . . . . . . . . . . 7.00
Poor Cinderella . . . 6.00
211 . . Barbie . . . . . . . . . . . . . . . . . 7.00
Cinderella Ball . . . 6.00
211 . . Ken . . . . . . . . . . . . . . . . . . . 7.00
Victory Dance . . . 5.00
211 . . Ken . . . . . . . . . . . . . . . . . . . 7.00
Roller Skate Date . . . 3.00
211 . . Barbie . . . . . . . . . . . . . . . . . 7.00
Red Riding Hood . . . 5.00
211 . . Ken . . . . . . . . . . . . . . . . . . . 7.00
King Arthur . . . 7.00
212 . . Barbie . . . . . . . . . . . . . . . . . 7.00
Guinevere . . . 7.00
212 . . Allan 1964 . . . . . . . . . . . . . 9.00
212 . . Ken . . . . . . . . . . . . . . . . . . . 7.00
The Prince . . . 7.00
212 . . Ken . . . . . . . . . . . . . . . . . . . 7.00
Arabian Nights . . . 7.00
212 . . Ken . . . . . . . . . . . . . . . . . . . 7.00
Mexico . . . 5.00
213 . . Midge . . . . . . . . . . . . . . . . . 7.00
It's Cold Outside . . . 5.00
213 . . 1964 Skipper . . . . . . . . . . . . 5.00
213 . . Skipper . . . . . . . . . . . . . . . . 5.00
Day At the Fair . . . 5.00
213 . . Midge . . . . . . . . . . . . . . . . . 5.00
Sparkling Pink . . . 5.00
213 . . Francie . . . . . . . . . . . . . . . . 5.00
Mexico . . . 3.00
214 . . 1963 Barbie Case . . . . . . . . 2.00
214 . . 1964 Skipper Case . . . . . . . 2.00
214 . . 1964 Ken Case . . . . . . . . . . 3.00
214 . . Skipper . . . . . . . . . . . . . . . . 5.00
Silk N Fancy . . . 3.00
215 . . Barbie . . . . . . . . . . . . . . . . . 7.00
215 . . Skipper . . . . . . . . . . . . . . . . 5.00
Coat . . . 2.00
215 . . Barbie . . . . . . . . . . . . . . . . . 7.00
Miss Astronaut . . . 4.00
215 . . Skooter . . . . . . . . . . . . . . . . 9.00
Outdoor Casual . . . 2.00
215 . . Twist, Turn Barbie . . . . . . 5.00
Flowers/Cooks . . . 3.00
215 . . Skipper . . . . . . . . . . . . . . . . 5.00
Can You Play . . . 1.00
215 . . Posable Skipper . . . . . . . . . 5.00
216 . . Skipper . . . . . . . . . . . . . . . . 5.00
Ship Ahoy . . . 1.00
216 . . 1965 Kiddle Case . . . . . . . . 2.00
216 . . Telly Viddle Kiddle . . . . . . 2.00
216 . . Calamity Jiddle . . . . . . . . . 2.00
216 . . Soapy Siddle . . . . . . . . . . . . 2.00
218 . . Tutti . . . . . . . . . . . . . . . . . . 6.00
Cookin Goodies . . . 4.00
218 . . Twiggy . . . . . . . . . . . . . . . 15.00
218 . . Tutti . . . . . . . . . . . . . . . . . . 6.00
218 . . Chris . . . . . . . . . . . . . . . . . . 8.00
Swing a Ling . . . 4.00
218 . . Barbie . . . . . . . . . . . . . . . . . 7.00
Dress . . . 7.00

218..Skipper ................ 5.00
Dog Show...2.00
219..Skipper ................ 5.00
Sledding Fun...2.00
219..Bunson Burnie .......... 2.00
219..Rosemary Roadster ..... 7.00
219..Baby Colleen ........... 8.00
219..Baby Liddle ........... 12.00
222..Sleeping Biddle ......... 8.00
222..Liddle Biddle Peep ...... 8.00
222..Little Middle Muffet ..... 8.00
222..Peter Paniddle.......... 8.00
223..Liddle Red Riding Hiddle . 8.00
223..Sizzly Fridle ............ 7.00
223..Howard Biff Boodle ...... 7.00
223..Freezy Sliddle .......... 7.00
225..Cinderiddles Palace...... 4.00
225..Sleeping Biddle Castle ... 6.00
225..Babe Biddle Car ......... 4.00
225..Lolli Lemon Kiddle ...... 3.00
226..Lolli Mint Kiddle ........ 3.00
226..Frosty Mint Kiddle ...... 3.00
226..Orange Ice Kiddle ....... 3.00
226..Violet Kiddle Kologne.... 2.00
227..Lily Of The Valley ....... 2.00
227..Rosebud ............... 2.00
227..Honeysuckle............ 2.00
227..Sweet Pea.............. 2.00
228..Apple Blossom.......... 2.00
228..Windy Fliddle .......... 8.00
228..Larky Locket ........... 3.00
228..Lou Locket ............. 3.00
229..Lorelie Locket .......... 3.00
229..Lorna Locket ........... 3.00
229..Lilac Locket ............ 3.00
229..Lucky Locket ........... 3.00
230..Heart Pin Kiddle ........ 3.00
230..Lorelie Bracelet ......... 3.00
230..Flower Pin Kiddle ....... 3.00
230..Suki Skediddle .......... 4.00
231..Teachy Keen ........... 8.00
231..Kiddle Kastle........... 4.00
231..Baby Small Talk......... 6.00
231..Alice In
Wonderliddle Castle...12.00
232..Valarie................ 4.00
232..Talking P.J. ............ 8.00
232..1967 Twist N Turn Barbie 5.00
232..Lavender Kiddle Case ... 1.00
233..Laverne Locket ......... 3.00
233..Louise Locket........... 3.00
233..Hearts Kiddles.......... 7.00
233..Hearts N Flowers ....... 3.00
234..Laffy Lemon............ 3.00
234..Luscious Lime .......... 3.00
234..Greta Grape ............ 3.00
234..Shirley Strawberry ...... 3.00
235..Anabelle Autodiddle ..... 6.00
235..Sister Small Walk ....... 5.00
235..Lickety Spliddle......... 6.00
235..Heather Skediddle ...... 4.00
236..Olivia Orange .......... 3.00
236..Lady Lavender ......... 6.00
236..Francie's Bed ........... 5.00
236..Rah Rah Teeny Boppin ... 4.00
237..Cherry Blossom ......... 5.00
237..Tessie Tractor .......... 4.00
237..Shirley Skiddle ......... 4.00
237..Harriet Helididdle ....... 5.00
238..Lickety Skediddle ....... 5.00
238..Tracy Skediddle......... 5.00
238..Anabelle Skediddle ...... 5.00
238..Captain Lazer.......... 10.00
239..Doug Davis............. 5.00
239..Sgt. Storm ............. 5.00
239..Major Matt Mason....... 5.00
239..Dainty Deer ............ 3.00
240..Baby Walk N Play ....... 9.00
240..Flossy Glossy ........... 3.00
240..Zoolery Kiddles..... 3.00 each
240..Lucky Lion ............. 3.00
242..Tiny Tiger............. 3.00
242..Miss Mouse............. 3.00
242..Funny Bunny ........... 4.00
242..Truly Scrumptious ..... 12.00
243..Barbie Family House .... 4.00
243..Mr. Potts Set ........ 9.00 set
243..Lenore Limosine ........ 7.00
243..Henrietta Carrage ....... 7.00
246..Snoopy Skididdle........ 3.00
246..Donald Duck Skediddle .. 3.00
246..Goofy Skiddler .......... 3.00
246..Lucy Skididdler ......... 3.00
247..1968 Kiddle Case ........ 4.00
247..Baby Go Bye Bye ........ 5.00
247..Kiddles Open House ..... 6.00
247..Small Talk Cinderella .... 8.00
249..Kiddle Living Room ..... 3.00
249..Callisto ............... 4.00
249..Cookin' Hiddle Set....... 5.00
249..Living Fluff ........... 7.00
250..Kiddle Mobile.......... 4.00
250..Twist N Turn Francie.... 5.00
250..1970 Living Barbie ...... 5.00
250..Barbie ................ 7.00
See Worthy...5.00
250..Barbie ................ 5.00
Yellow Mellow...2.00
251..Playhouse Kiddles....... 5.00
251..Rosemary Roadster ..... 9.00
251..Good Night Kiddle....... 5.00
252..Baby Din Din ........... 4.00
252..Lady Lace Tea Party .... 6.00
252..Baby Rockaway ......... 5.00
252..Nan & Fran ........ 10.00 set
253..Wet Noodles............ 1.00
253..Bugs Bunny Skediddle ... 3.00
253..1969 Barbie Case ........ 3.00
254..1969 Barbie Case ........ 2.00
254..Talking Baby Tenderlove . 4.00
254..Sing A Song .......... 12.00
254..Baby So High ........... 3.00
255..Tickle Pinkle ........... 3.00
255..Downy Dill ............. 3.00
255..Pocus Hocus ............ 3.00
255..Mother, What Now? ..... 3.00
256..Miss Information ........ 3.00
256..Red Hot Red............ 2.00
256..Nitty Nan .............. 2.00
256..Lilac Rockflower ........ 4.00
257..Heather Rockflower ..... 4.00
257..Barbie ................ 7.00
Prima Ballerina...3.00
257..Sun Buggy ............ 10.00
257..Rosemary Rockflower ... 5.00
258..Barbie ................ 5.00
Club Dress...2.00
258..Barbie ................ 7.00
Skate Mate...5.00
258..Barbie ................ 5.00
Salute to Silver...5.00
258..Walking Jamie.......... 9.00
258..Talking Stacey .......... 9.00
Maxi 'n Mini...7.00
258..Christie................ 7.00
Great Coat...5.00
259..Shoppin' Sheryl ......... 5.00
259..Baby Beans............. 3.00
259..Living Baby Tenderlove.. 4.00
259..Baby Love Light ........ 6.00
260..Talking Kip............. 4.00
260..Casper ................ 4.00
260..Cynthia ............... 8.00
260..Baby Play A Lot ........ 6.00
261..Malibu Ken ....... 6.00 (S.A.)
261..Living Fluff ........... 7.00
261..Living Barbie ........... 8.00
Fashion...4.00
Walk Lively Barbie .......... 7.00
262..Walking Jamie.......... 9.00
262..Ken & P.J. ............. 9.00
262..Pretty Hair Barbie ...... 7.00
262..Live Action Christie ..... 9.00
262..Pretty Hair Francie ..... 8.00
262..Living Barbie ........... 8.00
Silver Serenade...6.00
263..Malibu P.J. ........... (S.A.)
263..Malibu Francie ........ (S.A.)
264..Malibu Skipper ........ (S.A.)
264..Hi Dottie .............. 6.00
264..Barbie ................ 7.00
Silver Blues...5.00
264..Miss America .......... 15.00
265..Mod Hair Ken ..... 4.00 (S.A.)
265..Tiny Baby Tenderlove ... 6.00
265..Peachy............... 12.00
265..Sweet 16 Barbie......... 6.00
266..Sunshine Family....... (S.A.)
266..Barbie's 10 Speeder .... (S.A.)
266..Barbie's Horse ......... 12.00
267..Saucy ............... 20.00
267..Stacey ................ 9.00
Maxi N Mini...4.00
267..P.J. .................. 9.00
Fun Flakes...3.00
268..Tanya ................ 4.00

268 . . Action Jackson . . . . . . . . . . 4.00
268 . . Spiderman . . . . . . . . 2.00 (S.A.)
268 . . Tarzan . . . . . . . . . . . 2.00 (S.A.)
269 . . Batman . . . . . . . . . . 2.00 (S.A.)
269 . . Aquaman . . . . . . . . . 2.00 (S.A.)
269 . . Robin . . . . . . . . . . . . 2.00 (S.A.)
269 . . Superman . . . . . . . . 2.00 (S.A.)
270 . . Dinah-mite . . . . . . . . . . . . . 4.00
270 . . #1423 . . . . . . . . . . . . . . . . . . 2.00
270 . . #1431 . . . . . . . . . . . . . . . . . . 2.00
270 . . MS Fashion . . . . . . . . . . . . . 9.00
271 . . Riddler . . . . . . . . . . . 2.00 (S.A.)
271 . . Shazam . . . . . . . . . . 2.00 (S.A.)
271 . . Capt. America . . . . . 2.00 (S.A.)
271 . . Penguin & Joker . . 2.00 (S.A.)
272 . . Mr. Mxyzptik . . . . . 2.00 (S.A.)
272 . . Lainie . . . . . . . . . . . . . . . . 15.00
272 . . Cornelius & Zira . . . 3.00 (S.A.)
272 . . Astronaut, Dr. Zaius
And Soldier . . . 3.00 (S.A.)
273 . . New Born Baby . . . . . . . . . 6.00
273 . . Sweet & Cuddly . . . . . . . . . 6.00
274 . . 17" Monica . . . . . . . . . . . . 60.00
275 . . 21" Monica . . . . . . . . . . . . 75.00
275 . . 18" Monica . . . . . . . . . . . . 75.00
275 . . One, Two
Button My Shoe . . . 12.00
275 . . Polly Put Kettle On . . . . . 12.00
275 . . 5" . . . . . . . . . . . . . . . . . . . . 12.00
275 . . High Button Shoes . . . . . 12.00
276 . . 5" . . . . . . . . . . . . . . . . . . . . 12.00
277 . . Storybook Dolls . . . . . . . . 12.00
278 . . Storybook Dolls . . . . . . . . 12.00
278 . . 5½" . . . . . . . . . . . . . . . . . . 10.00
278 . . Muffie . . . . . . . . . . . . . . . . 10.00
279 . . Muffie . . . . . . . . . . . . . . . . 10.00
279 . . Lori Ann . . . . . . . . . . . . . . 10.00
279 . . Nappy . . . . . . . . . . . . . . . . . 3.00
279 . . Baby Sue . . . . . . . . . . . . . . . 3.00
280 . . Tracy . . . . . . . . . . . . . . . . . . 2.00
280 . . Theresa . . . . . . . . . . . . . . . . 2.00
280 . . Princess . . . . . . . . . . . . . . 22.00
280 . . Joan Palooka . . . . . . . . . . 10.00
281 . . Mousketeer . . . . . . . . . . . 22.00
281 . . Klinker . . . . . . . . . . . . . . . . 4.00
281 . . Playboy Bunny . . . . . . . . . . 8.00
281 . . Pebbles . . . . . . . . . . . . . . . . 3.00
282 . . Adventure Boy . . . . . . . . . 2.00
282 . . World Champion . . . . . . . 10.00
282 . . Laurel & Hardy . . . . . . . . . 1.00
282 . . Poppi Fresh Set . . . 2.00 (S.A.)
283 . . Puss & Boots . . . . . . . . . . 30.00
283 . . Drum Major . . . . . . . . . . . 20.00
283 . . Pin Up Girl . . . . . . . . . . . . 12.00
283 . . Sleepy Head . . . . . . . . . . . . 4.00
284 . . Jack & Jill . . . . . . . . . . . . . . 1.00
284 . . Bebe Jetpartout . . . . . . . . . 8.00
284 . . Little Audrey . . . . . . . . . . 25.00
284 . . Lucy Arnez . . . . . . . . . . . . 25.00
285 . . Bunny . . . . . . . . . . . . . . . . 20.00
285 . . Eloise . . . . . . . . . . . . . . . . . 30.00
285 . . 18" . . . . . . . . . . . . . . . . . . . 25.00
286 . . Danny . . . . . . . . . . . . . . . . . 5.00
286 . . Popeye . . . . . . . . . . . . . . . . 4.00
286 . . Crib Angel . . . . . . . . . . . . . 1.00
286 . . Tatters . . . . . . . . . . . . . . . 20.00
287 . . Hamburgler . . . . . . . . . . . . 2.00
287 . . Elsie . . . . . . . . . . . . . . . . . . . 8.00
287 . . Gas Genie . . . . . . . . . . . . . . 2.00
287 . . Dressy Bessie . . . . . . . . . . . 2.00
288 . . Little Lulu . . . . . . . . . . . . . 1.00
288 . . Mary, Many Face . . 7.00 (S.A.)
289 . . Dr. John . . . . . . . . . . . . . . 20.00
289 . . Liza . . . . . . . . . . . . . . . . . . 20.00
289 . . Judy . . . . . . . . . . . . . . . . . . 15.00
289 . . Libby . . . . . . . . . . . . . . . . . 15.00
290 . . L.B.J. . . . . . . . . . . . . . . . . . 20.00
290 . . Hildy & Herby . . . . . . . . . . 5.00
290 . . Spunky & Pip . . . . . . . . . . . 5.00
290 . . TV Jones . . . . . . . . . . . . . . . 3.00
291 . . Orphan Annie . . . . . . . . . . 18.00
291 . . Winkin Heidi . . . . . . . . . . . 4.00
291 . . Gingersnap . . . . . . . . . . . . 20.00
291 . . 19" . . . . . . . . . . . . . . . . . . . 18.00
292 . . Hug A Bug . . . . . . . . . . . . . 2.00
292 . . Laurie . . . . . . . . . . . . . . . . 18.00
292 . . Mimi . . . . . . . . . . . . . . . . . 20.00
Outfits . . . 4.00
293 . . Baby Lynne . . . . . . . . . . . . . 3.00
294 . . Roberta Ann . . . . . . . . . . . 22.00
294 . . Debutante Bride . . . . . . . 16.00
294 . . Dr. Casey's Nurse . . . . . . . 5.00
294 . . Dr. Kildare's Nurse . . . . . . 5.00
295 . . Granny . . . . . . . . . . . . . . . 22.00
295 . . Polly . . . . . . . . . . . . . . . . . . 5.00
295 . . Raggy Muffin . . . . . . . . . . . 2.00
295 . . Lisa . . . . . . . . . . . . . . . . . . . 6.00
296 . . Playgirl . . . . . . . . . . . . . . . 12.00
296 . . 22" . . . . . . . . . . . . . . . . . . . 12.00
296 . . Peter Pan . . . . . . . . . . . . . 18.00
296 . . Mother . . . . . . . . . . . . . . . 20.00
297 . . Carrie Cries . . . . . . . . . . . . 6.00
297 . . Maxi-Mod . . . . . . . . . . . . . . 4.00
297 . . Brother & Sister . . . . . . . 20.00
298 . . Nancy & Kim . . . . . . . 25.00 set
298 . . Malaika . . . . . . . . . . . . . . 10.00
298 . . Wanda . . . . . . . . . . . 6.00 (S.A.)
299 . . Lea . . . . . . . . . . . . . . 6.00 (S.A.)
299 . . Kim . . . . . . . . . . . . . . . . . . 20.00
299 . . Baby Ellen . . . . . . . . . . . . . 6.00
300 . . Cowgirl Annie . . . . . . . . . . 2.00
300 . . Miss Christmas . . . . . . . . . 2.00
300 . . Dorothy Collins . . . . . . . . 25.00
300 . . Baby Skin Doll . . . . . . . . . 12.00
301 . . Sunbabe . . . . . . . . . . . . . . 10.00
301 . . Peter Pan . . . . . . . . . . . . . . 5.00
301 . . Sun-Dee . . . . . . . . . . . . . . 15.00
301 . . Carrie . . . . . . . . . . . . . . . . . 4.00
302 . . Gene Autry . . . . . . . . . . . 165.00
302 . . Connie Lynn . . . . . . . . . . . 45.00
303 . . Cindy . . . . . . . . . . . . . . . . . . 8.00
303 . . Cycling Cheri . . . . 12.00 (S.A.)
303 . . Honest Abe . . . . . . . . . . . . 18.00
304 . . Needa Toodles . . . . . . . . . 15.00
304 . . Toodles . . . . . . . . . . . . . . . 12.00
305 . . Suzette . . . . . . . . . . . . . . . . 5.00
305 . . Bride Sue . . . . . . . . . . . . . . 4.00
305 . . Sunny Face . . . . . . . . . . . . 10.00
306 . . Wish Nik . . . . . . . . . . . . . . . 2.00
306 . . Impish Elfy . . . . . . . . . . . . . 1.00
306 . . Teenie Toodles . . . . . . . . . . 1.00
306 . . Hee Wee . . . . . . . . . . . . . . . 2.00
307 . . Dance Time . . . . . . . . . . . . 1.00
307 . . Bride Time . . . . . . . . . . . . . 1.00
307 . . Angeltime . . . . . . . . . . . . . . 1.00
307 . . Springtime &
Shoppintime . . . 1.00
308 . . Schooltime . . . . . . . . . . . . . 1.00
308 . . Moonmaid . . . . . . . . . . . . . 12.00
308 . . Baby Pee Wee . . . . . . . . . . 2.00
308 . . Batman Troll . . . . . . . . . . . 2.00
309 . . Pretty Portrait . . . . . . . . . 4.00
309 . . Educational PeeWee . . . . . 1.00
309 . . Kristina . . . . . . . . . . . . . . . . 3.00
309 . . Marika . . . . . . . . . . . . . . . . . 3.00
310 . . Fun Time . . . . . . . . . . . . . . 4.00
310 . . Beau Time . . . . . . . . . . . . . 4.00
310 . . Vacation Time . . . . . . . . . . 4.00
310 . . Prom Time . . . . . . . . . . . . . 4.00
311 . . Bride Time . . . . . . . . . . . . . 4.00
311 . . Winter Time . . . . . . . . . . . . 4.00
311 . . Date Time . . . . . . . . . . . . . . 4.00
311 . . Party Time . . . . . . . . . . . . . 4.00
312 . . Connie . . . . . . . . . . . . . . . . . 5.00
312 . . Littlest So Soft . . . . . . . . . . 3.00
312 . . Lovable Lynn . . . . . . . . . . . 3.00
312 . . Patti-Cake . . . . . . . . . . . . . . 3.00
313 . . Donna . . . . . . . . . . . . . . . . . 4.00
313 . . Magic Meg . . . . . . . . . . . . . 6.00
313 . . Miss Dollikin . . . . . . 3.00 (S.A.)
313 . . Lin . . . . . . . . . . . . . . . . . . . . 2.00
314 . . Loo . . . . . . . . . . . . . . . . . . . . 2.00
314 . . Weepsy . . . . . . . . . . . . . . . . 1.00
314 . . Thum-Fun . . . . . . . . . . . . . . 2.00
315 . . Janie . . . . . . . . . . . . . . . . . . 4.00
316 . . . . . . . . . . . . . . . . . . . . . . . . . 3.00
316 . . Calico Lass . . . . . . . . . . . . . 4.00
316 . . Ellie Mae . . . . . . . . . . . . . . . 4.00
316 . . Rusty . . . . . . . . . . . . . . . . . 15.00
317 . . Happi-Time Walker . . . . . 25.00
317 . . Dondi . . . . . . . . . . . . . . . . . 35.00
317 . . Roxanne . . . . . . . . . . . . . . 25.00
317 . . Luann Simms . . . . . . . . . . 30.00
318 . . Lucy . . . . . . . . . . . . . . . . . . . 5.00
318 . . Lucy . . . . . . . . . . . . . . . . . . . 8.00
320 . . Composition . . . . . . . . . . . 16.00
Early Non-Walker . . . 14.00
Early Walker . . . 12.00
Molded Lashes/Walker . . . 10.00
Bending Knee/Walker . . . 8.00
Add 2.00 for Brown Eyes
Outfits . . . 3.00 to 12.00
324 . . Ginny Bed . . . . . . . . . . . . . 18.00
327 . . Ginny Bed . . . . . . . . . . . . . 15.00
327 . . Jan . . . . . . . . . . . . . . . . . . . 15.00
329 . . Wardrobe Case . . . . . . . . 12.00
332 . . Pinky Toe . . . . . . . . . . . . . . 8.00
333 . . Littlest Angel . . . . . . . . . . . 6.00
333 . . New Baby Dear . . . . . . . . 30.00
333 . . Angel Baby . . . . . . . . . . . . . 6.00
333 . . Miss Ginny . . . . . . . 7.00 (S.A.)
334 . . Jeff . . . . . . . . . . . . . . . . . . . 15.00
334 . . Ginny . . . . . . . . . . . . . . . . . 10.00
334 . . Ginny . . . . . . . . . . . . . . . . . 10.00
334 . . Baby Dear . . . . . . . . . . . . . 25.00